Bonar Law

Bonar Law

R.J.Q. ADAMS

JOHN MURRAY
Albemarle Street, London

A catalogue record for this book is available from the British
Library

ISBN 0-7195-54225

Typeset in 11.75/13pt Garamond by Servis Filmsetting Ltd,
Manchester

Printed and bound in Great Britain by
The University Press, Cambridge

To John and Patricia Grigg

Contents

Illustrations

ix

The author and publisher would like to thank the following for permission to reproduce illustrations: plates 1, 2 and 3, Provincial Archives of New Brunswick; 4, 2nd Baron Coleraine; 5, 6, 8, 9, 10, 12, 13, 14, 15, 16 and 17, House of Lords Record Office; 7, National Portrait Gallery; 11, 18, 19, 20, 22, 23 and 26, Hulton Getty; 21, 24 and 25, Topham Picturepoint; 27 and 28, The Dean and Chapter of Westminster.

Preface and Acknowledgements

IN HIS LIFETIME Andrew Bonar Law showed little concern about his place in history and even less about the stuff of which history is made. He wrote understandable if idiosyncratic English, but wherever possible avoided making his case in print: his métier was the spoken word, the political speech. He never demonstrated the slightest interest in maintaining a diary or any other record of his judgements or motivations; had it been left to him, he would never have bothered to retain a scrap of paper that he wrote or received. It is a particular blessing to the historian that from quite early in his political career he employed secretaries to type his letters and memoranda, since his handwriting was never good, and grew worse. In addition to the keepers of official documents, it is to those secretaries, and to colleagues and friends who preserved his papers and correspondence, that scholars owe deep thanks. Without them, the biography that follows would have been impossible.

Bonar Law was a private man whom nature and experience had shaped so that he was largely unsusceptible to most worldly pleasures. Unlike Churchill he cared little for good food and drink, and unlike Asquith he was not seduced by 'society'. In contrast to his close friend Beaverbrook, he cared little for the accumulation of wealth (save for the fact that the fruits of his business success allowed him to pursue a political career); and unlike Lloyd George, he was not particularly vulnerable to the charms of beautiful women. The story has been told that a perplexed Lloyd George once enquired, 'Well, what *do* you like?' Without a second thought and to the then Prime Minister's amusement, Bonar

Law replied, 'I like bridge.' This, though the Wizard of Wales may not have recognized it, was one of Bonar Law's jokes – the grave Glaswegian was 'doing a Bonar'. To Austen Chamberlain he once said in pre-World War days that he cared only for two things in politics – Tariff Reform and the Irish Union. This, too, was not entirely correct.

Andrew Bonar cared for many things in the world beyond politics: certainly for his country and her Empire. His wife Annie was the great love of his life, and he was deeply fond of his children; he cared also for his many friends – with a particular penchant for those who could make him laugh. In his public life he was ferociously committed to the Conservative and Unionist Party, and he certainly embraced passionately if quietly the power he attained to affect the direction of his country. And these important things were among the few that he loved more than a good cigar.

Bonar Law has not fared well at the hands of historians, and the reason may be the publication little more than a decade after his death of one of the most influential books ever in any era of British history, *The Strange Death of Liberal England*, by my own teacher of thirty years ago, George Dangerfield. This incomparable limner painted a brilliant and dazzlingly biased picture of the last Victorian governors of Britain; and in his exasperatingly wonderful book dealt Bonar Law repeated body blows from which his reputation never fully recovered. Dangerfield wrote:

> He was a man *without unction* – so Sir Walter Raleigh has described him in one of his letters, adding unreasonably that he loved men without unction. If so, Sir Walter was one of the few people in England who could have felt anything much more than a liking for Andrew Bonar Law, who contrived to hide a mild and retiring disposition behind an appearance of rasping, uncomfortable self-consciousness. . . . His face was sad, his forehead crumpled, he had an unfortunate habit of saying the wrong thing in debate. He was absolutely honest, and he was excessively Tory in the matter of having no political imagination whatsoever: when attacked by men more subtle in dialectics than himself, he generally took refuge in a remarkably unpleasing rudeness.[1]

But Bonar Law had a doughty and powerful champion in the politician, financier and press magnate William Maxwell Aitken, Lord Beaverbrook, who also wrote history and commissioned others to write it for him, based upon the remarkable private archive he collected. Bonar Law was his friend and hero, and he wrote of him in 1921:

He is like a good deed in a naughty world – and the impeccable nature of his motives, his almost morbid pursuit of disinterestedness, are sinking into the public consciousness.[2]

Two biographies exist: the first, by the popular writer H.A. Taylor, *The Strange Case of Andrew Bonar Law*, appeared in 1932 and is little remembered today; more familiar is *The Unknown Prime Minister*, published in 1955 by Lord Blake, then a young Oxford don. This latter was the first book apart from his own memoirs to use Bonar Law's papers, which Beaverbrook owned. Beaverbrook was Bonar Law's literary executor and this is therefore the official life, a perspicacious and elegantly readable book in which Blake struggled mightily against the daunting image of Bonar Law as a moody, indecisive, Catholic-baiting Tory who was willing to violate the law of God and man to advantage his beloved Ulster. It has been widely praised, and continues to be read, and cited by historians. Yet it is true that what our time is pleased to call Bonar Law's 'image' continues to reflect Dangerfield's vision more than that of Beaverbrook or Blake.

What follows is not an attempt to save Bonar Law or his reputation, but an example of the undeniable fact that historians in each generation are driven to understand the past in their own terms. I took Bonar Law as my subject because his life is intrinsically interesting. His career encompassed those bitter struggles over the Irish Union which led to the constitutional structure which has been the centre of desperate controversy in our own time. He played a major role both in the debate over fiscal reform in those years and in the conduct of the Great War of 1914–18 and the peace which followed. He led and shaped his party for eleven turbulent years and held high office for eight; he unmade two of the most powerful Prime Ministers of our century, and himself ended his career at the top of Disraeli's 'greasy pole'. He was a defining figure in the development of the Conservative Party; and, though little attention was paid to the fact for years, most of the Tories who followed him as premier were more like him than like his predecessors. As dissimilar as they are, Baldwin, Heath, Thatcher and Major – perhaps even Macmillan – are all Bonar Law's spiritual heirs.

Forty years is a long dry spell between biographies – surely a singular case among the prime ministers of the first half of this century – and none has been in print for many years. The need for a study such as this is undeniable. Another major reason for this book addresses the matter of opportunity. H.A. Taylor wrote largely from secondary sources and

Lord Blake from a necessarily limited collection of primary sources: it has been my great fortune to have access to the public documents as well as private papers of virtually all the figures with whom Bonar Law shared the political stage – Baldwin, Balfour, Cecil, the Chamberlains, Churchill, Curzon, Hankey, Lansdowne, Long, and many others. It is not surprising, therefore, that this story should often differ from those told before.

There is a final reason: after writing a number of books about the political history of the early years of this century, like many historians I was inexorably drawn to the challenge of biography. Those who know me will be aware of my own peculiar and specific qualifications to understand a North American-born conservative with a taste for Carlyle and for 'low-brow' mystery novels, who worked in a horribly messy office (employing the floor as an extension of his desk) and was suspicious of the joys of nature but not of those to be found in his pipe or a cigar.

All historians depend upon others, and all histories are in that respect collaborative. It is also my pleasure to record here my gratitude to the many people and institutions who have supported my efforts. I gladly express my thanks to Lord Coleraine for his generous assistance in my researches into the life of his grandfather. I am also grateful to Bonar Law's American grandchildren, Mrs Ann Catherine Menninger and Mr David Colwell, and to the childhood friend of his children, Mrs Betty Boyd-Maunsell, for their insights into his private life. I must also thank Mrs Mary Sykes for her kindness and interest in my work. I am saddened to have to record my posthumous thanks to the late Bonar Hugh Sykes. He was a generous source of information about his grandfather and shared with me many valuable materials in his possession. He also became a valued friend, and I am deeply saddened that I am unable to place in his hands a book to which he much looked forward.

It is impossible adequately to thank all who aided me in the making of this book, but I cannot fail to single out Lord Blake, who encouraged me in my efforts from the outset. A number of historians have read and commented on all or parts of this manuscript, including Dr Paul Addison, Dr Charles Brooks, Mr John Grigg, Professor Peter Hennessy, Professor Thomas C. Kennedy, Professor William C. Lubenow, Professor John Ramsden, Dr J. Lee Thompson, Dr Larry L. Witherell and Professor David Woodward. Dr Jeremy Smith was generous with the produce of his own research into Bonar Law's battle against the third Home Rule Bill. The insights of Lord Skidelsky and Mr Kenneth Rose into the art of writing biography were very helpful and continue to ring true for me. Dr Thomas Ginn, MD, advised me on certain of the medical questions which arose as a result of research. Errors of fact or interpretation are, of course, my own, as are those which arise from the fact that I may have failed to take good advice when it was offered.

I am very grateful to the Master and Fellows of St Catherine's College, Oxford for electing me to a Visiting Research Fellowship in 1993; to the Department of History of the Queen Mary and Westfield College, London for electing me to a Visiting Professorial Fellowship in 1998; and to the Texas A&M University both for a Faculty Development Leave and a Scholarly and Creative Research Enhancement Fellowship which assisted me greatly in my researches.

All historians are dependent on the assistance of professional archivists and librarians, and I particularly wish to thank Ms Katherine Bligh of the House of Lords Record Office, whose knowledge of the Bonar Law, Beaverbrook and J.C.C. Davidson papers is profound. Lady de Bellaigue of the Royal Archives at Windsor, Mr Colin Harris of the Bodleian Library in Oxford and Dr B.S. Benedikz of the University of Birmingham were generous with their help to me in making use of the papers in their care. I wish to thank Dr R.A.H. Smith of the Manuscripts Department of the British Library for making available to me the Lansdowne papers recently acquired by the Library, and to Mr J. Graham Jones of the National Library for Wales for his assistance with the A.J. Sylvester Papers. I am also pleased to record my gratitude to the staffs of the many other institutions to which my researches have taken me. These include the Public Record Office; the Oriental and India Office Collections, British Library; the National Library of Scotland; the Scottish Record Office; the Imperial War Museum; the Libraries of Cambridge and Birmingham Universities and the University of New Brunswick; the British Library of Political and Economic Science; the University of Sheffield Library; the Churchill Archive Centre, Churchill College, Cambridge; the Liddell Hart Centre for Military Archives, King's College, London; the Provincial Archives of New Brunswick; the Reading University Library; the Harry Ransom Humanities Research Center of the University of Texas, Austin; the West Sussex Record Office; the Wiltshire Country Record Office; and the Liverpool City Library. My gratitude to the staff of the Sterling C. Evans Library, Texas A&M University, remains boundless.

I have to acknowledge the gracious permission of Her Majesty The Queen to quote from materials held in the Royal Archives. For their consent to quote from papers to which they hold copyright I wish to thank also Lord Astor; Mr and Mrs William Bell; the Hon. Mrs Charles Brand; Sir Simeon Bull; Lord Coleraine; Lord Crewe; Lord Derby; Lord Fisher; Viscount Hanworth; Vice-Admiral Sir Ian Hogg; Lord Long; Mr Edward Sanders; Lady Juliet Townsend; the Beaverbrook Foundation Trust; the Clerk of the Records, House of Lords; the Curators of the Bodleian Library; the Keeper of the Department of Documents, the Imperial War Museum; the Warden and Fellows of New College, Oxford; the Syndics of the Cambridge University Library; the Master, Fellows and Scholars of Churchill College in the University of Cambridge; the British Library Board; the Controller of H.M. Stationery Office; the Liddell Hart Centre for Military Archives; the University of Birmingham; and the County Archivist, West Sussex Record Office.

If I have infringed upon the copyright of any persons or institutions I hope they will forgive the oversight and inform me, so that the error may be corrected in any future edition of this book.

An American who has dedicated his professional life to a nation thousands of miles from his own encounters certain practical challenges. I am so very fortunate to have made over the years good and generous friends in Britain who have helped to make their country a second home for me. Certainly Professor Ian and Dr Sally Craig have for many years done so with generosity and kindness. St Catherine's College has welcomed me in Oxford over more than two decades, and I gratefully acknowledge my thanks to its Master and Fellows. In my own university, my friends and distinguished colleagues Dr Charles Brooks, Dr Joseph G. Dawson and Vice-President for Research Dr Robert A. Kennedy have been both interested in and supportive of this project. Without the encouragement of my publishers, Mr Grant McIntyre and, in America, Mr Norris Pope, and my literary agent, Mr Andrew Lownie, it is certain that this book would not now exist. My wife, Susan Charlotte Adams, continues to be the ideal historian's helpmate, critic and life support staff. She has read every word of this book many times and has so very often saved me from snares of my own creation. John and Patricia Grigg have been warm and generous friends for more than twenty-five years, and I have many reasons to be grateful to them. Friendship is not a debt and it is not correct to speak of repaying it, but I hope it will please them all the same that this book is dedicated to them with my gratitude and affection.

R.J.Q. Adams
Bryan, Texas
December 1998

I

Early Days

I

ON TUESDAY, 30 October 1923, King George V noted in his diary, so scrupulously kept and so unrevealing of either man or reign: 'Poor Bonar Law died this morning.'[1] The death was not unexpected, and preparations had been made. The body of the statesman was cremated, and four days later a private service was held at St Columba's, the Scottish Church in Pont Street.

The nation paid its official respects at a great state funeral on 5 November. The day was raw and cheerless, perhaps appropriate for the solemn service at Westminster Abbey. The magnificent Psalm XXIII was sung, and the readings were taken from the Gospel of St John and the Books of Job, First Timothy and The Revelation. Hymns included the glorious recessional by Bonar Law's old friend Rudyard Kipling, 'God of our fathers, known of old'.[2] The coffin was borne by soldiers of the regiments of his two sons lost in the Great War, but he did not want for the ministrations of the great. Pall-bearers included the Prince of Wales; the Prime Minister, Stanley Baldwin; the Speaker of the House of Commons, John Henry Whitley; two former premiers, Herbert Henry Asquith and Arthur James Balfour; and the Opposition leader and future Prime Minister, James Ramsay MacDonald. Also accompanying the casket were Bonar Law's political comrades-in-arms, Viscount Fitzalan, Lord Carson and Austen Chamberlain, as well as his closest friend, Lord Beaverbrook. Only his absence in America prevented former Prime Minister David Lloyd George from joining them. Among the principal mourners were the premiers of the self-governing Dominions, then assembled in conference in the capital of the Empire. It was, by any measure, a glorious send-off for the first Prime Minister since Gladstone to be buried in that hall of kings. As was often the case in Bonar Law's life, it may have been an honour he had earned, but it was not one which he would have cared for.

Despite the damp and cold of the cavernous and ancient minster, thousands – many of them Scots and Northern Irishmen – had filed silently past the small space allotted to their hero in the floor of the south nave, near the grave of the Scottish missionary David Livingstone. Ironically, eighteen years later another non-believing, dissenting premier, one whose career he had early nurtured, would be interred immediately next to the sceptical Presbyterian in that greatest of Anglican churches: the Unitarian Neville Chamberlain.

Bonar Law's ashes were buried close to the tomb of the anonymous representative of the glorious dead of the Great War, and Asquith is reputed to have remarked upon withdrawing: 'It is fitting that we should have buried the Unknown Prime Minister by the side of the Unknown Soldier.'[3] If said, it was a cruel but characteristic aphorism by the waspish Asquith, who always found a way to deprecate his rival and all his works.[4] What he meant, of course, was not that Bonar Law was unrecognized, but that he was unimportant.

Lord Curzon, who believed that his own ambitions had been frustrated by Bonar Law, wrote that he left the ceremony considering 'that in days to come people would ask who he was and how he ever got there.'[5] Like Asquith, Curzon meant less that Bonar Law's name would be a mystery to future generations than that he was of little consequence.

These men were quite wrong. Andrew Bonar Law was far from unimportant, either in his works or in his legacy. Yet he was most assuredly unusual – more so even than they. He was bred as far from the traditional stables of British statesmen as can be imagined. He had attended neither a famous public school nor an ancient university and had served in no distinguished regiment – the usual forcing-houses for prime ministers. Yet most of those who followed him in 10 Downing Street were more in his mould than in that of his predecessors. He was a pivotal figure in British political history, and if such significance is important, then his interment in the Abbey was not inappropriate. Yet the story of his life certainly demonstrates how unlikely a final resting place it was for this modest and private man, whose beginnings lay so far from Westminster.

II

Because of his North American birth, Andrew Bonar Law is often recalled as Britain's Canadian Prime Minister.[6] Technically this is not the case. He was born on 16 September 1858 in Kingston,[7] Kent County, New Brunswick; and in those days, nine years before Canadian federation, New Brunswick was a separate colony. The first Europeans to settle there were almost certainly French, followed in greater numbers by Empire Loyalists fleeing the American War of Independence. In the early nineteenth century the character of the colony was further changed by a large-scale migration of settlers from Scotland and Northern Ireland.

Bonar Law was the son of the Reverend James Law and Eliza Anne Kidston. His father was a Minister of the Free Church of Scotland, a native of County Antrim in Ulster, and a descendant of farmers of Scottish lowland stock. Soon after coming down from the University of Glasgow, in 1845 James Law accepted a call to New Brunswick and was settled into pastoral charge of St Andrew's Church at Kingston, in the parish of Richibucto.[8] He was twenty-three, and he ministered to that congregation until his retirement thirty-two years later.

Bonar Law's mother, Eliza Kidston, had been born into a family of Scottish and Empire Loyalist stock established in trade in the nearby Miramichi district of New Brunswick since late in the previous century. Her grandfather William Kidston had returned to Glasgow, where he established a highly successful merchant banking house; her father, also William, went back to North America to make his life in Nova Scotia. When he died prematurely, young Eliza and her two sisters were sent to her Kidston relatives in Scotland to be educated. As a young woman she returned to New Brunswick, probably to the home of her brother James in Newcastle. It is possible she taught school there briefly before marrying the thirty-year-old James Law in October 1852.[9]

The life of a rural clergyman in nineteenth-century New Brunswick cannot have been easy. James Law was the spiritual leader of several small townships which made up his parish, and contact between them was maintained by boat, on horseback or on foot. A minister's wages were modest, and James Law bought a small farm on the Miramichi

River to supplement the family income. A new manse was also required; it was simple, and is said to have been built in part by James Law's own hands.[10] Adjusting to the harsh winters and the isolation, James and later Eliza became popular and admired in the district.

Rural life on the edge of Empire was a little easier with a large family to provide a home-grown labour force. James and Eliza Law had four sons, Robert, William, John and Bonar, and a daughter, Mary, their youngest child. Most were given family names, but of his own Bonar Law often repeated a story told him by his father. According to this piece of family lore, his first and second names, justly famous in Scottish Presbyterian circles, were not given him to honour any of the more celebrated men who had borne them. Rather, his mother much admired the missionary Robert Murray McCheyne; and, because she had already called one son Robert, bestowed upon her fourth the name of the Reverend Andrew A. Bonar, biographer of the 'Saintly McCheyne'. Thoughout his life he was never called Andrew by family and friends, always Bonar. He signed his name A.B. Law until he was in his thirties when, perhaps to lend an air of dignity suitable to a success-ful young businessman, he altered it to A. Bonar Law. From this point the two names were universally treated as a kind of double patronymic – throughout his public life he was Bonar Law, and that is how he will be referred to in this book. A final point about his second name, and one which was important to him, is that it was – and should be – pro-nounced to rhyme with 'honour', rather than 'owner'.

Eliza Law died in 1861, soon after the birth of her only daughter. Bonar Law himself remembered little of his mother, but his father shared with him his memories of her as a loving wife and mother, uncomplaining about her austere life. James Law, though weighed heavily with grief, thereafter had as his main personal concern the upbringing of his five young children. He was fortunate in the Kidston family connection: Eliza's unmarried sister Janet, who had remained since girlhood with her Kidston relations in Scotland, set sail for New Brunswick upon receiving the sad news, to keep house and take charge of the children.

James and Bonar Law were no different from many fathers and sons: at once alike, and dissimilar. The minister possessed a dominating per-sonality and an imposing physique, his black beard and piercing dark eyes appropriate to a dynamic preacher. Founder and exemplar for the local Sons of Temperance, no doubt he frequently called down the wrath of God when trying to guide his flock along the paths of righteousness. He was remembered in his parish long after his retirement, and following his death a monument was raised to his memory by his parishioners. Though it is difficult to accept on the evidence of his sole surviving photograph, he was a loving, gentle parent, remarkably tolerant of his children's explorations and antics.

Young Bonar was by all accounts adventurous, curious, and as active as most small boys, but also distinguished himself in his studies at the village school, where the prodigious memory for which he later became famous first revealed itself. Years later, during the Great War, he reminisced about his father's pride when he recited without error the hundred lines of Joseph Sheridan Le Fanu's popular poem 'Phaudhrig Crohoore'.[11] He loved and admired his father deeply, and there is no doubt that the Reverend James Law influenced him greatly.[12] Apparently Bonar Law also found time for making mischief.[13] A boyhood friend vividly recalled

> . . . a stocky, eager boy, tirelessly active and apparently frivolous beyond cure. He was quick tempered but unresentful, and there was about him a kind of impudent frankness which was very engaging. He was noticeable for his courage. I remember how, when he was playing in the big barn into which he and his brothers and sister were turned on Sundays to amuse themselves out of sight and earshot of easily scandalized neighbors, he fell from a rafter fifteen or twenty feet from the ground. Dazed as he was, he immediately challenged his companions to leap as he had done from the roof.[14]

His memories of New Brunswick were not extensive, but he diverted his own children with tales of the winter play which is so much a part of a Canadian childhood.

There were two tragic parallels at least in the lives of father and son: each early lost a beloved wife and was left with the care of a large young family, and each suffered from what in later times would have been diagnosed as clinical depression. James Law, lonely in his responsibilities and his isolated New Brunswick village life without his beloved Eliza, fell into increasingly lengthy periods of crippling despair. He continued to lead his growing flock; yet as the years passed he drew less satisfaction from his parish work and found it ever more difficult to carry out his pastoral duties. His health suffered. In 1876 he took his family to Ulster for a visit, and apparently decided during that stay to retire from the ministry and from Canada. The remaining six years of his life were spent withdrawn from the world. Bonar Law too suffered from periods of depression, which grew worse as he grew older. This affliction attracted sympathy from those who cared for him and impatience in those who misunderstood, but was as much a part of his inheritance as his dark hair or brown eyes.

In 1865 James Law married again, and Sophia Wood, a local school-mistress, in time bore him two more daughters. Janet Kidston, who had developed a special affection for her youngest nephew, suggested that Bonar should return with her to her family in Glasgow. Comfortably circumstanced, the Kidstons could offer him an excellent education and a good start in life.[15] The young bride may well have been wondering what to make of her ready-made new family – James Law agreed to the plan.

As with so many events in Bonar Law's early life, there is no record of exactly when this decision was made. It has been generally accepted that his father's second marriage took place in 1870, and that Bonar therefore went to Scotland when he was twelve. However, James Law's remarriage was almost certainly five years earlier – since his two young-est daughters were born in 1866 and 1868 – and it is unlikely that Miss Kidston would have stayed on in Kingston for long afterwards. Furthermore, in a letter written many years later a cousin, John Kidston, recalled that the future Prime Minister was a small boy of about six when he and his aunt paused in their journey to Scotland to visit members of the Kidston clan in Springfield, Nova Scotia.[16]

More circumstantial is the evidence of Bonar Law's speaking voice, which revealed nothing of his place of birth. The journalist R.D. Blumenfeld, himself a transplanted American very sensitive to signs of 'colonial' origins, noted in his diary upon first meeting Bonar Law in 1900 that he seemed to have 'no trace of a Transatlantic accent'.[17] Typically, a childhood accent is more easily shaken off the younger a child is at the time of emigration, so Blumenfeld's observation seems consistent with his having left North America as a small boy.[18]

Whenever it was made, the decision to send Andrew Bonar Law from rural New Brunswick to bustling Glasgow was to change his pros-pects more profoundly than his father could have imagined. Thereafter his life was in Britain: he never saw Kingston again.

III

The rather brave little boy, separated from his family and his home, went to live with his Aunt Janet Kidston at Seabank, her house overlooking the Firth of Clyde in Helensburgh, some twenty miles to the west of Glasgow. Nearby were the homes of Bonar's first cousins, once removed. The middle-aged brothers Charles, Richard and William Kidston were partners in the firm of merchant bankers established by that William Kidston who had himself abandoned New Brunswick two generations earlier. Only the eldest, Charles, had married, and he had no children. Richard and William lived with their sister Catherine at Ferniegair, a large house not far from Seabank, Charles and his wife at Glenoran, an imposing villa a mile away on a hill above Helensburgh.[19]

There can be few better models of the Victorian Scottish *haute bourgeoisie* than the Kidston clan: hard-working, thrifty, proud of their family, and of their reputation as canny but scrupulous businessmen. Their prosperity was evident, yet they would have been decorously shocked by any hint of ostentation. Devout Presbyterians and faithful Conservatives, their orderly lives lacked only one thing: there was no immediate heir. Through no choice of his own, young Bonar had traded the spartan future of a poor preacher's son on the Gulf of St Lawrence for that of an adopted son of the banking house of Kidston. It was not the last time fate would intervene to provide the sort of opportunity no amount of effort could be counted upon to yield.

The Victorian middle class valued an appropriate education, and Bonar was immediately enrolled in a preparatory school, Gilbertfield House, in nearby Hamilton. At fourteen he was transferred to the justly famous Glasgow High School, where he read the 'modern' curriculum.[20] That he was sent to these local academies reveals something of the Kidstons and their ambitions for him. The cost of a school such as Eton or Harrow would not have been a barrier: the family clearly considered that a different sort of education was appropriate for their ward.

No doubt in part because of his remarkable memory, Bonar demonstrated a facility for languages. He had already begun to learn German as a small boy in Kingston, and at Gilbertfield he won a prize for Greek. At Glasgow High School he added honours in French to his record. His school reports were excellent, but Bonar was bound for business, not for one of the universities: the 'modern side' at Glasgow High School was for nascent capitalists. At sixteen his formal education ended, and he was bound for a clerk's stool in the imposing Queen Street offices of Kidston and Sons.

If the child is not necessarily father to the man, a strong case can be made that the youth is. During his years living with and among the Kidstons Bonar Law developed many of the tastes and habits which later characterized the public man. He remained, lifelong, a church-going Presbyterian, though in early manhood he seems to have lost his belief – which, he later explained with mock solemnity to Augustine Birrell, must have been due to an early taste for Carlyle.[21]

Reading brought him pleasure throughout his life. Books had been the constant companions of his boyhood, and he regaled his own children with confessions of his attempts to read under the bedclothes after bedtime. As well as his favourite Carlyle he read and reread the Scottish masters, devoured Scott's novels, and was often heard to recommend Dickens. History was another abiding interest, and he once astonished Austen Chamberlain by announcing that he had read Gibbon's entire *Decline and Fall of the Roman Empire* three times before he was old enough to vote. The subject of Bonar Law's ambition – or lack of it – has attracted comment from many of his contemporaries, as well as from later historians, and perhaps his love of Gibbon provides a clue: towards the end of his career he told the distinguished historian and Cabinet minister H.A.L. Fisher that he was eternally fascinated with the tales of soldier-commoners rising to the Roman imperium.[22]

Reading also provided Bonar Law – like many public men – with one self-confessed 'guilty pleasure': he consumed 'pulp' novels at a remarkable rate. A boyhood taste for escapist literature remained with him throughout his life, and his study was littered with detective stories and tales of adventure. In some respects at least his taste was impeccable, since there is no language to compare with English, and the British at that time were unequalled as writers of escapist fiction. He readily admitted that his predilections were not sophisticated. His restless mind required the distraction of books, particularly at the end of a long day of business or politics – but was more likely to find it in John Buchan or H. Rider Haggard than in Henry James or Joseph Conrad.

By the time Bonar Law was twenty-one he stood well above average height, with a slender but sturdy physique. He played tennis regularly at a Helensburgh club which he helped to found, and took up golf – the birthright of every Scot: he later won the Parliamentary golf championship. Both games were a source of pleasure throughout his life, and he gave them up only when forced to do so by declining health.

Three more sedentary pastimes also brought him lifelong pleasure: billiards, bridge, and chess. From the time he became master of his own house he owned an elaborate billiards table for which he insisted upon professional annual maintenance, while bridge always brought him relaxation, and he played literally until the end of his life. Chess, however, was closer to his heart than any other recreation. As a youth he got into the habit of carrying a miniature chess board about with him; on the train journey he made between Helensburgh and Glasgow every day except Sunday he played fellow commuters or, if no opponent presented himself, practised by himself. He eventually became a first-class amateur, competitive in play with opponents of international calibre. Bonar Law was introspective and serious even as a young man: the silent and absorbing gravity of a chess match suited him very well.

Though his benefactors intended him for a career in business, this did not mean an end to all intellectual or refined pursuits. Like other young self-improvers he went to early-morning lectures at Glasgow University given by eminent academics to broaden the horizons of young businessmen. In later years he recalled how he had tried never to miss the speeches of eminent men who passed through Glasgow, and loved to relate how, when he was twenty-one, he attended the installation of W.E. Gladstone as Lord Rector of Glasgow University. He left the ceremony fired, he said, 'with the hope and indeed the intention of one day occupying the position that was then filled by Mr Gladstone.'[23] Did the diligent young onlooker perhaps imagine himself occupying another of the Grand Old Man's posts?

Politics was a constant thread in the lives of the Kidstons and their circle. As an old Scottish friend of long acquaintance put it, 'Bonar Law took politics with his porridge.'[24] The Glasgow mercantile middle class numbered relatively few Tories, and it is likely that he met them all in the Kidstons' drawing rooms. An anecdote widely circulated after Bonar Law's time also has it that he met Benjamin Disraeli, Lord Beaconsfield, when the ageing statesman was speaking in the town. Perhaps apocryphal, it is not entirely beyond the realm of possibility – as a young man he certainly encountered a wide variety of Conservative notables who went to Glasgow to rally the faithful, and as certainly became particularly devoted to Beaconsfield, whose reputation was at its apogee during Bonar's youth. If the young man dreamed of leading the Party and the nation, he could have chosen a worse hero than the outsider who had become the darling of a party which valued insiders.

Certain fortunate young men destined for public life in those years learned the techniques of argument and debate in the Oxford and Cambridge Unions and the Inns of Court. Bonar, of course, could not. The next best thing, no doubt, combined with taking every opportunity to observe public speakers, was to join one or another of the various types of speaking society which were a feature of Victorian life.

Beginning with the literary clubs in his church circle, Bonar Law did just this. We do not know how halting his early attempts at public speaking may have been, but in 1878 he felt ready to join the recently-formed Glasgow Parliamentary Debating Association.

The Association conducted a mock parliament in which ambitious novices could try their hands at political debate. It was both school-room and practice field: little quarter was asked, even less apparently given. Members were assigned constituencies – Bonar's was North Staffordshire – for which they represented Conservative or Liberal party interests, and governments were formed; debates were held weekly on 'bills' before the 'House'. Organization of the mock parliament adhered as closely as possible to its Westminster counterpart, and in the hands of its able Speaker, James Turnbull, it thrived for many years.

In this company Bonar learned the rough and tumble of debate, developing a style which remained largely unchanged throughout his political career. His voice was naturally quiet, and he had frequently to be reminded to speak up. He never used notes, relying instead on his prodigious memory; initially he learned whole speeches by heart, but within a few seasons had discovered the trick of committing to memory a thorough outline of his address and improvising the actual presentation. In his third year as an 'MP' the Association's journal, *The Mace*, offered this review of Bonar Law's performance:

> Our Member has improved greatly since he first addressed the House. He has mastered to some extent his monotony of speech. There is one other little point he might try to get over. When he rises he makes a kind of a leap, which on account of his stature is peculiarly noticeable. But more – his style of standing is more slovenly than dignified. Altogether, he is a fair logician, possesses considerable judgment, has moderate self-possession, and speaks with much power and effect.[25]

In developing his own style he was bound, of course, to try on for size those of great parliamentarians of the time. If *The Mace* critic's assessment is accurate, he failed quite to master the manner of Lord Randolph Churchill, or the wit of Lord Beaconsfield:

> North Staffordshire, with alternative hand in pocket, went over in detail various paragraphs, not seemingly with any idea of amending them or with any clear objections, but rather with the good-natured intention of raising a laugh. In this he was very successful, though occasionally it was evident that

the laugh was against himself. His style of speech, introduction of subject, and leading to point are all remarkably good, but it was palpable that the weakness of his logical deduction resulted from the inability to find actual fault with the matter at hand.

... It is a great mistake for members who possess ability, as North Staffordshire undoubtedly does, to devote themselves to uttering common-places or jocularities. Frivolities, even from an able speaker, are still frivolities, and are of no assistance in furthering argument in debate.[26]

The Glasgow Parliamentary Debating Association neither created Bonar Law's appetite for politics nor made him a Conservative. He joined to hone his skills and test his mettle, and the ten years he spent as an active member served him well. The issues raised and powers exercised by the 'MPs' may have been imaginary, but the energy and skill displayed on the debating floor were very real; as a preparation for the realities of parliamentary debate, it was as thorough as any.

There is no doubt that Bonar Law aspired early to a public life. At the height of his career he recalled to Dr Thomas Jones, Assistant Cabinet Secretary, the frustrations and anxieties he had known in his youth – familiar to the young and ambitious of any era. He remembered musing, at the time of a local election in 1881, that 'Pitt [the Younger] at 23 was Prime Minister, and here am I at 23 and I am not even a member of the Glasgow School Board.'[27] He was fated to bypass the School Board and, unlike Pitt, to reach the heights of British politics at the end rather than the beginning of his parliamentary career.

IV

Joining the family firm at sixteen, Bonar Law applied himself to business with exemplary energy and a characteristic thoroughness which bespoke more than merely a sense of duty to his relations. He was paid a nominal salary at Kidston and Son and was, of course, a member of his Aunt Janet's household – his status that of a juvenile both in the family and while completing his commercial education.

Three morning trains carried the businessmen of Helensburgh into Glasgow's Queen Street Station, and the train he took was held to define a man's place in mercantile society. Habitués of the earliest train – which left at 7.10 a.m. and spent almost fifty minutes on the twenty-mile journey – were known as the Strivers; those who left an hour later, having enjoyed their morning tea, were the Drivers; and those prosperous gentlemen who took the last train, which did not arrive until nearly ten o'clock, were known to be the Thrivers. Bonar Law was a Striver, and so he remained long after he had quit business for public life.

In 1885 the Kidston brothers wished to wind up the affairs of the firm and retire; the Clydeside Bank had offered lucrative merger terms, but such a merger would have left young Bonar in a difficult situation. An often-repeated story that 'the family' found a new place for him is contradicted by a long-overlooked document among Bonar Law's papers which reveals that he himself identified the opportunity, but had to screw up his courage to ask for the help to take advantage of it.

William Jacks was a Helensburgh neighbour and a rather elderly Striver; he was also a Glasgow iron merchant, a respected member of the influential 'Iron Ring' of metal traders, and by 1885 he was ready to withdraw from active management of his own firm to pursue a parliamentary career.[28] Here was a common interest: Jacks wanted a younger partner to take over management of his firm, and Bonar was ambitious to 'get on' in business as quickly as he could. He had no capital of his own, and a very real sense of the debt of gratitude he already owed the brothers: it is easy to imagine how he must have felt as he wrote to William Kidston on New Year's Day 1885:

I have for a long time wished to speak to you but have not liked to do it & I write it now as I know I would not be able to say what I mean in speaking. Mr Jacks hinted more than a year ago that he would be willing to take me as a partner & I am told that he is now preparing to make a change in his business so that if I don't do anything about it now it will soon be too late. He has never mentioned the subject to me since & so of course I don't know if his offer would still be open.

I would like extremely to get into an active business & if Mr Jacks did not require a large capital, & if an examination of his books showed that the business was a thoroughly sound one I would consider it a greater kindness than any you have shewn me yet if you could see your way to advance the money necessary to enable me to join him. I know that this is a very large unreasonable request & if it were not that I feel I really *must* get some work to do I would never have the courage to make it.

It is this alone which makes me wish to change for if I could *make* anything like the income you have been giving me I would be more than content.

For years I have felt that my present position was very bad for me & I am quite certain that at my age none of you would have continued for a single year with no real work to do. As I said my reason for bothering you with this now is that if I put it off I am afraid it will be too late.[29]

William Kidston and his brothers were happy to advance Bonar the money to buy a partnership in Jacks's firm,[30] and from this point he set about building his own fortune in the Glasgow business community.

Ever the Striver, arriving early each day at his new premises in Royal Bank Place, Bonar Law's work ethic served him well. He was remembered by a subordinate of those days, Gray Buchanan, as a demanding superior who set his employees a high standard of probity – and long hours. There are indications that the delegation of responsibility did not come easily, and perhaps he was a somewhat isolated figure: 'He never asked for favours and therefore never expected to be asked for them. Perhaps because of that he stood more alone than most men.'[31]

It is difficult to argue with honest success in business, and Bonar Law made the firm of William Jacks extremely profitable. Jacks and Company were not manufacturers, nor was Bonar Law an ironmaster, as he was later so frequently described. These were the last great years of prosperity for the Scottish iron and steel industry, and Bonar Law and his colleagues of the 'Iron Ring' were factors – agents or middlemen between the makers of raw iron and the manufacturers who turned it into other products. Trading was carried on at the Royal Exchange building in two hectic daily sessions of two hours each which witnessed the exchange of millions of pounds weekly. In addition to participating in the 'Iron Ring' Jacks and Company also traded in iron ore and steel. Having prospered during Bonar Law's active business career and for some time thereafter, the firm did not long survive his departure and ceased to be profitable soon after the First World War.

Bonar Law strove hard in business, devoting his full energies to it for fifteen years. If, as his friend Max Aitken later noted, Bonar Law never became as rich as was often presumed, he certainly achieved comfort and security for his family during his lifetime. No earlier records of his earnings survive, but after he left Jacks and Company his annual taxable income in the years 1908 to 1913 averaged almost £6000, an impressive sum at the time.[32] As his business reputation spread he was offered various directorships, and eventually joined the boards of the Clydeside Bank, the Scottish Western Investment Company, the Caledonian Trust, and the Clyde Valley Electric Company.[33] He was also left money by the childless Kidstons: £30,000 each from Mrs Charles Kidston and Miss Catherine Kidston.[34]

Before his fortieth birthday Bonar Law had become a substantial man of property in a city which respected such men. He was neither a plutocrat nor – in view of the Kidston connection – an entirely 'self-made' man; but helped by the Kidstons' loan he had turned the company begun by William Jacks into a very successful enterprise, in large part through his own efforts. To make money, however, was never the overmastering desire of his life: the capital left him by his Kidston cousins allowed him, as he entered middle age, to consider the public service which he had had in mind since his days in the Glasgow 'Parliament'.

2

Enterprise and Ambition

N OW A SUCCESSFUL young man of business with independent prospects, Bonar Law at thirty established his own bachelor household. Janet Kidston gave him Seabank, and his sister Mary came to keep house for him. Of all Bonar Law's siblings the closest to him in sympathy as she was in age, Mary Law was a remarkable woman, singular and strong-willed and in many ways exceptionally self-sacrificing; she never married.

John Law, always called Jack, tried his hand at planting tea in Ceylon, then migrated to Scotland and eventually accepted Bonar's invitation to settle in Glasgow and join William Jacks. The next eldest, William, had preceded his father to Ulster and became a successful physician in Coleraine. Only Robert, the first-born, remained in Canada to work the small family farm. He apparently drank heavily and, constantly in debt, seems to have depended on the aid of his youngest brother.[1]

Robert's alcoholism and its results – the negative to the positive of the Reverend James Law's strict temperance views – perhaps had something to do with Bonar Law's life-long abstinence, though he never himself set it down to religious or moral principles, nor did he maintain a teetotal household. It seems rather that he simply had no taste for alcohol of any sort, throughout his life preferring ginger ale or milk to the ales and spirits which were the pride and prosperity of both his native and adopted homelands.

An indifference to the lure of grain and grape was matched by an almost total lack of interest in food. In an age which approved of robust appetites and well-rounded figures he maintained a slim physique with little effort. His favourite meal was boiled chicken, washed down with ginger ale and followed by rice pudding; and he always ate rapidly, allowing little time for conversation, which he thought more appropriate to after-dinner leisure and a cigar. Such tastes did not tend to a reputation for hospitality, and friends later recalled that dinners under his roof were more suited to a school refectory than a statesman's dining room: invitations to his table were accepted for reasons other than the pleasures of the feast.

Bonar Law's one significant weakness was tobacco. He smoked heavily throughout his life, and his room was invariably fogged with pipe smoke during the day. After meals he preferred cigars, and having rushed through lunch or dinner would fill the dining room with the heavy fragrance of his favourite Havanas. The thick cloud which always engulfed him caused Max Aitken's young daughter to christen him 'Mr Smoke'.[2]

Established in a house of his own but with no family calls on his time, Bonar Law was able to indulge in various self-improving pursuits. There was the Parliamentary Association, and he developed an interest in the local bankruptcy court, where he often represented his firm – and thereby polished his argumentative skills. He also supported good works of the kind considered appropriate to a prosperous businessman, including an annual concert series for the working classes.

That even in the interests of charity Bonar Law should have subscribed to these concerts is particularly ironic, as he was entirely unmusical. Any unavoidable exposure to music was suffered in excruciating boredom, albeit with admirable stoicism. Orchestral and choral music were a trial, but opera absolutely taxed his limits. As to dancing, he had been subjected to lessons at school, and as a gentleman bachelor apparently played his part at dance evenings; but from the time he married he seems never to have stepped on a dance floor again.

His enjoyment of tennis and golf notwithstanding, the out-of-doors in general Bonar Law could take or leave alone. Though born in a beautiful and unspoilt part of the world and brought up in a nation which was fashionably raising the appreciation of 'fresh air' and 'nature' almost to the status of a secular religion, he was indifferent to such pleasures. He was the last to respond when a country ramble was organized; he never fished, hunted or shot; and, save for bridge and the talk of politics, he found the country-house weekend an agonizing waste of time. When he walked – which he did daily – he did so purely for exercise and without the slightest concern for his surroundings. In later years, when he could easily have both afforded one and justified the expenditure, he gave not a moment's consideration to the purchase of a country house or estate. He preferred to holiday in hotels (frequently in France or Germany) which offered bathing, tennis, golf, bridge and his beloved chess. The politician Lord Winterton recalled in his memoirs a country-house weekend into which Bonar was dragooned during his years of power. Out walking, he asked his host the name of a bird their passing had flushed. Jaws dropped at the discovery that the leader of the party of the country gentlemen of Britain did not recognize a pheasant when he saw one – and he was begged never to mention the incident lest he deliver a rude shock to his Parliamentary following.[3]

In 1890, when he was thirty-two, Bonar Law met the daughter of a prosperous Glasgow merchant, Harrington Robley. Anne Pitcairn Robley, at twenty-four, with dark hair, large brown eyes and a lively manner, was considered quite a local beauty, and Bonar Law – a man whose frivolity had hitherto found its outlet in tennis and golf – seems to have fallen in love with her immediately. He paid his court, and was successful. An engagement was announced, and the wedding took place on 24 March 1891 at the West Free Church in Helensburgh. Bonar was attended by his brother Jack, and among Annie's bridesmaids was his Canadian half-sister, Janet Law.

Unfortunately, Annie Law is little known to history, and there is small chance of this being rectified. Her correspondence has been lost, and only a few of Bonar's early letters to her were preserved: what we are left with is the record of her impact on the lives of those who loved her. A single painting and a few surviving photographs reveal her to have been a beautiful young girl who became what the Edwardians decorously termed 'a handsome woman'. Despite giving birth to seven children – the eldest sadly stillborn – she remained slender, with the erect carriage the Victorians and Edwardians so admired. She was widely popular, both in Glasgow and later in London, much loved by her family, and worshipped by her husband. Her premature death left him devastated, and he never considered marrying again.

The young iron merchant took his bride home to Seabank, and a few years later bought his father-in-law's much larger house, Kintillo. Bonar Law enthusiastically embraced a growing family – by 1905 there were four sons and two daughters.[4] If Annie had no choice but to adjust to his work habits – by now both well-established and eccentric – they in turn seem to have accommodated themselves to family life. In his smoke-palled study he preferred to work in a favourite chair, often with a long leg thrown across the arm, his papers overflowing onto the carpet (which, he said, 'I also use as a desk'), apparently little or not at all perturbed by the near-anarchy of noisy young children and their pursuant mother, aunts, nannies and pets. As a statesman he was often thought to be stern and humourless: future colleagues and adversaries might have been startled to see him on the floor with several small boys astride his back, he the pony of their Wild West heroes. One need not be too imaginative to conclude that he meant to spare his own children the disrupted and truncated childhood he had known.

II

Mock parliaments, bankruptcy courts and debating societies were not ends in themselves. It was to the Palace of Westminster that Bonar Law looked for his future. By this time the Conservatives were coming to call themselves Unionists, and it was thus to the chairman of the Unionist committee in Bridgeton, then seeking a candidate for a traditionally Liberal seat, that Bonar Law wrote in early 1897, agreeing that he might try his hand there, '... if no man turns up & it is thought worth-while to contest the seat at all.'[5] Then the Unionists in a Glasgow constituency, Blackfriars and Hutchesontown, offered him the chance to stand in his own city. Financially independent and anxious to get into Parliament, he explained to the local chairman that he was not, however, enthusiastic about committing himself to the district unless an early election was probable, 'as I would very much dislike the trouble connected with being looked upon as a candidate for probably 4 years or so before an election takes place.'[6] With no better prospects in sight, however, within the year he pledged his troth to the Blackfriars Tories and began to speak regularly in the largely working-class neighbourhoods of the district.

Bonar Law was right to have reservations about his chances at Blackfriars. Since its creation in 1884 the constituency had returned only Liberals, and the incumbent was a popular Manchester merchant, A.D. Provand. The Unionists, led by the Prime Minister, the Marquess of Salisbury, had won the general election of 1895, and Bonar Law was concerned that he might have to wait until 1902, when the current Parliament had run its course.

These considerations were swept away when Britain became caught up in the Boer War: in the autumn of 1899 commandos of the Transvaal and the Orange Free State attacked the British Cape Colony. The nation on the whole rallied to the cause, despite – perhaps even because of – initial setbacks in the war, and the Government, sensing a political opportunity, took advantage of the mood of patriotism to call what became known as the 'Khaki Election' in the autumn of 1900.

The subsequent electioneering was particularly unpleasant, with strong words freely exchanged between pro- and anti-war partisans. If the local press is to be believed, the temper in Glasgow was milder than in many other districts. Nevertheless, well aware of the difficulties of wresting a seat from a sitting Member, Bonar Law campaigned hard, and soon earned himself the reputation of an extraordinarily well-prepared speaker who captured his audience with facts and common sense rather than flamboyant oratory. Furthermore, he showed himself a worthy adversary of the hecklers who inevitably dogged him, meeting their attacks with the ready humour which too many historians have forgotten was his. Some of his counter-blows became local legend, as when he was snarlingly asked whether he was in favour of the payment of electoral costs from public funds: 'I am not,' he responded promptly; 'but I do not object to an exception being made in my own case' (he in fact paid his own expenses in the contest). Did the candidate favour pensions for MPs retiring after twenty-four years' service? another questioner wanted to know. 'I shall be better able to answer that question twenty-four years hence!' came the reply.[7] If not as silkily elegant as Balfour nor as explosive as Lloyd George, Bonar Law went on to earn a fearsome reputation as a quick-witted and hard-hitting debater – and evidence of that style was manifest in October 1900.

Liberals squabbled among themselves about the rights and wrongs of the war, the national patriotic mood held, and the Unionists did well in the election. A few Unionist seats were lost, but in Blackfriars the electors reversed the pattern of fifteen years and chose the local man as their new Member: with a majority of 1,000 votes, he was now Andrew Bonar Law, MP.[8] He was forty-two, and he was ambitious for political success; he told his friends that if he were not in the Government in three years, he would return to the Iron Ring.[9]

With this first taste of electoral victory, Bonar Law displayed prudence as well as ambition: he wound up his mercantile life, ending his active participation in the firm of Jacks and Company so long (he intended) as his political career should last; but he retained his directorships. He also kept his Helensburgh home and rented a house in London – at different times over the next eight years he lived in Chelsea, Kensington and Wimbledon during the Parliamentary sessions.

He took the Oath of Allegiance to the Queen on 3 December, but the House sat for only a fortnight, intending to meet again in February. To a man eager to make his mark and accustomed to the pace of the business world, the ponderous workings of Parliament were a baffling revelation. Within a few months he was expressing his sense of frustration to Austen Chamberlain, encountered in the Smoking Room. He had been a member of the Parliament for many weeks, and it had yet to transact much in the way of business. Chamberlain, one of his first political friends, recalled his pensive mood: "'No, Austen [...] this is no place for me. It's all very well for men like you who came into it young; but if I had known then what I know now, I would never have stood for Parliament.'"[10] The disappointment lifted, however, as he began to learn the lesson of patience required of all new Members.

The death of Queen Victoria on 23 January 1901 hastened Members back to Westminster. Bonar Law paid little attention to all the ceremony involved, but was interested in the fact that the new King, Edward VII, opened his first Parliamentary session in person, contrary to his mother's practice. During the debate on the King's Speech, which began on 18 February, the audacious Pro-Boer David Lloyd George attacked the Government and their prosecution of the South African conflict with such vehemence that the Colonial Secretary, Joseph Chamberlain (father of Bonar Law's friend Austen), stalked out of the Chamber in fury.

The following evening, Bonar Law seized his chance. He spoke for only fifteen minutes, defending the Government and the Army with courage and a confidence that belied his status as a parliamentary tyro. In this first speech he brought into play a technique which was to serve him well over the years to come: with his letter-perfect memory and twenty years' dedicated reading of Hansard behind him, he was able to exasperate the Opposition leaders by recalling their own former speeches commending the men and the policies Lloyd George had so passionately denounced. Of the accusations levelled against the Government and the King's commanders by Lloyd George, Bonar Law said:

The Honourable Member said that we had exasperated the Boers. That is perfectly true, but he seemed to be under the impression that it would be our duty to make war in a peaceful manner! ... Of course we do not like [what is going on in South Africa]; the soldiers do not like it; and, above all, Lord Roberts does not like it. We don't like war, we don't like the horrors of war, but we are responsible for them only if the war is an unjust war, and that is a responsibility which this Government and country can bear with a clear conscience. If the Honourable Member had proved that in this war we had done anything contrary to the laws of war there might have been something in the charges he made which would have affected the Government and done discredit to the country. But he has not proved that, and no one could ...

I agree rather with Sir Wilfrid Laurier [the Canadian premier] when he said that the very fact that the war has proved so difficult, and that our enemies were so ready for it, while we were not, proved that the war was not our war, but that it was the war of those who were ready for it, and expected to beat us in it.

These were brave words for a maiden speech, and afterwards he sat down amid cries of 'Hear! Hear!' from fellow Unionists and jeering from the Liberal benches. His début did not amaze the House, as did that of F.E. Smith; nor did his first speech, like Winston Churchill's, capture the full attention of the press. But it impressed the party leaders as well as the grizzled veterans of the back benches. It was a warrior's speech, and it was as a warrior that he was to rise in politics.

III

The Unionists had governed Britain for all but three of the years since W.E. Gladstone had disrupted the Liberal party with his first Irish Home Rule Bull in 1886. Now they had profited from the Liberals' internal wrangles over the Boer War. Despite their victory in the 'Khaki Election', however, the Unionists themselves were soon faced with schism: they were the party of Empire, and with the new century the cause of Empire became intertwined with divisive questions of fiscal reform.

The central figure in this complicated tale was Joseph Chamberlain. A Birmingham manufacturer who like Bonar Law after him had given up business in mid-life to go into politics, Chamberlain had been a great radical Liberal, but broke with his party over Home Rule. In 1895 he and his colleagues, calling themselves Liberal Unionists, allied with the

Conservatives and accepted office under Salisbury. Still vigorous in his commitment to social reform, Chamberlain linked this with his new passion for the Empire. Now Colonial Secretary and convinced that if Britain wished to remain prosperous and retain her place among the Great Powers she would have to draw the diverse parts of the Empire more closely together, he began to develop the plan which was to occupy the last years of his career and shake the Conservative Party to its foundations.

In 1902 the need to adjust taxation to cover the costs of the Boer War drove Sir Michael Hicks Beach, Salisbury's Chancellor of the Exchequer, both to raise income tax and to revive small 'registration duties' – import taxes – on foreign grains, meal and flour. These unpopular tariffs had been abolished three decades earlier in the nation's passion for free trade, and 'Black Michael' emphasized that his only goal now was to raise necessary wartime revenue.[11] Free trader though he was, if Hicks Beach did not exactly light the fuse and throw the tariff bomb at his party, he at least held the taper. The explosive business was before them – where it was to remain for thirty years; it was also to become one of the two paramount issues of Bonar Law's career.

Bonar Law may have thought things a bit slow when first he arrived at Westminster, but the pace of political life quickened in the months that followed. With a new monarch came a new Prime Minister; in July 1902 the seventy-two-year-old Salisbury retired, his place taken – perhaps inherited – by his nephew, Arthur James Balfour. With Salisbury's place went his problems: a domestic agenda yet to be resolved, the aftermath of the recently concluded war, and a nascent intra-party debate on the tariff issue.

Also that summer, the leaders of the Great Colonies assembled in London for an Imperial Conference. Here the Canadian premier, Sir Wilfrid Laurier, let it be known that Canada would be pleased to enter into a mutually advantageous relationship of trade preferences, a prospect which showed itself to be popular among the colonial ministers and excited the blood of British imperialists.

Bonar Law again sensed an opportunity, and seized it with both hands: on 22 April 1902, he weighed into the fiscal debate with his first major speech in the House. The Member for Glasgow Blackfriars argued that much of the system of free trade then in place was still appropriate, and that a general revenue tariff was unnecessary and unwise at that moment. To the fury of the Liberals, however, he then went on to align himself with Chamberlain in insisting that the idea of an imperial customs union had merit in its potential to unite the trade interests of the Empire; given the strides which other nations were making, particularly such high-tariff rivals as Germany and the United States, perhaps there was as much danger in allowing the current system to remain forever unaltered as in the imposition of certain tariffs.

It was the second half of the speech which created something of a sensation on the Tory benches. Drawing on his business experience, Bonar Law made a plausible case for there being no empirical proofs that tariffs necessarily led to increases in the cost of living as borne by consumers. Skilfully parrying Sir William Harcourt's counter-thrust by quoting the elder statesman's own earlier words against him from memory, Bonar Law closed by suggesting that Liberals – self-proclaimed progressives – would be well advised to consider that the world had changed since the days of the Corn Laws.

The speech was an epitome of Bonar Law's future parliamentary performances. He spoke as he always would: without notes, but with the path of his argument and his evidence in order in his mind, while the presentation evolved spontaneously. Lloyd George's crony Tom Jones recalled many years later:

> B.L. told me that he had disciplined himself severely in the preparation of speeches to such an extent that he had never written a line of any speech he had delivered in the 20 years he had been in the House of Commons. In the early days he would sit down for 2 or 3 hours and not only meditate on the ideas of a speech but would frame every sentence precisely in his mind. After 2 or 3 hours of this he would be utterly exhausted.[12]

Like any ambitious new Member, he strove to give the impression of confidence – to seem well-informed, and at ease with his own argument. His remarkable memory was a potent weapon. When accused by Harcourt of wilfully misquoting him, Bonar Law was able to prove – supported by Hansard – that his recollection was absolutely correct. Sir Arthur Griffith-Boscawen noted afterwards that Bonar Law spoke with the knowledge of a businessman and the theoretical method of a 'Scottish metaphysician': 'Members were amused, but also greatly interested; and from that day Mr Bonar Law had the ear of the House.'[13] It was a moment of pure triumph.

Sir Ian Malcolm, himself a rising Unionist MP at this time, described Bonar Law's debating style in his memoirs:

[He spoke] rather like a clever young don lecturing a class of undergraduates, his hands clapsed behind his back, without a note to help him; terribly earnest and sincere, an unmodulated voice, a pronounced Doric accent, and rather clockwork gestures, when, if ever, these were needed. There was no attempt at humour and very little imagination. Always suffused with an atmosphere of business philosophy, his speeches were closely packed with figures and facts so admirably arranged and so lucidly presented that they were easy for the non-expert to follow.[14]

IV

Arthur Balfour was fifty-four when he succeeded to the leadership of nation and party in 1902. He was a curious man by any measure – a brilliant intellectual in a world of practical men, a great aristocrat come to lead in what was to prove the century of democracy. The first bachelor premier since the days of the Younger Pitt, he was elegant in a style already past, and cultivated an image at once charming and aloof. Even some who knew and admired him might have agreed, with Lord Beaverbrook, that 'Balfour had no human feelings.'[15]

A Government reshuffle inevitably accompanied Balfour's assumption of the premiership. The Earl of Dudley, Parliamentary Secretary to the Board of Trade, resigned to become Lord-Lieutenant of Ireland and, though the two had hardly spoken, the new Prime Minister offered the secretaryship to Bonar Law. Thus were his private aspirations met: he had achieved office in less than three years. The reason for his promotion was relatively simple: Bonar Law had been swift to distinguish his own as a powerful and technically masterful voice on economic and trade questions, at a time when such were in short supply. Though his Minister (Balfour's brother Gerald) was also an MP, and thus able himself to represent the department in the House, Bonar Law's growing stature as an expert on economic matters meant that he was often entrusted with the duty of concluding debates. His promotion marked Bonar Law as a coming man, a fact not lost on him, or on the House itself.

Balfour did not have an easy time of it with his new Government. In 1903 Joseph Chamberlain returned from a triumphant tour of South Africa to find that the new Chancellor, C.T. Ritchie, had struck Hicks Beach's registration duties from his Budget. 'Radical Joe' retaliated by declaring war on free trade in a ringing speech at the Birmingham Town Hall on 15 May. He described his dream of a united and progressive

Empire protected by a complex network of tariffs levied against non-Empire goods – a plan, which he called Tariff Reform, not authorized by the Government of which he was a member. Almost at once Balfour was caught in an inescapable tangle: one wing of his party (soon to be known as Free-Fooders) remained loyal to free trade, while the other, the Tariff Reformers, was increasingly enthusiastic for Chamberlain's programme.

There was no doubt which group claimed Bonar Law's allegiance: he was a Chamberlain man from the beginning. For many Tories, Tariff Reform became a political philosophy of renewal, of hope, and of world power. It would, Chamberlain preached, create a system which would enable British industry and agriculture to compete more equally with their most aggressive competitors, and would thus ensure British security and influence in a new century.

Bonar Law's concerns were somewhat less grand. Four years later he recalled that shortly after the famous Tariff Reform speech of May 1903, Chamberlain had said to him: 'I have taken this step, and I rely upon every one who, like you, believes in my policy, doing everything in his power to give it wholehearted support.'[16] The newest member of the Government had pledged his aid and stressed that his own primary desire was for retaliatory tariffs to make fairer Britain's trade with the other industrial powers. According to Bonar Law, Chamberlain had indicated his disapproval: 'That may be true,' he said, 'but if that were all, I should not have moved in this question. I should have left it to younger men. I have taken this step because I believe it is the one way by which it is possible for us to secure the real union of the British Empire.'

Joseph Chamberlain wished to reshape the British Empire into a united political entity which could both protect and prolong British institutions and also overawe Britain's rivals in the contest for world power. Bonar Law, former Glasgow iron trader, concerned himself more with practical matters – conditions of trade, and unemployment statistics. He backed Chamberlain's campaign, but it is no exaggeration to say that his motives and beliefs were more of this world – in the matter of Tariff Reform, he did not dream dreams or have visions equal to those of his new hero. Years later, when he was struggling against his final illness, Chamberlain said to L.S. Amery of Bonar Law: 'He is no Tariff Reformer.' To Amery, Chamberlain's adoring lieutenant, the meaning was clear: for Bonar Law the new programme 'was a question of trade figures and not a national and Imperial policy of expansion and consolidation of which trade was merely the economic facet'.[17]

In his assessment Amery overlooked a significant factor: Canada. The Dominion, self-governing and with seemingly limitless economic resources, was always close to Bonar Law's heart. He was sensitive to its potential and wary of the economic lure of the United States. His enthusiasm for Tariff Reform was certainly more businesslike than that of some of his fellow adherents, but it was not devoid of an intuitive side. He wished with all sincerity to ensure that Canada should remain joined by spiritual as well as economic and imperial links to Britain.

Chamberlain took his campaign to Glasgow in the summer of 1903 and there delivered a rousing address, inviting her sceptical sons to join his cause. Once again Bonar Law demonstrated no small courage when, a week later, he fully identified himself with Chamberlain's ideas. His constituents in Glasgow Blackfriars apparently received his declaration with only moderate enthusiasm: free trade, associated with a lower cost of living, remained popular in less prosperous, largely Liberal Scotland. Their Member advised them that twenty years earlier he would no more have criticized free trade than he would have questioned the Ten Commandments. But things had changed, he said, and now the realities of world commerce required an alteration in Britain's trade policy. The meeting reaffirmed its confidence in him by an overwhelming majority vote, but questions were many and applause perhaps somewhat subdued. Clearly, Bonar Law's political future in Blackfriars would depend upon the popularity of Tariff Reform.

Parliamentary success came quickly to Bonar Law in part through his good fortune in being a man in command of hard facts and possessed of real-world economic experience at a time when Balfour's front bench needed such a man. But he also laboured very hard at his new profession. He was diligent in attendance at the House, and worked relentlessly in his department. His hard-hitting debating style soon earned him the admiration of his fellow Unionists. He faced all comers with equal vigour, whether grizzled past masters like Sir Charles Dilke, newly-recruited Liberal heroes such as Winston Churchill, or the heaviest artillery the Opposition could muster – the former Home Secretary, H.H. Asquith, whose polished performances in the House were already legendary. Bonar Law was always well prepared, invariably it seemed primed with the precise date, name or fact needed to support his case, and never avoided battle on the floor of the House. His debating technique, Amery recalled, 'was like the hammering of a skilled riveter, every blow hitting the nail on the head.'[18] But with force, there was clarity. Lord Beaverbrook put down his success as a political speaker to 'an intense and sphinx-like straightforwardness';[19] R.D. Blumenfeld, the well-connected Anglo-American newspaper editor, declared that he was a 'mountain of common sense',[20] and Sir Ian Malcolm that on the most technical questions he made the 'involved seem intelligible'.[21] And always there was the power of his unfailing memory, as Tom Jones concluded:

> [Bonar Law was] a precise debater who had trained himself to pack his speeches, sentence by sentence, into his retentive memory like cubes in a box, by severe concentrated thought, which dispensed entirely with written notes. He took them out in perfect order, one after the other, when he rose to speak ...[22]

He also understood the value of a bit of theatre: his suits were made with a number of hidden pockets, and in the heat of debate he would sometimes reach into one to extract a small notebook or scrap of paper containing a fact significant to the question of the moment. This trick passed into legend – few knew that the papers were often unimportant or even blank, and that the datum was extracted not from his tail-coat but from some corner of his remarkable memory.

Yet even the cleverest junior minister could not save Balfour's Government. Dispirited by the disruption within his party caused by the Tariff Reform campaign as the Liberals – the scent of blood in their nostrils – were reuniting in their defence of free trade, Balfour finally resigned in December 1905. He had lost his grip on power, and now faced an extended struggle to keep his party together, and to hold on to its leadership. Bonar Law was destined to play a significant role in that drama.

V

The new Liberal premier, Sir Henry Campbell-Bannerman, promptly dissolved Parliament. Elections in those days were spread over several weeks,[23] and the first results in early January 1906 were disastrous for the Conservatives and Liberal Unionists. Many Tory notables fell, and in early polling Balfour lost his own seat in East Manchester, by 2,000 votes.

Bonar Law threw himself into defending his seat. His growing status in his party is illustrated by the fact that Balfour came to Glasgow to support him, while he was himself invited to speak in a number of other constituencies. His efforts in Blackfriars went unrewarded, however. The race was a three-cornered affair in which he faced his old adversary A.D. Provand as well as a Labour candidate, George Barnes. Working-class voters responded to the trade unionist, and both Provand (third, with 2,058 votes) and Bonar Law (2,974) trailed Barnes's poll of 3,284.

Bonar Law had suffered his first electoral defeat: 'You have gone down in the Labour wave,' Joe Chamberlain commiserated.[24] It is a further demonstration of his growing importance to his party that he was among the elect for whom efforts began immediately to find seats. Given the scope of the Liberal victory, it was no easy task. Leaving everything to the party managers, Bonar Law took advantage of his temporary retirement to go with Annie on a brief and long-promised trip to Canada – his sole visit to the Dominion since leaving Kingston.[25]

A seat was soon found for him with the retirement of Rutherford Harris from the safely Unionist south London constituency of Dulwich. When the by-election was held in mid May Bonar Law, despite facing a Liberal opponent who knew the district well, more than trebled the retiring Member's majority, claiming victory by 1,279 votes. His post-bag overflowed with congratulations from Tariff Refomers and Free-Fooders alike, attesting to his popularity and significance on the now-depleted Unionist benches.

The final figures for the 1906 General Election show the scale of the disaster the Unionists had suffered: the Liberals took 400 seats, the Irish Nationalists 83 and the infant Labour party 30; the Conserva-tives and Liberal Unionists had only 157 seats, a reduction of 245 in their representation.[26] To make matters worse, the combined Unionist side was itself divided into pro- and anti-Tariff Reform factions, with Chamberlain's followers outnumbering the Free-Fooders by 109 to 16, the remnant made up of those longing for a peaceful compromise.[27] The outlook was bleak.

The Victorian and Edwardian years in Britain were a time when political leagues and associations of all sorts seemed to proliferate, and the Unionist battles over fiscal reform, followed by an electoral defeat, provided stimulus of the richest sort for just such goings-on. After Chamberlain's great tariff speech his followers organized themselves as the Tariff Reform League, with Lord Ridley as its president, to plump for the programme. Bonar Law was an enthusiastic founding member and joined the governing committee. Other groups which came into existence at this time were less well known to the public. In early 1904, for example, L.S. Amery took the lead in forming the Compatriots, a group of a dozen self-proclaimed experts on various questions of the day. It was decidedly Chamberlainite in its approach to the tariff question, including among its members Lord Milner, former High Commissioner in South Africa, and Professor W.A.S. Hewins, both famous Pro-Tariff imperialists.[28] Though he declined their invitation to offer a theoretical lecture on fiscal reform to one of their meetings – as he tried to avoid all invitations to deliver non-political speeches – Bonar Law indicated his approval of the rather academic pursuits of the Compatriots.[29]

More colourful were the Confederates, a secret organization numbering perhaps fifty, its complete membership known but to a few leaders. This was the creation of several younger Unionists, who included Henry Page Croft, Lord Winterton and Thomas Comyn-Platt, in December 1906. Their principal purpose was to persuade their party leaders, by any means possible, to adopt the entire Tariff Reform programme, for they were among the most dedicated Chamberlainites, the 'Whole-Hoggers'. More ominously, they had the intention of ridding the Party of those, no matter what their rank or influence, whom they considered insufficiently committed to Tariff Reform.

The secrecy surrounding the group irritated their opponents, fascinated the press, and seems to have followed them to the grave: the list of members was never officially revealed.[30] The London *Daily Graphic*, disclosing the results of its own detective efforts in January 1909, concluded that among the members were Lord Duncannon and Lord Winterton, Jesse Collings, Sir Gilbert Parker, J.W. Hills, Page Croft and Bonar Law. In late 1907 Jack Sandars, Balfour's political private secretary, had reported to his master that the group included Edward Goulding, the journalists J.L. Garvin and Leo Maxse – and Bonar Law.[31] The following January, Lord Cecil wrote to his cousin Balfour with his own list of what he considered dangerous and disloyal conspirators – he too included Bonar Law.[32]

Such amateur investigators were often wrong in their conclusions, however. There is no doubt that many senior Tariff Reformers held views on fiscal and imperial matters similar to those of the Confederacy; certainly they worked closely with some of the members to advance the Chamberlainite programme.[33] The most recent research, however, indicates that Bonar Law was not a Confederate.[34] To judge from the few examples of correspondence between the two men and the scattered references in his letters to others, Bonar Law did not think highly of Page Croft, or of his friends. Furthermore, the Confederate leaders' own correspondence with Bonar Law indicates that he was little aware of many of their activities.[35] Perhaps, as it seems Austen Chamberlain did, he knew of and co-operated to some extent with them when their goals coincided with his, while maintaining enough distance to be able to preserve a 'plausible deniability' regarding their covert campaign.[36]

It is clear that tariff enthusiasts among the Unionists had already begun to look to Bonar Law as one of their greatest assets. In January 1907, for example, Lord Ridley of the Tariff Reform League – who was growing impatient with Balfour – expressed a wish to meet Austen Chamberlain and Bonar Law to request that the two take a lead in pressing the fiscal question in the House;[37] a month later Bonar Law summoned a meeting of MPs to encourage Balfour to maintain a strong pro-tariff line with the colonial premiers attending the forthcoming Imperial Conference.[38] By the middle of 1907 the Free-Food Tories had come to regard Bonar Law as one of their principal competitors for the soul of the Party.

The following year a group of Tariff Reformers led by Milner, Amery and Fabian Ware, editor of the Chamberlainite *Morning Post*, sponsored a document which they considered a new 'Unauthorized Programme' for their party.[39] This set forth a bold scheme which included preservation of the Union with Ireland, Tariff Reform, tax revision, restructuring of the House of Lords, social legislation and mandatory military training, and was submitted for the approval of both Austen Chamberlain and Bonar Law.[40] After some moderating influence, particularly from the sceptical Bonar Law, it was published in the *Morning Post* on 12 October 1908.[41]

A sad event following the electoral disaster contributed to push Bonar Law forward among the Tariff Reformers and strengthen his position in the Party. On 9 July 1906 a great celebration was held at the Bingley Hall in Birmingham to honour Joseph Chamberlain on his seventieth birthday, at which Tariff Reformers made up the majority of the Unionist parliamentary contingent. 'Radical Joe' was now the greatest figure in the Opposition party – and surely the achievement of their hearts' delight was only a matter of time. But their joy was cruelly dashed: two days later their hero was struck down with a cerebral haemorrhage from which he never recovered. Sequestered at his Birmingham home, Highbury, like a sort of Tariff Reform oracle, he lived on for eight years. His political career, however, was over.

With Austen Chamberlain, Bonar Law inherited a portion of Joe's mantle. The younger Chamberlain resembled his father right down to the eyeglass and the orchid buttonhole, and at just forty-two was already a Privy Councillor and former Chancellor of the Exchequer. Yet as a hard-hitting and technically masterful defender of the cause he was no match for the less experienced man. Following the Unionist disaster of 1906 Bonar Law, though neither a former Cabinet minister nor yet even a Privy Councillor, joined Balfour's Shadow Cabinet and became a leading Opposition spokesman. In November 1907 Lord Henry Percy, addressing a rally of Middlesex Unionists, summed up the conclusions of many within the party: in recent days, he declared, no one had done more yeoman service for their party, nor had anyone a more brilliant future than Andrew Bonar Law.[42]

There were many who agreed with Lord Henry that Bonar Law was precisely what was wanted. Leo Maxse, editor of the *National Review*, wrote to him immediately after the election débâcle: 'A good many people feel as I do as regards the present situation, and are agreed in looking to you for an independent lead on Tariff reform and many other questions.'[43] Such diverse observers from outside the House as Lord Milner and Alfred Deakin, the Prime Minister of Australia,[44] thought he was precisely the 'forceful lieutenant' which the uncombative Balfour needed to bring life to the Opposition.[45] At dinners in his honour in these years he was praised at the Constitutional Club by Austen Chamberlain, who longed for Tariff Reform, and at the Liberal Unionist Club by Lord Lansdowne, who did not.[46] In early 1907 Austen Chamberlain complained to Lord Ridley that Bonar Law was one of only a handful on the Unionist front bench who could be expected to fight effectively and vigorously for Tariff Reform.[47] Lord Balcarres, from his anxious vantage point in the Whips' Room, even feared in mid 1907 that an activist group of Tariff Reform MPs were preparing to advance the Member for Dulwich as a candidate for the Party Leadership.[48]

In opposition Balfour had continued to temporize on the tariff question, but at the annual party conference in November 1907, held in Chamberlain's Birmingham, he seemed at last to embrace the idea, to the point at least of endorsing retaliatory imposts to safeguard British industry.[49] Though some extreme tariff enthusiasts may have doubted the sincerity of his conversion, Bonar Law, who was most interested in such practical issues, appeared satisfied. He even allowed himself a certain optimism, writing to Deakin in January 1908: 'Balfour is now definitely fighting on the right side and I think he is going to carry his Party almost solidly with him and his leadership on the right side has always seemed to me the only thing necessary to make success assured.'[50] He may have been the darling of the Tariff Reformers, a party warrior admired by all loyal Unionists, but at this point Bonar Law still considered Balfour indispensable, and meant to concentrate on the task of holding up his arms.

3

'The coming man'

I

BONAR LAW'S GROWING political success required that he settle his family in London, and in the summer of 1908 he found the house which was to remain his home until high office brought him an official residence. For £2,500 he bought the lease on Pembroke Lodge in Edwardes Square, south of Holland Park.[1] Pembroke Lodge was a large house with a walled garden – and a tennis court, on which over the next eight years virtually every noteworthy Unionist enthusiast of the day tested his skill. Bonar Law's regular walks frequently took him along Kensington High Street, that agreeable thoroughfare of urban bustle which to him was as congenial as his dales to a country gentleman. Asquith later characterized the house as mean and rather *déclassé*; like its owner, however, Pembroke Lodge showed a modest and sturdy face to the world, but made a deeper impression on those who took the time to see inside.

After eight years in Parliament Bonar Law had become a popular figure in the House, particularly among the *habitués* of the Smoking Room, where his chess board and his pipe were familiar sights. An ambitious man and a fierce partisan in the Chamber, his quiet reserve and gentle sense of humour earned him friendships among Members of all parties which endured through his life and set him apart in the ego-driven world of national politics. Many years later he wrote candidly to the Liberal, Sir Donald Maclean: 'I always thought and fancy I said it to you more than once that your time of leading your party very much resembled my own experience and that in each case the success came because the House of Commons rather liked us.'[2]

Bonar Law continues to be remembered as 'unclubbable' (as his tee-totalism made him 'unpubbable'), a misconception reinforced by his annual entries in *Who's Who*, which were unrevealingly stark. In fact he had quite naturally joined the Carlton Club, as was expected of any Unionist Member, and probably also the Constitutional Club. He belonged to the rather athletically-inclined Bath Club, then located in Dover Street, and used its comfortable premises frequently in pre-war years. Though it was true that he found tedious the dinners which were an inevitable part of parliamentary life, Bonar Law always enjoyed inter-esting company and conversation – especially if the talk was about pol-itics. Hence he became a founding member of the rather glamorous Other Club, a dining society formed in 1911 by Winston Churchill, F.E. Smith, and forty other well-connected notables. They gathered monthly for lively conversation and splendid food, often at the Café Royal: Bonar Law invariably preferred the discourse and cigars which followed the extravagant meals and wines.[3]

Not surprisingly, his closest associates in these days were drawn from political life: they included Austen Chamberlain; the Tariff Reform Member for Worcester, Edward 'Paddy' Goulding; and the brilliant bar-rister and newly-elected MP Frederick Edwin Smith (known universally as 'F.E.'). He also became friendly with several Liberals, including the target for his maiden speech – Lloyd George, now President of the Board of Trade.[4]

Their initial engagement in 1901 was only the first of many duels in the House between these two combative spirits, fighting under different flags; but the mutual understanding which underlay their rivalry was not so unlikely as it may seem. Lloyd George was even more of an outsider than Bonar Law: he was cottage-bred, un-English, and possessed no more of the usual earmarks of political leadership than did the New Brunswick parson's son. When he became Chancellor of the Exchequer in 1908, Bonar Law congratulated him in a revealing private letter:

In one respect at least I am not a Tory (or what is supposed to be a Tory) – it always gives me pleasure to see success attained by merit alone & without any outside aids. Your success has been more rapid even than Mr Chamberlain's & you might now be thinking of the Scriptural warning about those of whom all men think well.[5]

Politics in 1909 was to be illuminated by the opening engagements of a ferocious political conflict which would continue until the outbreak of the Great War, and Bonar Law was to play first a supporting, ultimately a major role in it. On the eve of these important events, just as his public and private lives seemed to be so satisfying, he was struck by a personal tragedy that for a time rendered both totally empty. During the spring Annie Law had felt continually unwell, lacking her usual vitality. During the summer Bonar Law took a villa in a favourite family holiday spot near the Ayrshire coast so that she might enjoy the sea air and regain her strength, but it seemed to do her little good.

When her condition did not improve by the end of summer Annie reluctantly sought medical advice, and was referred to an eminent consultant in Leeds. An immediate operation for the removal of her gall bladder was prescribed, and the surgery was carried out on 28 October. Hopeful initial signs for recovery were misleading; her condition rapidly deteriorated, and Annie Law died suddenly on 31 October 1909, at the age of forty-two.

As she had wished, her funeral and burial were in Helensburgh. Many hundreds came to pay their final respects to the popular wife of a local hero, and the sad and stately procession stretched for some two miles from Ferniegair to the churchyard where she was laid to rest. Bonar Law said many times thereafter that he never forgot a single sad detail of that day.[6]

He was devastated, for the second time in his life. Annie had been his only love; their life together had been extraordinarily happy, and she had given him six children. He always praised her as his support in his business career and, though she was never comfortable in the public glare, as his helpmate and fellow campaigner in politics; she had lightly borne with his idiosyncrasies, and gloried in his successes. For several weeks he was simply unable to deal with the reality of her death. Unconsoled by religion and beyond the reach of friends and family, he fell for a while into a depression reminiscent of the dark times which had plagued his father.

He was retrieved from the edge, as he would be again, by the only palliative which could distract him: his work. The tragedy came at a time when it seemed his party – perhaps Conservatism itself – was at great risk, and he threw himself into politics more completely than ever. The public platform was now familiar ground to him, and he embarked on a demanding national speaking tour. He wrote to Lord Milner a month after Annie's death: '... though making speeches used to be a source of unhappiness to me I find that I am less miserable doing that than any-thing else & I have in consequence, rather foolishly I think now, placed myself in the hands of my committee ...'[7] Work provided distraction, fatigue and thus some measure of rest, and was to be his salvation.

Bonar Law had concerns which took precedence even over politics: his six children, the eldest fifteen, the youngest but four. Following the death of his own mother his aunt, Janet Kidston, had changed his life; his sister, Mary Law, once again took charge of his household, and sim-ilarly touched his children's lives. She came to be remembered by his intimates as 'Aunt Mary', though only her nieces and nephews would ever have dared address her thus. She cared for them and supported them, though perhaps she lacked the spontaneity of someone naturally at home in the company of children. It cannot have been easy for a middle-aged spinster, comfortable in her own life, to take on a large young family. She did so with great success, however, and was much loved in return.

Mary Law was fiercely dedicated to her brother and had a strong sense of his destiny – a conviction of which he gently made light throughout their life together. She had the gifts of all careful listeners, and he always valued her candid response to every issue on which he consulted her. He trusted her common sense and her honesty as he did those of few others in his career; in her turn, she seldom advised against a decision she sensed he had already made.

A strong-willed woman, Mary Law laid down certain conditions for her new life. She reluctantly agreed that when it was absolutely neces-sary she would act as Bonar Law's hostess at Pembroke Lodge, but it was a duty she gladly surrendered to her elder niece, Isabel, in later years. She enjoyed political talk and became very fond of several of her brother's associates, but she would not consent to accompany him in public or into the social life which accompanied his high political profile. When he became party leader and his social duties increased, she made it very clear that she intended to remain essentially invisible; and Bonar Law made sure that her wishes were respected.[8]

While it may be true that time often heals the deepest wounds, the shock of Annie's death left damage that was never truly repaired. Bonar Law had always been a grave man, but after this loss those who knew him commented that he habitually bore an air of sadness. It is not too melodramatic, then, to say that two things saved him from the worst effects of the second crushing loss of his life: his family – for the remainder of his life he was never truly happy unless surrounded by his children – and his deep commitment to his political work. The future Prime Minister Stanley Baldwin is reputed to have said of Bonar Law that: 'After his wife's death, ambition began to die.'[9] If ambition encompasses relentless effort and the pursuit of success, then Baldwin was quite wrong about his friend and patron. Bonar Law, to whom work was always congenial, from this point regarded his political career not only as a demanding task of national importance, but as an antidote to what sometimes seemed unutterable loneliness.

II

Few parliamentarians could recall a time when political battles were engaged with more bitterness than in these pre-war years. Unionists were not so wrapped up in their own differences over tariffs as to forget that the Liberals now controlled a crushing majority in the House of Commons and could, it appeared, do as they wished. Yet Balfour defiantly asserted that his party would continue to 'control, whether in Power or whether in Opposition, the destinies of this great Empire.'[10] What he meant, of course, was that the Unionists were prepared to use their own overwhelming majority in the House of Lords to block Government bills of which they disapproved – and they disapproved of much of the Liberal programme. In the sessions which followed the formation of a Liberal Government their Lordships vetoed or amended beyond recognition major bills dealing with education, plural voting, agricultural holdings, Irish farm tenants' rights and the licensing of public houses – all of which had passed through the Commons.

In June 1907 the Government majority in the Commons angrily passed a non-legislative resolution calling for the reform of the Upper House and recognition of the final authority of the House of Commons – and there the matter remained for a time. A change in Cabinet leadership in April 1908 weighed heavily on the debate: the ailing Campbell-Bannerman[11] resigned office and was succeeded by Herbert Henry Asquith. The new Prime Minister was most unlike his predecessor. Sophisticated, charming and sly, he had long since left behind his middle-class Yorkshire roots to become a doyen of the London Bar, and had made a socially brilliant second marriage. His debating skills had earned him the sobriquet 'the Hammer'; his intention was to remain in office for a long time, no matter what mischief the Tories might have in mind.

By this time the Liberals had other worries: in by-elections held between August 1906 and October 1909 they lost twelve seats to Unionists and another six to Labourites. Their Lordships' roadblock had become a serious problem, as had the challenge of financing, in good Free Trade order, an ambitious naval building programme inherited from their predecessors as well as their own social agenda, including the potentially expensive 1908 Old Age Pensions Act, with which the Lords had feared to tamper.

Lloyd George, now Chancellor, revealed his solution to the impasse in his famous People's Budget of April 1909. Through a combination of traditional tax increases and innovative duties, which included surtaxes on higher incomes and profoundly controversial taxes on land values, he sought to fund the new social programmes and regain the initiative for the Government. Centuries-long convention had it, of course, that money bills – Budgets – were never tampered with by the House of Lords.

The now legendary struggle over this Budget was waged in public and in Parliament through the summer and into the autumn of 1909. After it had staggered through some five hundred divisions in the Commons, the Unionist peers thundered in their own House their disapproval of a Budget they claimed would introduce a fundamental constitutional innovation disguised as a revenue bill. Finally, on 30 November, they plucked up their courage and overwhelmingly rejected it. A precedent had been challenged, and only the electorate could decide the issue.

Bonar Law was not enthusiastic about the use of their Lordships' axe to destroy the work of a Commons majority – even a Liberal one – yet also feared that the Liberalism envisaged by his friend Lloyd George was treading close to the socialist collectivism he himself so distrusted. Furthermore, like the Unionist peers he suspected that Lloyd George was using a money bill in order to slip past the Upper House a major constitutional change in the British political and economic system.[12]

When the Lords rejected the Budget, Bonar Law was still in deep mourning for Annie, and the election campaign which followed in December provided him with a reason for ceaseless, distracting, exhausting activity. He threw himself into the centre of the fight. It was the longest election in British history, with polling spread over twenty-six days, and Unionists were cautiously hopeful about the outcome. In November the party's Chief Agent, Percival Hughes, predicted gains, in the event of an election, in the Home Counties, the south-east and the west of England (the Midlands and the north looked less promising) and noted that, despite the important constitutional questions at issue, the warmest response to Unionist campaigning came at the mention of Tariff Reform and Imperial Preference.[13]

Balfour was ill during much of December and early January, so that Bonar Law, Austen Chamberlain and F.E. Smith were in demand as the most effective speakers on the Tory side. His secure seat allowed Bonar Law to spend much of his time campaigning up and down the country, and still hold Dulwich against his Liberal challenger, H.E. Cotton, by a generous majority of 2,418 votes.[14] The overall result, however, was more confused. The Liberals secured only 275 seats, a loss of 125 compared with 1906; the Unionists won 273 seats, gaining 116.[15] Despite this improved showing, the results were a disappointment to the Unionists: the Government majority remained secure, as they retained the support of 40 Labourites and 82 Irish Nationalists; and nothing less than a conclusive victory could have vindicated the action of the Unionist peers.

Though the Unionists had secured 300,000 more votes than the Liberals they had failed to carry the election, and now the Budget was quietly passed through the Upper House. The Parliamentary battle now progressed to a constitutional question: what was to be the role of the House of Lords regarding legislation passed by the Lower House? Asquith, determined to end the peers' interference and bruised by the recent election results, in late February introduced a Bill to eliminate altogether the power of the House of Lords to veto finance bills, and to ensure that all other bills which had passed through the Commons during three successive sessions within two years were presented for the Royal Assent regardless of the concurrence of the Upper House. The Tories, predictably, opposed the Bill, and partisan battle lines became more clearly drawn than ever.

While Balfour, Lord Lansdowne (the Unionist leader in the Upper House) and others led the fight over the powers of the House of Lords, Bonar Law's attentions in the following months were largely concentrated on the continuing party dialogue over Tariff Reform. If anything, the election had added fuel to the fiscal debate: as Hughes had also predicted, the Tories had had little joy in their hope of increasing their representation in traditionally Free Trade Lancashire. Some within the party took it as a sign that certain portions of the Chamberlainite programme required discreet and rapid interment. Bonar Law resisted such arguments, however, and in January 1910 wrote at length to Lord

Salisbury, son of the great Victorian Prime Minister, who had urged that tariff proposals be scrapped. To renege on the commitment to Tariff Reform, Bonar Law argued, would 'cause a division within our Party more complete and more hopeless than has existed at any time since the fiscal controversy was raised.' He stressed also that to his mind there was no electoral advantage to be gained by dropping the tariff programme; rather, that Tariff Reform was the paramount reason for their gains in the recent election. Finally, he emphasized to Salisbury that the abandonment of the call for food duties would neutralize all hope of further unity with the Empire.[16] Though Salisbury was sceptical, Bonar Law held to his conviction that Tariff Reform remained the 'first constructive work' of the party (words with which even Balfour had agreed), and that to abandon it would split the party from top to bottom.

More pressing political matters intruded, however: in April, Asquith announced that he would press forward with his plan to reduce the powers of the Lords and settle the unfinished constitutional crisis. Then, on 6 May, the nation was stunned by the news that King Edward VII had died after a brief illness. He was sixty when he came to the throne in 1901, and few seem to have expected much of him. Yet he had earned the affection of his people, and he was sincerely mourned. In the midst of a political stand-off, convention demanded a period of seemly mourning under the inexperienced new king. While some must have wondered what to do next, there came an unexpected suggestion from an unforeseen quarter: on 8 May 1910 J.L. Garvin, the editor of the *Observer*, published a leading article calling for an extraordinary conference of political leaders in which the most divisive constitutional issues should be openly discussed and settled 'before conflict is irrevocably joined on terms of war to the knife.'[17]

The bold suggestion of a 'Truce of God' proved irresistible, and just such a conference of party leaders met at Buckingham Palace some twenty times between mid June and early November. The Unionists were represented by Balfour, Lansdowne, Austen Chamberlain and the former First Lord of the Admiralty, Lord Cawdor.[18] Bonar Law played no direct role; nor did the Irish Unionist leader, Sir Edward Carson, who wrote in midsummer to Lady Londonderry: 'How dull everything is at present. I wish the conference was over or the king would fall in love or Arthur Balfour would get into the divorce court.'[19] Carson's mischievous hopes may have outstripped reality, but just beyond his purview certain events anything but dull were unfolding.

These events began in mid October with the presentation by Lloyd

George to Balfour of an adventurous proposal for the compromise of party differences and the creation of a bipartisan Cabinet with a hybrid programme encompassing Irish Home Rule, national insurance and poor law reforms, national military training, Imperial reorganization and perhaps even Tariff Reform.[20] The contents of the 'Lloyd George Memorandum' were known to the eight conferees and to a small number of other party leaders – perhaps some fifteen in all – but were discussed informally (and in secret) only between Lloyd George and Balfour. Balfour's political secretary J.S. Sandars preserved an empty envelope which once certainly contained either the document itself or notes on Lloyd George's explanation of it. On this is written:[21]

> N.B. Those who knew of this besides
> members of the conference were
> F.E. Smith
> Bonar Law
> Garvin

Though rumours of course circulated, the existence of the celebrated memorandum was never revealed either to the Cabinet or the Unionist Shadow Cabinet. Bonar Law was brought in to the secret almost from the outset, Lloyd George having expressly authorized F.E. Smith, his envoy to the Tories, to do so.[22] The episode is intriguing in all its parts but, given what lay ahead, at least one aspect of the proposal is of particular interest – the Chancellor's suggestion to Balfour that the knotty Irish problem might be settled through a kind of federal reorganization of the United Kingdom: not merely Irish Home Rule, but 'Devolution', or 'Home Rule All Round', as it came to be called. Equally interesting was the fact that as it was discreetly put about there were discovered members of the Unionist Party willing at least to consider the idea. These included Austen Chamberlain, Garvin, Goulding, Smith and Sandars (who knew of the memorandum) as well as Lord Milner, Alfred Lyttelton, L.S. Amery and Earl Grey (who probably did not). Bonar Law, with ties to federal Canada as well as to Ulster and Scotland, was certainly prepared to discuss the plan as an alternative to the desperate struggle over Home Rule which removal of the Lords' veto would make inevitable.[23]

The plan was, of course, doomed to be stifled at birth. Recalling for him the fate of Peel and his party in 1846, on 2 November Balfour informed Lloyd George that his scheme was simply impossible. A few days later the Conference dissolved, having accomplished nothing.[24] This meant a return to partisan business as usual, and Asquith announced that there was now no alternative but, for the second time in a year, to seek from the electorate a confirmation of his course. He had also made it clear to King George V, who had been reluctant to make any commitments of his own before another election, that a Government victory would necessitate His Majesty's agreement to the creation of a sufficient number of peers to ensure passage through the Lords of a bill reducing the powers of the Upper House.

III

During the summer of 1910 the idea had surfaced among certain influential Unionists that it would be a fine test of the electoral viability of the Chamberlainite programme if a notable Tariff Reformer were to fight a Manchester constituency in the coming election. The city polled early, and it was thought that a Tariff Reform victory in the historic home of Free Trade would be widely acclaimed and perhaps set off an electoral trend. Edward Goulding enthusiastically supported the idea, and wrote to Bonar Law on 4 August that he and Sandars had concluded: 'What was needed was for some front bencher to take his life in his hands & fight Manchester & give the lead to the country.'[25]

Goulding also announced that he had discussed the idea with Lord Derby and Garvin, and all were enthusiastically agreed that Bonar Law was the man for the important task. Derby, a Lancashire magnate with no love for Tariff Reform, wrote to him the same day: 'I shall not mention my own gratitude – but the gratitude of the party would be beyond description.'[26] Bonar Law considered the idea for a month, and his response (from Brittany, where he had gone for a weekend of golf) was guarded: he saw the logic behind the scheme and was prepared to consider it, though he wondered what would be the impact on Tariff Reform and on the party of a defeat.[27] Balfour, writing to Bonar Law, leapt at a notion which might settle the divisive fiscal debate one way or the other and which, after all, threatened him with no personal risk.[28] Bonar Law replied to Balfour that he was willing to take the plunge, though he intended to withhold a firm commitment until he had spoken to the Manchester Tories, which he planned to do early the following month. He pointed out once again his fear that a defeat would injure the party and, though he did not mention it to Balfour, Tariff Reform itself.[29]

Immediately following a Shadow Cabinet meeting on 8 November 1910, Bonar Law travelled to Manchester, where the Tory party managers enthusiastically endorsed what he now called 'the escapade'. In London five days later he was summoned to a late-night meeting of Unionist notables in a committee room of the Constitutional Club. In the chair was the Chief Whip, Sir Alexander Acland-Hood, and present were Lord Ridley, Smith, Carson, Goulding, Sandars and Garvin; the subject was the place of Tariff Reform in the election programme. Garvin, the influential editor with impeccable Tariff Reform credentials, surprised the meeting by declaring that the most controversial element of the 'Whole Hog' programme – duties on imported food – had to be shelved if the next election were to be won. Only Sandars and Carson immediately supported him, and when the meeting adjourned in the early hours of the morning, no decision had been reached as to what should be recommended to Balfour.

Bonar Law, having seen first-hand the discomfort among Manchester Tories at the mere mention of duties on footstuffs, had himself concluded that a commitment to such imposts was not absolutely necessary to initiate a first phase of Tariff Reform. He was equally certain that fiscal reform remained the party's most popular offering, but continued to fear the possibility of an upheaval among the Chamberlainites if they suspected that the programme was to be abandoned. The Unionist Whip Lord Balcarres noted his agreement in his diary of 16 November: pro- and anti-food duty party factions seemed primed for a struggle, and a summary jettisoning of food imposts from the electoral programme would probably split the party. 'Discomfort of the situation grows,' he noted.[30] The following day, at Nottingham, Balfour for the moment forestalled Chamberlainite anxieties by reiterating – in rather oblique terms – his commitment to Tariff Reform. Asquith's response, on 18 November, was to announce that Parliament would be dissolved on the twenty-eighth. Within those ten days, Bonar Law was to be drawn even deeper into the party scramble over tariff policy.

During this year of political deadlock the idea came under consideration in Westminster of employing a popular referendum as a means of settling, conclusively, issues which appeared to be insoluble by normal means.[31] It was particularly attractive to Unionists, who faced a Liberal–Labour–Irish parliamentary majority despite having themselves won more votes than any other party. If provision for a referendum could somehow be wedged into the Constitution, then perhaps their own proposals might be carried despite their recent disappointing electoral fortunes.[32]

The use of a referendum was also among the ideas the Unionist delegates at the abortive constitutional conference had put forward as a solution to House of Lords reform – not one which appealed to the Liberals. Provision for a referendum in cases of deadlock between the Houses of Parliament was included in Lord Lansdowne's bill for reform of the Upper House, debated in the Lords on 23 November 1910. Lord Crewe, the Liberal Leader, responded immediately: if the Unionists so strongly favoured referenda, let them submit their hearts' delight, Tariff Reform, to one.[33]

Balfour gave his answer to the challenge before a crowd of ten thousand at the Royal Albert Hall on Tuesday, 29 November, announcing: 'I have not the least objection to submitting the principles of Tariff Reform to a Referendum.' An optimist in the audience was cheered by the rest when he shouted, 'That's won the election!'[34] In explaining this bombshell to a stunned and angry Austen Chamberlain, Balfour referred to what came to be called his Referendum Pledge as 'Bonar Law's proposal', and Joe's son and heir found it difficult to forgive either of them.[35]

The Pledge was no more 'Bonar Law's proposal' than it was that of any number of Tories who rained advice on their leader in late 1910. More than anything else, it was a characteristic Balfourian tactic to escape an extremely difficult locus. Bonar Law had returned to Manchester on Saturday 26 November to meet Edward E. Marsden, the Unionist editor of the influential *Textile Mercury*. The two discussed party prospects for the election, and the editor found – as had the secret meeting at the Constitutional Club twelve days earlier – that Bonar Law was more open-minded on the subject of food duties than were certain other Tariff Reformers. According to Marsden, they agreed that an advance commitment to a popular referendum on any proposed Tariff Reform legislation might just win the Unionists the election. Emphasizing Bonar Law's agreement, Marsden had telegraphed the idea to J.L. Garvin, who was himself anxious for the party to escape the 'food tax' label. Garvin had trumpeted the idea in the *Observer* the next day, Sunday, and coupled it with a challenge for a similar pledge from the Liberals regarding Irish Home Rule.[36] He also worked assiduously through J.S. Sandars to bring Balfour to make a public announcement of his commitment to the plan. He need not have worried: the referendum idea was a perfect solution to Balfour's problem, and he seized it with both hands. He hoped it would allow him, on the one hand to placate the Chamberlainites by demonstrating that he stood by the spirit of Tariff Reform, yet on the other to conduct an election without the burden of what Free Traders damned as food taxes.

Inspired by Garvin, the Unionist press – the London *Morning Post* and the *Birmingham Mail* were exceptions – took up the idea, and Balfour's own correspondence began to turn heavily in favour of a tariff referendum. Meanwhile, Bonar Law had explained himself to his leader in a letter, written on the twenty-sixth but which did not reach Balfour until the morning of Monday, 28 November. To pledge a referendum, he asserted:

> ... would destroy the whole of the attack on the referendum as part of the proposals in regard to the relations between the two Houses which have been put forward by Lansdowne, and I cannot help thinking that it would make certain of securing the votes all over the country of people who still believe in Free Trade but are Unionist otherwise. From the point of view of Tariff Reform I cannot at the moment see that there is much objection to it, because we obviously could not carry a big change like this without a decent majority, and I doubt if we should want to carry it if we thought the country would give an adverse decision by means of the referendum.

However, he cautioned,

> Of course, if it is to be done it must be done quickly, or it would be of no use, and I can hardly say that I feel I have given enough thought to it even to recommend it; but I do think that it is worth your consideration.[37]

Bonar Law telegraphed to Sandars on the day of the Albert Hall address, clarifying his position still further:

> All wealthy Unionists, even strong tariff reformers, would say such declaration would mean victory but I find all working class audiences only interested in Tariff Reform and declaration would do no good with them and might damp enthusiasm of best workers ...

Finally, like J.L. Garvin, he preferred a pledge with certain strings:[38]

> Would there be any use in saying [that] if government undertake[,] in event of their obtaining majority[,] not to pass Home Rule without Referendum, we should give same undertaking regarding Tariff Reform[?][39]

Careful reading of this correspondence indicates that both Balfour and Marsden exaggerated Bonar Law's position regarding the referendum idea (and, in the case of Balfour's explanation to Austen Chamberlain, his paternity of it); and certainly overstated Bonar Law's influence over his leader. Balfour's closest associate at this time was Lord Lansdowne, an enthusiastic convert to the idea of a referendum as part of House of Lords reform and apparently the only party leader who saw much of Balfour in the two days before his Albert Hall speech. Furthermore, the impact of Garvin's press campaign and the large and steady influx of pro-referendum correspondence to Balfour were significant. Finally, it should not be forgotten that it was seldom Arthur Balfour could be jostled in a direction he did not wish to take – in politics, as in life. He chose to issue the Referendum Pledge because he thought it the best way of escaping the Liberals' accusation that a Tory victory meant food taxes; it was also the best plan on offer which had any chance of winning the coming election. Ascribing the credit for conceiving the idea to Bonar Law, one of their brightest stars, was a useful tactic for deflecting the anger of the Tariff Reformers.

At the Royal Albert Hall on 29 November Balfour did challenge the Liberals to submit Home Rule to such a plebiscite. Despite the advice of Bonar Law and Garvin, however, he failed to make his own referendum commitment contingent on any Liberal action. When polling ended, on 19 December 1910, the results left the major parties in virtually the same position as after the January election.[40] Despite all the excitement, the Referendum Pledge had had no effect on the election; but because of the debate, Tariff Reform would never be quite the same.

Bonar Law always insisted that the campaign in North-west Manchester was the hardest-fought of his career. His opponent, Sir George Kemp, was a popular local textile manufacturer, a hero of the Boer War and a former Lancashire county cricketer. A former Unionist (like Winston Churchill, who had once held it) who had crossed the floor over the tariff issue, he had himself narrowly won the seat in January. Manchester polled early, and Bonar Law gave the contest all he had. Churchill, now Home Secretary and ensconced in a safe seat at Dundee, began his campaign in the constituency. This looks like a response to the popular tale that Bonar Law had challenged Churchill to a direct fight for North-west Manchester, the loser to remain out of Parliament until the next general election.[41] In the event, the loser of such a duel would not have had another chance until 1918 – an outcome to ponder.

In the end, Kemp was victorious by 5,559 votes to 5,114. Bonar Law was disappointed, though in the end his defeat proved to be in many ways at least as good as a victory. Having sacrificed his safe Dulwich seat to lose narrowly on hostile ground after a monumental struggle against considerable odds – all widely covered in the press – he emerged as a genuine Tory hero. Despite the annoyance of some 'Whole Hoggers' who suspected him to have indeed been the true author of the Referendum Pledge, the aftermath of the December election saw his position in the party much advanced. Lord Derby did not love Bonar Law's Tariff Reform views, but deeply respected what he had done for the party. He wrote to a friend after the election that Bonar Law was '*the* coming man in the Party.'[42] Bonar Law did not exaggerate when he said in later years that the spirited defeat he suffered in North-West Manchester did more for him in the party than a hundred victories.[43] A final irony of this tale is that in February the party warrior was returned for the safe seat of Bootle, at the mouth of the estuary of the River Mersey: for the next eight years he was to represent a Lancashire constituency after all.

IV

The new Parliament met on 6 February 1911, and the first item of business on the Government agenda was to settle the question of the House of Lords veto. Increasingly bitter party battles since the 1909 Budget had taken a terrible toll of nerves on both sides of the floor. Nor can the realities of 1911 have eased Unionist frustrations: Asquith and the Liberals could command a renewed majority in the Commons, and a guarantee that the King would create a sufficient number of peers to overwhelm the Unionist advantage in the Upper House. In May the Prime Minister passed through the Lower House his Parliament Bill stripping the Lords of their unrestricted veto over legislation approved by the Commons. The new Bill also promised a comprehensive reform of the Upper House – a point of which Unionists took careful note.

Most Unionists, Balfour among them, concluded that the game was lost and declined to fight on – hence they were said to be 'hedging'. Irreconcilables followed the octogenarian former Lord Chancellor,

Lord Halsbury, who preferred to battle until the end and 'die in the last ditch', so the intra-party battle was said to be that of Hedgers versus Ditchers. On 21 July the Shadow Cabinet chose reality over romance: the Unionist Lords were commanded to let the Parliament Bill through. Bonar Law had hoped for a moderate, prompt and thorough reform of the Upper House,[44] but was content with the decision and far more concerned with matters of fiscal reform and Irish Home Rule.

On 26 July, Bonar Law revealed his conclusions in a letter to *The Times*: 'The bold course for any man', he wrote, 'is always the course which he himself thinks right.' But to pursue an uncompromising policy would lead only to disaster, and in a few months' time, 'if Lord Lansdowne had allowed the House of Lords to be swamped [with Liberal peers], and the Government are carrying in a single session bills to establish Home Rule, to disestablish the Church of Wales, and gerrymander the constituencies, then the Unionists of the country would not be praising the courage but cursing the folly of their leaders.' He had no time for the passionate rejectionism of the Tory Die-Hards and preferred the Parliament Act because – what would not have been the case if the Government had been forced to create regiments of peers – it offered the possibility of a two-year delay in the passing of contentious legislation. In his view this preserved a glimmer of hope. The letter concluded with words, the full portent of which perhaps even their author did not fully comprehend at this point:

> [The Lords] can delay for instance the Expiring Laws Continuance Bill or the Army Annual Act, and such action on their part would undoubtedly make the continuance of the Government impossible and compel an election ... It might or might not be wise to use this power, but if I am right in thinking that the House of Lords would have the means of compelling an election before Home Rule became law, that surely is not a power which ought to be lightly abandoned.

Rage though they might – and in an unseemly scene on 24 July the Tory Die-Hards in the Commons literally howled down the Prime Minister – the irreconcilables could not stop what had become inevitable.[45] On 1 August, the Parliament Bill passed the Lords by a vote of 131 to 114.[46] Not waiting for the outcome, Balfour had already taken the boat train to the Continent, *en route* to his favourite retreat in Bad-Gastein. For months to come, many in his party would find it difficult to forgive him for his acquiescence. Bonar Law had no time for Die-Hard recriminations: the passage of the Bill meant only that the fight lying ahead would be even harder – and now perhaps only another election could save the nation from Irish Home Rule.

V

In these difficult days the coronation of the new Sovereign, on 22 June, provided a brief respite from politics. In the Honours List customarily issued on such occasions, Bonar Law was appointed a Privy Councillor. It was indicative of his success in the House that this was at the behest of the Prime Minister – certainly no admirer of the new Member for Bootle – and warmly seconded by Balfour.[47] This was the only occasion on which Bonar Law's name appeared in an Honours List, and membership of the Privy Council was the only prize of its kind for which he ever felt any desire. The reason is enlightening: he was, as we have seen, an ambitious man who sought success first in business, then in politics. Membership of the Privy Council was evidence of party seniority and came usually to those who had already attained or could realistically aspire to high office. To be the Rt Hon. Andrew Bonar Law reflected the reality of the political power and recognition that he craved, not the decorative trappings, seductive though they were to many, then as now. He seems to have been simply unable to fathom the aspirations of those, whether in public life or not, who took pleasure in collecting titles or letters after their names. Years later, Lord Beaverbrook reached a similar conclusion:

> It was strange that he could not see in his desire to attain the front bench and to make successful speeches a parallel emotion to that of the well-to-do backbencher who wanted a Baronetcy or even sympathize with a Tory Brewer who had cast his eye on the Upper House. But the fact remains that from start to finish of his career he could not understand the desire for honours and would not make party profit out of it.[48]

The passage of the Parliament Act marked the end of eighteen months of intense struggle which had cost Bonar Law's party much in unity and perhaps in confidence. There was to be little time for rest, however, as the Government prepared to make good its promises to pass into law such contentious matters as Disestablishment of the Church of Wales and Home Rule in Ireland. The prospect stirred many loyal Unionists to paroxysms of fury, and it was clear that the corrosive fights which lay just behind them might be eclipsed in bitterness during the months

ahead. Given the bruises the party had collected in three straight electoral losses, in the debate over tariffs and in the political emasculation of
the Tory preserve of the House of Lords, it was understandable that
attention should come to focus on the party leadership.

4

Party Leader

DESPITE HIS IMPRESSIVE capacity for political work, Pembroke Lodge was more than ever the centre of Bonar Law's life after Annie's death. After he became Chief Whip, Lord Balcarres frequently complained of his leader's disturbing 'tendency to go home to dinner every night – "need I stay?" is a question put to me twenty times in thirty days!'[1] Yet despite the solicitous support of his sister Mary and the love of a houseful of bumptious children, in many ways Bonar Law remained a lonely man. Shortly before Annie's death, however, he had met a man to whom, to his great satisfaction, he was subsequently to grow as close as to a brother. This was William Maxwell Aitken, the future Lord Beaverbrook, and their initial acquaintance developed into a friendship which was to endure until they were parted by death.

Born in 1879, Max Aitken shared with Bonar Law antecedents both Scottish and Ulster; more remarkably, he too was the son of a Presbyterian minister in New Brunswick.[2] He took to business as easily as had Bonar Law, and his entrepreneurial gifts were such that he was a millionaire before his thirtieth birthday. Unlike his friend, Max Aitken found limitless pleasure in making money and exercising the power and influence it brought.

Encouraged by the City financier and politician Ion Hamilton Benn, the twenty-nine-year-old Aitken sought out his fellow New Brunswicker on his first short trip to London in September 1908, and managed to sell him bonds worth $5000 (Canadian).[3] In later years Aitken loved to quip that Bonar Law bought the securities only to be rid of his importunate younger self – but $5000 was a large sum of money in those days, and Bonar Law was anything but rash in matters of finance. He understood the Canadian investment market and knew an opportunity when he saw it – the gamble turned out to be a good one.[4] Aitken soon offered further financial proposals, and Benn replied in February 1909 that both he and Bonar Law were willing to put a substantial amount of money into his hands 'to be in your inner circle'.[5] Accordingly, early in the following October Bonar Law bought a £5000-interest in Aitken's latest investment project, the Royal Securities Corporation. Having set aside his business career but with a young family to provide for, he was not averse to a sizeable low-risk investment with an entrepreneur who was rapidly earning a reputation as something of a financial wizard.

When the two met again in 1910, the lives of both were much changed.[6] Aitken's business and political ambitions had convinced him to make Britain his permanent home; Bonar Law was a solitary widower, much wrapped up in Westminster politics. This was Aitken's chance to make an impression on an influential politician with Canadian roots and imperialist credentials who could act as the patron he needed to establish himself in Britain. In the early autumn they met for the third time, at a luncheon given by a mutual friend, Edward Goulding. The conversation on this occasion turned as much on politics as on business, and the two got on very well. Aitken soon afterwards offered his new friend membership in a select investment syndicate. The entrance tariff was $100,000 (Canadian), a fortune in the money of 1910, which Bonar Law was happy to remit.[7] When the enterprise was wound up two years later, he took away $200,000. Thereafter, the business correspondence between the two men was constant and voluminous, and Aitken's financial acumen profited Bonar Law handsomely throughout his career.[8]

While the getting of money was a strong force in bringing the two men together, it soon became secondary to the friendship which rapidly developed. Despite their similarity of background, by any other measure the two were thoroughly unlike. Aitken was brilliant, energetic and impulsive: Montreal had proved too small a field for his financial buccaneering and political aspirations. Bonar Law was steady, thoughtful and, particularly since his bereavement, grave. He understood and respected ambition and success, however, with which Aitken was superabundantly endowed. He recognized in the younger man warmth, excitement, and a kind of sympathy which touched him. Each had a characteristic sense of humour – Aitken's rather puckish and outgoing, Bonar Law's gentle and in a lower key – that complemented the other's, and each was at the time quite lonely. Aitken saw in Bonar Law a man of stature, probity and Empire-mindedness, and of adamantine stability, amply qualified to be the political and personal hero he sought. Bonar Law was touched by Aitken's dedicated loyalty, and found him a trust-worthy outlet for his innermost thoughts, while his ready humour was often able to bring the older man out of the periodic depression which plagued him.

Aitken wished to launch himself on a political career, and his energy, commitment to Tariff Reform and, not least of all, his great wealth made him an attractive catch for the Unionists. Bonar Law encouraged his ambition, and in early October wrote to him that he had alerted the party managers to keep an eye out for a suitable seat.[9] A month later Bonar Law wrote to the Unionist Chairman in Ashton-under-Lyne, who had tried to interest him in the constituency, suggesting Aitken instead: 'He is a man of really exceptional ability, who without any outside help has made a large fortune; he is a keen imperialist, and for that reason, now wants to stand for Parliament.'[10] The Ashton commit-tee adopted Aitken as their candidate; quite against informed predic-tions, he carried the Lancashire seat in the December 1910 election and held it until he was offered a peerage in 1916. Consistency of viewpoint meant little to Max Aitken during his long career, but he never wavered in his loyalty to Bonar Law, and only Mary Law's rivalled his confidence in his friend's greatness.

Despite his own attitude to honours and to others who coveted them, Bonar Law was aware in Aitken's case of his craving not just for the status but for the legitimacy which he thought they conferred. He therefore supported the offer, in the same Coronation Honours List which made him a Privy Councillor, of a knighthood for the financier and fledgling MP – in the face of objections on the part of the Canadian Governor-General[11] and probably of Lord Derby, the leader of Lanca-shire Unionism.[12] Aitken wrote to his friend:

[Chief Whip Alexander Acland-] Hood did me the kindness but you made it possible and in my selfish way I want you to know that I am always ready to serve you not because of what you've done for me but because you are your-self.[13]

Often the two men did not agree on the correct political path for the nation, or the party. Despite legends to the contrary, it is also true that Bonar Law often did not seek – and as frequently rejected – Aitken's political advice. Their friendship, however, became a constant of his life. Cherkley Court, the Surrey house Aitken purchased in 1911, became a regular retreat for Bonar Law and his brood, where Gladys Aitken lavished maternal affection on the children while the men talked politics or played golf. 'You know it takes a good deal to make me willing to go anywhere, but I wish to make an exception in this case,' Bonar Law teased Aitken in 1911.[14] He made the 'exception' again and again, as his elder daughter recalled years later: 'My father was a constant guest. Lunch on Saturday or Sunday, a game of tennis or bridge – often both – and back to London for dinner.'[15]

Bonar Law was soon describing Max Aitken as his 'most intimate friend', and so he remained.[16] Aitken responded with unfailing fidelity and admiration, and prided himself on always turning up when needed. As it happened, he was soon able to help further Bonar Law's rise to the topmost place in the Unionist Party.

II

As we have seen, Arthur Balfour's leadership of the Unionist Party in the years following the 1906 election had been much criticized. He had been mistrusted almost from the outset of Joe Chamberlain's campaign, and was finally judged a roadblock by the Tariff Reformers. Zealots of the Tariff Reform League and the Confederacy had concluded that he was insufficient in his vigour for the cause that, in their view, was the only electorally viable policy the party had on offer.

At the same time, Balfour's attempts to co-opt and tame the Tariff Reformers irritated the Free-Food Tories. In mid 1910 Lord Robert Cecil, a tariff sceptic and Balfour's own cousin, wrote in exasperation to his wife: 'I think pretty soon I must write & tell AJB that I no longer regard him as my leader & then maybe I can be quite friendly with him. At present I don't much like meeting him.'[17] The prickly Lord Robert was not alone in his annoyance.

A further source of trouble for Balfour was his resistance, even after three successive electoral defeats, to modernizing the machinery of the party.[18] The hierarchy of Central Office – the leaders in the two Houses, Chief Agent and Whips – had been in place since Disraeli's time, and from the earliest days of Balfour's premiership there had been widespread criticism of it from the back benches and in the party press.[19] He had successfully resisted all suggestions for administrative reform until, following the December 1910 electoral defeat, a meeting of Tory notables led by another Cecil cousin, Lord Salisbury, delivered a stinging ultimatum demanding a thorough-going review of the entire apparatus of party management. Balfour capitulated: in February 1911 he appointed a Unionist Organization Committee chaired by a former Chief Whip, Aretas Akers-Douglas.[20]

In April 1911 the Committee recommended the appointment of a party chairman and a treasurer, an expanded Central Office staff, and a revamped Whips' Room. The committee 'had prefaced each section of their reports with trenchant criticisms of existing systems. Publication or implementation of the reports would thus endorse these criticisms, which is exactly what Balfour had hoped to avoid.'[21] Balfour had no choice but to embrace the recommendations – though he never fully implemented them; he survived the episode, but it did nothing to slow the erosion of his position.

Defeat in the struggle over the House of Lords veto turned a vociferous minority on the right wing of his party adamantly against Balfour. Among them were certain restive younger Unionist partisans who, led by the tireless Page Croft and in sympathy with their Die-Hard elders, had in 1910 formed the Reveille Movement.[22] In 1911 some fifty of these so-called Die-Hard peers and MPs formed the Halsbury Club, named after their ancient hero. Their denials of hostility towards him notwithstanding, this was anything but welcome to Balfour.[23]

Although Balfour was readily acknowledged to possess one of the greatest intellects Parliament had seen in many a year, the mental processes which led him to make decisions remained a mystery to his colleagues, and his cool superiority impressed his followers but did not inspire them. Furthermore, his brilliance could not compensate for the fact that he had lost three successive elections and showed no sign of having any idea how to avoid losing a fourth. The Member for Hammersmith, William Bull, expressed the thoughts of many Unionists when he wrote in his diary in July 1911 that, despite his vaunted brilliance, Balfour simply was not a battle chieftain: 'He does not lead – He is like a sleepy lion who has to be poked up to roar occasionally.'[24] Many frustrated and angry back-bench Tories, bruised and humiliated in defeat, quietly agreed with outspoken extremists like Lord Willoughby de Broke and Page Croft that they were led by a man who simply refused to show much fight. Bull had not lost his respect for Balfour as a great parliamentarian, but he concluded ominously that 'People [in the party] were getting sick of AJB.'[25]

Replacing a Unionist leader in 1911 was no easy feat. The party had no established procedure for choosing its leader when in Opposition, much less for expelling an unsatisfactory one. Perhaps more important in this case was the fact – which had certainly protected him in 1910 and 1911 – that there seemed to be no obvious alternative to Balfour. In the midst of the 'Truce of God' episode, J.L. Garvin had written to Balfour's most vehement antagonist in the press, the editor of the *National Review*, Leo Maxse: 'For heaven's sake don't revive at present the movement against him ... there is nobody else.'[26] The party Whip, Balcarres, wrote early in 1911: 'When somebody complains of Arthur Balfour's attitude a simple query as to his possible successor brings the conversation to an abrupt close. There is no available heir to the throne ... to talk of a change of leadership is futile when no potential substitute can be named.'[27]

Even this stark reality, however, could not save Balfour. Maxse was particularly infuriated by Balfour's capitulation over the Parliament Bill; in September 1911 he threw caution aside and began his brutal 'B.M.G.' (Balfour Must Go) campaign in the *National Review*. He further announced that at the mid November meeting of the National Union of Conservative and Constitutional Associations – the annual national party conference – he would offer a motion of 'warm and unstinted admiration for the conduct of the "No Surrender" Peers led by Lord Halsbury ...'[28] This was unquestionably a studied insult designed to embarrass Balfour and, Maxse hoped, drive him from the leadership.

As early as 26 July 1911 Bonar Law had warned Balcarres, newly-elevated to the post of Chief Whip, that if the votes of a substantial number of Tory peers were required to get the bill through the Lords, it would bring Balfour down.[29] In the end, more than thirty Tory peers had voted for the bill; and, as Balfour fled to the Continent, his leadership was already mortally wounded. By the end of September he was confiding to Steel-Maitland (the recently-installed party chairman) and Balcarres that he was contemplating resignation.[30]

Bonar Law was not among those who longed either for a different leader or even for a particularly different Arthur Balfour. In his 'Hedger' letter to *The Times* of 26 July 1911 he had commended his leader for his prudence in the final stages of the struggle over the Lords. Three months later a group of party luminaries came together at the London house of the Duke of Devonshire to consider how Balfour's position might be strengthened in the face of the growing Die-Hard insurrection. Bonar Law was a prominent participant, and he and the former Irish Secretary, Walter Long, were deputed to meet Sir Edward Carson, the Irish Unionist leader, and attempt to form an alliance to shore up Balfour's leadership.[31] Carson, fully occupied with Ireland, was uninterested, however, and the meeting was without issue.

According to Aitken, by this point Bonar Law believed that Balfour's position had become very tenuous and considered that, while his own loyalty remained firm, circumstances beyond his control might direct it elsewhere very soon.[32] Austen Chamberlain's thoughts were following a similar path: at precisely the same time he wrote to his stepmother of the plausible rumour that Balfour was contemplating resignation.[33] While the punctilious Chamberlain would not yet admit it, perhaps even to himself, possible successors were beginning to manoeuvre for position.

Understandably, among senior Unionists the possibility that Balfour might resign pushed aside all other considerations. It was already obvious that the chief contenders for his crown would be the two senior former ministers, Chamberlain, Balfour's last Chancellor, and Long, former Chief Secretary for Ireland. Two other names heard in connection with the possible contest were those of Carson and Bonar Law, yet all was mere surmise until the vacancy existed. By early November it was accepted it soon would, and the supporters of the potential candidates made ready to jockey their men into the first place.

The two favourites could hardly have offered a greater contrast. Like Lord Lansdowne, the Unionist leader in the Lords, Austen Chamberlain officially remained a Liberal Unionist and technically an ally of the Conservatives who made up the majority of the Unionist contingent in the House. The great Joe's elder son was a complex man, rather thin-skinned for a politician and haunted by two personal daemons: the dominating reputation of the father he worshipped, and the fear lest somewhere in British public life there should exist a man who considered him to be guided by anything other than the motives of a gentleman. He was also highly intelligent, generous and loyal – if faintly ridiculous in the orchid and eyeglass which parodied as much as they echoed his father's style. The major difference between these two Chamberlains was that the son lacked both the father's drive and his ruthlessness. Yet when the leadership contest began, Chamberlain commanded the allegiance of the majority of the Tariff Reform contingent in the House. His major drawbacks in the eyes of his detractors were his roots in the 'Birmingham gang', his party affiliation, and his surname.

For Walter Long, the leadership was scarcely short of a birthright. His lineage and his broad acres in Wiltshire, his governorship of Harrow School, honorary studentship of Christ Church, Oxford and colonelcy of the county yeomanry – all were the stuff of which Tory dreams were made. Like Chamberlain he was also a former Cabinet minister, and a long-term fixture on the front bench. As Irish Chief Secretary under Balfour, he had led the Ulster Unionists in the House between 1907 and 1910. But Long, too, possessed significant failings: though notoriously easily offended himself, his own brash plain-speaking often inflicted pain; he was quick to anger and to attack, yet his willingness to pacify and even to flatter former adversaries was sometimes perceived as insincerity; his intellectual gifts were far from admired, he was only six years younger than Balfour and, appearances to the contrary, his health was frequently indifferent. Yet Long was loyal to friend and party, and the bluffness which repelled some appealed to others tired of Balfourian finesse. If Long lacked Chamberlain's cleverness and subtlety, to many in the party his thirty years of tireless service in the House and his traditional antecedents made him an attractive candidate.

Of the two others whose names were mentioned one, Sir Edward Carson, promptly announced his absolute refusal to be a candidate for the leadership.[34] The other, Bonar Law, kept his counsel. He was certainly not the absolute outsider many historians have been quick to label him: he was widely respected by the party rank-and-file as a man who in a remarkably short time had earned his place on the front bench. He was one of the most widely sought-after speakers among the party luminaries and clearly destined for high office in the next Unionist Government. It was not surprising that Bonar Law's name should have been mentioned in discussions of a possible successor to Balfour: Austen Chamberlain himself wrote on the eve of the leadership contest that he considered him a possible aspirant for the place, though a confident Walter Long took his candidacy less seriously at this point.[35] Certainly, if the prize were to elude either or both the two favourites, Bonar Law had to be considered a logical alternative.

As Balfour drew closer to resignation, Aitken encouraged Bonar Law to make a serious run for the leadership: there is little reason to believe that he required much convincing. He had entered Parliament with a keen ambition for high office, and he had reached the front bench in near-record time. The leadership appealed to him, and by mid October he seems to have made up his mind to offer his candidacy. His most energetic advocates were his friends Max Aitken and Edward Goulding, who first laid their plans on board the *Lusitania*, bound for Canada in the second week of October.[36] They rushed through their business and were back in London on 7 November, the day before Balfour's official resignation, and ready for the political contest. While Bonar Law's qualifications for the post of leader were allowed by many among the Unionist faithful, Aitken soon found that he was the first choice of no more than forty supporters – the remaining 230 MPs were divided between the other candidates.[37]

In early November Long was told by his closest advisers in the House that he commanded more support among Unionist MPs than any possible rival. Long's forces, however, were largely confined to the back benches, while the party whips, most of the Shadow Cabinet and even Balfour himself seemed to prefer Chamberlain.[38] Chamberlain, who certainly desired the leadership very much, none the less wished it to be thought that he viewed it as a mixed blessing at best, and preferred to be seen as being carried along by the enthusiasm of his supporters.

The exact way in which the contest would be settled remained unclear in the absence of established procedures for selecting a leader under such circumstances.[39] A Unionist Prime Minister of course led the entire Parliamentary party and, as in Balfour's case, retained the leadership role when the party passed into Opposition. If a leader was chosen when his party was out of office, however, he technically led only in the Commons or the Lords. All agreed, therefore, that the choice should rest with Unionist Members – interpreted in this case to mean both Conservatives and Liberal Unionists – of the House of Commons.

Balfour finally announced his resignation on 8 November, and the Chief Whip, Lord Balcarres, taking the initiative, announced a meeting of Unionist MPs at the Carlton Club five days later.[40] There was little time for further delay, as the annual party conference was to begin in Leeds on 16 November. What remained unclear was whether the victor should be determined on the basis of a plurality on the first ballot, or whether there were to be several rounds of voting until one aspirant achieved a true majority – a question which remained unsettled, and was eventually obviated by the course of events.[41]

Bonar Law considered his possible candidacy for the leadership very seriously. At fifty-three, he was of suitable age – ten and four years younger, respectively, than Balfour or Long, and five years older than Chamberlain. Though he lacked Cabinet experience, his position in the

Parliamentary party demanded that he be taken seriously as a candidate – particularly in light of the fact that support for the two favourites appeared to be so nearly even. Allowing his name to go forward at this point could at the very least be considered an excellent way of announcing his availability for the leadership at some future time,[42] while a graceful and strategic withdrawal in the event of one of the front-runners rapidly amassing a majority might also be a useful way to ensure the respect and gratitude of the successful candidate.

Attractive as the prize was, trying for the leadership was not without risk. Bonar Law was friendly with both Chamberlain and Long, and wished to keep those relationships unimpaired. Of the two, however, it is clear that he himself preferred Chamberlain as a potential leader. From the *Lusitania* in October Aitken wrote to him that it was Goulding's understanding that 'you promised Austen you wouldn't contest first place with him. I ridiculed this statement, if made, having any effect on your friends, using the obvious arguments.'[43] Some observers have taken at face value this statement by Aitken which repeated the contention of Goulding, who was at the time still backing Chamberlain.[44] As early as mid August, however, when Balfour's leadership was already in decay, Bonar Law had remarked to Chamberlain that the two of them were 'more or less rivals' for the succession.[45] Chamberlain wrote to his stepmother two months later that after a discussion with Bonar Law he had concluded that his friend felt 'that if Balfour retired and I were too unpopular with a section of the Party to be chosen to succeed, the leadership must fall to himself, and I have no doubt that he would like it in exactly the same sense I should. And indeed he practically said as much to me last August; but he is thoroughly straight and will do nothing underhand.'[46] Desiring the leadership – or at least establishing his credentials for some future contest – was one thing, but negotiating the dangerous path that led to the prize was another.

On the day of Balfour's resignation Aitken was summoned to Pembroke Lodge to hear the news for which he longed: Bonar Law would allow his name to go forward for the first round of balloting. As he had in the past and would in the future when major decisions were to be resolved, he pondered and, having decided, then sought the endorsement of those he trusted. Aitken understood this, and played his part. Following a great Tariff Reform dinner that evening, at which both he and Chamberlain spoke, Bonar Law announced his decision to his closest associates. By the following day they, like Long's friends, were energetically canvassing Members for their support.[47] Chamberlain, repelled by the thought that he might be perceived as grasping at the prize, kept a tighter rein on his admirers.[48]

He did not, however, keep his supporters from making discreet attempts to ensure his victory. Garvin, for example, called on Bonar Law on the morning of 9 November 'to persuade him not to allow his name to be put forward. He reported that he found Law inflexible, quite determined to get the position if he could and quite satisfied that he was fully qualified for it.'[49]

On 10 November Bonar Law received a letter in which Goulding reported that he had informed Balcarres that 'you had decided to comply with the request of many friends and stand and serve if the Party so desired next Monday.'[50] Goulding enclosed with this a letter sent him by James Fitzalan Hope, MP for Sheffield Central and a strong Chamberlain man. A friend of both the rivals, Hope expressed his apprehension at Bonar Law's decision to seek the leadership and, like Garvin, made his bid to dissuade him. Of Bonar Law Hope wrote: 'I like and admire him immensely, but I do not think that he has a chance of election, and his standing may gravely prejudice Austen's chances and in any case cannot fail to leave a nasty taste. I am hardly intimate enough with him to beg him to desist, but I hope that you will use your influence in that direction.'[51] While committed now to the contest, Bonar Law was understandably troubled by these views, coming as they did so soon after Garvin's visit. He went to see Aitken the following morning to take his advice.

Bonar Law seems not to have been particularly influenced by Garvin's pleas, but the firm position taken by an influential back-bencher like James Hope was quite another matter. He read Aitken his draft reply to Hope, in which he first argued the usual case of ambitious men who seek preferment: he did not openly seek the position, and accepted nomination only in response to the requests of Members made to him after the Tariff Reform dinner on the evening of 8 November. The draft continued: 'Goulding was one of them and I told him that I was not a candidate, but when I was further asked, "would you accept it if it were offered to you?" I said, of course I would. I cannot see what other attitude I could possibly take.' Neither he nor Hope wanted Long as leader, he agreed, but he rejected the idea that his own candidacy was somehow a particular threat to Chamberlain's ambitions. He added: 'If I find at the meeting that the question is not to be settled in favour of the candidate who in the first vote obtains an actual majority, then, if in my opinion my nomination is likely to damage C. and help L., I should be quite ready to say that I would not allow myself to be nominated.'[52] There is, of course, no record of his private discussion with Aitken, and all published versions of the episode reflect the latter's recollections.[53] Aitken passionately wished for Bonar Law to win the contest and feared the effects of the gentlemanly tone of the last paragraph, so he argued for a less qualified version of an answer. In his memoirs he recalled his talk with his friend as resulting in a heated argument, with a dramatic climax in which he threw Bonar Law's draft letter on the fire and, when passions had subsided, drafted another himself.[54] A.J.P. Taylor summed up what has become the consensus when he wrote that 'Aitken's real task was to hold Law steady.'[55] An examination of the letter eventually sent to Hope suggests that this view – like Aitken's own recollection – is overly dramatic. In the letter Bonar Law wrote:

> I have not sought and do not seek the leadership, but friends of mine have asked me whether I would accept the position, if it were offered to me, and I have said that I would.
>
> I do not see what else I could do.
>
> I may add that I am quite satisfied that the fact that my name is put forward will not affect Chamberlain any more than it will affect Long.[56]

While perhaps less generous in tone, it makes clear Bonar Law's rejection of the idea that his own candidacy was a threat to Chamberlain's chances and, without going into the details included in the initial draft, his determination that he – Bonar Law – would himself decide any question of withdrawal, if this seemed necessary. Whether this modification grew from the melodramatic scene described by Aitken it is impossible to say, but it is obvious that the difference between the first and second drafts of Bonar Law's letter was not so great as has usually been reported.

Meanwhile, although Long may well have had more pledges of support than his principal rival, it had appeared to the Chief Whip, Balcarres, that the two front-runners were nearly equal in strength.[57] He had therefore, on Thursday, 9 November, called on each to discuss the dreadful prospect of deadlock: in the morning Chamberlain indicated to him that in such a case he was prepared to withdraw, 'assuming W. Long did the same.'[58] Long, wavering now and fearing that his health might not stand the strain of the leadership, agreed in principle.[59] After an anxious day of sifting conflicting information, Balcarres called on

Chamberlain again at lunch time on 10 November, when Chamberlain repeated his earlier offer: in order to prevent a divisive result, he would withdraw from the contest – subject to Long's doing the same.[60] Balcarres once again went to Belgravia to see Long, who seconded the plan.[61] The leadership contest was over.

Balcarres took the news to Bonar Law at the House of Commons, but his reception was not precisely what he expected. As his diary relates,

> [Bonar Law] was very frank. Said that he had definitely determined to stand, even though it would involve his defeat. He almost indicated that refusal to stand at this juncture when being pressed to do so by his friends would remove him from the list of potential candidates when a subsequent vacancy might occur.
>
> Said that he did not really feel himself fitted for the post from experience. I replied that as he had entered on a candidature, ex hypothesi, he had considered his claims of some weight. He agreed, but repeated that his shortcomings were numerous – that as a widower and humble in means he could not entertain etc.
>
> At one moment I wondered if he lacked courage for the immediate crisis – which brought my mind back to an earlier impression that his candidature was to establish a qualification for the future.[62]

Bonar Law withheld his acceptance until he had spoken to Chamberlain, who wrote to his family that he had advised his rival that he had no choice but to take the offered post, despite Bonar Law repeating to him the suggestion of Chamberlain's supporters that Long be allowed to have the job in order to prove his incapacity.[63] Chamberlain, as his version of the interview indicates, saw his talk with Bonar Law as critical to the other man's willingness to take the post, and himself as virtual 'king-maker'.[64] Bonar Law, however, without Chamberlain's knowledge, went also to Long, who warmly encouraged his acceptance, writing later in the day: 'You are the only man who can unite the whole Party.'[65] With the blessings of his rivals, then, Bonar Law saw Balcarres once again, in the evening, and accepted the arrangement.

Bonar Law had little expected to win the leadership, but it is obvious that he saw himself as leadership material. Why did he tread so warily when it seemed that fortune was to deliver him the prize? Chamberlain had been his first friend in the House, and carried great weight among Unionists, especially among Tariff Reformers: to make an enemy of him would have been a great mistake. Long was likewise a friend, and popular among Tories of all stripes – Bonar Law had no desire to see him succeed Balfour, but nor did he wish to offend the outspoken squire any more than was absolutely necessary.

There were other reasons: the method by which the field was reduced from three runners to one was certainly curious, and the tortuous creation of a semblance of unanimity was bound to annoy some ordinary back-benchers. Familiar as he was with the Smoking Room of the House, he knew back-bench opinion would *make* the next leader – or break him, as it had Balfour.

Finally, we must recall that Bonar Law realized fully what a dark horse he was in this race. He did not expect to win the leadership at this time, and had every reason to fear that if he accepted it under these circumstances, it would prove a poisoned chalice. He understood too that, now the offer had been made, refusal could end any hope of it ever being repeated. His acceptance was an act of courage, all the same, and he took every means of assuring himself that it was not one of foolhardiness. It is not surprising that he should have sought reassurance from Balcarres, Chamberlain, Long and, of course, Aitken.

Agreement among leaders was no absolute guarantee, however, that the Parliamentary party would acquiesce, and as the Junior Whip William Bridgeman noted in his diary on the evening of the compromise, 'there is now a greater feeling of discontent about than at any previous time, and many of the supporters of each protagonist think their man has been jockeyed out. I fear that Monday's meeting may now be a stormy one.'[66] His fears, however, proved groundless. Tempers cooled, and the weekend provided sufficient time to rekindle the flame of Unionist solidarity.[67]

At midday on Monday, 232 MPs assembled in the Smoking Room of the Carlton Club, and the friendly atmosphere filled Balcarres with relief: 'By this time all doubts and hesitations had vanished.'[68] The veteran Tory former minister, Henry Chaplin, took the chair, and Walter Long made a warmly received speech nominating Bonar Law for the leadership. Chamberlain – who reputedly had never before been inside the club – ungrudgingly seconded the nomination. After a hearty voice vote unanimously electing the new leader, Sir Edward Carson was deputed to bring the waiting Bonar Law before his followers.

He was hardly prepared for his reception: the assembled Parliamentary Unionist Party – some standing on their chairs and waving handkerchiefs, agenda papers or whatever else came to hand – hailed him with tumultuous cheering.[69] He was overwhelmed, and struggled to control his emotions. In few words, spoken quickly and in a low voice, he paid tribute to his predecessor, the absent Balfour, and acknowledged the generous sacrifice of his rivals. Coming quickly to the business at hand, he addressed it in a way both characteristic and candid:

> All my intimate friends told me yesterday that at the meeting I was to avoid saying anything depreciating myself, but I cannot pretend that I am not afraid of this task. I am afraid of it. If I were quite sure that I am incapable of filling it, no power on earth should make me touch it. I am not quite sure, for no man can know accurately either his capacity or his limitations. But I am sure of this, that with the disadvantages under which I labour, which every one of you will understand – the disadvantage of never having been in the Cabinet, the disadvantage too of having had comparatively small experience even of the rough and tumble of the House of Commons – that under those disadvantages I cannot possibly succeed unless I receive from you all a support as generous and perhaps more generous than has ever been given to any leader of your Party.[70]

The brief speech was well received, though few thought it so fine as the nominating addresses. In fact it was vintage Bonar Law, modest, self-deprecating and absolutely frank. He expected them to labour and sacrifice both for him and, more importantly, for the party. There was no bombast, there were no fulsome phrases. Perhaps his listeners might have gained an insight into the character of their new leader had they known the tale told often over the years by Max Aitken: in his car on the way to the meeting, Aitken advised his friend, 'Remember you are a great man now.' Bonar Law smiled and replied: 'If I am a great man, then a good many of the great men of history are frauds.'[71] The results of the momentous day were well summed up by Bridgeman, whose anxieties over party harmony had passed away: 'Bonar Law was very nervous & very modest, but made a good impression, & we all parted with the feeling that "we are jolly good fellows" & so we really are.'[72]

III

After the long reign of the Cecils, Bonar Law's elevation came as something of a shock to some Tories. The great political hostess Lady Londonderry, according to Jack Sandars, "fulminat[ed]' at the idea of a Glasgow merchant leading the party of English gentlemen.[73] The socially ambitious Arthur Lee, MP for South Hampshire, himself married into an American fortune, sniffed that the party was behaving like a gentlemen 'who is conscious he has married beneath him'.[74] Lady Londonderry became reconciled to the new leader and even enthusiastic about him once she convinced herself that he had allowed her to 'take him up';[75] Lee simply fell into line and brooded.

It is impossible to say how many of his Liberal colleagues agreed with Lloyd George, who wrote to Bonar Law of his election that 'had the Unionist party always shown the same wisdom in their decisions, I should not have been writing this letter in the Chancellor of the Exchequer's room.'[76] The irrepressible Margot Asquith took a different view, writing to St Loe Strachey that: 'Politically [Bonar Law] is the most sophistical untrue unsound gerry-built quick clever affectionate vulgarian I've ever seen.'[77]

Bonar Law began his task with an abundance of good will within his own party, however. Long's close friend William Bull concluded: 'I am glad [he] has got it [as] he is better than all the others.'[78] Lord Derby, who distrusted Bonar Law's commitment to Tariff Reform and longed for Balfour's return, wrote to his friend and sovereign, King George V, that he doubted Bonar Law's 'personal magnetism': 'But his election has done good and our party is quite united in loyalty to him.'[79] The tariff zealots showed their 'esteem and confidence' in Bonar Law by promptly disbanding the Reveille movement.[80] Even the legendarily outspoken Admiral Lord Fisher wrote to a friend: '*I am in the 7th Heaven at Bonar Law's being Leader* ... As a rule I *hate politicians*. They are all "opportunists" – but I don't believe Bonar Law is one!'[81] The Die-Hard editor H.A. Gwynne seemed to agree with Lloyd George, writing to Lady Bathurst that 'we have blundered on the right man.'[82]

A letter from Balfour's antagonist Leo Maxse made clear what many Unionists longed for, and expected of Bonar Law: 'The one demand of the Party outside parliament is that the white flag which has so long waved over our front bench shall be hauled down ... and that the Party in the country shall receive a clear and unhesitating call to arms, so that we may know precisely where we are.'[83] Balfour, for all his glittering talents, had failed as a battle leader; and if his successor expected a long tenure, he would have to rally his troops and lead them against the well-entrenched forces of the Government. John Ramsden has written:

> [Bonar] Law conceived of the role of the leader in an exactly opposite sense from Balfour: he sought to foster unity by placing himself at the head of the

discordant elements where Balfour had thrown the leadership on the side of restraint ... Much of his leadership was thus a form of pragmatic extremism, extreme action and the threat of more extreme action to come, but used in the cause of more limited objectives.[84]

His first concern had to be for the party machine, the rejuvenation of which Balfour had failed to complete. Bonar Law retained Balcarres and the other party whips, and the chairman, Steel-Maitland. For his parliamentary secretaries he disappointed his cronies Aitken and Goulding, and chose less controversial men with impeccable Tory credentials: George Stanley, Lord Derby's younger brother, and John Baird, an old Etonian and son of a baronet. Both served him well, and their choice delighted traditionalists in the party, whom Bonar Law realized he would have to win over.

He inherited a Shadow Cabinet which was aged, often divided, and weighed down with supporters of his predecessor and of his former rivals, Chamberlain and Long.[85] He began almost immediately to invite younger men – F.E. Smith and Lord Robert Cecil were the first – on to the front bench to alter the mix. It was his practice to summon his whole cabinet only when necessary, preferring to gauge the feeling of the party through the back-benchers and to consult the leaders individually or in smaller working groups.

Finally, Bonar Law the former businessman, unlike Balfour, embraced the need for a more efficient organization of better executive talent in Central Office. John Boraston became Principal Agent in 1912, and Malcolm Fraser, a former journalist, became the party's first professional press director. Steel-Maitland as Party Chairman with his lieutenants departmentalized the operation of the party and constituted the first professional executive staff in its history. Similar efforts at modernization were begun by the newly appointed Party Treasurer, Lord Farquhar, who initiated a hugely successful fund-raising campaign: on the eve of the Great War the party war-chest had risen to £671,000, more than twice what it had been in Balfour's time. As a result of these innovations the party became more efficient, and financially stable; and its relations with the constituency committees and the national and regional press became more effective than ever before.[86]

The Unionist Party of which Bonar Law had become the leader was a difficult entity to pin down. There were in this period two parallel Conservative organizations: Central Office in London, the rapidly developing 'brain' of the party, made up of the professional staff and parliamentary leaders; and the National Union, of constituency representatives. A further complication was the fact that, while all Conservatives were Unionists, not all Unionists were Conservatives, since the broader, informal appellation usually encompassed Chamberlainite Liberal Unionists as well. The touchy matter of this division had been sidestepped by the 1911 Organization Committee; but the fact that the Unionist leader in the Lords, Lansdowne, and the popular candidate for leadership of the party in the Commons, Austen Chamberlain, were both Liberal Unionists was a reminder of what a curious anomaly the division was.[87]

Bonar Law's pragmatism provided an opportunity to cut through this Gordian knot of overlapping designations, loyalties and responsibilities. The complicated business of uniting the two organizations was accomplished at a meeting of senior Conservatives and Liberal Unionists at Pembroke Lodge on 12 February 1912.[88] The remodelled party machine was given the somewhat awkward title of the National Unionist Association of Conservative and Liberal-Unionist Organizations, and the merger was ratified by separate meetings of the two amalgamating parties on 9 May.[89] The term Liberal Unionist died out soon thereafter, and those who had borne it were finally welcomed into that Conservative bastion, the Carlton Club. All were officially Unionists now, and remained so until after the ratification in 1922 of Lloyd George's Irish treaty, when the name Conservative came once again into common use.

Dr Vernon Bogdanor has written of the principal tasks which confront any leader of the Conservative Party:

> First, he must display competence and efficiency at his task; secondly, he must be perceived as an electoral asset, and have a reasonable prospect of carrying the country in a general election; thirdly, he must retain the allegiance of the Conservative back-benchers; and fourthly, he must retain the support of the party in the country. Above all, a Conservative leader must not split the party.[90]

Arthur Balfour had failed materially in several of these duties, and as a result had come dangerously close to splitting his party. Bonar Law, the compromise choice as his successor, now faced the task of leading his battered party against an entrenched Government majority and into what promised to be the most bitter partisan conflict in living memory. This sober and modest man brought to his daunting task a zeal which left even his most committed followers breathless. Before the end of the year, Balcarres was to note in his diary: 'So far as Bonar Law's leadership is concerned, all or nearly all look upon it as an unqualified success.'[91]

5

Unfinished Business

A T THEIR ANNUAL conference in Leeds on 17 November 1911, Bonar Law addressed his party for the first time as leader. In a seventy-minute speech this most unphilosophical of statesmen defined his understanding of conservatism. Under his lead, he promised, the Unionists would never take office as a party of reaction. Neither, however, would they compete with their opponents in pursuit of what he saw as change for its own sake. 'Do not touch anything', he advised, 'unless you are quite certain that you are going to improve it.' What would be his benchmark of leadership? 'A disposition to preserve, and an ability to improve, taken together[,] would be my standard of a statesman.' This aphorism of Edmund Burke's, which Bonar Law never tired of quoting throughout his career, was perhaps as close as he came to enunciating his own political first principles.

As for the Government, he made it clear that it was his intention to make their way as hard as possible. Referring to recent criticism in the Liberal press of his combative debating style, he said:

> The advice given to me was that I should in the future be less rude than I have been in the past. That is possibly good advice. I shall at all events remember it; but in the bitter fight which lies before us, a fight for everything we hold dear, I have no hope of being able to act in such a way as to be able to satisfy the writer of the article.[1]

These contentious words aptly foreshadowed the rough-edged parliamentary atmosphere of the years preceding the Great War. In April 1912, after a bitter exchange with the Opposition leader upon the introduction of the Third Home Rule Bill, Asquith denounced Bonar Law for his remarks in Belfast a few days earlier, quoting him as having accused the Liberals of making government a 'market-place where everything is bought and sold'. Casting his eyes up and showing his famous profile, the Prime Minister thundered sarcastically: 'This, Mr Speaker, is the new style.'

Asquith confidently pursued his theme, extracting an acknowledgement that Bonar Law had in fact hurled such a slander: 'Let us see exactly what it is. It is that I and my colleagues are selling our convictions.' Bonar Law's split-second response stunned the Liberals and delighted his followers: 'You have not', he said, 'got any.' Denied his triumph, the Prime Minister concluded wearily: 'We are getting on with the new style.'

From this developed the Liberal article of faith that Bonar Law pioneered the so-called 'new style', and that this technique of combative politics characterized by harsh accusatory rhetoric debased a previously higher order of political manners.[2] The harsh turn which political practice took in these years is not so simply explained, however. Bonar Law had become leader of his party because the manner in which his predecessor led had failed. Arthur Balfour, for all his remarkable qualities, had suffered three successive electoral defeats, and appeared to many to be incapable of ever taking his party to victory at the polls. He had failed to keep the party, with its Tariff Reformers and Free-Fooders, sufficiently united. Many Unionists had concluded that Balfour was not a warrior, at a time when a warrior was needed. Bonar Law stood now in Balfour's place at least in part because many thought he was that warrior. His manner was tougher, and he dared not wait long to demonstrate it. If it were true that his style was 'perilously far from the masterly witticisms of Mr Balfour',[3] then it was equally true that this was precisely what many in his party wanted.

It was also true that this bellicose political climate not only preceded his leadership, but originated less with Bonar Law than with Lloyd George and his radical Liberal followers on the one hand, and the angry Unionist Die-Hards on the other. Bonar Law had not been in the forefront of the angry skirmishes precipitated by the 1909 Budget in which the brilliant Chancellor had taunted their Tory lordships to their political demise – or at least towards the Parliament Bill which had compromised their political power. It should not be forgotten that in this significant struggle Bonar Law had been among the Unionist moderates, a Hedger rather than a Ditcher, arguing in the House and on the platform against the most extreme measures.

Finally, it must be recalled that the political climate which produced the Parliament of these last few pre-war years was unlike any other previously known. It was an age of political and social disorder, of dramatic demonstrations by women's suffragists, widespread work stoppages among trade unionists, and dire threats from partisans on both sides in the struggle over Irish Home Rule – all in an increasingly democratic time when the reins of political power were passing from the hands of the traditional leadership classes. In addition, the 1910 elections had left the major parties in uncomfortable balance, with the Government dependent upon the support of the Irish Nationalists and Labour, and the Opposition (soon to be the largest single party in the House) correspondingly frustrated and quarrelsome. F.E. Smith is said to have called it the 'Mad Parliament' – not entirely without justification.[4]

In early 1912 the fastidious Chief Whip, Lord Balcarres, addressed this matter of Bonar Law's authorship of the 'new style'. Writing to an aunt, he noted that the philosophical Balfour simply could not 'hate the thing that is evil'. The times, he regretfully acknowledged, required a fighting chieftain who would hit hard and rally the party: 'Our friends in the country like B.L. because his attitude is uncompromising and because it conforms to their belief in his genuine distrust of the Radical Party.' Yet, Balcarres concluded, such combativeness gave the new leader little pleasure:

> His mind is strict and precise in logic, the construction of his argument seems based on a geometrical thesis, his whole style is that of a keen logician who desires the issue settled upon the merits of argument. It is in this sense that his parliamentary career began, with a quiet deferential voice, and a retiring manner. Now, with real reluctance he feels that the world is not governed by the reasonable marshalling of fact and figure before an impartial jury – and he is driven to employ the bludgeon as well as the rapier.[5]

Bonar Law's hard-hitting style was intended to bruise those opponents who had humbled Balfour and who held so many, if not all, of the parliamentary cards. It was also intended to unite the sometimes fractious Tories around a single battle standard, and to give heart to those whose frustration had perhaps contributed to make his predecessor's leadership impossible. Instead of identifying himself with restraint, as Balfour had, his aim was to lead as if from a war chariot, binding to it the most angry and dynamic Unionists and inspiring his more moderate followers. In this way he would control and direct them all. One keen observer has noted that

> His strategy was rather to canalize the enthusiasm of the diehards into party channels, to articulate their views, and to create unity from the sense of movement ... As a result of this he was labelled as a diehard and a bigot, when in fact he actually distrusted the diehards and was himself distrusted by the bigots.[6]

Many years after these struggles were ended, Asquith recalled that as he and Bonar Law walked together to the State Opening of Parliament in February 1912, the latter had said: 'I am afraid I shall have to show myself very vicious, Mr Asquith, this session. I hope you will understand.'[7] If this rather notorious declaration was ever made – and Asquith's memoir is the sole source for it – Bonar Law doubtless meant that he had no other choice.

Bonar Law's approach, according to the Unionist Whip and old Etonian William Bridgeman, earned the former New Brunswick farm boy the 'warm admiration' of back-benchers.[8] Electoral politics is an uncertain game in which success counts for much when leadership is judged, and no small part of this regard was due to the fact that in by-elections held between his elevation to the leadership and the outbreak of war, the Unionists wrested no fewer than fifteen seats from the Government side, losing only one in return.[9] Many Unionists were inclined to attribute much of this success to Bonar Law and the 'new style'.

II

As a compromise choice for leader, Bonar Law's position was not ideal – and he inherited both failed strategies and unresolved quarrels. The 1910 elections had left the Liberal Party without an overall majority but, with Irish and Labour support, still in control of the House of Commons. Furthermore, the 1911 Parliament Act, which left the Upper House unreformed but now empowered only to delay legislation which had passed through the Commons, had wrested from the Unionists a powerful weapon. Hence, Bonar Law quite rightly considered it essential to choose carefully the battles he would fight – or, more accurately, those he would not.

Several of the issues which divided political opinion at this time simply did not engage his interest. The struggle for women's suffrage, for example, he merely evaded. It is true that few Unionists – and few of their Liberal opponents – supported any of the various efforts to grant some form of suffrage to women. Bonar Law considered the issue merely unprofitable, writing in January 1912: 'It seems to me ... that from our point of view – which is naturally the desire to defeat the Government – the less part we take in this question the better.'[10] He left his party unwhipped on the issue, and said only that he would support a national referendum to decide it, if the Government would take the initiative to propose one. On this point he carried with him a Shadow Cabinet equally happy to avoid the matter.[11]

The question of social reform – legislation designed to ameliorate conditions among the poorer classes – was more complicated, but he attempted to deal with it in almost the same way. As we have seen, though he was identified with the Tariff Reform and self-declared constructive wing of the party, he had some years earlier advised caution when his friends published an 'Unauthorized Programme' calling for re-establishment of an energetic Tory activism reminiscent of the days of Disraeli and Lord Randolph Churchill. By 1912 a Unionist Social Reform Committee, chaired by F.E. Smith, had been established under the protection of the party chairman, Steel-Maitland, at Central Office.[12] Though he wished to avoid an open struggle with such USRC enthusiasts as Steel-Maitland and the MPs F.E. Smith and Arthur Griffith-Boscawen, the dynamic proconsul Lord Milner and editors such as Garvin and Gwynne, Bonar Law was unenthusiastic about what he saw as their desire to compete with the Liberals in a sphere in which Unionists could never prevail. As leader, he could be counted upon to insert the necessary references in his speeches and to appoint the necessary committees, but he had never believed that this was a profitable seam for Conservatives to mine.[13] As early as November 1907, when pressed by Garvin to propose a bold programme of Unionist social legislation, Bonar Law had advised caution:

> This does not mean we should do nothing, and what I think we ought to do is to try to agree upon two or three things which we would constantly speak of in our addresses and not to try to cover the whole ground; and another thing which I think equally important is, we must not try to do too much at a

time, and therefore our first business is to press for Tariff Reform and Social Reform in every direction in which the two can be shown to be connected. What I mean by this, for instance, is not merely the connection through employment, which is by far the most important of all, but also the general idea that Preference does not mean merely a fiscal rearrangement, but [the reorganization] of the whole Empire for the benefit of the citizens of the Empire. Among the ideas connected with this, I think one of the most important and [one] which I believe would be popular also, is to press the importance of meeting periodical time[s] of distress through unemployment by a system of migration to the Colonies.[14]

Bonar Law remained ambivalent, even took contradictory positions in private from time to time, on such 'social' matters as the appropriateness of the payment of salaries to MPs (included in the Parliament Act) and the 1912 National Insurance Act. This latter legislation, which was in train when Bonar Law became leader, caused him momentary embarrassment when he allowed himself to be drawn by the Prime Minister into a misleading 'admission' in debate. On the opening day of the 1912 Session, in response to Bonar Law's criticisms of the bill, Asquith turned on him: 'Is the Right Honourable gentleman, if and when he comes to power, going to repeal it?' Startled, and conscious of the challenge, the Opposition leader growled angrily: 'Certainly.'[15] In fact, neither he nor his party had any such intention; and in the end allowed the bill through the Lords in December without requiring the Government to resort to the Parliament Act. Chagrined by a slip which made him look rather a parliamentary tyro, Bonar Law had publicly to climb down a few days later. No lasting harm was done, but it was an experience he neither enjoyed nor repeated.[16]

When Balcarres tactfully pressed his leader for direction on the matter of social programmes he was told 'that as the Radicals refuse to formulate their policy in advance we should equally be absolved.'[17] This curt response masked Bonar Law's own lack of both interest in and resolution on these questions. His unwillingness to concentrate on social issues may indeed have ultimately strengthened his hold over the party faithful, most of whom were at least as ambivalent or uninterested in them as their leader.[18]

Bonar Law's first great public speech as leader, before an audience of 10,000 at the Royal Albert Hall on 26 January 1912, revealed much about what he did consider important. He attacked the Government as a 'revolutionary committee' determined to overturn the constitution and committed to Home Rule only as payment for a corrupt bargain which kept them in power. They excelled, he said, at political 'trickery'; they bartered honours; they had 'put themselves into the pockets' of the Irish Nationalists. The speech was delivered, according to reports, 'quietly and deliberately', without passionate outburst or overt emotion. Its resolute, icily purposeful tone thrilled and delighted his audience – he eschewed the 'subtle dialectic' of Balfour without embracing the theatricality of Lloyd George or F.E. Smith. He meant, as an admirer noted, 'business'.

In this speech he drove home the three concerns which were to occupy his attentions as leader in the next few years: the first was an attack on the legitimacy of a Government which remained in power, he believed, by refusing to submit its most controversial policy, Home Rule, to an election. Second, he reiterated his party's commitment to Tariff Reform and Empire, and pointed out that on this important matter wavering Unionists had but two alternatives: tariffs, 'which they dislike, and Lloyd Georgeism, which they detest.' Finally, he revealed much in few words by reminding his listeners that his party would not permit the rights of Irish Unionists to be trampled upon, and that a truly just Home Rule – acceptable to all sides – might thus prove impossible of achievement.[19]

In later years Austen Chamberlain recalled of Bonar Law: 'He once said to me, before the War had stirred deeper emotions, that he cared intensely for only two things: Tariff Reform and Ulster; all the rest was only part of the game. The success of such a man as leader of the Tory Party presents one of the paradoxes of our political life.'[20] In fact Bonar Law cared for much more, and Chamberlain knew it; yet in the two and a half years of almost constant political engagement that followed, these two matters dominated his mind. It is also true, however, as we shall see, that in the end he was to compromise over both for what he became certain was the good of nation and party.

III

The unfinished business of Tariff Reform provoked the first serious crisis of Bonar Law's leadership, and almost brought it to a premature end. Balfour's fall called attention to his November 1910 commitment that the next Unionist Government would submit this contentious policy to a plebiscite. The Referendum Pledge had soothed those Unionists who feared a popular reaction against 'food taxes'; but it had failed to win the election. Whole-Hoggers in the party, the Tariff Reform zealots, meant to be quit of it, while Free-Fooders wished to impress upon the Tariff Reformer who now led them their own resolution to retain the Pledge.[21] More than a year before assuming the leadership, Bonar Law had suggested in a letter to the tariff sceptic Lord Salisbury that Unionists would do well to accept that imposts on foodstuffs were an integral part of their programme. To his mind, protection was the only progressive economic proposal they had which would interest both the agricultural and the industrial voter: 'To propose, therefore, to leave out these food duties would, in my opinion,' he reasoned, 'be to run a serious risk of losing the advantage we have gained in the Counties, without any guarantee of securing an equivalent advantage in the towns.[22]

Neither was the question of Empire unity lost on the transplanted North American:

> The whole Imperial side of the Tariff Reform movement is bound up in the mind of the public with the food duties ... For us to give up the food duties after we had definitely accepted them as part of our programme, would seem to the Colonies like the abandonment of the only side of the Tariff reform movement which could be of value to them.

It would also, he added, betray the increase in imperial sentiment he sensed among the electorate since the South African War.

Important as he considered these matters of policy to be, Bonar Law also thought it instructive to point out to Salisbury what was to him a crucial matter of real-world politics:

> The Unionist Party is now committed to the whole policy of Preference, including food duties, and there is a large section of the party – and I believe one of the most earnest and energetic sections – which regards Preference not as a political opinion but as something almost sacred. If, therefore, Mr Balfour, Mr Chamberlain and Austen Chamberlain were to propose this Part of the proposal, even then there would, in my opinion, be a whole sale [*sic*] revolt among the rank and file which would cause a division in our Party more complete and more hopeless than has existed at any time since the fiscal controversy was raised. If this view is correct, and I am convinced that it is, then this consideration is in itself absolutely decisive; for it is only by means of a united Party that there can be any hope of making headway against the revolutionary schemes which threaten everything both in the constitution and in our national life which we all prize.

After becoming leader, he made his position clear to Lord Derby, who himself believed that food imposts constituted an albatross around Unionist necks: 'I think there is nothing for us but to go straight forward with the programme as it is . . .'[23] Early in 1912 he reiterated to another correspondent an article of faith from his Albert Hall speech: after the 1910 elections, he believed, Unionist Free-Fooders 'had no choice between supporting a Tariff Reform party and supporting the methods of the present Government.'[24] To these correspondents, Bonar Law seemed ready to nail his Tariff Reform colours to the Unionist mast.

Lord Lansdowne, who had never previously expressed any particular enthusiasm for Tariff Reform, appeared to agree. Writing to Bonar Law on 19 February 1911, he enclosed a lengthy memorandum addressing the questions both of the 'millstone of food taxes hanging on our necks' and of Balfour's Referendum Pledge. He concluded that while import duties on foodstuffs were not an attractive electoral policy, neither were they impossible – and they were best dealt with openly and with a public commitment to keep them small until 'the question of the tariff had been again before the country.' Of the Pledge, Lansdowne concluded by observing that Balfour's challenge to the Liberals – to submit Home Rule to a plebiscite, as the Unionists had offered to do with Tariff Reform – had not been taken up. Furthermore, the use of referenda to settle issues of constitutional import seemed to have little in the way of public support. Hence, he argued, '. . . we remain free to deal with the constitutional question on our own lines, to use it or not to use the referendum according, as we may decide when the time comes.'[25] The dropping of the Pledge, then, seemed to trouble him not at all. A large landowner in Ireland, Lansdowne had abandoned the Liberal Party over Home Rule; and the idea of laying to rest the divisive matter of tariff policy and concentrating Unionist energy and ingenuity on Irish considerations much appealed to him.

Bonar Law immediately called together a small group of party notables, including Lansdowne, Curzon, Balcarres and Long, to discuss the proposal to abandon the Balfour Pledge and embrace the full Tariff Reform programme, including food duties, once and for all. Conclusions were mixed, with Lansdowne favouring abandonment of the Pledge, and Long advising the public disavowal of imposts on foodstuffs. The lack of unanimity was not encouraging: 'B. Law nervous and low,' Balcarres recorded in his diary, '[and] says he won't hedge. If pressed to hedge he would prefer to resign, etc. Uncomfortable conference.'[26]

Seeking a resolution, Bonar Law summoned the Shadow Cabinet to grasp the tariff nettle, and on 29 February 1912 the first meeting of the full parliamentary leadership since Balfour's day was held at Lansdowne House in Berkeley Square.[27] Bonar Law left the initiative to Lansdowne, who could not be accused of being a doctrinaire Tariff Reformer. As Lansdowne observed, though there might be electoral advantages in dropping any commitment to food duties, to do so would lead only to accusations of 'poltroonery' and bad faith. Balfour's Referendum Pledge, he continued, had failed as a step towards constitutional revision, and the Liberals had not agreed to a similar pledge regarding Home Rule – hence, the Unionist offer could be withdrawn with impunity. Even Balfour, he reported, now agreed. Sir Robert Finlay endorsed this position, as did Lord Selbourne, George Wyndham and Austen Chamberlain. Lord Londonderry alone argued uncompromisingly for immediate deletion of any mention of food imposts from the party programme. Long and Alfred Lyttelton – and, most strongly, Derby – all expressed a desire for some suitable escape path from the food taxes stigma, but agreed there seemed at the moment to be none. The others remained silent.

Bonar Law enthusiastically endorsed Lansdowne's position, which was of course his own: in the first place, with Balfour's referendum offer the party had entered into no explicit long-term commitment; in the second, any attempt to escape food taxes would not only delight the Liberals but initiate a bloody internecine struggle between Unionist Whole-Hoggers and Free-Fooders. Finally, he reminded his colleagues that Canada, the most highly developed economy among the Dominions, would never agree to full tariff union with the mother country without a British commitment to food duties. Despite their cost, there was no honourable escape from food imposts: 'We must', he stressed to his colleagues, 'carry our handicap honourably and boldly.' In the end, the waverers gave in, and the Shadow Cabinet endorsed their leaders' position: the Referendum Pledge was dead, and food duties now an integral part of the party programme.[28] From a wish to avoid embarrassing Balfour so soon after the change in leadership, Bonar Law advised that it would be best, however, to withhold any announcement of the new policy for the time being.

Asquith introduced a new Home Rule Bill in April 1912, and in the months that followed the Irish issue was to extend its hold over British politics. Unionists, of course, placed this crisis above all others; and, as we shall see, Bonar Law became totally embroiled in the struggle. It was a time when party unity was an absolute necessity, and the assertive (though unannounced) new tariff policy disturbed some of the Unionist leaders. Derby, though he had acquiesced in the Shadow Cabinet, remained troubled by the decision and wrote to Bonar Law only a fortnight later that 'to drop [food duties] now would probably split the Party absolutely'. Yet, he pleaded, without the Referendum Pledge behind which to shelter, the party's prospects in the next election were dangerously impaired. Even if they did win, he continued, '[then] I honestly do not believe you will get the food taxes through the House of Commons however big our majority and if we split and went out we should be in the wilderness for 20 years ...'[29] Bonar Law remained unmoved, though he was no doubt horrified by Derby's allusion to a party sundered 'absolutely'.

Several weeks later, Salisbury similarly tried his hand again, and received a strong and immediate reply.[30] Bonar Law argued that it would be impossible to separate duties on foodstuffs from other elements of the Tariff Reform programme, as Salisbury suggested, for submission to a referendum. Besides, given the escalating costs of defence and social programmes, 'it would be simply impossible for us to do otherwise than raise the additional money at once by a tariff reform Budget.'[31] Tariff Reform, he remained convinced, was the only possible Unionist alternative to the Lloyd Georgeian vision of the confiscation of wealth.

Finally, Bonar Law reminded Salisbury of the danger he feared most: any alternative to the Shadow Cabinet policy would lead to a destructive split in the Party, driven by the angry Tariff Reform wing, who would (he thought) have every right to feel betrayed. Though a committed Tariff Reformer himself, he told Salisbury that if Unionists chose to fight it out among themselves, he would gladly stifle his own desires, embrace the majority view and work for party unity. He made one thing clear, to Salisbury's horror: 'I could not possibly, if such a split did take place, continue as Leader and oppose those with whom I have all through been working.'[32]

Despite Lansdowne's increasing impatience, throughout the spring and into the summer of 1912 Bonar Law withheld announcement of the decision to abandon the Referendum Pledge.[33] He delayed in part because of the planned visit to London in mid July of the Canadian Prime Minister. Sir Robert Borden's Canadian Conservatives had driven their Liberal opponents from office the previous September, and in the name of Empire unity had cancelled a recently negotiated trade 'Reciprocity Treaty' with the United States. What Bonar Law desired of

Sir Robert was a public statement of the necessity of a British Tariff Reform programme, including food duties, to Anglo-Canadian co-operation.[34] Borden agreed to make just such a statement, including the promise of reciprocal Imperial trade preference, upon the implementation by Britain of a tariff favouring Canadian foodstuffs. He also agreed to stress that failure by London to do so would create an 'irresistible pressure' for Canada to make terms with other countries – meaning, of course, the United States.[35]

It is unclear how much, if any, of the proceedings of the February Shadow Cabinet meeting had by this time become known to the pro- and anti-tariff Unionist partisans. Certainly the party grew more restless through the summer, as rumours began to circulate that the Referendum Pledge was to be jettisoned. The secret brotherhood of Confederates renewed their harassment of those Unionist candidates they considered 'unsound' on Tariff Reform, and Austen Chamberlain and his friends continued to speak out against the Pledge, as they had at every opportunity since the end of 1910.[36]

To Bonar Law these were ominous signs that he had been right in suspecting that the greatest danger to party unity lay in the potential anger of the Tariff Reformers. He wrote to Hicks Beach, now Lord St Aldwyn, on 3 September that, despite the wishes of some within the party, renewal of the Referendum Pledge was impossible because there was no Unionist fiscal policy apart from the Tariff Reform programme. As he had pointed out to Salisbury and Derby, so he reminded St Aldwyn of his opinion that renewal of the Pledge would lead to open revolt by the Tariff Reformers. To emphasize his point, he added: '... and I am inclined to think that it would be justified from their, or perhaps I should say our, point of view.'[37] Then, to re-establish his claim to moderacy, he suggested that a public commitment to a small tariff on imported food ('5 shillings [per quarter] on wheat and 5 per cent on other food stuffs') might well calm the Free-Fooders; but he also cited Borden's view that without food duties, Imperial preference was no use to Canada – and that without Canada, Tariff Reform was meaningless.[38] In a letter to Aitken enclosing copies of this correspondence, he dwelt on the absolute necessity of keeping Sir Robert Borden stalwart in his demands for full Anglo-Canadian tariff co-operation: yet, as Bonar Law concluded wistfully, in electoral terms, 'the food taxes are only a handicap to us here.'[39]

In early October Lansdowne suggested that the November party conference would provide the ideal opportunity to announce the repeal of the Referendum Pledge; and that, since he had been leader in the Lords when Balfour made the Pledge in 1910, it was appropriate that he should announce the revised policy.[40] The plan appealed to Bonar Law, not least because of Lansdowne's low profile in the tariff controversy.[41]

The party convention opened on Thursday, 14 November at the Royal Albert Hall, and the rumour-laden air of politics was highly charged. The previous day, the first anniversary of Bonar Law's election as party leader, a scene had erupted in the Commons which in its passion and violence demonstrated how jittery the nation's governors had become. On 12 November the Opposition had narrowly defeated the Government in a snap division on a minor financial amendment to the Home Rule Bill. The following evening Asquith, backed by the full complement of his Liberal–Labour–Irish majority, attempted to introduce a resolution to reverse the vote, and was met by hysterical shouting and vituperation from the Opposition benches. According to one observer, it 'would have taken very little to make a general fight.'[42] Perhaps the most outrageous incident occurred after the exasperated Speaker, Lowther, had declared the tumultuous House adjourned. As Members filed out Winston Churchill taunted the Opposition by waving his handkerchief, and an infuriated Unionist MP, Ronald McNeill, inappositely but with stunning accuracy hurled the Speaker's own copy of the *Standing Orders of the House* at Churchill's head.[43]

What must have seemed to some amazed observers like sheer cabaret could not be taken lightly: the House was adjourned for a week. Tempers eased somewhat during this interval, but the passions involved and the resultant strain on these men kept the temperature of political discourse at a dangerous level. It should also be noted that while the Tory outrage had not precisely been orchestrated, neither was it entirely spontaneous. Bonar Law had taken no hand in the planning of the fracas; however, the rough outline of the scene – though not its intensity – had apparently been considered in the Unionist Whips' Room, and it is difficult to imagine that the Leader of the Opposition was completely unaware of the strong measures being contemplated to make the Prime Minister regret his error.[44] Whatever his private feelings, Bonar Law delighted the most warlike in his party by refusing to condemn the perpetrators of the ugly scene. His Liberal critics were even more outraged when at the opening of the party conference the following night he observed that he 'had not tried to interfere with these proceedings ... and would never in similar circumstances think it his duty to do so'.[45]

On 14 November, then, Lord Farquhar, Chairman of the National

Union, opened the conference and had the honour of introducing the leader of the Upper House. The diminutive Lansdowne, raising himself to his full height, promptly declared his rejection of the idea that the commitment to Tariff Reform had in any way weakened the party. Then he dropped his bomb: equally incorrect was the presumption 'that we shall be precluded by engagements into which we have entered from dealing with Tariff Reform, should we come into power, until we have made a further reference to the constituencies.' Conveniently disregarding Balfour's own ambiguity of November 1910, he insisted that the Liberals had ignored the proffered arrangement under which the Unionists had agreed to submit tariffs to a referendum if the Government would subject Irish Home Rule to a similar plebiscite. Hence, he concluded, when the Unionists next took office, they would do so with a free hand to deal with tariffs as they saw fit. As Bonar Law had suggested to St Aldwyn, Lansdowne promised that the Unionist leadership would propose a moderate tariff and undertake not to exceed it without reference to the voters in a subsequent election. Thus was the Referendum Pledge revoked; from its apparently enthusiastic reception, Lansdowne presumed the revocation to be popular.[46]

Farquhar then struggled to introduce Bonar Law. The audience cheered themselves hoarse at the mere mention of his name, and it was some minutes before the leader could make himself heard.[47] Bonar Law had agreed that Lansdowne should take the lead in the new aggressive stance on tariffs, and he held to this: his own sole reference to the subject was the simple statement, 'I concur in every word which has fallen from Lord Lansdowne ...' Even this brought more wild cheering, and demands by the Chairman for 'Order! Order!' Bonar Law went on in his brief address to condemn the Government in both broad and narrow terms (yet more cheers), and to promise that after the next election the nation could anticipate reversals of the Liberals' disastrous policies regarding Welsh Church disestablishment, land taxes and, of course, Irish Home Rule. He concluded by explaining what had led him to gamble on dropping the Referendum Pledge in the first place: he had had anxieties upon accepting the leadership, he told them, but on balance he thought he had succeeded, due in unequal measure to the attacks of their enemies and the friendship and encouragement of Unionists of all stripes. 'We are, in my opinion,' he said, 'more united at this moment than any political party has been in my time.'[48] Amid more cheers, he sat down – and no doubt hoped that his remarks about unity were to prove no less than the truth.

Within a remarkably brief time, however, he was to discover that the warm reception he had received did not reflect any broad popularity in the party for the reversal of policy Lansdowne had revealed. Bonar Law's attention was now much directed towards Ireland; meanwhile a storm quickly gathered over the remains of the Referendum Pledge. Archibald Salvidge, the powerful Liverpool party manager, was quick to point out to Walter Long that their leaders had erred in failing first to consult the constituencies – and the crisis which soon engulfed the party indicated that he was correct.[49] The centre of disquiet was Lancashire – home to both Salvidge and Lord Derby – where a meeting of the county Party was planned for 21 December.

Bonar Law was both surprised and disappointed by the reaction within his party, but continued to believe that his approach was the correct one for the moment; further, that even if Lansdowne and he had erred in their timing or method, there was little hope that a recantation now would rectify any past mistakes. He wrote to St Loe Strachey, editor of *The Spectator*, on 16 November, defending the decision: 'It was a case of a choice of evils, and all that one could do was to take the lesser of these two, and that I am sure we have done.'[50] After a fortnight spent reading letters addressed to him, the majority of which appealed for a return to the Referendum Pledge, Bonar Law clarified his position to Carson, Smith, Chamberlain and Balcarres: he regretted that this issue was paralysing the party at a time when Unionist energies were critically needed elsewhere. Furthermore, since his advocacy of the new position to a large measure depended on its potential to stave off party division, he was not philosophically averse to a return to the old position, if this was the necessary price of unity. Balcarres noted, however, that Bonar Law was adamant that he would make no change 'in response to active and open pressure.'[51] Yet another redirection, he made quite clear, must lead to a full meeting of the Unionist Party and to his and, probably, Lansdowne's resignations – precisely the course he had outlined to Salisbury five months before.

Bonar Law wrote to Strachey early in December that he continued to believe the new policy to be the correct one: 'I think the Union [with Ireland] more important than Tariff Reform; but the Union can only be preserved by the action of a United Party, and now at least there is no chance of a United Party in any other way than by adherence to the policy laid down at the Albert Hall.'[52] His final effort to save the situation, a speech made a few days later in Aitken's Lancashire constituency of Ashton-under-Lyne, was a distracted performance which perhaps betrayed the strain under which he laboured. Promising his audience complete candour – 'I want to tell you exactly what it is we propose in regard to food duties' – he explained that no such imposts were inexorably intended by the next Unionist Government, but rather that a conference with the self-governing colonies would be held to ascertain whether food duties were necessary to their participation in a system of imperial preference. Though roundly cheered by the audience Aitken had carefully gathered, this seemed less a clarification than yet another varient of the tariff programme.[53] Whole-Hoggers were quick to sense a weakening in his commitment to food taxes, while tariff sceptics wanted nothing less than a renewal of the Referendum Pledge.

An impatient Austen Chamberlain spoke the very same evening at Carlisle, once again rejecting all compromise over the full tariff programme and threatening that it would 'split the party from top to bottom and shake the confidence of their countrymen in their honesty, good faith, and courage if they postponed consideration of this great subject.'[54] It was plain for all to see that the Unionists were not, as their leader had so recently asserted, 'more united at this moment than any political party has been in my time'.

Bonar Law soon realized that he had misjudged the balance in his party: the Whole-Hoggers were well organized, boasting much energy, talent and commitment, and he had feared their potential to disrupt the party if they judged that Tariff Reform was being betrayed from within. He had failed, however, to understand that far more Unionists, including even moderate Tariff Reformers, feared that dropping the Referendum Pledge would endanger the electoral prospects of the party.[55] He knew his Ashton speech had not succeeded in defusing the crisis, and explained his discomfort to the Die-Hard Lord Selborne: 'What I am sure of is that while the great bulk of our Members are agreed in desiring to get rid of the food duties, none of them have any idea as to what the policy of the Party would then be ... For the moment all that we can do is to have patience and see how things develop.'[56] '[We] must', he wrote to Strachey, 'just do the best we can.'[57] Candid though his evaluation was, it was not a policy for action, and party leaders who do not act in a time of crisis often do not remain leaders.

It appeared that 'things' would 'develop' most immediately in Lancashire. The local Unionist organization were to meet on 21 December under the chairmanship of Lord Derby, whom Bonar Law was coming to number among his difficulties. Edward George Villiers

Stanley, seventeenth Earl of Derby, was forty-seven, and at the height of his powers. He was round of physique and sanguine of constitution, as well he might be: he was the 'King of Lancashire', perhaps the last great aristocrat more powerful for what he was than what he did. So unlike the Tory leaders who had preceded him, lacking their inherent or acquired perceptions, Bonar Law never fully understood the great landed class in their last generation of power – but he certainly knew that he neither trusted nor particularly liked 'Eddie' Derby.[58]

On the tariff question, Derby's mind had been settled since the election of December 1910. On the day that Bonar Law became leader, Derby wrote to him of his own conviction 'that Tariff Reform as presently advocated will not do for us here and by hook or by crook we have got to make such alteration as will prevent our opponents having the very taking cry that we are taxing the people's food and I am in hopes that you may see a way out of the difficulty.'[59] Derby sincerely believed that Tariff Reform meant electoral disaster in Lancashire; yet it is also true that in the Shadow Cabinet he did not protest against the decision to abrogate Balfour's Pledge.

At their meeting the Lancashire Unionists roundly condemned food duties, and called for a renewed Referendum Pledge. After a brief public session visitors were sent away, and the meeting – under Derby's supervision – endorsed a three-week recess, as a sort of 'cooling-off' period, presumably in lieu of a motion demanding restoration of the Pledge. Bonar Law was incensed: though it stopped short of a public challenge to his policy, this could hardly be seen as anything less than a passive censure of his actions – an ultimatum with a three-week deadline. Later that day Derby wrote him what was intended to be a soothing letter, inviting him to a luncheon to meet a delegation of men from the County Palatine and hear their complaints.[60] Bonar Law's refusal, polite but firm, nevertheless demonstrated his resentment of the local party's pretensions:

> I believe that a way out might be found if things were allowed to rest for the present, but if resolutions were adopted by the Lancashire Association contrary to the declared policy of the Party, it would, I expect, be necessary to summon a Party meeting, and in my opinion, a complete split in the Party would result.[61]

Bonar Law thought the atmosphere of crisis might be stilled by respite, and to him it seemed clear that what he was getting instead was Derby stirring up his loyal troops; as he wrote to Balcarres, 'This shows that Derby is the sole cause of all the trouble, as I suspected.'[62] Derby may have acquiesced in the majority Shadow Cabinet desire to drop the Balfour Pledge, but he seized every opportunity thereafter to criticize this revision of party policy – and Bonar Law considered this both unprincipled and treacherous. Derby, however, was a symptom more than a cause: he may have been disloyal to his leaders, but opposition to jettisoning the Referendum Pledge did not originate with him. Neither was it the creation of the Northcliffe press, the other bugbear angrily blamed by Bonar Law for his troubles.[63]

Bonar Law was correct, however, in his conclusion that Derby constituted a genuine problem. Immediately following the Lancashire party meeting Derby had, he learned, circulated among local Unionists a mischievous questionnaire which included queries Bonar Law judged to be 'leading': 'Do you think the abandoment of the referendum will do harm?', for example, and 'Do you think we could carry the election with food taxes?'[64]

Bonar Law also suspected that Derby, despite his assurances to the contrary, longed for the return of Arthur Balfour. At the time of Bonar Law's election to the leadership, Derby had indeed written to the King that 'six months from now ... the party will want [Balfour] back and wonder at their disloyalty to him and I hope be ashamed of themselves.'[65] On 22 December 1912, the day following the Lancashire party meeting, he went further, writing to Balfour: 'I know you are loyalty itself but could you not come back with a policy that did not include food taxes? If you did I believe the country would rally to you in a marvellous way and many of those who would come in are those who are now loudest in proclaiming their belief in Tariff Reform.'[66] Balfour had no time for such fantasy; he replied, 'If there are members of the Party who cannot see eye to eye with the Leaders on this subject the time may come, I suppose, when they will have publicly to express dissent. I earnestly hope it will *never* come; but I am sure the longer the fateful moment can be deferred the better.' But whatever the event, Balfour emphasized: 'Remember that *if Bonar Law goes the Party, as far as I can see, is doomed.*'[67] In Derby's view, whether Bonar Law went or stayed, party unity was lost 'unless the food taxers give way'.[68]

Bonar Law took his young family to Aitken's country house, Cherkley Court, for Christmas, but it cannot have been altogether a pleasant interlude. Balcarres summed up the gloom in the Unionist camp at the end of the year: 'Unquestionably we are in a parlous state.'[69]

Returning to town immediately after the holiday, Bonar Law wrote on 31 December to the Unionist elder statesman Henry Chaplin, acknowledging that the Albert Hall policy now seemed to have few friends. The letter reveals little optimism about his own position:

> Politicians are not the most stable people, but the change which has taken place is really remarkable – even for politicians. The strongest Tariff reformers are all coming to me saying it is impossible to fight with food taxes. The position, therefore, as you will see is a very difficult one, and I really have no idea how it will end, but so far as the present is concerned, I am not going to depart in the least from the policy we have laid down, though (between ourselves) I am concerned that it must in the end be modified. I doubt whether this modification will be possible under my leadership, and that is a bridge which I need not cross till we come to it.[70]

He wrote similarly to Lord Roberts on the following day: the Albert Hall programme might have won in the end 'if the party had supported it, but [he concluded] it cannot win if the party are hesitant and do not believe in it.' To this he added that if another reversal of policy proved necessary, it must be made under another leader.[71]

Bonar Law met the Lancashire Unionists on 2 January – in a committee room of the House, rather than under Derby's roof – and demanded that when they reconvened in nine days, they must pass a vote of confidence in him and drop any proposed resolution condemning food duties. Otherwise he would resign.[72] Balcarres as Chief Whip calculated that by this point no more than forty Unionist Members continued actively to support abandoning the Pledge,[73] and confided to his diary on 6 January his conclusion that Bonar Law's threat to resign was no bluff.[74] In a memorandum of the following day, Bonar Law wrote of Lansdowne and himself: 'It seems to me that we have only two alternatives: one is to go forward without hesitation with the policy which we have announced [at the Albert Hall], and the other is to resign.'[75]

He surmised that, because of the dread within the party of choosing another leader after such a short interval, he could summon a party meeting and possibly 'succeed in carrying a majority of the Party in favour of steady adherence to our present policy.' To those who had already encouraged such a bold step – including the Confederates Page Croft, Amery and George Lloyd – he had suggested that coerced adherence would be temporary and ultimately unhelpful.[76] 'I think', he concluded in his memorandum, 'we must adopt the second [alternative], and for us the sooner that course is taken the better.'

Bonar Law favoured a full party meeting at which he would explain that, while dropping the Balfour Pledge remained to his mind the correct approach, evidence indicated that the party did not agree. There remained, therefore, only one option: 'after the declarations made by Lord Lansdowne and myself it would be simply impossible for us to announce a [further] change in policy and to continue to lead the Party.'

Into this bleak picture a small glimmer of light was about to be introduced, however. On Monday, 6 January, encountering both Bonar Law and Lord Lansdowne at the funeral of the Duke of Abercorn, Sir Edward Carson learned to his horror that, though both appeared ready to bow to the majority over the Referendum Pledge, they were resolved, in such a case, on resignation. As an Irish Unionist Carson cared little for disagreements over tariffs and pledges and referenda; what concerned him was the need for a united party to combat the spectre of Home Rule.[77] According to the party whip Robert Sanders, Carson inspired Edward Goulding to organize a petition among the Tariff Reformers beseeching Bonar Law and Lansdowne to compromise over the Albert Hall policy and also remain as leaders.[78] This picture of a chance encounter with Carson and his subsequent brokering of an unlooked-for solution to the deadlock has proved attractive to historians.[79] It is likely, however, that the appeal placed before him shortly thereafter, always known as the January Memorial, was not unexpected by Bonar Law, either in form or in content.

Following his conversation with Bonar Law and Lansdowne at the funeral, Carson immediately sought out his loyal confidant, the Ulster leader Captain James Craig, MP for East Down. Apparently the two Irish Unionists approached Aitken, and Craig went late that night by prior arrangement to Aitken's house to meet Bonar Law. The three searched together for a compromise which would allow Bonar Law a decorous retreat from the Albert Hall policy while somehow enabling him to stay in place as leader. They agreed 'that a memorial should be sent by MPs to B.L. recapitulating the crisis of Church, Union and Constitution, begging him to harmonize the party, and to accept the tariff compromise.'[80] Bonar Law indicated that such a compromise would be acceptable to Lansdowne and himself *only* if a large majority of Members were to sign the memorial.

When apprised by Balcarres the following afternoon of the progress of the scheme, Bonar Law demonstrated that his Glaswegian common sense remained in good order: tiring of the talk of catastrophe, he announced he was going out to order a new overcoat, 'which he says [noted Balcarres] is long overdue.'[81]

The January Memorial was ready in two days, the result of long and hard negotiation among the partisans on both sides of the tariff issue who took part in several drafting sessions on 7–8 January.[82] Circulated immediately, the document paid rich tribute to Bonar Law's leadership, and reiterated the party's commitment to Tariff Reform and Imperial Preference. It called attention to the Ashton-under-Lyne speech and its formula for an imperial conference to decide the future of tariffs. Getting to the point, it continued:

> The question which is agitating the Party resolves itself into this – as to whether, in the event of the British Government finding it desirable, as the result of such conference, to impose duties upon foodstuffs with a view to the mutual advantage of the Colonies and ourselves, the proposals formulated should be forthwith brought before Parliament or first submitted to the electors for their decision.
>
> By the adoption of the latter course we feel that no abandonment of principle is involved. It should involve a modification in procedure which could be accepted for the sake of closing our ranks. We should in any event be prepared to follow your leadership, which we believe to be indispensable to the Party.

Noting the primacy of the Home Rule battle and party members' collective agreement that he was their only possible leader in it, the document concluded:

> In these circumstances, affirming our loyalty to you and our willingness to follow any course that you may think proper, we appeal to your devotion alike to the country and the Party not for one moment to entertain the idea of resigning at the present juncture.
>
> For the reasons we have mentioned we hope you may find it possible in this grave emergency, like many of the signatories to this document, to sink your own views as to the best methods and procedure in relation to one point, however important, in our policy, so that we may end all controversies and under your leadership oppose an absolutely united front to the disastrous proposals of the Government.[83]

Within two days, 231 of the 280 Unionist Members in the House had signed the Memorial. The Speaker and twenty-seven front-bench Unionist Members were not invited to sign; other non-signatories were seven Members who were ill or abroad, five who were absent from London, one who was vacating his seat, and a scattering of others who were unaccounted for. Only eight MPs actually refused to sign:[84] Lord

Winterton, L.S. Amery, Lieutenant-Colonel Archer-Shee, the cousins Allen and Charles Bathurst, William Burdett-Coutts, George Lloyd and George Touche.[85]

Bonar Law's official response was made public on 13 January 1913, in the form of an open letter to the Chief Whip which left no doubt who was the leader and who the followers in the Unionist Party. He offered the commitment of the next Unionist Government that, in the event of food duties proving necessary and desirable to both the Imperial and Dominion parliaments, no such duties would be implemented until they had been placed before the British voters at a second election.[86] Bonar Law explained why Lansdowne and he were willing to accept this, despite their recent public pronouncements to the contrary:

> This modification does not seem to us to involve any principle, the adoption of which would have prevented us from loyally supporting the course of action desired by the majority of the Party. It would, nevertheless, have been more agreeable to ourselves, and in our view more for the interest of the Party, that the change in method should be accompanied by a change of leaders.
>
> The memorial, however, which has been presented to me, and which has been signed not only by those who desire that the method of procedure should be modified, but by those who prefer that it should have remained unchanged, urges upon us that in the opinion of those who signed it a change in the leadership 'would be fatal to the best interests of the Party and of the country.'
>
> We feel that in view of such an expression of opinion from such a quarter, it is our duty to comply with the request which has been addressed to us, and this we are prepared to do.[87]

Comments elicited by the text of the letter were collected informally by Balcarres in the lobbies of the House and reported to Bonar Law. They were numerous and wide-ranging, from 'very dignified' and 'awfully good', to 'a little stiff necked' and even 'faulty grammar'. The Chief Whip, his nerves badly frayed by the crisis, probably found himself most in agreement with the unnamed MP who described the solution as 'a perfect godsend'.[88] When Bonar Law summoned the parliamentary party to the Carlton Club later on the day his letter appeared, the compromise was endorsed with enormous relief and he and Lansdowne were heartily cheered – the Whole-Hog programme had been mortally wounded, but the Unionist Party was saved to fight another day.[89]

Bonar Law knew the cost of what he had done, and anticipated criticism for abandoning his own closest friends. As he wrote to Austen Chamberlain, the son of his first political hero:

> You cannot fail to look upon it as if it were going back upon your father's life-work, and though I believe that the tendency towards closer union on the part of the Colonies is the direct result of what he did, yet that cannot at the moment soften the blow much.
>
> It is to me a great misfortune that I should be in such a position that it is I who seem to deal the blow at his policy. I have told you, and I am sure you believe me, that if you or your father wished it I should gladly resign my position [,] but I have not the courage to go on and be responsible for a policy which, with the feeling in the Party such as it is, I am sure is bound to fail. If I had been your father, I might have carried it through successfully, but I cannot.
>
> In this crisis as in the earlier one, you have acted as what I know you are, a great gentleman.[90]

The conclusion is unavoidable: this crisis was largely the outcome of a misjudgement on the part of Bonar Law. At the time he replaced Balfour, Unionist policy over fiscal reform was unclear. Zealous Tariff Reformers obviously intended to kindle the party's commitment to import duties, and he was certain that, better organized and more ruthless, they were more dangerous to party unity than the Free-Food Tories. A Tariff Reformer himself, his sense was that they would become uncontrollable if import taxes, including food duties, were not placed in the forefront of the party programme. Yet, in the end, this turned out not to be the case. Unionists were not ready to risk all for tariffs: to judge from their actions once the crisis was under way, none but the most dedicated Tariff Reformers were prepared to throw all electoral caution to the winds in the interests of the Chamberlainite programme.

The reasons behind Bonar Law's actions throughout the crisis are neither difficult to discover nor inconsistent with his values. Like many Unionists, his mind was already more concentrated on the Home Rule struggle than on the fiscal reform debate; he needed little reminding that a divided party would be a useless weapon in any fight to preserve the Union. In addition, it should be remembered that while Bonar Law was a Tariff Reformer, he was not so committed to the full Chamberlainite vision as the most doctrinaire believers. He had embraced the Referendum Pledge in 1910, but two years later saw it not as a philosophical but as a political matter. Furthermore, as the crisis played itself out, he came to see that he had misjudged the relative strengths of the wings of the party: despite the blustering of such Whole-Hoggers as Amery, Lloyd and Page Croft, and the lofty pronouncements of the son and heir, Austen Chamberlain, they proved in the end not to represent the strongest element within the party. Finally, Bonar Law was an ambitious man whose ultimate goals were yet to be reached, and he was not averse to taking a political risk when the stakes were high enough and the odds tempting. Abandoning the Referendum Pledge was a dangerous game. When that failed, only an additional risk – threatening resignation while proposing compromise – seemed to offer the hope of recouping what he had lost.

The compromise of the January Memorial was a curious one, for through it the party leaders' publicly announced policy was rejected by the rank and file, while the leaders themselves not only retained their places but were even able to announce that their reversal involved no matter of principle. It was no accident, no eleventh-hour miracle sprung on Bonar Law and Lansdowne by Carson as a surprise. Bonar Law was from the outset in the confidence of the Unionists who crafted the compromise, and was kept informed as the document was refined. Despite being manifestly a device providing for the tergiversation of their leaders, the Memorial was received by most party members with, as we have seen, a degree of feeling ranging from relief to sheer ecstasy and rejected by only a tiny handful – indicating just how welcome a stratagem it was. Bonar Law's personal popularity remained high throughout the episode, despite his obvious role as the partial cause of the trouble.[91]

Finally, it should not be overlooked that Bonar Law was well aware how strong a hand he was playing. Although technically leader only in the Commons, he had wasted little time in demonstrating his primacy over the ageing Lansdowne.[92] Furthermore, his readiness to threaten his own resignation demonstrated with small margin for doubt his confidence that he was the only possible leader. Unionists knew that to expel a second leader within thirteen months would be disastrous. Were they so foolish as to do so, Balfour would not return – and of the two rivals of the previous year, Chamberlain was even less compromising on tariffs, while Long's health was more uncertain and his reputation for instability unimproved. Among the other party chieftains, Alfred Lyttelton inspired small confidence, Selborne's supporters were few, Curzon's even fewer, and George Wyndham's fewer still. The formidable Carson was completely wrapped up in the struggle against Home Rule, and thoroughly pledged to Bonar Law – as his role in the drama demonstrated.

Close examination of this crisis, John Vincent has written, 'reminds one how a chess-player's skill may avert the fate of Peel.'[93] The destroyer of the Corn Laws, while certainly a greater figure in history than Bonar Law, did not begin to equal him as a party leader. Through a miscalculation Bonar Law threatened both party unity and his own place as party leader; but he recovered almost immediately and, if anything, strengthened his party and his own hold over Unionism.

6

Ireland: 'We are in for troublous times'

WITH THE EXCEPTION of a very few of the truest of believers, Bonar Law's Unionist followers forgave and forgot his miscalculation over Tariff Reform; and the primary reason was that a much older and greater struggle began anew in 1912, over the granting of political autonomy – Home Rule – to Ireland. In no way did the tariff question – or matters of economic, military and foreign policy – became unimportant to them; it was rather that the question of Irish Home Rule had the power to push these other matters into the background.

Ireland was Britain's first imperial possession. Since the days of the Norman kings Englishmen had engaged from time to time in attempts to conquer that second island, and over the centuries the land and the law of Ireland came gradually under British control. The advent in Tudor times of Protestantism, not through the revelations of any latter-day prophet but at the behest of a line of practical and ruthless monarchs, drove governors and governed further apart and exacerbated their mutual dislike and lack of understanding. With the Stuarts came a policy of managed immigration – the 'Plantation' – into the north-east of Ireland of a people unlike either the native Irish or the 'Ascendancy', the transplanted English ruling class who controlled much of the rest of the island. These newcomers, largely Scottish and thoroughly Calvinist, were installed to foster Protestantism and provide a cadre on Irish soil absolutely loyal to the Crown. They fulfilled all expectations. They throve and they multiplied, and they established control over the ancient province of Ulster, which they came to think of as their own.

At the time of the French Revolution and the wars against Napoleon, many on both sides of the Irish Sea were reminded of the ancient Irish maxim, 'England's peril – Ireland's opportunity'. At the turn of the eighteenth century, after the latest in the long series of rebellions against English rule, the Younger Pitt proposed his solution. To accompany his Act of Union making of the two islands one nation, he proposed what was then called Catholic Emancipation – the removal from Catholics of limitations to full citizenship. But, great as Pitt was, his plan misfired. In the end, the 1801 Act uniting Britain and Ireland disappointed both the Prime Minister and the Irish Catholics: in the face of stubborn Protestant protest on the part of King, Parliament and people, Catholic Emancipation was dropped. Rather, Ireland was Jonah to Britain's whale; the pitifully weak Irish Parliament ceased to exist, and Irishmen no longer had a country – even a conquered country – of their own. Whatever else it might have meant, the Act endorsed the mastery of Briton and Protestant over Irishman and Catholic. In doing so, it became a totemic object of hatred for Irish Nationalists.

By the middle of the nineteenth century, as legal disadvantages to Catholics and Nonconformists finally began to drop away, a pivotal event came upon Ireland. The Great Famine of 1845 to 1850 not only halved Ireland's population, through death or distressed immigration (and dramatically changed the demographic make-up of many other countries, including both Britain and America); in doing so, this horror injected further poison into ancient wounds. British policy over the Famine was not a shadowy form of genocide, as the black legend would have it, but neither was it a catalogue of human compassion. The Government embraced the *laissez-faire* Benthamite economic wisdom of their time – and who, Britons consoled themselves, could have done more? Many Irishmen thought they knew the answer, and only the dissolution of the Act of Union would satisfy them. Increasingly generous Land Acts in the fifty years which followed orchestrated the creation of a growing class of Irish small-holders, yet neither the Famine nor the rule of the Ascendancy, many of whom were themselves ruined by the calamity or bought out under the Land Acts, were forgiven or forgotten.

In the final decades of the nineteenth century the southern Irish peasantry found a party and a political hero of their own: the Irish National Party, led by the formidable 'Green Lion', Charles Stuart Parnell, thoroughly Irish in all but blood and religion. W.E. Gladstone concluded that educational and land legislation were not enough to uplift Catholic Irishmen, and in 1886 he dropped the political bomb of his age: Britain's second island must have the autonomy of which the Parnellites dreamed, embodied in the First Home Rule Bill – which in fact offered only the most limited sort of self-rule. The attempt failed, famously, splitting Gladstone's party and driving Joe Chamberlain's anti-Home Rule Liberal Unionists into partnership with the enraged Conservatives.

The failure of the Bill disappointed Irish and British Home Rulers, but the Liberal Party committed itself to try again. In 1893 Gladstone, now the Grand Old Man of British politics, saw his Second Home Rule Bill pass through the Commons. That was as far as it got, of course, for it was then promptly throttled by the overwhelming Unionist majority in the Upper House. When Gladstone laid down his burden his successor, Lord Rosebery, shelved the Liberal Party's commitment to Home Rule; for a time it slept, but it did not die. Neither did the Unionists counter-resolve to stop Home Rule again, when the time came.

The 1910 elections had wiped away the great Liberal majority of 1906, and by the time Bonar Law came to his party's leadership, the Unionists were by a small margin the largest single party in the House.[1] To maintain their Government, the Liberals depended upon the eighty-four Irish Nationalists, led by John Redmond; and this ensured that even the most reluctant among them rediscovered a commitment to Home Rule – Redmond's price for keeping the Government in power. As significantly, perhaps, the Parliament Act of 1911 provided in its awkward way for the absolute primacy of the House of Commons. Struggle as they might, Unionists knew that a Home Rule Bill introduced in 1912 would become law by 1914, unless they could either somehow sabotage it during its required three passages, unaltered, through the Commons, or secure a Dissolution of Parliament. Under the rules of politics as revised by the Parliament Bill, they had no other options.

Most of Ireland's million Protestants – about a quarter of the island's population – lived in Ulster's six north-easternmost counties. In Antrim, Armagh, Down and Londonderry they formed a clear majority, while in Fermanagh and Tyrone the numbers of Protestants and Catholics were approximately equal; in the remaining counties of Cavan, Monaghan and Donegal Protestants were in the minority. According to the 1911 census, Protestants accounted for 56 per cent of the total population of the province's nine counties, a balance reflected in the returns following the December 1910 election: seventeen Ulster Unionist Members and sixteen Irish Nationalists.[2] The Southern Unionists – those living outside Ulster – made up no more than ten per cent of the population of the rest of Ireland, and the majority could be found clustered around the cities of Dublin and Cork. Apart from the constituency known as Dublin University, Ireland beyond Ulster was, electorally, a Nationalist preserve.

Bonar Law's knowledge of the south and west of Ireland was neither deep nor personal, but Ulster was another matter. He was born of an Ulster father who had educated his son in his country's culture, and his religious heritage – from both New Brunswick and Glasgow – was soundly Presbyterian. He had spent much time in the province and knew it well, and his elder brother practised medicine there. He understood the gulf between Ulstermen and Irish Nationalists, and he judged it to be one which, realistically, could not be bridged. He also accepted that it was not for nothing the Tories now called themselves Unionists and had in 1912 accepted into their fold Chamberlain's anti-Home Rule Liberals.

Despite these sympathies, before late 1911 Bonar Law had said little about Ireland, either in the House or on the platform. Two events changed this. The first was the Parliament Act, which he dubbed the 'Home Rule in Disguise Bill'.[3] Only days after its passage he announced in the House a position from which he did not retreat over the long course of the fight: if the British electorate clearly wished to sanction the 'experiment' of Home Rule for Ireland, his command to Unionists was, 'You have got to submit'.[4] His counsel, however, did not end there:

> On the other hand, I say equally deliberately, if this or any other Government try to force through a measure on which there is good reason to believe that the people of this country are not agreed ... I would never, if I were one of those Irish loyalists[,] consent to have a system forced upon me as part of a corrupt Parliamentary bargain.[5]

The Ulsterman's son fully understood the connection between Home Rule, the powerful Parliament Act and the possible need for the Opposition to force an election.

The second event was Bonar Law's elevation to the leadership of his party. In a series of speeches culminating at the famous January 1912 meeting at the Albert Hall, he had much to say about a new Home Rule Bill. At Bootle in early December he took up a theme to which he would often return, asserting that 'The attempt of the Government to carry this measure in a Parliament where the majority was obtained on other issues is one of the most dishonest things which has ever been done by any political party in this country.' The former businessman turned next to the question of what exactly his Irish policy would be:

'My Irish policy is to treat Ireland precisely as I treat England, Scotland and Wales.' That was the truth, but not the whole truth. We have treated Ireland far more generously than we have ever treated any other part of the Kingdom ... What Ireland needs and what we have given her is less politics and more industries. What our opponents, led by Mr Redmond and his band[,] are promising to Ireland is more politics and less industry.

He closed with strong words (and perhaps a hint of self-parody), aimed at a Government which, he warned, must not underestimate the dedication of the Unionists to the fight against Home Rule:

Now, I have spoken as I always try to speak, with restraint, but restraint does not mean weakness ... I speak, as I believe I am entitled to speak, not only for myself but for the Unionist party in the House of Commons – that when the time comes there will be no shrinking from strong action. There will be no shrinking from any action which we think necessary to defeat one of the most ignoble conspiracies which has ever been formed against the liberties of free-born men ...[6]

At the Albert Hall in January his major themes lay elsewhere, but he returned briefly to the Home Rule question, particularly to the reality which most troubled Asquith and his colleagues: the Ulstermen. 'We who represent the Unionist Party in England and Scotland', he said, 'have supported, and we mean to support them, not because we are intolerant but because their claims are just.' Roughly belabouring Asquith's Cabinet as Gadarene swine, foolishly 'running down a steep place into the sea', he warned the Liberals, who had won less than half the votes polled in the last election, that:

If they really seriously attempt to carry out their programme when at least half of the nation is against them, it will not be representative government – it will not be government at all; it will be the tyranny of a revolutionary Committee. If they make the attempt they will impose a strain upon our Parliamentary institutions which I am sure these institutions cannot bear.[7]

From the outset of his leadership Bonar Law understood that the existence of an Irish Protestant minority vociferously loyal to the Union constituted his party's strongest anti-Home Rule weapon. As this speech indicates, he also determined that it would be unwise for him, as the Unionist leader in this debate, to allow any colleague to manoeuvre him out of his position as possessor of the boldest voice in his party.

While many in Britain at this time equated the enactment of Home Rule with the abandonment of loyalists throughout all Ireland, the well-organized Protestant population of the north-east had no intention of allowing them to forget that most Irish Unionists were Ulstermen. By this time, much of their hope lay with their leader, Sir Edward Henry Carson, QC, MP. Imposing, hawk-faced and brilliant, he was a dynamic force in Unionist politics both in Ulster and outside it. Pitiless to his enemies, he was also generous to friends, vain about both his age and his appearance and, upon occasion, very funny. Though he lacked nothing in the way of worldly success, his nature remained saturnine. Curiously, this charismatic and powerful man suffered from persistent hypochondria, and regularly peppered his correspondence with complaints about his delicate constitution: in the end, he lived to be over eighty.

A Trinity College man and the son of a successful Dublin architect of Scottish stock, Carson had inherited no Ulster ties.[8] He was a communicant of the Church of Ireland, had lived most of his life in Dublin and London, and represented Dublin University in the House for a quarter of a century. He became one of the most famous barristers of his generation, taking silk both in Ireland and England and serving as Solicitor-General under Salisbury and Balfour. He well deserved his reputation as one of the greatest of cross-examiners – duelling with and finally destroying Oscar Wilde in the celebrated Queensberry criminal libel case of 1895 – and by his mid forties was a Bencher of the Middle Temple, wealthy and comfortable at the apex of his profession.

Carson was fifty-six when, in 1910, he succeeded Walter Long as leader of the Ulster Unionist MPs. Though he had refused to have anything to do with the party leadership race in 1911, Bonar Law understood that Carson's brilliance, magnetism and independent position as Ulster leader made him something of a rival, none the less. Something else should be remembered about Edward Carson: his undoubted talent shone best when attacking an entrenched position – he was a natural destroyer of other men's works. He proved restless, inefficient and easily frustrated in office, but he was unequalled when in fighting opposition.

Given the political complexion of the years 1910 and 1911 – the lost elections, the battle of 'Hedgers' and 'Ditchers' followed by the passage of the Parliament Act and the rejection of Balfour – there is no doubt that Bonar Law inherited a bad-tempered party moving towards the political Right.[9] If Unionists were in a rigid and recalcitrant mood, for the time being he was willing to lead them in the direction in which they were inclined to go. He both disliked and distrusted most of the leaders of the Government, and meant to test them with heavy blows.

Such a climate of opinion combined with the burden of centuries of Anglo-Irish animosity was perfectly designed to stir the ever-glowing coals of religious aversion into a fire-storm of hatred. If Bonar Law was exposed to anti-Catholic intolerance as a boy, it did not survive in the man, yet he believed (with George Bernard Shaw) that when Ulsterman sang 'O God, Our Help in Ages Past', 'they meant business'.[10] He said once to his friend, the newspaper proprietor Sir George Riddell: 'It may seem strange to you and me but [the Ulster debate] is a religious question. These people are in serious earnest. They are prepared to die for their convictions.'[11] His commitment to Ulster was undeniable, and his language remained throughout these years unabashedly combative. His feelings, however, were not those of the average Ulsterman: his rhetoric was aimed at the men of power in Westminster, not at the Irish people and certainly never at their religion.

Bonar Law believed that Irish Protestants had reason to fear subjugation to a Parliament in Dublin, and supported without reservation the right of the Ulster community to safeguard their identity, whatever the outcome of the Home Rule debate. However, he had no sympathy for their undoubted religious intolerance towards their Catholic neighbours. In his speech at Bootle in December 1911 he told his audience: 'I am not fond of talking about religion. When I came down here as your candidate I was told that I must not talk politics, that I must abuse my Roman Catholic fellow-subjects. I do not believe it.'[12]

He wrote similarly to the distinguished Anglican layman, Sir Charles Cripps: 'I hate bringing in religious bigotry as much as you do, and I think I have always avoided it in my speeches, and shall certainly try to do so in future. Of course, religion is the main factor in Ulster; but there is no reason, in my opinion, why our attack upon Home Rule should take the form of an attack upon the Roman Catholic religion.'[13] Bonar Law was quite prepared to play the Orange card of Ulster to stop Home Rule, but he would never beat the Orange drum of anti-Catholic hatred.

It is irresistible to conclude that had the Government at this point brought in a bill which exempted Protestant Ulster from Home Rule, the Unionists would have had their most promising ground cut from beneath their feet. The Liberals knew what the Ulster challenge was to be, and on 23 September 1911 Carson reminded them. At Craigavon, his friend Captain Craig's estate on the shores of Belfast Lough, he told a crowd of 50,000:

> I now enter into a compact with you, and every one of you, and with the help of God you and I joined together ... will yet defeat the most nefarious conspiracy that has ever been hatched against a free people ... We must be prepared ... the morning Home Rule passes, oursleves to become responsible for the government of the Protestant Province of Ulster.[14]

Unmoved, Asquith informed the King in February 1912 of the Government's conclusion that the Home Rule Bill should apply to the whole of Ireland. Yet he kept one card up his sleeve: if, in the light of 'fresh evidence of facts, or the pressure of British opinion',

> ... it becomes clear as the Bill proceeds that some special treatment must be provided for the Ulster counties, the Government will be ready to recognize the necessity either by amendment of the Bill, or by not pressing it on under the provisions of the Parliament Act. In the meantime, careful confidential inquiry is to be made as to the real extent and character of the Ulster resistance.[15]

Asquith did not of course reveal this line of thinking to his opponents. However, the harsh strategy planned by Bonar Law was precisely intended to prove that Gladstonian Home Rule was impossible because the 'real extent and character of the Ulster resistance' could not be overcome. In the end he meant to make the Liberals' political nightmare come true.

II

The 1912 Parliamentary session opened on 14 February, and the King's Speech proclaimed the Government's intention to implement Home Rule. The storm warnings for the coming political season proved themselves accurate as the two parties wasted little time in beginning to tear at one another over Welsh Church disestablishment, National Insurance and Trades Union regulation. None of these issues, however, generated such heat as the new Government of Ireland Bill.

The Bill was to be introduced on 11 April, and Bonar Law travelled to Ulster on Easter Sunday, four days before, for a flying tour of the province. He was received as a favourite son, and tumultuous crowds pressed to hear and acclaim him in Larne, Comber and Belfast. The zenith of the visit came on 9 April, in the grounds of the Royal Agricult- ural Society at Balmoral, near Belfast. Seventy Unionist MPs adorned the platform, as did the Protestant Primate of All Ireland and the Moderator of the Church of Scotland. The Ninetieth Psalm was sung, reminding those assembled that all flesh was as grass, while overhead perhaps the largest Union Jack ever made – some forty-eight feet by twenty-five – waved from a towering staff more than ninety feet high. Bonar Law, astounded by the size of the meeting,[16] addressed the crowd of more than 100,000 silent Ulstermen:

> Your are a besieged city ... The Government by their Parliament Act have erected a boom against you, a boom to cut you off from the help of the British people. You will burst that boom. The help will come and when the crisis is over men will say of you in words not unlike those once used by Pitt, 'You have saved yourselves by your exertions and you will save the Empire by your example.'[17]

Carson followed with a speech less eloquent and more angry, and at the conclusion of the meeting strode once again to the centre of the platform: 'Raise your hands,' he demanded. 'Repeat after me: "Never under any circumstances will we submit to Home Rule".' Bonar Law joined his friend and raised both his hand and his voice, further cement- ing the tie between British Unionism – and its leader – and the welfare of the Ulstermen.

Developing a plan to combat the Bill was no easy task for Bonar Law, as the options available to him were both few and dangerous. In the first place, the Government majority combined with the Parliament Act made the Bill's passage appear all but unstoppable. Leader and Whips were tireless in their efforts to delay procedure on the floor of the House and, with each division, to press the Government majority relentlessly.[18] Though the clanging division bells might bring every Unionist running, and though one after another Opposition Member risked suspension for the extremity of his language, the Bill could not be derailed in the normal course of things – barring the unlikely event of a break-up of the Government majority.

Second, Bonar Law was faced with the fact that while all Unionists in Britain and Ireland opposed Home Rule, they did not necessarily oppose it in the same way or to the same degree – or even to the same end. The Ulstermen, closely and militantly united, attracted the support and admiration of many British advocates. The Southern Irish Unionists, far fewer in number, and their supporters in Britain faced possible division between those resigned to 'inevitable' Home Rule and willing to see Ulster drive the best bargain she could, and anti-Home Rule absolutists, ready to condemn any signs of desertion by Ulster – a situation which encompassed dangerous possibilities and demanded close watching.

Third, facing all partisans was the terrible tradition of violence which lurked just below the surface of Irish politics. Ulstermen had begun to enroll in paramilitary units sponsored by the Orange Lodges as early as 1910, and in January 1913 these were united to form the Ulster Volunteer Force.[19] Home Rulers in the South soon followed their lead and formed the Irish National Volunteers.[20] The resources and manpower of the Royal Irish Constabulary were limited, and if wide-spread civil disturbance arose, the military would be the only hope of restoring order. This placed a peculiar pressure upon the British Army, for which Ireland and especially Ulster traditionally supplied a disproportionately large number of officers and other ranks – the majority of whom were Protestant, and presumably therefore unsympathetic to Home Rule.

So the 1910 elections and the Parliament Act had made of Home Rule, once a distant concern, a present danger; and Bonar Law intended that Ulster should be the anvil on which it would be hammered to bits. On 16 April 1912, in his first formal response to the Bill, he reminded the House that Ulstermen had said they would never accept its provisions, and that he believed them. 'How', he asked the Prime Minister, 'are you going to overcome that resistance?' If the Prime Minister meant to depend upon the Army to break them, Bonar Law advised that he should think again.

He also attacked the moral dilemma inherent in the Government's latter-day Gladstonian Bill: inclusion of the Protestant north-east in an autonomous Ireland with a Dublin-based Parliament. If, he argued, it was somehow right that Ireland should acquire self-governance because she was by history, religion and race unlike the rest of the United Kingdom, then Ulster, for similar reasons, merited similar treatment in Ireland. As he reminded the House:

> In Belfast and the surrounding counties – where the feeling is overwhelmingly Unionist – they are a million of people – something like a fourth of the

whole population of Ireland. If, therefore, there is any ground upon which you may say that the Nationalists of Ireland are entitled to separate treatment as against us, the ground is far stronger for separate treatment of Ulster ..

Another element of Unionist opposition carried the ethical argument a step further, Bonar Law stating plainly in this same speech that it was impossible peacefully to force one-quarter of the population of Ireland into estrangement from the United Kingdom if they did not wish to be so estranged. Only coercion could deliver all of Ireland into a Home Rule Parliament, he thundered; only force and almost certainly blood-shed could divide Ulstermen from the Union with Britain. This brought his followers to their feet. Glaring at the uncomfortable gentlemen on the Treasury Bench opposite, he painted a picture of what he said would be the result of their policy: did they plan to hurl the full majesty and power of the law, supported on the bayonets of the British Army, against a million Ulstermen marching under the Union Jack and singing 'God Save the King'? Would the Army hold? Would the British popula-tion – would the Crown – stand for such a slaughter? He gestured angrily: 'The thing is impossible. All your talk about details, the union of hearts and the rest of it, is a sham. This is a reality. It is a rock, and on that rock this Bill or any Bill like it will inevitably make shipwreck.' While Mr Speaker struggled to restore order in the Chamber, the reality of what they had heard no doubt struck Honourable Members: the Leader of the Opposition had openly warned the Government of the possibility of civil war in Ireland.

Bonar Law revealed a third powerful component of the Unionist campaign in this speech: the complaint that the Government had not submitted the issue to the people in an election. Since becoming leader, Bonar Law had stated repeatedly that Unionists would accept Home Rule if the electorate sanctioned it. With the bill now before the House, he was able to taunt the Government that the most controversial legis-lation of recent memory was going forward without being tested at the polls. Unionists had struggled to make Home Rule a key test in the 1910 elections, while Government supporters had wisely preferred to take up the constitutional challenge of the Lords veto.[21] In the House on 16 April, Bonar Law further warned the Government: '... you will not carry this Bill without submitting it to the people of this country, and, if you make the attempt, you will succeed only in breaking our Parlia-mentary machine.' By March 1914, after two years of rough-and-tumble politics, he had not retreated one step from this position:

I said to the Prime Minister: Make certain – and surely, in face of all of this trouble it is worthwhile making certain – that you have the will of the country behind you, and, so far as the Unionist party are concerned, we will absolutely cease all unconstitutional opposition to the carrying of your measure.[22]

One final element of the Unionist campaign against Home Rule was less emotive, but significant all the same: this involved the Government pledge, in the Preamble to the Parliament Act, to reform the Upper House and 'to substitute for the House of Lords as it at present exists a Second Chamber constituted on a popular instead of a hereditary basis.' As Carson, at his lawyerly best, said in the same debate: 'You are bringing [Home Rule] in, while the Constitution of the country is in suspense … while the lying preamble [of the Parliament Act] remains unrepealed.'[23] The Unionists were to argue throughout the course of the lengthy debate over Home Rule that so long as this commitment to change the very structure of Parliament held, the introduction of legislation of fundamental constitutional importance was inappropriate until the constitution itself had been clarified.[24] Throughout the Home Rule crisis Asquith repeatedly renewed this commitment, saying on 10 March 1913, for example: 'Not only are we under a distinct obligation to fulfill this intention, but we have the strongest possible interest in doing so …'[25] Such promises – which the Cabinet had no intention of fulfilling at this time – simply drove the Unionists to further fury and encouraged them to argue with greater force that the constitution itself was 'in suspense'. Asquith and the Liberals, of course, remained unmoved.

In those two and a half years between Asquith's reintroduction of Home Rule and the coming of the Great War the British parliamentary system was placed under a stress as great as any in modern times. Bonar Law's relentless campaign to drive an unwilling Government to submit their Home Rule policy to the electorate spared no one in public life whom he thought had a role to play, and this included the King. In a few moments of private conversation with King George following a state dinner at Buckingham Palace in May 1912, Bonar Law revealed to His Majesty, whom he hardly knew, both the depth of his determination in the Home Rule crisis and his profound antipathy towards the Government. Austen Chamberlain recalled Bonar Law's version of the encounter:

'I think I have given the King the worst five minutes he has had for a long time,' he observed; and this is his account of their conversation as noted by me as soon as I got home.

The King began, 'I have just been saying to Sir E. Carson that I hope there will be no violent scenes this session.'

'May I talk quite freely to Your Majesty?' asked Law.

'Please do. I wish you to.'

'Then, I think, Sir, that the situation is a grave one not only for the House but also for the Throne. Our desire has been to keep the Crown out of our struggles, but the Government have brought it in. Your only chance is that they should resign within two years. If they don't, you must either accept the Home Rule Bill or dismiss your Ministers and choose others who will support you in vetoing it – and in either case half your subjects will think you have acted against them.'

The King turned red and Law asked, 'Have you never considered that, Sir?'

'No,' said the King, 'it is the first time it has been suggested to me.'

Law added, 'They may say that your assent is a purely formal act and the prerogative of veto is dead. That was true as long as there was a buffer between you and the House of Commons, but they have destroyed the buffer and it is true no longer.'[26]

The King was stunned by what his most recent biographer has called this 'unamiable crudity'.[27] Bonar Law, always an uneasy courtier, had not intended offence to his Royal host, but with kings and commoners alike he 'consciously believed that he owed it to his principles and his party to call a spade a spade on every possible occasion.'[28] His blunt speaking understandably annoyed King George, who did not forget it. Within the year, however, he had grown more receptive to Bonar Law's logic, if not to his charm.[29]

Asquith decided to meet broadside with broadside. He travelled to Dublin in mid July – the first Prime Minister do so in more than a century – to make a rousing speech of his own. He ridiculed Unionist demands for yet another election and then turned to the claims of the Ulstermen: their campaign against Home Rule, he said, was 'purely destructive in its objects, anarchic and chaotic in its methods', and he poured further scorn on their predictions of dire consequences if the Bill passed. His audience cheered ecstatically when he roared: 'Ireland is a nation, not two nations, but one nation.'[30]

In bitter response, the Unionists staged a meeting on 27 July, at Blenheim Palace, hereditary seat of the Churchills and birthplace both of Lord Randolph, who first played the 'Orange card', and of his son Winston, Asquith's First Lord of the Admiralty. The rally crowded the quadrangles and gardens of the Palace with more than 13,000 of the faithful and curious. More than forty peers joined the Duke of Marlborough on the great terrace, including Lansdowne, Derby and Londonderry, and the Duke of Norfolk – the leading Roman Catholic layman in the country. All the Unionist notables of the Lower House attended, including Carson, Chamberlain, Long, Smith, and the Cecil brothers, as well as most of the parliamentary party. Bonar Law was of course the principal speaker, and he did not disappoint those who came to hear fighting words. His speech lasted an hour and, with two by-election victories over the previous fortnight to fuel his rhetoric,[31] surpassed for sheer fire even his performance in Belfast. His words were harder-edged than any he had used before:

> [The Prime Minister] has returned from Ireland and he has told us that the Parliament Bill was not carried for nothing. It was to force through Parliament the Home Rule proposals which at the election were carefully hidden from the people of this country, and which they did not dare to even mention in their election addresses – proposals which they are trying to carry, not only without the consent, but as we know, and as they know, against the will of the people.
>
> The Chief Liberal Whip has told us also that the Home Rule Bill will be carried through the House of Commons before Christmas. Perhaps it will . . . I do not know. But I do know this – that we do not acknowledge their right to carry such a revolution by such means. We do not recognize that any such action is the constitutional government of a free people. We regard them as a revolutionary committee which has seized by fraud upon despotic power. In our opposition to them we shall not be guided by the considerations, we shall not be restrained by the bonds, which would influence us in ordinary political struggle . . . We shall use any means to deprive them of the power which they have usurped and compel them to face the people whom they have deceived.

As much for the ears of the Liberal Cabinet as for those of his audience he explained, in terms of menacing simplicity, precisely what he thought would happen if the Government continued on its stated path:

> [The people of Ulster] say, rightly or wrongly, that under a government dominated by men who control the Ancient Order of Hibernians, neither their civil nor their religious liberty would be safe. They say it and believe it. They say also that they will never submit to such a parliament, and no one knows better than I how firmly they mean it . . .
>
> Nations, and great nations, have indeed taken up arms to prevent their

subjects from seceding, but no nation will ever take up arms to compel loyal subjects to leave their community. I do not believe for a moment that any government would ever dare to make the attempt, but I am sure of this – that if the attempt were made, the Government would not succeed in carrying Home Rule. They would succeed only in lighting fires of civil war which would shatter the Empire to its foundations.

On this subject I shall say one word, and one word more only. While I had still in the party a position of less responsibility than that which I have now, I said that in my opinion if any attempt were made, without the clearly expressed will of the people of this country, and as part of a corrupt parliamentary bargain, to deprive these men of their birthright, they would be justified in resisting by all means in their power, including force. *I said so then, and I say so now, with a full sense of the responsibility which attaches to my position, that if the attempt be made under present conditions, I can imagine no length of resistance to which Ulster will go, in which I shall not be ready to support them, and in which they will not be supported by the overwhelming majority of the British people.*[32]

Of the millions of words Bonar Law uttered in speeches throughout his public life, the words emphasised are surely better remembered and more often criticized than any others. Many historians have agreed with George Dangerfield that this was a 'crude step into rebellion.'[33] For Lord Jenkins, 'From behind the sad eyes of Bonar Law the tide of quiet violence poured out.'[34] More recently, Professor Jalland has concluded that 'The Unionist leader's more menacing and irresponsible remarks haunted him for the next two years.' His 'public recklessness in 1912', she writes, 'cannot be justified.'[35] Such serious rebukes cannot simply be put aside.

Bonar Law believed that the Liberal Government was not playing the political game by the received rules. He could not forgive the fact that they had brought in a bill of major constitutional significance without making it the central issue of an election, and that they were proceeding with their controversial programme despite being a minority party in the House dependent for success upon the Irish Nationalists – whose sole purpose, he believed, was the break-up of the United Kingdom. The steady loss of by-elections to Unionist challengers convinced him all the more that his view was shared by the electorate. 'Representative Government does not, in my opinion,' he wrote in 1913, 'mean the uncontrolled will of a Cabinet.'[36] To doubt the sincerity of these opinions would be to misunderstand the man.[37]

Furthermore, Bonar Law believed that Ulster was the key to Home Rule: if the resolution of Ulstermen could prevent passage of the Bill, then he would use it to do so. Throughout, his plan was to use the Ulster crisis to force an election concentrated on Home Rule, which the voting trend of by-election victories convinced him the Unionist Party would win. Failing that, his next best hope was to save Ulster from the clutches of a Dublin legislature through some plan of exclusion. He believed that a Government dependent on Irish votes would have to be bludgeoned into understanding the depth of British distaste for and the obduracy of Ulster resistance to Gladstonian Home Rule.

He marvelled at the Government's determination to press on, and raged at what he thought was Asquith's belief that 'some miracle' would save him from the worst: 'But in any case we are in office, and sufficient unto the day is the evil thereof.'[38] To his mind, harsh words like those at Blenheim placed before the premier the choice which could not be avoided: election or resistance, perhaps even armed civil conflict. He believed that his own public position embraced this terrible responsibility, while that of the Government – blinkered, he thought, and misled – avoided it. In 1913 he wrote to J.P. Croal, editor of *The Scotsman*, of his conviction that if Asquith brought in Home Rule on the authority of the Parliament Act without submitting it to the electorate,

> ... something very nearly resembling civil war will result ... He must realize this, and therefore nothing but compulsion of the most extreme kind would make him submit to an election before his Bills are carried; and there is a great danger that rather than face that risk he will go straight on and land the country in something like disaster.[39]

What could have been clearer, he thought, than his pledge in the House on the first day of 1913:

> ... if you attempt to enforce this Bill, and the people of Ulster believe, and have a right to believe, that you are doing it against the will of the people of this country, then I shall assist them in resisting it. But if you put it before the people of this country as a clear issue, then it is a problem for Ulster, and not for me ... So far as I am concerned, if it is submitted to the people of this country as a clear issue, so long as I speak for the Unionist Party I shall do nothing to encourage them in resisting the law.[40]

It was Bonar Law's absolute conviction throughout the Home Rule fight – even when, later, he came to consider stratagems for compromise – that this dilemma had to be kept before the Government. He clung to it utterly and without regret, and to understand this is to understand much about his leadership of the Unionist campaign and the remorselessness of his personal style. He knew his path was littered with dangers, but he could see no other. To shrink from it, in his judgement, was to allow the use of Government power to expel from the national community people whose fervent desire it was to remain a loyal part of it – as if, in some madder world, Lincoln had wished to send his armies in 1860 to drive the southern states out of the American Union. Such catastrophe he could stomach only if it were the unequivocal decision of the national electorate.

III

Despite the war of words, the Home Rule Bill made its halting way through Parliament, the Unionists doing all within their limited power to impede it. Introducing the Bill, the Prime Minister had promised that he had no intention of using his majority to invoke the Parliamentary 'guillotine' to limit debate; hence the Bill passed its Second Reading only on 9 June, progressing two days later to the Committee Stage, where it was caught up in an unanticipated controversy fraught with implications for its political future. This episode was the work of a young independent-minded Liberal, Thomas Agar-Robartes, who on 11 June inspired a three-day debate on his amendment to exclude the four solidly Protestant counties of Antrim, Armagh, Down and Londonderry from the authority of the proposed Dublin Parliament.[41] It was impossible for the Government to accept such an amendment at this time in the face of Nationalist hostility – hence Asquith's rousing remarks in Dublin a few weeks later.

Agar-Robartes' amendment put the Unionists in a delicate position, given Bonar Law's primary desire to bring about an election on the question of Home Rule, at the very least to exclude Ulster from its provision. A few weeks earlier he had indicated to the newspaper proprietor Riddell that a system allowing each Irish county the right to 'remain outside the Irish Parliament' would meet his personal concerns regarding Ulster. Yet, as he also explained, he was not sanguine about any compromise without Ulster's complete co-operation: 'We are in for troublous times.'[42]

Regardless of what in the end might have been acceptable to him, Bonar Law was on record as opposing Home Rule without qualification, and he could not now overlook the grim determination of absolutist anti-Home Rulers, led by the Southern Unionists and their sympathizers, including both Lansdowne and Long. For him to embrace an exclusion amendment so early in the fight could be interpreted as his abandoment of the Irish Unionists outside Ulster.[43] Other possibilities, however, inclined him to the amendment: first, it might be carried, cause a fissure between Liberals and Irish Nationalists, upset the Government, and cause a Dissolution of Parliament. Second, for Unionists to win the election which would follow a dissolution, it would be necessary to demonstrate to the electorate their dignified willingness to listen to reason (and consider compromise), combined with a stance of principled courage. Third, despite all efforts a compromise of some sort might become necessary, and therefore irresistible, if Ulster were to be preserved without bloodshed.

After long consideration, Bonar Law did therefore support the Agar-Robertes plan, telling the House on 11 June that, though still adamantly opposed to Home Rule, Unionists would 'support any amendment which, bad as the Bill seems to us to be, would make it less bad than it was before the amendment was introduced.' Even Carson, sneering that he hoped the innovation would wreck both Government and Bill alike, announced his intention to vote for the amendment. It did not pass, but Bonar Law and his followers were pleased to see the normal Government majority fall by 40 votes, to 69, and delighted to observe Government whips having to trawl for votes to defeat a compromise measure put forward by a Liberal Member. As Bonar Law concluded when speaking at St Dunston's Lodge a fortnight later: '... things are going very well with us ... for it seems to me that every day shows more clearly that the Government are getting tied up into a knot which cannot be severed by any method except suicide.'[44]

The Agar-Robartes debate also provided the Unionist leadership with an opportunity to combine their usual condemnations of Home Rule with the more uncharacteristic language of compromise. Carson offered an amendment of his own on 1 January 1913, proposing the exclusion of all nine Ulster counties from the Home Rule Parliament – intended as much to test the resolve of the Government as to alter the Bill. As in the earlier case, Unionists seized the opportunity to accuse the Government of being the recalcitrants in the contest of wills, and to claim for themselves the role of compromisers.[45] Predictably, Carson's amendment did less well than Agar-Robartes's, and was defeated by 97 votes; but it was not soon forgotten.

In this super-heated political atmosphere, Bonar Law did not commit the error of allowing his opponents to view such Unionist tactics as concessions, or signs of weakening resolve. He warned the Government to take absolutely at face value both the determination of the Ulstermen and the Unionist Party's commitment to them. Soon after the Agar-Robartes debate he turned once again to the tactics of the closed fist. Gesturing angrily at the Treasury Bench, he declared:

> They are putting themselves in a position from which they cannot recede ...
> They are deliberately shutting off from themselves the right to go back on the
> decision which they are now taking. That means that they know that if Ulster
> is in earnest, if Ulster does resist, there are stronger things than Parliamentary
> majorities. They know that in that case no Government would dare to use
> British troops to drive them out. They know as a matter of fact that the
> Government which gave the order to employ troops for that purpose would
> run a greater risk of being lynched in London than – [prolonged cheers].
> What are the Government doing? ... What these Right Honourable gentle-
> men are doing deliberately now is this: they are saying, and have said it in so
> many words to the people of Ulster, 'convince us that you are in earnest,
> show us that you mean to fight, and we will yield to you as we have yielded to
> everybody else.' They talk about incendiary language: what they are doing is
> inviting the people of Ulster to show not by language but by acts that they are
> in earnest.[46]

The Ulstermen did not disappoint Bonar Law: in the previous autumn at a meeting at the Rosemary Hall in Belfast, four hundred delegates of the Ulster Unionist Council had declared that they would back their leaders and their British allies in the face of any danger caused by their fight against the Government. Furthermore, they had portentously endorsed a motion to authorize a secret Commission of Five to join Carson in drawing up a constitution for a 'provisional Government of Ulster ... to come into operation on the day of the passage of any Home Rule Bill, to remain in force until Ulster shall again resume unimpaired her citizenship in the United Kingdom.'[47] The intention was to frighten the Liberal Government, but no one knew with absolute certainty if it was also, should the situation arise, to do exactly what the motion said.

A clue was offered on 28 September 1912, 'Ulster Day', which witnessed perhaps the most romantic gesture of this entire drama. Carson and 237,368 of his Ulster followers signed – some reportedly in their own blood – a new 'Solemn League and Covenant' modelled on the

Scottish Remonstrance of the seventeenth century.[48] Its language and sentiments were unmistakable:

> Being convinced in our consciences that Home Rule would be disastrous to the material well-being of Ulster as well as the whole of Ireland, subversive of our civil and religious freedom, destructive of our citizenship, and perilous to the unity of the Empire, we, whose names are underwritten, men of Ulster, loyal subjects of His Gracious Majesty King George V, humbly relying on the God Whom our fathers in days of stress and trial confidently trusted, do hereby pledge ourselves in Solemn Covenant throughout this our time of threatened calamity to stand by one another in defending for ourselves and our children our cherished position of equal citizenship in the United Kingdom, and in using all means which may be found necessary to defeat the present conspiracy to set up a Home Rule Parliament in Ireland.
>
> And in the event of such a Parliament being forced upon us, we further solemnly and mutually pledge ourselves to refuse to recognize its authority.
>
> In such confidence that God will defend the right we hereto subscribe our names.
>
> And further, we individually declare that we have not already signed this Covenant.
>
> The above was signed by me . . . . at 'Ulster Day', Saturday, 28th September 1912.
>
> GOD SAVE THE KING.[49]

In his Dublin speech Asquith had told a cheering throng that he refused to believe British subjects would stand against 'the supreme authority of the Imperial Parliament'. Even in the face of the melodramatic 'Solemn League and Covenant', he insisted that he had not changed his mind. Bonar Law's response was simply that such demonstrations were evidence that if peace were to be maintained in Ireland, Home Rule must be submitted to the electorate. The extravagance of his language and his complacent attitude to promises of Ulster resistance were intended to press the Government to a similar conclusion. As Parliament rose in August, the bill remained bogged down in committee.

In September, during the recess, Bonar Law was invited by the King to Balmoral, the Royal retreat in Scotland. His aversion to country-house weekends had, if anything, intensified over the years; summoned by his Sovereign, however, to Balmoral he went – though not without complaint. He wrote to H.A. Gwynne: 'This place is endurable but if I had to spend a great deal of time either here or in any country house I should long for a movement that "BLMG" [Bonar Law Must Go!] so that I could escape.'[50]

The King's diary entry of 27 September reveals little about his conversation with the Opposition leader: 'After luncheon, had a talk with Mr Bonar Law about politics.'[51] Perhaps His Majesty was reminded of their previous unpleasant encounter: Bonar Law drove home his forecast of events and, as he had four months earlier, left the King feeling decidedly anxious. If the Home Rule Bill made its way through the Commons and then came before him for the Royal Assent without having passed in the Lords, the King would find himself in a difficult position, as Bonar Law noted in his own record of the conversation:

The Unionist party will hold that as the Constitution is admittedly in suspense (for the duty of carrying out the Preamble of the Parliament Act is acknowledged by the Government) & as it is at least doubtful, & in view of the bye-elections hardly doubtful, whether the Govt have the support of the Country, the position is precisely similar to what it would be if the Govt supported by the House of Commons asked the Sovereign to use the Prerogative to overcome the opposition of the House of Lords.

In such circumstances Unionists would certainly believe that the King not only had the constitutional right but that it was his duty before acting on the advice of his Ministers to ascertain whether it would not be possible to appoint other Ministers who would advise him differently & allow the question to be decided by the Country at a General Election.

The last precedent prior to the Parlt. Act which Mr Bonar Law could recall was the Reform Bill of 1832. He believes, without having the opportunity of confirming his recollection, that though an election had been fought specially on the Reform Bill the King [William IV] did not consent to the creation of the new Peers till he had sent for the Leader of the Conservative Party & ascertained from him that he was not prepared to take the responsibility of forming a Government. Such would be the view of the Unionist Party.

The Government, Bonar Law acknowledged, would insist that the Sovereign's duty was at that point to assent to the bill. Then he returned to a theme with which His Majesty was all too familiar:

In reality it does not matter much which of these views is constitutionally sound. In any case whatever course was taken by H.M. half of his people would think that he had failed in his duty & in view of the many bitter feelings which by that time would have been aroused the Crown would, Mr Bonar Law fears, be openly attacked by the people of Ulster & their sympathizers if he gave his assent to the Bill & by a large section of the Radical Party if he took any other course.

Such a position is one in which the King might not be placed & Mr Bonar Law is of opinion that if H.M. put the case clearly to the Prime Minister he would feel that it was his duty to extricate the King from so terrible a dilemma.

Mr Bonar Law also ventured to suggest to H.M. that when any crisis arises it might be well to consult informally Mr Balfour[,] Lord Lansdowne or himself & he assured His Majesty that any advice given under such circumstances would not be influenced by Party considerations.[52]

The King continued to dislike both Bonar Law's message and his manner, but as time passed he came to see that there was substance in the warning. A few months later, in March 1913, Lord Knollys retired and Lord Stamfordham became the King's sole Private Secretary;[53] Knollys's sympathies were Liberal, Stamfordham's decidedly Conservative.[54] For this and other reasons, in the course of the following year the King became increasingly sensitive to the logic of Bonar Law's unvarnished and unavoidable conclusions.

When the House reassembled in October 1912 there was no respite from the Irish imbroglio for the Sovereign, his Parliament or his people. Asquith jettisoned the promise he had made in March: to hasten the Bill's first passage through the House, the 'guillotine' was employed – only six of the remaining fifty-one clauses were debated, and twenty-seven partly discussed.[55] Bonar Law, Carson and their colleagues fulminated to no avail, as the Government majority held. On 16 January 1913 the Third Home Rule Bill passed through the Commons with the anticipated hundred-vote majority. Predictably, the Upper House took only nine days to reject it – on a vote of 326 to 69 – on its Second Reading. From this point, if the Bill were to become law in the next session but one, under the provisions of the Parliament Act not so much as a comma could be altered.

Although the Unionists wrested two more seats from the Liberals in by-elections,[56] the final weeks of the year were for Bonar Law a period of stress as the Referendum Pledge crisis briefly pushed even Home Rule aside. The horror expressed by his followers at Bonar Law's threat of resignation and their immediate willingness to embrace the Memorial compromise certainly owed much to their reluctance to so much as consider the loss of his fierce leadership in the Home Rule battle.

With the irresistible machinery of the Parliament Act now in motion, Unionists must have wondered what was to be done next. Lord Milner, the coldly brilliant exponent of Empire, articulated the way: 'To my mind there is only one road to salvation for Unionists now, and it is to shout "Ulster, Ulster", all the time ... No running after Lloyd George, no mention of Tariff reform ...'[57] Bonar Law agreed; and if there had been any doubt in the past, after January 1913 the matter, for most Unionists, came down to Ulster.

7

'Ulster, Ulster, all the time'

I

BONAR LAW MARKED the end of 1912 with a sense of relief. It had been a year of political struggle and risk inside his party, of bitter strife with the Government majority in the House. The Tariff Reform zealots had accepted but were certainly not pleased with the Memorial compromise, and Austen Chamberlain wrote early in 1913: 'I will do my best for him but I am not called upon to shoulder his mistakes to the same extent that I defended Balfour.'[1] Staunch Free-Fooders, like Lord Derby or Lord Robert Cecil, were as sceptical – though from the opposite perspective. Proponents of the Established Church, like Lord Hugh Cecil, or of military reform, like the parvenu millionaire Arthur Lee, taxed their leader regularly for the insufficiency of attention he gave to their favourite causes.[2] Asquith's Government pressed on with their promised and controversial programmes, including Welsh Church disestablishment and abolition of the system under which certain university graduates and property holders were entitled to more than one vote, and Lloyd George readied his 'Land Campaign' to achieve his dream of the restructuring of the land-holding system in the countryside – something Unionists were prepared to oppose root and branch.[3]

Yet the strife which characterized his first year as leader notwithstanding, so long as the Third Home Rule Bill remained the principal interest of their party, most Unionists realized that Bonar Law could hardly be bettered as a fighting chief. J.S. Sandars, an adroit observer who had no reason to love him, agreed; as he wrote to Lord Stamfordham,

> The simpler methods of Bonar Law; his neat and incisive style; his familiarity with, and his use of the modern and unpolished weapons of political combat[,] attracted the fighting elements in the Unionist ranks. He tripped occasionally but he was quickly on his feet and was quickly forgiven. His speeches that [were] lacking in literary finish were fighting speeches. His courage was undoubted. He had the great virtue of being very unaccepable to his opponents in the House of Commons. It was the hour, and he was the man.[4]

One curious business did push the Irish debate aside in Parliament for a time in 1913: what is remembered as the Marconi Scandal preoccupied even Bonar Law for a time.[5] The origins of the affair lay in a contract in March 1912 between the Government and the British Marconi Company to establish a worldwide wireless transmission network. Soon afterwards the managing director of Marconi, Godfrey Isaacs, offered shares in his subsidiary American Marconi Company (which was unrelated to the British contract) to his brothers, one of whom was the Attorney-General, Sir Rufus Isaacs. Sir Rufus in turn laid off 1,000 shares each on his colleagues Lloyd George and Alexander Murray, the Master of Elibank and Chief Liberal Whip. Murray, 'a past master at concealed investments', also secretly purchased another 3,000 shares with Liberal Party funds.[6] It was these covert arrangements, once revealed, which constituted the scandal.

Criticism of the contract began in the press during the summer of 1912, and by August *Eye-Witness*, a monthly known for its anti-Semitic flavour, was suggesting in lurid fashion that impropriety was afoot. The Prime Minister, who by this time knew of the purchases made by Isaacs and Murray (though apparently not yet of Lloyd George's acquisition), decided on a strategy of counter-attack and offered the appointment of a Select Committee of the House to examine the entire business of the Marconi contract. In the debate on the proposed committee, on 11 October, Sir Rufus denied that either his colleagues or himself had had 'one single transaction with the shares of *that* company' – which, in the case of the British concern was, strictly speaking, quite correct.[7]

In February 1913 the Paris daily *Le Matin* joined in, retailing an untrue rumour that the Isaacs brothers and the Postmaster-General, Herbert Samuel – who had negotiated the contract, but had purchased no stock – had traded in British Marconi shares. The injured parties quickly mounted a libel action.[8] Though Bonar Law had characterized the Liberal Government as a 'corrupt committee' he was referring to their political principles, not to their personal financial dealings, and he was shocked to learn early in 1913 of his friend Lloyd George's American Marconi stock purchases. Veteran of the Glasgow Iron Ring that he was, Bonar Law always believed that profit legally obtained by private citizens was fair gain; at the same time, he knew also that these ministers of state had acted foolishly, even irresponsibly, and that the longer Lloyd George – Chancellor of the Exchequer – remained silent about his own involvement, the worse time he would have. In March, as the *Le Matin* case proceeded, Sir George Riddell wrote in his diary:

> ... Bonar Law had spoken to [Lloyd George] in a friendly and manly way regarding the Marconi incident. He said that he was quite sure that there had been no moral wrong on LG's part, but that he would have to raise the question in the House. LG offered to produce to him all his private books and papers relating to his own affairs, but BL said there was no occasion for this, as he had no doubt on the subject.[9]

The infamous libel action which followed provided Bonar Law with some discomfort of his own, for when it opened in the court of Mr Justice Darling all three leading counsel were seen to be prominent Tories, and leaders in the Ulster Unionist movement: James Campbell, Carson's fellow MP for Dublin University, represented the newspaper, F.E. Smith appeared for the Attorney-General, and Carson himself for Samuel.[10] Many Unionists disapproved of the involvement of the party's most famous lawyers, and those who were annoyed in March grew positively furious a few weeks later: a second charge of libel was brought, against the editor of *Eye-Witness*, Cecil Chesterton – brother of the celebrated G.K. – and Carson and Smith combined their talents to hammer him, in the interests of the Liberal ministers. Their brilliant performances earned them the condemnation of many Unionist colleagues – who leaned heavily upon Bonar Law to do something about the outrage.[11] Bonar Law kept his head, accepting the fact that the customs of the Bar prevented a barrister from refusing a legitimate client – even if he was a prominent Liberal. Bad party politics it may have been, but the two distinguished litigators had centuries of legal precedent behind them.[12] None the less, in some Unionists the trials engendered a resentment towards Carson and Smith which only a return to the Irish battles could counteract.[13]

Meanwhile the Select Committee soldiered on, and as its full details became known the Marconi affair plummted towards its nadir.[14] Unsurprisingly, given the Committee's conventional Government majority, its report issued in June exonerated the ministers. The report was debated in the House on 18 and 19 June, and for two days of blistering argument all other business ceased.[15] The offending ministers admitted to having acted thoughtlessly, but neither acknowledged wrong-doing. Unionists railed against their failure to reveal the full truth months earlier, but the Government majority benignly accepted mere 'expressions of regret' from Lloyd George and Isaacs.

Bonar Law's concluding remarks expressed his disapproval, but demonstrate too a generosity much at odds with his reputation as a brutal partisan. He tabled a resolution:[16]

> That this House, having heard the statements made by the Attorney-General and the Chancellor of the Exchequer, acquits them of acting otherwise than in good faith, and reprobates the charges of corruption which have been proved to be wholly false, but regrets their transactions in shares of the Marconi Company of America and the want of frankness displayed by them in their communications with the House.

While he expressed understanding – he had a black-sheep brother of his own – Bonar Law focused on the issue he could not ignore:

> You do not examine with the same suspicion something which comes from the brother, and a brother whom, as the Attorney-General showed, he trusted ... but it does not alter the position of his public actions as a public man ... You can never truly make a distinction between a contractor who is a relation and who is not. That is impossible. You must judge of these things not by motives but by what people do.

Even before becoming party leader, Bonar Law had refused certain lucrative directorships and resigned others which he feared might reflect upon his integrity and that of Parliament and party.[17] Responsible ministers of the Crown had now brought criticism – he stopped short of suggesting dishonour – upon themselves because they had violated a cardinal principle of men in such positions: they had not only employed privileged information to speculate in stocks, but had purchased shares in a concern which was 'certainly indirectly, and in my belief directly, interested in the company which was making a contract with the Government.' What, he queried, was the wish of his party and the duty of the House?

All we ask is that the House of Commons should express in the mildest terms you like its disapproval of what has been done ... and we shall in my belief be only expressing what is the almost universal feeling in the United Kingdom.

Like the Committee report itself, the resolution adopted by the House reflected partisan realities: a tepid Liberal version was passed by a majority of 78 votes, and the two ministers were not reprimanded in any way. 'Marconi' was over, but the Opposition was further enraged when in the autumn Sir Rufus Isaacs was appointed Lord Chief Justice of England and, at the New Year, to a peerage.

It is untrue that Bonar Law moderated his attack and aided the ministers' escape from censure (or worse), either because of his friendship with Lloyd George, or for some other unknown reason.[18] Already in mid 1912 he had said of Lloyd George to Riddell: 'I like him personally, but as I am attacking him, think it wiser to avoid him.'[19] Churchill too was wrong when, musing about whether the Unionists had been simply too dull-witted to use the Marconi scandal to overturn the Government, he told his friends: 'Some of them were too stupid, ... [but] frankly some of them were too nice.'[20] He included in the latter category the Leader of the Opposition. Yet although Bonar Law the former businessman never feigned a superior disapproval of profit-seeking he did denounce, vigorously and fairly, the ministers' speculation in 'tainted' stocks and their disingenuous conduct in revealing the truth slowly, incompletely and, finally, only from necessity. Under the less demanding standards of those days, he did not consider that they had behaved criminally; but he had no intention of providing even his friend Lloyd George with an easy way out of his difficulties.

One last point should be made: While 'Marconi' never captured wide public attention, it gripped the House of Commons, largely because of the angry partisan atmosphere that already existed. The Irish Question receded only briefly, and the scandal at once reflected and added to the acrimonious political climate. Riddell, who had friends in all parties, noted in August 1913: 'The feeling between the two parties is very bitter. This is due in great measure to the new regime adopted by Bonar Law ... Now it is war to the knife.'[21] Bonar Law's own last word on the matter was illustrative both of the man and the affair. He wrote to a friend: 'I did not like my job about the Marconi business, because it was so personal, but it could not be helped.'[22] If Bonar Law was never among the most savage during this nasty affair, neither was he guilty of the political crime of being 'too nice'.

II

The Marconi affair flashed brightly and then subsided in 1913, and politics soon returned to business as usual. At the end of January the Unionists were surprised to lose Londonderry City to the Liberals – the new Member was a popular local Protestant and moderate Home Ruler – but otherwise by-election results continued throughout the year to favour them.[23] The progress of the Home Rule Bill was less encouraging: it completed its second circuit through the Commons on 7 July, to be crushed once again in the Lords eight days later. The bruised and battered Parliament rose on 15 August for six months, leaving Unionists to ponder whether with the Parliament Act and the Government majority still in place, the floor of the House of Commons was the most promising place to turn back Gladstonian Home Rule.

As we have seen, Bonar Law had endeavoured to convince the King to take a hand in the Irish imbroglio, a prospect which His Majesty viewed with extreme reluctance but which he was coming to conclude might prove unavoidable. In late July 1913, Lord Lansdowne and Bonar Law submitted for Royal consideration a powerful six-page memorandum outlining the official position of the Unionist leadership.[24] Reiterating their call for the decision regarding Home Rule to be put before the electorate, they stressed that the timetable of the Parliament Act required any such decision to be made promptly. Continued Government reliance on the 1911 Act, they warned, would place the Crown in a difficult position, '... and the seriousness of it will become increasingly evident as the crisis approaches.' As Bonar Law already had on two previous occasions, they urged His Majesty to withhold his Assent from such constitutionally significant legislation, untested in any election and passed under the aegis of the Parliament Act. This was contentious advice: it horrified Bonar Law's distinguished legal adviser Professor A.V. Dicey, and was risky in a constitutional monarchy. Only the poverty of options available to the Unionists can explain their attraction to it.[25]

More practical, they thought, was their second critique: that by bringing such a controversial bill forward without seeking the endorsement of the electorate, and assuming receipt of the Royal Assent, the Government were guilty of placing the Sovereign in an impossible position. The Unionist leaders reminded King George of the disturbed state of public opinion, and predicted more to come. Their conclusion he had heard before: 'So far as the position of the Crown is concerned, it will not matter which view is right; the result will be that, whatever course is taken by His Majesty, half his people will think he has failed in his duty.'[26] There was, they argued, only one solution:

> ... His Majesty should address a memorandum to his Prime Minister, pointing out that the Crown would be placed in an impossible position, that it is the duty of His Ministers to save him from such a position, and that they can save him from it, without any risk to themselves (except that of discovering that they have misread the opinion of the country), by submitting their Home Rule Bill to the decision of the people.

The King recognized his predicament, and this captious analysis cannot have eased his anxiety. After consulting several elder statesmen including Lord Cromer, Lord Loreburn and Lord Rosebery, King George decided to act. Asquith, Harold Nicolson once wrote, habitually 'allowed sleeping scorpions to lie' and had not discussed the Irish situation with the King for months;[27] he must therefore have been surprised when on 11 August his Sovereign handed him a memorandum six hundred words long, written in his own hand and demonstrating how deeply Unionist arguments had cut.[28]

King George had come to the conclusion that the possibility of civil conflict between Protestant and Catholic in Ireland was quite real. He now reiterated the dilemma that had once so antagonized him: whatever he did, he was in danger of alienating at least half his people. 'No Sovereign', he complained, 'has ever been in such a position, and this pressure is sure to increase over the next few months.' Was it not possible to reach a settlement – perhaps through a conference of all parties – leading to 'Home Rule all round, Reform of the House of Lords etc., not on Party lines, but by agreement?' The King, it appeared, had become a devolutionist, and it was not particularly agreeable to his Prime Minister.

Asquith responded a few weeks later with two separate papers.[29] In the first, he refuted the Unionists' contention that it would be constitutionally admissable for the Sovereign either to withhold his assent to the Home Rule Bill or to dismiss the government in order to force a dissolution. In his second memorandum, Asquith argued that a Home Rule election would solve nothing. A Liberal victory would not end Ulster recalcitrance; a Unionist triumph was possible, he asserted, only on issues such as the Insurance Act or 'Marconi', and would not be accepted by supporters of the current Government 'as a verdict adverse to Home Rule'. As for the King's suggestion of an all-party conference, Asquith insisted that for it to be fruitful 'there must be some definite basis upon and from which its deliberation can proceed. I fear that at present (it may be different nearer the time) no such basis can be found. I shall be only too glad if that fear can now or hereafter be satisfactorily dispelled.'

The apprehensive King prolonged the exchange by pressing his case in a long letter a few days later. Asquith once again rejected his anxieties, as he rejected all the Unionist arguments which – he was displeased to see – were creeping into the Sovereign's consciousness.[30]

Determined to press his hope for a compromise, King George summoned various political leaders to a series of weekends at Balmoral in early autumn. Bonar Law arrived on 13 September – two days after the publication in *The Times* of a letter by Lord Loreburn, the former Liberal Lord Chancellor, appealing for 'a conference or direct communication' among the parties.[31] He found Churchill already in attendance, and a curious episode unfolded. Bonar Law neither liked nor trusted the young First Lord; it is doubtful whether he would have gone on a tiger shoot with him – but he would play golf with almost anyone. In the chill and damp of 17 September they played and, as Asquith had charged his young colleague to do, talked politics. Bonar Law wrote of their conversation to Lansdowne, who had left Balmoral only a few days before:[32]

> The substance of what I said was simply this: that it seemed to me that the position for both parties was becoming impossible. I thought their programme was absolutely impossible without civil war; and on the other hand, we would be driven in resistance to their policy to take such action, including rendering Government in the House of Commons impossible, with the direct result that the Army encouraged by us will not obey their orders. I spoke to him of the only two grounds on which I thought discussion was possible ...[33]

These 'grounds', Bonar Law recalled, he had already laid before the King the previous day:

> The first[,] that an attempt should be made by the Government to carry out their declared intention of preparing a scheme of devolution which would apply not only to Ireland but to the whole of the United Kingdom. The dis-

cussion of such a proposal would present no difficulty to us for no vital principle was involved in it, as it was entirely a question of expediency and we should be quite ready to consider it with open minds.

The second possible basis of discussion was that N.E. Ulster shall remain an integral part of the United Kingdom, and that some form of Local Government be given to the rest of Ireland.

The practical difficulty of such an arrangement did not seem to me insurmountable, and it would no doubt prevent the armed resistance of Ulster. I made it, however, clear to H.M. that in my opinion no such solution was possible unless it secured a large measure of approval from the Unionists of the South and West of Ireland, for I was sure that the leaders of the Unionist Party would not give their consent to any scheme which would be regarded as a betrayal of the loyalists of Ireland.

Bonar Law had pointed out once again to the King, and reiterated to Churchill, his belief that if the Government continued to resist an election fought over the Home Rule Bill, the Army would almost certainly reject any orders from the Government to enforce the Bill in Ulster, and that British Unionists would support them.[34] He also reiterated the commitment of his party to give 'every possible support to the people of Ulster', but also that, 'if there were an election and the people decided in favour of Home Rule, [Unionists would not] encourage or support the resistance of Ulster.'

This series of private conversations is important to our understanding of both the progress of the Irish crisis, and Bonar Law's place in it. His references to the Army's likely reluctance to enforce Home Rule against Ulster and the warning that Unionists would spontaneously support such reluctance, indicate how profound were the feelings involved in the Irish Question. Of this, David Dutton has written perceptively:

> This is not a case of political metamorphosis, of democratic politicians transforming themselves into anarchists. What Unionists did and said in these years accurately reflected the intensity of feeling on the Unionist side against the plans of Asquith's government. In the British parliamentary system, based upon a confrontational and often ritualized debate between government and opposition, the sincerity of a politician's stance is sometimes open to question. But no element of feigned passion was involved in the struggle over Ireland.[35]

His prognostications were strong medicine indeed, which Bonar Law did not dispense lightly. He knew his party, the depths of their hatred

for Home Rule and the parallel antipathy to be found among many
officers in the Army. He understood that worst sometimes did come to
worst, and that for him to ignore the possibility of tragedy would
impede it not at all. His harsh warnings of what he thought a very real
possibility were however always tempered with compromise: if the
people were consulted and endorsed Home Rule, Unionists would not
resist it or support those who did.

Equally important are two other conclusions: like the King, Bonar
Law had no fear of a compromise based on some sort of constitutional realignment. The exclusion of Ulster from some measure of
Irish Home Rule would be personally acceptable to him *if* it were
acceptable to the Ulstermen and the Southern Unionists, and to their
antagonists, the Irish Nationalists. This door he left decidedly ajar.
Second, he confined all discussion of compromise to a small circle of
senior leaders: he knew that if the idea of inter-party discussions took
the nation's fancy and an offer of some such dialogue were to be made
publicly and in the name of the King, his party would be unable to
resist it, regardless of the conditions attached to it.[36] For the time
being, therefore, he made certain that the Unionists remained focused
on the demand for an election.

Despite these small and discreet signs of thaw, the public face of
Unionism continued to be set hard. On 23 September the Ulster Union-
ist Council met in Belfast to flesh out their plan to create a Provisional
Government in the event of Home Rule becoming law.[37] Soon the
Ulster Volunteer Force, under the command of a retired British officer,
Lieutenant-General Sir George Richardson, were being reviewed by
Carson and his deputies. Yet only a few days before these provocative
steps were taken, another ray of hope had appeared. Carson laid aside
his revolutionary clothes and wrote candidly to Bonar Law on 20 September:

> As regards the position here I am of opinion that on the whole things are
> shaping towards a desire to settle on the terms of leaving 'Ulster out' – the
> difficulty arises as to defining Ulster & my own view is that the whole of
> Ulster shd be excluded but the minimum wd be the 6 plantation counties &
> for that a good case cd be made. The South & West would present a
> difficulty & it might be that *I* cd not agree to their abandonment tho' I feel
> certain that it wd be the best settlement if Home Rule is irresistible.
> Probably some more generous treatment could be dealt out to safeguard
> their interests, but with British rule in Ulster I don't think there would be so
> much to fear . . .[38]

If Bonar Law and Carson were moving towards consideration of Ulster exclusion, the chief British ally of the Southern Unionists decidedly was not. In the same post which brought him Carson's temperate communication, Bonar Law received a letter from Lord Lansdowne, master of broad acres in County Kerry. Having read Bonar Law's recent memorandum to the King, Lansdowne reminded him of those in the party who were sceptical: 'the practical difficulty of an arrangement under which "a sort of Home Rule" would be given to Ireland, while North-east Ulster would remain an integral part of the United Kingdom, would be greater than you suppose.'[39] He followed this with other similar letters over the next few days, all of which indicated that he and his friends were willing to consider Ulster exclusion only if Home Rule were to become 'inevitable', and this he refused to believe would be the case.[40]

Lansdowne and his friends – including Salisbury, Willoughby de Broke, Curzon and Long – were a small but formidable force within Unionism, and they were unwilling at this point to accept the implication that Home Rule was merely an Ulster question. If Bonar Law meant to put compromise on the table, he would have to convince these men first. In response, and as something of a corrective to a colleague who perhaps needed to be awakened to the dangers of narrow-minded reactionism, Bonar Law reminded Lansdowne that all possible alternatives were fraught with danger: 'The prospect before us is either the Government go on[,] with, as I fully believe, the certainty of disorder approaching at least civil war; or, that we compel an election which we are not certain of winning, and even if we win, there will be I think the certainty of lawlessness in Ireland on the other side[,] encouraged to the utmost by the whole radical party in this country.'[41] Another letter to Lansdowne three days later was slightly softer in tone, but he continued to insist that by no means could the party openly reject all consideration of compromise. Though he was aware that certain influential Unionists would be hostile towards it, some discussion of Ulster exclusion from Home Rule might have to be faced, he said; he accepted, however, that if there was legitimate hope of finding a negotiated settlement, the surest way to destroy it would be to reveal in advance Unionist willingness to settle. If grounds for negotiation could be established, invitations to do so should originate with the Crown, which 'would in the eyes of the public save us from responsibility for every one would recognize that if such an invitation were sent we [would have] no choice but to accept it.'[42]

Lansdowne remained unconvinced, and indeed no conference came about for many months. Yet this correspondence underscores the fact that Bonar Law, though well aware that there were many sides to be satisfied, was cautiously willing to discuss the possibility of a compromise encompassing some form of Home Rule. He had not forgotten the disaster caused in 1912 by a premature announcement to the Shadow Cabinet of his Tariff Reform policy, however: with few exceptions, on this occasion he kept his ratiocinations to himself.

III

By early October, fending off Royal pressure for a prompt all-party conference, Bonar Law was ready to take the views of his senior colleagues on recent developments.[43] Both Balfour and Smith had already come down in favour of examining the possibilities for compromise.[44] Lansdowne remained unmoved, but certain of his most powerful allies seemed prepared to desert him. Having spoken with Curzon, Long and Lord Robert Cecil, Bonar Law informed Balfour on 9 October: '... all of them (including Walter [Long]) I think would welcome a settlement much as in other conditions they would have objected to it.'[45] The volatile Long, thought to be a bell-wether of Southern Unionist opinion, surprised Bonar Law with his understanding: '... it is a very difficult time for you and Lansdowne and the only thing your colleagues can do is to assure you of our cordial support whatever you decide to do.'[46]

On 5 October Bonar Law met Carson to discuss the matter of greatest concern to Lansdowne and others sceptical of Ulster exclusion: the attitude of the Southern Irish Unionists. Carson had just returned from a meeting in his Dublin house with a group of their leaders. According to H. Montgomery Hyde, Carson related that he asked his visitors:

'Is it your decision that I am to go on fighting for Ulster?'
The Southern Unionists answered 'Yes.' Carson made a note and went on. 'Will my fight in Ulster interfere in any way with your fight in the South?' 'No.'
Carson made another note. He then pointed out that, if the Southerners lost and the Ulstermen were now asked to fight, only to surrender in the end with them, it would take the heart out of the Ulster movement. 'If I win in Ulster,' he continued, 'am I to refuse the fruits of victory because you have lost?'

The logic of Carson's case was clear. 'No,' they answered emphatically.
From then on the paths of the two sections of the Irish Unionists tended
to be more and more divergent.[47]

Bonar Law related this to Lansdowne and offered it as his opinion
that the '... leading men of Ulster do desire a settlement on the basis of
leaving Ulster out, and Carson thinks such an arrangement could be
carried out without any serious attack from the Unionists in the South.'
Lansdowne, chief advocate of Southern Unionism, must have winced at
Bonar Law's conclusion that Unionists outside Ulster had 'become
more or less reconciled to the idea of Home Rule'.[48]

Bonar Law attached to this letter a lengthy analysis of the crisis:
failing some sort of compromise, he wrote, the Home Rule Bill would
pass into law under the auspices of the Parliament Act. This would
surely be followed, he concluded, by an outbreak of violence in Ulster
'which would in effect be civil war.' Carson's Provisional Government
would seize control and be faced, inevitably, with the British Army. The
results, he feared, would be costly to all sides:

> In view of the fact that the action of the Ulster Prov. Govt would be openly
> supported by the whole Unionist Party in GB it seems to me doubtful
> whether the Army would obey the orders of the Govt and certain that the
> Army would be divided and that its discipline would be destroyed.

If the Government were able to command a loyal force they would
put down Ulster resistance, and the resultant bloodshed would be followed by political revulsion in Britain and, of course, an election. 'That
as I believe would be the position of the Govt, and what', Bonar Law
enquired, 'would be the position of the Unionist Party?'

If they were defeated in such an election, the Unionists' situation
would be 'desperate'; and 'If we won it by a small majority, the position
would not be much better.' A large majority, however, would solve
immediate problems and allow a Unionist Cabinet to carry out a programme of coercion combined with conciliation not unlike that of the
Salisbury Government following the failure of the 1886 Home Rule
Bill, 'and we could pass a Redistribution Act which by reducing the
number of Nationalist Members would finally kill the H.R. agitation. If
however we had a small majority our position would I think be impossible.'

Unionist policy up to this point had been concentrated on forcing an
election, Bonar Law noted, with little discretion shown in pledges of

support for Ulster. Was the party not bound, he extrapolated – if things remained as they were and the Home Rule Bill passed through the Commons a third time – to carry things to their logical conclusion and make the conduct of business in Parliament impossible? He spelt out clearly how repugnant he found such a prospect: 'In my belief it would be possible by such means to force an election, but the consequences of using such means is appalling for even if successful it would destroy perhaps for a generation our whole Parliamentary Institutions.' The persistent image of Bonar Law as an uncompromising extremist, embracing 'a course that for violence and extremism had no parallel in modern British history',[49] should be tempered by noting his confidential recommendation to Lansdowne: 'These considerations,' he wrote, 'which I do not think are exaggerated[,] make me feel that if it is possible to secure a settlement by consent we ought to secure it even if it should be a settlement which we dislike.'

Setting aside as probably impractical any devolutionary or federal multiple-parliament scheme, Bonar Law considered in detail only the possibility of the exclusion 'of Ulster, or part of Ulster'.[50] He again burdened Lansdowne with the conclusion he and Carson shared: that the majority of Southern Unionists were not prepared to resist Home Rule as in Gladstone's day:

> The change is due to the fact that [they] ... have come to look on H.R. as inevitable, and that they realize that owing to the extension of Local Govt they could not have less power under H.R. than they have now – that in fact, apart from sentiment, which of course counts for a great deal, their position would not be materially altered ... On the whole, therefore, if the Govt were to propose an open conference with the undertaking that the discussion would be on the basis of excluding Ulster and of making in their H.R. proposals the modifications which in that case would be necessary[,] we ought to agree to such a conference, and to do our best to secure a settlement in that way.[51]

Many difficulties remained, of course, and the most troubling was the lack of agreement as to what constituted 'Ulster'. If the Government would consider for exclusion only four or even six counties, Bonar Law concluded, 'the Ulster Unionists would surely refuse such a limitation [, in which case] we ought not to enter a conference, for nothing could be worse for us than that we should be put in the position of having to refuse an offer which the people of this country would regard as fair and reasonable.' Lansdowne's reply demonstrated that while he continued to find exclusion distasteful, he at the same time found his colleague's logic compelling; it also indicated that he would think very carefully before rejecting any compromise which had earned Bonar Law's full approval.

The Liberals were engaged in their own manoeuvres: on 29 September Lloyd George dined with F. Harcourt Kitchin, a Scottish journalist who could be trusted to tell all to Bonar Law. Claiming that 'all his cards [were] on the table', the Chancellor recoiled from any suggestion of the coercion of Ulster, and suggested that perhaps the best solution for all parties lay in allowing Ulster to 'contract out' of Home Rule. If the Unionists would propose an exclusion scheme, negotiations over terms could begin.[52]

Churchill, who knew his father's Irish speeches by heart, played the next hand. A week later, before his constituents at Dundee, he addressed Unionist concerns over the rights of Ulster and declared that the design of Home Rule could still be altered to encourage a settlement – 'But only upon one condition – there must be agreement.'[53] The hint of exclusion was obvious, but Churchill found himself far in advance of his colleagues, and his public declaration was not taken up by the Liberals.

Asquith, as it turned out, had an initiative of his own in mind: he wrote to Bonar Law on 8 October – the day on which Bonar Law wrote his detailed analysis to Lansdowne, and Churchill flew his Dundee 'kite' – in the rigidly impersonal tone he always employed towards the Leader of the Opposition. Noting that Churchill had reported his conversation with Bonar Law at Balmoral in September, and that a formal conference seemed inopportune at that moment, he proposed another plan:

> I understand, however, the suggestion thrown out by you to Churchill to be that an informal conversation of a strictly confidential character between yourself and myself – with perhaps another colleague on either side – might be useful as a first step towards the possible avoidance of danger to the State, which all responsible statesmen must be equally anxious to avert.
>
> I write, therefore, to say that (if you are still in the same mind) I should be happy to take part without delay in a conversation so conditioned.[54]

Bonar Law had anticipated that such an invitation might result from his talk with Churchill, and replied immediately: 'I thank you for your letter & think that such a meeting as you propose may be useful.'[55] Lansdowne, suspicious but unwilling to bear responsibility for vetoing the proposal, agreed that the meeting should take place but wanted no part of it.[56] Bonar Law wrote to the Prime Minister suggesting that they confer at Aitken's house, Cherkley Court; Asquith agreed, and the date set was 14 October.[57]

With Lansdowne's ominous warning that any Home Rule compromise would be 'odious to most of us'[58] fresh in his mind, Bonar Law met Asquith on the appointed morning. The two spoke alone for an hour, after which the Prime Minister hurried off to meet a Cabinet unaware of this encounter. Bonar Law immediately dictated an eight-page *aide-mémoire* of the conversation and sent copies to Lansdowne and Balfour. In an accompanying letter he spelled out to Lord Lansdowne the danger that Asquith might yet manoeuvre the Irish Nationalists into accepting a scheme to exclude from Home Rule the four Protestant Ulster counties, carry out a plebiscite in 'the two doubtful' counties (Fermanagh and Tyrone) and subject the remainder of the province to a Dublin Parliament. In his idiosyncratic style, Bonar Law's words poured out:

> I dont [*sic*] believe Carson could possibly accept this solution; and yet it would be so reasonable that I think we would be in a hopeless position if we had to refuse it. I hope, therefore, that there will be no conference; and the best thing that can happen for us is that he [Asquith] should find that the Nationalists are irreconcilable in the matter; for even if we did decide to enter a conference (which would be very difficult)[,] when they had made up their minds with the consent of the Nationalists to exclude Ulster they could then definitely make that proposal public and appeal to the country with this proposal, and I should have very little hope of winning an election under such conditions. I think therefore the position is very serious for us and we must be very careful.
>
> The Nationalists [he added in a postscript] are Asquith's only difficulty, for I am sure that the Radical Party, if the Irish were squared, would be delighted to exclude Ulster.[59]

At their meeting, Bonar Law reported, he had told Asquith of the difficulties faced by his party: the first was their commitment to the welfare of the Southern Unionists. The second was the political consideration that compromise over Ulster would deprive them of 'one of the strongest points in our favour in an election' and appear to the Die-Hards as 'a second climbing down', which might drive them to bolt. A third obstacle mentioned by Bonar Law cannot have much impressed Asquith and was little more than a debating point: that a Home Rule settlement would hasten passage of disestablishment of the Welsh

Church, a cause, he argued, which was more important to 'a very much larger number of our Members in the House of Commons' even than Home Rule.

Next, he recorded that he had renewed his demand for a Dissolution, and brushed aside Asquith's contention that the Carsonites would resist Home Rule regardless of the results of an election. He had informed the Ulstermen unequivocally, he insisted, that once Home Rule was placed before the electorate, the British Unionist Party would abide by the result: '... I added', he wrote, 'that Mr Asquith must understand as well as I did that [this] made all the difference, and that it was really the certainty of British support which made the strength of the Ulster resistance.' He had rejected Asquith's offer of an election *after* the passage of the Bill and insisted that, if the Government had faith in their mandate, they must go forward with their Bill. If they did not, he had emphasized, they were honour-bound to call an election immediately.

Bonar Law had promised Asquith no rest in the interim: it was his duty, he had reminded him, to press without quarter for a Dissolution: 'and in saying that,' he added, 'I hinted at the possibility of disorder in the House of Commons, of using the letter of the Parliament Act, and as a result of all this of his finding that the Army would not obey orders.'

Though he had reminded the Prime Minister that the parties were not yet agreed about what actually constituted the Ulster they were discussing, Bonar Law had sensed, he told Lansdowne, that it was too early to wrestle with this troublesome matter. He noted in his memorandum: 'I passed from that subject without going into it at all, for it was quite evident to me that he had in his mind only the four counties.'

After an hour, Asquith had paused and offered a summary of the Unionist position: barring outcry from the Southern Irish Unionists, and once there was agreement on which counties actually constituted Ulster, the Unionists would accept the passage of Home Rule if the province were excluded. No doubt with the sensibilities of Lansdowne and his friends in mind, Bonar Law had demurred:

> I replied that that was not quite the position, as I had made it clear that the first thing we should have to do would be to make sure that we had the support of the colleagues whose adhesion to any scheme would be essential, as in my opinion it would be quite impossible to go on with any proposal if we found that any of the prominent leaders of our Party would be disposed to fight against it. He accepted this and then repeated his declaration of our position, as far as I can remember, in these words: 'Subject to the agreement of your colleagues whose concurrence is essential to you, if there were not a

general outcry against you in the south and west of Ireland, if Ulster (which we can at present call X) were left out of the Bill, then you would not feel bound to prevent the granting of Home Rule to the rest of Ireland.' I accepted that statement as correct, and that is where the interview ended.

The Prime Minister was a seasoned campaigner, and left their meeting confident that Bonar Law's problems were greater than his own.[60] His brief record of the meeting reveals his sly optimism: in it he recalls that he asked Bonar Law if he was prepared to throw the Southern Unionists 'to the wolves', and noted that the answer was in the affirmative, unless the majority of the 'sheep' protested.[61] Asquith clearly had much more to learn about his adversary.[62]

The two leaders, no doubt each hoping he had seized the initiative and left the other off-balance, agreed to reveal the Cherkley meeting to as few colleagues as possible. Without actually mentioning the interview, Bonar Law subsequently analysed the situation carefully in a letter to J.P. Croal: if Asquith could square the Nationalists, he would almost certainly propose an inter-party conference and a scheme for exclusion from Home Rule of only the four Ulster counties; whereupon Carson would reiterate his public commitment to reject any exclusion which did not cover Fermanagh and Tyrone, and thus doom the plan to failure. The way would then be clear for Asquith to counter with the offer of a plebiscite in the two mixed-religion counties, and thus force the Unionists into the position of either accepting, or publicly rejecting, what would appear to be a thoroughly reasonable proposition. Furthermore, in such a scenario the Southern Irish Unionists might raise a cry of betrayal, with a 'violent echo' in Britain.[63]

For Croal's benefit, Bonar Law then turned to his own reading of the situation:

> Personally, and this is entirely for your own guidance, for I should hardly say it so distinctly even to my own colleagues, I do not look upon such a solution as absolutely inadmissible ... in my view if the question were left to the electors I think they would decide that Ulster must not be coerced; but I think also that they are so sick of the whole Irish question that they would vote in favour of trying [a Home Rule] experiment so long as the Ulster difficulty was solved.

He continued to suspect, he admitted, that Redmond and his Nationalists would not in the end swallow Ulster exclusion in any form, and considered that it therefore remained of the utmost importance for the

Unionists to preserve the appearance of moderation. This, he wrote, was a posture which could be profitable in the end, as Asquith appeared to him to be inclined to negotiate: 'and he ought to be. His position is I think a pretty desperate one.' Asquith's commitment to the passage of the Home Rule Bill by means of the Parliament Act and without reference to the electors might lead to violent civil disturbance; on the other hand, he was likely to lose any election held in the near future. 'He must realize this,' Bonar Law concluded to Croal, 'and therefore nothing but compulsion of the most extreme kind would make him submit to an election before his Bills are carried; and there is a great danger that rather than face that risk he will go straight on and land the country in something like disaster.'

Bonar Law knew the Unionist leaders were pursuing a hazardous course, but he was also confident that the Government could be forced to resort to an election before they had embraced calamity – and the Cherkley meeting strengthened his resolve. He would continue to keep up both public and private pressure on the Government, driving into the heart of their programme what he hoped were the twin stakes of, first, the Government's refusal to refer the matter to the electorate, and second, the Ulstermen's determination, supported by the Unionist Party, to defend the integrity of their community by whatever means they could. At the same time, he would at every opportunity remind the electorate that the Unionists were open to a just and practical offer of compromise by the Government – in the knowledge that any workable agreement might well drive the Nationalists to desert the Government and so bring it down. Finally, he would himself remain open to the possibility of some form of Ulster exclusion if it were acceptable to a majority of the various elements of opinion within the Unionist Party. It was a complex and even dangerous policy, but one to which he adhered – until a greater conflict forced all Britons to lay the Irish Question to one side.

Soon after their Cherkley meeting, both Asquith and Bonar Law spoke in public – the Prime Minister at Ladybank and the Leader of the Opposition four days later at Wallsend – but neither mentioned their recent discussions. Bonar Law, sharing the platform with Carson, confined himself to familiar themes: the accustomed demand for an election, the pledge of Unionist support for Ulster, and the possibility of civil disorder if the Home Rule Bill were pushed through. In referring to the Prime Minister's Ladybank speech, however, he had a message both for the electorate and for Asquith. Noting that the press had treated the speech as a rejection of compromise over Home Rule, Bonar Law uncharacteristically took a softer line:

> I understood it ... to be an invitation to us, the Unionist leaders, to enter with him into an interchange of views and suggestions in a spirit free, frank without prejudice ...
>
> All that is necessary for me to say, and it can be said in a single sentence, a sentence which I think is not ambiguous. If I have correctly understood Mr Asquith, if he does mean to extend to us the invitation which I have indicated, then I say we shall not decline to respond to it. We shall carefully consider any proposals he may make to us and consider them with a real desire to find a solution, if a solution be possible.'[64]

Asquith did respond with an invitation, but only for a second private talk; and the two met once again at Cherkley on 6 November, just days before the Unionists secured two more by-election victories, in Linlithgow and Reading.[65] Though Bonar Law warned, with only slight exaggeration, that there were already in place 'elements of a die-hard movement against us if any compromise were effected', the conversation turned again to the possibilities of such a solution.[66] Asquith raised three alternatives: the plan favoured by Sir Edward Grey, of 'Home Rule within Home Rule', or limited Ulster autonomy under a Dublin Parliament; Ulster exclusion for a limited term of years, with ultimate reversion to a Home-Rule Ireland; and Ulster exclusion with the option to 'come in' to Home Rule at some future time. As he noted in his memorandum of the meeting, Bonar Law made it clear to the Prime Minister that the first two cases would be absolutely unacceptable. Taking up the third possibility, he outlined a plan of exclusion 'only to be terminable by a plebiscite by the people of Ulster in favour of joining the Irish Parliament', suggesting that 'the term of years ought not to be too short of time, and that it ought to be at least ten years, to which he replied that that was a matter of detail which could be considered later.'

The leaders then finally faced the vexed matter of the geographical delineation of Ulster, and Bonar Law reminded Asquith that Carson always referred in public to the traditional Ulster province of nine counties. In the face of an attractive alternative, however, he believed Carson 'would see his people and probably, though I could not give any promise to that effect, try to induce them to accept it.' Bonar Law came away from the meeting thinking that Asquith, 'though he did not definitely say he agreed to that', recognized, as he himself did, that 'Ulster' meant at the least the six counties, including Fermanagh and Tyrone. Next he turned to other perils which lay in the way of compromise:

> I then said to him: It is obvious that any settlement of this kind is out of the question if the Nationalists are determined not to have it; for the Unionists do not wish it, and you cannot impose a settlement which nobody wants. To this, of course, he agreed, but added that Redmond and the 'Old Guard' realized that this was their last chance, and that they must choose between such a settlement and nothing.

As the discussion continued, he recorded, Bonar Law had emphasized that even if a workable compromise were possible, the Unionists would make no promise that Asquith could count on their votes to pass *any* Home Rule plan through the Commons. The most they would do was 'say that we disliked it but we were willing to submit to it rather than face civil war.' Bonar Law recalled that Asquith countered that the Government expected of the Opposition that Lansdowne should agree to allow a modified Home Rule Bill through the Upper House, and that they 'should give it a fair trial, and would not if we [the Unionists] succeeded in the general election immediately upset it. "These conditions", the Prime Minister concluded, "seem to me essential if there is to be any settlement."'

Bonar Law's memorandum finally turned to what was later to become a point of controversy: he enquired of Asquith what he would do next. He recalled the premier as saying:

> '... The next step will be taken at once. I shall definitely make this proposal at my Cabinet on Tuesday, and I think that I can carry my Cabinet and my own Party with me. I have had no communication with the Nationalists, and what they will do I do not know. As soon, however, as I have got the agreement of the Cabinet [Chief Secretary for Ireland Augustine] Birrell will approach the Nationalists.'
>
> I then said, 'I am not in the least afraid, Mr Asquith, of your trying to jocky [*sic*] me, but I am afraid of your colleagues.' To this he replied: 'You need have no fear; I shall say nothing to them except that I put this proposal before you and that you replied that you could of course say nothing about it until you had an opportunity of consulting your friends.'
>
> Mr Asquith has not therefore tried to do even what I certaintly expected he would try to do, and that is, to get a conditional acceptance from me. He has left us perfectly free, and my impression is that he has definitely made up

his mind that a settlement on these lines is the only alternative to a general election.

Bonar Law added a postscript to his memorandum in which he noted that he had pressed upon Asquith a final time his conclusion that the best solution lay in turning to the electorate. If an election were held, they had agreed, and the result was 'something like a stalemate', as Bonar Law believed possible, then a compromise would become irresistible. But, the Prime Minister had insisted, if the Liberals and Home Rule were victorious, and the British Unionists submitted to the result while the Ulstermen forcibly resisted, 'even if there were not much bloodshed[,] any settlement arrived at after coersion [*sic*] of Ulster could not possibly be a real settlement and would be a deplorable result.' The Unionist leader had made no reply, and on that ominous note the meeting had ended.

Bonar Law once again sent his *aide-mémoire* of the meeting only to Lansdowne and Balfour,[67] but on this occasion he also wrote separately to Walter Long. Rumours of compromise had made the former Irish Chief Secretary even more ill-at-ease than he already was about the welfare of the Southern Unionists. Bonar Law explained that discussions of a possible compromise solution could only increase the possibility of an election, as they were likely to weaken Nationalist adherence to the Government. 'From a Party point of view I hope the Nationalists will not agree, for if they do I am afraid that our best card will have been lost.' To keep Long more or less tractable, he reminded him, as he had Lansdowne, that party leaders could not always do as they wished: 'On the other hand, if [Asquith] makes us a definite proposal on these lines I don't see that we could possibly take the responsibility of refusing it.'[68] In a second letter written the following day he acknowledged that others shared Long's anxieties, but explained his conviction that a bold step had to be taken:

They probably don't realize that by refusing to negotiate with the Government we would only make our position worse; for undoubtedly if Asquith can square Redmond, and we refuse to assist him in making arrangements [about] the exclusion of Ulster, they would do it on their own account and go to the country on that issue. In that case we should equally lose our best card for the election; and worse than that, we should seem, at least I think so, to the majority of people unreasonable in the attitude we take. So far we are committed to nothing, and every step must be taken with the utmost caution.[69]

If Bonar Law believed that Asquith would offer an exclusion scheme 'at once', he was to be disappointed. The explanation was two-fold: whatever Asquith may have said, he had no intention of presenting as his own any four- or six-county exclusion plan. Equally importantly, Lloyd George had turned his mind to the resurrection of an option which would appeal more to Liberals than anything Bonar Law might suggest.

As the Unionist leaders waited for a response from Downing Street, the weeks passed. Bonar Law was inclined to believe a Lobby correspondent's conclusion that the Cabinet would 'make no overtures to us'.[70] He suggested to Balfour and Long that the silence was perhaps evidence that the Nationalists would 'not have exclusion at any price'.[71] The Prime Minister finally broke his glacial silence on Wednesday, 3 December, proposing yet another private meeting for the following Tuesday – an invitation which Bonar Law found 'funny',[72] but could not refuse.[73]

What he could not know was that as early as 12 November Asquith had sought the advice of the Cabinet on the subject of Ulster exclusion. He revealed few details of the two Cherkley discussions; nor did he mention the scheme he had outlined in principle to Bonar Law – an omission which Bonar Law considered a breach of faith when he learned of it subsequently. Asquith, however, in his own recollection of their Cherkley *tête-à-tête*, made no reference to having promised to place such a proposal before his Cabinet. Historians have drawn differing conclusions,[74] but it seems plausible that the wily Prime Minister, as Professor Gilbert has written, 'soon thought better of putting this plan to his colleagues.'[75] It is certainly the case that Bonar Law had nothing to gain from putting such words into Asquith's mouth and then having to admit to his restive senior colleagues that he had been taken in by them.

The evening of the Cabinet meeting Asquith, Lloyd George, Grey, Lord Crewe and Lord Haldane were present at a small dinner party, at which the Chancellor resurrected the idea of temporary Ulster exclusion from Home Rule – he posited a period of six years – with automatic reversion to the authority of a Dublin Parliament. This scheme was presented at a second Cabinet meeting that week, and it was decided that Asquith should take it up with the Nationalist leader, John Redmond.[76] As yet another Cabinet, on 24 November, the Prime Minister revealed Redmond's answer: while he was willing to countenance Ulster autonomy within a Home Rule Ireland, at present 'no [other] arrangement as to Ulster was thinkable'.[77] Asquith, however, was not entirely in agreement.

The third Cherkley meeting, on 10 December, produced only agreement to disagree. Still angry that Asquith had failed to proceed with the exclusion plan discussed a month earlier, Bonar Law sent his recollections of this latest sterile discussion to Lansdowne and Balfour. He reported Asquith's latest overture – Lloyd George's plan of temporary exclusion, which Bonar Law had, of course, already rejected at their last meeting:

> I at once told him that this proposal would not be accepted, and could not possibly lead to an agreement; and I added that when I had seen some suggestion to that effect in the Press I had felt that he (A. himself) must realize that that was a hopeless solution, for it would leave all the agitation and ill-feeling in Ulster to go on during the [exclusion] period. He admitted he did not think this a feasible plan.[78]

Next Asquith had again tried – and, predictably, failed – to interest Bonar Law in Ulster 'Home Rule within Home Rule' and, finally, in the long-cold idea of United Kingdom-wide devolution – which continued to fascinate Churchill and, once again, Chamberlain.[79] Bonar Law had impatiently brushed these notions aside and reminded the Prime Minister of what he insisted was the only idea worthy of the slightest hope.

> The end of our interview was a statement by [Asquith] that he understood that nothing could be considered by us except the exclusion of Ulster, and he would carefully consider whether a settlement on that basis was possible.
>
> My feeling, however, is that he has no hope whatever of making such an arrangement, and that his present idea is simply to let things drift in the meantime.

'I really do not understand', Bonar Law wrote to Lansdowne, 'why he took the trouble of seeing me at all. The only explanation I can give is that I think he is in a funk about the whole position and thought that meeting me might keep the thing open at least.' Lansdowne, only slightly less suspicious of the secret talks than he was of the idea of exclusion itself,[80] shared his pessimism in a letter to Chamberlain: 'At this moment I can see nothing ahead but rocks – reefs and reefs of them!'[81]

Chamberlain himself, feeling frustrated and shut out since the time of the January Memorial, put his own oar in the water that day by suggesting to the anxious Lord President, Viscount Morley, that the Prime Minister might meet directly with Carson.[82] An invitation was promptly issued and accepted, and a meeting was scheduled for 16 December. Bonar Law found the idea curious, but did not oppose it.[83]

The old antagonists met at the South Kensington house of the Under-Secretary for India, Edwin Montagu, and Asquith promised to send Carson a proposal for his consideration. This plan proved to be no more than the already twice-rejected 'Home Rule within Home Rule' idea, and, if anything, had even less appeal for Carson than Lloyd George's design.[84] Bonar Law and Carson met and promptly drafted an outright rejection.[85] Displaying marked insight, in view of what lay ahead, Bonar Law reported to Lansdowne that he found the suggestions '... utterly fantastic and [they] have no sense to them at all I think except as the preliminary to exclusion of Ulster which I think he must have in his mind.'[86] Asquith prevailed on Carson to meet him a second time in early January but could not budge him from his position that only complete Ulster exclusion was worthy even of discussion.[87]

Bonar Law had insisted on the need for these negotiations to be allowed to play themselves out; as he cautioned Lansdowne, 'our main object has been, and I think still should be, to act in such a way that we cannot be accused of unreasonableness or unwillingness to consider any possible settlement, and therefore it would not I think do for us to break off anything in the nature of negotiations with too great haste.'[88] Perhaps more fascinating is the fact that, true to his word that the Unionists should remain open to 'any possible settlement', Bonar Law had a secret meeting with the Independent Nationalist MP William O'Brien. Little came of it; as he wrote to O'Brien, 'I have seen Carson and am sure you will expect that he agrees with me in thinking that there is nothing we can do as the result of my conversation with you the other day. It was a pleasure to me to meet you.'[89]

In early January 1914, after his and Carson's fruitless meetings with Asquith, Bonar Law informed the Prime Minister of his intention to reveal the fact that the negotiations had occurred.[90] In Bristol on 15 January he told his listeners that 'There have been conversations between party leaders, but so far they have been without result; and I am grieved to say ... – for nothing can be gained by cherishing vain illusion – that, so far as I can judge, there can be no result.'[91]

A week later he wrote to the King's Private Secretary, Lord Stamfordham, explaining that while Unionists remained opposed to the principle of Irish Home Rule, in the interests of avoiding civil strife they were ready to discuss a settlement based on the exclusion of Ulster and 'including the consideration of safeguards, for the minority in the rest of Ireland.'[92] Bonar Law's conversations with Asquith had left him little reason to share the King's continuing hope that through '"give and take" by *all* parties concerned an amicable solution may yet be found'; and he prepared the Palace for bad news:

> I now despair of any agreement between the two Parties ... I am convinced, therefore, that unless definite proposals are made which would prevent the armed resistance of Ulster[,] any further conversations would serve no other purpose than to continue the policy of drift, which can only have the most disastrous results.
>
> In our belief there are only two courses open to the Government: They must either submit their Bill to the judgment of the people, or prepare to face the consequences of civil war.

He closed this long letter with the earnest request that His Majesty should call upon the Prime Minister to submit to an election, as he thought might have been the King's own wish in the autumn. Stamfordham's prompt reply indicated that King George was not prepared to play such a bold hand at that time. Nevertheless, as Kenneth Rose has written, and contrary to what has often been assumed, 'The King had not abandoned his desire to see Home Rule put to the test of a general election, even if that required so hazardous a measure as the dismissal of the Government or the withholding of the Royal Assent.' But nor had His Majesty changed his opinion in one respect: 'Yet in his heart of hearts he was unwilling to change his advisers, least of all at the prompting of Bonar Law. He admitted to [Lord] Esher that he liked Asquith ... For the dour and abrasive Leader of the Opposition he felt no such regard.'[93]

There is no doubt that throughout this episode Asquith and his colleagues were under tremendous pressure, since Liberal hopes of remaining in power depended upon the votes of an Irish National Party consumed by the desire for Home Rule. Bonar Law, though he had no Government to preserve, was equally taxed by this contest of nerves. To have any hope of success, he believed, he had to maintain an intricate web of contingencies, each dependent upon all the rest. If at all possible, the United Kingdom had to be preserved as it was; therefore, the Unionist Party had to be held together; therefore, the Ulster minority had to be kept firm, but not allowed to tumble over the brink of commitment into open violence; therefore, to keep Unionist election hopes alive, the possibility of a compromise based on mutually acceptable terms had to be nurtured; and finally, unrelenting pressure had to be maintained on the Government. All this had to accomplished as Bonar Law preserved his mastery over his party and its mercurial stars – Lansdowne, Carson, Long, Balfour, Chamberlain, and the rest.

He had agreed to the Cherkley 'summit meetings' in order to discover whether an agreement with the Government acceptable to Unionists was in fact possible, and also to prove once again that his party was open to 'reasonable' compromise – which is why he finally made the meetings public in mid January. By now Bonar Law was convinced that the Prime Minister had displayed his weakness. As he wrote to Lord Selborne,

> ... the one impression which I had derived from my interview with [Asquith] was that he [was] in a funk about the resistance of Ulster, and I am convinced that he will not face that when it comes to the point. In my opinion, at present he is quite at sea and does not in the least know what he can do ...[94]

The new Parliamentary session was scheduled to begin in early February, and under the terms of the Parliament Act Home Rule would almost certainly become law by the summer. Therefore, Bonar Law intended to dispense a course of stronger medicine to the Government.

8

To the Brink

I

WITH THE FAILURE of the Cherkley talks, Bonar Law saw little immediate hope of a compromise between the political parties over Home Rule.[1] In his Bristol speech in mid January 1914 he again insisted that his party was prepared to make every sacrifice for a settlement:

> We are opposed utterly to Home Rule. We think Home Rule is a great evil, but we think that civil war is an evil infinitely greater, and if the Government could make to us any proposal which would do away with the prospect of civil strife, we should not only be ready to consider it, but we should be ready to consider it with a real desire to accept it, if acceptance were possible without ... the sacrifice of honour ...[2]

Honour, he reminded his listeners and the Government, encompassed the unshakeable commitment that Ulster should not be forced under the authority of a Dublin government: 'We intend, with the help of the Almighty, to keep that pledge, and the keeping of it involves more than the making of speeches. It involves this, that we are bound in honour to Ulster to use every means – any means – which seem to us effective, to prevent the coercion of Ulster.' The Government, he demanded, must 'realize that we are in earnest as they realize today that Ulster is in earnest – then they will see that what they propose is impossible, and that they must appeal to the people.'

Bonar Law was well aware of how deeply this commitment was felt by many British Unionists; not the least of these was Lord Milner, who was now drawn back into politics by it.[3] The great imperial administrator lent his incomparable organizational talents to the anti-Home Rule movement and, borrowing a page from the Ulstermen's book, with his friends promulgated a British Covenant. Written by L.S. Amery, the pledge was perhaps not so finely worded as the Ulster document, but its burden was clear enough:

> ... we do hereby solemnly declare that, if the Bill is so passed, we shall hold ourselves justified in taking or supporting any action that may be effective to prevent it being put into operation, and more particularly to prevent the armed forces of the Crown being used to deprive the people of Ulster of their rights as citizens of the United Kingdom.[4]

Bonar Law was uneasy about this, writing to Lansdowne in mid January that it would be helpful to their cause only if it elicited an overwhelming response.[5] He need not have worried: the Covenant, announced in March, was launched on 4 April with a massive rally in Hyde Park 'Against British Forces being used to Shoot Ulster Loyalists'; hundreds of thousands gathered to hear Carson, Chamberlain, Milner, Long and most of the party's other notables – though not Bonar Law or Lansdowne – speak, from fourteen different platforms.[6] By midsummer Walter Long was able to claim that more than two million had signed; unlike some of their Ulster cousins, however, all seem to have been content to express their enthusiasm in ink, rather than blood.[7]

Bonar Law kept his distance from the Covenant campaign: if his commitment to Ulster was as real as that of these zealots, as Leader of the Opposition his responsibility was far greater. Convenants might hearten his followers and frighten the Liberals, but his mind remained concentrated on the problem of identifying a way to derail the Home Rule Bill. Time was growing short: the Parliamentary session would begin in February and unless another path were found, Home Rule would soon become law. His greatest anxiety was lest Asquith concoct a settlement offer which, though hostile to the goals of Unionists and Ulstermen, would capture the imagination of an electorate wearying of the Irish quarrel. Worse still, Asquith, whose political skills Bonar Law deeply respected, might then carry the election which would surely follow.

At this point almost any option appeared to Bonar Law to be worthy at least of examination; as a consequence, he gave consideration to the possibility of amendment of the Army Annual Act in the House of Lords, a curious episode which has earned him the disapproval of generations of historians. 'Bonar Law realized that recourse to such tactics violated a basic and ancient principle of the constitution,' one distinguished critic has written; another has referred to the very idea as an 'almost incredible plot.'[8]

Since the Bill of Rights following the Glorious Revolution of 1688 the subjection of the military power in Britain to the civil had not been questioned, and each year an Army Annual Act was passed to legalize the existence of the forces for the twelve months following. This has been called the 'cornerstone of the constitution',[9] although, unlike most other modern states, Britain of course has no written constitution. Placed before Parliament each April as a bill, technically the Annual Act could, like any bill, be rejected or amended. To prevent its passage, however, would nullify the legal status of the Army, in effect destroy it. Even to consider its amendment in the Lords was a heady political gamble; for the Unionists to have acted on the idea would certainly have been a mistake. However, the constitution was whatever Parliament said it was, as the passage of the Parliament Act proved, and to suggest that amendment would have been judicially unconstitutional was to go too far.

As we have seen, Bonar Law had raised the issue of amendment of the Army Act in public three years before, following the Unionists' defeat over the Parliament Act, his point being that the Unionists were not without weapons to counter-attack an all-powerful Commons majority.[10] Lord Selborne agreed, and wrote to him in mid 1912 that vetoing the Act in the Lords would topple the Government and bring about an election.[11] The idea had surfaced again among Unionists as the divisive events of 1913 played themselves out. Milner certainly was considering it, and in June 1913 Lord Hugh Cecil had outlined a plan of his own to amend the Act; he sent copies to Bonar Law and to Selborne, his brother-in-law.[12] In December, Bonar Law had received from a former Unionist MP, Sir Ailwyn Fellowes, a detailed legal justification for amendment.[13] In February 1914, Lord Willoughby de Broke threatened to offer his own amendment to the Act.

Bonar Law believed that forced alienation of the loyalist Ulster minority from the United Kingdom and their subjection to the power of an unsympathetic authority they did not recognize – a Dublin Parliament – would do violence to the constitution of the United Kingdom;

he concluded that amendment of the Army Act to prevent the use of troops to coerce Ulster – he never advocated, as is sometimes suggested, a veto of the Act – would not.[14] He was certain that the majority of the Army, with its large proportion of Ulster-bred and other pro-Union officers and men, were unlikely to obey any Government command to turn their guns upon the province, and had plainly said as much, privately, to Asquith and Churchill.[15] It was likely, he considered, that any order to march on Ulster would effectively tear the Army apart.

He also believed that the Government were contemplating – even preparing – such orders. Field Marshal Lord Roberts, heroic Boer War Commander-in-Chief, now in his eighties, warned him: 'To insist on their [compelling Ulster] would, I believe, strain discipline to almost the breaking point, and have a most disastrous effect on the Army generally.'[16] 'Little Bobs' had scant sympathy with party politics but was apparently willing – had Bonar Law wished it – to publish an open letter expressing his fears.[17] These men believed that amendment of the Act to prevent the use of troops to enforce Home Rule in Ulster might save the Army from the terrible choice which American soldiers had faced in 1860. To Bonar Law, the proposed amendment was a 'fail-safe' device which would have no effect unless the Government was indeed prepared to coerce Ulster.

By early 1914, as his other options dwindled and passage of the Home Rule Bill loomed closer, Bonar Law was seriously considering the amendment scheme.[18] He raised the subject in late January with Lansdowne, who apparently recoiled from it.[19] The two leaders did agree, however, that the possibility had to be considered, and that expert legal advice was needed.

While Lansdowne retreated to Bowood to nurse an infected eye, Bonar Law took soundings of their senior colleagues. Within a few days he was able to report that those he had managed to contact – Selborne, the three Cecil brothers, Chamberlain and Carson – were agreed that the scheme required careful evaluation. He explained to Lansdowne:

> It is indeed a very serious step; but after all, it is not so serious as allowing the Government to drift into a position where force is used in Ulster; and it is the only step I see which we can take to prevent that result within the letter of the Constitution ...
>
> So far as I can judge if we take that action we shall compel an Election ... If we miss this opportunity then really no other is left except to put pressure on the King, and of the two I am sure you will agree that the latter would be the greater evil.[20]

Bonar Law recapitulated for Lansdowne his worst fears: Asquith might yet engineer Nationalist agreement to a settlement scheme moderate in appearance yet unacceptable to the Unionists; such a ploy could conceivably win an election, which the Government would then declare gave them a mandate for forcing the scheme on the province – and all would be lost. He reminded his friend that options were few:

> It seems to me, therefore, that it is a question between an Election more or less forced by us on what we will try to represent as the plain issue: Shall the Army be used to coerce Ulster without the consent of the electors? Or on [Government] proposals for Home Rule which to moderate men will not appear unreasonable.

Lansdowne remained gloomy about laying hands on the Act, and Balfour and Curzon expressed similar reluctance.[21] After soliciting an amendment proposal from the former Attorney-General, Sir Robert Finlay, Bonar Law grew more convinced that it might be necessary to put the plan into action – if the Government continued to refuse to call an election before the final passage of Home Rule.[22] On 4 February he presented Finlay's blueprint to the Shadow Cabinet: were Home Rule to be passed under the provisions of the Parliament Act, the Army Act should be amended in the Lords by stipulating that the Army should not

> ... be used in Ulster to prevent or interfere with any step which may thereafter be taken in Ulster to organize resistance to the enforcement of [the Home Rule] Act in Ulster nor to suppress any such resistance there unless & until the present Parliament shall have been dissolved and a period of three months shall have lapsed after the meeting of a new Parliament.[23]

The anxious front-bench Unionists gladly acceded to the suggestion of Lord Robert Cecil that they withhold any decision until a panel of distinguished lawyers had offered advice.[24] The committee, chaired by Finlay, included Lord Halsbury, George Cave, Carson and Cecil, and reported to the party chieftains at Lansdowne House on 12 March.[25] The lawyers came down unequivocally in favour of action, and Bonar Law and the still-chary Lansdowne announced their agreement ('reluctantly reached') to the Shadow Cabinet.[26] With only Curzon, Derby and Selborne (who had now changed his mind) expressing dissent, the Shadow Cabinet decided 'provisionally to agree to amendment of army act, but to leave details and decision as to the moment of acting to

Lansdowne and B.L.' None the less, the Earl of Crawford – as the former Chief Whip, Balcarres, had become in January 1913 on the death of his father – noted that the meeting was unenthusiastic, and theorized: 'This [conclusion] I fancy was against the general desire of those present.'[27]

There is little reason to doubt that among this company, Bonar Law was the strongest supporter of the scheme. However, in the week which followed the meeting the possibility dissolved of such an amendment ever being put before the Upper House. Lansdowne remained suspicious of the idea, and Curzon and Selborne worked assiduously to change Bonar Law's mind. Balfour, whose opinion his successor always considered carefully, agreed with them. Outside that charmed circle but men whose opinions carried weight in Unionist counsels were the constitutional sage Dicey and the editors Croal, Strachey, and Geoffrey Robinson of *The Times*, all of whom opposed the scheme. In the end, no amendment to the Army Act was offered – but it was not the urgings of these advisors that turned their leader from it.

Bonar Law had risen from the back benches; the men of the back benches had made him leader of their party and sustained him through his greatest trials; one day, they would make him Prime Minister. More than the grandees of the front bench, it was they who stayed his hand. Bonar Law received many visitors and innumerable letters from party loyalists agitated by rumours of the Army Act scheme: even so violently a pro-Ulster back-bencher as Ian Malcolm raged that amendment of the Army Act would drive him from the party.[28] The new Chief Whip, Lord Edmund Talbot, was ordered to sound parliamentary party opinion on the question, and this was discreetly done on 18–19 March. Junior Whip Robert Sanders noted in his diary:

> Most of the whips are against it, and on the whole the feeling in the party is against it. The Scotchmen say it would be fatal to Unionist hopes in Scotland. Curiously enough Ronald McNeil says it would be most unpopular with the Orangemen who say they have no quarrel with the army. The one strong point is that it must force an election, and it is rather hard to see how to enforce one otherwise.[29]

This was the kind of advice Bonar Law understood, and heeded throughout his political career.

On 19 March he summoned J. St Loe Strachey to Pembroke Lodge. An ardent free-trader, Strachey had set aside his quarrel with the Tariff Reformers in order better to oppose Home Rule, and Bonar Law both liked and trusted him. Aware that he hated the Army scheme, Bonar Law had sought him out to ask that he refrain from taking up the matter in the columns of *The Spectator*. As Strachey wrote to Curzon later that same day, Bonar Law had told him that

> ... he could not honestly say he thought there was much chance of the [Army] Bill being amended because it would obviously be impossible to do so unless there was a completely unified party, and as at present advised, he did not think it at all likely or possible that there could be an undivided party.[30]

Strachey's summary was correct. Bonar Law wrote to Croal of the *Scotsman* in similar vein the following day:

> As regards the Army Annual [Act], I think there is a great deal to be said for and against the idea of having an amendment forbidding the use of troops in Ulster until after an election; but it would be quite fatal to do it if there were any serious opposition to it in our ranks, and I think there is a sufficient amount of that feeling at present to make it impossible to do so.[31]

Later that same evening, and after he had made his decision, word reached Bonar Law and his colleagues of the incident at the Curragh camp, south of Dublin, in which officers tendered their resignations under the impression that they were on the point of being ordered to 'coerce' Ulster. At once, the Army Act amendment scheme became irrelevant. Like Sanders, Bonar Law had seen value in the scheme, 'warts and all', because of its potential to force an election on the Liberals. He was wise enough, however, not to attempt to resist the strength and unity of party sentiment, though it is likely that it surprised him. It was an attitude rooted in part in a feeling for the Army as a gallant and unique national institution which ran deep among Unionists,[32] combined with an aversion felt by many party loyalists to what might be considered 'tampering' with the Army and the constitution. A third reason was that the scheme courted the possibility of arousing public disapproval of further interference by the Lords, and most Unionists dreaded a second 'Peers versus People' campaign. Finally, it was no accident that rumours of the amendment scheme were circulating, for they had been carefully leaked in order to cause the Government anxiety. In this way, perhaps the proposal had already accomplished whatever good it might for the Unionist cause.[33]

Another event also influenced the judgement of the Unionists, leaders and rank-and-file alike. In mid February Asquith had commissioned Lloyd George to prepare a formal version of his proposal for temporary exclusion of those Ulster counties wishing to 'opt out' of Home Rule, and by early March it was being discussed in the Liberal press. Even Carson admitted that this hated scheme might, as Bonar Law had long feared, appear to the electorate to be 'plausible' and thus give the Government the upper hand in the struggle for public sympathy.[34] Asquith outlined the plan on 9 March as he moved the Second Reading of the Home Rule Bill, announcing his intention to bring in a parallel amending bill to allow a six-year exclusion for those Ulster counties which wished it.

This innovation, though unacceptable to the Ulstermen or their British allies, opened the first public debate among the party leaders over a possible exclusion compromise. Bonar Law had long stressed that his party could not afford to appear to the electorate to be rigid and unreasonable, and despite the fulminations of a small knot of irreconcilables most Unionists agreed with him. Unsatisfactory though Lloyd George's plan was, the idea that the Government had (as it seemed) embraced the principle of Ulster exclusion and were apparently able to carry Redmond's Nationalists with them was enough to drive many Unionists away from any consideration of interfering with the Army Act.[35] The scheme was never mentioned again.

Asquith's six-year exclusion offer raised the stakes in the Home Rule struggle, and the bidding passed to the Unionists. The main speech on 9 March rejecting the plan was rightly left to Carson, the voice of Ulster, who thundered that the Protestant Province would embrace no 'sentence of death with a stay of execution for six years.' Bonar Law held his fire, offering only a low-intensity attack on the lack of details in the brief White Paper on Asquith's offer published the same day.[36] He also added another element to the debate by resurrecting the referendum idea, suggesting that the Ulster exclusion question be submitted to a national plebiscite. This offensive he expanded in the House on 19 March. Unlike Carson, he struck a moderate pose and, though he rejected the time limit on Ulster exclusion, made the following pledge:

> [The Government] have suggested that this question should be settled[,] so far as Ulster is concerned, by taking the opinion of the people of Ulster. If that is a right method in regard to Ulster, it cannot be a very wrong method when applied to the whole of the electors of the whole of the United Kingdom. I am going to make to the Government, on behalf of the Opposition ... an offer

which I hope the [Prime Minister] will not reject without at least some consideration.

If he chooses to put his new suggestions into his Home Rule Bill, and if he submits these suggestions to the country by a Referendum and the country decides in favour of them, then I have the authority of Lord Lansdowne to say now that, so far as his influence in the House of Lords goes, that body will offer no impediment to carrying out completely, without alteration and without delay, the decision of the will of the people of this country.[37]

Asquith, knowing well Redmond's contempt for such proposals and having lost five seats to his rivals in by-elections over the previous year, had no intention of trusting the future of his Government to a referendum. However, once committed to compromise, he could not cling to any particular proposal if another could better gain him the desired result. Without consulting Redmond he therefore sent Bonar Law two days later an offer to jettison county referenda in favour of exclusion of the six Ulster counties, subject still to the six-year time limit. Bonar Law maintained his refusal to consider any compromise tied to a time limit, and the proposal was rejected. None the less, his national referendum proposal was a useful tactic in that it troubled the Liberals and cast upon the Unionists and himself a glow of democratic compromise – a particularly remarkable feat since it was a tactic that entailed stepping over the still-warm body of the Army Act scheme. All, however, was soon pushed aside by events in Ireland.

II

Among Unionists during these years, whenever the question of the disposition of Ulster in a Home Rule Ireland arose, the subject of coercion soon followed. Ulstermen and their British allies were always ready to suspect the Government of planning to force Home Rule on the unwilling north-eastern counties – an imputation which was unfailingly denied – and suspicions always centred on the possible role the Government might have in mind for the British Army. The Unionist Party included many former officers for whom it was an article of faith that the Army would almost certainly break up rather than obey orders to force Ulster under a Dublin Parliament, and contacts between Unionists and serving officers tended to reinforce this belief. Field Marshal Lord Roberts though it likely; so, probably, did the King.[38] Bonar Law agreed; before a Unionist audience in Dublin in November 1913, he had outraged Liberals by comparing Asquith to the unfortunate James II: 'In order to carry out his despotic intention the King had the largest paid army which has ever been seen in England. What happened? There was no civil war; there was a revolution. The King disappeared, and why? Because his own army refused to fight for him.'[39]

By mid March 1914, as Unionists considered amending the Army Act, rumours were circulating that the Government had obtained warrants for the arrest of the Ulster leaders and that a pre-emptive strike against the province was being planned. In this volatile atmosphere, Churchill challenged the Unionists in a fighting speech at Bradford: 'If all the loose, wanton and reckless chatter we have been forced to listen to in these months is in the end to disclose a sinister revolutionary purpose, then I can only say to you "Let us go forward and put these grave matters to the proof."'[40] In the House five days later, Bonar Law returned the First Lord's fire:

> What about the Army? If it is only a question of disorder, the Army, I am sure, will obey you, and I am sure that it ought to obey you. But if it is really a question of civil war, soldiers are citizens like the rest of us. It never has been otherwise in any country at any time.[41]

Carson, himself no stranger to the melodramatic, spoke briefly and threateningly in the debate, and finally – after a rebuke from the Speaker – grumbled that his place was with his followers in Ulster. He strode to the top of the Chamber, paused near the Speaker's Chair and with a wave of his arm declared, to the cheers of his admirers: 'I am off to Belfast.' Within an hour he had leapt aboard the 17.55 Belfast mail train, and by morning was at Craigavon, headquarters of the Ulster Volunteer Force. This was a grand gesture by a great actor: but what did it portend? Did the Government intend to arrest Carson?[42] Did he think the time had come to declare the Ulster Provisional Government? Neither Bonar Law in London nor Carson in Belfast would comment; almost certainly they did not know; but all agreed that it further raised the level of axiety.[43]

While the Unionists pondered their difficulties, Bonar Law's question 'What about the Army?' engaged the attention of a Government grown weary of both Unionist rhetoric and the growing danger of the Ulster Volunteer Force. On Saturday, 14 March, the day of Churchill's Bradford speech, the War Office had sent an encrypted message to the Commander-in-Chief in Ireland, Lieutenant-General Sir Arthur Paget. The cable indicated that 'attempts may be made in various parts of

Ireland by evil-disposed persons to obtain possession of arms, ammunition, and other Government stores ...' and that he should at once 'take special precautions for safeguarding depots and other places where arms or stores are kept, as you may think advisable.'[44] Thus began the notorious Curragh affair.[45]

On Wednesday, 18 March Paget hastened to London for talks with Asquith and Churchill, and with his War Office superiors: the Secretary of State for War, Colonel J.E.B. Seely; the Chief of the Imperial General Staff, Field Marshal Sir John French; and the Adjutant-General, Lieutenant-General Sir John Spencer Ewart. A subject not overlooked in these discussions was that of the possibly conflicting loyalties of officers in the event of armed trouble in Ulster. Paget, understandably uneasy about the impact of sudden troop movements in the overheated political climate of Ireland, expressed to Seely his concern in particular regarding officers having 'direct family connection with the disturbed area of Ulster', and suggested 'that in the event of serious trouble arising [, since] their future private relations might be irretrievably compromised if they were engaged with our troops, they should be permitted to remain behind either on leave or with details.'[46] Other officers dissentient from action in Ulster, he concluded, should simply be decommissioned without pay or pension. 'Jack' Seely, whom Asquith ridiculed to his inner circle as the 'Arch-Colonel', inexplicably agreed to these strange innovations.

In anticipation of trouble Major-General Sir Nevil Macready, Director of Military Planning and considered neutral on Irish matters, was secretly given a 'sleeping' commission as Military Governor of Belfast. The uneasy Paget returned to Dublin the following day with orders to redeploy two battalions to protect warlike stores held in Omagh, Armagh, Enniskillen and Carrickfergus. Also on the nineteenth, and with Cabinet approval, Churchill ordered the Third Battle Squadron of the Royal Navy to steam from Spanish waters for Lamlash, on the Isle of Arran; ships were also designated to be prepared to transport troops to Ireland, and a cruiser was despatched to Carrickfergus in Ulster.[47]

Sir Arthur Paget's reputation was irretrievably damaged by the events which followed. A gallant and able officer (and a grandson of Lord Uxbridge, who gained fame and lost a leg at Waterloo), he was also emotional, and notoriously prone to speak without having considered the weight of his words.[48] In the light of events, it is clear that he was sorely misplaced in his Irish command in the month of March 1914.

Calling together his senior commanders on the morning of 20 March, he explained that operations would soon begin to make safe the military stores held in Ulster. Insisting that he would do all possible to avoid bloodshed, he apparently gave the impression that the Army would soon be engaged with the UVF and that the country might at once be 'in a blaze'.[49]

Paget then explained the novel options agreed upon in London: officers domiciled in Ulster would be excused, but any others who refused to participate in the operation would be summarily dismissed. The generals were then released to place these conditions before the officers under their commands. Disaster immediately followed: within hours Brigadier-General Sir Hubert Gough and fifty-seven of the seventy officers of the Third Cavalry Brigade stationed at the Curragh camp in County Kildare indicated that 'if duty involve[d] the initiation of active military operations against Ulster' they would choose dismissal. By the end of the day, as word of these events reached London, many Unionists were concluding that their fears of a Government plan for a pre-emptive strike – the 'plot against Ulster', 'the pogrom', as many called it – had been all too justified.

The bizarre tale was far from over: Gough and his three senior sub-ordinates were called to London on the Sunday in an effort to prevent a split in the Army and embarrassment for the Government. Incredibly, Gough demanded and received from Seely the following day a written document pledging that the Government 'had no intention of taking advantage of this right [to use the Forces to maintain law and order in Ireland] to crush political opposition to the policy or principles of the Home Rule Bill.'[50] When it was shown to him, Gough added at the end of the paper: 'I understand the reading of the last paragraph to be that the troops under our command will not be called upon to enforce the present Home Rule Bill on Ulster, and that we can so assure our officers',[51] and Sir John French initialled it, signifying his agreement. This extraordinary document, while it allowed Gough to withdraw his own letter of resignation, ensured that not only Seely and French but also the Adjutant-General, Ewart, would soon be writing theirs. Thus ended the military phase of the affair.

Bonar Law almost certainly knew of these Government decisions – Macready's appointment, the naval manoeuvres and the anticipated troop movements – even before Paget's return to Dublin. He knew of the crisis at GHQ Dublin almost from the moment of Gough's announcement of his resignation, for on the afternoon of 20 March he received at the House of Commons an anonymous telegram informing him of it.[52] More importantly, a caller who was the source of much of this information called at Pembroke Lodge at 9.30 the following morning, though he probably hoped no one had noticed his arrival.[53] This was the Director of Military Operations at the War Office, Major-General Henry Hughes Wilson, exceedingly tall and gangly, whose prominent nose and long face had earned him in youth the sobriquet 'Ugly' Wilson, which stuck to him for life. The scion of an old Ascendancy family, his politics were right-wing Unionist, and his contempt for the Liberals – particularly for the Prime Minister – was without limit. A natural and ruthless intriguer, Wilson was also a brilliant conversationalist and possessed charm, wit and a rather boisterous sense of fun. Although his military career had not been without controversy, it had nevertheless been remarkably successful, as his rank and responsibility indicated.

Wilson had been introduced to Bonar Law in 1912, and the two got on well together; thereafter, few matters of Army policy remained long unknown to Bonar Law.[54] They shared a commitment to the Irish Union; but Bonar Law cared nothing for Wilson's other passion, the imposition of mandatory military service, and resisted his requests to support it.[55] Despite his apparent solemnity, Bonar Law enjoyed the company of a mixed circle of friends, including such picaresque characters as Wilson, particularly if they possessed wit and humour and brought him useful political information. Though Wilson hated most politicians, he found Bonar Law 'quiet and unostentatious', and straight as a die. It is not surprising that they got on.

Henry Wilson was Bonar Law's best but not his sole source of information on the Curragh incident. Among others, Lord Derby, Amery, Walter Long, and the editors Robinson and Gwynne – each with his own sources of information – deluged him with reports, of varying degrees of accuracy.[56] After meeting his senior colleagues on Sunday evening, 22 March, Bonar Law wrote to the Prime Minister demanding that normal parliamentary business be put aside to consider the Army emergency – and Ulster. His proffered solution remained unchanged: there must be permanent Ulster exclusion, or an election, or a national referendum. The Opposition would raise the matter in Monday's session in the House.[57]

Debate in the House in the days which followed was predictably bitter, and the Unionists discharged their heaviest artillery at Seely and Churchill. Seely was accused of having bungled his own 'secret plan' for the 'pogrom' against Ulster; the First Lord (whose orders to the Fleet had been cancelled by Asquith on Saturday) they denounced for stealthily manoeuvering his warships in order to menace a Belfast guilty only of loyalty to King and country. The burden of Bonar Law's attacks centred on Government preparations to coerce Ulster; on 25 March he even dredged up the unpleasant spectre of 'Marconi':

> What we complained of chiefly at that time was not what those colleagues had done – which was quite pardonable. What was not so easily pardonable was the action they took to conceal from the House and the country what they had done. It is the same now. The Government are concealing something. What it is we do not know, but we do know that they are ashamed of it.[58]

On this same day, Asquith announced both the quashing of the now-public pledge to Gough, and the resignation of Colonel Seely, the War Secretary – the latter was initially refused as a face-saving gesture but was quietly accepted five days later. To the astonishment of the Opposition and the delight of his supporters, on 30 March Asquith revealed that he would himself take the War Office portfolio. Following the practice of the day, he immediately resigned his seat to stand for re-election in East Fife.[59] Bonar Law was furious at what he considered a mere theatrical gesture, intended to provide the Prime Minister a fortnight's respite from the line of fire.

A brief White Paper published by the Government on 25 March, followed by a more comprehensive version on 22 April, was ostensibly intended to explain the misunderstanding that had provoked the Army crisis.[60] Neither document, however, served to placate those who believed the Government desired a 'pogrom' against Ulster. The enmity brought about by the episode smouldered for weeks without dying: Unionists raged against the Government 'plot' to dragoon loyal Ulster, while Liberals condemned Unionist 'inspiration' of what they inaccurately described as mutiny at the Curragh.

Both sides were wrong. The Government had had no plan for a pre-emptive strike to break Ulster, although the military and naval manoeuvres, in the wake of Churchill's provocative speech at Bradford and Paget's bungling in the tense atmosphere of early March, made it seem to supporters of Ulster that Asquith intended the very worst. By the same token, the Unionists had played no part whatsoever in inspiring the threatened resignations at the Curragh camp, and it should be recalled that the term 'mutiny' was an emotive misnomer: no actual refusal to obey orders occurred. High-ranking Liberals did however know that the Shadow Cabinet were considering amendment of the Army Act, and were deeply resentful of the open and close contacts between senior Army officers and the Unionist leaders.[61]

It is not necessarily what is true that moves men and women, but rather, what they believe. Each side in this affair, nerves frayed by years of corrosive struggle, sincerely believed the worst of the other. Bonar Law's words in these days were not as extreme as those of some other Unionists, but they were bitter, and they were condemnatory. He had from the outset believed that the Army would resist any 'plot' against Ulster by refusing to obey orders. Here was hard evidence that the Government, for whatever reason, had issued commands to invest Ulster with additional troops. Whether he truly believed that the intention was to put matters 'to the proof' before the Ulster Volunteer Force became armed and operational cannot be known. It is clear, however, that he was shocked that the Government should be willing to attempt anything so provocative; and he was contemptuous of what seemed to him attempts by ministers to hide the full extent of their plans.[62] He could not forget the apparent willingness of Churchill, Seely, and perhaps Asquith, even to contemplate firing the first shot; and it was difficult for him to forgive. Liberal certainties that Unionists were in league with disloyal high-ranking officers in the Army will have been as profoundly felt.

On Sunday 22 March, as this incident was building to its climax, Bonar Law met the Archbishop of Canterbury. The Archbishop, Asquith's curious choice as emissary, repeated the Prime Minister's offer of exclusion of the six counties with the familiar six-year time-limit, but with the additional provision that the arrangement would be subject to a plebiscite at the end of the period, with similar referenda to follow periodically thereafter as necessary. Bonar Law told Archbishop Davidson that he had already offered to lay before his party a proposal for permanent exclusion, but only for that.[63] On Tuesday he reminded the House that if the Prime Minister were to prove by means of a referendum that the country supported his Home Rule plan, Unionists would cease at once all opposition to it. Each leader continued to find the other's offer equally unappealing.

Too-close concentration on the Curragh incident alone tends to obscure a point about the Army and the Irish Question which is worth noting. The threatened resignations which sparked the crisis almost certainly represented only the first trickle of what was likely to have developed into a torrent throughout the Army. While the resignations actually tendered – not voluntarily – and accepted were limited to those of one minister and two very senior officers holding Government jobs, the War Office subsequently estimated that as many as one-third of the entire officer corps would be likely to resign rather than obey orders to enforce Home Rule in Ulster. The Army in Ireland, GHQ Dublin reported, would, as a result, be useless in any such plan – and this was advice the Government had little choice but to accept.[64] It was a humiliating turn of events for Asquith and his Government; it is remarkable, given the grotesque mishandling of the affair, that the outcome was not worse.[65]

III

In what were to prove the last months of peace in 1914, the small world of British politics had become a veritable bear garden. Bonar Law announced his intention to move yet another vote of censure against the Government, and this was scheduled for 28 April. As otherwise reasonable statesmen seemed prepared to let passions rule them, late on the night of 24 April word arrived in London of the successful landing at Larne in Ulster of 35,000 rifles and three million rounds of ammunition. The gun-running was the work of a Major Frederick Crawford, a former Militia officer and fanatical Ulsterman, one of those who had signed the Covenant in his own blood; his adventures rivalled the most lurid and swashbuckling fiction. Bonar Law knew nothing beforehand of the operation but was quick to align himself with Carson (who almost certainly did) to defend this provocative action on the part of the UVF as a necessary act of resistance against a Government whose violent 'plot against Ulster' had been thwarted.[66]

Predictably, the censure debate on the 28th was once again bitter and pointless; Asquith, returned from his by-election hiatus, further infuriated Unionists by announcing that he would respond to no more questions about the Curragh incident. Wounding accusations flew on all sides, but more significant was the fact that the Home Rule Bill was due to complete its third and final passage through the Commons on 25 May. No one knew precisely what would be the outcome: surrender or compromise for one side or the other, or civil war for both.

Yet if the Bill was unstoppable in Parliament, now more than ever it appeared to be unenforceable on an unwilling Ulster. Neither violent speeches in the House nor ominous machinations on the part of private forces outside it could break the deadlock; only agreement between bitterly opposed parties could do so. Attempts were made in varied quarters to resurrect the possibility of devolution – 'Home Rule All Round' – or United Kingdom federalism as a possible compromise. Milner's circle lobbied diligently to raise enthusiasm for such a solution, and it was given a hearing by Churchill and Lloyd George among the Liberals, as well as by Bonar Law, Chamberlain and even Carson among the Opposition.[67] Several supporting memorials were circulated among MPs of both major parties;[68] and in late April even that hardened realist Robert Sanders thought he sensed the will for a settlement among his party.[69] But the federal schemes came to nothing, and Sanders's hopes soon faded. In early May he concluded: 'The party opposed to compromise on Home Rule is in the ascendant just now ... [and the federalists] a hopeless minority.'[70] Bonar Law, while keeping on the pressure in the House, could think of little more to do at this moment than wait upon events.

With his own party no less disturbed by the situation, Asquith tried to seize the initiative by inviting Bonar Law and Carson to meet him on 5 May, once again at Montagu's house. Shortly before the meeting Bonar Law convened the Shadow Cabinet, but they could muster no new plan which might save the situation: Chamberlain and Lansdowne plumped for federalism, Bonar Law and Carson counselled against action and expressed continued suspicion of Liberal motives, and others present divided between the two positions.[71] Carson in his frustration was heard to bark: 'I don't care a damn ... Only a fool would fight if there is hope of accommodation. And what a great thing it would be if this long-standing controversy could be settled once and for all.'[72] But neither he nor Bonar Law was at all optimistic.

Bonar Law and Carson found this latest meeting with Asquith as sterile as those that had preceded it. The Prime Minister announced his determination to see the Home Rule Bill through under the Parliament Act and then to deal with Ulster by means of his proposed Amending Bill. Predictably the two Unionists were adamant that they could not co-operate unless there was settlement on the terms of the second Bill in advance of passage of the first. Bonar Law reminded Asquith of his own view of the Government's position: they had, he maintained, three options: to attempt to coerce Ulster – now clearly impossible; to exclude the province from Home Rule without conditions; or to call an election. The Prime Minister demurred, and the men parted.[73] In the

House the following week Asquith announced that he would push the main Bill through before the Whitsun recess, and only then turn to the Amending Bill.

The death in mid May of Bonar Law's stepmother Sophia[74] brought him a momentary distraction from these struggles, but no more. The final Third Reading debate on 21 May triggered an extraordinary explosion of anger on all sides as Unionist back-benchers provoked a disorderly scene of shouted accusations and insults.[75] In the midst of the tumult the harried Speaker, J.W. Lowther, pointedly enquired of the Leader of the Opposition if the scene had his 'consent and approval'. Bonar Law, sensing an opportunity, momentarily silenced the House by replying immediately and with frigid gravity: 'I would not presume to criticize whatever you consider your duty, Sir, but I know mine is not to answer that question.' The quietus was brief: Bonar Law resumed his seat, and Opposition Members exploded in wild cheering. Appropriate or not, this inspired and spontaneous dramatic turn did much both to hearten the unruly Unionists and to burnish his reputation among them. Such a powerful retort spoke to their bruised pride and recalled their tradition of leaders set apart, above the parliamentary party – neither Disraeli nor Balfour could have done better. The Clerk of the Privy Council noted in his memoirs that the comment won Bonar Law 'more fame than three years of laborious tactics.'[76] For days afterwards his letter bag overflowed with congratulations like those of Sir Robert Finlay: '[If] you had a year to think it over, your answer to the Speaker could not have been improved.'[77] The humiliated Lowther briefly contemplated resignation, but wisely settled instead for the generous apology offered a few days later.[78]

Satisfying as such cabaret was for the Unionists, it did not solve their problems. Asquith carried the Home Rule Bill for the third time on 26 May, and only the Royal Assent now lay between it and the statute books. At the same time he announced that the anticipated Amending Bill would soon be introduced in the Lords. Bonar Law wrote subsequently to Lansdowne, Balfour and Carson that this manoeuvring put the Unionists 'in a position so difficult that whatever course we take we will be open to the gravest objections, and is almost certain to produce great differences of opinion among our own friends.'[79] He was sure of several things: first, that the Liberal–Irish Nationalist partnership was doomed if Asquith offered any exclusion compromise acceptable to Ulster; second, that if the Liberals were somehow able to square the Redmondites and offer a tolerable settlement, the Ulstermen would be well advised to accept it; and, third, that the best policy for the moment was for the Lords to alter the proposed Amending Bill to suit Unionist requirements 'and leave it to the Government to accept or refuse these amendments.'[80] He was also confident that, barring any Asquithian magic, if the Unionists hung together they would win the next election – and three more by-election victories in May reinforced this conviction.[81] Perhaps the waiting game would prove to be the winning one.

On 23 June the Lord Privy Seal, Lord Crewe, introduced the Amending Bill in the House of Lords. It offered to each Ulster county the option (through a plebiscite) of a six-year exclusion from Home Rule, with ultimate reversion to the authority of the proposed Dublin Parliament. By the time it reached its Third Reading on 14 July, the Unionist peers with their decisive majority in the Upper House had amended the proposed legislation to exclude indefinitely from Home Rule all nine counties of Ulster; and a week later it came in this form to the Commons.

Progress towards a solution still appeared to be deadlocked, with the Unionists, buoyed up by recent by-election successes, further hardened against compromise.[82] Asquith's situation was difficult. His proposed solution to the stalemate was the main Bill, combined with and modified by the Amending Bill – yet he knew full well that he had no hope of enforcing the former without the latter, and that the all-important second bill would languish through two more Parliamentary sessions unless he was able to secure the co-operation of the Unionists who controlled the House of Lords.[83]

The Prime Minister therefore once again suggested informal negotiations, initially through the former Chief Whip Alexander Murray (now Lord Murray) and the newspaper proprietor Lord Rothermere.[84] Bonar Law and Carson agreed to meet Murray on 1 July for 'a long conversation with the view of finding out what was the minimum which Ulster would accept, or whether it would be possible to grant it.'[85] At the meeting Bonar Law indicated that the Unionists would consider the exclusion of a portion of Ulster; he later recorded Murray's proposal in the name of the Government:

> The area suggested included the four [Protestant]counties with the exception of part of South Armagh and a strip of South Down. It included also a strip of Donegal[,] and the discussion showed that if it was possible they were willing also to put within the excluded area a strip of Monaghan and possibly of Cavan.

An 'exclusion Ulster' of this magnitude might have been acceptable to the Government; but Carson also demanded Tyrone, religiously mixed and the largest and most central county of the province, and Bonar Law supported that claim. Murray saw immediately that it would doom any proposed settlement. In fact, the negotiations stalled at once in any case, as Redmond immediately rejected any talk of indefinite exclusion. Carson sailed for Belfast, for the annual celebrations marking the anniversary of the Battle of the Boyne – and to settle with the Ulster Unionist Council the final arrangements for the proclamation, 'in trust for His Majesty', of the provisional government. Bonar Law remained in London, waiting for the negotiating ball to be returned by the Liberals.

Honourable Members were called upon at this time to mourn the death on 2 July of Joseph Chamberlain. Bonar Law spoke with feeling in the House a few days later, recalling of his own early days in Parliament that '... for me at that time the essence of my political faith was belief in Mr Chamberlain.'[86] But those days were long gone; and Bonar Law led the Unionist Party, as the great Joe never had. It was unclear what would happen next in the record-breaking heat of that summer of 1914, and in precisely what direction he would choose to lead.

He had not long to ponder: on 16 July he and Carson again met Lord Murray.[87] Murray dismissed any hope of settlement so long as Carson held fast to his claim on all County Tyrone. In fact, compromise over this territory was unlikely, even had Carson wished it, 'for he was certain that even if he were to make such a proposal there would not be even the smallest possibility of its being accepted [by his supporters].'[88]

Murray then tried another tack: given Asquith's public commitment to seek the Royal Assent for the Home Rule Bill before the end of the parliamentary session, perhaps the time had come to encourage the King to summon the multi-party conference he had long sought. Though Bonar Law and Carson both expressed suspicion of what could only be a delaying tactic, they knew they had nothing else to offer. If His Majesty wished for a conference, they grumbled, they could not openly reject his command. Later on the afternoon of 16 July, Bonar Law received a note from Asquith requesting a private interview in the Foreign Secretary's room in the House.[89]

Conceding for the moment abandonment of the six-year time limit, Asquith concentrated on the possibility of dividing Tyrone between Home Rule Ireland and Ulster. Predictably, Bonar Law would not rise to the bait. Asquith then turned to the inter-party conference, which Bonar Law indicated had little chance of success so long as important issues of geography remained unsettled. The Prime Minister could only sigh at the possibility of civil war 'over so small a difference'. To the people of Ulster, Bonar Law suggested, it was no small matter; and, since the Government seemed to be in no position to enforce its will, it was no small matter to Asquith, either. With this they parted. Asquith had no option left except the conference – but with the Amending Bill due to be debated in the Upper House in four days' time and no sign of co-operation from their Unionist Lordships, and no other ideas to offer, he had little to lose.

Later that evening Lord Murray again contracted Bonar Law, this time through Aitken, indicating that Asquith would ask the King to summon the party chieftains to Buckingham Palace. Bonar Law held to his position: so long as the disposition of County Tyrone remained unsettled, he thought a conference useless. However, 'if the Prime Minister on his responsibility gave such an invitation in the name of the King we should be bound to accept it.'[90] In truth, like Asquith he was uncertain what to do next, and he had little to lose by further delay.

The conference opened on Tuesday, 21 July, with Asquith and Lloyd George representing the Government, Bonar Law and Lansdowne the Unionists, Redmond and John Dillon the Nationalists, and Carson and Craig the Ulstermen.[91] After the King's brief welcome in the ornate '1844 Room' (so-called from the time of the visit of Czar Nicholas I, and once a bedchamber), Speaker Lowther took the chair. The nine men met for three days; the heat was stultifying, and it was clear from the outset that agreement would be impossible. Bonar Law's note of the initial day of negotiations reveals the fatal conundrum: Asquith and the Nationalists seemed willing to give way on the time limit, but would not say so openly until the geographical extent of the excluded area was settled – what, therefore, was to be done about County Tyrone?[92] Carson and Craig made it clear that Ulster – they themselves, therefore – would not tolerate the loss to a Dublin Parliament of any of Tyrone ('that most damnable creation of the perverted ingenuity of man', as Asquith called it).[93] Redmond and Dillon demonstrated complete disagreement with the Ulstermen, and equal tenacity. There the conference began, and there it ended – the next day, and that which followed, changed nothing. To the delegates from Ireland, Nationalist and Unionist alike, the question to be addressed concerned not merely the disposition of territory, but what kind of compromise they could justify to their people. All present were under enormous pressure, but Redmond and Carson bore the heaviest burdens as each, ultimately, was expected to speak for his nation. Asquith described the dilemma to his beloved friend Venetia Stanley:

> The Speaker[,] who incarnates bluff unimaginative English good sense, of course cut in: 'When each of two people say they must have the whole, why not cut it in half?' They wd neither of them look at such a suggestion ... I have rarely felt more hopeless in any practical affair: an impasse, with unspeakable consequences, upon a matter which to English eyes seems inconceivably small & to Irish eyes immeasurably big. Isn't it a real tragedy.[94]

To the Lord President, Lord Morley, the reason for the impasse was clear: 'The issue of Tyrone is narrow enough, but then, as history so abundantly shows, when men want to fight, a narrow issue will do just as well as a broad one.'[95] Old Gladstonian that he was, Morley was too harsh: Redmond and Carson did not simply 'want to fight'. Their intractability over County Tyrone coruscatingly illuminated the hopeless position in which each as a leader found himself: neither could afford, politically, to leave behind – abandon – any of his people under the sway of the other. Though they differed in detail, Bonar Law wanted a solution as much as Asquith – but neither man could proceed further than his Irish allies were willing to go. And neither Redmond nor Carson could range one step beyond the limits of conscience of his own followers.

In any event, the discussions had failed. Asquith marvelled at the final scene, as Carson and Redmond, Craig and Dillon parted with warm handshakes and generous words. Describing it in a letter on the same day to Miss Stanley, Asquith was characteristically superior but not far off the mark: 'Aren't they a remarkable people? And the folly of thinking that we can ever understand, let alone govern them!'[96]

Other men had other ideas. Two days later, on 26 July, an attempt by Irish Volunteers, the Nationalist counterpart of the UVF, to run guns of their own into the port of Howth north of Dublin in broad daylight tragically miscarried. The authorities intervened – no doubt stung by the earlier successful escapade at Larne: the police called upon the Army for support, and the result was riot, three civilian deaths and the wounding of thirty-eight others. Infuriated by the apparent willingness of Dublin Castle to use deadly force in the South while turning a blind eye to the mischief of the UVF, Home Rulers raised such a cry that Redmond demanded a further delay in consideration of the Amending Bill. This was now rescheduled for 30 July.

The debate never occurred: greater and incomparably more destructive events now, for a time, pushed aside the Irish issue. On 28 June the heir to the throne of Austria-Hungary, Archduke Francis Ferdinand, was murdered in a provincial backwater of his exhausted empire. On Friday, 24 July, as the Unionists waited at Buckingham Palace to take their leave of the King, a newspaper was brought in which contained details of the harsh Austrian demands on the Serbian government, collaborators in the murder. At this, in Churchill's matchless phrases, 'The parishes of Fermanagh and Tyrone faded back into the mists and squalls of Ireland, and a strange light began immediately, but by perceptible gradations, to fall and grow upon the map of Europe.'[97] There would be no civil war; neither, for the time being, would there be a solution. The Irish question had severely tried these statesmen, and they had failed to find the answer. It is little wonder that they were prepared to give their full energies to the new challenge of war, and leave the old one alone.

9

The Liberals' War

I

ON THE MORNING of Thursday, 30 July 1914, Bonar Law telephoned the Prime Minister (something he had never before done) and asked him to come to Pembroke Lodge. Asquith described to Venetia Stanley his arrival at 'a rather suburban looking detached villa in a Bayswater street, with a small garden & furnished & decorated itself after the familiar fashion of Glasgow or Bradford or Altrincham.'[1] His superior tone was intentional, as was the mislocation of Edwardes Square by a mile – both designed to emphasize his disdain for the man he later referred to as the 'gilded tradesman'. It was an attitude which it pleased Asquith to maintain – ultimately, to his cost.

The Prime Minister found Carson with Bonar Law, and learned that he had been invited to listen to the Unionist case for postponement of the final step which could place Home Rule on the statute books. Asquith agreed with the general logic of suspending domestic strife during the inevitable international crisis, and heightened the moment by reading aloud from the latest alarming diplomatic telegrams. But he did not agree to any specific proposal as to how a 'moratorium' might be implemented.

Within an hour of this meeting Asquith had gained the agreement of Lloyd George, Grey and Redmond to accept the offer of at least a temporary Home Rule truce. Confronted as he was with the very real possibility that a decision in favour of Britain entering the war would split his Cabinet, he must have been delighted to reduce by one his inventory of anxieties.

On the following day, 31 July, Bonar Law travelled to Henley, to Wargrave Manor, Edward Goulding's Thames-side house, to meet Carson and F.E. Smith. Aitken completed the party; as he recalled later, Bonar Law and Carson seemed particularly reluctant 'to turn from Ireland and confront the realities of war'.[2] 'The realities' prevailed, however; soon the conversation became focused on the possibility of a European conflict: what position, they wondered, should the Unionist party adopt? Furthermore, what was the proper attitude towards a Government which rumours indicated might fragment over the decision between peace or war?

Of course, foreign policy was not one of Bonar Law's principal political interests. Though he was not unfamiliar with the world beyond Britain, his speeches indicate that over the years he had offered scant advice on international relations, beyond steady support for the various *Ententes* and for a strong defence establishment. During the current crisis, however, he had kept in close touch with Grey and was fully apprised of the tense European situation.

Smith, who as a great friend of Churchill had knowledge of the Liberals' divisions, brought to the meeting an informal query from the First Lord: would the Unionists consider taking any places which might be vacated by resigning anti-war Liberal ministers?[3] Bonar Law brought Smith up short with a firm negative. If war came, and especially if the Germans ignored the international treaty of 1839 guaranteeing the neutrality of Belgium, Bonar Law could promise the Government the Unionists' complete support. But of inter-party government he would hear nothing at this time – especially nothing at second hand: if the Liberals desired some sort of collaboration, then it was for Asquith to propose and Bonar Law to dispose. Smith was silenced, and all talk of coalition quashed.

On Saturday 1 August, with no news to clarify the state of affairs in Europe, the four men agreed to remain in the country until the afternoon. Carson and Smith went on the river, and Bonar Law was playing tennis with his host when the Unionist MPs George Lloyd and Admiral Lord Charles Beresford arrived, to find that he, '... like another Drake, insisted on finishing his set before discussing matters.'[4] Lloyd shared what he had learned from his contacts at the French Embassy and Beresford, a former commander of the Channel Fleet, filled the party in on French naval priorities. Recognizing that the country was no place to be, Bonar Law and his colleagues returned immediately to London.

Once there, Bonar Law and Lloyd went to Lansdowne House and a meeting of those Unionists who were in town on this Bank Holiday weekend; besides their host these included the Duke of Devonshire and A.J. Balfour, as well as the Chief Whip, Lord Edmund Talbot. Remarkably, also present was Bonar Law's unofficial military adviser, Major-General Henry Wilson. Lloyd and Wilson criticized the Government's lack of action, but senior Unionists were unsure how they might appropriately influence the Cabinet.[5] In lieu of other suggestions, it was agreed that Bonar Law and Lansdowne should contact the Prime Minister and place themselves at his disposal; and this they did.

Early Sunday morning Austin Chamberlain (who had himself hurried back to London at the behest of Leo Amery) called on Lord Lansdowne and found the former Foreign Secretary convinced, as he was, of the need to support France immediately.[6] Nothing had been heard from the Prime Minister, and Chamberlain therefore quickly drafted a letter strongly urging support of Britain's *Entente* partners and promising. Opposition endorsement of such a policy. While Lansdowne breakfasted, Chamberlain drafted a second note calling for immediate mobilization, and for a British demand for an absolute German undertaking to respect the neutrality of Belgium.[7] The past and future foreign ministers then set out for Pembroke Lodge to see Bonar Law.

Judging that it was not the place of the Opposition to participate in Government policy-making, Bonar Law argued that it was up to Asquith to accept or reject the offer of counsel which Lansdowne and he had made. Following a lengthy conversation many times interrupted by telephone calls, telegrams and messages, Bonar Law, as Chamberlain later recalled, eventually allowed himself to be persuaded: 'I am not sure that after all Austen is not right. I think we ought to write to the Prime Minister.' Using Chamberlain's original draft as the basis for the communication, Bonar Law immediately despatched this message to Asquith:

Lord Lansdowne and I feel it is our duty to inform you that, in our opinion, as well as that of all the colleagues whom we have been able to consult, it would be fatal to the honour and security of the United Kingdom to hesitate in supporting France and Russia at the present juncture; and we offer to His Majesty's Government the assurance of the united support of the Opposition in all measures required by England's intervention in the war.[8]

It is unlikely that this letter influenced a Cabinet whose members were, in the face of the crisis, by degrees composing their differences.[9] It is equally unlikely that Bonar Law himself believed the message did much to hasten the Government toward doing what he saw as their obvious duty. Perhaps, however, it served in some small way to ease the minds of those in the Cabinet who favoured intervention in Europe, as it did those of the Unionists.

Asquith's initial response, received the same day, was non-committal: Britain's obligations to her *Entente* partners in the crisis were few, he noted, but the Government would take into account the welfare of France, the German naval threat in the Channel and the North Sea, and the neutrality of Belgium.[10] Bonar Law took the letter to Brooks's Club, where Lansdowne, Devonshire and Chamberlain were awaiting him, and it was quickly agreed that the two senior Unionist leaders should see the Prime Minister as soon as possible. This they did the following morning, Monday, 3 August, by which time it was certain that German troops were on the point of violating Belgian neutrality – the prospect which most troubled waverers in the Government – and that British intervention in the struggle was assured. At the Cabinet meeting immediately following their interview with Asquith, these matters dominated the discussion – the Government did not split, but found themselves instead united, and preparing for war.[11]

Later in the afternoon Grey, in the most famous speech of his life, explained to a silent House Britain's narrowing range of options. Bonar Law followed, making the Unionists' position clear: 'The Government already know, but I give them now the assurance on behalf of the party of which I am leader in this House, that in whatever steps they think it necessary to take for the honour and security of this country they can rely upon the unhesitating support of the Opposition.'[12] Redmond and Carson spoke in similar vein: the nation had recently been engaged in a terrible struggle; now, they declared, that debate must be put aside in the face of the greater crisis. These pledges all fell due the following night: Germany rejected the Government's ultimatum for withdrawal from Belgium, and Britain was officially at war from 11 p.m. on 4 August. 'Patriotic opposition' – the suspension of normal criticism of the Government – became the Unionist order of the day.

While it is going too far to suggest that with this the 'life went out of politics',[13] party leaders did wish to make public the new atmosphere of co-operation. The Liberal, Unionist and Labour whips hammered out a truce by which normal confrontational politics were suspended until 1 January 1915, or for the duration of the conflict. At the same time a Parliamentary Recruiting Committee was formed to organize the politicians' efforts to encourage enlistment in the Forces.[14] With this began the period of 'patriotic opposition'.

On 4 August, for the first time in their careers, Asquith and Bonar Law shared a platform, delivering at the Guildhall their first great speeches of the War – a particularly striking circumstance given the untoward bitterness of politics recently in the Irish controversy. Perhaps Bonar Law thought some symbolism was called for. He had agreed to spend that Monday night, 3 August, at Hackwood, with what remained of Curzon's bank-holiday weekend party. Given his deep dislike of such country-house parties, he may have felt like a human sacrifice to the new harmony. Asquith was there as well, and the two were seen in cordial – probably uncomfortable – conversation. On the evening of 4 August, for the first time in many months and giving another sign of the new spirit of things, Bonar Law attended a dinner of the Other Club, where he chatted amiably with, of all people, Churchill and Jack Seely. None of this can have been easy for him.

It was not long before the nascent truce came under strain: on 6 August Unionists learned that Asquith had acceded to Redmond's demand for the Home Rule Bill to receive the Royal Assent and be put on the statute books. Bonar Law wrote to Grey that if the Government were to follow such a course,

> ... under no circumstances would we take a factious part in hindering the Government in circumstances such as exist today; but if that course were taken we should have to say that in our opinion the Government have acted dishonourably, that we cannot trust them, and that though we will not hamper them it will be impossible for us to co-operate with them.[15]

Following a rapid exchange of letters between himself and Asquith over the next two days,[16] Bonar Law had a stormy discussion with the Prime Minister and Lloyd George in which the efforts of Lewis Harcourt, the Colonial Secretary, to arbitrate signally failed.[17] Bonar Law wrote to Asquith demanding to know how the Government intended to proceed, and his letter crossed in the post with one from Asquith indicating that action was absolutely necessary and there were in his view only two possible ways in which to proceed: the Bill could be placed on the statute books, with accompanying legislation to suspend its operation in the current emergency (the course he thought the Cabinet preferred); alternatively, the Bill could be made law with a six-month delay and with provision for the exclusion of Ulster for three years before Parliament reconsidered that status. The Shadow Cabinet met on 9 August and declared that a moratorium *in statu quo* on the Bill was the best solution – failing that, they informed the Prime Minister, they would accept the second option he had outlined.[18] When Asquith announced in the House on 7 September that the Home Rule Bill would receive the Royal Assent and then immediately be suspended for the duration of the war, the Unionist leaders concluded that he was little interested in compromise.

Bonar Law knew well that he could not stop this process. However, he thought it a mean trick on Asquith's part to go forward with the Home Rule and Welsh Church Bills (this was to be treated similarly) to appease what he saw as merely the fringe elements of the Government's supporters, while the Unionists were silenced by their pledge of patriotic opposition.[19] His colleagues agreed: 'How is it possible', the usually philosophical Balfour railed, 'to let political warfare run riot within the [Commons] and proclaim a truce of God everywhere else. Such a policy is unthinkable.'[20] Bonar Law wrote to Asquith on 10 September: '... I learn with the deepest regret that you have determined at such a time as the present to revive party controversy in Parliament ... [Your decision is a] breach of the definitive pledge given by you in the House of Commons & repeated by yourself in conversation.'[21]

On 14 September, a day before the scheduled debate on Asquith's suspensory legislation, angry Unionists met at the Carlton Club. Bonar Law reiterated his condemnation of Asquith's decision, concluding:

> Gentlemen, we cannot fight the Government now. They have tied our hands by our patriotism. But when the War is over the fight will be resumed, and it will, in my opinion, not be less successfully resumed because we put our country now before our party. But whether my expectation in that respect is correct or not it does not matter. We are doing what I ask you to do not because we think it will pay but because it is right.[22]

Bonar Law's intention was that in the next day's debate he alone would speak for his party, and the Unionists would then retire from the Chamber.[23] The gesture was certainly dramatic – which is perhaps what made it so powerful. His speech denounced Asquith for misleading the Opposition with his declarations about the suspension of party struggle for the duration of the conflict. He inveighed against Redmond as the true author of the scheme and against Asquith for giving in to Irish Nationalist demands, and closed with these words:

> Now I have only this more to say. The Government have treated us abominably. But we are in the middle of a great struggle. I said the other day at the Guildhall that until that struggle was over, so far as we were concerned, in everything connected with it there would be no parties, there would openly be a nation. What the Government have done will make no difference whatever in our action in connection with everything regarding the war ... I give that pledge, and I give it with the full approval of all the members of our party. In regard to this debate I have made protest as well as I could, but when I have finished we shall take no further part in the discussion. You cannot debate this subject without inflicting injury. We shall not do it.
> ... We leave the House not under protest and still less as a demonstration. We leave it because, in my belief, to have forced us to debate this subject at all under present circumstances is indecent, and we will take no part in that indecency.[24]

The Unionists then silently left the Chamber.[25] It was an angry and powerful speech, though perhaps not as bitter as many delivered in the days of the Ulster campaign. To combine condemnation of the Government and a pledge of continued patriotic co-operation with silent retirement from the Chamber was so effective as to cause even Asquith to admit in private that 'it was unique in my or I think anybody's experience.'[26] But the grand gesture was only a protest: the controversial bills went to the King, received the Royal Assent, and by means of accompanying legislation were suspended for the duration of the War.

These men could not foresee in 1914 the many twists and turns the Irish question had yet to make; neither could they foresee the political upheavals which lay ahead of them. Even in the early months of war, however, there were some in Westminster apprehensive of the grim determination behind these angry exchanges. Walter Runciman, President of the Board of Trade, wrote to a friend some weeks later: 'The political truce is very thin ... If things go wrong we shall be flayed.'[27]

II

Unionists soon began to chafe at the fact that 'patriotic opposition' meant no opposition at all. Many wished for the freedom to attack the

1. The Reverend James Law, MA

2. Bonar Law's childhood home, Rexton, New Brunswick, Canada

3. The successful candidate, 1900

4. 'He was always happiest surrounded by his children.' The Law family, 1908:
(*left to right*) James (Jim), Bonar, Isabel (Tizzie), Harrington (Tony),
Charles (Charlie), Annie holding Catherine (Kitty), and Richard (Dick)

5. A rare moment of
recreation. Bonar Law
on the links, 1908

6. Bonar and Annie Law campaigning in North-west Manchester, December 1910

7. Bonar Law as
seen by Sir Francis
Carruthers Gould

8. 'I use the floor as a
desk.' Bonar Law poses
with pipe and papers, 1911

9. With Austen Chamberlain, Bonar Law emerges from the Carlton Club moments after being elected leader of the Unionist party, 13 November 1911

10. Bonar Law in academic dress after receiving the honorary degree LL D from the University of Glasgow, June 1912

11. The Unionist annual conference at the Royal Albert Hall, 14 November 1912, at which Lord Lansdowne and Bonar Law repudiated Balfour's 'Referendum Pledge'. (*Left to right*) Sir Edward Carson, Austen Chamberlain, Sir William Crump, Bonar Law, Lord Farquhar, Lord Lansdowne, Miss Alice Lakin, Arthur Steel-Maitland, Walter Long and Lord Curzon

12. 'Never will we submit to Home Rule!' Bonar Law and Carson arrive at
the Balmoral show grounds in Belfast, 9 April 1912

13. The great Unionist rally at Blenheim Palace, 27 July 1912

14. The warrior for Ulster: Bonar Law speaking at the Blenheim rally.
To the left is the Marquis of Londonderry, and to the right,
at the front of the platform, Sir Edward Carson and F. E. Smith

15. The Theatre Royal, Ashton-under-Lyne, 16 December 1912:
Bonar Law attempts to clarify the abandonment of the Referendum Pledge.
To his left is the local MP, his friend Max Aitken

16. Bonar Law calling for Sir Edward Carson on their way to the
Buckingham Palace Conference, July 1914

17. Accompanied by Major-General C.H. Powell, Bonar Law inspects a
contingent of Ulster Volunteers at Ballykinlar Camp, 1914

18. The Man Who Won the War:
David Lloyd George, here with
Edwin S. Montagu, 1914

19. The uncrowned Prime Minister:
Lord Curzon, with Viscount Peel

20. The squire: Walter Long

21. The party chairman:
Sir George Younger

22. Predecessor: Arthur James Balfour. Bonar Law thought him the greatest man in Parliament

23. Successor: Stanley Baldwin at the time he became Prime Minister

24. J.C.C. Davidson: he wrote the mysterious Davidson memorandum

25. Lieutenant-Colonel Sir Ronald Waterhouse (1899, as 2nd Lieutenant of the Seaforth Highlanders): he delivered it

26. Bonar Law's 'most intimate friend', Max Aitken, Lord Beaverbrook

27. The simple stone marking Bonar Law's grave in Westminster Abbey

28. The wreaths honouring Bonar Law at his State funeral, shown heaped upon the monument to Lieutenant-General William Hargreaves by Roubiliac

Government, as the initial nine months of hostilities revealed to Unionist eyes a mare's nest of mismanagement, shielded from public obloquy only by the political truce. The Army, unprepared for conflict on such an unprecedented scale, was under-equipped, under-armed and under-manned. From the outset the generals called for more and ever more men, a demand which intensified as they became bogged down in the trenches that soon characterized the war on the Western Front. The Royal Navy suffered almost unbearable embarrassment: the German cruisers *Goeben* and *Breslau* were allowed to escape from them in the Mediterranean, then three cruisers and the battleship *Audacious* were lost to German arms – all in the first weeks of war.

Understandably, Unionists took their disquiet into Parliament – where, since they were barred from a concerted attack on policy, they resorted to criticism of individual ministers: Asquith; the Lord Chancellor, Viscount Haldane, whom they accused of being far too enamoured of German culture; and the Home Secretary Reginald McKenna, whom they considered 'too tender to aliens' – these were repeatedly singled out for criticism, as, of course, were the war ministers.[28]

At the onset of hostilities Field Marshal Lord Kitchener of Khartoum, widely considered Britain's greatest living soldier, was appointed Secretary of State for War.[29] The Prime Minister thus divested himself of the responsibility he had assumed in the wake of the Curragh incident, and at the same time indicated, he hoped, how serious were his Government's intentions. It was a remarkable appointment; Kitchener, at sixty-four, became the first serving officer officially to take political control of the Army since General Monck at the Restoration of Charles II. The lustre of his reputation remained publicly undiminished up to his death in 1916, but criticism of his management of the War Office was common in Westminster by early 1915. Unused to having his orders in any way questioned, 'Lord K' bore the grievances of the Unionists and a small number of Liberals with an outward stoicism – which may have masked but failed to lessen his contempt for politicians whom he little respected and never understood. From the outset he assumed complete responsibility for Britain's part in the land war. By the spring of 1915, as the conflict dragged on against most people's expectations, certain powerful statesmen were beginning to search for ways to rid themselves of him.

The other favoured Opposition target was Winston Churchill. Bonar Law considered him unsteady, untrustworthy and provocative;

and his role in the Home Rule furore had sharpened that opinion. Many Unionists – who had not forgiven him for abandoning their party a decade eartlier – held similar views, and insisted that the Admiralty was not safe in his hands. In the first months of hostilities he had sponsored a gallant but hopeless defence of Antwerp, using naval personnel who when the city fell were interned for the remainder of the War – a misfortune compounded by the naval disasters noted earlier. Not long afterwards, of course, he became the principal champion of the Dardanelles campaign, which ultimately led to further costly failure. Most Unionists soon became determined to drive him from the Admiralty, if possible from the Government – a determination shared by Bonar Law.

By Christmas of 1914 the War was still popular with the British people, but a deep-seated and growing anxiety was beginning to be felt among the Opposition. It was not, they considered, going well, yet they were confined to such unfulfilling duties as making recruitment speeches and serving on committees. They accounted themselves the party that 'knew' about war, yet they were powerless to affect its direction. In addition, their day-to-day representation in the House of Commons was much reduced: by January 1915, as many as 139 Unionist MPs had volunteered, compared with 41 Liberals.[30] Most of the remaining 100 Unionists were beyond military age, but though they were denied the excitement and fulfilment of active service the desire to help defeat Britain's enemies burned as brightly in them as in any young man in uniform, and appeared destined to go unrewarded. This must be kept in mind if we are to understand the remarkable turn of events of May 1915 which led to the restructuring of the Government.

In late January a group of Unionist MPs led by Basil Peto, Ernest Pollock and Professor W.A.S. Hewins came together to form the Unionist Business Committee, a 'ginger group' who met periodically in order to consider ways of encouraging a more energetic prosecution of the War. On the very day of their first meeting, Bonar Law received a fiercely-worded letter from Walter Long (whom he had urged to take the chair of the UBC) which demonstrated that frustration with the political truce was felt as keenly on the Opposition's Front Bench as among their back-benchers. After verbally flaying the Government for their indifferent leadership, he hinted at what was at the back not only of his mind but of certain other senior colleagues': 'Here not only has there been no coalition – personally I do not favour it, and I gravely doubt its success – but the Government have persistently pursued those party aims which occupied them before the War.'[31] On the same day came a letter from Lord Curzon, who complained similarly of the Liberals having 'all the advantages [of a coalition] while we have all the drawbacks ... They tell us nothing or next to nothing of their plans, and yet they pretend our leaders share both their knowledge and their responsibility.'[32]

Bonar Law understood that the real subject of these letters was not so much Government failures as the feasibility of coalition. Though it was all but impossible at the moment to discuss it openly – and both Curzon and Long had punctiliously denied any interest in it – the idea of participating in the direction of the War was much in the minds of these men. There were already useful precedents: despite party differences Asquith had retained Balfour as a member of the Committee of Imperial Defence and included him in his War Council, the Cabinet's chief war policy committee, while the Government had been making certain secret telegrams from the War Office available to Bonar Law and Lansdowne. With this in mind, Lord Crewe had written to *The Times* on 9 January indicating that the Unionist leaders possessed 'preliminary knowledge' of events on the Western Front, and that their opinions had been solicited. Bonar Law wrote immediately to contradict the implication inherent in Crewe's letter, that in some way the Unionists were party to decision-making.[33]

At about this time, Bonar Law and Lloyd George met privately to discuss the idea of a possible inter-party coalition at some point in the future – rather as Lloyd George had suggested in 1910.[34] Apparently Bonar Law advised that regardless of what others might think, his backbenchers were suspicious of such notions and rather in a mood for increased opposition than amalgamation. It is not known whether he revealed that those 'others' to whom he referred included important members of the party leadership. In any event, he insisted, the time for any fruitful discussion of such things was not yet.

Bonar Law did not tell either Curzon or Long of his meeting with Lloyd George; instead, he warned them against any immediate consideration of coalition. If there was so much disapproval of Liberal leadership, he argued, 'I am not at all sure that we should not openly declare that the truce is at an end ...'[35] He too had misgivings about the Government's conduct of the War, but if open party conflict was to be avoided, the only viable options available were '[to] go on as we are, or face a coalition.' For the time being, he advised, the party truce was the best alternative. This left the two restless Unionists necessarily silent.

In fact, Bonar Law was far more receptive to the possibility of a coalition Government than has previously been indicated by historians. Late in 1914 he had a long private talk with the editor of *The Times*, Geoffrey Robinson. Their conversation ranged far and wide over questions related to the conduct of the War and, just as he had to Curzon and Long, Bonar Law spoke of his disappointment in the Government. To him it appeared that 'There was no co-ordination and no one was in supreme control.' Although he was not prepared at that moment to accede to any plan to share responsibility with the Liberals, his frank assessment of what the future might hold, as recorded by Robinson, is interesting: 'He thought [a coalition Government] would come in time – indeed the Liberals themselves must turn to it when they came to clearing up the mess at the end of the war. Meanwhile', Robinson continued, 'he defended his attitude of "No criticism" by pointing to the disaster which has befallen every political party in the past when it has opposed a popular war.'[36]

Far from being absolutely antagonistic to the idea of coalition, then, Bonar Law thought it a probability, given what he saw as the Liberals' shortcomings in fulfilling their responsibilities. However, he was equally certain that for the time being – and for so long as his parliamentary party were suspicious of the idea – his best policy was to keep coalition at arm's length. On the other hand, he believed that Unionist firebrands must not be allowed to force a return to open opposition to a Government engaged in directing a war which the nation supported. Hence he waited, struggling to curb his followers.

Two other well-known events of early 1915 have sometimes been seen as portents of coalition: the attendance of Bonar Law and Lansdowne at a meeting of the War Council, and the proposal by Lloyd George that the manufacture of and traffic in alcohol in Britain be taken over by the state. On 10 March 1915, at Churchill's urging, the two Unionists were invited to be present when the War Council discussed Russia's ambitions regarding Constantinople. It was an uneasy meeting, and Bonar Law, a true Tory where Russian aspirations were concerned, spoke out against a plan which had the rather distracted support of the Liberals. The experiment in co-operation was not repeated:[37] Asquith thought the visitors fairly useless, while Churchill, disappointed, concluded a few days later that the Cabinet had succeeded only in inviting 'a lot of ignorant people to meddle in our business.'[38] Bonar Law and Lansdowne also thought the experiment a failure, and would have declined a further invitation, had one been forthcoming. Many back-benchers also disapproved, and might well have agreed with Major-General Wilson, who when he had heard the full story wrote to Bonar Law: 'I am sure you are very wise, as, later on if things go wrong, you would be tongue tied.'[39]

As regards Lloyd George's proposal to nationalize the liquor trade, Lord Beaverbrook has suggested that because certain of the Opposition leaders saw merit in the idea, 'A feeling of friendliness was restored – and though the issue passed, the impression it had left behind did not. The "Drink" problem smoothed the way towards Coalition.'[40]

The initiative was based on Lloyd George's conclusion that the efficiency of industrial workers was being seriously impaired by the easy availability of cheap, strong alcohol. He solicited a wide range of opinion, and found it favourable in some quarters. Bonar Law was a tee-totaller who knew from both private and business experience the impact alcohol could have upon a work force; he expressed approval for Lloyd George's goal, as did Curzon and Long, but certain other senior Unionists were extremely hostile.[41] Perhaps most important was the fact – not recorded by Beaverbrook – that it was unpopular with ordinary Unionist MPs. Whether it was because of the party's long connection to 'the trade', the prohibitionist overtones of the proposal or its imposing cost (estimated to be at least £250,000,000), Unionist back-bench opinion was vociferously opposed – and the lead was taken by the UBC. By April 1915 Bonar Law had concluded that the inherent 'difficulties' negated whatever personal sympathies he might have felt for the plan.[42] This was one game which, when risks were weighed against possible benefits, was not worth the candle.

It requires some effort to see how this quixotic proposal should have worked to restore that 'feeling of friendliness' between the front benches which 'smoothed the way towards Coalition'. The episode is, however, a useful reminder of the influence Unionist back-benchers had on their leaders. Had senior Unionists openly pressed for Lloyd George's scheme, it is not inconceivable that tension between leaders and followers might have led to a crash – something Bonar Law, who had not forgotten the Referendum Pledge affair of 1912, knew had to be prevented. While this minor business had nothing to do with the upheaval which later created a coalition, the Unionist Party rumblings it gave rise to were remembered by the Shadow Cabinet.[43] When crisis came in May 1915, fear of losing control of their party played an important part in causing Unionist chieftains to co-operate with their former enemies on the Liberal front bench.

III

Any explanation of how an inter-party administration came to be formed in the spring of 1915 must begin with a recognition of the impatience felt by the Opposition – as also by a small group of Liberals – with the Asquith Government's performance in directing the War.[44] Historians have long agreed that two events brought matters to a head in May 1915: reports of munitions shortages at the front – the so-called 'Shells Scandal' – and the resignation of the First Sea Lord, Lord Fisher. Yet these episodes would not have been enough, either singly or together, to topple the last Liberal Government had it not been for the long-smouldering frustration of Unionists bound hand and foot by the party truce.

The Shells Scandal had been many months developing.[45] As the presumption grew among critics in Westminster that the Government had failed to organize British industry adquately for munitions production, this became linked in the minds of many Unionists with the idea that the state should take control of manpower for industrial and military needs – that is, introduce conscription. Such thinking brought many Unionists closer to Lloyd George than did any discussion of state purchase of the liquor trade, for he had taken the lead in efforts to accelerate munitions manufacture and control labour. His Pro-Boer past was forgotten as in March 1915 he secured control of a so-called Treasury Committee which was theoretically empowered to increase war production; but within a few weeks, he found that his committee was no match for Lord Kitchener and the War Office with their traditional procurement methods. Lloyd George had made useful friends, however: as 'Paddy' Goulding wrote at this time to Aitken,

> L.G. has again been acting as a big man over this crisis with labour and the sooner Squiffy [the Unionists' nickname for Asquith] clears out and lets him take the lead of a coalition the better.[46]

The munitions question began to gain momentum in Parliament. Inspired by Professor Hewins and the UBC, who demanded that 'resources of all firms capable of producing munitions of war should be enlisted under a unified administration in direct touch with the producing firms', a debate over munitions supply took place on 21 April.[47] It was a relatively tame affair: Bonar Law preferred a businesslike enquiry into methods of munitions acquisition to the UBC's frontal assault, and struggled to keep his restive troops in check.[48]

The day before the debate, Asquith gave a major speech in Newcastle designed to ward off the coming attack. Praising the efforts of Government and workshop alike, he said: 'I do not believe ... that any army has ever either entered upon a campaign or been maintained during a campaign with better or more adequate equipment.'[49] As his most recent biographer has noted, however, 'His critics, who had more reliable sources of information, were not persuaded.'[50] These sources included such high-ranking officers as Major-General Wilson and Sir John French, back in favour after the Curragh incident and now commanding the British Expeditionary Force; and Unionists were not only not persuaded – they were furious.[51] The Prime Minister, thinking to scotch the threat, had stumbled badly.

Over the days which followed, pressure upon the Unionist leaders increased and the party truce was seriously endangered. Hewins noted in his diary on 6 May: 'I have never believed that this Government could carry the War through successfully. It is quite discredited and the sooner it is reconstituted the better.'[52] Within a week, the UBC was threatening to throw over the party truce and mount an open attack over the munitions question. Bonar Law was not prepared to support the Business Committee in this, and faced them on 12 May. He demanded their agreement to withhold any action *for the moment*, and they backed down.[53]

Shortly after Bonar Law had thrown a wet blanket over the sparks emanating from these putative rebels, the embers flickered to life elsewhere. In *The Times* on Friday, 14 May appeared a leading article which attributed the British Army's failure at the recent battle of Neuve Chapelle to a shortage of artillery ammunition. It was the product of a conspiracy between the newspaper's proprietor Lord Northcliffe and its military correspondent Colonel Charles à Court Repington, and also Field Marshal Sir John French, and the intention was twofold: to shift the blame for failures in the field from the generals to Kitchener and the War Office; and to force the Government to provide more and better armaments.[54] At the same time, French took the dangerous step of sending two aides to London to furnish Lloyd George, Bonar Law and Balfour with confidential information to bolster his case that his army was being starved of artillery ammunition.[55]

The appearance of this provocative leader in *The Times* stirred up back-benchers so recently stifled by Bonar Law, and their promises of good behaviour were much strained by the revelations. Professor Hewins, for example, wrote directly to Asquith the following day, announcing his intention to ask questions in the House related to the alleged munitions shortage.[56]

In such a turbulent atmosphere something approaching revolt on the back benches was not impossible, and the Shadow Cabinet met that same Friday to decide upon a course. The leaders sounded very like their followers: things could not go on as they were, and Bonar Law and Lansdowne proposed to write to the Prime Minister demanding (and promising support for) consideration of military and industrial conscription and of redoubled efforts to enhance munitions production.[57] They wished to move the Government towards a more aggressive policy and to do so in positive terms – thus maintaining the appearance of constructive, non-partisan co-operation.[58] The most important passages of the draft by Lansdowne and Bonar Law insisted that:

> In our view, therefore, it is impossible to exclude the possibility that it may become necessary, and perhaps at a very early date, to adopt some form of compulsory organization with the object of inducing men in some cases to join the Army, and, in others, when they are specially qualified, to render not less valuable service in our factories and workshops.
>
> ... [We] think it right to add that whenever the Government decide that such a step is necessary they can rely upon our support, and we believe that they will also have the support of the nation.[59]

Both this letter, with its implication of co-operation rather than censure, and the assault in the House threatened by Hewins and his friends were overtaken by events at the Admiralty, where tensions regarding the Dardanelles campaign were erupting into a crisis. This Allied effort had its roots in the Russians' request in January 1915 for a British attack which would relieve Turkish pressure on the Czarist armies in the Caucasus. It also held out the possibility of breaking Turkey, thereby providing a southern route by which to engage Austria-Hungary, and thus an alternative to the stalemated Western Front. Kitchener, initially unwilling to commit ground troops, suggested a naval demonstration instead, and this was begun in February. Easy success eluded the Navy, however, and the War Council decided upon a larger combined operation of naval and ground forces, initiated in April. The invaders established a foothold on the beaches of the Gallipoli Peninsula, but secured little else. As on the Western Front, they dug in, and there they remained: 'They could not go on,' Captain Liddell Hart has written, 'and national prestige forbade them to go back.'[60]

Churchill soon became the greatest proponent of the Dardanelles

Campaign, but it was bitterly opposed by his own First Sea Lord, Lord Fisher. An innovative reformer who had reshaped the Navy earlier in the century, Fisher at seventy-four was a hero to the Unionists and also much admired by Churchill, who had summoned him out of retirement to his old post in October 1914.[61] On 14 May 1915 Churchill obtained the approval of the War Council – over Fisher's objections – to press the attack in the Dardanelles. Though the two had worked well together for a time, Fisher could bear it no longer, and in the early hours of the following morning he wrote in his habitual breathless way to Churchill:

> After further anxious reflection I have come to the regretted conclusion I am unable any longer to remain your colleague. It is undesirable in the public interests to go into details – Jowett said 'never explain' – but I find it increasingly difficult to adjust myself to the increasing daily requirements of the Dardanelles to meet your views – as you truly said yesterday I am in the position of continually vetoing your proposals. –
>
> This is not fair to you besides being extremely distasteful to me.
>
> I am off to Scotland at once so as to avoid all questionings.[62]

Alas for Churchill, it soon became clear that he and the aged admiral were chained together; and, just as fatally, that Churchill was shackled to the Cabinet. When the one threw himself into the sea, he unquestionably dragged the other in after him – and together they pulled Asquith's Liberal Government down into the depths.[63]

Asquith saw that Fisher had to go: he had abandoned his post in wartime, and his legendary self-confidence was verging now upon megalomania. It was clear also, in the poisonous political atmosphere, that Churchill would have to go as well. Over the next forty-eight hours Asquith tried to bring Fisher (who had remained in London) to heel and listened to Churchill's pleas to retain his office – and, as was his wont, waited upon developments.

There is little doubt that Bonar Law had heard rumours of the ructions at the Admiralty before he took his breakfast on the morning of Saturday, 15 May. When he opened his morning post, he found a strange communication – an undated newspaper cutting of some antiquity from the *Pall Mall Gazette* reporting that 'Lord Fisher was received in audience by the King and remained there about half an hour'.[64] Since the envelope was addressed in Fisher's unmistakable hand, it could mean only one thing – that the First Sea Lord had resigned. The political situation was now surely reaching crisis, and Bonar Law had to act quickly if it were to be prevented from spinning out of control.

With his back-bench contingent already on the war-path over munitions shortages and rumours of poor War Office management, over the need for military conscription, and the futility of the Dardanelles campaign, Bonar Law knew the vision of Churchill and a crew of tame Sea Lords sitting tight at the Admiralty was enough to drive the Tories over the brink; this in turn would destroy the party truce and almost certainly lead to a bitter and divisive election that would shatter public morale. He knew Fisher well and respected his great work as father of the Dreadnought fleet, yet he now made a considerable effort to keep the Admiral at arm's length, refusing his pleas for a meeting. He was confident that it was better – for Fisher, and for the country – that he should accept retirement.[65] By the same token, he thought Churchill too should go, and was quite prepared to act without mercy to drive him from the Admiralty.

On Monday morning, 17 May, Bonar Law went to the Treasury to see the Chancellor. It is understandable that in this crisis he should have sought information from Lloyd George, with whom he had been friendly for a decade, rather than from Asquith, who treated him stiffly and with condescension. Possibly the businessman in him respected the way Lloyd George had fashioned himself into the Cabinet's most energetic advocate of increased national organization for war production. He certainly knew him to be unafraid of daring solutions to difficult questions – and it seemed to be the time for a bold response. The two spoke very briefly, as Bonar Law laid out his analysis of the crisis. Lloyd George recalled in his memoirs that:

> He was especially emphatic as to the impossibility of allowing Mr Churchill to remain at the Admiralty if Lord Fisher persisted in his resignation. On this point he made it clear that the Opposition meant at all hazards to force a Parliamentary challenge. After some discussion we agreed that the only way to preserve a united front was to arrange for more complete co-operation between the parties in the direction of the War.[66]

Lloyd George left Bonar Law at the Treasury and walked to Number 10 to confront Asquith with the bones of this conversation. The premier, it appears, sensed immediately the weight of both Bonar Law's threat and Lloyd George's solution, and readily accepted the conclusion. In their memoirs both Lloyd George and Beaverbrook describe a dramatic scene in which the Chancellor returned to collect Bonar Law, and the two met Asquith in the Cabinet Room, where they sealed their agreement: 'In less than a quarter of an hour', Lloyd George wrote years later, 'we realized that the Liberal Government was at an end and that for it would be substituted a Coalition Government.'[67] This is the version accepted by historians and retold many times.[68]

However compelling the accounts, the scene may not in fact have been played in quite this way.[69] While Bonar Law left no record of that day, Austen Chamberlain did. As he recounts events, when Lloyd George went alone to Number 10 to speak to Asquith, Bonar Law also left the Treasury, going by prior arrangement to meet Lord Lansdowne in Berkeley Square,[70] where Chamberlain was summoned to join them.

During their meeting, Bonar Law and Lloyd George had drafted a letter to the Prime Minister in the name of the Unionist leadership, citing the Fisher controversy and calling for an inter-party Government.[71] Apparently Lloyd George showed this to Asquith, who approved of its general purpose – to be displayed before the Cabinet as evidence of the need for a Government reshuffle. In Berkeley Square, meanwhile, Bonar Law, Lansdowne and Chamberlain rewrote the draft, omitting any mention of coalition and suggesting instead a change 'in the constitution of the Government':

> Lord Lansdowne and I have learnt with dismay that Lord Fisher has resigned, and we have come to the conclusion that we cannot allow the House to adjourn until this fact has been made known and discussed.
>
> We think that the time has come when we ought to have a clear statement from you as to the policy which the Government intend to pursue. In our opinion things cannot go on as they are, and some change in the constitution of the Government seems to us inevitable if it is to retain a sufficient measure of public confidence to conduct the War to a successful conclusion.
>
> The situation in Italy makes it particularly undesirable to have anything in the nature of a controversial discussion in the House of Commons at present,[72] and if you are prepared to take the necessary steps to secure the object which I have indicated, and if Lord Fisher's resignation is in the meantime postponed, we shall be ready to keep silence now. Otherwise I must today ask you [in the House] whether Lord Fisher has resigned, and press for a day to discuss the situation arising out of his resignation.[73]

According to Chamberlain, it was only at this stage that Bonar Law was called by telephone to Downing Street to talk to the Prime Minister. He personally (and probably alone) delivered the Unionist version of the letter to Asquith, who accepted it in this form.[74] Whatever the actual movements of the party leaders on 17 May, it is of greater importance to enquire how they arrived at their conclusion.

For Lloyd George, a restructured Government offered the opportunity to wrest the management of munitions production from Kitchener and perhaps even manoeuvre 'Lord K' out of the War Office. For the Prime Minister, who had only a few days before denied in the House any interest in coalition, a hybrid Cabinet would be distasteful – but the alternative might be a political explosion which destroyed his premiership.[75]

It is worth noting that two more personal dramas were also played out at this critical time: one involved Bonar Law, and may be safely left to one side for the moment. The other touched Asquith deeply, and several historians have suggested that it may have affected his judgement.[76] On 12 May, Venetia Stanley had informed him that she intended to bring their alliance to an end and marry Edwin Montagu, now Chancellor of the Duchy of Lancaster. Though the precise nature of their love affair must remain conjectural, there is little doubt that Asquith genuinely cared for Miss Stanley, and felt her loss keenly. It is also possible that, coming on top of his other worries, the first throes of disappointment made him more inclined to clutch at the easiest solution on offer. Yet his actions in the week following the decision in favour of coalition indicate that, however emotionally wounded he may have been, neither his political craft nor his instinct for survival were much damaged.

Why, after opposing even discussion of the idea for many months, did Bonar Law now agree to a coalition? In the first place, as we have seen, his day-to-day parliamentary following was now largely made up of men too old to fight but too energetic to sit quietly and allow a Government in which they had no confidence to run the War. Following the lead given by the UBC in the Commons and Lord Milner and his friends in the Lords, they were in contentious mood, and on the very edge of once again turning Parliament into a battle-ground. In Bonar Law's view, this could lead only to a dissolution and the nationally divisive election campaign he dreaded.[77] As explained to Lord Buxton, Governor-General of South Africa, a month later: 'From the outbreak of the war, I had set my face against anything in the nature of party criticism. This policy was not very easy to carry out in practice, but we had succeeded very well.' However, the munitions debate and the struggle at the Admiralty changed everything. He continued: 'I feared, therefore, that nothing would prevent full-blooded debate in the House, and I looked with absolute dismay at the prospect of ordinary party warfare at such a time.'[78]

There was another reason. Bonar Law, as has been demonstrated, was never as resolutely opposed to the idea of coalition as he declared to others in the party – like F.E. Smith – whom he considered were all too ready to save the Government from themselves. Whatever others might think, he would take no step towards coalition until he was certain it was the only and obvious solution. By mid May the party truce was in shreds, and an inter-party administration seemed the only way to prevent a break-up of Parliament. It remains unclear which of the three men – Asquith, Bonar Law or Lloyd George – first suggested coalition as a solution to the problem which faced them. Perhaps it does not matter, as by this point it seemed to each of them his only alternative.[79]

While Asquith was left to deal with his shocked Cabinet, Bonar Law met his senior colleagues the following morning, 18 May, and outlined these events. According to Chamberlain, there was ready agreement to the idea of coalition – demonstrating, perhaps, how hungry for participation in the War the Unionists had become – and discussion settled immediately on the distribution of offices. Unsurprisingly, his old adversaries thought it would be well for Asquith to step down; and Bonar Law told them that, while he had suggested to Lloyd George that he himself, Balfour or Grey could ably lead the new Government, the Chancellor found this politically impossible.[80] Asquith and Bonar Law now exchanged coldly polite letters – the one putting forward, the other accepting, the offer to the Unionists to enter Government.[81] In the evening of 18 May the Prime Minister and the Leader of the Opposition jointly announced the coalition to an amazed House of Commons.

IV

With agreement to construct an inter-party Government came the difficult task of allocation of offices. Asquith knew he would have to sacrifice loyal friends and include some of his bitterest critics. Yet, while capable at times of the most egregious sentimentality, he could be as ruthless as any successful party leader has sometimes to be.

In their conversations of 17 May, Asquith, Lloyd George and Bonar Law had agreed on two key points: Kitchener, whom they thought ill-placed at the War Office, had to go; and the Unionists were to receive fair representation in the new administration. Asquith indicated initially that Lloyd George should take Kitchener's place, while Bonar Law should go to the Exchequer, Balfour to the Admiralty in succession to

Churchill, and Chamberlain to the Colonial Office. Lansdowne was to become Lord President of the Council. Surprisingly, the Prime Minister also seemed willing to include Carson but to exclude Curzon, and to accept the Unionist black-balling of Haldane.[82] Within a very short time, however, most of these arrangements had been jettisoned – possibly Asquith never intended to honour them in the first place.

The Northcliffe press began a series of attacks against Kitchener on 21 May, and the resulting expression of popular support for him convinced the three coalition-makers that he simply could not be sacked.[83] In order to retain Kitchener and at the same time remove his hand from munitions supply, it was decided to create a new government department with full responsibility for the provision of 'warlike stores' – and it became a question of the highest importance who would head this department. Closely linked to this was the matter of who would be Chancellor of the Exchequer in the new administration, since Lloyd George, munitions zealot, was widely touted for the new ministry. Unionists – who by this time had an almost thirty-seat edge over Liberals in the Commons, as a result of by-election victories in the years preceding the War – were agreed that if Lloyd George chose Munitions, Bonar Law should be offered the Exchequer.

It was not to be. Lloyd George did become Minister of Munitions, but Bonar Law rather than Chamberlain took the Colonial Office and McKenna – despite the enmity of Lloyd George and the Unionists – the Exchequer. Such an unexpected ordering demonstrates that Asquith, despite all, was still able to manipulate circumstances thrust upon him, to his own advantage. On 24 May, when senior Liberals and Unionists met to discuss the distribution of offices, Bonar Law's colleagues pressed for him to have the Exchequer, or, failing that, Munitions.[84] Asquith insisted that the results of the last three elections made a Tariff Reformer at the Treasury impossible. Furthermore, he argued, with Kitchener (whom he counted as a Unionist) remaining at the War Office and Balfour destined for the Admiralty, Bonar Law at Munitions would put the three military departments in Unionist hands. Pressed by his colleagues and angered by Asquith's stratagems, Bonar Law indicated to Lloyd George the following day that he was contemplating withdrawing his agreement to coalition.[85]

According to one insider, Asquith sent Lloyd George to Bonar Law on the morning of Friday, 25 May with a simple message: 'There are my terms, you can take them or leave them.'[86] Beaverbrook has insisted that Lloyd George made an appeal 'to [Bonar Law's] shining qualities of disinterestedness and patriotism[,] which [he] could never resist even though he ought to have done so.'[87] Bonar Law, however, did not care for Asquith's message or his method, so he was not particularly susceptible to Lloyd George's charm on this occasion. The Colonial Office, important in peace time, did not in time of war invest its holder with the dignity appropriate to an Opposition leader in a coalition government. It seems more likely that Bonar Law was as determined as he had always been to maintain political peace and improve the conduct of the War, and considered that a battle over office at this point might result in control of his parliamentary party being transferred from his own hands to those of Unionist firebrands. Hence, to the annoyance of many of his colleagues, Bonar Law went to the Prime Minister and agreed to accept the Colonial Office.

Each of the three principals had his reasons for acting as he did in these negotiations. The Prime Minister was disdainful of Bonar Law, and they were most certainly horses bred in different stables. 'A few months before,' Asquith's biographer has noted, 'he had come across Bolingbroke's remark about Bishop Warburton: "Sir, I never wrestle with a chimney-sweep"; and had commented: "A good saying, which I sometimes call to mind when I am confronting Bonar Law." '[88] He also disliked him – they had, after all, been engaged in hurtful political combat over several years – and there is no doubt that he intended, as he wrote soon afterwards, 'to prevent B. Law taking either the office of Munitions or the Ex[chequ]er.'[89] It is not difficult to suppose that it gave Asquith pleasure to depreciate his old enemy by manipulating him into an office of less significance than his rank as Opposition leader demanded. More important was the fact that he intended to prevent Bonar Law establishing a power base from which he could command real authority – and to demean him thus before his own colleagues would be helpful in disarming both him and the entire Unionist Party.[90]

Although Lloyd George valued Bonar Law more highly than did Asquith, this did not deter him from pursuing his own agenda. He anticipated that he would return to the Exchequer after he had set munitions production to rights, and McKenna was willing to take the job on a temporary basis, with reversion to the previous incumbent; Bonar Law would not have agreed to such an arrangement. Thus Lloyd George joined with Asquith in manoeuvring Bonar Law to one side, thereby also retaining his own position as the second man in the Government. As a result, relations between himself and Bonar Law were cool for some time thereafter.[91]

It is rather hard to imagine Curzon, Chamberlain or Long behaving as Bonar Law did in this episode. His legendary modesty – which was real as well as apparent – no doubt played a role, but it must not be exaggerated. He remained despite it an ambitious man, and there seems every reason to believe that he wanted and felt that he deserved the Exchequer, once the War and Munitions offices were settled. J.C.C. Davidson, who became his private secretary at this time, recalled:

> Bonar Law accepted the situation and consented to go to the Colonial Office. But he remained bitter at being given such a second-class post when he had been led to believe he could expect a major post, and commented very sharply on it. Asquith, of course, resented deeply the need to bring the Conservatives into Coalition at all.[92]

Bitter he may have been, but Bonar Law was certain from the outset of the War that after years of the most corrosive inter-party controversy, it was essential that partisan political struggle be suspended for the duration.[93] To this policy he had adhered since August 1914, forcing his colleagues to behave accordingly even when this seemed to endanger his hold on his party. It explains why coalition was at the back of his mind although he fought shy of it until the time seemed right to him, and why he cast his party's lot with the Liberals only when that time came. It is the only explanation for the way he swallowed his ambitions and accepted the difficult task of leading his party from an inferior office.

Bonar Law, like Asquith, was troubled by a deeply personal misfortune at this time; unlike Asquith, however, he was made to bear it in public. This was the Jacks Case, which concerned a Crown prosecution brought against the Glasgow firm of which Bonar Law had once been a senior partner.[94] A consignment by the firm of 7,000 tons of iron ore to the Continent, destined for a German customer, was *en route*, at sea, as war was declared. Its delivery a few days later put the company technically, though apparently unwittingly, in violation of the Trading With the Enemy Proclamation of 5 August.

Bonar Law's brother Jack was one of five partners in the firm, and it was thought for a time that all five might be charged; but in the event, only two of the principals were indicted. In June 1915 they were tried, convicted and sentenced to terms of six months' imprisonment, while the company was fined £2,000. It may have seemed a sound business decision to deliver goods and receive payment for an order placed months earlier, and it was almost certainly taken in ignorance of the fact that almost as it was made it became an offence against the Crown; but in the climate of opinion of 1915, it simply could not be overlooked. The men served their sentences, and afterwards returned to the firm.

While relieved that his brother was exonerated, Bonar Law knew it would be impossible to avoid being tarred to some extent at least with the brush so liberally applied to the Jacks Company; and he was prepared for the onslaught. In early May the socialist journal *Justice* carried a letter from the veteran British Marxist H.M. Hyndman in which he virtually accused Bonar Law of implication in the affair. In fact, Bonar Law had ceased to be a partner in the firm in 1902, his sole connection since that date being an interest-bearing deposit account he had maintained with them.[95] He was hurt by the accusation and prepared to counter-attack with a lengthy statement in the House. In light of the Marconi affair two years before, it is interesting that a draft of this statement shows Bonar Law proposing to make the following pledge: '[My brother] has been accused of this great crime, but to be accused does not necessarily imply guilt, and if it should be proved that he has been guilty I should not be willing to continue in public life and I should at once resign the position I now hold.'[96] As it was, Jack Law was not prosecuted, and this dramatic gesture proved unnecessary.

The hysterically patriotic fervour of those days, both in and out of Westminster, made it impossible that the affair should not have a political fall-out. Asquith himself smiled knowingly, and wrote to Venetia Stanley when rumours of the case first circulated: 'It will be one of the ironies of fortune (after what we innocently suffered over Marconi) if B.L. (equally innocent) were to encounter a like injustice ...'[97] By mid May, however, details of the case were well known in Westminster, and it was widely accepted that Bonar Law was not personally involved.

While he was much troubled by this humiliating affair, there is no evidence to suggest that Bonar Law's behaviour in his negotiations with Asquith in May 1915 was affected by it.[98] He was certainly angry and hurt by the false accusations against his brother, and the unfounded rumours that somehow he was part of the scandal. The Jacks case, however, was not responsible for making a frustrated Colonial Secretary of a potential Chancellor of the Exchequer – any more than the ending of a love affair caused the Prime Minister to overturn his Government.

More than any other politician, Asquith was the victor in these events of May 1915. Yet in his triumph and in its result the seeds were sown for a humiliating defeat which would cast him down and break his party, and Bonar Law had a great role to play in that coming drama. Asquith was a gifted politician who kept his party together and in power through many challenges over many years. Had he been a greater man, he might have abandoned his *hauteur*, made a genuine ally of Bonar Law, saved his party and himself, and earned a place as one of the saviours of his nation. As it was, for nineteen months following May 1915 Bonar Law struggled to make the coalition function as a successful war government. Once he was convinced that it was impossible for it to do so, however, he destroyed it almost without a second thought.

10

Colonial Secretary

I

THE NEW CABINET consisted of twenty-two members: twelve were Liberals, one was a Labourite (Arthur Henderson), another (Lord Kitchener) was without party affiliation, and the remainder were Unionists. While hardly an equitable division of the spoils, it was an apportionment which Bonar Law and his colleagues accepted and one with which they thought they could live until the War was won and the political parties returned to business as usual.

Several significant changes in his small personal staff followed Bonar Law's appointment. From his predecessor, Lewis 'Lulu' Harcourt, he inherited as an unpaid private secretary J.C.C. Davidson, then twenty-six, son of a distinguished Scottish physician. Despite his youth, Davidson was experienced in the ways of Whitehall, and Bonar Law soon found he had gained a resourceful assistant. Before long the much-burdened minister had developed a high professional regard and an almost paternal affection for Davidson, who was efficient, discreet and fiercely loyal.

During this period Bonar Law saw much less than had been his custom of Aitken, who had taken up duties as an 'Eye Witness' or observer at the Front on behalf of the Canadian Government.[1] At the same time his tireless parliamentary secretary John Baird finally managed to side-step Bonar Law's entreaties and join the Army.[2] Their absence made Davidson all the more valuable, and Bonar Law prevailed on him to remain at his desk rather than accept the commission he too longed for.

Bonar Law's own two elder sons were in uniform by this time, and the two younger were at Winchester School. At Pembroke Lodge were a butler (Pitts) and a chauffeur (Sweeney), as well as a cook and housemaid. In charge of Bonar Law's younger daughter was the governess, the formidable Miss Duggan: fiercely proper and a devout Roman Catholic, she had soon discovered that the irrepressible nine-year-old Kitty Law, the apple of her father's eye, required a good deal of governing.[3] Mary Law must have been glad of Miss Duggan's help as she continued to supervise the domestic arrangements at Pembroke Lodge, but was happy to surrender her duties as hostess to twenty-year-old Isabel.

A new addition to the household at this time was John Berry who, like Davidson, soon became a fixture. Berry, officially a Treasury Messenger, became Bonar Law's personal attendant and was, according to Davidson, 'as perfect a "gentleman's gentleman" as anyone could have wished for.'[4] An experienced servant, Berry was well versed in the handling of Whitehall gentlemen, and developed a special affection for this melancholy man whose demands were so frugal. He kept Bonar Law's tobacco and cigar boxes filled and made sure the evening gingerbread and glass of milk were close at hand at the end of the inevitable evening's work. Berry was one of that nearly extinct class of servants who understood the utility of intimidation of his social betters, and woe befell any senior civil servant or under-secretary who unduly troubled his master. Under the combined demands made on a party leader and wartime minister, Bonar Law soon became quite dependent on Berry, who stayed with him for the remainder of his ministerial career. The unfailing support of this tightly-knit circle, and of Max Aitken, of course, was to prove indispensable in the trying period which lay ahead.

During the nineteen months of the Asquith coalition the Government faced three major difficulties which in essence laid the groundwork for its destruction: the question of manpower for the Army, a renewed Irish crisis, and the very controversy which had provoked the Government restructuring – the Dardanelles campaign.

Bonar Law had from the outset been supremely sceptical about the expedition against Turkey, and the military advice of the commanders in Asia Minor had not changed his mind. His perception of the generals was different from that of Asquith or Lloyd George. Asquith saw them as technicians plying their trade while he got on with the serious business of running the nation; Lloyd George was beginning to conclude that the 'brass hats' were men of limited vision, and that his own dynamic though hitherto pacific genius was quite capable of conducting a war. Bonar Law got on well with generals, though he was not, unlike Lord Derby, either overawed by or particularly committed to them. He saw them as experts who deserved to be allowed to get on with their business; if they proved themselves incapable, however, he was prepared to abandon them utterly and turn to other professionals.

The fact that Asquith now refashioned his War Council into a Dardanelles Committee indicated the significance of this campaign. The premier took the chair, and the members included Kitchener, Balfour, Lloyd George, Bonar Law, Grey and Churchill, as well as Lords Lansdowne, Crewe, Curzon and Selborne; McKenna attended frequently, and Carson became a member in August 1915. It was a typical Asquithian creation, designed to defuse political tension and involve potential critics in responsibility for policy. At their first meeting on 7 June, Kitchener and Churchill carried the day for continuation of the Dardanelles offensive, and the Committee recommended that the British force there be strengthened.

In a candid letter to Selborne the following morning, Bonar Law indicated the inability he felt either to accept the optimistic arguments of the generals, or to counter them. Kitchener and General Sir Ian Hamilton, the commander on the scene, had advised that reinforcement would turn deadlock into victory; Bonar Law was no soldier, and he felt ill-equipped to combat their arguments.[5] He was, however, deeply troubled by what he had heard:

> That we can force the Dardanelles by frontal attacks from our present positions I do not believe and I fear that even the additional troops we have sent are not sufficient to put ourselves astride the peninsular [*sic*] and cut off the Turkish communications which I fear is the only way to force the position.[6]

In the end, he acceded to the request for additional troops – which had in any case been agreed in principle weeks earlier.[7]

Five divisions commanded by Lieutenant-General Sir Frederick Stopford landed at Suvla Bay in early August, to augment the seven already in position. Their brief initial success soon gave way to rising casualties among the mixed British and colonial forces – and to further stalemate. When the Dardanelles Committee met on 18 August, Bonar Law led a spirited resistance to this 'forward' policy.[8]

Asquith voiced his own annoyance, indicating that it was difficult to understand, after Suvla Bay, how Hamilton could remain confident of victory; and he wrote to Kitchener that Stopford and his staff 'ought to be court-martialled and dismissed from the Army.'[9] When it was suggested in committee that Hamilton was close to victory Bonar Law, increasingly impatient, snarled that 'he was always *nearly* winning.'[10] Only the French promise early in September to send troops to Asia Minor, it seems, deflected a decision in favour of withdrawal.[11]

The hybrid Government was put under strain by this crisis – yet Asquith often achieved success from his deft balancing of contending sides in his Cabinet. In pre-war days he had managed a Government of radicals and moderates, big Navy men and pacifists, pro- and anti-suffragists, by offsetting one group against another – first backing one side to the other's cost, then reversing the process, and succeeding far more often than he failed.

In the new Cabinet he carried on in the old way and apparently intended one key to his programme of controlling factions to be Bonar Law – the former antagonist he had manoeuvred into accepting an inferior office and cajoled (it seems) into submitting to the status of a some-thing-less-than-equal partner. In his efforts to diminish Bonar Law and thus better control the Unionist contigent, Asquith found co-operation not lacking, least of all from the ambitious and brilliant Lord Curzon.[12] Though in May he had shown little enthusiasm for giving him office, Asquith was soon treating the self-important Earl as a rival to Bonar Law. A useful example of how he played one against the other is the appointment in August of a War Policy Committee to consider precisely how large an army Britain should put in the field.[13] It was an important body whose conclusions would have much bearing on the looming con-scription question, and Bonar Law was furious when he discovered that Asquith meant neither to include him, nor even to seek his advice on which Unionists to appoint. Asquity blandly explained on 12 August that

> I, of course, included your name in the first list of the Committee which I showed to Curzon. We both thought it looked too long. So I left out you and Simon as being heavily occupied with departmental work. But I need not say that I shall be very delighted if you will serve on the Committee, and I have given instructions accordingly.

Bonar Law's reply was immediate, and curt:

> I have your note but my object in writing to you was not to ask that I should
> be added to the Committee, and in the circumstances I prefer not to serve on
> it.[14]

He considered it a purposeful slight – which it clearly was – for the
leader of the Unionist party not to be consulted or included in perhaps
the most important *ad hoc* Cabinet committee of the hour. It strained his
loyalty to the coalition and to Asquith, and his respect for Curzon –
though it did not yet break them.[15]

A similar incident occurred a month later when Asquith apparently
told Lloyd George that Bonar Law had demanded the title of Deputy
Leader of the House, which Lloyd George had held for some years. It is
not difficult to imagine the leader of the largest single party in the
Commons seeking the title to strengthen his position within his own
party – especially among those who thought he had acquiesced too
quickly in accepting the Colonial Office. Had the office been available,
Bonar Law certainly would have taken it – but to try to deprive Lloyd
George of it behind his back would have been a dangerous mistake, one
he seems unlikely to have made. Lloyd George wrote angrily to Bonar
Law that he was welcome to the prize, but ought to have written to him
first.[16] Bonar Law replied that he had made no such demand, but had
merely remonstrated once again at being unconsulted. He continued:

> I said that I had been placed in a false position because I was still supposed
> to have been the Leader of one party & that when a [coalition in the past] was
> formed the Leader of the other party has been the deputy leader of the
> House. I did not ask for [the Deputy Leadership] then and have not men-
> tioned it since.[17]

The two met the same day to compose their quarrel, and each took away
from the episode the conclusion that Asquith had at the very least mis-
handled the affair – and at worst, fomented it to divide two potential
rivals.[18] Bonar Law then had a meeting with the Prime Minister who,
quickly turning the conversation to his own problems, blamed Lloyd
George as a mischief-maker and the new and undeserving darling of the
masses. Bonar Law's advice to Asquith was characteristically unambiguous: the two Liberals would do well to compose their differences, and
Asquith must gather himself for a more energetic prosecution of the
War, starting with the deposition of Kitchener.[19]

Asquith's pinpricks made Bonar Law's Cabinet and party responsibilities that much more onerous. Considering the alternatives in May 1915, the Colonical Secretary had concluded that for the time being there was no other possible Prime Minister. Asquith was sly and difficult, but Bonar Law continued to believe he was the only man who could hold the coalition together and stave off a divisive general election. The conviction did little to make his lot easier.

By the autumn, the Dardanelles Committee – unlike the public – was receiving little in the way of encouraging news: the summer offensive on the Western Front had led to Joffre's failure to break the Germans in Champagne, and by mid October to an additional 50,000 British casualties. Neither had prospects in the eastern Mediterranean improved: French promises of assistance had come to nothing, and Hamilton's forces remained pinned down in their disadvantageous positions. In late September Bulgaria threw in its lot with the Central Powers, and a few weeks later King Constantine dismissed his pro-British premier and reasserted Greek neutrality. In order to salvage something from their crumbling position, the British and French agreed to establish a position in western Thrace, at Salonika – but where would the troops come from?

On 11 October the Dardanelles Committee met to consider a grim picture: Serbia was doomed, its capital already lost to Austrian and German troops and its eastern provinces on the point of being overrun by the Bulgarians. The plan to occupy Salonika offended pro-Dardanelles ministers, who wished to salvage the campaign at the Straits. Churchill and Curzon vigorously defended this position, while Bonar Law, Lloyd George and Carson argued that the campaign was lost and the only suitable place in the area for British troops was at Salonika. The divided Committee could agree only that 150,000 men should be moved from the Western Front to Egypt, with their final destination – the Dardanelles or Salonika – to be decided only after advice was received from Hamilton's newly-appointed successor, Lieutenant-General Sir Charles Monro.

Bonar Law was unhappy with the compromise, fearing that the abandonment of the Salonika initiative and of Serbia would open up a route from Germany through the Balkans to Turkey. His own conclusion was that the Dardanelles campaign should be ended immediately.[20] Carson agreed, so strongly that he sent in a letter of resignation on 12 October. Bonar Law was well aware that this matter, as well as the growing debate over the imposition of conscription, was beginning to turn the minds of certain other Unionists towards resignation.[21] His

Chief Whip, Lord Edmund Talbot, advised on 16 October that this would surely destroy the coalition and make an election inevitable: 'Better than this I suggest it is better to keep Asquith, with all his faults, where he is at present . . .'[22] This was precisely Bonar Law's thinking, so he did not resign, the Dardanelles affair remained unresolved, and the Government staggered on.

Carson could not be dissuaded from his resignation, which caused Bonar Law some disquiet. He knew there was a risk that Carson, as a disenchanted free lance, could become a magnet for Unionist critics of the coalition, and that damaging criticism of the Government would intensify. Carson and Bonar Law were still agreed in their opposition to the Dardanelles campaign, however, and shared with others the desire to be rid of Kitchener. In fact on 21 October the Cabinet – chaired by Lord Crewe, as Asquith was indisposed – recommended dissolution of the Dardanelles Committee and substitution of a war executive council made up of the premier and three or four colleagues only.[23] When this meeting broke up, ministers remained behind after Kitchener's departure and expressed an almost unanimous opinion that he had to go.[24] Asquith seemed to agree, and Bonar Law, wishing fervently to strengthen his resolution, wrote to Lloyd George a week later:

> Have you any objection to my telling the P.M. that you said to me that you were satisfied that nothing but disaster lay ahead for us as long as Lord K was War Secretary & that you were going to write to the P.M. that you could not continue to share the responsibility for the continuance of the present arrangement at the W.O. & that I had replied that if that issue were definitely raised I must take the same course.[25]

The rather confused events of the next few days, however, did nothing to promote co-operation among the three key members of the coalition. Confronted with a potentially dangerous alliance, Asquith saw each of the two others separately, and Lloyd George concluded merrily that they would soon be rid of 'Lord K'.[26] To Bonar Law, Asquith proposed the curious solution that he should take on the War Office himself, as he had following the Curragh affair. Shocked by the proposal, Bonar Law at first expressed no objection; but silence did not necessarily imply consent. Decisiveness in a crisis is much praised, but Bonar Law feared leaping to a wrong conclusion more than he feared the criticism of those who resented the time he took to reach what he thought was a correct one. After a day's thought, he put a stop to the plan by writing to Asquith:

The criticism which is directed against the govt and against yourself is chiefly based on this – that as Prime Minister you have not devoted yourself absolutely to co-ordinating all the moves of the war because so much of your time and energy has been directed to the control of the political machine. Now you are proposing to undertake duties which in the view of the country, as I believe, ought to be performed by a man who does nothing else, and thinks of nothing else ... I am sorry that I did not express my view to you at once, but for the moment I overlooked the disadvantages and was disposed to welcome your presence at the War Office without taking into account the other considerations.[27]

To buy time, Asquith quickly produced another plan. Though Monro had reported in favour of evacuating the Dardanelles, the Prime Minister – after apparently securing Lloyd George's agreement – proposed to the Cabinet on Thursday, 4 November that Kitchener himself be sent to Asia Minor to formulate his own recommendation.[28] Bonar Law was unprepared for this, and annoyed that it appeared to be supported by Lloyd George – who, he had thought, was of his own mind regarding evacuation – but in Cabinet he once again raised no objection.[29] After considering the matter for a few hours, he concluded that he could not accept any further delay in abandoning the Dardanelles; and wrote promptly to Asquith setting forth his objections. To Asquith, it appeared that the Colonial Secretary was again reversing his opinion after further thought. Such a method of proceeding earned Bonar Law Asquith's contempt – for which, it must be said, he cared little. As he explained to the Prime Minister, he had held his peace while a final decision awaited Monro's recommendation, which was unequivocally in favour of evacuation; and now the process was to be repeated:

> If, as is at least possible, this delay may result in the destruction of our force [in the Dardanelles], a weight of responsibility will rest upon the Cabinet, which I am reluctant to share. I therefore earnestly request you to call at once a meeting of the cabinet so that a definite decision may be taken on the subject.[30]

He circulated his letter to other members of the Cabinet, and was granted his hearing the next day.[31]

The Cabinet discussion was arid: Kitchener had already embarked; Asquith had announced the winding-up of the Dardanelles Committee; the generals were preparing to plunder as much of Kitchener's authority at the War Office as might be possible in the absence of a Secretary of State in whom they had lost confidence – and no minds were changed.

The spirit of the meeting seemed to be that if Bonar Law remained patient, he would have his way; even the other anti-Dardanelles ministers mustered little energy to support him. This he found unsatisfactory, and for the first time since taking office he threatened to resign. He wrote to Asquith on Monday, 8 November:

> I fully admit, as I did Saturday, that I ought to have presented my views on Thursday and when the times [*sic*] comes for the discussion of the grounds of my resignation I shall for that reason be exposed and justly to the most severe criticism; but from my point of view the fact that when the subject was unexpectedly raised I failed to grasp the situation in all its bearings would not justify me after I had time for full consideration in accepting a decision which I truly believe is not only a mistake but a fatal mistake ...
>
> The facts of the position as I see them are that now that the Germans have free communication with Constantinople the position of our forces at Gallipoli is untenable, that we sent General Munro [*sic*] to give us a report on the situation from a purely military standpoint and that he has reported in the most definite way in favour of evacuation. Instead of acting on his report we are sending Lord K. to make another report which means further delay at a time when in my opinion delay may be fatal ...
>
> In these circumstances it would be absurd for me to continue in the Cabinet until Lord K. has reported and I feel [compelled] to place my resignation at once in your hands.[32]

Yet in the end there was no resignation. In a brief note to the Prime Minister written later the same day, Bonar Law indicated that he had now 'determined to postpone the consideration of my position in relation to the Gallipoli policy until after Lord Kitchener's report has been received.'[33] Almost certainly he had concluded, since writing his first letter – perhaps Asquith had assured him – that the Dardanelles campaign would soon be wound up.[34]

As all expected, on 15 November Kitchener cabled his initial recommendation that the troops in the Dardanelles should be evacuated.[35] The old hero's days were numbered, however. His popularity remained too great for him to be shunted off into some honourable sinecure, but by the end of the year he was to lose many of his remaining powers to a new Chief of the Imperial General Staff – General Sir William Robertson, known universally as 'Wully'.

There remains only one further detail of this ill-starred episode to be noted: Asquith had accepted the Cabinet's recommendation that he restructure his council of war, and had announced it to the House on 2

November, the eve of the Dardanelles evacuation crisis. Though he would have preferred merely to reshuffle the Dardanelles Committee, Asquith now promised its replacement with a committee of 'not less than three, and perhaps not more than five'. His plans had embraced himself, Lloyd George and Balfour, then he added McKenna and, of all people, Lansdowne. Knowing he could not acquiesce in a further snub, Bonar Law had coolly informed Asquith that it was probably sensible not to include him as he was already close to resignation over the Dardanelles. Asquith took the point: he abandoned his consideration of Lansdowne (who was in his seventies, and in any event refused to serve) and, insisting that his mind had 'swerved about it', implored Bonar Law to join the committee.[36] Despite the fact that he was evolving rapidly into Britain's most prominent figurehead, Kitchener was added upon his return from the Near East.[37] The membership of the new War Committee was made public on 11 November.

Kitchener returned to London on 22 November and duly confirmed his recommendation for evacuation of the Dardanelles. Curzon's best efforts in Cabinet to save the campaign were unconvincing, the other members preferring Bonar Law's round condemnation of it as a gamble which had failed. The withdrawal began in mid December at Suvla Bay and Anzac and ended in early January with Cape Helles – all without the swingeing casualties soldiers and civilians alike had feared. The Dardanelles campaign was over.

Beaten in this struggle and denied membership of the War Committee, Churchill embraced his fate and resigned – but only after Asquith had refused his brazen request to be made governor and military commander in East Africa.[38] He was already a major in the Oxfordshire Yeomanry: he now determined to take up his commission. Bonar Law's response to Churchill's resignation speech of 15 November was kind, but he stopped well short of saying he preferred that he should stay. For Bonar Law, getting his way over the Dardanelles was what mattered, and the eclipse of Churchill was simply an added benefit, though he considered no backwater too far removed from Westminster for the former First Lord.

II

The Dardanelles episode soon came to seem a minor skirmish compared with the battle for mandatory military service which next broke over Westminster. Put most simply, by mid 1915 Unionists, to a man, were in favour of conscription, while most Liberals remained profoundly suspicious of it: Lloyd George, Churchill and a small band of their party colleagues were the exceptions.

Compulsory service had not to date been a part of British military practice in modern times, but the Great War shattered all precedents. Almost without realizing it the nation was swept into war on an extended Western Front, and few at first understood it would require armies of unparalleled size. By early 1915 the professional force which had stepped off so smartly the previous August had been all but destroyed, to be replaced by reserves and recruits. For the remainder of the War, the Army would require continual renewal and augmentation with fresh manpower, on a prodigious scale: and it was these demands for ever more men that created the conscription controversy.

Questions about the possible imposition of compulsory service were asked in Parliament early in the War, but Asquith assured the House that this was not contemplated. Alone among ministers, Churchill raised the issue in Cabinet in the first weeks of the conflict, and received a similar reply. It hardly seemed necessary: Lord Kitchener called for recruits on 7 August 1914, and hundreds of thousands of young men responded. Throughout August and September and into early October the mass of volunteers literally overwhelmed the recruiting stations. Thereafter numbers fell off, and concern began to surface in the War Office that Britain might not be able to build a force suitable to her developing role on the Western Front.

In these months there was one man in Britain who could virtually alone have imposed conscription on the nation, and that was Lord Kitchener.[39] His popularity was at its apogee; his famous poster was everywhere, and his reputation exceeded that of politicians and soldiers alike. Had he demanded compulsory service, it almost certainly would have been implemented – yet Kitchener was sceptical about its value, and would not endorse it until he thought it absolutely necessary.[40] Walter Long was quite correct in his belief that, as he wrote to Kitchener on 2 December 1914, '... if you were to insist upon Compulsory Service ... you would be supported by every loyal man in the Country, and this means the vast majority.'[41] Yet entreaties from mere politicians did not move Lord Kitchener of Khartoum.

With more than a hundred of their parliamentary colleagues in uniform, the Unionists were subjected to a barrage of testimonials to the need for conscription. 'Johnny' Baird now acted as Bonar Law's eyes and ears at the Front, and most Unionist MPs on active service called on their leader when they took leave in London. He also regularly received information on conditions in France through such high-ranking officers as Major-General Wilson and the Commander-in-Chief himself, Sir John French or, after December 1915, his successor, Sir Douglas Haig.[42]

In pre-war years Bonar Law, like Balfour before him, would have nothing to do with calls for mandatory service, rightly fearing popular opposition to the idea, and resisted any attempt to include it in the Unionist programme. By 1915, however, he had concluded that the needs of a general war simply could not be met from volunteers alone. In his early struggles with munitions supply, Lloyd George had complained to Bonar Law that the unregulated recruitment of large numbers of skilled artisans was a principal reason for the undersupply of armaments. Bonar Law appreciated the problem, and explained at this time to F.S. Oliver that he thought trusting to the voluntary system led to the Army attracting the wrong men – those with irreplaceable industrial skills – while others who might more easily be spared for military service were overlooked. The party truce remained uppermost in his mind, however, and he knew that if Unionists were to press the issue of mandatory service they would almost certainly upset the delicately poised armistice between the parties. 'I dont [*sic*] think however', he wrote, 'that it would have been either possible or wise to raise the question of compulsion until the voluntary system has failed.'[43]

Conscription was seldom out of the minds of party leaders in the months preceding the 1915 coalition. Only Churchill among the Liberal ministers dared mention it, however, and Bonar Law carefully resisted efforts by Lord Midleton and Lord Selborne in the Upper House and by Long and the Unionist Business Committee in the Commons to plump for it openly.[44] Only after May 1915 did the issue begin to become unavoidable in Westminster and in the Unionist press.[45] It should be recalled that the inventory of complaints drafted by the Unionist leaders on 14 May – overtaken by events and never sent – had, on the very eve of coalition, included a demand for military and industrial conscription.[46]

Some Liberals had anticipated that conscription would be the price Bonar Law would demand for co-operation, a prospect which heartened many politically-minded soldiers.[47] Colonel Thomas Bridges, for example, had written to Bonar Law on 18 May: 'The Army will expect that compulsory service will be a condition of your participation in the

Government.'[48] Long went even further: 'We must have compulsion for Army & Labour. I believe we ought to have Martial Law.'[49] Yet conscription was not introduced in May 1915: so long as the Liberals remained opposed to it and Kitchener could not be persuaded to endorse it, Bonar Law remained unconvinced that it was worth a political struggle which might too easily lead to that divisive election he so feared.

Ironically, it was Kitchener himself who hastened the introduction of mandatory service. On 6 July 1915 he and Asquith met their French counterparts for a conference at Calais. Asquith came away convinced that the French had been accommodating on most major points – and well they might have been: in a meeting alone with the French generals, Kitchener had delighted them by committing Britain to place an army of seventy divisions in the field – nearly double the force she could muster at the time.[50] If any single decision sounded the death-knell for the volunteer Army, this was it.

The War Policy Committee appointed in August had a decided pro-conscription majority of Selborne, Chamberlain, Churchill and Curzon. Only Crewe, the chairman, and the Labour Member, Arthur Henderson, opposed its immediate imposition. Since each side remained immovable, in the end they presented to the Cabinet on 8 September not one but three reports. The official finding simply reiterated the choices open to the country: to maintain the Army at its current size, to increase it through further voluntary enlistment, or to adopt compulsion. The conscriptionists produced a report demanding mandatory service, while Henderson issued a paper warning that this would lead to 'insuperable difficulties, accompanied with a divided Cabinet, a divided Parliament, and a divided nation.'[51] A few days later, the Trades Union Congress met in Bristol and strongly endorsed both Henderson's recommendation and voluntary service.

Asquith was not so philosophically committed to voluntary service as many of his followers; but he remained convinced that both the public and the Liberal Party opposed conscription, and he had no intention of endangering his premiership by bringing it in before it became absolutely necessary.[52] Bonar Law had concluded as much, yet was very conscious that his party wanted conscription. Like Henderson, however, he dreaded the possible political fall-out from fighting the controversy to the finish at that time. Henderson believed compulsion would never be accepted by labour until it was proven to be unquestionably essential for the maintenance of the Army. It is no wonder that the politicians looked to Kitchener for a lead: so popular was he still that it was inconceivable the nation would deny him compulsory service if he declared it to be imperative.

In early October 'Lord K' circulated a paper which indicated that he had moved closer to the conscriptionists, for in it he called for consideration of a strange amalgam of voluntarism and compulsion: conscription by lottery.[53] A few days later he reiterated what he had told the War Policy Committee and demanded the intake of 35,000 volunteers per week through to the end of 1916, nearly double the average of late 1915 – a daunting challenge.[54] The Cabinet, as they met almost daily, ensnared in the conscription question, must have been dumbfounded by this requirement. On 12 October Long wrote to Bonar Law predicting immediate disaster,[55] while Lloyd George confided to C.P. Scott, the editor of the *Manchester Guardian*, that no fewer than eight ministers were prepared to resign over conscription – including Carson, Churchill, Curzon, Long, Lansdowne, Kitchener, Bonar Law and himself.[56]

In the end there was only one resignation – that of Carson, who gave the Balkan situation, not conscription, as his explanation – and the coalition was saved once again. Henderson's ominous words were heeded, and the conscription zealots accepted one last compromise: a final 'big push' for volunteers, led by Lord Derby, Kitchener's newly-appointed Director-General of Recruiting (and, ironically, a confirmed conscriptionist). What is remembered as the Derby Scheme was announced on 19 October and called on men to either enlist or 'attest' – pledge to come when called – in sufficient numbers to meet Kitchener's demands.

The Unionist ministers accepted the Scheme only as an insurance policy against a rupture of national unity, and as a device to force the Liberal and Labour parties and the TUC to embrace what they saw as inevitable. This was Bonar Law's view. His Chief Whip agreed, reasoning that if Asquith were to resign over conscription his place was likely to be taken by Lloyd George, who would then enjoy the support of the Unionists, but of few Liberals and Labourites. In the election which would surely follow, the conscriptionists would win but only after a campaign which would divide the nation. Better, he concluded, to wait for the almost certain failure of the Derby Scheme and then have united support for conscription – or at least acquiescence.[57]

To ensure that Asquith understood what was required of him, Bonar Law wrote on 16 October, seeking an undertaking that 'if by the end of November [the terminus of the Derby Scheme] it is evident that the required numbers cannot be secured by voluntary means he will on behalf of the Government propose that compulsion should be adopted.'[58] The Colonial Secretary revealed his determination a few days later, telling the Cabinet: 'In this war we must risk everything . . .'[59] Asquith complied, and in a 'Secret Note' sent to his colleagues testified to his general acceptance of conscription if Derby's effort did not succeed.[60]

In the House on 2 November Asquith outlined his conclusions: if after the Scheme had run its course there remained a sizeable number of men of eligible age who had failed to enlist or attest, this would 'force the country to the view that they must consent to supplement by some form of legal obligation the failure of the voluntary system.' The Prime Minister also clarified exactly which men he thought ought to be subject to compulsory service, adding that so far as he was concerned, 'the obligation of the married man to serve ought not to be enforced or held to be binding upon him until – I hope by voluntary effort, if it be needed in the last resort, as I have explained, by other means – the unmarried men are dealt with.'[61] This 'pledge to the married men' was soon to prove a mistake.

Preliminary results of the Scheme, available on 14 December, were disappointing, and the final figures discussed in Cabinet ten days later confirmed that this method would not raise the numbers demanded by the generals. The case for conscription seemed confirmed, and the Army Council drove an additional nail into the coffin of voluntary service by demanding on 16 December yet another increase, of a million men – which Asquith endorsed a week later.[62] In fact, Asquith had privately given permission to initiate the drafting of a conscription bill on 7 November.[63]

Bonar Law took no pleasure in a series of events which could well be interpreted as a political victory for him, writing to St Loe Strachey at this time that: 'The situation has never seemed to me all round, since the war began, so difficult as it is now.'[64] His awareness of what conscription meant in human terms was almost certainly made more acute by the fact that both his elder sons were in uniform – Jim training as a pilot with the Royal Flying Corps and Charlie in the King's Own Scottish Borderers.

On 29 December 1915 a sombre Cabinet met to approve the so-called 'bachelors bill' providing, subject to Asquith's pledge in Parliament, for the conscription of unmarried men only. With the exception of Lloyd George Liberal ministers remained unhappy about the bill, but in the end only Sir John Simon resigned. Bonar Law and the

Unionists were troubled by the limited scope of the plan, and remained convinced that general military conscription was necessary. Yet they realized that in a delicate political situation in which all seemed to depend on a unified nation, they had to take what they could get – and that was conscription for unmarried men between the ages of eighteen and forty-one.[65]

The National Service Bill, introduced on 5 January 1916 and shepherded through the House by Bonar Law and Long, became law on 27 January. Despite baleful predictions, public reaction to this first dose of compulsion was so stoical that some conscriptionists wondered whether mandatory service for married men would not be accepted with similar equanimity. Britain's most powerful soldiers were in complete agreement: the strong-willed Chief of the Imperial General Staff 'Wully' Robertson, and General Sir Douglas Haig who in December 1915 had replaced French as commander on the Western Front. Both believed fervently in carrying the struggle through to the end. They were also agreed that the Army required all the men it could possibly obtain – regardless of marital status – and Robertson wasted little time in reminding the Government that this was his wish.[66] There were few in Parliament who openly disagreed with them.

In February Asquith appointed a Military Finance Committee, which set the projected size of the Army at sixty-seven divisions, sixty-two at the Front with full reserves.[67] This effectively doomed the experiment in limited compulsion, as 'bachelor conscription' could not possibly raise enough men; furthermore, Haig was planning a great offensive for the summer of 1916. A second round of debate on national service began almost immediately.

Bonar Law may have been uneasy that the conscription debate was far from over, but his personal position in the House and in the country had never been higher. He had skilfully led his followers through the initial battles of the manpower crisis, replacing his reputation as Ulster warrior with that of a man of probity who put national unity before party.[68] Clementine Churchill, the former First Lord's wife and one-woman intelligence service, had been asked to keep a close watch on Bonar Law. She cared little for her husband's old enemy, but admitted on 21 January: 'If tomorrow the P.M. disappeared Bonar Law would be the successor. He has made a great impression in the House during these last weeks by his skilful handling of delicate topics and this impression will spread to the country.'[69]

Within a few weeks, however, Bonar Law's anxieties about the effectiveness of bachelor conscription had been confirmed, and the danger seemed to emanate from within his own party.[70] In the same week that the conscription bill was introduced a Unionist War Committee was formed, with Carson as chairman, and soon almost all the Unionist back-benchers were attending its weekly meetings.[71] The formation of the UWC would have been significant even without Carson; with him in the chair, the Committee had the potential to become a possible alternative party organization, he a rival leader. It was also known that Carson dined regularly with the 'Monday Night Cabal' of Lord Milner and his admirers – Amery, Robinson, Oliver and Waldorf Astor, the proprietor of the *Observer* – who cared little for Bonar Law's struggle to save the coalition.[72]

In early March Bonar Law wrote to J.P. Croal that he could not support limited conscription indefinitely, merely to keep the Government afloat. He had only refrained from demanding general conscription three months earlier because he had feared 'that we would lose more by dissension at home than we would gain by increased military efficiency ...' However, he added:

> If an examination shows that with the present system we cannot get the men which the country can afford, taking into account the need of keeping up our financial strength, then I should not agree to continue in the Government unless the changes were made ... You probably realize, however, that apart from this definitive question there is so much general discontent with the Government, and particularly with the Prime Minister, that the continuance of the present Government may for that reason alone become impossible.[73]

Yet until the results of such 'an examination' were clear, he would not act. Later in the month he chastised the intemperate Sir Henry Wilson, who had pressed him to overturn the coalition:

> I wonder whether you have ever thought out what would be the consequences of such a step as you propose? If we broke up the present Government, it is obvious that a new Government could not exist in the present House of Commons. There would, therefore, be the immediate necessity of a general election; it would be fought, in spite of the war, with almost the usual amount of party bitterness; and if our Party succeeded in getting a majority we would be faced with an opposition of precisely the same nature as that at the time of the Boer War.

If the Government took a step for which the people were not ready, however,

... we should find that the first effect of such a change, when it was obvious that instead of even the appearance of unity the nation was bitterly divided, would be to discourage our Allies and make our enemies feel certain that we could not stay the course.[74]

Propelled by the Unionist ministers the Cabinet met on 30 March (without Asquith, who once again was ill) and agreed that the Military Finance Committee should be recalled to consider the manpower question. This was done, and Bonar Law – awaiting the conclusive 'examination' of which he had written to Croal – advised a stormy Carson in clear terms that the UWC would simply have to remain patient a little longer.[75] On 13 April the committee reported that they could agree only on recommendations to extend the service of time-expired men, absorb into the Army men from the Territorials, and lower the age of call-up.[76] Bonar Law knew his back-benchers would not accept this. The generals could not, and responded with a memorandum of terrifying simplicity which changed the situation conclusively:

> The [Army] Council, then, still hold the opinion that it is absolutely necessary that every man of military age who is physically fit and can be spared from Naval service or industrial or other indispensable employment should be made available for service in the military forces. This represents the only maximum which the Council has ever contemplated ... The Council therefore wish to point out that any such postponement of a decision as that contemplated by the Committee would involve serious consequences to the successful prosecution of the war.[77]

On 16 April Lord Stamfordham sought out Bonar Law, who offered a sober analysis: if conscription were not promptly expanded he would be unable to hold his party, and an election was all but certain to ensue. It would be an election preceded by a bitter campaign and resulting in a Unionist victory – but also, quite probably, in a deep fracture of national unity.[78] The Unionist Whip William Bridgeman advised: 'If you support the Government and have to admit that it is against the opinion of the Army Council, I do not think a quarter of the party would go with you.'[79]

Bonar Law was certain the time had come for Asquith to do the right thing. He wrote immediately to remind the Prime Minister of the calamity that would follow an election and subsequent return to single-party government. He reminded him also that the Unionist ministers, who were agreed on the necessity for general conscription, had been prepared to try to hold their party to the 'bachelor' compromise only in the interests of national unity. The insistent demands of the Army Council had drastically altered the situation, however, and to ask Unionists to resist the Council's conclusions would surely cause a break between the party rank-and-file and their leaders:

> If I thought [the Army Council] view was wrong, or if I thought that it was impossible for you to go farther than you propose, I should be ready to face the Party and lay upon them the responsibility of breaking up the Government. But I do not take that view. I think it is easier for you to carry your supporters in favour of [general] compulsion than it is for us to obtain the support of our Party against it.
>
> In these circumstances, I feel that the attempt to carry our Party in favour of your proposals would fail, and that it would be impossible for me to acquiesce in those proposals.[80]

Asquith's response to this pressure was to create yet another panel: the Committee on the Size of the Army, which included himself, Crewe, Kitchener, Bonar Law, Lloyd George, Balfour, Long, Henderson and General Robertson, met on 18 April 1916. Two possible solutions were discussed: Lloyd George, strongly supported by Bonar Law, demanded a general conscription bill, with the proviso that it would not be enforced if volunteers came forward in sufficient numbers to satisfy the Army Council's manpower demands. Henderson suggested that the three-part plan of the Military Finance Committee, revealed five days earlier, be given a six-week trial, with general conscription held up as the price of failure.[81] Only Robertson's indication (which was less than candid) that he did not care how they were obtained so long as the Army got its men kept Bonar Law from threatening a Unionist withdrawal from the Government.

On the following day Henderson, who in what Lloyd George called 'an engineers' war' was now much listened to as the voice of the working classes, encouraged his Cabinet colleagues to accede to the Labour Party demand for a Secret Session of the House of Commons in order that the most confidential information on manpower might be aired. Meanwhile, as Labour Members met privately to condemn general compulsion, a hundred and twenty-five UWC men convened under Carson's leadership to renew their demand for it.[82] More intimidated by the representatives of the working classes than by Carson, over the protests of Lloyd George and Bonar Law the Cabinet on 20 April endorsed both Henderson's request for a Secret Session and his proposal for another six-week delay.[83] The only appeal of this latter expedient, essentially very like the failed Derby Scheme, seemed to lie in its supposed power to mollify a population thought to be hostile to a broadening of compulsory service. The Liberals and even most of the Unionist ministers appeared to agree on it, nevertheless, and the two dissenters uneasily acquiesced in the majority opinion.

The Secret Session was scheduled for Tuesday, 25 April 1916. This followed the Easter weekend, for which Asquith, crises notwithstanding, was in the country. He returned to London very late on Monday night, and a more superstitious man might have sensed an ill omen in the news which greeted him. Lieutenant-Colonel Sir Maurice Hankey, Secretary to the War Committee, who accompanied him, recalled that '... on arrival in Town we got the first news of the Dublin outbreak. Asquith merely said "well, that's something", and went off to bed.'[84] The Easter Rising was indeed 'something', but Asquith had more immediate problems.

The Secret Session was nothing short of a disaster for the Prime Minister. Asquith in the Commons and Crewe in the Lords explained the Government's case for a final test for limited conscription, as proposed by Henderson.[85] Supporters of the Government were then savaged by spokesmen of the well-prepared Unionist War Committee and their noble allies in the Lords. A few days earlier Sir Henry Wilson had written to a friend: 'Have we got the sodden old brute [Asquith] by the throat at last? Steady now; Thumbs down.'[86] Such was the brutal spirit of the attack: Asquith emerged from the Chamber with his legendary confidence for once shaken.[87]

Having no other policy in hand, Asquith insisted that Long go ahead as planned and place the Henderson compromise before the House the following day; it was promptly cut to bits by Carson and his friends,[88] and never heard of again. Prime Minister and Cabinet surrendered to general conscription – the Liberals reluctantly, the Unionists and Lloyd George jubilantly. Asquith announced the fact in the House on 2 May, and the following day introduced a bill which extended conscription to married men. It received the Royal Assent on 25 May, and Britain's conscription policy thereafter paralleled those of the other combatant nations.

If Asquith had been wounded by the conscription battle, Bonar Law had also suffered short-term injury. While he emerged from the struggle more or less at one with Unionist ministers, his standing had been weakened with the impatient UWC: they cared little for his trials in Cabinet, and thought he had been dilatory in pressing the case for general conscription. For the time beng Carson was their darling, and on 4 May more than a hundred Unionist MPs honoured him at a luncheon. Milner took the chair; the leader of the Unionist Party was conspicuous by his absence. Carson's speech lauded the efforts of the UWC and revelled in their victory over the Prime Minister. Though there was no overt criticism of Bonar Law or of the Coalition, this celebration and the events it commemorated represented a barely-veiled threat to the Unionist leader – as he knew very well.[89]

III

As the Dardanelles controversy had overlapped the conscription debate, so was this latter dispute resolved only as another Irish crisis arose to tear at the heart of the Government. Before plunging into this tortuous episode, however, it is important to note the passing of Lord Kitchener. In May he had been invited to Russia to consult with the Czar, and his colleagues were pleased at the prospect of having him out of London for a time. On 5 June the cruiser *Hampshire*, carrying Kitchener to Archangel, was cut in half by a mine only a mile and a half off Marwick Head in the Orkneys. All but fourteen aboard were lost, including the War Secretary, and a stunned nation was plunged into deep mourning for the obsolete hero in whom they had never lost faith.

Asquith swiftly announced that he would once again take temporary charge of the War Office until a regular appointment was made. 'Wully' Robertson, who had exacted control of strategy as the price of becoming CIGS, had no intention either of compromising his powerful position or of serving under a War Secretary with too many ideas of his own. The soldiers therefore favoured Derby for the post, and considered Chamberlain to be almost as harmless.[90] Neither man, however, could possibly be acceptable to Bonar Law. At this point he could not allow himself to be passed over in favour of any other Unionist and still retain credibility as party leader.[91] Asquith himself, although he loathed the prospect, realized the job had to go to either Bonar Law or Lloyd George.

The relationship between the Colonial Secretary and the Munitions Minister had been strained from time to time since the beginning of the war, yet there was no doubt that Bonar Law considered Lloyd George at once the most effective and the most nakedly ambitious of his colleagues. The two saw eye to eye over conscription, and also came together over Lloyd George's audacious attempt – just then unfolding –

to settle Ireland. On Whit Monday, 11 June, they met at Cherkley and, after some wrangling, agreed that Lloyd George should become Secretary of State for War.[92] Bonar Law, while believing that he had every right to the job, now accepted the fact that Lloyd George was better suited to it – and that the Unionists would be content with his appointment. He undertook to convey the news to Asquith.

Bonar Law was scheduled to travel to France the following morning, 12 June, but was forced to delay his departure after learning from a telephone call to Downing Street that Asquith had no intention of returning to London from his Oxfordshire country house in order to see him. Accompanied by Max Aitken, Bonar Law therefore motored to The Wharf, near Sutton Courtney, to confront the Prime Minister. Their encounter was the subject of a celebrated anecdote, published first by Lord Blake in 1955, which described Bonar Law's fury at being made to wait while Asquith finished a hand of bridge with three ladies.[93] Though he did not publish the tale in any of his own books, the source of the story was Max Aitken (then Lord Beaverbrook). When controversy arose as to the accuracy of the tale, Beaverbrook said to his secretary: 'You can tell Blake that Bonar Law told me, and he always told the truth' – which may well have been the case.[94] However, an undated note in Beaverbrook's own hand admits: 'B-L may not have been right about the bridge game or the ladies, but he did believe that A. had time to snub him.'[95]

In the end, the veracity of Aitken's tale is of little importance.[96] More germane is Bonar Law's annoyance at being summoned to the country to suit the Prime Minister's convenience on a morning when he was scheduled to travel to the Continent on official business, and at being made to wait while Asquith completed some private business, whatever it may have been. Coldly resolute by the time he saw Asquith, Bonar Law brusquely waved aside the Prime Minister's offer to him of the War Office and laid down his ultimatum: Lloyd George must have it. Asquith agreed.[97] He cannot have looked forward to advancing the career of the colleague who was fast becoming a serious rival. Lloyd George (handing the Munitions Office to his second-in-command there, Dr Christopher Addison) got the prize – with Derby as his Under-Secretary, but without any restitution of the powers which had been surrendered by Kitchener to General Robertson, the Commander of the Imperial General Staff.

Of far greater immediate importance was the chain of events in Ireland. Led by a former schoolmaster, Padraic Pearse, a rag-bag republican government had declared itself and run up its tri-colour flag over the General Post Office in Dublin on that fateful Easter Monday afternoon. The rebels' brief glory exacted a high price: within the next few days sixty-four had been killed and two hundred wounded. Yet 134 soldiers also died and another four hundred were wounded – virtually all of them Irishmen, as were the more than two hundred civilians killed and six hundred injured – in the suppression of the insurrection.

The rebellion did not impress Dubliners, nor did it spread beyond the capital. In the weeks which followed, however, public perception of the rebels changed. Fifteen presumed leaders of the Rising were tried by drum-head court and summarily shot as the traitors to the Crown they undoubtedly legally were (as most did not deny). Charges and punishments appeared haphazard, confused and unjust, however; some key conspirators were spared the firing squad, and at least one innocent was shot on the authority of an officer later judged to be mad.[98] Thus were they raised from the level of violent cranks to that of heroes of Irish freedom – Anglo-Irish relations would never be the same.

The Chief Secretary, Augustine Birrell, was a likeable academic lawyer sadly mismatched to his task. After nine years in office he was weary of the Irish struggle, and had wished to retire with the coming of the coalition – after the Rising, Asquith was pleased to allow him to do so.[99] On 12 May Asquith crossed to a subdued Dublin to assess the situation for himself. He returned in a week convinced that Home Rule could await the end of the War, but that the machinery of Irish governance required prompt overhaul.[100] Someone would have to broker a settlement if Ireland were to be saved from the extremists, and he concluded that the man to do it was Lloyd George. Sidestepping an offer of the Chief Secretaryship, Lloyd George agreed to make an effort to identify possible terms of a settlement, and the Unionist ministers agreed that he should do so, subject to Asquith's assurance that no Home Rule settlement would be imposed during wartime.[101]

Lloyd George began his negotiations on 23 May and for a fortnight shuttled back and forth between Redmond's Irish Nationalists and Carson's Ulster Unionists. Throwing over his limited fact-finding mission, he soon began discussions aimed at identifying terms for the prompt implementation of some variety of Home Rule. Carson, of course, remained committed to permanent Ulster exclusion, while Redmond stood by his offer of temporary partition only, and many Southern Unionists – fearful of republicanism since the Rising – dug in their heels over any form of Home Rule. By early June Lloyd George was able to present a draft scheme combining immediate implementation of the extant Home Rule Bill with exclusion of the six Ulster counties and continuation of the current Irish representation at Westminster. While the settlement was to be subject to review by the London Parliament after the War, Lloyd George assured Carson that permanent exclusion was guaranteed.[102]

Carson presented the terms to the Ulster Unionist Council as the best deal for which they could hope, and Bonar Law and most Unionist ministers seemed to agree – convinced by Lloyd George's arguments that the successful prosecution of the War required swift decisive action, and that America, neutral in the War so far, favoured Home Rule. Lloyd George apparently allowed both sides in Ireland to think that the plan had Cabinet endorsement, which was not the case. Details of the supposedly secret negotiations inevitably leaked out, however, and certain Unionist leaders and their back-bench friends were infuriated to learn that Lloyd George seemed to be brokering a deal without the full authority of the Cabinet; worse still, that Asquith appeared to be ready to reward treason by reneging on his pledge to withhold Home Rule until the War should end. The prime movers in this party revolt were Lord Lansdowne and Lord Selborne and, most importantly, Walter Long, who was determined to undermine the Lloyd George scheme.[103]

Long and his friends – including Salisbury and Midleton, who joined Lansdowne and Selborne in an effective rear-guard action in the Upper House – would not budge. Asquith, though aware that Lloyd George had disingenuously hawked his plan about as a Cabinet proposal, could scarcely repudiate the man who was now his War Minister. Nor could Carson climb down, having brought the Ulstermen to acceptance. Redmond, though he hated the idea of exclusion, understood that a prompt settlement was the last hope for his party – faced as they were with the new separatist movement inspired by the Rising. Along these lines the parties divided.[104] Eighty Unionist MPs, meeting on 22 June to voice their hostility to the idea of 'rewarding' the Rising with immediate Home Rule, were mollified only by Bonar Law's promise, brought by Bridgeman, that he would assent to no Home Rule formula without consulting the party.[105] For Bonar Law the choice was no choice at all, as he indicated to Lord St Audries (the former Sir Alexander Acland-Hood):

> ... it seems to me that now that the negotiations have reached this stage[,] if our Party turns them down we shall simply have the whole of Nationalist

Ireland in hostility to us instead of, as has been the case up to now, having for the first time in our history Nationalist Ireland divided and the official section of it on our side. We are getting the exact terms which would have been accepted at the time of the Buckingham Palace conference . . .[106]

The Cabinet met twice on 27 June, when Lansdowne and Long argued emphatically against the settlement and Bonar Law opposed his long-term comrades in the same terms as his letter to St Audries.[107] Privately he told the Chief Whip, Lord Edmund Talbot, that any further postponement would not only fail to bring better terms but was likely to break up the Government and lead to the election which he wished to avoid.[108] Bereft of any other idea, Asquith took the familiar step of appointing a small committee, of himself, Lloyd George, Lord Robert Cecil and Sir George Cave, to make a last attempt at saving the proposal. The Cabinet then adjourned for a week.

The committee endorsed the settlement (to satisfy the Unionists, the primacy of Westminster for the remainder of the War was emphasized) and pacified Cabinet rebels for the time being; Bonar Law put the proposal before his party on 7 July.[109] He explained the position he had taken in Cabinet: he regretted the circumstances which had made the Lloyd George plan necessary, but thought Home Rule was now inevitable. To the Southern Unionists he spoke frankly: their position would 'not be made worse by a settlement now than a settlement at any future time.' To counter those who might have been inclined to doubt his determination, he added:

> Since [the beginning of the War] we have been sailing on an uncharted ocean with no compass to guide us except this, that we are bound to do what we think is right in the national interest without regard even to the interests of our Party. Whether I am right or wrong[,] that is what I am doing now. I am bound to do what I think right[,] and as long as I am in the position in which you placed me I am bound to tell you what my conviction is, and it is this, that if we go back on these negotiations now as a Party we shall make a terrible mistake.

Perhaps Carson made it somewhat easier for the troubled Unionists by admitting that while his own sympathies were against the proposal, 'I find my judgement bringing me along to the goal reached by Mr Bonar Law.' There was no vote taken, but Bridgeman was certain Bonar Law would have carried a majority.[110]

In the end, it did not matter. On 11 July Lansdowne, suspicious of the settlement, told the Lords that it was unacceptable without an absolute guarantee of permanent Ulster exclusion and equally specific safeguards for the interests of Southern Unionists. Redmond, with all Irish eyes upon him, could not ignore the challenge: he responded in kind with an equally angry demand for recognition of the provisional nature of any exclusion agreement.[111] This exchange of absolutes mortally wounded the Lloyd George proposal, and again the delicate hope of compromise was crushed. Lord Robert Cecil was merely intoning words over a broken corpse when he implored the Cabinet to postpone any attempt at settlement until the end of the War.[112]

By the end of July Asquith had abandoned the plan; government from Dublin Castle was restored, as was the Lord-Lieutenant, Lord Wimborne. Bonar Law had insisted at the time of Birrell's resignation that either the Lord-Lieutenant or Chief Secretary must be a Unionist.[113] He got his way: Asquith appointed H.E. Duke to be Wimborne's Chief Secretary, with an English Roman Catholic, Sir William Byrne, as Under-Secretary. Thus ended another attempt at settlement; after the conclusion of the War, the price of peace in Ireland was to prove much higher.

With the failure of the compromise he had supported, Bonar Law's position in the autumn of 1916 was hardly encouraging. His relations with the Unionist sceptics – including Lansdowne, Selborne and Long – were cool. To his brother Long wrote angrily that his old comrade Bonar Law had 'led us into the mess in which we find ourselves now'.[114] Selborne was equally harsh.[115] Invited to speak plainly, Bridgeman told his leader of the unhappiness within the party, and went away certain that Bonar Law had learned a painful but useful lesson about the continuing power of Ireland to divide the Unionist rank-and-file.[116]

Aitken, however, saw the silver lining to the dark cloud:

> So the July of 1916 closed sadly for Bonar Law. Yet there were several significant aspects of the Irish crisis which were prophetic. For the first time Bonar Law, Lloyd George and Carson had worked together as a team.
>
> In this Irish question Bonar Law had ... definitely disassociated himself from what might be justly described as the main current of Tory thought when it was manifestly wrong and out of date.[117]

This pronouncement by Bonar Law's closest friend has been widely credited, and certainly his latter point is inarguable: Bonar Law had stood against Die-Hard rejection of the best settlement for which

Unionists could have hoped; while according to his whips his position as leader was unchallenged, a minority in the Lower House and a large number of peers thought him wrong in so doing.

Of the first contention, it would be more correct to say that for their own reasons Bonar Law, Lloyd George and Carson had on this occasion worked in parallel, but not yet as a team. More heat in the crucible of Westminster would be required to fuse the three together, and this lay nearer in the future than even they realized.

11

The December Crisis

I

THE POLITICAL STRUGGLES of the spring and summer of 1916 left the Government weakened and divided, but it would almost certainly have survived indefinitely had the military efforts of Britain and her Allies been successful. Had the generals delivered victories, Asquith might have re-established his authority and silenced his critics. As a result of a combination of patriotism, dogged determination and censorship, the British civilian population remained remarkably supportive and even optimistic about the War. So long as the party leaders and back-benchers in Westminster shared at least a portion of that resolve and remained convinced that the Asquith coalition was the best achievable Government, the party truce would continue. This was Bonar Law's view; and had the crushing military disappointments of 1916 been avoided, he would have continued to support the coalition against its critics. But this was not the case, and in December he abandoned Asquith and played a pivotal role in destroying the coalition he had once laboured to preserve.

Hopes for a decisive British victory were raised on 31 May 1916, as the German Navy at last came out into the North Sea to engage the Grand Fleet under Sir John Jellicoe. Yet the Battle of Jutland was a pale victory at best, for the German fleet quickly abandoned the field and steamed away into what proved to be permanent cold storage in the waters at the mouth of the Elbe. Though the Royal Navy lost fourteen ships to the Germans' eleven, they were able to claim that they held the field at the end of the day. Nevertheless, the war of the great surface ships was over; Asquith and his colleagues enjoyed no reflected glory; and the brief excitement passed, leaving only frustration behind.

In contrast, the Battle of the Somme, begun on 1 July, was a national tragedy of unprecedented proportions. The Somme offensive had been approved by the War Committee – including, of course, Bonar Law – when the Battle of Verdun was at its height, as a measure to relieve pressure on the French Army.[1] Haig, who had come to believe (incorrectly, as events were to prove) that the German Army was fatally vulnerable, considered a decisive breakthrough possible. The 57,000 casualties of the first day represented the greatest loss in history to a British force; over the next four months, the operation claimed 360,000 more.[2] In the end there was no breakthrough. There were, however, many thousands of families who suffered, and among them were the Asquiths. On 15 September the Prime Minister received the news that his eldest son, Raymond, had been killed leading his troops 'over the top'.[3] There can be no proper time for tragedy; but given the challenges which lay before Asquith, this affliction could not have struck him at a worse period.

France and Britain did not suffer alone: the Russian General Alexei Brusilov predicted a breakthrough in the East, and in June audaciously led his huge armies in the last-ever Czarist offensive. After some initial success, by mid September Brusilov's forces had sustained more than a million casualties, and thus prepared the way for the collapse of the dynasty he served. Romania also tasted disaster after joining the Allied cause in August: within three months most of that unhappy nation was in German and Austrian hands, and Bucharest fell on 6 December. Romania's war was over: Russia's soon would be.

The Battle of the Somme did not drive Britain out of the War, but its horrible reality destroyed what was left of the popular belief that the end of hostilities would come soon. And its effect was even more far-reaching: 'Nothing that happened during the Somme campaign', Professor Wilson has written, 'provided clear proof ... that the direction of the country's affairs was in the best possible hands.'[4]

II

If the climate of popular opinion remained remarkably sanguine despite all this, that within the political world at Westminster did not. The Somme was only the latest blow to be dealt a Government that had survived the conscription controversy, the Dardanelles failure and the Easter Rising. To this must be added the humiliation of demands from Members for enquiries into the Dardanelles failure and similar reverses in Mesopotamia (where General Townshend had surrendered his small force at Kut-al-Amara to the Turks in April 1916) – met with the creation of commissions which must have brought to mind the angry scrutinies of Crimean War days. Asquith's agreement to such 'acts of self-mutilation' on the part of the Government – which he later tried unsuccessfully to retract – certainly indicated that he was operating with less than his usual skill and craft.[5] The commissions were constituted in the late summer and pursued their embarrassing investigations, reporting in the spring of 1917.

Asquith's life was made no easier by the criticisms of certain elements of the London press, particularly those controlled by Lord Northcliffe. The great press lord had by this point decided that Asquith had to go, and his press machine – within the limits of the censorship apparatus – relentlessly attacked his leadership. At least as ominous was the fact that even the great Liberal editor C.P. Scott, of the *Guardian*, had concluded that Asquith was unfit for his task and deserved to be 'dead and buried – politically!'[6]

Aitken failed in his efforts to bring Bonar Law and Northcliffe together, but the Colonial Secretary was drawing close to the editor of the Liberal *Daily Chronicle*, Robert Donald, with whom he found it easy to talk 'off the record'. He remained on intimate terms with Croal of the *Scotsman* and was in frequent touch with R.D. Blumenfeld, editor of the *Daily Express* (which Aitken now controlled), as he was with Scott. Sir Edward Carson was supported and Asquith denigrated at every turn by Gwynne in the *Morning Post*, and Carson also co-operated with Northcliffe during these weeks.[7] It is easy to exaggerate the role of the press in the downfall of the coalition – Asquith certainly did – but it is true to say that 'The press caught and reflected Britain's mood in late 1916.'[8] By December it had certainly caught the mood of much of the House of Commons.

The spark which set all this political tinder alight was struck on the evening of 8 November, when a minor bill to offer captured German assets in Nigeria for sale to the highest bidder unhinged the House quite unexpectedly. Carson, in restive mood, used this seemingly secondary business to attack the Government in the name of patriotism and property – he sought to limit bids to those of British interests only – and all but shattered it.[9]

At the time the coalition was formed, Bonar Law was speaking for his Unionist Cabinet colleagues when he pledged to the party that 'because we feel that you have allowed us to speak for you – it is for that reason, and for that reason only, that we have entered this Government.'[10] In December 1916 he went further, pledging that if he lost his party's confidence, he would resign office immediately and end the coalition.[11] The debate over the Nigeria policy grew rapidly from spirited to bitter, with Carson and Bonar Law – who as Colonial Secretary was presenting the Government case – as the principal antagonists. Carson and his friends could not defeat the bill, but they came close to forging a majority of Unionist Members and calling in Bonar Law's promise.[12]

When supporters came to his room afterwards to congratulate him, Bonar Law saw no cause for celebration. He lost no time in seeking the reason for the uprising, setting his whips to work gathering opinion and then speaking individually with as many rebels as possible to discover their true motives. He was soon reassured, he told Donald, that the insurrection 'was simply a symptom of discontent with the Coalition, rather than hostility to myself.'[13] Yet he knew menace when he saw it. Had things remained as they were, he recalled only a few weeks after these events, 'their hostility would [have made] it impossible for me ... to continue in the Cabinet.'[14] Sixty-five of the 138 Unionists voting on the bill – a majority, if those in party or Government office were subtracted from the total – had rejected the call of their official leader. This alone made Carson a rival for Bonar Law's place.

The tribulations of a year in office had not changed Bonar Law's opinion that Asquith was indeed, as he appeared to be, irreplaceable: he enjoyed the loyalty of his party, mastery of the House and, despite all, wide approval in the country. As a figurehead, therefore, Bonar Law judged him second to none. Yet in those parlous months there were few who suggested that even so admirable a symbol was conducting an efficient war administration, and several statesmen in and outside the Cabinet were coming to the conclusion that what was needed was a war council with executive rather than merely advisory powers. Bonar Law was one of these.

Sensing danger, he warned the Prime Minister following the Nigeria debate that a 'radical change in the Government must be made, and made at once.' Asquith waved this aside, and Bonar Law unsmilingly promised that he would return *when he had a definite plan.*[15] Soon afterwards he spoke to Carson, and although they were uneasy with each other after their recent clash, they soon found common ground in the need for an executive war council. Bonar Law emphasized his view that 'under a Constitution such as ours the control of the political machine, even from the point of view of the conduct of the war, was as essential as the preparation of big armies; and', he recalled, 'I added that in the present House of Commons no one I thought could control that machine so well as Mr Asquith.'[16] Carson noted enigmatically that he did not 'altogether disagree'; a *rapprochement* had begun.

Lord Lansdowne took the next step towards overheating the political atmosphere: on 13 November he circulated a highly controversial memorandum to the Cabinet which questioned the substance of a recent dramatic call made by Lloyd George for a 'fight to a finish – to a knock-out',[17] and suggested that a compromise peace might be the only alternative to endless slaughter.[18] Bonar Law was horrified by the memorandum – just as Lansdowne had been repelled by Bonar Law's endorsement of Lloyd George's sentiment.[19] Shared disgust at what they considered the 'defeatism' of Lansdowne's arguments fuelled the engine that ultimately drove Bonar Law, Carson and Lloyd George together.[20]

Already seeking co-operation among these three statesmen was Sir Max Aitken. The thirty-six-year-old financier, Member of Parliament and now newspaper proprietor had been much occupied as Canadian 'Eye Witness' at the Front and was, as usual, paying little attention to parliamentary business. By 1916 he was seeing more of the new War Secretary, Lloyd George, and less of his own overburdened leader than at any time since the beginning of the War. Yet among his intimates Bonar Law still trusted few more than Aitken, and used his services whenever an absolutely loyal, dedicated and discreet lieutenant was required. In the weeks following the Nigeria debate Aitken reclaimed his former place at Bonar Law's side and once again assumed the roles he so valued, as tactician and agent to his friend and political hero.

On Sunday, 12 November Bonar Law visited Aitken at Cherkley, where he found Churchill and F.E. Smith engaged in an angry discussion about the coalition, the Liberal denouncing and the Unionist defending it. Depressed by the news from the Somme and still smarting over the Nigeria debate, Bonar Law rounded on Churchill: 'Very well,' Aitken recalled him barking, 'if that's what the critics of the Government think of it – we will have a General Election.'[21]

This was certainly within Bonar Law's power: Did he mean what he said? If he were pushed too far, he could quite well advise Asquith to join with him – with all loyal Unionists and Liberals, and the party machines behind them – and go in unity to the people for relief from their antagonists' attacks. It was a terrible threat to Churchill and to the malcontents of the Nigeria debate; but it also disquieted Aitken, who wanted to end the reign of Asquith and initiate that of Bonar Law and Lloyd George. Immediately he resolved to encourage what already seemed more plausible than it had hitherto: a collaboration between Bonar Law, Lloyd George and Carson.[22]

In London the following morning Lloyd George revealed to Aitken the depths of his impatience with Asquith's management of the War. More significantly, he indicated that he and Carson were in agreement on the need for a small war council to replace Asquith's system of Cabinet committees. He well knew that this conversation would be relayed to Bonar Law, and confided to Frances Stevenson his hope that the Colonial Secretary was near the 'end of his tether'[23] and ripe for co-operation. The next morning Lloyd George left London for Paris, while Bonar Law called twice during the day on Aitken, who in his London *pied-à-terre* at the Hyde Park Hotel had taken to his sickbed. They discussed more than his health, Aitken recounting – probably they came as no surprise – Lloyd George's hopes for a revised war executive and his communications with Carson.[24]

Bonar Law's feelings for Lloyd George were ambivalent during these anxious days. He found him insensitive to the problems posed by certain of his more difficult Unionist Cabinet colleagues – particularly the ambitious Curzon. He had not forgotten Lloyd George's behaviour in the matter of the Deputy Leadership of the House, and was hurt by his absence during the Nigeria debate – Carson he credited with at least fighting openly. Indeed, at the time of Carson's resignation in October 1915, Bonar Law had said of their mutual suspicions about Asquith, 'There's one man I distrust more.' He meant Lloyd George, and he did not confine this sentiment to Carson's ear alone.[25] Only later did he learn that Carson and Lloyd George had dined together just hours before the Nigeria debate.

While admiring Lloyd George's brilliance, Bonar Law thought him capable of selfishness and ruthless in his ambition; he was suspicious of his continuing quarrel with the Chief of the Imperial General Staff, and of his faith in his own gifts as a strategist. Yet, unlike Asquith, he also saw that Lloyd George was emerging as the greatest figure of the War, and unreservedly admired his creation of the Ministry of Munitions. Because he knew him to be the best man for the post, he had driven the sceptical Asquith to appoint Lloyd George to the War Office; and he had supported him in his recent Irish negotiations. From his own austere standpoint Bonar Law regarded Lloyd George as he always had and always would – with tolerance of his foibles and admiration for his great gifts, yet always with a certain measure of the disapproval of the natural puritan. At this point, however, he had not yet overcome his distrust, feeling uncertain of the man's motives.[26]

Stifling his wariness, Bonar Law took the first step – as with Asquith and Carson – by inviting Lloyd George to dinner, on 17 November. The evening went on without Lloyd George, however. Though he told his secretary and mistress Frances Stevenson the invitation had been withdrawn, suggesting that Bonar Law was in a 'wobbly state of mind', actually it was he who was unready: he fought shy of the meeting when he discovered there were to be other guests, and rebuffed Bonar Law's offer to meet him privately afterwards.[27] A start had been made, none the less, and Aitken, now restored to health, shuttled back and forth between the two Cabinet ministers over the next two days, making certain that each knew the other's mind regarding a revised war administration.

On Monday 20 November Bonar Law, Lloyd George and Carson at last came together, over dinner in Aitken's hotel suite. Bonar Law wrote a month later: 'By this time I had got a scheme sketched out. My idea was a War Council consisting of ministers without portfolios, with the Prime Minister as President and Mr Lloyd George as chairman.'[28] Bonar Law wished Asquith to hear first-hand of his concerns about his leadership, and had therefore called on him the afternoon of 19 November and told him bluntly 'that unless he acted on his own initiative things would get serious.' The Prime Minister, he advised, had to be seen to take action or he would 'find himself in a humiliating position.'[29] To his eventual cost, Asquith showed little interest.

The dinner meeting apparently skirted specific proposals, as the three men each had reasons for caution: Bonar Law admired Carson's initiative and courage but remembered the Nigeria debate and rightly saw him as a threat to his leadership. He thought Lloyd George the most effective member of the Government but distrusted his personal ambition. The conversation was wide-ranging but guarded, though Bonar Law made one point with absolute firmness: he had no intention of taking part in any mere conspiracy to displace Asquith. What they most notably shared was an eager desire to replace the existing War Committee with an efficient war executive, and Bonar Law held out

hope that Asquith could be driven to take the step himself.[30] He continued to be wary of Lloyd George, telling Aitken later that Monday
evening: '... I am not going to be drawn into anything like an intrigue
against Asquith. I have had experience of what flows from this sort
of conversation with Lloyd George.' He wanted the talents of both
Liberals in a revised administration, and he wanted them to compose
their differences: 'Lloyd George himself', he added, 'would do far better
to go quite openly to the Prime Minister and tell him what he has told
us.'[31]

The tide, however, was running against Asquith. On 21 November
Bonar Law and Lloyd George met again, when the latter suggested an
alternative plan, of a three-man council with the Prime Minister in an
external supervisory role – a prospect which again raised Bonar Law's
suspicions of Lloyd George's motives.[32] On 22 November, however, the
Cabinet discussed Lansdowne's memorandum. Bonar Law sensed what
seemed to him an undertone of sympathy among some ministers for
what was to him sheer defeatism: how, he wondered, could victory be
secured by such men? The resolve of the Unionist leader for change
grew firmer after this painful afternoon.[33]

On Saturday, 25 November Bonar Law welcomed Carson and Lloyd
George at Pembroke Lodge. Doubts were cast aside, and the three
quickly produced for Asquith's signature a memorandum announcing a
change in the political administration of the War:

> ... I have decided therefore to create what I regard as a Civilian General Staff.
> That staff will consist of myself as President & of three members of the
> Cabinet who will have no portfolios & who will devote their whole time to
> the problems which arise in connection with the prosecution of the War. The
> three members who have undertaken to fulfill [*sic*] these duties are ————
> & I have asked Mr Lloyd George & he has consented to act as Chairman &
> to preside at any meeting which owing to the pressure of other duties I find
> it impossible to attend. I propose that this body should have executive
> authority subject to this[:] that it shall rest with me to refer any questions to
> the decision of the [full] Cabinet which I think should be brought before
> them.[34]

Aitken's own persuasive version of the episode establishes him as the
author of this statement. Yet although he was present in the house, it is
unlikely – notwithstanding his role as go-between – that he was in the
room during the discussions between the three men; Bonar Law himself had dictated the draft memorandum to Aitken before the others

arrived. His aim was to combine Lloyd George's desire to decrease Asquith's role in a streamlined war council with his own insistence that the premier must be closely identified with it.[35] The others understood that without Bonar Law's co-operation they had little hope; and that if they pushed too hard and drove him into Asquith's corner, the two acting together would almost certainly be able to destroy the malcontents.

Though historians continue to discount Bonar Law's role at this time, it should be remembered that it was he – not Lloyd George or Carson – who confronted Asquith that afternoon with the document. He now told Asquith once again that a reorganization could be made without any loss of dignity on his part *if he acted quickly* – otherwise a smooth transition would be 'impossible'.[36]

Only on Monday did Bonar Law receive Asquith's formal response, though he had been forewarned that it would be a rejection.[37] Lord Jenkins has speculated that Bonar Law perhaps 'failed to inform Asquith of the full significance of the demand he was presenting.'[38] It seems more likely that the failure was Asquith's, in misapprehending the magnitude of what was put before him.

A recent and powerful study of the period has suggested that Bonar Law at this point lost his nerve, and started to work for a compromise between Lloyd George and Asquith.[39] What Bonar Law wanted was a new war council, with Lloyd George and Carson as members. Like Lloyd George (though perhaps not Carson), he wanted Asquith to remain Prime Minister, and he had sought a workable compromise on this basis from the first days of the crisis.

Upon receiving Asquith's rejection Bonar Law went to see him again, insisting that he must accept the proffered advice: he had no idea how unpopular his Government had become; he must compromise to avoid a total collapse. Asquith had to co-operate with Lloyd George, he told him; and, he believed, 'the best way was for the two of them to have a frank talk together and see to what extent they could come to an agreement.'[40]

Bonar Law promptly summoned Carson and Lloyd George to the Colonial Office to discuss Asquith's disappointing reaction, and they agreed that the two senior Liberals should meet. Miss Stevenson noted in her diary her concern that Bonar Law was the 'only weak spot ... who cannot make up his mind to strike.'[41] For 'weak spot' one should apparently read *someone who she feared might disappoint Lloyd George*.

Up to this point, Bonar Law had confided nothing of these negotiations to his Unionist Cabinet colleagues: now rumours of a possible Government reshuffle had made their way into the newspapers, and it could no longer be avoided. Moreover, Lord Robert Cecil had circulated a plan of his own, calling for the creation of two executive committees – one for war and the other for domestic affairs.[42] Any further division of authority was precisely what the 'triumvirate'[43] of Bonar Law, Lloyd George and Carson did not want, though the proposal found some favour in Cabinet on Wednesday, 29 November. The two triumvirs who were there withheld their fire because they intended that their own initiative should push this proposal aside. None could know, of course, that this was the final meeting of the Asquith Cabinet.

Unable to avoid it any longer, Bonar Law met the Unionist ministers on Thursday afternoon in his room in the House. He outlined the plan for a small executive council and, ignoring the rumours that Carson was involved, proposed only the name of Lloyd George as chairman – both suggestions were coolly received.[44] Bonar Law reiterated his belief that Asquith should be retained if possible but added that, whatever the Unionist ministers' intentions, he himself would not remain in the Government if a restructuring plan was not speedily adopted.[45] The meeting broke up without harmony and without resolution; in Bonar Law, sceptical by nature and apparently denied the support of his senior colleagues, it cannot have engendered much peace of mind.

Asquith and Lloyd George met the following day, 1 December. Lloyd George explained his latest plan for a war council free of departmental duties, with the premier relegated to an external supervisory role – Asquith, not surprisingly, received it coldly. When Bonar Law heard Lloyd George's report of this later in the day, he had his own reservations about the speed and direction of events. He was suspicious of the reasons behind Lloyd George's eagerness to separate the Prime Minister completely from the vital centre of war administration, and of his obvious desire to replace Balfour at the Admiralty with a more energetic minister.[46]

'I became alarmed,' he recalled, 'from the fear that Lloyd George was counting upon me to back him in whatever steps might be necessary, and I therefore asked to see him on the Friday night; and we met again at the Hyde Park Hotel.' Bonar Law was in a mood to have the air cleared: 'Now I want to know', he demanded, 'exactly to what extent you consider I am committed to you.' Lloyd George, no doubt wary in his turn of what this meant, replied that he did not consider him committed in any way. Bonar Law explained, as he recorded later, that

I was committed to support him to the fullest extent in securing a small War Committee of which he would be Chairman, but ... I did not feel justified in dictating to the Prime Minister precisely the way in which that Committee should be constituted, and, therefore, I must be free to take whatever action I thought right if the small Council were agreed to; and if the Prime Minister suggested other names to constitute it. Lloyd George agreed to this, and, indeed, added that he himself had not made the names a condition in his conversation with the Prime Minister.[47]

This was apparently enough for Bonar Law. Despite all odds, he was prepared to force the issue of the three-man war council in co-operation with Lloyd George; but he continued to believe that the Prime Minister should remain prominent in a revised administration.

Predictably, Asquith rejected the proposal;[48] upon which Lloyd George prepared to call in Bonar Law's promise, sending to him a copy of Asquith's letter and adding: 'The life of the country depends on resolute action by you now.'[49] As Lloyd George grew more agitated, the press – sustained on leaks, many of them from Aitken – erupted over the prospect of a change in Government, and Asquith dug in his heels. Bonar Law realized it was time to take the senior Unionists more fully into his confidence.

III

The political snowball now proceeded ever more rapidly downhill. On 3 December Bonar Law saw Carson, who insisted that he was prepared to jettison Asquith altogether and take his chances with a Lloyd George administration.[50] Earlier that Sunday morning, Bonar Law had gathered what Unionist ministers he could muster on short notice at Pembroke Lodge.[51] The Tory grandees were irritable, certain the press knew more of what was afoot than did they, several citing a well-informed weekly which had declared that morning: 'Mr Lloyd George has arrived at the definite conclusion that the methods of dilatoriness, indecision, and delay which characterize the action of the present War Council are such, in his opinion, as to endanger the prospects of winning the war.'[52]

Bonar Law informed them of Asquith's rejection of Lloyd George's latest proposal. Lord Crawford's notes of the meeting indicate that because of Asquith's procrastination and the apparent stalemate, Bonar Law was prepared to resign.[53] After an hour, they determined to advise

Asquith to submit the resignations of the entire Cabinet – if he refused, they would retire from his Government.[54] According to Crawford, they thought it 'dangerous to let Ll.G. force Asquith's hand by resigning this afternoon', but were willing to provide an opportunity for him to form a more efficient Government *if he could*. 'The point at issue', Crawford concluded, 'is whether Ll.G. can stand without Asquith.' Bonar Law presumed that they 'did not wish [it] to seem that their position was forced by the action of Lloyd George.'[55]

Chamberlain argued that Asquith had lingered too long, while Lloyd George had 'made the Government impossible [and] should be faced with his responsibilities.'[56] Bonar Law, patience spent, had a slightly different agenda:

> What I wished to do [he wrote later] was to say to the Prime Minister that we considered it absolutely necessary that there should be a change in the conduct of the war, and that as Lloyd George was the only alternative then change should consist in practically putting the direction of the war in his hands; and that if the Prime Minister could not see his way to adopt this course then we [Unionists] should resign.

Though perhaps not so dramatic as his original plan of resigning alone, this 'would have the same effect of producing a crisis which would put an end to what seemed to me an impossible situation.'[57] To this end, they concluded that Bonar Law should communicate to Asquith their terms:

> We share the view expressed to you by Mr Bonar Law some time ago that the Government cannot continue as it is.
>
> It is evident that a change must be made, and in our opinion, the publicity given to the intention of Mr Lloyd George makes reconstruction from within no longer possible. We therefore urge the Prime Minister to tender the resignation of the Government.
>
> If he feels unable to take that step, we authorise Mr Bonar Law to tender our resignations.[58]

Aitken argued in his version of events that the resolution was intended to strengthen Asquith's hand against Lloyd George – an interpretation which has now been convincingly overturned.[59] Certainly the principals never made such a claim and at least two, Chamberlain and Cecil, categorically denied it.[60] Lord Jenkins has referred to the motives of the Unionist chieftains as 'the greatest mystery of the whole crisis', but there seems to be little mystery.[61] What they wanted was to make something happen – the War was going badly, Carson the wrecker was restive, Bonar Law was ready to move – and Lloyd George appeared to be ready to act with the other two, if necessary, to push the Unionist ministers to one side. They sensed that great events were about to unfold, and they feared being overtaken by them unless they acted; so act they did.

Aitken, who had been waiting in another room while these deliberations were in train, remained at Pembroke Lodge for lunch; Bonar Law showed him the resolution, and brushed aside his pleas to delete the reference to Lloyd George and 'publicity' – the very upheaval in the press which Aitken had helped to generate.[62] Bonar Law then hurried off with the document to Downing Street where, he recalled, he 'communicated its contents' verbally to Asquith.[63] Asquith's official biographers have reproached Bonar Law for omitting to hand over the resolution itself, and thereby misleading the premier;[64] Lord Jenkins concludes that he 'neglected his duty – which was to show Asquith the resolution and let him decide for himself what it meant.'[65] Lord Blake leaves the question open;[66] Aitken simply does not mention it.[67]

What happened – and why? Several weeks later, Bonar Law read over his *aide-mémoire* of the events of the day and amended the line which said that he 'did not actually hand him the document' to read 'I forgot to hand him the document.'[68] His explanation was: 'The Prime Minister was not only greatly shocked but greatly surprised by our communication, and *asked me to treat it as if it had not been made until he had an opportunity of discussing the matter with Lloyd George.*' This is also what Bonar Law told the Unionist ministers on 3 December when he returned from Downing Street.[69] Whatever passed between the two party leaders, there is no reason to believe that after he had spoken to Bonar Law it was unclear in Asquith's mind that the Unionists were set on a restructuring of the Government or, failing that, on unilateral resignation.[70]

Had Bonar Law engaged in sharp practice? His amendment of his memorandum may simply have been a truthful correction of an oversight resulting from confusion, or it may have been a clumsy justification of his actions, or a subterfuge to shade his conduct. Perhaps, despite Aitken's insistence to the contrary, Bonar Law withheld the text of the resolution to save Aitken himself or Lloyd George from the embarrassment of being accused of trafficking with the newspapers. Lord Jenkins and other critics, even Aitken in his own way, prefer versions which suggest he withheld that single sheet of paper either through neglect of duty, or through artifice.[71] Austen Chamberlain wrote soon after these events that what the Unionist ministers wanted was to stabilize the situation, with either Asquith or Lloyd George in the topmost place: 'Accordingly, we drew up a statement expressing our concurrence with the views expressed by Bonar Law about a fortnight previously, that reconstruction was inevitable.'[72] Chamberlain and his friends thought their leader ought to have left the paper with Asquith, but none of them 'then or afterwards charged Bonar Law with bad faith or suspected him of it. We thought he had blundered.'[73]

Far from blundering, he very nearly got what he desired: critics miss the point that Bonar Law – unlike Carson – wanted the two great Liberals yoked together in a revamped war administration. Asquith, his instinct for survival piqued, had within two hours struck a deal with Lloyd George to remain as premier while the War Secretary chaired a small war council – a plan that suited Bonar Law completely. The issue of what Bonar Law did with the paper itself should not detract from the more important matter of what he said to Asquith. He left him in no doubt as to what the Unionists wanted; and, to judge from the actions of all parties afterwards, reassured that they had not simply 'gone over' to Lloyd George. Probably he again plumped for the compromise solution that both he and Lloyd George wanted at this point.[74]

Leaving the Prime Minister to meet Lloyd George, Bonar Law returned to Pembroke Lodge to find Crawford, Cecil, Chamberlain, Smith and the Irish Secretary, H.E. Duke, anxiously awaiting his news.[75] An hour later he was summoned once again to Downing Street and when he rejoined the Unionists afterwards – they had now moved to Smith's house in Belgravia – at 7 p.m. it was to announce a compromise. Asquith, Lloyd George and he had agreed that there would be a small war council, the membership to be arranged, to be chaired by Lloyd George and externally supervised by the Prime Minister. At Bonar Law's urging, the newspapers were informed that Asquith was to reconstruct his Government.[76] Bonar Law retired to his bed at the end of that long Sunday thinking he had achieved his goals: 'This was a great relief to me,' he recalled, 'for I had throughout worked with the one object of securing greater efficiency in the conduct of the war whilst retaining Mr Asquith as Prime Minister.'[77]

His confidence was premature, however, and his efforts to achieve a settlement soon fell apart. On Monday, 4 December *The Times* carried a leading article by Geoffrey Robinson which was critical of Asquith, disclosed much of the negotiations behind the proposed war council, and named Bonar Law, Lloyd George and Carson as the forces at work. The Prime Minister, certain Lloyd George was its source, was angered and hurt by the message of the article – that he was to be reduced to a figurehead and his powers put into the hands of his rivals.[78]

Later that morning Asquith explained to the King that the Government could not go on as it was. Aitken has indicated that (perhaps before his audience of the Sovereign) Asquith saw several important Liberals – all of whom advised resignation and a straight fight against Lloyd George.[79] According to this version of the story, Asquith also found time on this remarkably busy morning to see the 'Three Cs' – Curzon, Cecil and Chamberlain – and was told by them of their estrangement from Bonar Law and Lloyd George and their willingness to support a Government without the two conspirators.[80] According to Lord Samuel, however, Asquith did not see his Liberal colleagues until Monday evening,[81] and it seems unlikely that he saw more than one Unionist, Lord Lansdowne.[82] It does seem to be true that the 'Three Cs' met Lansdowne, Crawford and Long in Chamberlain's room at the India Office in the early afternoon to share their suspicions about Lloyd George and Carson, and their annoyance at being kept so long in the dark.[83]

Bonar Law spoke to Asquith only briefly, in the early afternoon, and was disappointed to hear that he was 'not quite so decided as to the appointment of the small War Council as he had been the previous evening.'[84] Having spent several hours pondering this danger signal, in the evening he pursued the Prime Minister from the House of Commons to Number 10, and demanded to see him. He stayed only a few minutes, and must have left Asquith rather breathless; as he noted,

> I told him that in my opinion the only way to save the Government was to carry out the arrangement made the previous day. I added that the position had become extremely difficult, partly through the action of the Press, and partly through his own delay in carrying out this arrangement which had made it more difficult for it to be brought into effect without loss of dignity for him. I told him, indeed, that as the position then was, there would be a certain amount of humiliation, but added that he had gone through this sort of thing before, and in my opinion he was a big enough man to live it down.[85]

Bonar Law then returned to the Colonial Office to meet Lansdowne, Crawford, Curzon, Cecil, Chamberlain, Long, and Smith. He had little new to tell them, however; nor had Lansdowne, of his own meeting with Asquith. The consensus among them was that, subject to continued wrangling between Asquith and Lloyd George, the compromise would hold.[86]

The following day, however, Tuesday, 5 December, the entire attempt at settlement collapsed. Lord Derby gave Bonar Law, Lloyd George and Carson breakfast at his house in Stratford Place; there was then no additional news, and they dispersed to their offices. Only later in the morning did Lloyd George learn, and inform Bonar Law, that Asquith had backed out of the arrangement. He sent on the Prime Minister's letter:

> After full consideration of the matter in all its aspects, I have come decidedly to the conclusion that it is not possible that such a Committee could be made workable and effective without the Prime Minister as its chairman ...
>
> I have only to say, in conclusion, that I am strongly of opinion that the War Committee ... ought to be reduced in number so that it can sit more frequently and overtake more easily the daily problems with which it has to deal. But in any reconstruction of the committee, such as I have, and have for some time past had, in view, the governing consideration, to my mind, is the special capacity of the men who are to sit on it for the work which it has to do.
>
> That is a question which I must reserve for myself to answer.[87]

The letter was a challenge; Lloyd George accepted it, and promptly sent in his resignation. Bonar Law's hope for a compromise was now in tatters, and he had to choose one side or the other: Asquith and continuity, or Lloyd George and innovation. With the murderous deadlock on the Western Front no closer to resolution than it had ever been, he did not hesitate:

> Up to this point [he later recalled] I had been in a very difficult position – of being friends with both sides, and I was throughout greatly worried by the fear that each side might in the end think I had proved false to it. After reading the Prime Minister's letter, however, I came definitely to the conclusion that I had no longer any choice, and that I must back Lloyd George in his further action.[88]

Would his senior colleagues do the same? At 11 a.m. the 'Three Cs' and Long met at the India Office, the beginning of an episode Aitken famously characterized as a 'court of enquiry' into Bonar Law's actions.[89] In fact it was not that at all, but neither was it particularly helpful to him. The four thought themselves justified in their annoyance with Bonar Law: he had ignored them in the run-up to the crisis, he had negotiated with Asquith in a manner which they thought most awkward and, worst of all, he had co-operated with the highly suspect

Lloyd George and Carson, rather than with them. Yet, disgruntled as they were, they recognized that a Government without Bonar Law and Lloyd George was impossible.[90] This was no court, but a company of the frustrated and – in their view – the unrepresented.[91]

Long was sent to invite Bonar Law to meet them at the India Office – Aitken's 'court' – and he was soon sorry that he had undertaken the mission. Much of Bonar Law's popularity at Westminster was due to the generous and soft-spoken style of his personal dealings with men, so much so that there were those who wished him harder and more ruthless. Yet when angered he could be coldly severe; and Long felt the full force of the storm.[92] Bonar Law declined to be summoned by any four of his followers, no matter how senior. Long returned with a message: their leader would receive the entire company of Unionist ministers that afternoon at the Colonial Office, at 4.30. Bonar Law suspected Curzon and perhaps even Chamberlain of having been trying on his crown while he was distracted – he might have compromised with Carson in the wake of the Nigeria affair, but these men were not so formidable as Carson.[93] Long hastened back to his friends, and the Unionist mountain came to Mohammed.

Contrary to Aitken's version, when Asquith finally saw the 'Three Cs' in the early afternoon, the uncomfortable hour and a quarter turned on one question: would they serve under him if Lloyd George and Bonar Law refused? Explaining that they bore him no hostility, their answer had none the less to be a 'perfectly definitive negative'.[94] They would provide no lifeline for the beleaguered Asquith.[95]

Asquith now consulted his Liberal colleagues (and Arthur Henderson), while the 'Three Cs' went to join the other Unionists at the Colonial Office.[96] The testy correspondence exchanged between Asquith and Lloyd George was read out by Bonar Law, as were Balfour's letters to Asquith refusing to abandon his colleagues and remain in office.[97] There was little sympathy for Asquith's conclusion that the Unionists had 'deserted' him.[98] The Unionists understood that Lloyd George's resignation was irrevocable, and that their leader had taken his side rather than the Prime Minister's. They saw also that Bonar Law meant to push the matter through to a conclusion, and that they dare not stand in his way. The 'Three Cs' had told Asquith there was no hope for him without Lloyd George and Bonar Law; there was little else to do but communicate to him that, as things were, the Unionists were as one in their determination to resign. They deputized Curzon to take the news, over Bonar Law's signature, to Number 10:

Lord Curzon, Lord Robert Cecil and Mr A. Chamberlain have reported to a meeting of all the Unionist Members of the Cabinet, except Mr Balfour who was unable to be present, the substance of their conversation with you.

After full consideration we are of opinion that the course which we urged upon you on Sunday is a necessity and that it is imperative that this course should be taken today.

We hope that you have arrived at the same conclusion, but if this is not so, we feel that we have no choice but to ask you to act upon our resignation.[99]

Curzon arrived as the Liberal ministers were in conference, and sent in the letter.[100] He was soon ushered into the Cabinet Room and told that Asquith would resign; and after expressing decorous regrets he turned on his heel and went back to the Colonial Office and his waiting colleagues. Crawford recorded the consensus among the Unionists:

Everything that has transpired since our meeting on Sunday has explained the justice of our view. We are where we were that afternoon, but with 48 hours of scandal and bitterness added: all might have been avoided had Asquith taken our advice, but he is unable to discern that the respect felt towards him by the H. of C. is not the same thing as the vexation he arouses in the country. He harps on one, is blind to the other. He thinks that he has a great following – so he has but it is insufficient, and though there will be a reaction in his favour before long, many thousands of loyal and patriotic men no longer associated with party politics, will rejoice when they learn tomorrow that he has at length resigned.[101]

IV

This was the climacteric of Asquith's Government; as Leader of the Opposition, Bonar Law was summoned to his Sovereign at 9.30 p.m.[102] Doubtless King George held Bonar Law in large part responsible for the political crisis; they clashed immediately over the relative merits of Asquith and Lloyd George. Then, when His Majesty turned to business and asked the Unionist leader if he would undertake to form a Government, Bonar Law raised the question of a possible Dissolution of Parliament. Though he had long struggled against the idea of a wartime election, he knew that he, Lloyd George and Carson had now gone so far that a popular mandate might be a necessity. The King declared himself against the idea, Bonar Law promised to 'consult his friends', and they once again parted as they had in the past, in unsettled disagreement.[103]

After leaving the Palace Bonar Law saw Lloyd George, and informed him of his own extremely slim hopes of fulfilling his pledge to the King to attempt to form a Government including both Asquith and the War Secretary. With Lloyd George's blessing, he set out immediately for Downing Street.

Characteristically, Bonar Law came straight to the point: would Asquith serve with Lloyd George under a 'neutral' Prime Minister? Asquith enquired who this latter might be.

> I said that as His Majesty had sent for me I was the natural person, but that if he thought it would be easier for him to serve under Mr Balfour I would be delighted to fall in with such an arrangement. Mr Asquith, after a moment's consideration, said that he could not agree to this.[104]

Thus did Asquith put an end to Bonar Law's original plan of harnessing the two great Liberals together; he made no further effort to form an administration. The following morning, after a brief meeting with Carson, Bonar Law and Lloyd George called at Carlton Gardens to seek the advice of the convalescing Balfour – which was that Bonar Law should recommend the King to call the party leaders together at Buckingham Palace.

Hoping still for a compromise, at 3 p.m. the following day King George welcomed Asquith, Lloyd George, Bonar Law, Henderson, and the last Unionist premier, Balfour, who had temporarily abandoned his sickbed.[105] The discussion was courteous and formal – wounds kept hidden and bitterness under wraps – but it was fruitless: Asquith refused to serve under any other Prime Minister and insisted that the Prime Minister (whoever he might be) must preside over the proposed war executive, while Lloyd George and Bonar Law remained firm in their agreement that no matter who was Prime Minister, Lloyd George must chair the new council. After ninety minutes it was concluded that Asquith should in his turn 'consult his friends' and, if his position remained unchanged thereafter, that Lloyd George should then endeavour to form a Government. The Liberal chieftains advised Asquith to stand his ground, and in less than two hours Bonar Law had Asquith's final word: 'They are unanimously of opinion that I ought not to join your Government. They think, & I agree with them, that I, and probably they, can give more effective support from outside.'[106] The responsibility then passed to Lloyd George.

Bonar Law and Lloyd George appeared at the Palace at 7 p.m. The

Unionist leader was received first, and reported that he had been unsuccessful in his attempt to form a Government. His Majesty promptly sent for Lloyd George, who was waiting impatiently in an anteroom. Within an hour of their arrival, the two men set about making a Government.

Did Bonar Law sincerely attempt to form a Government, or was he merely clearing a path for Lloyd George? At the time, Lord Crawford questioned whether 'he ever seriously thought of it.'[107] Dr Thomas Jones, writing Bonar Law's entry in the *Dictionary of National Biography*, asked the question twenty years later of Stanley Baldwin, who reported that Davidson, Bonar Law's secretary, thought he did not make a real effort.[108] Bonar Law himself explained that he had accepted the King's commission because he hoped that Asquith and Lloyd George might be willing to serve together under him, but in any event,

> ... I have no doubt I could have formed a Government, for I should have had at the outset the support of the whole Unionist Party with Lloyd George and his friends in addition. I did not do so for two reasons: First, that I was not at all sure that I was equal to such a position at such a time, and though I should not have hesitated to face it if circumstances had seemed to force it upon me, I did not think that such a situation had arisen[, but rather] that Lloyd George was marked out in the public mind as the alternative to Asquith for the conduct of the war, and though I felt sure that he would have accepted the situation yet I could not refrain from feeling that he would think it a false position, and sooner or later would regret it.
>
> The second and principal reason was that I felt sure that the Unionist Party could be relied upon to support the Government with Lloyd George as Prime Minister, and that I could not rely, as the Unionist head of a Government, on receiving anything like the amount of support from the Liberal Party which there was reason to hope would be given to a Government of which a Liberal was the head by the Unionist Party.[109]

There seems little reason to doubt that with men and circumstances as they then were, his judgement was absolutely correct on all counts.

The two partners – as now indeed they were – left the Palace, each to do his part in forming the new administration. By prior arrangement Bonar Law and his Chief Whip, Talbot, went straight to Balfour to offer him the Foreign Office. It is possible that at Buckingham Palace in the afternoon Bonar Law had hinted that such an offer would be forthcoming; whatever the case, he now required a firm answer. He recalled saying:

'Of course you understand that I have come from Lloyd George to ask you on his behalf to become Foreign Minister.' Mr Balfour rose from his seat, and without a moment's hesitation, said: 'That is indeed putting a pistol to my head, but I say at once yes.'[110]

Bonar Law thought that Balfour, in view of his great prestige, was the most important acquisition for the new Government. Yet Balfour alone did not a Government make: despite what blandishments Lloyd George might muster, no senior Liberals were prepared to join, and Bonar Law had made it clear that Churchill – who certainly would have – continued to be unacceptable to the Unionists. The new administration would have to be constructed largely from among Bonar Law's followers.

Now that he was to be Prime Minister, Lloyd George modified his original vision: in the interests of efficiency the war council and the Cabinet must be one and the same, with all other ministers excluded and subject to its authority. There was another innovation: the membership grew from the original three envisaged, to five. The addition of a fourth man was the price of Labour support, with Arthur Henderson offered a place in the inner circle. Henderson had seemed to be an Asquith man in the crisis but agreed to serve, and after he met Lloyd George on the following day the Labour MPs pledged their support. The fifth member of the council was, in many ways, really second in importance: Bonar Law readily agreed at first to forgo full membership in order to lead the Treasury and the Commons. As we shall see, this proposal survived only a day, and when the Government was announced his name was included as a member of the War Cabinet.

Though Lloyd George and Bonar Law swiftly learned that they would have to depend on the Unionists for experienced ministers, it is also true that they may not have found it so difficult to secure their services as was for many years believed.[111] As early as 5 December Lord Crawford was recording that while Chamberlain seemed disinclined to join a Lloyd George Government, the ambitious Curzon and Cecil were 'anxious to do so as a public duty if required'.[112] Walter Long also sounded quite available when he wrote to a friend on Wednesday, 6 December: 'I don't care who leads, or who composes the Gov. so long as a stable Gov. is set up and this war work is carried on with vigour.'[113]

According to Aitken's version of events, Lloyd George and Bonar

Law 'made no headway' with the senior Unionists on Thursday 7 December and Lloyd George himself was rebuffed by Long.[114] Yet as Long later recounted the story, he met Lloyd George and Bonar Law at the War Office on Thursday morning and was offered virtually any departmental office;[115] accepting readily, he chose the Colonial Office, which he much coveted and Bonar Law hoped never to see again. However, as he revealed to Chamberlain seven years later, Long refused to allow his acceptance to be divulged immediately to the others.[116] On the same day (and without specifically consulting his colleagues), Curzon agreed to join the new War Cabinet and serve as leader in the Upper House. Crawford's pointed comment of two days earlier indicates that few Unionists should have been surprised by this *volte-face*.

Once they had Long and Curzon in the fold, Lloyd George and Bonar Law met them with Chamberlain and Cecil in the early evening, hoping to bring in the remaining 'Two Cs'. It was known that Cecil had already recognized his 'public duty' to serve, and this left only the reluctant Chamberlain – so the meeting was essentially for his benefit. Lloyd George announced that he was considering a War Cabinet of himself, Carson, Henderson and Curzon, all without departmental duties; and that Bonar Law would combine the Exchequer with the Leadership of the House of Commons and attend the War Cabinet *ex officio* only as his time allowed; he also, now, disclosed that Long would take the Colonial Office, and requested that Cecil, Minister for Blockade, and Chamberlain, Secretary of State for India, should retain their portfolios.[117] The discussion – and the revelations – allowed the super-principled Chamberlain to announce his conversion, and all fell into place.[118] Within an hour, all four had formally agreed to serve. Lloyd George had his Government, and hurried to the Palace to inform his uneasy Sovereign.

The Government finally put in place, however, was not precisely as indicated by Lloyd George to Chamberlain and his friends. Though Bonar Law's work-load as Chancellor of the Exchequer and Leader in the Commons would be daunting enough, he and Lloyd George were agreed that it was impossible for him to avoid full membership in the War Cabinet – particularly with such energetic and ambitious colleagues as Curzon and Carson among its members. Bonar Law thus took on no fewer than three demanding jobs.

When the War Cabinet met for the first time on 9 December, yet another surprise was unveiled: not Carson, but the brooding and brilliant figure of Lord Milner joined Lloyd George, Bonar Law, Curzon and Henderson.[119] Carson had ceased to be a co-equal with the other two Government-makers: he had played his part as a catalyst, and the immediate future depended on a partnership of Lloyd George and Bonar Law. Additionally, the 'Three Cs' and Long were not on good terms with Carson; and Bonar Law, by playing a prominent role in crushing Asquith, had restored his own prestige among the Unionist back-benchers and now at least had less to fear from him. King George's most recent biographer has noted that he too had openly opposed Carson's membership in the War Cabinet,[120] while Lloyd George recalled that his inclusion was made impossible by the 'personal prejudices of the majority of the Conservative leaders'.[121] Carson went instead to the Admiralty, where his tenure was undistinguished, while in the place originally intended for him Milner burnished his reputation.

In his Cabinet-making Lloyd George was able to secure the services of several Liberals, though none were of the rank and experience of those who had either turned him down – as did Lord Rosebery, Edwin Montagu and Herbert Samuel – or been black-balled by the Unionists – like the frustrated Churchill. Lloyd George, erstwhile pro-Boer, radical, and scourge of the Lords, now faced his momentous responsibilities with a Government made up largely of Unionists.[122]

While the once-popular fiction that Aitken was the ghost in the machine which destroyed Asquith has now been laid to rest, it is true that he played an important role. He provided the triumvirs with a discreet and willing ear. His houses offered them secure meeting places. He accepted the roles of go-between and 'fixer', and he used his influence in the press in their interest. In his own account of events, Aitken insisted that Lloyd George and Bonar Law had marked him down for the Board of Trade, then snatched the prize away and given it to the businessman Sir Albert Stanley.[123] There is no evidence to substantiate the claim, however, and all prospective lists of appointments which survive omit his name.[124] What he was offered, and accepted, was a peerage.

At the time Aitken had no future in high politics to risk, and Bonar Law wrote to him on the day his barony was proposed: 'I hope you will accept L.Gs [*sic*] offer.' The man repelled by the honours system added as a post-script: 'It would be a delight to me if I felt that this would give you pleasure.'[125] In the end, it did.

The puckish figure of Max Aitken continued to play an important part in Bonar Law's life – as he must in this book – but hereafter he will be known by the title under which he became far more famous: Lord

Beaverbrook. Though he wished it to be thought otherwise, he was pleased by his new status – and Bonar Law was pleased for him.

The un-making of Asquith was neither a palace coup nor 'revolution, British style'. The Prime Minister depended upon the majority of the gentlemen of Parliament, as greater ministers than he had learned in their time. The faith of that majority in Asquith's leadership had been shaken, and the appearance of a logical alternative destroyed him. He might have continued in a position of influence, either as Prime Minister outside a remodelled war council or in a prestigious post under another Prime Minister – certainly Lloyd George and Bonar Law would have been satisfied with either arrangement. He rejected these alternatives, and in doing so shattered his Government and, as it turned out, his party. From this point on he belonged to the past; the central figure of the challenging present was David Lloyd George. He would not, however, have become 'The Man Who Won the War' and made the peace without Bonar Law at his right hand for the next five years.

12

Partnership

I

F<small>OR THE FOUR</small> years which followed the establishment of the new administration, Bonar Law remained its second most important member. In addition to leading both the House of Commons and the Unionist Party and heading the Treasury, as Lloyd George's deputy he often presided over the War Cabinet during the Prime Minister's frequent absences. He was a member of virtually every other important Cabinet committee, and was usually called on to attend even those to which he had escaped appointment. It was an astounding work-load for any one man.

He seldom missed debates in the House, and more often than not was principal spokesman for the Government, as Lloyd George's appearances on the Front Bench also became increasingly rare. Bonar Law was absent only when it was unavoidable; and despite the grinding fatigue to which it led, it was his habit to remain until each day's sitting was adjourned.

Such a demanding regimen took its toll, and Bonar Law's already spare frame grew thinner, his face more deeply lined. The habitual gravity of his demeanour became even more pronounced. Whatever the demands of public life, he had usually slept well – but after the end of 1917, even this gift often deserted him. Despite late nights and long working days, he escaped any serious physical illness, although throughout the War he was disinclined to take any but the briefest of holidays –

and even the bouts of depression which sometimes almost crippled him in 1917 did not keep him away from his work for long. This way of life exacted its price, and the end of the War found him both physically and spiritually close to exhaustion.

In carrying out this gruelling schedule Bonar Law leaned heavily on his personal staff. When he moved to the Treasury he refused to leave behind the indispensable J.C.C. Davidson, despite strong protestations from Walter Long, the incoming Colonial Secretary,[1] Miss Edith Watson, who replaced Miss Tugander as Bonar Law's principal clerical secretary and remained with him for the balance of his career,[2] was also stolen from under Long's nose. Patrick Gower, seconded from the Inland Revenue staff, like Davidson and Miss Watson served Bonar Law until his retirement in 1923. Among the Treasury staff, the new Chancellor came to depend heavily on Geoffrey Fry, who at the end of the War joined Bonar Law's personal staff where he too remained a trusted confidant for the remainder of his master's life.

Ever since his days in the Glasgow Iron Ring Bonar Law had believed that an efficient office functioned best in an atmosphere of trust, and slowly he had come to learn the importance of delegation. The great affection he developed for this small circle was reciprocated, and his refusal to deal with strangers in confidential matters was the stuff of which civil service legends are made. Davidson recalled many years later that, however endearing, such limited vision had its perils for the master of the nation's purse strings:

> Bonar hated new faces, and it was only with the greatest difficulty that I was able to wean him from the appalling habit of telling his official Private Secretaries when they answered the bell that he wanted me. I really believe he thought I alone could fulfill his wishes, but gradually I was able to persuade him that Treasury files were beyond me, and that Their Lordships appeared to cover a field of activity far beyond the intellectual grasp of understanding of an ordinary degree man.[3]

The man whose prodigious talents saved Bonar Law from the dangers lurking among the Treasury files was the ingenious young economist John Maynard Keynes, who soon became another loyal aide. Just thirty-three, Keynes had been plucked from his Cambridge fellowship to head the newly-organized 'A' Division of the Treasury, in charge of foreign finance. The two men were decades apart in age and in what would today be called 'life-style' – on the face of it they seemed an unlikely pair, but they got on well and became fast friends.[4] The young don soon came to admire his new chief, preferring his unembellished manner to that of the more flamboyant Lloyd George. Bonar Law found himself with a new bridge partner and a life-long admirer, while Keynes gained a sympathetic chief and in short order appointment as a Companion of the Order of the Bath, an honour he much wanted and Lloyd George had denied him.[5]

A remarkable example of Bonar Law's confidence in the economist occurred in March 1918. Keynes, learning that the contents of the studio of the painter Edgar Degas were to be auctioned in Paris, went straight to the Chancellor and begged for funds to buy pictures for the National Gallery. Bonar Law cared little for art, but he trusted the young economist's sense of value and immediately provided £20,000 to add to the national collection paintings which are today beyond price.[6]

Bonar Law's former Parliamentary Secretary, John Baird, returning from the Front with the DSO, joined the Government as Under-Secretary at the new Air Ministry. Bonar Law turned instead to a Worcestershire back-bencher little known outside the House: Stanley Baldwin. Like Bonar Law, Baldwin was a wealthy iron merchant; he had stood with his leader during the Nigeria debate, and held the same views during the political crisis of December 1916.[7] Baldwin was well liked in Westminster, and his reputation had been enhanced by his tireless attention to wartime committee work. It probably did him no harm that he too loved his pipe and a good game of tennis; soon after the formation of the new Government he was invited to Pembroke Lodge for a Sunday afternoon's tennis, and the appointment was made.[8]

Baldwin's rise proved to be meteoric. Sir Hardman Lever, the new Financial Secretary to the Treasury and one of Lloyd George's businessmen of 'push and go', refused a seat in Parliament.[9] As a result, Baldwin found himself almost immediately on the Front Bench, to provide the Treasury with an additional voice in the House. Lever soon left for New York to establish the new British War Mission, whereupon Baldwin was promoted to Joint Financial Secretary. Thus began a career in office which was scarcely interrupted for the next two decades. Bonar Law found Baldwin congenial, competent, unaffected and scrupulous; within a very short time he too had become a trusted member of the Chancellor's inner circle.

Bonar Law's private life did not escape change: as Chancellor of the Exchequer he was expected to live at Number 11 Downing Street. He hated alterations to his personal routine, but he and his family soon adjusted to life in the cavernous official residence. After the Asquiths, who had no London home of their own, declined Bonar Law's offer of Pembroke Lodge, the house became a military hospital for the balance of the War.[10] Bonar Law never returned to Edwardes Square, for when he retired from office in 1921 he no longer required such a large house.[11]

With its heavy Victorian scheme of decoration, Number 11 must have been a gloomy place. It was certainly under-occupied by the Law family, with the two elder sons in the Army and the younger boys away at school. Miss Mary Law continued to lead the retiring life she preferred, and Bonar Law's elder daughter, Isabel – still called 'Tizzie' by her father – became a nurse in a London hospital for wounded servicemen. Only eleven-year-old Kitty appears to have much enjoyed the move, as the ample gardens and numerous rooms provided her and her playmates with endless potential for adventure and mischief. Kitty frequently insinuated herself into the company of important callers at Number 11, and became a particular favourite with Lloyd George, his secretary Miss Stevenson, and the Beaverbrooks.[12]

There was another significant addition to the family at about this time. In 1916 Isabel Law brought home and nursed back to health a large black Labrador dog which had been struck on the head by an aeroplane propeller and badly injured. He was named Farman, after the plane's French manufacturer, and became a valued member of the family. Bonar Law was particularly fond of him – he had not enjoyed the companionship of a dog since his New Brunswick childhood – as were the children; but Miss Law, in her capacity as housekeeper, seldom failed to point out that Farman was a considerable nuisance.[13]

Bonar Law bore his new responsibilities in the House with an air of stoical patience which surprised friends and opponents alike who had witnessed the slashing warrior of earlier days. As one contemporary recalled,

> ... the old Bonar entirely disappeared and made way for quite a different person of the same name, who served with the utmost fidelity and success under the very man who had been, but a few years before, his most inflexible political enemy ... [Lloyd George] must often have said to others what he said to me many times in Paris, during his frequent absences abroad on Conferences between 1917 and 1919: namely[,] that he felt he could never have carried on if he had not had the fullest confidence in Bonar's power to manage the House of Commons while he was away.[14]

Many in the Government came to depend on the new Chancellor's parliamentary skill, not least of all the businessmen and academics Lloyd George brought into government who had no experience of the workings of the House. 'When they got into an extra bad tangle,' Arthur Griffith-Boscawen recalled, 'the invariable practice was to send for Mr Bonar Law to get them out of it, and this he always did with consummate skill and in the shortest possible time. When a minister got into this sort of trouble, poor Mark Sykes used to say that he had "done a Bonar" ...'[15]

Bonar Law found the new Government easier to deal with than the old. As Asquith's Colonial Secretary he had been in a decidedly secondary position which did nothing to improve his authority over self-confident Unionists like Curzon or Chamberlain. Even worse, he had hated that Government's desultory style, with which he was neither comfortable nor, he thought, particularly effective. The War Cabinet functioned in a more business-like way: printed agendas were circulated, a professional secretariat under Colonel Maurice Hankey provided the administration with a precise institutional memory, and the impatient Prime Minister sought decisions from his colleagues, rather than debate.[16] Hankey, who had previously little admired Bonar Law, came to change his view: in 1917 he concluded that only when the Chancellor was in the chair did the Cabinet meet his own high standards of efficiency.[17]

As much as anything else, it was the co-operation between Lloyd George and Bonar Law which held this innovative machine together and gave it focus. On most mornings Lloyd George would enter Number 11 through the private entrance from his own official residence and go straight to the Chancellor's study, where he invariably found Bonar Law already at work, engulfed in a thick haze of pipe smoke. The usual practice was for Lloyd George to loose off volleys of military or political strategies, to which Bonar Law would return fire, outlining what were to him obvious weaknesses. If Lloyd George did not always yield, he invariably paid attention to what he called Bonar Law's remarkable 'creative common-sense', describing him as 'the most constructive objector that I have ever known.'[18] In such a way did the two leaders reach agreement on tactics.[19] Of their alliance, Peter Rowland has written:

> Bonar Law ... was theoretically Lloyd George's second-in-command but, in effect, his partner. They proved to be a combination, offering a formula for

success even greater than the one offered by Asquith and Lloyd George during the six years preceding the war. They admired and liked each other and their harmony increased with the passing of the years. It was, in truth, the perfect partnership. So long as they held together, the Government would be invincible.[20]

Bonar Law was fully aware that Lloyd George's new war administration was a personal enterprise to a greater degree than that of any premier since the days of the younger Pitt; and he meant, as he wrote to Long, 'to back him to the fullest extent I can.'[21] Yet he knew too that Lloyd George's enthusiasm and genius could be as destructively explosive as they were creative, and he made it clear to the Prime Minister that he would not hesistate to put the brakes on any strategies he was certain were dangerous. He once joked that his main war work consisted of 'hanging on to the coat-tails of that little man', and on occasion, this was precisely the case.

In the two years which followed, however, Bonar Law held on neither too often nor too tightly. The partners sometimes disagreed – even quarrelled – yet in almost every significant matter affecting the waging of war, Bonar Law supported Lloyd George's final decision, even if he was alone in doing so. Hankey, who was in almost daily contact with both men throughout the War, recalled that this loyalty '... gave Bonar Law an influence over Lloyd George which was wisely exercised and exceeded that of any other member of the Government.' This intimacy, Hankey concluded, was an asset of the greatest importance to the Government, and the nation.[22] Stanley Baldwin called it simply the most perfect partnership in political history.[23]

II

Unlike the Prime Minister, Bonar Law did not emerge from these years with a lofty reputation as a wager of war. His provinces included the conduct of parliamentary business, the management of the largely Unionist Government majority in the House, and the administration of fiscal policy. Financial questions claimed much of his energy in 1917 – as well they might, for the nation's financial vigour was one of the Allies' major weapons.

Britain was the fiscal backbone of the Alliance. Since August 1914 she had been forced to raise enormous sums through taxation and by means of domestic and foreign credit, and to make huge loans to her allies.[24] By the time Bonar Law became Chancellor, 40 per cent of British war purchasing – and a similar percentage of total borrowing – was carried out in North America, while spending by the War and Munitions offices proceeded without regulation by the Treasury.[25] To make matters worse, at the end of 1916 the US Federal Reserve Board tightened credit on foreign borrowers; as a result, Britain was expected to back her loans with gold, and her precious reserves were soon disappearing at the rate of $5,000,000 per day.[26]

The problem of foreign indebtedness dogged Bonar Law throughout his tenure at the Treasury and after. His immediate reply to the American crisis was to increase domestic borrowing, and at the Guildhall on 11 January 1917 he announced a new War Loan campaign to raise £600,000,000 – a staggering sum in those days. This decision initiated a definitive struggle between the Treasury and the Bank of England for primacy over national finance – a dispute in which many presumed the Chancellor to be overmatched by his opponent, the Bank's Governor, Lord Cunliffe. Notwithstanding the centuries-old privileges which made it the Government's banker, the Bank of England in those days was a private company controlled by its directors, or Court, and Governor. Cunliffe had largely had his own way under Asquith, and had secured the additional privilege of meeting the Chancellor only in the presence of the Prime Minister.[27] Convinced that high fiscal matters were beyond the capacity of a former provincial iron merchant, Cuncliffe had no intention now of compromising his control over Britain's international credit.

Governor of the Bank since 1913, Lord Cunliffe was self-confident, even bullying in his manner; and he presumed that Bonar Law would be guided by his advice.[28] He was wrong, however; Bonar Law announced that the new war loan would be floated at 5 per cent – one point below the prevailing interest rate – which Cuncliffe insisted would ensure its failure. Bonar Law believed that patriotism would carry the bond issue in the financial community, and he was proved right: the loan was much over-subscribed, and had raised more than £1,000,000,000 when it closed in mid February.[29]

At a time when Britain was expending £67,000,000 a month in America, even this victory did not win the finance war for Bonar Law.[30] Nor did tensions between the Treasury and the Bank of England end when the United States, exasperated by Germany's submarine campaign, entered the War in April 1917. American financial assistance was now assured, but as a result of the countervailing pressures of short-term needs, and fears of post-war indebtedness, it became all the more important for the Treasury to manage carefully the terms of that indebtedness. In the Chancellor's view, control of British borrowing in America could not continue to be governed by the London Exchange Committee (of Cunliffe, his deputy, and two City bankers) created for that purpose in November 1915. In the Governor's view, it was too important to be in the hands of a Glasgow politician and a Cambridge don.

In April the Chancellor ordered Sir Hardman Lever in New York (as was Cunliffe, at the time) to take control of British financial matters in North America.[31] In the early summer Lever was instructed to support the dollar–sterling exchange only so long as the supply of British-held dollars lasted; thereafter convertibility was to be suspended, Bonar Law's intention being to hold fast to the remaining British gold stores in North America as the Treasury's last liquid reserve there.[32] Furious with this policy, Cuncliffe returned to London in June and protested tactlessly to Bonar Law that the Treasury was interfering with the powers of his Exchange Committee.[33] Convinced that Keynes and the Joint Permanent Under-Secretary at the Treasury, Sir Robert Chalmers, were the malefactors, Cunliffe was resentful when they were not sacked at his demand. He sent Lloyd George an ultimatum: 'I cannot remain a mere figurehead acting under men in whom I have no faith, unless the Cabinet after this warning is prepared to accept the entire responsibility.'[34] But in this he overplayed his hand: by appealing to the Prime Minister over the head of the Chancellor, he had made a test of strength with Bonar Law inevitable.

Nor was it long in coming. A few days earlier the Treasury had ordered that some £17,000,000 in gold deposited in Canada by the Bank of England be placed at Lever's disposal; the Chancellor, aware of Cunliffe's disapproval, wrote to Lever reassuring him of his powers as Financial Secretary to the Treasury.[35] On 5 July Bonar Law was informed that on his own authority as Governor of the Bank Cunliffe had ordered the Canadian Government instead to place the gold at the disposal of J.P. Morgan & Co., Britain's financial agents in America since 1915.[36] Bonar Law summoned the Governor immediately and demanded an explanation. Cunliffe admitted that in the normal course of things he ought to have consulted the Treasury first, but asserted that this 'was not the principle on which we were now working.'

Cunliffe had sealed his own fate, and Bonar Law had reached the end of his very short rope. Immediately he telegraphed to Ottawa and New York to reverse the Governor's decree. Then he presented the Prime Minister with a choice of three solutions to this problem: he offered to resign; or the Governor could retire at once. There was also, he suggested,

> ... a third possible alternative[,] which is that Lord Cunliffe should agree to work with me in a reasonable spirit and with a full knowledge that the Chancellorship of the Exchequer is not in commission and that the views of the British Government, as represented by me, must be carried out ... I am therefore only willing to allow the present arrangement to continue on the condition that Lord Cunliffe sends to me in writing a declaration that he will at once resign the Governship of the Bank of England if he receives a request from me to that effect.[37]

Bonar Law and Sir John Bradbury, the other Joint Permanent Under-Secretary at the Treasury, met the Prime Minister on 13 July to draft a letter of surrender to Bonar Law's terms for Cunliffe's signature.[38] The Governor resisted, appealing to the Prime Minister and to his friends in the City; but they could not save him. Lloyd George admired Cunliffe, but a substitute for him could be found easily enough – Bonar Law was irreplaceable. The Governor, again summoned to Number 11, was required to write out his resignation, which Bonar Law held for future use.[39] Baldwin took control of the London Exchange Committee (it was dissolved in November), and in August 1917 Bonar Law created a committee of Lord Buckmaster, Austen Chamberlain and Keynes to oversee the entire matter of Government expenditure in America.[40] Shortly afterwards, Cunliffe was quietly retired.[41]

Essential though it was, most Exchequer business during the War was devoid of such pyrotechnics as these. In a wartime Government so unusually constituted, even the presentation of the Chancellor's annual budget lacked the potential to enflame the House. Bonar Law's Budget Speech of 1917 announced the greatest combination of expenditure and taxation to date, and his 1918 Budget exceeded even that, yet neither inspired controversy of much note.

During his years in opposition Bonar Law had burnished his reputation as a Unionist champion by savaging the annual estimates of two successive Liberal Chancellors, Asquith and Lloyd George. He faced no similar treatment when he presented his own Budgets. Points were certainly raised, but they were usually uncontroversial and almost always technical – from Labourites seeking greater taxation of what

they considered war wealth, and ever-greater state control over industry; from Liberals and Unionists questioning the wisdom of expenditure on such a scale; and from Unionists and Liberals craving an
explanation for the upward spiral of taxes (increased by some 500 per
cent by the end of the War) and what appeared to them to be naked
confiscation of capital. Bonar Law's major fiscal concerns were not
political – the financial problem which most interfered with his rest
was the unending need to find the funds to pay for the greatest war in
history.

Not the least of Bonar Law's worries was his fear of the corrosive
long-term effects of a mounting national debt. In his desire to minimize
the liabilities to be left to future generations he ensured that Britain paid
a higher percentage of war costs from taxation and lower interest rates
on internal borrowing than did any other belligerent power. Combined
with his incurable habit of speaking his mind, this caused a controversy
which must have left many within the business community – and the
Unionist Party – in doubt as to his economic orthodoxy.

The origins of this largely forgotten episode lay in a private meeting
he had with the Parliamentary Committee of the Trades Union Congress 14 November 1917. With many thousands of their comrades
dying in the trenches, these trade unionists stressed their conviction
that the heaviest part of the fiscal burden of the War should be borne
by the wealthiest part of the population. Bonar Law pointed out that
receipts from indirect taxation had fallen from 42 to 18 per cent of the
state's income, while those from direct taxation, primarily income tax
and wartime excess profit taxes, had risen from 58 to 82 per cent. As to
fortunes increased or created by the War, he indicated that his mind was
open regarding the imposition of a compulsory levy on such accumula-
tions of capital. He spoke plainly to the delegation:

> The question of whether or not there should be conscription of wealth, then,
> is entirely a matter of expediency, and I think it is a matter which concerns,
> mainly, not the working classes, but the people who have money. In my
> opinion, it is simply a question of whether it will pay them best, and pay the
> country best, to have a general capital levy, and reduce the National Debt as
> far as you can, or have it continued for 50 years as a constant burden of taxa-
> tion.
>
> Perhaps I have not thought enough about this to justify me in saying it,
> but my own feeling is that it would be better, both for the wealthy classes and
> the country, to have this levy of capital, and reduce the burden of the
> National Debt. That is my own feeling.[42]

Bonar Law spoke candidly in what he took to be a confidential forum, though he might have expected that his comments would be leaked to the press. And they were, to the worst possible effect: many Labourites were sceptical, while the business community – men hitherto content in the knowledge that the former iron merchant was 'one of them' – were stunned and angry.[43] A Scottish shipbuilder put it simply: 'I read your speech to the Trade Unionists ... and my gullet struck work at once.'[44]

Bonar Law, straightforward as ever, made no effort to deny his comments when the matter came up in the House on 29 December. He explained that whatever passions this particular idea might excite, the long-term fiscal problems resulting from the War required that his mind remain open to all options. To him, it seemed that a single levy on private capital with the object of reducing the war debt had in principle certain advantages over the annual extraordinary taxes being levied on upper incomes. He reminded Members that he had expressed only his willingness to consider the idea, as it was being considered, in one form or another, in all the belligerent nations. Then, with the firmness to which the House had become accustomed, he announced that he would say no more about the subject. His brief closing statement told as much about the man as about the question at hand:

> All I can say is this: I do claim the right to look at any problem of that kind with a perfectly open mind, and if it ever does become a practical question, if I am still in political life I will oppose or support it simply from the point of view of whether I believe it is or is not in the national interest.

Of the episode, Bonar Law wrote to his friend Croal:

> You probably know how this has arisen. In dealing with any political question I have only two methods: one is to say what I think, the other is to say nothing. In this case I thought I was saying nothing because what I said was addressed to a private deputation and hitherto I have had no example of confidence being given away. Of course I should not have dreamed of saying it if I had thought it would have been published, not because I have any hesitation in saying what I think about it but because I do not think the present an opportune time.

Yet, he continued, he had few regrets, and his discomfort was a small inconvenience when compared with his apprehensions as to the stifling effect on economic recovery of the many years of wartime-level income taxes that might be required to retire the war debt. Regardless of the criticism it brought him, he said, the responsibility was his. His last words on the subject were no doubt a comfort:

> I hope, however, that you will not think that even in my own mind I am at all committed to it. All I ask is that it should be treated not as a terrible heresy but as a question to be judged on its merits when the time comes.[45]

Once the War ended, Bonar Law in fact came to the conclusion that a capital levy was a political impossibility, although he continued to believe that abnormally high income taxes – on 'earners' rather than 'owners' – destroyed the creation of new capital and would retard recovery and economic growth. He went on wrestling with the question of war debts long after he had left the Treasury, and he found no solution. The search for an answer was of course destined to be abandoned only after a crippling world depression and another world war – disasters which the Chancellor did not live to see.[46]

By the end of 1917 Bonar Law was beginning to conclude that to combine the Chancellorship with his other demanding responsibilities was all but impossible for any one man.[47] Yet he continued to do so, a hostage to public, political and City confidence, since his reputation as a kind of surety of fiscal good sense rendered him irreplaceable. When the Great War ended, he left the Treasury behind without regret.

III

Bonar Law's many public obligations almost certainly made it easier for him to push his fears for his two soldier sons to the back of his mind. His children brought this retiring man without wife or mistress or any taste for material comforts his greatest personal satisfaction. Like countless other parents, in the terrible year 1917 he suffered losses which almost destroyed him.

In 1915, at the age of eighteen, Bonar Law's second son, Charlie, had enlisted in the King's Own Scottish Borderers. In early 1917 he was posted to Egypt, and on 19 April there arrived at Number 11 the telegram all families dreaded: Charlie was reported missing, following the Battle of Gaza.[48] Bonar Law was devastated by the news: 'When I heard of it,' he later told C.P. Scott, 'I felt at first that I must give up everything.'[49] No more than after his wife's death was he able to draw solace from the Calvinist faith of his fathers, but withdrew into himself: for days his family could not comfort him, and the demands of high office were ignored. Balfour had his philosophy and Churchill his painting, but Bonar Law's few avocations had largely been suspended for the duration. As he had when Annie died, and would again in future, he threw himself even more completely into his work.

There appeared a flicker of hope in mid June, when the Papal Apostolic Delegate in Constantinople forwarded information that Charlie might be a prisoner of war: 'He is a different man since the news came,' a colleague noted.[50] This small hope, however, was cruelly destroyed days later when the report was proved to be false – it was almost as though he had lost the same beloved son twice. Charlie's body was discovered only in late November – still recognizable after so many months because of the dry heat of the desert.[51]

For months afterwards, on the rare occasions when he spoke of the tragedy his characteristic stoicism came close to deserting him, as he struggled to maintain his composure.[52] Long before the horrors of the Great War were even imagined, he had had too much of death in his life. To bury a child, however – a son he was only to coming to know as an adult of great promise – struck him even harder than those other afflictions.

After a week of mourning, he returned to the task in hand; his already extended working day began to grow longer, and he seldom left his room in the House before the small hours of the morning. As Lord Cunliffe was to discover, Bonar Law's personal experience of the dreadful human costs of the War brought out in him an unyielding hardness in his dealing with anyone he judged to stand in the way of a swift and successful conclusion to the conflict.

Many Unionists had similar feelings, and that often made all the more difficult the task of managing the party which supported the hybrid Government. Most of the men who remained behind after their younger party colleagues had joined the Colours could only observe from an impassable distance their brothers and sons at the Front. It should not seem surprising that in their frustration they often became exercised not only over war strategy but also over agriculture policy, House of Lords or franchise reform – and, as we shall see, about the unresolved problem of Ireland. Leading such men was difficult when affairs ran smoothly, but in mid 1917 an unexpected storm broke over

Bonar Law and put his authority to a severe test. The first rumbles were heard in May, when it was rumoured that the Prime Minister meant to find a place in the Government for the Unionists' *bête-noire* – their former colleague who had crossed the floor, antagonist of Home Rule days and architect of the Dardanelles campaign, Winston Churchill.

The irrepressible former minister had returned from active service in the middle of 1916, and by the spring of 1917 had begun his campaign to re-establish himself in politics. At a Secret Session of the House on 10 May held to discuss the conduct and prospects of the War, he made a powerful speech against a further offensive in France and in favour of a holding operation until American forces could be brought to bear. Lloyd George concluded not only that such undoubted energy and brilliance would be an asset to his Government, but that they could become dangerous if Churchill was left with nothing more constructive to do than stir up the listless Opposition – better to gather him in and bind him to the Treasury Bench.

Lloyd George knew only too well that Bonar Law disagreed. The Chancellor remained antagonistic to Churchill – the man he had once described as the 'only Machiavelli in politics' – and was certain that to give him office would be to ignite an explosion among the Unionist rank-and-file.[53] Proof was soon to hand: on 8 June, three hundred delegates at the annual party convention unanimously carried a resolution that the admission of the former First Lord to the Government would constitute nothing less than an insult to the Forces.[54] These Unionists had not forgotten that during the Cabinet-making of December 1916 their leaders had refused to serve with Churchill; on 4 June Curzon had reminded Bonar Law, quite unnecessarily, 'It is on record, and to the pledge I and I think all my colleagues [still] adhere.'[55]

Yet six weeks later Churchill replaced Addison at the Munitions Ministry, and did so with Bonar Law's reluctant imprimatur. Unlike Lloyd George, Bonar Law neither thought Churchill's genius particularly necessary at that juncture nor feared his potential as an adversary of the Government – he stood by the pronouncement he had made to the Prime Minister when the Government was formed: 'I would rather have him against us every time.'[56] When he acquiesced in the prodigal's return, he did so for a different reason.

In mid July, having decided to go forward with Churchill's appointment, Lloyd George sent Beaverbrook to talk Bonar Law round; and Beaverbrook it was who delivered the inflammatory news to the Chancellor on the evening of the seventeenth, thinking silently, 'This will put his pipe out.' Perhaps it did, but Bonar Law did not direct his anger at Beaverbrook: 'Lloyd George's throne will shake,' was his tight-lipped reply.[57]

Beaverbrook also told Bonar Law that Lloyd George was at that moment announcing his decision to the press, which only intensified the Chancellor's anger; once the newspapers had the story, even he could scarcely orchestrate a reversal of the situation. He *could*, almost certainly, bring down Lloyd George by his own resignation – but this, he was well aware, would only put a less capable Government in place. The Unionists were likely to emerge from the resultant election as the largest party, and it was equally likely that Bonar Law would succeed to the pre-miership. He believed, however, that he would not be a better war min-ister than Lloyd George – nor, if he stood aside, would Asquith, or Carson, or any other imaginable alternative. Lloyd George had gone about this business in an unfortunate, perhaps in a sense a cowardly manner; but once he had made his decision public, he had to be allowed to have his way. Bonar Law was angry with his colleague, and the two certainly quarrelled; but in the end he had no choice. As he himself had often said: regardless of all else, it was Lloyd George's Government.

The ancitipated wave of indignation broke immediately over Bonar Law; the back-bench 1900 Club – of which he had been a founding member – passed a unanimous resolution of protest, and on 19 July he received a delegation of the enraged Unionist Business Committee. He was sympathetic to their distrust of Churchill, and told them so. At the same time, however, he defended Lloyd George's right to appoint whom he wished, and spelled out his own responsibility, as Chancellor, to support that right or resign. It was for them to make a similar deci-sion – and if they chose to abandon Lloyd George, he reminded them, then they abandoned Bonar Law as well: he would resign the party leadership immediately.[58]

The threat was real, and it was understood: if Bonar Law could toler-ate Churchill, presumably so could they; and by his firmness the Chancellor made certain that for the time being they would. Never-theless, Bonar Law knew the affair had been costly for Lloyd George and for himself; he wrote to Croal, '... as regards the Government as a whole, and especially as regards the Prime Minister, I confess I am surprised that after six months during which nothing has gone particularly well in the war the unpopularity has not become greater than it is.'[59] Sanders put it more simply: 'our party is sullen and annoyed.'[60]

There were other changes at this time among the political chieftains. Hurt by criticisms contained in a report of the Mesopotamia Commission, Chamberlain characteristically insisted on resigning from the India Office, and Lloyd George took the opportunity to bring another Liberal, Edwin Montagu, into the fold. Dr Addison, making way for Churchill at Munitions, became the first Minister for Reconstruction.

The War Cabinet also saw changes: the Labour MP George Barnes took the place of Henderson, who resigned when he was barred from attending an international socialist meeting in Stockholm; Carson, at best an indifferent first Lord, handed that office over to Sir Eric Geddes and joined the War Cabinet, as did the South African Defence Minister Jan Christian Smuts, bringing the total membership to seven.[61]

The three Liberal appointments were far from popular among Unionists: in addition to their dislike of Churchill, they considered the radical Addison to have been a failure at the Munitions Ministry and foresaw his new Ministry being used as a platform for an expensive programme of social reforms. Montagu was suspect for having clung to Asquith in December 1916, and also because of his enthusiasm for Indian constitutional reform.[62] These appointments added to the resentment on the right wing of the party among those who disapproved of Lloyd George's wrangles with the generals – and, in their hearts, of coalitions, and of radicals. They became increasingly suspicious of their own party leaders, men who were willing to compromise in such matters.[63] Bonar Law's former antagonist, the Die-Hard Page Croft, went so far as to announce the formation of an independent National Party.[64] Supported only by a handful of Die-Hards and extreme Tariff Reformers, and by the *Morning Post* and the *Globe* among the press, he made little impact.[65] Potentially more dangerous were those mainstream Unionists who, while disapproving of Croft's histrionics, thought that positive results from Lloyd George and his Government were long overdue.[66]

The Prime Minister's own frustration equalled that of any of his critics, and was based largely on his disappointment with his own generals. Early in 1917 he had succeeded in mustering support in the War Cabinet for the experiment of subordinating Haig and the British Army to the new French Commander-in-Chief, General Robert Nivelle, in his spring campaign.[67] The plan backfired: Nivelle promised a breakthrough on the Aisne, and failed miserably; all he broke was his own career, and the will of the French to continue for the time being with anything more than an 'active defence'. Haig, now a Field Marshal, was however encouraged by the Canadian success at Vimy Ridge in April and that of the British Second Army at Messines Ridge in June, and began to plan yet another offensive for later in the summer. He was certain that, supported by Robertson, he could break the deadlock on the Western Front.

The decision lay with the War Cabinet, and they relied for advice on the War Policy Committee of Lloyd George, Curzon, Milner and Smuts established in early June.[68] Bonar Law had declined an appointment to the Committee but – predictably – attended most of its meetings. Fruitlessly Lloyd George pressed his own plan, of shifting the centre of attack to the south, against Austria. Several factors tipped the balance in the Committee towards Haig: the military high command were unified behind him and Smuts, the only member with combat command experience, argued that the generals must have their chance. Furthermore, Professor Woodward has written,

> As Robertson had predicted, the civilians, faced with a united front of their military advisers, dared not overrule the technicians of warfare. With great foreboding, they acquiesced ... The majority of the War Cabinet did not believe in Haig's plans. But were Lloyd George's paper schemes any better? That was the alternative with which the ministers were faced if they vetoed the Flanders offensive.[69]

The War Cabinet, including a reluctant Bonar Law, gave way; and so, finally, did Lloyd George. On 22 July Haig's artillery began the bombardment which launched the Third Battle of Ypres, and nine days later the greatest fighting force Britain had ever placed in the field went 'over the top'. After more than three terrible months of fighting, plagued by foul weather, poison gas and a dogged German resistance, the British forces reached the ruins of what had once been the village of Passchendaele – which gave its name to the entire battle. Though they had succeeded in relieving the pressure on the beleaguered French, there had been no breakthrough, and the cost had been numbing: Britain sustained losses of some 300,000 men, the Germans probably as many.[70]

Passchendaele had run only half its dreary course when, in mid September, Bonar Law was notified that his eldest son, Captain James Law, had been reported missing in France.[71] Like many fathers in 1914, no doubt, Bonar Law had counselled caution; but like many sons Jim, then twenty-one, had promptly accepted a commission in the Royal Fusiliers, and was a combat veteran by 1915. (When Charlie, barely out of school, enlisted some months later, Bonar Law was distressed but knew better than to oppose him.)[72] In August 1915 Jim transferred to the Royal Flying Corps to train as a pilot officer.[73] In July 1916 he was injured in a crash during training in Britain, but soon made a complete recovery. On 17 September 1917 Jim's 60th Squadron was posted to France; only three days later, his aircraft was shot down in combat. His body was never identified.[74] With Charlie's death only five months behind him, Bonar Law fell into a deep depression and once again was inconsolable.[75] There were few who cared more for him than Beaverbrook; he suggested that Bonar Law go to France where he could be closer to any news and meet the members of Jim's squadron. It proved to be excellent advice.

Accompanied by Beaverbrook, Bonar Law crossed the Channel immediately. He met Jim's commander, Major Cochran Patrick, and his fellow flying officers. He asked to see an aircraft of the type Jim had flown; shown to a small, battle-scarred plane, he folded himself into its cramped cockpit and sat silent and alone for more than two hours. Then he reappeared, composed and once again resigned. He thanked his hosts, and returned with Beaverbrook to London. He responded gratefully to the many expressions of sympathy which poured in but, as in the case of Charlie's death, hardly spoke of it again until the end of the War.[76] He threw himself once more into his work; when his devotion to his responsibilities was remarked upon, he often replied, 'My sons would have wished it.'[77] One can only begin to imagine the emotional trial he endured in the autumn of 1917 when he accepted the decision of his third son, Tony, to enlist in the Tank Corps and, later, to undergo pilot training.[78]

IV

Bitter and humiliated over his acquiescence in what proved to be the carnage of Third Ypres, Lloyd George planned to gain control over the generals by creating an Inter-Allied Supreme War Council with final authority over strategy.[79] Supported once again by Bonar Law – whose faith in the commanders and in great offensives was gone – he had argued the War Cabinet into agreement with the plan by early November. Similarly, in early December he established a Cabinet Manpower Committee to allocate human resources between the services and necessary domestic industry.[80]

The next element of his plan was the expulsion of Robertson, and this he accomplished in February 1918 – once again with Bonar Law's support. Like Curzon and Balfour, the Chancellor would have accepted a restriction of the powers of the CIGS through a revocation of the 1915 Kitchener–Robertson agreement, but Lloyd George would not have it. 'Wully' dug in his heels at the Prime Minister's proposal to place large reserves of Allied troops under the authority of the new Supreme War Council, headquartered at Versailles, but the first British representative on the Council was General Sir Henry Wilson, who allied himself with Lloyd George.[81] In February Robertson gave in, and his humiliation was deepened when he was replaced by Wilson. Typically, the announcement of the arrangements to the House was left to Bonar Law.[82]

In late November 1917, as the struggle between Lloyd George and his generals was raging, Bonar Law at last chose to face the National Union and confront the disquiet within his party, having resisted the call for a party meeting during the summer at the time when feeling about Churchill's appointment was running high. The new party chairman, Sir George Younger, was in agreement with him on this, observing in October that to have met then would have put the Unionist ministers 'properly in the soup'.[83]

For several reasons the late autumn was a good time for this sobering task: the furore over Churchill had died down, and the results of Third Ypres had subdued the noisiest back-bench supporters of the generals. Another factor was purely coincidental: on 29 November, the day preceding the meeting, the *Daily Telegraph* carried Lord Lansdowne's notorious 'peace letter', which essentially reiterated the message of his Cabinet memorandum of 1916: that victory was beyond the grasp of either side in the Great War, and that continued conflict could lead only to irreparable damage to European civilization. It is unclear whether Bonar Law knew in advance of the publication of the letter – certainly Balfour had seen a draft, but there is no indication that he informed his leader of it.[84] In any event, the letter having exploded into the political landscape, Bonar Law made repudiation of its sentiments a key element of his address to the Union.

This particular meeting was noteworthy in several respects. It was usual for local journalists to be engaged to record the minutes of Unionist conferences, which were then published. The conference on 30 November 1917 was open only to party officers, the parliamentary party and representatives of the constitutuency organizations, and minutes were taken by a Central Office stenographer.[85] Hoping to rally his audience, Bonar Law gave only a brief address, and then took the unprecedented step of opening the meeting to questions from the floor. He was aware that there was discord among the parliamentary party, aware too that this innovative approach had every potential to backfire. In the end, however, his candour and his willingness to come out from behind the dignity of great office carried the day.

The meeting was a great success for Bonar Law.[86] Avoiding any personal attack on his former colleague,[87] he began by making clear his absolute condemnation of the Lansdowne letter.[88] 'I disagree absolutely,' he said, 'not only with the arguments, but with the whole tone of his letter. I think it is nothing less than a national misfortune that it should have been published, now of all times.'[89] So powerful and unambiguous a rejection of Lansdowne's sentiments must surely have been magnified in its effect by his hearers' awareness of his own recent losses.

In responding to questions, he patiently explained the negotiations which had brought the Government into existence, and reviewed the efforts made by Unionist ministers the year before to hasten the introduction of compulsory military service. He reiterated the commitment of the party to Tariff Reform, and expressed his support for the Milnerite strategy of seeking a post-war alliance with the 'patriotic' (i.e., non-socialist and pro-Government) elements among the working classes. Bonar Law once again explained the contentious episode of Churchill's restoration to office and asserted, according to Sanders, that Lloyd George had left him 'a free hand as to [the] choice for Unionist members of the Cabinet and claimed [the] same right for himself.'[90] Finally, he identified the issues he thought would affect the future of the party, advising the delegates that those who opposed the forthcoming Representation of the People Bill, which would radically increase the electorate, were not only wrong but foolish. For the party, survival in post-war years lay in co-operation with the millions of new voters – the sole alternative was extinction. A distinguished observer has noted that:

In this single speech, Law foreshadowed the development of the party for the next fifteen years: the strategic dilemma over relations with other parties after the war, the need to make real concessions to make a coalition workable, the openings that could be created by a national leader of independent reputation . . .'[91]

In party political terms, this was perhaps Bonar Law's most remarkable hour of the War. As the veteran Whip Sanders recalled, 'Bonar was quite admirable. He took the meeting into his confidence and ... spoke quite openly on one subject after another. The effect was excellent.'[92] In his unadorned candour he reduced the distance between leader and followers, earned the overwhelming approval of the delegates, and moved the Unionist Party significantly closer to a more representative and modern style.

V

In the New Year Lloyd George once again stirred up controversy, this time with his decision to bring several of the press lords into the Government. In February Beaverbrook was appointed Chancellor of the Duchy of Lancaster and Minister of Information, while Northcliffe took charge of an independent Department of Propaganda in Enemy Countries.[93] The arrangement was much criticized: Northcliffe wavered, the King strenuously objected to Beaverbrook, and many Unionists, habitually suspicious of powerful newspaper proprietors, complained to their leader through the Unionist War Committee. Following as they did his efforts to neutralize restiveness on the back benches, the appointments undoubtedly left Bonar Law in a difficult position – not least because of his well-known friendship with Beaverbrook; when Chamberlain, who was not in the Government at the time, attacked the nominations, Bonar Law sensed fresh trouble brewing and in his own hand drafted a letter of resignation for Beaverbrook's signature.[94] Beaverbrook's biographer has suggested that Bonar Law 'lost his nerve', and perhaps that was so.[95] However, it is more likely that he loathed the prospect of defending Northcliffe's appointment, yet felt he could not support Beaverbrook's case without inviting unanswerable accusations that he was putting friendship before duty. It was a difficult personal situation, and one which seemed beyond political solution.

Lloyd George and Bonar Law decided to lop the head off a possible anti-press-lord campaign in Parliament by bringing Chamberlain into the War Cabinet in place of Carson – who, always unhappy in office, had conveniently created a vacancy by resigning in January 1917.[96] Though relations between the two had cooled temporarily since Chamberlain's resignation, it was Bonar Law who invited him – successfully – to rejoin the Government.[97]

In March yet another press lord in the Government caused Bonar Law further annoyance. A quarrel erupted between the first Secretary of State for Air, Northcliffe's brother Lord Rothermere, and the Chief of the Air Staff, Sir Hugh Trenchard. Both were rigid men: the general demanded to be consulted, the minister to be obeyed. To no one's surprise Trenchard resigned, on 19 March, and his case was widely supported both in the House and in the anti-Government press.[98] Trenchard was extremely popular among the Unionist back-benchers and Rothermere, foolishly attempting to defend himself by attacking the general, succeeded only in bringing down a storm on his own head. Among his detractors were John Baird, his own Under-Secretary, who threatened resignation; and J.C.C. Davidson, who took the case to the Chancellor. By early April Bonar Law had concluded that Rothermere was a liability to the Government; he therefore, according to Davidson, took matters into his hands and confronted the erring minister – uncharacteristically, over the telephone. In order to save embarrassment to himself and to minimize the damage he had caused, the air minister (Bonar Law inisted) must resign.[99] Such a forthright approach no doubt surprised Rothermere; but in the end he accepted Bonar Law's injunction, and was able to soothe his wounded pride with a viscountcy. Though he wrote a brief letter of thanks to Bonar Law for his 'kindness' in extricating him from the affair, later events suggest that Rothermere nursed some resentment against him.[100]

These disputes were soon pushed into the background. At dawn on 21 March 1918 the Germans launched what was to prove their final offensive. His forces strengthened with fifty-two divisions released from the Eastern Front by the Russian collapse, Ludendorff ordered his 6,000 guns to open against the British Third and Fifth Armies a barrage which exceeded even the awesome displays of 1916 and 1917. This was the great Kaiser Offensive. By mid April Haig was commanding his troops to dig in for what seemed a last desperate defence. Every available man was rushed to the Front, every possible gun and shell delivered to the Army. By June even Sir Henry Wilson's faith was shaken: 'I find it difficult to realize [he noted in his diary] that there is a possibility, perhaps even a probability, of the French Army being beaten. What would this mean? The destruction of our Army in France?'[101] Well might he worry: by this point Haig's forces had already sustained 350,000 casualties, and had fallen back forty miles.

The military drama in France provided the backdrop for the last significant political episodes of Bonar Law's war. Because of the desperate need for military manpower, the first raised once again the issue of the Union with Ireland; the second involved the most serious accusations of his long career against Bonar Law's personal integrity.

The Home Rule Bill of 1914 was a dead letter, and Lloyd George's efforts to broker an agreement followng the 1916 Easter Rising had also failed. In the spring of 1917 he resolved to make another attempt, by means of a convention of representatives of the Irish constitutional parties. In July 1917 the Nationalists, the Ulster Unionists and the Southern Unionists took up the debate at Trinity College, Dublin, with Sir Horace Plunkett in the chair, and the Convention continued to meet until the spring of 1918.[102] Ironically, Redmond – the last great champion of Gladstonian Home Rule – died in March, and the Irish Convention survived him by only a few weeks. The delegates brought forth a compromise plan for a single Irish Parliament, in Dublin – and then dispersed. Their design remained unloved and unimplemented, scorned by fervent Nationalists and Unionists alike.

Now free of the responsibilities of office, Carson once again led the Ulster Unionists, no friend either to the Convention or to their proposal. Since leaving the War Cabinet in January he had repeatedly warned Bonar Law of the Unionist explosion which would occur were he so foolish as to endorse any Home Rule plan before the end of the War.[103] The Chancellor soon realized that he might have to do precisely that.

What brewed up was not simply another Irish crisis, for the Convention's plan appeared as the Allies were reeling under Ludendorff's attack. The Army's needs were paramount, and on 25 March the War Cabinet agreed to expand the available manpower pool. Ruthless 'comb-outs' of exempted men in agriculture and industry were approved, and a new conscription bill was to be introduced to broaden the age limits for service; unlike previous acts, it would apply to Ireland.[104] It was this extension of conscription to Ireland which lay behind Lloyd George's attempt to identify an Irish settlement. He was desperate for men – he hoped to raise 50,000 in Ireland – and in his desperation he was prepared to grasp an obvious nettle: on 5 April the War Cabinet endorsed his plan to combine the new Military Service Act with the promise of swift passage of a new Home Rule Bill.

It was an audacious gamble. On 9 April the Prime Minister announced the so-called dual policy of conscription combined with the pledge of 'a measure of self-government in Ireland'. Only three days later, Haig issued his most famous order of the War: 'Every position must be held to the last man: there must be no retirement. With our backs to the wall, and believing in the justice of our cause, each one of us must fight on to the end.'[105] The new Bill was rushed through all its parliamentary stages in a few days, with Lloyd George's accompanying promise hanging over the Unionists like a pall. The Unionist War Committee met on 16 April: predictably, their support for compulsory service was balanced by their distrust of any wartime Home Rule Bill.[106] The Irish Nationalists, infuriated by what they saw as nothing less than extortion, voted against the Bill in the House and then marched out of the Chamber. In Ireland the Catholic Church, the Nationalists and the revolutionary Sinn Féin party found themselves in agreement in their utter contempt for the new conscription law. A general strike which paralysed commercial activity in the South was the result, demonstrating that, with the exception of Unionist Ulster, Ireland was united in rejection of the 'dual policy'.

On 11 April the War Cabinet authorized the creation of yet another committee to seek a workable compromise scheme. Chaired by Long, who himself disliked the dual Home Rule–conscription policy, they began their work four days later.[107] From the outset it was clear that, influenced by Long and Chamberlain, they leaned towards the old panacea of a federal United Kingdom. The harried War Cabinet took up the question on 23 April.[108] Long and the federalists were opposed by a sceptical Balfour; the argument raged around Bonar Law. His position on Home Rule had changed little from pre-war days: he could accept Home Rule so long as Ulster was excluded, and the rights of Southern Unionists were protected. Federalism no longer seemed workable to him, and he knew that prompt passage of any Home Rule Bill would be dangerous; but he was willing to tolerate either, or both, so long as they did not break apart the Government at this critical point of the war.

Carson was beside himself at what he saw as a threat to Ulster. Writing to Bonar Law on 27 April, he raged against the dual policy, contrasting what was to him the open sedition in the South with the patriotic loyalty of Ulster.[109] He went so far as to threaten to publish his letter. Angered by these implicit intimidation tactics, Bonar Law embraced Wellington's policy of 'Publish and be damned': if Carson insisted on publicity, he could expect a hard-hitting riposte and 'the beginning of conflict between us'.[110] Carson shrank from the battle, and no more was heard of his threat.

In this fractious atmosphere, Bonar Law proposed what seemed to him a realistic solution: in Cabinet on 23 April he suggested that the wisest thing would be to set the problem aside until such time as Long offered up a draft bill. Recognizing a lifeline when they saw it, the Cabinet seized this one. Irish conscription was unenforceable, Unionist suspicions doomed any further wartime consideration of Home Rule: Lloyd George – the author of the exercise – abandoned the matter. Though Long did circulate a draft bill, the War Cabinet decided to postpone consideration of the dual policy until the time was right to implement it.[111] That time, of course, never came. Bonar Law and his colleagues can have felt nothing but relief.

The Chancellor had no time to enjoy his escape from this difficulty. Soon he and Lloyd George found themselves embroiled in a clamorous political controversy which could have destroyed the Government as well as their public lives and reputations. The so-called Maurice affair began on 7 May with the publication of a letter in which the recently-deposed Director of Military Operations, Major-General Sir Frederick Maurice (who had been sacked by Sir Henry Wilson when the latter became Chief of the Imperial General Staff), contended that both the Prime Minister and the Chancellor of the Exchequer had lied in recent speeches in the House.[112] Lloyd George he accused of having knowingly misled Parliament when he said on 9 April that the Army was stronger on 1 January 1918 than it had been a year earlier. Bonar Law, he claimed, had been disingenuous when, in response to a parliamentary question by the Liberal, George Lambert, on 23 April, he said that a recent extension of the British sector at the Front had been agreed between the British and French commanders and not forced upon Haig by the Supreme War Council at Versailles. To a second query, by William Pringle, as to whether 'this matter had been entered into at any time' by the Council, he had responded that 'this particular matter was not dealt with at all by the Versailles War Council.' Referring to Maurice's letter, Lloyd George joked to Baldwin some days later: 'Poor old Bonar, he felt it very much. He doesn't like being called a liar. I don't mind. I've been called a liar all my life.'[113] He was right on both counts.

The origins of Maurice's accusations against Bonar Law lay in a request made the previous autumn by the French, that the British Army relieve them of some of their burden. In September Lloyd George had agreed to this in principle, and in October – before the Versailles Council had come into being – Haig and the French commander, General Philippe Pétain, had settled between themselves that the British would defend an additional twenty-eight miles of the Western

Front, as far as Barisis. While Paris – supported from early winter onwards by the new Supreme War Council – pressed for a greater commitment, Haig, backed by his own Government, would not budge from the agreement on Barisis. Haig's forces made the move, and there the matter rested until the German Offensive began.[114]

Defending this territory fell to Gough's Fifth Army, which unfortunately took the full force of the German assault in March. Haig had agreed to the extension in the first place only because it was difficult to deny the French assistance (their line at the time was more than three times longer than the British); and he feared that if he resisted any change an even less palatable solution might be forced on him.[115] Through March and April the Germans pounded the British Army, and the critics who believed that the War Cabinet had failed to give adequate support to the generals pummelled the Government. To the disgruntled patriots of the right-wing press, responsibility for the peril of the Army lay with the 'frocks', and on 22 March the *Morning Post* openly demanded 'Bring Robertson back'. This was the dangerous climate of opinion in which the Maurice affair was played out.

At the War Cabinet meeting on the morning of 23 April it had been agreed, in preparation for Lambert's question, that Bonar Law should emphasize that the extension of the British line had resulted from agreements 'made entirely by the British and French military authorities',[116] and it was this reply which prompted Pringle's follow-up.

Were Bonar Law's responses truthful? With regard to the extension of the line to Barisis, absolutely: it had certainly been agreed between Haig and Pétain. The veracity of his reply to Pringle about the involvement of the Supreme War Council turns on a technical point: in early February the Council had considered extending the British line, and recommended an extension beyond Barisis. In at least one sense, then, the Versailles Council had indeed discussed 'this particular matter', and thus Bonar Law's remark was less than strictly accurate. There seems to be little doubt, however, that in his reply he was addressing the point regarding the authorship of the extension. Those later deliberations at Versailles changed nothing – Haig and Pétain had made a deal, and Lloyd George backed Haig.[117] Bonar Law had no intention of misleading his interrogator, and gave a truthful answer on a precise point. The object of the parliamentary attack by Lambert and Pringle was to demonstrate that the Government had compelled Haig into over-extending his forces, and were thus responsible for the recent disasters; furthermore, that the Cabinet had starved the British Army of manpower.

These, then, were General Maurice's accusations.[118] At Question Time on the evening of 7 May, Asquith rose to ask a Private Notice Question of the Leader of the House. The subject, of course, was the Maurice letter, and the House held its collective breath. Lloyd George had advised Bonar Law to face the 'miasma of lies' with defiance, but his advice was unnecessary: the Chancellor felt both insulted and infuriated by Maurice's accusations[119] and had already formulated his counter-attack. In the War Cabinet that morning Lloyd George had suggested that the accusations should be dealt with in a statement to the House, followed by a debate. Bonar Law absolutely refused, insisting that 'in his opinion, it was essential that a Judicial Enquiry should be held, as this letter reflected on his personal honour.'[120] Lloyd George's proposal would not do,

> ... as the charges made against the two Ministers were that they had made misstatements, and if their defence was only to be made in the House of Commons, when General Maurice, who had made the charges, could not be present, it would be considered that an *ex parte* statement only had been made.

Bonar Law had not lied, and he refused to deflect the accusations with political argument; he meant to have his name cleared. He demanded a judicial enquiry – a Court of Honour of two senior judges – into the matter, to report within one week. The Cabinet preferred Lloyd George's plan, but Bonar Law would not be dissuaded. Finally, having agreed that the only other alternative – a House Committee of Enquiry – was unacceptable, they uneasily acceded to Bonar Law's demand.[121]

That evening, in response to Asquith's barb, Bonar Law put forward the proposal he had wrung from the War Cabinet – and it was categorically declined by the former premier, supported strongly by, of all people, Carson.[122] Historians have sometimes suggested that in insisting on a judicial enquiry Bonar Law blundered, in the heat of the moment. He did not: rather, in his indignation he was determined upon an honourable strategy, but one so politically dangerous that Lloyd George, Balfour, even Churchill had begged him to abandon it. There was little reason for the two coalition leaders to fear a debate on the accusations: among the greatest parliamentary tacticians of their time, they were backed by an overwhelming majority and would be armed with data amassed by the resourceful Hankey. Yet Bonar Law could not bear the idea of entrusting his honour to a political debate. It would not be enough to win such a debate; he wanted it proved, as he believed it would be, that he had been falsely accused.

In the end, it was Asquith who blundered. In refusing to agree to a judicial enquiry (disdaining even Bonar Law's offer to allow the Opposition to choose the judges), he threw away any chance there might have been of putting the ministers in the dock. In a sense, Bonar Law's demand was for Asquith a lifeline – perhaps unwisely thrown. Had he accepted it, the Chancellor would assuredly have emerged from the episode unscathed – but some of the mud of the accusations might well have stuck to Lloyd George, whose own case was not so iron-clad.[123] At the very least, a judicial enquiry into the veracity of the nation's two most powerful men might have damaged the Government's credibility. As it was, Asquith swept this opportunity aside. He demanded instead the appointment of a Select Committee of the House; when Bonar Law refused, he announced that he would offer a resolution to create one. He was promised his debate two days hence.

Lloyd George's enemies in this contretemps were an odd collection with little in common: the Asquithians; a clique of right-wing Unionists (supported by their friends in the press) who believed that the Prime Minister's amateur strategy-making was damaging the war effort, and had not forgiven him for removing Robertson; and the former member of the War Cabinet Sir Edward Carson, trailing behind him a long list of grievances which included the recent muddled Irish negotiations and Lloyd George's treatment of senior generals and admirals. Their fortunes hung on two questions: could it be proven that Lloyd George and Bonar Law had lied to the House? And could anyone offer a credible alternative Government? In the end, the answer to each was 'No'.

The Unionist War Committee met on 8 May to discuss their position; the coalition was doomed if they were to turn solidly against its two senior ministers. Lord Salisbury, Carson, or H.A. Gwynne and the *Morning Post* might perhaps have been willing to stomach the return of Asquith, the only alternative Prime Minister – but these Unionist back-benchers would not.[124] The meeting rejected Carson's inflammatory proposal for neutrality on the Asquith resolution; and Amery recorded that following heated speeches, the majority were agreed: 'whatever happened, we were not prepared to let Asquith come back.'[125]

The debate in the House on the late afternoon of 9 May disappointed those hoping for a classic battle of parliamentary giants. Asquith's speech lacked fire and conviction. Veering away from his best ammunition, Maurice's accusations, he avoided too the obvious fact that he had engineered what was in effect a vote of confidence in the Government, and merely spoke to the virtues of a Select Committee.[126] Nor was Bonar Law up to his usual fighting standard. Speaking only briefly, and reflecting his sense of injury and outrage, he confined himself largely to addressing Asquith's motion for a House Select Committee. By prior agreement, the main defence of the Government was left to the Prime Minister.

The day belonged to Lloyd George. There was in the end no 'Maurice debate': what the packed House witnessed was a stunning solo display by the greatest rhetorician of his age. He thundered that Bonar Law had in no way misled the House in April regarding the extension of the British line, and that the transfer of responsibility had been agreed between Allied commanders before both the creation of the Supreme War Council and the onset of the German offensive. Eyes blazing, he pounded his fist into his open palm and declared that 'There was not a single yard taken over' as a result of deliberations at Versailles. As for Maurice's infamous letter, he demolished both the undisciplined general and his charges by pointing out – with something less than complete candour – that the figures he had cited in the House on 9 April had been provided to the Government under Maurice's authority during his tenure as Director of Military Operations.[127] Then he played his trump card: regardless of Asquith's attempt to evade the issue, the House faced a vote of confidence against the Government. Those who marched into the 'Aye' lobby, he declared, were publicly committing themselves to replace the Government with one made up of the Opposition. Beside that fact, all argument paled.

The debate lasted less than three hours; when it was over, one observer noted, 'You couldn't find [Asquith] with a magnifying glass.'[128] For the first and last time he had divided the House against Lloyd George's wartime Government – his resolution failed by 295 votes to 108, and the Liberals never recovered. Carson returned eventually to the Unionist fold, and the anti-Lloyd George, pro-military faction in the House were humiliated. Bonar Law's integrity was never questioned again.

Few observers in Britain could have guessed that as this parliamentary fracas was being fought out, the Great War was drawing to a close. Though his men fought on for three more months, Ludendorff's gamble had failed. The German offensive stalled in early June in the Nyon–Montdidier sector, and failed utterly on the Marne in mid July.

The initiative passed to the Allies, and Rawlinson's Fourth Army broke the German line at Amiens on 8 August, 'the black day of the German Army'. It was the beginning of a very sudden end: the later success of German myth-makers notwithstanding, only the Armistice saved them from being completely crushed.

The governments of the Central Powers were everywhere in collapse. Military and political victory seemed complete for the Allies, as the greatest conflict yet known came at last to an end. Yet even before the triumphal ceremonies had begun, the problems of reconstruction and recovery were already demanding the attention of Britain's leaders. His country, his Party, and certainly Lloyd George expected that Bonar Law would bear a great part of the burden. Only those closest to him understood that, like so many of his countrymen, he was close to exhaustion.

13

The Challenge of Peace

———————•————————

I

THE STRAIN ON Bonar Law of the war years was obvious, and by late 1918 some of his friends feared he was close to collapse. In September he travelled to Danny Park, Lord Riddell's house in Sussex, for a meeting of senior ministers. Riddell noted in his diary that 'Bonar Law is very broken and obviously on the edge of a breakdown.' Lloyd George added more detail: 'He won't go for a holiday. He does not even care for golf or bridge. He just reads and smokes and works.' With tears coursing down his cheeks, Bonar Law himself admitted to Riddell, 'It is useless to conceal that I am nearly at the end of my tether.'[1]

Soon after Armistice Day, the Liverpool Unionist leader Archibald Salvidge met Bonar Law at 11 Downing Street. In the distance they could hear a military band and a cheering crowd. Salvidge later recalled:

> Suddenly I realized that Bonar Law was crying. He put his head in his hands and a sob shook him. I was terribly moved. I patted his shoulder and said, 'For God's sake, don't give way like that. The Empire still needs you. Your work is not finished yet. The strain must have been unbearable, but you helped to deliver your country.'

Bonar Law had said little of his personal losses in the War. Now, to this old companion, he spoke of the death of young men in battle and the tragedy of those left behind; of his own lost sons, the ambitions he had had for them, and what they would not live to see. Of himself he admitted:

> This is what the victory means to me – time for a moment to mourn my dead. You are an old friend ... I have had some great sorrows. It has done me good to speak of these things.[2]

Yet, like so many others at this time, he pulled himself together. Although he regularly scoffed at those who insisted he was indispensable, he was certain that important tasks lay ahead for the Government, and that much would be expected of him. He believed the greatest work would be demanded of Lloyd George, and that to abandon him at this point was unthinkable. He had also concluded that it was nothing less than a national necessity that his party should hold fast to the coalition and to the Prime Minister, and that it fell to him to ensure that it did so.

He did suggest to Lloyd George that now was the ideal time for the two of them to retire and leave the treaty-making to others, but it is unlikely that he expected to be taken seriously.[3] So, despite his fatigue and spiritual desolation, for the next two and a half years party leadership once again became Bonar Law's principal responsibility. It is difficult to avoid the conclusion that, quite apart from the promptings of conscience, he equated inactivity with the melancholy which never now seemed far away.

As early as March 1918 the Lloyd George Liberals and a Unionist committee led by Bonar Law had begun in private talks to consider arrangements under which the coalition partners would co-operate in the impending election campaign.[4] By July a plan had been proposed to set aside a certain number of constituencies for the Prime Minister's followers, but Bonar Law was reluctant to reveal any details of these preliminary discussions to his party at this point.[5]

His reasons are not difficult to discover: he was convinced that it would be a grave mistake to allow 'the little man to go',[6] but certain senior Unionists, among them Long and Derby, were less so.[7] Even Sir George Younger, who favoured it, feared party criticism of any apparent rush into electoral co-operation.[8] Further on the political right, Selborne, Midleton and Salisbury represented pockets of resistance; and Page Croft's 'cave' of Die-Hards had already declared a rather shaky autonomy. Such familiar issues as House of Lords reform, tariff policy and Welsh Church disestablishment were divisive so long as they remained unresolved; and the unsettled Irish question continued to dominate the minds of Unionists in Britain and Ireland.

In September at Danny no conclusion had been reached on the election question, and a week later Bonar Law wrote at length to Balfour: while it would be unjust to accuse the Asquithians of failing to support the war effort, he reasoned, the Maurice affair demonstrated that they were 'taking every opportunity of attacking the P.M. Looking at it entirely from this point of view, therefore, I do not think he would be wrong in having an election as soon as possible, but our position is more difficult.' Following a coalition victory, the 'old questions' would demand immediate attention, and the Unionist leadership would be well advised to have their responses prepared. Bonar Law's first priorities included the tariff question and the future of the Welsh Church; then there were thornier matters still: 'Questions of this kind are, for example, land, [the] liquor trade and the general conditions of industrial life.'[9]

Nevertheless, the life of the Parliament elected in December 1910 having been prolonged by special legislation during the War, a prompt election was necessary, and the Unionists were in a position to extract considerable compromise from the Lloyd George Liberals. Bonar Law believed that if nature were allowed to take its course, Lloyd George would inevitably become another Joe Chamberlain – a partner inseparable from the Unionists, but with no Salisbury to block his way as leader. This, he confided to Balfour, was perhaps not a 'bad thing for our Party and a good thing for the nation.'

Yet, Bonar Law continued, he was convinced, in the first place that he could not long delay reaching a decision on the election question; and in the second that the old Toryism of land and deference had little future in a post-war world, where 'a rational solution' to Britain's problems would be found only in co-operation between practically-minded Unionists and coalition Liberals. Failure to forge such an alliance, he believed, would drive the coalition Liberals into partnership with the socialists: the Unionists, therefore, had to hold to Lloyd George.

By mid October party negotiators had concluded that Lloyd George's followers might contest 150 seats without official Unionist opposition; but agreement to lay aside the old battles came harder. When the divisive question of import duties threatened to derail co-operation, Carson stepped in. At his lawyerly best, he arranged an agreement between Lloyd George and Bonar Law under which economic development could be emphasized in the forthcoming campaign without resort to the old fighting terms 'Free Trade' or 'Tariff Reform'.[10]

Yet the compomise remained fragile, and nearly collapsed altogether on a quite unrelated issue. Lloyd George, judging him to be hopelessly incompetent, wished to be rid of the Unionist President of the Local Government Board, William Hayes Fisher, and on 28 October angrily decided to sack him. Bonar Law saw the inflammatory text of the letter Lloyd George intended to despatch; he was able to intervene and save the condemned minister's feelings, but warned him to prepare for the worst.

Hayes Fisher was popular within his party, and complained loudly of his treatment: Bonar Law was soon faced with the prospect of party revolt in the top ranks. Letters and telegrams supporting Hayes Fisher poured in to Number 11, and final agreement on the coalition election appeared to be in danger of collapse.[11] As a Unionist, Hayes Fisher was technically Bonar Law's appointment; yet the Chancellor accepted that no premier could lead a Government from which he was unable to dismiss ministers in whom he had lost confidence.[12] What was wanting was discretion, so Bonar Law orchestrated an exchange of painfully correct letters between Lloyd George and Hayes Fisher, and the latter's temporary, face-saving transfer to the Duchy of Lancaster;[13] finally he was placated with a peerage, and a lucrative seat on the Suez Canal Company board.[14] Political equilibrium was restored, and Lloyd George was rid of Hayes Fisher with the parting shot to Bonar Law: 'The P.M. does not mind if he is drowned in Malmsey wine, but he must be a dead chicken by tonight.'[15]

Having prevented this row from derailing the negotiations for coalition co-operation, on Friday 25 October Bonar Law obtained the agreement of his senior Unionist colleagues to a coalition election campaign, and a joint Unionist–coalition Liberal election committee was appointed. Two days later the Cabinet gave formal approval.[16] The Labour Party, optimistic about their future and wary of being tied to Lloyd George's chariot, had long made it clear that they wanted nothing to do with any future coalition.[17]

In their negotiations the Unionist and Liberal leaders had found much common ground: there was little controversy, for example, over the inclusion of progressive-sounding declarations regarding education, taxation, housing and public health.[18] Hoping to scotch any wrangling over more divisive questions, Bonar Law seized the initiative by drafting a letter for the Prime Minister's signature setting forth terms for electoral co-operation. The draft letter was dated 2 November, and Lloyd George took it with him as he departed for Paris, leaving his fledgling coalition Liberal organization under Bonar Law's command.

The premier agreed to the terms of the document without alteration, and on 8 November Bonar Law convened the senior Unionists to secure their adherence.[19] He read out his draft, which called for co-operation in the election 'of candidates who undertake to support the present Government not only to prosecute the War to its final end and negotiate the peace, but to deal with the problems of reconstruction which must immediately arise directly an armistice is signed.'[20]

The Unionists had every reason to be pleased with Bonar Law's letter: the coalition's first commitment, it declared, was to the 'unity and development of the British Empire'. To this was linked commitment to 'the imperative need for improving the physical conditions of the citizens of this country through better housing, better wages and better working conditions.' The path to achievement of these laudable goals was 'pure Bonar':

> In the first place[,] in regard to economic policy: I have already accepted the policy of Imperial preference as defined in the Resolutions of the Imperial Conference, to the effect that a preference will be given on existing duties and on any duties which may subsequently be imposed. On this subject I think there is no difference between us. I have at the same time stated that our policy does not include a tax on food, but that it does not of course interfere with the granting of a preference on any article ... on which, for our purposes[,] we have imposed a duty.

This was, of course, the core of Bonar Law's 1913 escape from the onus of 'food taxes'; the conclusion of the coalition's electoral policy on economic development was equally familiar:

> As regards other aspects of this problem, I am prepared to say that the key industries on which the life of the nation depends must be preserved. I am prepared to say also that in order to keep up the present standard of production and develop it to the utmost extent possible, it is necessary too that security should be given against the unfair competition to which our industries have been in the past subjected by the dumping of goods below the actual cost of production. Beyond this I should say that we must face all these questions with new eyes, without regard to pre-war views or to pre-war speeches ... without any regard to theoretical opinions about Free Trade or Tariff Reform.[21]

In his draft Bonar Law trod lightly around the subject of Ireland, and fell back on the old plan of Home Rule combined with exclusion for the North. He thought, however, that moving forward with such a scheme 'must be postponed until the condition of Ireland makes it possible.'

The letter also indicated acceptance of the 1914 Act disestablishing the Church of Wales, but embraced the plea of the Welsh bishops that the impending penury of their Church deserved amelioration. While this disappointed the party's High Churchmen, the majority of Unionists agreed with Bonar Law that, while Welsh priests must not be driven out into the road to beg, the Church (like the three remaining Welsh Unionist MPs) would simply have to adjust.[22]

Bonar Law's letter put these words into the mouth of the Prime Minister: 'I am prepared at once to agree that the election should be contested on the basis of this letter, and after you have consulted with your colleagues I should be glad to know definitely whether we may consider an arrangement on these lines as concluded.' The Unionist ministers agreed, and Younger wrote to Bonar Law later that day: 'no one can ever accuse you of not having thoroughly safeguarded the party interests.'[23]

On 5 November 1918 the King had granted a dissolution, and the eight-year-old Parliament was finally at an end. On 12 November the two coalition parties held separate meetings to put the seal on their collaboration. At the Connaught Rooms Bonar Law read out the Lloyd George letter as the basis for continued coalition, and there followed unanimous endorsement of Balfour's motion of confidence in both the leader and his message.[24] Many Unionists were displeased to learn subsequently that at the coalition Liberal gathering Lloyd George had made only a passing reference to 'his' letter of compromise while putting a decidedly traditional Liberal twist into his remarks – all promptly leaked to the press.[25] To heal wounded feelings, a widely-publicized joint coalition meeting was staged on 16 November, addressed by Lloyd George, Bonar Law, and the coalition Labourite George Barnes. The 2 November letter was made public, and the coalition manifesto based upon it was distributed.[26]

His part in these arrangements and in the election campaign itself has brought much criticism down on the head of Lloyd George.[27] At its heart were the so-called 'coupons', letters of endorsement signed by the party leaders which were sent to approved coalition candidates.[28] Bonar Law's actions have caused less dispute: he insisted to his followers that the independence and identity of their party were not in question and, in the end, made a reasonable and profitable bargain for the Unionists.[29] Of the 531 'couponed' candidates, 362 were Unionists and most of the balance were Lloyd George-ites.[30] In a few constituencies (where

Unionists thought they were being asked to surrender certain victory in favour of a 'couponed' Liberal) local Unionist resistance prevented recognition of the 'coupon' candiate, while in others, as Professor Ramsden has pointed out, 'It was only the fear of Labour and strong pressure from Central Office, including the withdrawal of financial aid, that kept the local parties in line ...'[31] Most Unionists, however, apparently accepted the reality of the situation – or at least maintained a discreet public silence regarding their misgivings. Like Bonar Law, they believed that Lloyd George's popularity in November 1918 was an undeniable electoral advantage.

For the first time polling was confined to one day – 14 December. The preceding three-week campaign – at least, as conducted by the leaders – was not quite so bloodthirsty as legend would have it. Neither Lloyd George nor Bonar Law called for the Kaiser to be hanged, as tradition relates, though such sentiments were not doubt felt, if not invariably expressed, by many candidates in all parties.

His old constituency of Bootle had been disadvantageously divided as a result of the new franchise act, so Bonar Law returned to Scotland, to contest the new district of Central Glasgow.[32] Most of his electioneering was confined to the very opening of the campaign and to the eve of polling, for he was struck down by what was probably a relatively mild case of the murderous influenza which killed more than 150,000 Britons (and tens of millions world-wide) in the winter of 1918–19.

This was a milestone election: the 1918 Representation of the People Act had enfranchised most men over 21 and women over 31, and more than 10,000,000 voted. Despite his illness and his therefore limited campaigning, Bonar Law's own contest resulted in the annihilating defeat of his Labour opponent, D.J.M. Quin, by 17,653 votes to 4,736. Results overall were nearly as agreeable: the coalition returned 335 Unionists, 133 Liberals and 10 Labourites (or National Democrats, as the coalition Labour MPs came from this point to call themselves) holding the 'coupon'. In addition, the Government could generally count on the support of 23 un-couponed independent Conservatives and 25 Irish Unionists. The Opposition side was divided, with 63 Labourites, 28 Asquithian 'Wee Free' Liberals, 7 Irish Nationalists and a smattering of independents. Members of the revolutionary Sinn Féin organization won 73 Irish seats once held by Redmond's Nationalists, but they refused to take their places in the House. In practice the Opposition totalled little more than 100, led for the first time by Labour.

It was with relief and gratitude that Bonar Law now took on the largely ceremonial office of Lord Privy Seal, surrendering the Treasury to Chamberlain; to the new Chancellor's annoyance, however, he did not vacate 11 Downing Street.[33] His other important offices – *de facto* deputy premier, Leader of the House and Leader of the Unionist Party – he of course retained, and in effect took charge of the Government while, peace-making in Paris, Lloyd George 'practically disappeared from domestic politics.'[34] Even after the treaties had been completed months later, the Prime Minister's appearances in the House continued to be infrequent, and Bonar Law remained the visible head of the machinery of government.

The Peace Conference began soon after the election, and Bonar Law was of course designated a member of the British delegation.[35] With himself, Balfour, Bonar Law and Barnes scheduled to be in France for an extended period, Lloyd George wished to suspend normal cabinet government during the peace-making, and Bonar Law to divide his time between Paris and the supervision of ministers in London. As it was, Bonar Law's membership of the British delegation proved little more than nominal, since his responsibilities as functional head of the Government required him to spend most of his time in London.

Lloyd George's dubious plan did not survive a furious challenge by Chamberlain, and in early January Bonar Law suggested that the pre-election War Cabinet might simply be left in place.[36] In practice Lloyd George's scheme prevailed none the less, for its absentees left the War Cabinet no more than a rump, and Bonar Law soon fell into a routine of consulting with Lloyd George in Paris, then hurrying back to London to communicate their conclusions to the various ministers. War Cabinet meetings, such as they were, usually consisted of Bonar Law, Curzon and Chamberlain discussing with various interested ministers decisions the Prime Minister and the Lord Privy Seal had already made. As he had begun to do in 1917, when time was one of the things he had too little of, Bonar Law (usually helmeted, and swathed in a fur-lined leather flying suit) made many of these journeys by aeroplane, which earned him the unsought distinction of being the first British statesman regularly to employ air transport.

This peculiar form of governance could not long survive the Peace Conference. Lloyd George had to abandon his hopes for a streamlined administration modelled on the War Cabinet, and normal government was reinstated in October 1919 – to Bonar Law's immense relief. His senior Unionist colleagues in the new twenty-one-member Cabinet included Chamberlain; F.E. Smith (now Lord Birkenhead) as Lord

Chancellor; Milner as Colonial Secretary; and Long as First Lord of the Admiralty. Crawford became Chancellor of the Duchy of Lancaster; Robert Horne, Minister of Labour; Sir Eric Geddes, Transport Minister; and Lord Lee, Agriculture Minister. Curzon became Foreign Secretary, and Balfour Lord President of the Council. Among the Liberals, Churchill took the War Office (combining it with the Air Ministry); and Dr Addison the new Ministry of Health. H.A.L. Fisher remained at Education and Montagu at the India Office, while Barnes continued as Minister without Portfolio. Shortt passed the poisoned chalice of the Irish Chief Secretaryship to Ian MacPherson and became Home Secretary. The former CIGS, Sir John French, had been created Viscount French of Ypres in 1915 and now entered the Cabinet as Lord-Lieutenant for Ireland.

The coalition was a curious conglomeration which required close watching by the Leader of the House. While friendly relations, made easy by wartime co-operation, prevailed at the top levels,[37] there were age-old reasons for Liberals – even Lloyd George Liberals – and Unionists to be suspicious of one another. Questions of fiscal and social policy, quite apart from the unsolved Irish question, always held the potential to divide them. Tradition also played its part: some coalition Liberals longed for reunion with the Asquithian remainder, while there were Unionists who – like Lord Raglan, reputedly referring to the Russian enemy in the Crimea as 'the French' – continued to distrust their Liberal allies as a matter of course.

Many of these men particularly distrusted Lloyd George. He may have been 'The Man Who Won the War', but they were true Tory blue at heart. Nothing less than a full-dress conversion on the part of the former radical could make them love him – and perhaps not even that. Bonar Law valued Lloyd George's personal friendship, admired his genius, and remained convinced that only he could lead a credible Government at this time. Yet he was equally convinced that the day was not long distant when Unionists would be called upon to steer the nation away from the false path leading towards socialism. He meant to ensure that the party was both strong and independent when that day arrived.

II

Few Governments in British history had faced a greater panoply of challenges:

... the problems of demobilization; of brief boom and rapid slump; of whether or not, and how, and how fast, to dismantle wartime controls; of how to cope with the intellectual and social ferment stirring in the Labour movement and among the industrial workers; of violence in Ireland, Egypt and India; and the complex tasks of reconstruction in Europe and the Middle East after the simultaneous collapse of all the world's greatest land-empires.[38]

Yet peace was the first priority, and on 28 June 1919, the fifth anniversary of the Sarejevo murders, Allied and German representatives gathered in the magnificent Hall of Mirrors at Versailles to sign the most important of the Paris treaties. Precisely at three o'clock in the afternoon the brief ceremony began, and Bonar Law added his signature to the document just below that of Lloyd George. As soon as the ceremony ended he took his leave of the Prime Minister and made for the door, Davidson energetically opening a way through the crowds – pausing in the struggle only long enough to discover that their hats had been stolen. Within the hour, however, they were in an aircraft bound for London. Though there were more treaties to be signed, the Lord Privy Seal was to find he had no more time to devote even to the ceremonial aspects of peace-making. At home, the politics of the post-war period had begun in earnest.

In his few interventions in the election campaign Bonar Law had endorsed both the culpability of the Kaiser – if not his hanging – and the obligation of Germany to pay just reparations to her enemies. At Versailles the Kaiser was soon forgotten, but the other matter was enthusiastically supported: an Inter-Allied Reparations Commission was to be created to deal with the question of how much could and should be paid. Bonar Law had acquiesced in the appointment of both a Treasury committee (which took its lead from Keynes) and an advisory commission of bankers from the Allied Powers (Lloyd George's choice as principal British representative was Lord Cunliffe, now considered to be rehabilitated). The expression of polarized opinions which inevitably accompanied any mention of reparations ensured that the two committees disagreed fundamentally, with estimates of what Germany could pay ranging from Keynes's £3 billion to Cunliffe's £24 billion.

Bonar Law's view was that the Germans owed a great debt for a war caused largely by their ambitions, but also that European recovery required an economically sound Germany. He thought the best path between these two undeniable facts lay in presenting the Germans with a reasonable total sum representing their indemnity, payable in annual increments of perhaps three hundred million pounds, to be raised through the sale of bonds.[39] He became, therefore, a 'notable force for moderation' within the British delegation.[40] Regrettably, Lloyd George's own resistance to immoderate demands deteriorated in the face of the righteous anger expressed by the French and Belgians, and the ravings of the popular press at home; and Bonar Law left the Government before a policy had been firmly settled. There is no evidence that he was determined to flex all his political muscles to ensure that Britain should spare nothing to force a temperate settlement. While Bonar Law would have been startled to hear that in three years he would be premier, he would not have been surprised to learn that the reparations issue would be waiting for him – still unresolved.

Among Bonar Law's concerns in domestic politics – shared by all in his party, and by many other Britons besides – was the sudden rise of the Labour Party and of trade union discontent following the hard years of war. The new party was committed to a socialist programme, including the nationalization of industry – alike odious to Bonar Law. Though in Britain there was no 'Red Scare' on the level of that in America, there was much anxiety as the newspapers described in lurid detail the excesses of the new Russian Soviet regime and of leftist uprisings across central and eastern Europe.

However, the seeds of workers' restiveness in Britain were more practical than ideological. Demobilization deranged the labour supply; raw materials and industry had been ruthlessly geared to war needs while traditional British export markets had fallen to other nations. Post-war demand for goods created an immediate inflationary impetus, and prices rose more quickly than wages. This false boom crashed most cruelly in 1920, when the first signs of deflation and of an economic slump were characterized by widespread and extended unemployment. While the Prime Minister had promised a 'fit land for heroes', the economic orthodoxy of the day stipulated that the correct treatment was a return to the old ways of the market place – to reduced taxation and expenditure. Understandably, many workers turned to traditions of their own – to confrontation, and the threat (and, in many cases, the reality) of labour stoppages.

The miners, railwaymen and transport workers had reforged their pre-1914 trade union Triple Alliance at the close of the War; the Government feared a great national strike movement to solidify and improve upon the gains made during wartime, and evidence on which to base such fears was not lacking. In September 1918, even before the Armistice, Bonar Law had met union leaders and played a key role in averting a national rail strike;[41] but he was unable to prevent bitter and sometimes violent work stoppages in his own Glasgow in January 1919. The War was over, yet troops with bayonets were parading in his home city.

Unlike Churchill (at that time, if not later in his long career), Bonar Law had no faith in the power of the nationalization of industry to cure the ills either of workers or of business.[42] He overruled the suggestions made by Churchill during the election campaign for nationalization of the railways; and, having publicly committed the Government to abide by their findings, he was relieved by the garbled advice regarding state ownership of coal mines offered in June 1919 by the Sankey Commission.[43] Veteran of the Glasgow Iron Ring he might be, but he was no economic reactionary: on 4 February 1919 he told the War Cabinet that in the labour disorders of that strike-plagued year, the trade unions might well have been the only thing standing 'between us and anarchy'.[44] Yet he also thought that if met, the miners' demands for a 30 per cent wage rise combined with a six-hour day and nationalization of the pits would prove economically ruinous. Though he was willing to meet the miners' leaders privately in order to seek a compromise, he told the Cabinet that he was not opposed to freezing union funds in the case of illegal strikes.[45]

Late 1919 brought a major rail strike and 1920 witnessed further stoppages in the mines; both actions were settled with limited gains for the strikers. Lloyd George's announcement that mines and railways were to be handed back into private control, coupled with the mine owners' decision that the slump in coal exports necessitated a drop in wages, led the miners to strike on 1 April 1921. There was fear of a general strike, but the miners' partners in the Triple Alliance shrank from confrontation, and the coal strike movement abated, nor did it recur during the remainder of Bonar Law's career. The TUC was no more able than the Government to solve the economic woes of these years, and failure likewise awaited the Conservative, Labour and National Governments of the balance of the inter-war years.

At least as painful to Bonar Law as the economic situation was the unsettled condition of Ireland. Few things were as they had been in pre-war days: the Irish Nationalist Party was ruined, and so was their political agenda. In their place were the Sinn Féiners who, declaring Irish independence in January 1919, boycotted a London Parliament they considered irrelevant to Irish affairs. Only a few Unionists now thought it possible to prevent some arrangement for Irish autonomy – but what might it be? What was clear was that the 1914 Home Rule Act, suspended since that time, satisfied no one.

Understandably, the Government dreaded having to face the Irish issue, but by the middle of 1919 it could no longer be avoided. The island was in the grip of a brutal guerrilla war between the British Army and the Royal Irish Constabulary (reinforced by the notorious 'Black and Tans' and Auxiliaries – the 'Auxies') on one side, and the Irish Republican Army of Eamon de Valera's outlaw 'government' on the other. By June the newspapers were full of Irish outrage and counter-outrage and even supporters of the Government were pressing Bonar Law as Leader of the House to consider imposing on all parties a settlement based on a plan of federal devolution. Walter Long, still a believer in a federalist solution, responded for the Government and admitted in the House that they had 'no formal position on the matter' at the moment.[46] Carson, soon to withdraw to the relative calm of the Law Lords' bench, reminded all who would listen that Ulster's agenda had not changed: in July, he roused himself to snarl that he would 'call out the Ulster Volunteers' if the Government weakened even one of their pledges to the province.[47]

Another Cabinet committee on Irish policy was appointed in early October 1919 to 'advise the Cabinet as to the policy they recommend for adoption'; it was chaired by Long and included the Viceroy and Chief Secretary, French and MacPherson, as well as former and future chief secretaries, Shortt and Laming Worthington Evans.[48] Bonar Law was concerned by what he sensed to be desperation within the Cabinet, writing to the absent Balfour to disregard what would inevitably appear in the newspapers: the Cabinet had come to no decision. Though prepared, he added, to support any new legislation which 'would work', he dreaded any new bill drawn up in unseemly haste which might only make matters worse.[49]

Long's committee issued their initial report on 4 November, recommending the creation of 'one Parliament for the three Southern provinces and a second parliament for Ulster, together with a Council of Ireland composed of members of the two Irish parliaments'.[50] They met regularly until February 1920 and issued several more reports, but this remained at the heart of their advice. Finally on 24 February the Cabinet agreed on a bill proposing one parliament for a Northern

Ireland consisting of the six counties, and another for the remainder of the island.[51] The bill had its first reading the following day and was passed a second time, with Bonar Law and Long leading for the Government, on 31 March 1920.

It then languished until autumn, both Government and Parliament apparently wishing to hear as little as possible about it. Perhaps the Prime Minister expressed the opinion of many on all sides in Britain when he declared in a private letter that 'Ireland is a hell's broth.'[52] But ministers were not to be spared the last step on the road to Home Rule: the bill struggled through its final passage on 9 November 1920, and received the Royal Assent six weeks later.

Ireland now had a new constitutional structure – one which, it soon appeared, did not please everyone. A six-county Northern Ireland granted separation from the rest of the island left a small knot of the most implacable Southern Unionists angry at their abandonment; the South had finally achieved Home Rule, but this was no longer enough. Bonar Law had played a significant role in bringing about the new arrangements, but the ensuing atmosphere of discontent ensured that he would find no joy in them. Those who had hoped that the wrenching fracture of the Union would at least bring an end to strife must also have felt betrayed; the violence in the South did not abate.[53] Outside the six counties, the Act was a dead letter.

III

Bonar Law and his colleagues never ceased in these months to be troubled by the divisions which sometimes boiled to the surface of the coalition. A remedy much discussed at the time was that of bringing the separate wings of the coalition permanently together – 'fusion', it came to be called. The party committee chaired by Bonar Law in March 1918 to negotiate a possible coalition election also considered the possibilities for long-term partnership. Ignoring grumbling among party Die-Hards, Bonar Law quietly encouraged discussion of the question because he thought Lloyd George the necessary premier for the foreseeable future; his conception was of a loose 'united front' not unlike that between the Liberal Unionists and the Conservatives of Joseph Chamberlain's day.

No doubt he thought also that ultimately the result would be similar, with the Lloyd George Liberals being absorbed into an expanded

Unionist Party. However, the matter of his own party's identity would, he realized, require careful handling. He told Riddell in September 1919 that he believed the vast majority of his followers were prepared to go along with Lloyd George 'step by step', but did not think 'they would agree to scrap their party organization and give up their powers of defence and offence should he propose something with which they totally disagree.'[54]

Most of the Unionist chieftains agreed with him, then, that to abandon Lloyd George was unthinkable. It was also true, as Professor Morgan has pointed out, that the coalition Liberal and Unionist ministers worked extremely well together despite the suspicions that existed among the 'other ranks' of the parties, and that '... the Cabinet's inner coherence compares favourably with that of most British governments during the course of the present century.'[55] So long as Lloyd George appeared to most Unionists to be irreplaceable, and while the threat of the Labour opposition was new and worrisome, it seemed obvious that the two parties needed each other.

The rapid recovery of the Labour and Liberal Opposition following the 1918 electoral rout was another source of considerable anxiety at Unionist Central Office. In the course of two years from March 1919, thirteen seats that had been won by 'couponed' coalitionists were lost in by-elections, eight of them to Labour.[56] Concern over this trend fuelled the enthusiasm of many Government supporters for the idea of fusion, and as early as the spring of 1919 a coalitionist New Members Committee, consisting largely of Unionists, was formed to press the idea on their leaders.[57] While the Committee had the blessing of the party hierarchies, many veteran Unionists grew 'rather up in arms' against it, particularly when they noted that some of its more enthusiastic members were using the term 'Centre Party' to describe their group and their goal.[58]

The New Members Committee was looked on with special benevolence by the Liberal luminaries Churchill and Addison and the senior Unionists Balfour, Birkenhead and Chamberlain. More importantly, Lloyd George seemed supportive, and Bonar Law intimated that he was not averse to the sort of fusion which might revitalize Unionism and free it from Die-Hard reaction. 'I am perfectly certain,' he wrote to Balfour in the autumn of 1919, 'indeed, I do not think anyone can doubt this, that our Party on the old lines will never have any future again in this country.'[59]

In mid October Bonar Law had tested the waters, suggesting to a meeting of party workers consideration of a single 'fused party'.[60] At the party conference in November he took as his theme the necessity for greater coalition co-operation: 'In the House of Commons', he argued, '... we are working as one party. In the constituencies I am sorry to say that it is not true.' He warned his listeners of the increasingly credible threat of Labour, and admonished the faithful: '... do not let us assume that the Government which is working together is going to fall to pieces, and [let us] prepare for the next election ... on the assumption that we are going to fight it in support of the Government which we are supporting now.'[61]

Momentum seemed to favour fusion: on 7 December Lloyd George declared that 'National unity alone can save Britain', and Churchill and Birkenhead energetically supported him on the platform and in the press.[62] In early March 1920, the New Members Committee garnered almost a hundred signatures, mostly of Unionists, on a pro-fusion memorial;[63] and a few days later Balfour lent his great prestige to the movement, proposing to recommend fusion in an open letter to his constituency chairman.[64] In Cheshire later in the month a squabble among the local coalition party committees over a by-election in Stockport, hinting at division in the provinces, drove the party leaders to give further consideration to the fusion question.[65]

'Fusion', Lord Crawford mused in mid March, 'is the order of the day. We are to fuse Lloyd George or Ll.G. is to fuse us – I am not sure which ...'[66] The wry diarist must have been one of many who felt equally confused. Clearly it was time for the two leaders to state publicly whether 'we intend to go on with it': Lloyd George was expected to do so before his parliamentary followers on 18 March, and Bonar Law in an address at Worthing the following day.[67]

Lloyd George conferred privately with the Liberal ministers on 16 March and with his MPs two days later, and the result of these meetings was to stop the fusion movement in its tracks – before the Stockport by-election, contrary to what has sometimes been suggested. The senior Liberals, no doubt disinclined to go the way of the old Liberal Unionists, rejected the idea root and branch; Lloyd George, master of improvisation, backtracked with all his customary dexterity. The following day, details of the meeting – supposedly conducted in confidence – were exposed in the press.[68] Made wary by the Liberal ministers' revolt, to his parliamentary contingent on 18 March the premier recommended not fusion but a vague 'closer co-operation'. Apparently, as he told Miss Stevenson, 'the time was not quite propitious' for fusion.[69]

Bonar Law had no choice but to follow Lloyd George's lead. Speaking on 19 March he too merely stressed renewed coalition team-work. 'Fusion seems off,' Crawford noted, 'and a closer co-operation between the two wings of the coalition now seems our ideal.'[70] Bonar Law, writing again to Balfour, indicated that his disappointment was limited:

> I do not like the idea of complete fusion if it can be avoided, but I had come to think, as you had also, that it was really inevitable if the Coalition were to continue. But it always seemed to me more important from L.G.'s point of view than from ours. As a Party we are losing nothing and, since the necessity of going slowly in the matter has come from L.G.'s own friends, I do not regret it . . .[71]

Failing to perceive that they had no real political future, the coalition Liberals killed the fusion movement out of fear of being gobbled up by the larger Unionist Party. Foremost among the reasons why most of the Unionist leaders, including Bonar Law, readily accepted this development was the difference of opinion over fusion which was evident between the party leadership on one hand, and the constituency organizations on the other. The scepticism felt in the constituencies showed itself vividly at the June Meeting of the National Union. Within the Unionist Party its leaders were all-powerful in the making of Cabinets and the shaping of electoral campaigns; but they could not revise the structure and content of the party without the acquiescence of the hundreds of delegates from the constituency committees. It was made very clear at this party convention that the men and women of the local organizations were not keen for amalgamation with the coalition Liberals.[72]

The new Executive elected at the conference were hostile to the idea of fusion, and the discussion among delegates demonstrated that many were in agreement with them. Robert Sanders, now Deputy Chairman of the party, noted in his diary his own estimate that only a slight majority of the delegates favoured even continuation of the coalition.[73] A provocative anti-fusion motion was declared out of order, but the point was made. Bonar Law, who supported a resolution endorsing 'closer collaboration' with the coalition Liberals, found that his speech was not received with the usual warmth. In the end, a tepid compromise resolution at once extolled co-operation among all who opposed socialism, but roundly endorsed the independence of the Unionist Party.

Bonar Law also came away with the distinct impression that Lloyd

George's reputation with the party rank-and-file had grown a bit shop-worn. As Sanders recalled,

> After the meeting [Bonar Law] said to one of the local people that it was very unlike the last Conference in 1913 when he attacked L.G. for 45 minutes amid great applause. The local man replied: 'There would have been just as much enthusiasm if you had done the same tonight.' Bonar told me he narrated this to L.G.![74]

Bonar Law did not of course attack Lloyd George, however much some Unionists might have relished such a scene. His loyalty to the Prime Minister and the coalition remained unshakeable throughout his tenure of office in this Government. He favoured fusion as a seemingly necessary development, but understood that such an arrangement would be possible only if and when the men and women who made up the parties wished it. As it was, the time was never 'propitious' – to use Lloyd George's term – and party fusion never came about.

IV

The final months of Bonar Law's career as chief supporter of the Lloyd George coalition mirrored the remaining life of the Government: they were strained, exhausting, and afflicted with incessant political troubles. Most Unionists had reacted violently against Bonar Law's wartime 'kite' suggesting consideration of a limited capital levy, and cared as little for Chamberlain's extension of the Excess Profits Duty. They brought their complaints to Bonar Law.[75] Post-war foreign policy had to deal with new or resurgent problems or worries: the gradual dissolution of the sultanate in Turkey and the rise of the Nationalist strong man, Mustafa Kemal (later more famous as Atatürk, 'Father of the Turks'); the retreat of the United States into a renewed isolationism, and Franco-German quarrels over reparations; and the withdrawal of the former ally, Russia, now the USSR, into civil war and a bitter seclusion punctuated only by forays into fomentation of international revolutions. The domestic economy continued its downward slide, and by midsummer the Government found themselves preparing for a general strike – which, bless-edly, never materialized.[76]

Many Unionists had acquiesced only ill-temperedly in the 1920 Irish Government Act. Depressed by the bloody 'Troubles', Bonar Law had stayed the course because there seemed to be no other option: he had kept his party in line and seen the legislation through.[77] Now he was resolved that the new system should have its trial. But it soon proved to be unenforceable beyond the borders of Northern Ireland – nor had it done anything to lessen the vicious twilight war between Britain and the Irish republicans.

Though it was of shorter duration, Bonar Law faced another explosive political crisis with the Dyer debate of July 1920, the origins of which lay in the movement led by Mohandas (later Mahatma) Gandhi and the Indian National Congress to demand self-rule. The policy of Congress combined mass demonstrations and civil disobedience; the response of the Raj was the assertion of authority. In Amritsar in April 1919 the resident commander, Brigadier-General R.E.H. Dyer, had ordered his troops to fire on a demonstration he considered riotious: more than a thousand people were wounded, and 379 killed. Dyer was disciplined by his military superiors, and this was upheld by the Indian Secretary, Montagu, and the Government. The incident eventually made its way to the floor of the House on 8 July 1920.

Not surprisingly, an element within the Unionist majority rushed to Dyer's defence – some because they thought that though the results were regrettable he had acted correctly against perceived rebels, others because they simply disliked Gandhi and Congress. The ever-observant Sanders noted other reasons: 'There has been more excitement over the Dyer debate on Thursday than there has been since the War. A lot of Conservatives absolutely saw red about it ... Government really had a good case; a good many men voted against merely because Montagu had made them angry.'[78] He might have added that some of these backbenchers were equally annoyed with Lloyd George for putting the supercilious Montagu in such a high place.[79] Once again it fell to Bonar Law to maintain discipline in his ranks, and the Government was upheld.

After two years of peacetime office, optimism for the future of the coalition was beginning to wear thin. By-elections continued to be lost – three in 1921 to the independent candidates of the Anti-Waste League which campaigned for cuts in budget spending and was supported by the resources and the newspapers of Lord Rothermere. This begat the notorious 'Geddes Axe' which fell on Government expenditure both good and bad and led to the once-praised reconstruction programmes of Dr Addison being abandoned by the Prime Minister, out of a cold-blooded mixture of necessity and disloyalty.[80] Unionists were also exercised about the distribution of honours under Lloyd George – both because they believed them to be unfairly dispensed to his own friends (to the presumed disadvantage of deserving Unionists), and because of the thinly-disguised system of cash payments to National Liberal coffers which they generated.[81] For each of these crises, of course, there were inevitably many lesser annoyances which upset the Unionist host. By March 1922 the National Union, led by its chairman, Sir Alexander Leith, was close to open insurrection against the continuance of the coalition.[82]

Bonar Law's intimate personal circle also underwent change, but in this case for a particularly happy reason. In June 1920 Isabel Law, now twenty-four, married Major-General Sir Frederick Sykes, the Controller-General of Civil Aviation and former Chief of the Air Staff. Beaverbrook wrote of Bonar Law's beloved Tizzie that 'She was his comforter and shield all through the war'; certainly he much depended on her. She was equally devoted to him: by this time she had taken many responsibilities from the shoulders of Mary Law, acting as her father's hostess and seldom failing to accompany him to unavoidable social engagements.

Perhaps not surprisingly, he seems to have been oblivious of the attraction between the lovers: 'The secret,' a friend later noted, 'such as it was, was no secret to anyone except her father.' When he finally learned what everyone else in the household knew, he teased his daughter: 'Oh Isabel, how could you, when you knew I was so worried about Ireland!' Yet 'Sykey', as he came to be called, was rapidly absorbed into the family circle, and Bonar Law soon developed a deep affection for him and respect for his advice.[83]

If Bonar Law lost a daughter and gained a son, he also lost a secretary and gained a parliamentary follower: in 1920 Davidson announced that he wished to try his hand at electoral politics, and his place as private secretary was taken by Colonel Ronald Dockray Waterhouse. A professional soldier who had served honourably in the Great War, Waterhouse had known Bonar Law's aides Davidson and Baird since before the War, and had been Sir Frederick Sykes's secretary at the Air Staff. Clearly he was more than a mere secretary, for when Sir Frederick married Isabel Law, Waterhouse stood at his side.

Historians encountering Waterhouse have generally been critical – both of his character, and of his suitability for his new appointment – and it has been reported more than once that he was personally disliked by Bonar Law.[84] The ebullient officer seems indeed to have had an undoubted taste for intrigue, and to have been a social climber of remarkable agility; he enjoyed a wide circle of friends, many of whom were very highly placed.[85] Sykes recalled that 'He was a first-class organizer and was invariably helpful. He had a chameleon-like quality of immersing himself completely in the life and interests of anyone with whom he was for the moment serving.'[86] When he retired in 1921 Bonar Law wrote to Waterhouse: 'I want to tell you in writing what I said to you personally, how much I value the unselfish and affectionate help which you have given me.'[87] Had he disliked Waterhouse, as has been suggested, it is highly unlikely that when he returned to office in October 1922 Bonar Law would have immediately recalled him to his service,[88] yet this is precisely what he did; nor, when he retired finally in May 1923, would Bonar Law have included Waterhouse in his very short Resignation Honours List.

Throughout his career, often to the disapproval of others, Bonar Law indulged his taste for picaresque characters who were clever, amusing and useful to his ends – such as Beaverbrook, Goulding, McNeill, even Sir Henry Wilson. His association with such men unsettled some of his colleagues, but to Bonar Law they were good company and helpful aides. Waterhouse might be added to this list. Perhaps he was another like the friend, years earlier, in whose cause Bonar Law protested to a disapproving loved one, 'Do let me like him.'[89]

By 1921 Bonar Law had been continually in office through five turbulent years, and signs of his fatigue were obvious to those close to him: Tom Jones, Assistant Cabinet Secretary, mentioned it to the Prime Minister in January. Lloyd George agreed, offering his own mischievous remedy: 'B.L. ought to take a drink. Unfortunately he is a teetotaller ... Failing drink, the only remedy for Bonar is a wife.'[90] There was no prospect of the Lord Privy Seal taking this advice, nor is it likely that either option would have prevented the rapid decline of his health.

In March he turned to the pleasure of an honour long delayed. In 1914 he had consented to be a candidate for election to the Lord Rectorship of the University of Glasgow but, like so many agreeable things, the election had been subsumed in the War and its aftermath. In the autumn of 1919 the Glasgow undergraduates finally cast their ballots and Bonar Law was elected, soundly defeating two famous scholars, the Liberal classicist Gilbert Murray, and the Socialist philosopher Bertrand Russell.[91] Not until 11 March 1921 was he able to deliver the traditional Rectorial Address.

Forty years before he had stood at the back of the University's Kibble

Palace to hear Gladstone's Rectorial, and as a young clerk he had risen early to attend lectures there. Now Lord Rector himself, he wished his own address to be a success, and friends noted that he seemed more anxious about it than about any other public speech he had ever given.[92] The theme of the speech may have surprised those who knew little except the reputation of the tired statesman who stood in front of them, for he spoke about the nature of success.[93] In a low, strained voice barely audible at the back of the hall, he extolled to his young listeners the plain virtues of work, concentration and ambition to 'win the game', at the same time cautioning them that such victories had their price and could 'narrow the heart'. Well aware that his own public life was nearing its close, this melancholy man granted his listeners a look deeper into his heart than perhaps they realized. He might well have been explaining why he had not fled his crushing responsibilities at any point in the previous few years when he told them that apart from the matter of religion, 'of which I do not speak', the best life could give consisted of only two things:

> They are very simple things, and perhaps not simple but commonplace. The first is human affection; this gives us always in our daily life a zest and interest outside ourselves. The second is work – work which in itself is worth doing, and which we can do with all our heart; and I shall conclude by quoting on this subject the words of a great Scotsman ... Thomas Carlyle: 'Man's highest and sole blessedness is that he toil and know what to toil at: not in ease, but in united victorious labour, which is at once evil and the victory over evil, does his freedom lie.'

While it was received with generous applause, the address left many admirers in the large crowd anxiously troubled. Bonar Law looked grey and drawn, and his voice broke several times during the discourse. He spoke, as he always did, without a text; and at one point his marvellous memory failed him entirely, while he stood at the lectern in painful silence for almost two minutes before recapturing his train of thought. He was obviously not well.[94] Sanders recorded in his diary two days later:

> Bonar Law is really tired out and wants a thorough rest. We have had a very strenuous time in the House lately. There are an awful lot of supplementary estimates, and a good deal of criticism of them [because of the 'anti-waste' mania]; the result has been many latish sittings, and yesterday a sitting on Saturday.[95]

None the less, Bonar Law felt better at the weekend, and insisted he was well enough to play tennis on Sunday, 13 March. Later that evening he collapsed. Lady Sykes, who happened to be present at Number 11, overruled her father's characteristic reaction that he was merely tired, and insisted that a doctor be summoned immediately.[96] The distinguished medical consultant Chichester Gould May found his patient in a state of thorough exhaustion, his temperature elevated and his blood pressure dangerously high; he feared the onset of pneumonia.

Other consultants called in confirmed both diagnosis and treatment: any hope of recovery lay in retirement from office and six months of complete rest. Lloyd George, who came to him the next day, was horrified at the prospect of Bonar Law's retirement and hoped that he would simply take an extended holiday, returning to duty when his strength was renewed; Balfour entertained similar hopes.[97] The position of those who loved Bonar Law was very difficult. Lady Sykes held her tongue, but feared her father would speedily regret a premature retirement; Mary Law, Davidson (now MP for Hemel Hempstead and Bonar Law's Parliamentary Private Secretary) and Waterhouse agreed that immediate resignation was the only course.[98]

There was no doubt in Bonar Law's mind, and he embraced the doctors' recommendation without a moment's hesitation. Writing to Balfour on 15 March he explained that while he regretted the necessity of abandoning his colleagues, it could not be avoided:

> While the War lasted I did not think of giving up but ever since I have longed for release ... I have felt that as long as it was only a question of my feelings it would be unfair to L.G. and perhaps rather cowardly to run away while the difficulties are so great, but Dr May today after examining me for blood pressure told me definitely that unless I could take immediately at least a three months' holiday a breakdown is quite inevitable.[99]

He seized the opportunity for release from work which once had given satisfaction but to which he no longer felt equal. It has been suggested that his retirement may have been tactical, some critics offering his later brief return to politics as a proof that he used it merely to effect a strategic retreat from a decaying coalition, or from the assaults of Unionist Die-Hards.[100] Certainly he was relieved to escape these, and the other burdens which troubled him.[101] Yet there is little reason to doubt that he was close to complete physical collapse, perhaps also that his illness presaged the cancer which, though his physicians had not yet discovered it, finally ended his life two years later.

Bonar Law retained his parliamentary seat but formally resigned all his offices on 17 March 1921.[102] The news stunned Parliament and the nation. Lloyd George was deeply depressed, and Miss Stevenson confided to her diary in May that, notwithstanding all the strains their relationship had been subject to, 'Since Bonar left, [Lloyd George] has lost an ideal companion with whom he could laugh & joke and enjoy himself. He cannot do that with Chamberlain.'[103]

In an emotional speech the Prime Minister announced Bonar Law's retirement in the House on the thirteenth, and letters of sympathy from the mighty and the ordinary alike poured into Number 11. Bonar Law was a true House of Commons man, and no expression of regret touched him more deeply than that of the editor of the Official Report of the House, W. Turner Perkins, who captured the feelings of many:

> Since I came here in 1881, to the House of Commons, I have witnessed no demonstration of more sincere sympathy than that which the Prime Minister's statement in relation to your health evoked.
>
> No leader could enjoy the love and esteem of all parts to a larger degree than you have done since you became the Leader [of the House], and the prayers of everyone will be that, after the peaceful rest which your present condition involves, you may be spared to continue work which has been of such benefit to the whole country.[104]

Lord Crawford regretted the loss for many reasons:

> [Bonar Law's resignation] is a great blow to us. His departure weakens the Coalition as a parliamentary force. His debating power, his conciliating attitude, his candour and disinterestedness, all combined to make him an invaluable asset at any time, most particularly during these years of danger. Moreover he exercised great influence on the prime minister, and was a useful link between the two wings of the Coalition.[105]

Two days later the former party leader stood on the platform at Charing Cross Station surrounded by a small knot of well-wishers consisting of his family, his friend Beaverbrook, and his aides Miss Watson, Davidson and Waterhouse, waiting to begin his journey to recuperation on the Continent.[106] The newspapers paid only scant attention to the departure, and doubtless few of the other waiting travellers on the railway platform had any idea of the identity of the stooped man in the heavy overcoat. Such anonymity pleased him, however, for he presumed – incorrectly, as it turned out – that his life in the spotlight was over.[107]

Bonar Law was glad to take his physicians' advice to flee an English

March for the warmth of the South of France. Accompanied by Sir Frederick and Lady Sykes and his youngest son Dick, he quickly embraced an uncharacteristic regimen of rest, mild exercise and insulation from the anxieties of public life. He played chess and bridge, and as he regained his strength added golf and tennis; for the first time since the War began he had time to read novels instead of state papers. By the standards of the preceding decade, his routine was pleasantly uneventful. He encouraged few visitors from home and avoided the more fashionable hotels where he might have met political acquaintances – thus the task of amusing their father fell on Isabel and Dick. Isabel had been married less than a year: her devotion of time to him speaks both to her affection for her father and the understanding of Sir Frederick, whose own duties required his prompt return to London.

Bonar Law did not want for political news; his former secretaries Miss Watson, Geoffrey Fry and Patrick Gower, who now all served his successor, as well as Beaverbrook, Tom Jones, Davidson and a host of other friends, kept up a steady flow of information. He resisted all efforts to draw him back, however. A decade after he had presumed his ambitions to have been broken Austen Chamberlain now led the Unionist Party, and the responsibility for maintaining the coalition became his. Bonar Law wished him well, but in no way envied him.

The swiftness of his recovery surprised and pleased both his doctors and himself, though his strength was not what it had been.[108] The reaction of his former followers was uniform: the back-bencher Sir James Remnant, for example, wrote that he spoke for many in hoping that Bonar Law was enjoying his respite from Whitehall, '[but] all I can say is that your friends are not enjoying your absence! Come back and lead us. Your successor won't do ... We want you back badly.'[109] A few days later Birkenhead wrote from the Woolsack:

> You cannot allow yourself to be permanently exiled ... You may prolong your stay but you cannot make it indefinite. And as you have to come home I should come whenever you want. Surely it is a mishandled delicacy to think you cannot return without causing embarrassment. You can only avoid this
> (1) By a permanent exile
> (2) By dying
> As a whole I suspect that you would think either price too high[:] you will have to come and might as well come now or soon.[110]

Sanders sent a similar message through Lady Sykes,[111] and as early as the end of April Beaverbrook was imploring: 'Come home now.'[112] Bonar

Law replied to his 'dear Max' as to other well-wishers: 'Though I know that I shall be terribly bored before long for want of occupation I am still very glad that I am out of it . . .'[113] In writing to Lloyd George, he could not resist contrasting his current life with the recent past:

> I am leading a life which if I were young would be perfectly disgraceful. I get up late, play bridge . . . for three hours & after dinner go to a second-rate café & play chess till bedtime. So far I am not bored but this will not amuse me indefinitely . . . I have of course been following everything in England closely & I have quite understood that you have been passing through & are still passing through a worse time than any I had.[114]

On 15 June Bonar Law succumbed to his friends' entreaties for a brief visit to Britain, and soon found himself being pulled in opposite directions by two powerful forces longing for his return – in anticipation of which, perhaps, he stayed in London with his former secretary Geoffrey Fry, rather than at Cherkley or Number 10.[115] Beaverbrook beseeched him to come home and lead the Unionist Party out of the coalition, and Lloyd George tried to lure him back to shore up the Government.[116] Die-Hards, Tariff Reformers, anti-Home Rulers and anti-coalitionists conveniently forgot the difficulties they had caused him and now looked on Bonar Law as a free agent capable of bringing Lloyd George and the coalition to book. Immune to all blandishments, within five days he was back in France.

From his exile Bonar Law kept a close watch on events in Ireland. Despite the failure of the 1920 Irish Government Act and after many months of terrible violence, by August 1921 a fragile cease-fire was in place, and Lloyd George was in secret communication with de Valera – a considerable political gamble, of course, and it is not surprising that the inestimable service Bonar Law might be to him in assuring Unionist support for yet another Irish settlement should have entered his calculations. He therefore summoned his former coalition partner to England, late in the month, to Lympne, the Kent home of his parliamentary secretary Sir Philip Sassoon.

The meeting and its purpose were of course not publicised: Bonar Law confided to Beaverbrook on 20 August: 'I think now that he wishes to see me not for any special thing but because he is going away to Scotland & if he did not see me now there would be no knowing when we should meet.'[117] Lloyd George did however have a 'special thing' in mind – to try to gain Bonar Law's support for his negotiations with the Irish rebels, and for a definitive settlement. He was worried about

Ulster opinion, but the solutions he put forward elicited no commitment from his friend. Though the two-day visit was amiable, Bonar Law is unlikely to have let pass the opportunity of reminding the premier that whatever might be negotiated between the Government and the Irish rebels, no attempt must be made to coerce Ulster into an all-Ireland Parliament.[118] By 25 August he had returned to France, where he remained for what was left of the summer.

In September he was ready to return permanently to Britain, and to limited political activity. Having sold the lease on Pembroke Lodge a year earlier, he now had no London home; in late summer Lady Sykes found a suitable house, 24 Onslow Gardens in South Kensington, and took on the task of preparing it in his absence. He was delighted with the result, and it was his home until his death.[119] In the early days of autumn he brought his self-imposed exile to an end.

14

Renewal

I

B ONAR LAW WAS delighted by how much good his rustication had done him, and joked to J.P. Croal in November 1921:

> I am really in far better health than I have been for years – so much so that there is some point in what I see the papers say, that I could never have been very ill and went away simply to get out of the mess.

He suspected, however, that his respite was nearly over:

> All the same, I did not intend, whatever I might have done ultimately, to have had anything to do with politics till the beginning of next session. But it looks now as if I might.[1]

Not at all surprisingly, what brought Bonar Law back to day-to-day politics was the Irish question, and particularly the welfare of Ulster. Lloyd George having responded to the failure of the 1920 Irish Government Act by establishing contact with the outlawed Irish republican movement, Bonar Law feared that he might throw over the autonomy of Northern Ireland guaranteed under the Act, in a desperate bid for a final Irish settlement.

The overture to the Irish revolutionaries had grown out of King George's address to the opening of the new Belfast Parliament in June 1921, in which he appealed for 'forbearance and conciliation', for his people 'to forgive and to forget', at a time when 'the eyes of the whole Empire are on Ireland'.[2] These generous words seemed to touch all who had grown tired of violence, and Lloyd George – who was wavering at this time between coercion and negotiation – acted quickly. First a cease-fire was negotiated, as we have seen; then, on 11 October, secret talks began between the British Government and agents of the outlawed republican parliament, the Dáil Eireann.

Though these negotiations were no direct part of Bonar Law's life, what does require exploration is the perception of them formed by him, by the British electorate, and particularly by members of the Conservative Party – as Unionists were now again beginning to call themselves. Once he had come down on the side of negotiation, Lloyd George knew that failure would mean public humiliation, possibly political ruin. The Irish delegates' aim was to slip as much as possible of the spirit of an independent Ireland into any agreement; if they could not immediately achieve the republic of their dreams, they wished at least to return home with all Ireland under a single Dublin government. The traditional third element in this tangle – the Protestant Ulstermen – chose to take no part in the secret negotiations. Such was the combination of forces and men which set the scene for Bonar Law's return to the centre stage of politics.

By early November Lloyd George believed that the two principal Irish representatives, Michael Collins and Arthur Griffith, were prepared to accept the status of self-governing Dominion for Ireland, with the King as Sovereign – but subject to the familiar Nationalist demand for a single Dublin Parliament whose writ should run in Ulster as well as in the South. Lloyd George turned next to Sir James Craig and the Ulstermen.[3] He first met Craig on 5 November, and five days later proposed to him that the new Northern Ireland Parliament be subordinated to an all-Ireland legislature; Craig refused to have anything to do with the plan.[4]

Lloyd George expressed surprise at the rebuff, having emerged from their talk on the fifth believing Craig to be reconciled to such an arrangement.[5] Frances Stevenson gathered, presumably from Lloyd George, that the reason for what seemed to be a volte-face was that '[Craig] is apparently taking heart from the fact Bonar is with him.'[6] It is true that when Lloyd George – former defender of Ulster exclusion – (and, likewise, Birkenhead and the Irish Secretary, Sir Hamar Greenwood) indicated his readiness to put the new Belfast Parliament under Dublin's authority, Craig went straight to Bonar Law. There is no record of this meeting, but it is not difficult to surmise the tenor of the conversation; and it is useful to bear in mind that it was after leaving his old friend that Craig drafted his letter of rejection of the proposal.[7]

Bonar Law had no desire to take a lead in politics again – but the welfare of Ulster was perhaps the one issue capable of derailing his hope for a quieter life. Lloyd George certainly did not wish to see Bonar Law become exercised over the Irish question, fearing he might lead a Die-Hard movement against the negotiations, and went so far as to appoint a confidential go-between to keep him informed of the progress of the talks.[8] He had good reason to be anxious, for as Bonar Law wrote to Croal in November,

> ... I have made up my mind ... If L.G. goes on with his present proposals I will oppose them. I shall try to get the Conservative party to follow me. If I succeed we will simply be back on the old lines. If I fail to get the majority[,] which means of course the control of the organisation, I will simply drop out ... If the majority of the party go with me I think there would be [a] fair chance of winning. On the other hand if I cannot carry the majority of the party it is obvious that I could not do anything effective now, and I am certainly not going to do what Disraeli did after the [repeal] of the Corn Law – attempt to build up a new Conservative party.[9]

Bonar Law had said as much to Lloyd George himself when the two old friends dined together on 10 November, and the significance of his words was unequivocal: the Prime Minister was dependent on a Conservative majority utterly opposed to any such coercion of Ulster as was proposed. The Government would collapse either when the policy was announced or soon thereafter, as Conservative ministers were driven to resignation by their own followers.[10]

Bonar Law was right, and Lloyd George knew it: the attitude of Conservatives in and outside Parliament was everything in this crisis. It is true that the climate of opinion among them in 1921 was a far cry from the rejectionist mind-set of 1914.[11] They wanted peace in Ireland – but not necessarily at any price. Lord Derby warned the Prime Minister that any attempt to force the six Ulster counties of Northern Ireland under a Dublin Parliament would provoke a Conservative backlash, and he spoke for many when he wrote to the party chairman, Sir George Younger:

> I myself shall stick to Lloyd George as long as he does not use any compulsion with regard to Ulster though I do not like this sort of purchasing of loyalty from the Sinn Feiners ... I should not agree with Ulster [should she

stand in the way of peaceful settlement] but at the same time seeing what our pledges are I personally should have no alternative except to go with the Party ...[12]

The test came a few days later at the annual party conference in Liverpool, the seat of Ulster Unionism in England. Bonar Law did not attend, but he had made his position known to the party through Younger and others. Lord Salisbury wrote to tell him that among the 1,800 delegates there was absolute firmness on the matter of the integrity of Northern Ireland, but also sincere hope that the Anglo-Irish talks would 'secure peace with honour'. At the same time, there was little sympathy for Lloyd George but much of 'the old deeply-rooted desire not to break up the Party – that is the Conservative & Unionist Party, not the Coalition.'[13]

In the face of rumblings of revolt led by Colonel John Gretton and a knot of Die-Hard MPs, Chamberlain, Birkenhead, Worthington-Evans and the powerful Liverpool party chairman, Salvidge, renewed the old pledge: there would be no coercion of Ulster, regardless of the talks with the Irish.[14] The Die-Hard challenge died away, and Lloyd George acccepted that there must be two separate parliaments in Ireland, as laid down in 1920.

Bonar Law, certain that he was close to the heart of the party on the Irish matter, had written to his confidant J.P. Croal a few days before that the conference 'will be a revelation as to what the feeling of the party is.' Of Ulster he added: 'I feel as strongly about it as I did [before the War]. So you will not be surprised, I am sure, that if this issue is raised nothing will move me from my position.'[15]

Lloyd George had most senior Conservative ministers on his side, and he did not fear the attacks of Asquithians or Labourites. But how was he to deal with a figure *of* but no longer *in* the Conservative leadership – a man deeply admired by the rank-and-file Tories whose votes supported the coalition? The answer was that he would have to climb down;[16] and behind his surrender stood the figure of Bonar Law, who was able to trump 'Lloyd George's ace because he was a credible alternative Prime Minister'.[17]

Tom Jones was sent to Collins and Griffiths with the message that they must allow Northern Ireland the choice of accepting the authority of a Dublin Parliament or retaining her present identity. If they did not, the alternative was the fall of the Government and its replacement by a 'militarist' regime led by Bonar Law – who became in the negotiations a sort of bogeyman, 'hated traditionally in the South and himself supposed to reciprocate the abstract hatred in a sick Canadian-Ulster brain.'[18] Perhaps the Irish agents believed Lloyd George's argument that economic realities would eventually bring Belfast and Dublin together.[19] In any event, a treaty was signed in the early hours of 6 December, and to no one's surprise Belfast announced that she wanted nothing to do with the new Irish Dominion (or 'Free State'), or with her parliament.

Bonar Law had no idea, of course, that his name had been used as a synonym for reactionary extremism to move the Irish delegates to compromise.[20] Lloyd George knew perfectly well what his position really was: on 10 November Bonar Law had told him in plain terms that he should say to Collins and Griffiths that Northern Ireland had to be guaranteed the right to decide her own fate, but

> 'For your own part of Ireland frame your own constitution, and if it is within the Empire we will accept almost anything you propose ...'
>
> If the Sinn Feiners refuse the plan I have sketched I would say to them 'Very well: go to the devil in your own way – govern your own part of Ireland as you please.[21] If you form a constitution within the Empire and behave decently to Protestants there and make no attempt against Ulster, we will not interfere with you. We will allow trade to go on as at present. On the other hand if you don't behave decently we will spend no more British blood in Ireland. We will fight you by economic blockade.'[22]

Such was the extent of Bonar Law's 'militarism'. Had he known, however, that his name had been employed – no matter how unfairly – to advance an Irish compromise, he certainly would have approved. When the terms of the agreement which created the Irish Free State (without Northern Ireland) were considered by the House on 21 December, Bonar Law spoke out for the first time in many months. 'When I say I am in favour of this Agreement ...,' he said, 'I do not pretend to like it, but I ask myself this: What is the alternative? ... It looks really as if the men who signed it intend loyally to carry it out, and is it not worth our while giving them the chance?' The House agreed.[23]

II

Ireland having apparently been settled by Lloyd George, 'the solver of the insoluble', ministers turned to the question of the next election.[24]

The Irish treaty had improved the Prime Minister's popularity in the country, and he and his fellow party 'fusionists' thought they perceived that the atmosphere was favourable at last for uniting the wings of the coalition. The parliament was three years old: an election now would take advantage of the first circumstance, and perhaps facilitate the second.

With such heady stuff in mind, on 20 December Lloyd George summoned to a dinner at Birkenhead's Belgravia house the Liberals Churchill, McCurdy, the coalition Liberal Chief Whip, and T.J. McNamara, the Minister of Labour; among the Conservatives present were Birkenhead, Chamberlain and Worthington-Evans, as well as Salvidge and Beaverbrook (whose newspapers had warmly supported the Irish negotiations). Notable for their absence were the Conservative Chairman, Younger, and Chief Whip, Colonel Leslie Wilson.[25] As telephoned reports of the debates on the Irish treaty in the Dáil were relayed to the diners during the course of the evening, Lloyd George joyously predicted that the coalition would be swept back into power if an election were held promptly. Chamberlain was sceptical, the Liberals generally enthusiastic, but Birkenhead and Churchill, though much in favour, uncharacteristically quiet.[26] The party reached no conclusion, and Lloyd George postponed a decision until his return in a few weeks from what he presumed would be a triumphant performance at a forthcoming international conference at Cannes.

Salvidge wrote privately to the Prime Minister that he favoured continued partnership between the coalition parties – with one important condition, as he recalled later:

> It was that, if the Coalition wished to continue, they must bring back Bonar Law. His health seemed to be better and he could be persuaded to take up office again. Whilst he remained out of the Cabinet there existed an alternative Prime Minister to whom discontented Tory elements could turn in case of open revolt. In that lay the one weak spot in the Coalition front, and I said that 'Bring Bonar back' was the best watchword I could give them if they had me up to London a dozen times.[27]

This was advice Lloyd George understood – and had foreseen. The recent Irish crisis had convinced him both of the danger posed by the unmuzzled Tory hero, and of what a priceless asset he could prove to the Government, particularly if there were to be an early election. He therefore pursued a complicated agenda: he would revive the party fusion campaign, press for a prompt election, and lure Bonar Law back into office.[28] Meanwhile, Chamberlain fretted over the election question and sabotaged his whips' Christmas holidays by setting them to work assessing party opinion on the prospect.[29] Lloyd George, unimpressed by this, 'longed for those good old days of the Coalition when Bonar Law was both his loyal and his resolute partner!'[30]

In mid January the thirtieth of the great post-war international congresses (the 'summit meetings' of their time) was scheduled to begin in Cannes, and Lloyd George intended to score a great victory over French 'revanche-ism' and in favour of European accommodation. Yet he also needed to settle his domestic political problems, so in the week preceding the conference he gathered around him in France several of his senior colleagues, including Birkenhead, Churchill and Worthington-Evans. Bonar Law was also enjoying a brief holiday in Cannes. So was Beaverbrook, and by his own account he brought Lloyd George and Bonar Law together in his hotel suite. The premier, Beaverbrook recalled, spoke enthusiastically about closing ranks and appealing to the electorate, and without warning offered his former partner the Foreign Office. This held no appeal for Bonar Law, and was immediately declined; he added that, with Ulster secure, the Government need not fear him.[31] It would have amused him to know – perhaps he did – that the incumbent Foreign Secretary, Lord Curzon, had installed himself in another hotel less than a hundred yards away.

Meanwhile, the election genie Lloyd George had released from its bottle was rapidly growing into an unmanageable monster. Pro- and anti-election forces – all theoretically still coalition compatriots – battled in the Conservative press.[32] Heeding warnings from the Central Office professionals, the party chairman, Younger, sent a circular letter to all constituency chairmen in which he mildly endorsed coalition but emphasized that 'there seems to be no justification whatever for precipitating an Election'. To do so, he insisted, would lead to 'an emphatic protest against an appeal to the people before the electoral programme on which the Coalition was elected is completed'. More ominous for the leadership was his conclusion that an 'electoral upheaval' would probably destroy coalition co-operation and reanimate demands for an independent Conservative Party.[33] Younger also gave a series of press interviews and, to complete his campaign, in a speech to his constituents on 11 January 1922 outlined what he considered the threat to the party inherent in an early Dissolution.[34] Derby correctly surmised that Younger's attacks ensured that any proposal for a coalition election would split the Conservative Party.[35] Bonar Law was sceptical about the desirability of an early election, but indicated his disapproval of the way Younger had taken matters into his own hands: however, he wrote to Miss Watson, 'when I know the whole story I may take a different view.'[36]

The plan for an early election was now dead. Chamberlain wrote to his sister Ida of Lloyd George having put the 'fat in the fire' by raising the subject without suitable preparation, and complained that, as a result, his own letter-bag was 'heavy with protest and threats' from Conservatives of all stripes.[37] 'I most earnestly press you', he implored the Prime Minister, 'not to pursue the idea.'[38] Bogged down in his wrangles with the French and shaken by the reaction to his election idea, Lloyd George agreed to drop it for the time being.

The Cannes Conference broke up on 13 January 1922 with little accomplished, and its failure deeply depressed Lloyd George.[39] He publicly shelved his plans to recommend fusion and an early election in an address to his supporters on 22 January in which he denied that he favoured an immediate election, and advocated – in terms of 'more restraint and less eloquence' – continuity, and national and international co-operation.[40] In fact, he was in deep trouble.

In early February Chamberlain met senior Conservatives to discuss the situation, but the meeting reached no useful conclusion. He followed this with another, at which Tory ministers confronted some twenty-nine concerned MPs, including Lord Hugh Cecil, Banbury, Gretton, Page Croft, Sir William Joynson-Hicks, and Ernest Pretyman.[41] Middle ground was hard to find, and Sanders drew an ominous conclusion: 'Our leaders', he wrote, 'do not realise and cannot be made to realise how very fast the main body of the Tory party is slipping away from them.'[42]

Certainly Chamberlain did not. By this point, perhaps the only gesture that might have stilled Conservative back-bench feeling and saved the coalition would have been for Lloyd George to step aside in favour of a Tory premier. The Prime Minister told Riddell that he had made such an offer both to Bonar Law and to Chamberlain, provided they would pledge to continue his Irish and European 'pacification' policies.[43] In Bonar Law's case, if the offer was made, it can have been nothing more than a symbolic proposal: he was not the leader of his party, and had made it clear that he wished never again to hold office. Lloyd George did offer to stand aside for Chamberlain – and received in reply the refusal he certainly anticipated.[44] Chamberlain remained until the bitterest of ends 'obsessively loyal and perhaps too mesmerized by Lloyd George's talents to think of replacing him'.[45]

In March Lloyd George fell ill, and disappeared from London to convalesce at Criccieth. In his absence – and following four recent successive Government by-election defeats – Goulding and the Birmingham MP Sir Patrick Hannon organized a meeting of Conservative Members to express their confidence in both Lloyd George and Chamberlain.[46] To their embarrassment it quickly deteriorated into an unseemly row between pro- and anti-coalitionists, and was hastily adjourned to avoid the likely defeat of a resolution endorsing the coalition.[47] The coming spring offered but a grim prospect:

> For most Unionists, the government seemed to be doing nothing right ... Unionists felt that the government's foreign policies were reckless in the extreme, with their flirtations with Bolshevism. There was chaos in Ireland ... At home there were expensive hazards of Lloyd George's 'swing to the left'. Reform of the Lords was totally ignored. Salvidge was a lone supporter of the government on the National Union's executive committee ... In March 1922, with Lloyd George incommunicado in Criccieth, grievances from farmers and others continued to fester, to the government's discredit.[48]

Lloyd George returned at the end of the month, prepared again to attempt to recoup his fortunes on the international stage. In April he sailed off to the Genoa Conference, where he planned to civilize the Bolsheviks, reconcile his former allies and enemies over reparations and, not incidentally, embrace the role of last great World Statesman. He was again disappointed: America sent no representatives, rendering war debt settlement an impossibility. Poincaré stayed away, and his tame delegation rejected any compromise over reparations. Then, on Easter Sunday, the ostracized Soviet Union and Germany announced their own Treaty of Rapallo, agreeing to mutual recognition and the cancellation of wartime monetary claims. It was a humiliation for the Allies, and one for which the London press – particularly the Northcliffe papers – pounded Lloyd George without mercy, or concern for accuracy. The Prime Minister must have wondered whether any possible catastrophes had been spared him: only three days earlier, armed Irish anti-Treaty extremists had occupied the Four Courts in central Dublin. Neither the British Army nor the interim Free State administration had acted immediately to dislodge them, and Ireland seemed once again on the edge of civil war.

Another violent act soon occurred to enrage Conservatives: on 22 June Field Marshal Sir Henry Wilson was assassinated on the doorstep of his Eaton Place home. A Die-Hard and a strong voice for armed resistance to anti-Treaty terrorism, he had entered Parliament as MP for North Down only four months before, and had been acting as military adviser to Sir James Craig. The assassins were members of Collins's own Irish Republican Brotherhood and were swiftly captured, tried and executed.[49] Public and Parliament alike were stunned by the shooting in broad daylight of a Field Marshal in full uniform, let alone a Member of Parliament.[50]

Conservatives were infuriated, and many joined Wilson's grieving mother and widow in blaming the Government. Chamberlain, badly shaken, wrote to his sister Hilda: 'Henry Wilson's murder & all the circumstances connected with it besiege my thoughts & I cannot get [away] from them ... I really cannot write a letter. It makes me think & think & think all round what I would most wish to forget.'[51] Alas for the troubled party leader – he had all too much to think about.

On the day of Sir Henry's funeral, 26 June, once again the House took up the Irish situation. 'Bitter things were said ...,' Sanders noted, 'but Winston really took the wind out of their sails to start with by saying the Government would now insist on Collins & Co. standing for no more nonsense.'[52] Though he had sometimes lost patience with him, Bonar Law had liked Wilson, and was outraged by his murder. He went straight from the funeral to the House, and all waited to hear what he would say. Directing his eyes towards the Treasury Bench, he said that while he continued to have hopes for the Irish Treaty, had he been able to see into the future, he doubted now that he would have voted for it. Not only had it been necessary already to defend the guarantees so recently pledged to Northern Ireland but, in addition, 'I assumed that the men who had signed the Treaty not only meant to keep it in good faith but meant to run risks, and all risks, in order to carry it out. I understood they meant to govern.'[53] He referred, of course, to the presence still in the Four Courts of the rebel force of Rory O'Connor – unmolested and mocking the authority of the Irish Free State government. Bonar Law sat down to widespread cheering, not this time confined to the Conservative benches. Afterwards Lloyd George and Churchill met him outside the Chamber, and the latter recalled that 'he manifested an intense passion. As far as I can remember he said, "You have disarmed us today. If you act up to your words, well and good, but if not ——!!"'[54]

These were words spoken in anger. Sanders recalled that later in the evening Bonar Law was 'very disturbed at the way things had been going, but agreed with me that it had been hard to point out the precise moment at which interference would have done good.'[55] The earlier passionate exchange in the Lobby must have stirred Lloyd George's fear that Bonar Law was preparing to challenge the Government. He seems to have been willing to allow the two Liberals to think so, perhaps as a catalyst to move them to act over Ireland. Nothing could have been further from his mind, however; he had indicated to Lord Derby a few weeks before that he had no intention of entertaining a return to office in *any* Government.[56]

In any event, heavy pressure was brought to bear on the new Irish government, and between 28 and 30 June Michael Collins's Free State Army suppressed the Dublin rebels. This marked a new phase of civil war in the Irish Free State, as pro- and anti-Treaty Irishmen turned their guns on each other while a horrified Britain stood by. Within two months Arthur Griffith, reluctant architect of the Treaty and President of the Dáil, was dead of heart failure. So too was Collins – cut down in his turn by assassins' bullets.

When it must have seemed impossible that any remained, further humiliation descended upon the Government as the so-called 'honours scandal' captivated newspaper readers throughout the summer. The exchange of decorations or titles for political services or contributions to party coffers had long been a lucrative privilege of the party in power. Political professionals knew that the operation of such a system required discretion above all – Lloyd George seemed unwilling to exercise the necessary finesse, and his Tory allies were particularly annoyed and embarrassed by the result.[57]

Like Bonar Law, Lloyd George personally cared nothing for the honours system; but unlike his old friend he led a splinter party without funds, or even an established party machine. If his faction was to survive, it needed money; and he had at his disposal a commodity for which there was endless demand. He ran the system too hard, however; and, his Conservative partners believed, he ran it to their disadvantage. Worse still, his agents themselves gained rather sordid reputations. The greatest of these was the infamous honours tout J. Maundy Gregory, a parson's son and sometime theatrical producer turned proprietor of London's opulent Ambassador's Club, where he practised his persuasion game.[58] The open secret of Gregory's activities was that the lion's share of the money he raised went into a fund controlled by Lloyd George.

The 1922 Birthday Honours List published on 3 June made it clear that Lloyd George had finally gone too far in the blatant unsavouriness of his recommendations. The King balked, Chamberlain supported him, and Lloyd George backed down.[59] Once exposed, the worst abuses of the old system were corrected – but not before they had damaged the Government's reputation.

Many of the London newspapers reported a Cabinet crisis at this time, but they misinterpreted Lloyd George's problems: in July, Crawford noted in his diary, 'So far as I can judge, no crisis exists. Nothing at any rate at the cabinet meetings provokes any serious controversy: our proceedings are harmonious and rather dull.'[60] The crisis was in fact developing outside the Cabinet. On 19 July Chamberlain met Younger and Leslie Wilson, who spoke in strong terms: the disquiet within the parliamentary party could not be ignored. The same was true in the middle ranks of the Government; so Chamberlain agreed to meet the unhappy junior ministers and whips on the twentieth, and Sanders presented their case.[61] He pointed out what Chamberlain should already have known: the problem in the constituencies was not that the coalition parties could not co-operate, it was that the Prime Minister had become tarnished goods. The party rank-and-file wanted a Conservative premier and a larger number of Cabinet offices – it was time for Lloyd George to go.[62] Sanders was surprised by the mildness of Chamberlain's response: 'he seemed to think it quite likely that the P.M. would step aside quietly, and advise his colleagues to go on.'[63]

Chamberlain took these concerns straight to the Tory chieftains, who were piously horrified at the very idea of Lloyd George's retirement. When they heard of this, the under-secretaries met alone on 2 August and requested an urgent meeting with the full complement of Conservative ministers: this took place the following day in the famous Moses Committee Room in the House. Chamberlain and the recently ennobled Earl of Balfour spoke soothingly, counselling patience; Sanders and Sir Ernest Pollock, the Attorney-General, replied with equal moderacy for their friends. Birkenhead then took the floor and destroyed the polite atmosphere by scolding the junior ministers in the same haughty tones in which he had derided Younger in February, demeaning their anxieties and insisting that they were motivated by mere 'gossip'. Pollock recalled later:

> It is idle to pretend that [his] attitude and language did not create animosity. I have seldom seen men so stirred. They had refrained from words of recrimination, but the very fact that they had done so deepened their feelings of injustice and resentment.[64]

On the following day, as the House rose for the summer recess, many Conservatives must have wondered at the rumours which swirled around them: what was to become of the coalition and, for that matter, of their leaders?[65]

Historians cannot resist indicating watersheds — points at which this or that important trend had its inception. The break-up of the coalition no more began in the Moses Room on 3 August than it did with the Maundy Gregory case, or the assassination of Sir Henry Wilson. This meeting was a symptom, as they were, but significant none the less: it marked the beginning of the end of the loyalty of most of these mid-level Tories to the coalition and to the leaders who continued to embrace it.

Derby, free of the constraints of office since 1920, had also lost faith in the coalition. He wrote to Chamberlain in September 1922: 'The more I see and hear from people the more convinced I am that the Coalition as constituted at the present moment cannot go on ... It certainly cannot survive a general election.'[66] Chamberlain replied that these sentiments surprised him, but it is difficult to see why, by this point, they should have done so.[67] Derby renewed his warnings in stronger terms a week later:

> ... there is no disguising the fact that [Lloyd George] is looked on with the greatest distrust by the Conservative party as a whole; and if anybody, who would be likely to be a real leader (and Salisbury [leader of the Die-Hards] is not one) came forward at the present moment, in opposition to him, I believe he would secure the majority of the Conservative party to follow him.[68]

Perhaps even the well-informed Derby did not know that a fortnight later Lord Salisbury wrote to Bonar Law in hope that the former leader would come forward to reclaim his place and free the party from Lloyd George.[69]

On 17 September the coalition leaders assembled at Chequers, the Prime Minister's country retreat, to assess their chances of survival. Finally they made the decision they had avoided in January: Parliament would be dissolved, and the Government would appeal to the electorate. It was a disastrous conclusion, and none present should have seen this more clearly than Chamberlain. He had been warned by elder statesmen and by party managers, junior ministers and back-benchers. Younger had cautioned him that the rank-and-file demanded a Conservative premier, and Sir Leslie Wilson had warned that more than 180 constituency organizations were prepared to support independent Conservative candidates in the next election.[70] Chamberlain, while admitting that there was pressure for a Tory Prime Minister, that the party would convene in November, and that the official leaders might be unable to control that assembly, was yet convinced that an early election was necessary to save both the Government and his leadership of the Conservative Party, and that it could not be won without Lloyd George. He knew there was risk involved, however:

> No Govt is possible without coalition. No Coalition on present lines & *in present conditions* is possible with Co-Libs except under Ll.G. premiership.
> *And* the Natl Union in Novr may declare
>   (a) against coalition of any sort
>   (b) against coalition except under a Unionist P.M.
> What a kettle of fish! Envy me my job![71]

A second danger in which the Government now became ensnared involved their policy in Asia Minor, a fascinating episode which turned on several key points. Despite the War and the Treaty of Sèvres of 1920, which essentialy dismantled the Ottoman Empire and awarded Smyrna to Greece, Conservatives remained as they had always been – pro-Turkish; Lloyd George, impressed by their charismatic and ambitious premier, Eleuthérios Venizélos, favoured a pro-Greek policy. In October 1920, before Sèvres had been ratified, the Anglophile King Alexander of the Hellenes died suddenly and was replaced by his father and predecessor on the throne, the anti-British King Constantine. Venizélos was promptly exiled, and relations between London and Athens became uncertain.[72]

Also significant was the fact that the ancient sultanate of the Ottomans was nearing its end, and power in Turkey was now in the hands of the Nationalists of Mustafa Kemal, who was determined – in the teeth of the Treaty – to drive the Greeks from Asia Minor. By the late summer of 1922 his forces had done precisely that, and even threatened the token inter-Allied force maintained at the Straits under the terms of Sèvres. Regardless of the Treaty, Britain's allies, France and Italy, now wished to accommodate Turkey, leaving Greece supported only, and uneasily, by Britain. What Kemal's rapidly expanding army faced at the village of Chanak on the Asian shore was an Anglo-French-Italian force of only 7,600 men, representing three governments who were not of one mind regarding what was expected of them.

Such was the situation when the Cabinet met on the afternoon of Friday, 15 September, 1922. Lloyd George made it clear that his policy would be to stand against the Turks: they should not be allowed to violate Sèvres and have their way in the Straits. If the Turks were to engage the Allied force, it meant war with the Allies and, he presumed further, with the British Empire. Churchill provided the text of a message to the Dominion capitals sent, hastily, shortly after midnight, advising that 'The announcement of an offer from all or any Dominions to send a contingent even of moderate size would undoubtedly exercise in itself a most favourable influence on the situation.'[73]

On Saturday a communiqué was handed to the press, to inform the public of the decisions made the previous day. The reaction was not at all what the Cabinet had anticipated. The British having failed to take account of the time differences between the various capitals, some Dominion leaders learned of the request for aid not through official channels but from the newspapers. Australia and Canada replied that no action could be considered until their parliaments had been consulted; South Africa was silent; only Newfoundland (still at this point a separate Dominion independent of Canada) and New Zealand responded favourably. The British press reaction was swift, and overwhelmingly negative: unflattering references to Churchill's previous connection with the Gallipoli peninsula abounded.[74]

The significance of the Chanak Crisis, as it was known, was considerable, both in the long and the short term. It is no exaggeration to suggest that the terrible path to Appeasement, Munich, and a second world war passed through Chanak. Yet to leave it at this is unfair. Though it is difficult to maintain that any head of government acts at any time without any political motive, the intention of Lloyd George and his colleagues was to take a stand against armed threat and in favour of the international treaty system. They failed because they acted precipitately, without adequately preparing the way in Westminster, or with the international community, or in the Dominions. They also failed to convince the British public that their decision was either logical or correct. Considering Chanak in the context of post-war politics, however, it is difficult to avoid the conclusion that no amount of preparation by the men then in power in Britain could have made a success of this policy.

Lloyd George was determined. The disappointing reaction of the Dominions did not deter him, neither did the sterile replies of the other regional powers who were called upon for help. Additional British troops were moved to Asia Minor. Then on 20 September came a much heavier blow: the French and the Italian contingents at the Straits lowered their flags and marched to Constantinople. Britain stood alone at Chanak.

On 27 September Colonel Plastiras and the army deposed King Constantine once again, replacing him with yet another son, George II. Venizélos, hastily recalled, was sent to London to renew Graeco-British friendship. By this time the Turks had violated the neutral zone at the Straits created under the Sèvres Treaty. At midday on 29 September the Cabinet decided to order the British commander at Chanak, Lieutenant-General Sir Charles Harington, to issue a stern ultimatum: the Turks were immediately to withdraw all forces from the neutral zone of the Straits, or face the consequences. The message, of course, meant war: 'The soldiers at Chanak had kept their heads, but the statesmen in Downing Street had pulled the trigger.'[75]

'Tim' Harington declined to issue an ultimatum he could not enforce, and instead established contact with the Turks in the hope of resolving the incident peacefully. The Cabinet passed over his disobedience and followed his lead: talks began in early October. At Mudanya, with the battleship *Iron Duke* as a backdrop, generals and diplomats slowly hammered out terms which ultimately led to an armistice on 12 October. There would be no war: Greek ambitions perished, and Turkey and Britain struggled to recapture their former state of amity. A year later, at Lausanne, the Treaty of Sèvres was overturned and the episode at Chanak officially closed.

This affair weighed heavily on the minds of coalition leaders already determined to appeal to the electorate: they found themselves committed in Asia Minor to what appeared for a time to be an unpopular policy of war. The Prime Minister was a Liberal and pro-Greek, the majority on the Government benches Conservative and pro-Turk. It was unclear who exactly were the governments in Athens or in Constantinople. The British military commander on the scene had advised against Government policy and, when his orders arrived, ignored them and successfully pursued his own course. Furthermore, Conservative ministers had been advised from all sides that Lloyd George's popularity among Tories was spent. There was no doubt that the decision to schedule an election was a gamble of striking proportions – but it was a gamble that Chamberlain was now more than ever convinced had to be taken. To do nothing was to watch the Government wither and die.

There was one man whose opinion of all this – the proposed election and the crisis in Asia Minor – was much sought-after: Bonar Law. Though he had played little part personally in the creation of the Treaty of Sèvres he had been a member of the Government who made the peace, and hence accepted responsibility for it. Furthermore, he too had been impressed by Venizélos, and had seemed content with the Government's pro-Greek policy.[76] During the height of the Chanak crisis, Bonar Law maintained silence – in fact, he was not himself certain what his position should be. In a letter to Derby on 25 September he described himself as feeling grateful that the 'Turkish business' was over. Though the Government's confused handling of the crisis had escaped disaster, he anticipated much trouble about it within the party and doubted that he could avoid taking a stand:

> The centre of gravity politically will I think rest in the National Union meetings in November.
>
> I do not myself know what I ought to do then but I hope that before it comes the right path will be plainer than it is now.[77]

III

By this point, the Chanak crisis and the likelihood of an immediate election had become hopelessly intermingled in the minds of many Conservatives. Those who opposed another coalition election generally resisted the Prime Minister's Turkish policy, and vice versa. Stanley Baldwin, the President of the Board of Trade, was far from alone in thinking that Lloyd George and Churchill were courting war so that they could '... call a General Election at once and go to the country which, they calculated, would return them to office for another period of years.'[78] Bonar Law told the Conservative Chief Agent, Malcolm Fraser, that he suspected as much.[79] Griffith-Boscawen, the Agriculture Minister, warned Chamberlain on 2 October that the electorate simply would not support a Government which threatened war in support of Lloyd George's pro-Greek sentiments, and that Conservatives 'generally would prefer to see the Turks [have the disputed territory] rather than the Greeks.'[80]

Despite efforts to convince him to take a hand in the matter,[81] Bonar Law refused: he had several times advised Lloyd George to retire gracefully, presumably in Chamberlain's interest, but he would not go beyond this.[82] As the world awaited the beginning of the talks at Mudanya, Beaverbrook again tried to coax his friend to position himself publicly in opposition to the Government; and again Bonar Law resisted.[83]

Bonar Law seldom acted on impulse; when he did, he often had to rely on the help or the foolishness of others to rescue him from the consequences – as with the Memorialists of the pre-war Referendum

Pledge crisis, or Asquith's stumbling in the Maurice affair. In October 1922 he was determined not to be guilty of taking a reckless decision: he did not wish to bear the burden of overturning the Government from the outside, and he had not forgotten that he bore part of the responsibility for the Government's post-war policy in the Near East. He did, however, take issue with the actions of what he saw as the war party within the Cabinet – Lloyd George, Birkenhead, Chamberlain and Churchill. They were courting an unnecessary conflict, he believed, which neither the British people nor the Conservative Party wanted; and, as in the case of the Irish negotiations of 1921, after long pondering he decided that the time had come to break his silence.

According to Beaverbrook, Bonar Law surprised him on the evening of 6 October by announcing that he had decided to take the very public step of writing to *The Times* to stress the importance of preserving the partnership with France and Italy: 'Failing joint action,' he said, 'we must decline to do anything on our own account.'[84] Bonar Law had informed Derby and Wickham Steed, the editor of *The Times*, beforehand, and the letter appeared on Saturday, 7 October.[85]

In the letter he acknowledged that he thought the Government quite right in wishing to prevent the Turks from sweeping through the neutral zone of the Straits and perhaps into the Balkans; such approval, however, led only to the sharp edge of his criticism:

> It is not, however, right that the burden of taking action should fall on the British Empire alone. The prevention of war and massacre in Constantinople and the Balkans is not specially a British interest. It is the interest of humanity. The retention also of the freedom of the Straits is not specially a British interest; it is the interest of the world . . .
>
> The course of action for our Government seems to me clear. We cannot act as the policeman of the world. The financial and social condition of this country makes that impossible. It seems to me, therefore, that our duty is to say plainly to our French Allies that the position in Constantinople and the Straits is as essential a part of the Peace settlement as the arrangement with Germany, and that if they are not prepared to support us there, we shall not be able to bear the burden alone, but have no alternative except to imitate the Government of the United States and to restrict our attention to the safeguarding of the more immediate interests of the Empire.

Members of the Government endeavoured to view the letter in the best possible light. Chamberlain congratulated him, and Churchill wrote to the Dominion premiers: 'Bonar Law in a timely letter today expresses a very general view.'[86] Crawford followed suit: 'It is a remarkable letter in its effect rather than striking in its form, and will exercise a good deal of influence. Substantially it reflects the broad opinion of the cabinet.'[87] Bonar Law himself indicated to Chamberlain that his intention was entirely constructive: to strengthen the hand of Curzon, who had just arrived in Paris to attempt to salvage some sort of co-operation 'in [his] talk with Poincaré[,] & I felt also that it could not do any harm.'[88] The letter should not therefore be seen simply as an assault on the Government.[89]

In Whitehall, however, it provoked other sentiments as well. Curzon, Lord Lee (now First Lord of the Admiralty) and Hankey agreed with Beaverbrook that Lloyd George, Birkenhead and Churchill (Lee added Chamberlain and Horne) wanted a showdown with Kemal.[90] For all these men, regardless of their differing viewpoints, Bonar Law's 'studiously moderate' letter raised danger signals. For the restive back-bench Conservatives, however, the fact that *any* such public communication had been made carried another meaning: scores of letters poured in on Bonar Law from those who longed to consider him an alternative leader of their party.[91] Birkenhead, who knew well and feared Bonar Law's popularity among back-bench Conservatives, viewed the letter in no other way from the moment he read it.[92]

Bonar Law's full intentions at this point are more difficult to gauge. He was well aware of the disquiet in the party over the Cabinet's obvious desire for an early election, and he made no secret that he opposed it as a potential disaster for Conservatives. He was in regular communication with Derby, Salisbury, Younger, Sanders and Leslie Wilson, all of whom also opposed another coalition election. As we have seen, he had told Lloyd George privately that he would be well advised to resign in favour of Chamberlain and retire temporarily from politics – as he himself had done – allowing the coalition parties to fight the next election independently.[93] Given his long experience, Bonar Law could not have failed to realize that, in such a volatile atmosphere, to send even so temperate a letter to *The Times* would encourage anti-coalition Conservatives to perceive him as one who could save them from the force which had seduced their official leadership.

Chamberlain and the Tory ministers now found themselves in a precarious position as the dissentient murmuring among their followers threatened to become a roar. The party managers Younger, Wilson and Fraser, as well as certain members of the Government – the ministers Baldwin and Griffith-Boscawen and the under-secretaries Sanders and

Amery – had concluded that the link with Lloyd George had to be broken. Lord Derby agreed with them, having come to the view that a coalition election campaign would forfeit Lancashire to Labour; so did the Die-Hard leaders, Salisbury and Gretton, who had relatively few followers but commanded considerable sympathy within the party. They were soon to find on their side the formidable Curzon, whose loyalty to the Government was finally shattered by what he considered to be Lloyd George's Turkish adventure. Furthermore, they could count on the press support of Beaverbrook, who was now dedicated to bringing down the Lloyd George coalition and restoring Bonar Law to the Conservative leadership.

With the Chanak crisis over and his party scheduled to convene in November, Chamberlain's faith in a prompt coalition election remained unshaken; and in this frame of mind he met the Conservative leaders on 10 October.[94] He and Birkenhead spoke passionately of the need to retain Lloyd George's leadership, Balfour of the necessity of dissolving Parliament before the November party conference. Curzon and Crawford opposed Balfour's advice, and Griffith-Boscawen regretted any further continuance of the coalition. The most unequivocal terms were used by the usually silent Baldwin, who apparently 'said Ll.G. was the albatross round our neck and we ought to get rid of him.'[95]

Baldwin, now fifty-five, was certain that this would be his only grand gesture: 'I am resigning from the Cabinet,' he told his wife. 'I shall never get a job again.'[96] He reiterated his position when the ministers met again two days later, and this time he was supported by Curzon and Lord Peel, Secretary of State for India, as well as Griffith-Boscawen and Wilson.[97] Yet the pro-election policy held. Now, like Baldwin, Wilson reached the limit of his accommodation: after informing Younger, Fraser and Bonar Law, he declared to Chamberlain that if he adhered to the coalition election plan, 'I must publicly dissociate myself from such action'.[98] Younger warned Chamberlain similarly and, as its chairman, summoned the Executive of the National Union to lay plans to call a party meeting on their own authority.[99]

Chamberlain was angry, but cautious: he advised Lloyd George to delete from the text of a speech scheduled for 14 October all references to a forthcoming election; in the meantime he himself would tighten discipline within his own party. To Birkenhead he explained his intentions:

I am not sure that it may not be necessary to call a Party Meeting & to tell them bluntly that they must either follow our advice or do without us[,] in which case they must find their own Chief & form a Govt *at once*. They would be in a d——d fix.

The malcontents assume that they can reject our advice & use us for their own purposes. They make a mistake and it may be well to prove it to them.[100]

He almost certainly was unaware how closely his sentiments echoed those of Asquith in December 1916.

Bonar Law was kept apprised of events by Younger and Wilson and a host of party stalwarts, including Davidson and Sir Samuel Hoare. Beaverbrook and Davidson were hopeful that he was prepared to come forward to save the party,[101] but Hoare related that in conversation after a tennis match on the twelfth Bonar Law had seemed disinclined to take part in an ugly battle against old friends and comrades.[102] On Friday, 13 October Chamberlain spoke in Birmingham, declaring himself an 'unrepentant coalitionist' while accusing those who opposed the Government of 'criminal folly'. This was followed the next day by Lloyd George's scheduled speech, in Manchester. It was a great speech, in which, the Mudanya talks notwithstanding, he renewed his attacks on the Turks, and questioned the loyalty of the French to the Allies' cause. The two speeches caused Conservative insurgents to redouble their efforts – Curzon considered Lloyd George's remarks positively treacherous.[103] By the end of the day he was prepared to resign rather than face another election under him.[104]

Bonar Law was much troubled, and a steady stream of callers at Onslow Gardens on the thirteenth, the day of Chamberlain's Birmingham speech, said nothing to ease his mind. Hoare portentously declared to him that the fate of the party was in his hands;[105] and Amery and Griffith-Boscawen sought but did not receive his approval for their immediate resignation.[106] In the afternoon Baldwin, by now very much a ringleader of the insurgency, arrived for a long chat. Bonar Law liked and trusted the unassuming former ironmaster and patiently explained what he had already told the others: he was anxious for the welfare of the party and certain that his differences with the Government were now well known. Yet he had no wish to lead an uprising against Chamberlain, nor was he at all certain – if it came to that – that he was strong enough in resolution or in physique to lead a Government. Like Amery, Baldwin thought Bonar Law would agree to lead again if he were to be convinced that only he could save the party. He argued his case with his usual quiet conviction, and left with Bonar Law's promise that he would at least consult his physicians about his fitness for office.

Gaining confidence every hour, Baldwin forgot his plan to retire and devoted his energies to his new vocation of full-time revolutionary. After leaving Bonar Law he met several like-minded colleagues and planned a luncheon meeting of junior ministers and under-secretaries for Monday, 16 October.[107] The talk was much about Bonar Law and what he might or might not do.

Well aware of this dissent, Lloyd George and his senior ministers determined to put a stop to it, and dined together (without Curzon or Baldwin) at Churchill's house in Sussex Square on Sunday, 15 October, to lay their plans. The election issue and the troublesome matter of who ruled the Conservative Party and the Government, they decided, should be settled in four days' time at a meeting of Conservative MPs at the Carlton Club.[108] Wilson, the *de facto* representative of the anti-election forces, was pointedly asked if such a procedure was acceptable – he assented, and all dispersed for four days of furious campaigning.

On Monday, as planned, Amery assembled the Chief Whip and fifteen junior ministers and under-secretaries for luncheon at the Metropole Hotel, where they resolved unanimously

> That the Unionist Party, while welcoming the co-operation, during and after the forthcoming General Election, of any party with which it may be in sub-stantial agreement, shall go to the country as an independent party, and the leader of the Unionist Party shall be prepared to accept the responsibility of forming a Government if the Unionist Party after the election should be the largest party in the House of Commons.[109]

They then joined a meeting of the full complement of Conservative ministers at which, Amery recalled, Chamberlain explained his odd formula of going 'to the country as a Coalition Government, Members individually, however, going as Conservatives or Liberals, without a Coalition label, and leaving the question of the reconstruction of the Government quite vague.'[110] The so-called 'revolt of the under-secretaries' was frankly anti-Lloyd George, while their seniors were pro-Lloyd George: co-operation between Conservatives and Liberals after an election was not an issue. Both sides were well aware that the atmos-phere of the forthcoming party meeting was going to be hostile to con-tinued co-operation with Lloyd George – before or after an election.

Clearly there would be revolt, but would it lead to surrender? The answer seemed clearly to lie with Bonar Law. Though such prestigious Conservatives as Salisbury, Long, Derby and – though it was unknown to his Cabinet colleagues – Curzon were now associated with the 'anti' movement, they were members of the Upper House and hardly suited to lead a popular insurrection against the Prime Minister. This was made clear to Bonar Law by Wickham Steed, who called on him on Tuesday, 17 October.

Bonar Law, as he had promised, twice saw his doctor, Sir Thomas Horder, during these days. On Tuesday afternoon he visited Baldwin at his house in Eaton Square to discuss the forthcoming party meeting. Baldwin enquired about Horder's advice, and later reported it to his wife: 'It's no go; [Bonar] can't join us; he says that the doctor's verdict is bad but won't tell me what it is.' While Baldwin was sitting alone in deep gloom, Davidson arrived with news of the medical examination gleaned from another source: 'When I called at Onslow Gardens to learn the news, Aunt Mary [Law] told me that she had seen Horder and that he had said that Bonar could resume work and that it was *this* that had so depressed Bonar.'[111]

Sir Thomas's conclusion was that his celebrated patient could resume full political activity for perhaps two years – hardly an endorsement calling for unlimited celebration, given Bonar Law's collapse eighteen months previous. At a time when he was unsure of his own strength, Bonar Law hated the prospect of having to choose between loyalty to the official party leaders, his friends and former colleagues, or responding to the pleas of the rank-and-file, insistent that only he could save the nation and the party from irreparable harm. It is understandable that he would be saddened when his physician refused to make the painful decision for him.

On Wednesday, the day before the Carlton Club meeting, Bonar Law found it impossible to escape his many counsellors. He spoke to Beaverbrook on the telephone early in the day and recounted his fears that any action he took might only make matters worse and could even break up the party.[112] Beaverbrook, himself ill and miserable, took to his bed. The first caller of the day at Onslow Gardens was Curzon, who surprised Bonar Law by announcing that he had resigned, and that Lloyd George had been unable to persuade him to change his mind.[113] They were soon joined by Hoare, who again pleaded with the former leader to come forth and re-claim his throne. Bonar Law heard them out and, to be rid of them for the moment, suggested mildly that he might instead give up his seat, retire from public life and live quietly for what time remained to him. Curzon was perplexed, Hoare shattered.

There were many other callers. As Beaverbrook recalled of that Wednesday, '… he was hustled and bustled and pushed this way and that by ardent and hysterical advocates. All this activity was of no account. There was nothing doing with Mr Bonar Law.'[114] His determination to avoid doing the wrong thing for his nation and his party, as well as his uncertainty about whether he had the physical stamina to lead a Government, led him to draft a letter to Archibald Craig, his Glasgow constituency chairman. His situation was impossible, he wrote: 'After thinking over the position most assiduously, I have come definitely to the conclusion that I am not in a condition to play this active part in the controversy which would be expected of me & that in these circumstances it is my duty to make it clear that I am not a factor in the situation.'[115]

Hoare took this sobering news to Baldwin and Davidson at the Board of Trade, as the two were on the point of leaving for luncheon in Onslow Gardens. Bonar Law, as always, rushed them through their meal, but their arguments continued for three hours. His position, he insisted, was impossible: *must* he chose whether to betray friends, or party, or even nation? He read his draft letter to them, and Baldwin – the most even-tempered of men – reached the end of his tolerance. He drove home his point with imagery which would not have been out of place in the sagas of Empire of his cousin (and Bonar Law's friend and admirer), Rudyard Kipling: 'Well,' he said, 'you are leaving all the white men on the beach. They can't get on without you to lead and it means we shall just all sink out of politics and we shall leave it to those who are not as honest.'[116] Shepherding the flustered Davidson before him, he turned sadly and withdrew.

Callers continued to arrive throughout the late afternoon and early evening: Colonel Gretton brought the encouragement of the Die-Hards. Hoare returned, accompanied by George Lane-Fox and Ernest Pretyman (who had been canvassing the back-benchers) and bringing with him the results of a well-attended meeting of Conservative MPs favouring revolt against Chamberlain and coalition.[117] Wickham Steed, the former editor of *The Times*, and Arthur Mann, editor of the *Yorkshire Post*, came to press Bonar Law to lead it. Even Austen Chamberlain himself called briefly – perhaps to gain a glimpse of his own fate. He was told unhelpfully by Bonar Law: 'I expect that if I had remained in your place, I should have acted like you.'[118] Thus did the reluctant rebel pass his day.

The object of all these people's hopes and anxieties had reached his decision, however. It was fitting that Beaverbrook, still suffering from a bad cold but hoping for the best, should be the first to know: he was summoned to Onslow Gardens at eight o'clock, and found there a party which included Mary Law, Sir Frederick and Lady Sykes, and Davidson. Bonar Law took Beaverbrook into his small study and laid out the worst possible case before him, reading his proposed resignation letter and outlining the disasters which might accompany his attendance at the Carlton Club. Beaverbrook later recalled remaining silent as long as he could, then blurting out his own arguments. Bonar Law cut him off: 'He calmly refilled his pipe and said quite simply: "I am going to the meeting."'[119] Finding suddenly that he had never felt in better health, Beaverbrook went off to inform the Press Association.

Curzon returned, to be told the news, and was delighted to be asked to retain the Foreign Office in the likely event of a Bonar Law Government.[120] Davidson rushed off to share the good tidings with Baldwin and their fellow insurgents. The morning newspapers carried the all-important story, and most assumed that it meant the end of the coalition – as did most of their readers. They were, of course, correct.[121]

Bonar Law left no personal record of his decision to attend the Carlton Club meeting and thereby declare himself an alternative leader of his party, save for a brief reference in a letter to Sir Robert Borden: '[If] my own family – my sister and children – had not been so strong against my giving up, I believe that is the course I should have adopted.'[122] There is no doubt that Miss Law, Sir Frederick and Lady Sykes, and Tony, Dick and Kitty Law supported his decision – though it is equally certain they would have supported him had he decided instead to retire from public life. In his view, there were powerful reasons on both sides of the question, and even late on the night of 18 October he was still wrestling with his conscience and his sense of duty.[123]

The question of Bonar Law's health is clearer now than it was at the time: he was a dying man, with only twelve months to live. Even his physicians did not know this in October 1922, however: they had advised him – and perhaps the time-frame was in response to his query – that he could return to politics for at least another two years. He was more active and felt better than he had since taking office in wartime, and he and his family had no reason to disbelieve his battery of distinguished physicians.

The question of Bonar Law's health is related to another matter which made his decision difficult and must not be overlooked. Although he occasionally used the threat of retirement from Parliament to silence obtrusive admirers, he felt reasonably fit, and clearly had as yet no desire to abandon politics completely – otherwise he would have given up his seat much earlier. His intervention in the Irish treaty negotiations demonstrates that the role of elder statesman appealed to him, as it frequently does to those who have once held great responsibility. He viewed the question of a return to the cares of office rather soberly, however, writing candidly to Lord Long only a few months earlier: 'I am now very well but I am not going back to the old life which I look back on as a nightmare ...'[124] There is no reason to disbelieve the sentiments of this letter: Bonar Law had been an ambitious man, and had enjoyed remarkable success in opposition and in office: but the ambition to be the King's first minister he once felt was gone. What awaited him at the Carlton Club was hard duty.

Yet it was duty all the same. That is why he went and why, sadly for him, he drove many of his oldest comrades into the political wilderness. The appeals of his protégés Baldwin, Davidson and Hoare; of the grandees Curzon, Derby and Salisbury; of the party managers Younger, Wilson and Sanders; and of scores of earnest back-benchers – these proved irresistible. It had all become clear, and they were right: only he could save the party from Lloyd George, and only the Conservative Party could save the nation. Perhaps Baldwin's plea had touched him most of all – Bonar Law simply could not leave them 'on the beach', or 'leave it to those who are not as honest'. He did not clear his house of well-wishers and retire to his bed until the early hours of Thursday, but when he finally did, he slept well.

The meeting at the Carlton Club, in those days located in Pall Mall, was scheduled for 11 a.m., but the excitement began earlier, with the news in the morning papers that the previous day's three-way by-election at Newport had been won by the Tory, Reginald Clarry. Despite this result's reputation as 'one of the most exciting boomerangs in English politics',[125] it was not exactly what it has seemed to many historians: only in Westminster – certainly not in Newport – did it appear to be about the coalition.[126] Neither Clarry nor the Liberal candidate, Lynden Moore, had paid it the slightest attention in their campaigns. Chamberlain, however, had insisted that this would be a great test for the coalition, and saw much value in the fact that the split between its parties would surely throw the election to the Labour man, J.W. Bowen. He actually put back the Carlton Club party meeting for a day in order that the polling results should teach his followers a valuable lesson.[127] Having seen the surprising outcome, anti-coalition Tories now absolutely agreed that Newport was significant – and the professionals at

Central Office grew confident that the Conservatives could win the next election against 'all comers'.[128] For the coalition ministers, it was an ominous beginning to what was to prove a ruinous day.

Bonar Law, arriving at the club accompanied by Derby and Davidson, was surprised by the loud cheers he received from the crowd assembled on the pavement – in vivid contrast to the cool reception accorded Chamberlain and Birkenhead, who arrived only moments before him, a contrast reflected once the great figures stepped inside.[129] It was nevertheless 'a thoroughly good-humoured crowd', Crawford recalled. In a bit of fun at the expense of the bibulous Birkenhead, a prankster had ordered that two immense tumblers of brandy and soda be brought out, 'to lubricate Chamberlain and F.E.'[130]

From the chair, Chamberlain delivered the first (and by far the longest) speech of the morning, declaring resolutely that there were no significant policy differences between the coalition parties, and that the coalition must continue under the leadership of the Prime Minister.[131] His speech was received politely, but without enthusiasm. This was not the case with the brief address that followed, in which Baldwin neatly savaged both the coalition and its leader:

> [Lloyd George] is a dynamic force [he said], and it is from that very fact that our troubles, in our opinion, arise ... It is owing to that dynamic force, and that remarkable personality, that the Liberal Party, to which he formerly belonged, has been smashed to pieces; and it is my firm conviction that, in time, the same thing will happen to our party.[132]

The cheers which greeted this told the tale. Baldwin's speech was followed by a motion made and seconded by Pretyman and Lane-Fox, that the party, 'whilst willing to co-operate with the Coalition Liberals, should fight the election as an independent party with its own leader and its own programme.'[133] Balfour spoke rather inappositely against the motion, and several lesser lights supported it;[134] but the meeting had grown impatient, and shouts of 'Bonar Law, Bonar Law' from the floor indicated the will of the assembly.

Good-humoured those present may have been, but the meeting was by this point beginning to look very like a revolt. The question whether the insurrection had a leader was answered immediately Bonar Law rose to speak. Crawford, who supported Chamberlain, recorded in his diary: 'He looked ill, I thought ... His voice so weak that people quite close to him had to strain their ears – but his matter was clear and distinctly put. After his speech the issue was unmistakable ...'[135] Bonar Law's remarks took no more than a quarter of an hour: he would support the motion, he said, reasoning that to follow Chamberlain's lead would bring on a deep split in the party and leave Conservative identity in the hands exclusively of the 'reactionary element'. If the motion were rejected, and the coalition continued therefore,

> ... I will tell you what I think will be the result. It will be a repetition of what happened after Peel passed [*sic*] the Corn Bills. The body that is cast off will slowly become the Conservative Party, but it will take a generation before it gets back to the influence which the Party ought to have.

He anticipated that if the motion passed, Chamberlain and his friends might go to the electors as a splinter party, separated if not divorced from the mainstream of Conservatism. The thought of this saddened him, but he knew what it would mean – that

> ... the great bulk of our supporters would say they refuse to leave their organisation, and would continue as members of the Unionist Party.
> That is the position ... I shall vote – and for the reason that it is the best chance of keeping our Party as an integral Party – in favour of our going into the election as a Party fighting to win ...

In his most hard-hitting words he reminded his fellow Tories of the fundamental question which brought them together:

> This is a question in regard to which our system (and a good system it has been) has hitherto gone on this principle: that the Party elects a leader, and that the leader chooses the policy, and if the Party does not like it, they have to get another leader.[136]

It was all that was needed: the question was called, ballot cards distributed and promptly counted: 187 MPs supported the motion, 88 opposed it, and there was one abstention.[137] Chamberlain promptly adjourned the meeting, his leadership and the Government itself in ruins. There is no doubt that all had turned on Bonar Law's intervention. William Bridgeman, who voted in favour of the motion, recalled: 'His speech made a great deal of difference in the result. If he had not come I think we should have won [anyway]. If he had spoken for Coalition I am pretty sure we should not.'[138]

Events now moved quickly: the Cabinet – without Curzon and Baldwin – met immediately, and Lloyd George announced he would resign at once. At 4 p.m. King George received the Prime Minister, who recommended that His Majesty send for Mr Bonar Law. Lord Stamfordham immediately telephoned to Onslow Gardens, only to be summoned himself to the Prime Minister-designate and told that Bonar Law – ever the good party man – would not attempt to form a Cabinet until he had been once again elected leader of the Conservative Party.

Stamfordham's arguments that the King had to have ministers and that the sentiments expressed at the Carlton Club meeting were unquestionable were brushed aside. At six o'clock Bonar Law had his first audience of the King since leaving office, and firmly explained his reservations. King George's anxiety over the ratification of the Irish Treaty, which by law had to be carried out before early December, was eased by Bonar Law's promise that he would ensure this took place.[139] With that, he withdrew to await the endorsement of his party.

The Parliamentary Conservative Party – 152 peers, 220 MPs and 67 candidates – met at the Hotel Cecil on the afternoon of Monday, 23 October to elect a new party leader.[140] Lord Curzon presided and made the speech of nomination; Baldwin seconded; and Bonar Law was elected by a unanimous vote. Accepting, he expressed his thanks, and briefly reiterated his remarks at the Carlton Club meeting.[141] At 5.30 p.m., at the age of sixty-four and after twenty-two years in the House, he became Prime Minister of Great Britain.

When a deputation of Derby, Salisbury and Amery went to see him on Friday morning, 20 October, to request formally that Bonar Law accept their nomination for the leadership of the party and, by implication, the premiership, Derby recorded the historic event: 'We went down and had a short talk – quite satisfactory – but all the same although he was excited and therefore more energetic than he had been, his health did not seem to me so particularly good.'[142]

15

'A real old Tory Cabinet'

———————◆———————

I

WHEN A CENTURY earlier Lord Melbourne failed to leap at the offer of the premiership, his raffish secretary Tom Young is reputed to have burst out: 'Why, damn it all, such a position was never occupied by any Greek or Roman, and if it only lasts two months it is well worth while to have been Prime Minister of England.'[1] Given his love of the histories of great men, it is unlikely that Bonar Law failed to recall this tale in October 1922. He had indeed gained a prize that no Greek or Roman had ever held, but in many ways it had come too late. Yet achieving it at last gave pleasure, all the same: Lord Derby met Bonar Law privately a few hours after the Carlton Club meeting and noted: '... I found him an entirely different man from the night before, and quite full of fight.'[2]

The talk was of offices, the first duty of any new Prime Minister. Bonar Law's initial thought was to announce to the forthcoming party conference that he would lead a Government for only one year, and this did not trouble Derby in the slightest. Bonar Law's reasoning was based upon realistic reservations about his health, as well as his hope that with this act of self-denial he could lure back to office many former coalitionists. After the unsettling political events of 1922, however, to fight an election under a self-proclaimed caretaker Prime Minister might have led to electoral disaster. As it was, only Derby thought it a good idea, and the pleas of Curzon, Davidson and Amery carried the day: there was no public talk of early resignation by the new Prime Minister.[3]

Bonar Law wasted no time reassembling his staff. He recalled Davidson, who again became his Parliamentary Private Secretary, and his secretaries Miss Watson, Gower and Fry. During Bonar Law's absence from office Colonal Waterhouse had served as aide to the Duke of York: coincidentally, he arrived in London with the Duke on the very day of the Carlton Club meeting. That afternoon Bonar Law summoned him to Onslow Gardens and restored him to his post as Principal Private Secretary. The incomparable John Berry also returned to his master's side, now with the lofty title of Office Keeper to the First Lord of the Treasury and head of the personal staff, the Messengers, attached to Number 10. Of Lloyd George's plethora of secretaries the incoming Prime Minister particularly wished to retain the services of Tom Jones, but otherwise kept on only the shorthand wizard A.J. Sylvester, as a senior secretary.[4]

Fiscal and constitutional conservative that he was, Bonar Law had no intention of keeping in place the elaborate team of secretaries and advisers Lloyd George had gathered together. In his first speech as premier, in Glasgow on 26 October, Bonar Law announced to great cheers: 'We have decided to bring the Cabinet Secretariat in its present form to an end.'[5] In Whitehall Sir Maurice Hankey, of course, was piously horrified, and his deputy Tom Jones made ready to take his talents to the Welsh Department of the Board of Education. Their anxieties were misplaced, however: it was Lloyd George's huge personal secretariat, the so-called 'Garden Suburb', which Bonar Law distrusted. The 'Suburb' was quickly sent packing, but Bonar Law had never entertained any idea of destroying the bureaucratic machinery created by Hankey to serve the Cabinet itself. The Cabinet Secretariat was retained, but Bonar Law insisted that it be both leaner and cheaper: Hankey had to make do with a budget reduced by two-thirds and a staff of forty, rather than the 102 in place in October 1922.[6]

More important to Bonar Law, of course, was the matter of assembling a Cabinet. His hope that the solidarity of the Tory former coalitionists might waver went unrealized, and he set about making his Government from the materials at hand – the anti-coalition forces.[7] He did not accept that there was truth in the gibe that he was faced with a shortage of talent, but he did fear he would be unable to recruit ministers with sufficient Front Bench experience. Certainly rumours were soon circulating in Whitehall that he was even trying to effect a compro-

mise with the 'Wee Frees', the Asquithian Liberals.[8] It was true that
Bonar Law tried to cast his net a bit further than he might have wished:
he offered the Colonical Office to Viscount Ullswater, the former
Speaker, James Lowther,[9] and the Exchequer to his own one-time arch
opponent who had since become a good friend and regular bridge
partner, Reginald McKenna.[10] At sixty-seven, however, the erstwhile
Speaker shrank from the rigours of office, and the former Chancellor
was reluctant to surrender his new life as Chairman of the London, City
and Midland Bank.

On record as being against the excesses of the Lloyd George
years, Bonar Law finally assembled what has proved to be the smallest
peacetime Cabinet of the century, some sixteen members, including
the former coalition ministers in the Upper House – Cave (Lord
Chancellor),[11] Curzon (Foreign Office), Derby (War Office) and Peel
(India Office) – as well as Baldwin (Chancellor of the Exchequer) and
Griffith-Boscawen (Ministry of Health). Among those who joined them
were the Duke of Devonshire (Colonial Secretary), Lord Salisbury (Lord
President), the former whips Sanders (Agriculture) and Bridgeman
(Home Office), and the future Lord Halifax, Edward Wood (Education).
Often characterized by their opponents in the ensuing election as a lack-
lustre 'Government of peers', the Cabinet contained nine Members of
the Commons and only seven of the Upper House (fewer than Asquith's
or Lloyd George's peacetime ministries). Although they were also condemned, particularly by the former coalitionists Birkenhead and
Churchill, as a Government facing 'first class problems' with 'second
class brains', in fact they were not short of academic distinction: among
them were three Fellows of All Souls (Curzon, Amery and Wood); three
former Presidents of the Oxford Union (Curzon, Griffith-Boscawen
and Hoare); and the present and two future Chancellors of Oxford
University (Curzon, Cave and Wood). The Bonar Law Government also
produced two future premiers (Baldwin and Neville Chamberlain) and
the ministerial core of most of the Cabinets of the inter-war years. While
it was perhaps not a Government of exceptional talent it had more than
its share, particularly given its size, and certainly compared favourably
with many that followed. The new Prime Minister put it simply to the
House:

> ... I would not like to assert that we have ... a monopoly of first-class brains,
> but we are, I hope, and I believe, a Government composed of men of good
> judgment – and what is perhaps not less important, we are a Government of

first-class loyalty. We are working together, and I am sure will continue to work together as a team, without personal ambitions or jealousies, in the desire to serve the country.[12]

Such comparisons aside, perhaps the electorate found themselves more in sympathy with Lord Robert Cecil's retort to Birkenhead: 'It is better to have second class brains than second class character.'[13]

It was not a dearth of talent among his ministers which concerned Bonar Law but the scarcity of star performers and, because of the retreat of the Chamberlain 'cave', of men with administrative experience.[14] Though all but one of his fifteen new colleagues had held office, only six had headed Cabinet-level departments of state.[15] This convinced him that the Carlton Club breach must be healed quickly, and the prodigals brought back into the fold. His team did not remain in place long enough to establish a lasting identity, however, and – whatever else they were – they will always be remembered as Sanders described them: 'a real old Tory Cabinet.'[16]

Bonar Law had viewed Lloyd George's style of management with a mixture of admiration and disapproval. He acknowledged his predecessor's prodigious energy and genius in running what often seemed to be a one-man administration; he also believed that to try to rule Britain in this way was to half-govern, and to half-govern badly. Bonar Law believed that tranquillity and good sense were what was called for – if these were, as Lord Crawford described them, the principles of a chartered accountant, then he was content to have it so.[17] As Asquith had been willing to settle nothing, so Lloyd George had wished to decide all things himself. 'That is not my idea,' Bonar Law told the Conservative women's organization at Drury Lane. 'My idea is that of a man at the head of a big business who allows the work to be done by others and gives his general supervision. That is my idea of the work of the Prime Minister.'[18]

The Cabinet once again reverted to being a committee of governors – each with his own province – with the Prime Minister not an emperor but *primus inter pares*. Cabinet meetings reflected this, and those who had enjoyed the wide-ranging and sometimes brilliant discussions which characterized the Lloyd George era must have been sadly disappointed. Lord Peel noted that Bonar Law's Cabinets were often 'simple and almost perfunctory affairs', prompting Crawford, to whom this comment was made and who well recalled the Lloyd George Cabinets, to soften his own earlier sarcasm by adding: 'Lucky people! ours were terribly long and serious functions too.'[19]

With an election campaign before him, political questions arose to test the new premier from the outset, and the first of these was the unfinished business of Tariff Reform. Most of the members of the incoming Cabinet met at Onslow Gardens on 23 October, and demonstrated that hard lessons had been learned. The Government was to be led by the greatest champion of the policy, and included as First Lord of the Admiralty L.S. Amery, the keenest Tariff Reformer among the younger generation; but also among its members were Derby and Salisbury, who would not have tariffs at any price. There would be no repeats of the 1912 Referendum Pledge fiasco, however: in 1922, the Tariff Reform lions seemed almost anxious to lie down with the Free Food lambs. Of the tariff issue, Amery recorded in his diary: '... with one accord they all wanted to say nothing at all.'[20] The election manifesto, it was decided, would simply leave the matter 'open'; and Bonar Law pledged to the voters that there would be no change in the fiscal system for the life of the Parliament.[21] Thus was the still-dangerous issue carefully side-stepped for the duration of his premiership.

The Irish Question, too, seemed to have lost most of its sting. As we have seen, the December 1921 treaty which recognized the twenty-six counties as a Dominion or 'Free State' required prompt action. Bonar Law had supported the treaty, and had promised the King he would see it ratified – and his colleagues agreed that following an immediate election, Parliament should be convened promptly to enact the necessary enabling legislation. Die-Hard sensibilities remained alive and well in the party and (in the person of Salisbury) in the new Government; so long as Northern Ireland remained secure, however, pragmatism overruled the suspicions deep in Unionist hearts. The same could be said of the other divisive issues which had exercised Conservatives in the previous four years, particularly House of Lords reform and arrangements for the disestablished Welsh Church. These too were virtually ignored in the official programme of the party – and the other parties generally avoided them with equal vigour.

With what, then, did the new administration go to the voters? Amery, who was charged by Bonar Law with drafting the party manifesto, argued that they would be well advised to stress the change in Government as their central theme: it was a good time to offer themselves to the electorate on the basis of *not* being Lloyd George. Initiating the campaign in Glasgow on 26 October, Bonar Law stressed that his would be a Government of 'tranquillity', in foreign and in domestic policy – which promptly drew from his opponents, as he had anticipated, the gibe that his policy was to do nothing.[22] At Drury Lane a week later he reminded the Tory ladies of some favourite words of one of his heroes:

> Let me read what Disraeli said about it – 'The Conservative Party are accused of having no programme or policy. If by a programme is meant a policy which assails or menaces every institution, every interest, every class, and every calling in the country, I admit we have no programme. But if to have a policy with distinct aims, and these such as most deeply interest the great body of the nation, be a becoming programme for a political party, then I contend we have an adequate programme.'
> ... What Disraeli said I, too, say. I want tranquillity and stability. I mean as little as he did. But that does not mean that I am satisfied with the world today; that I wish no change. I mean what Disraeli meant. There are times when it is good to sit still and go slowly.

He cared little for criticism that he was offering a 'do nothing' policy:

> When I say we want quiet and tranquillity and stability, that does not mean that I am unconscious of the terrible suffering now going on through unemployment, through the high cost of living, and through the state of housing. It does not mean that we are leaving out that which had been arranged by the last Government. But I do have at the back of my mind this feeling, that though we must not neglect palliatives, in a condition so critical the real cure must come from better trade and better industry, and that is the way to deal with it. I don't come before you with any hope of being able to work any miracles. I think we have a capable sincere Government and we shall do what we can to face the difficulties of our position.[23]

From his vantage point in the political wilderness, Lord Crawford thought this struck just the right note: 'the country is tired of the "brilliance" of F.E. and the rest of us!'[24]

Parliament was dissolved on 26 October and polling day set for 15 November. It was in many ways a most perplexing election, of which Professor Kinnear's summing-up hits the mark precisely: 'The election of 1922 was characterized by a systematic effort by the leaders of all three non-socialist parties to present as few policies as possible.'[25] After the break-up of the coalition, any official co-operation between Conservatives and National Liberals, as the Lloyd George-ites had become, was out of the question. However, Central Office left it to the constituency committees to sort out their relationships with former coalition Liberals – after all, they had been yoked together for seven years – and in many districts the old partners co-operated precisely as they had before the October disruption.[26] The Labour Party at this time was so decentralized as to be almost leaderless and, save for broad socialist sentiments, left policy largely to individual candidates.

Labour's major contribution to the debate of 1922 was the endorsement of a capital levy, which caused Bonar Law some embarrassment in view of his own announced willingness during the War to consider it as an expedient. Labour spokesmen such as J.R. Clynes and J.H. Thomas were quick to remind their audiences that the premier had himself 'endorsed' such a programme – but the aspersion did not stick. Bonar Law quoted his speeches, patiently explaining that he had endorsed nothing of the kind but merely indicated that his mind was open to the possibility of employing a levy in lieu of extraordinarily high post-war income taxes: Labour, he pointed out, desired both. As ammunition for an election controversy, the capital levy proved a dud shell. The same could be said of attacks on the new Government's Anglo-Turkish policy – once again in the headlines, as Curzon made ready to meet Allied and Kemalist representatives in Lausanne. The voters seem to have paid little attention.

In a manner modern voters would recognize, the election of 1922 was one of personalities rather than issues. With many of the Conservative 'stars' sulking in their tents, the remarkable record and well-known reputation for probity of Bonar Law were perhaps the strongest 'arguments' the Tories could put forward. Though recurrent throat trouble sometimes made speaking uncomfortable for him, he fought harder from the platform and with greater wit than he had in any election since 1910. The historian of the contest has noted that the success of his personal campaign 'defused the Coalitionists' claim that they had a monopoly of brains.'[27]

While Labourites dithered and non-socialist candidates vied in extolling the virtues of 'tranquillity' and 'safety first', it is not surprising that the Conservatives should have emerged with a victory. Nevertheless, the outcome seemed far from predictable at the time. Though he had been given the proverbial 'clean bill of health', the difficulties of Cabinet-making, disquiet over the impending Lausanne Conference, and the barrage of advice, demands and queries about the election caused Bonar Law great concern; and he was troubled by fatigue and what appeared to be laryngitis throughout the campaign. He was an inveterate worrier, and this all sharpened his usual sceptical caution. He joked to his old friend Sir James Campbell, now Lord

Glenavy: 'You remember the life I led at the time of the first Coalition: this is worse.'[28]

One of the most unpleasant crises with which Bonar Law had to deal, though unknown to the public, offended him beyond measure. On 24 October Viscount Rothermere went to him and, in reply to the Prime Minister's expressed hope for support from his newspapers, apparently suggested that it was available in exchange for an earldom for himself and a promising Government appointment for his son Esmond. Bonar Law, never an admirer of the senior Harmsworths, had already thwarted Rothermere's ambitions during the Great War. He said nothing after Rothermere had dropped his bomb, merely picked up the telephone and summoned his visitor's car: a firm rejection and a humiliating dismissal in one. Rothermere stormed from the Prime Minister's presence – without his earldom, and without the appointment for his son.[29] Bonar Law had always been repelled by the negotiations which inevitably accompanied the dispensing of political largesse, but this remained for him the most unpleasant example of such bartering of his long career.[30]

Polling Day dawned cold and rainy across the nation. Bonar Law was once again contesting Central Glasgow, and he had become anxious about his ability to hold a seat in a city troubled by unemployment and labour unrest. His huge majority of 1918, he believed, was no indicator of what this day might bring. He and his immediate circle gathered in his office at Number 10 to await the results, and the cautious optimism he had exhibited in October seemed to melt away. By this point his voice had grown weak and his throat hoarse and painful, which he blamed on a bad cold and on the many speeches he had made.[31]

The initial results were not encouraging, showing both Labour and the 'Wee Free' Liberals to have captured more urban seats than seemed at all healthy for the Government. Bonar Law's result in Glasgow was not reported until the early hours of the morning: his 10,000-vote majority had melted away, but he was victorious by a safe margin of 2,514 votes over his Labour opponent.[32] The sun staunchly refused to shine on the morning of 6 November, but the news was bright for loyal Tories – the reports of late returns (mainly from the counties) were very good. Though four discrete parties had taken the field, the Government was returned with a comfortable parliamentary majority. Of the 615 seats at stake, the Conservatives captured 345, with 38.2 per cent of the total vote; Labour came next with 142 seats (29.5 per cent); Lloyd George's National Liberals won only 62 seats (11.2 per cent), and the Asquithians a mere 54 (17.5 per cent). The total poll was the largest to date, with more than 14 million votes cast by 71.3 per cent of the eligible electorate. With the inclusion of the various independents and small-party winners, the Government held a working majority of 77 over all others. After an odd campaign, it was a satisfying victory.

The triumph was not universal, however: one Cabinet minister and two under-secretaries were defeated: Griffith-Boscawen, the Minister of Health, and J.W. Hills and Sir Leslie Wilson (the latter also Chief Whip).[33] However, with the exception of Birkenhead the Conservative former coalitionists conducted themselves as promised and, at least publicly, supported Bonar Law. This was certainly true of Austen Chamberlain, who behaved with the utmost correctness towards those who had driven him from office – although Beaverbrook somewhat oversold his man in writing later that 'He did not nourish or cultivate animosities and hostilities.'[34] The proud and thin-skinned former leader expressed his displeasure to his brother Neville when the latter joined Bonar Law's Government, and took absolute delight in the defeats of those whom he thought had personally betrayed him.[35] 'I'm glad', he wrote to his sister, 'that Leslie Wilson is out & I chuckle every time I think of Boscawen's defeat.'[36]

Chamberlain's ambition to return to high office was matched by Bonar Law's longing to accommodate him, but this same letter makes clear that he nursed a lingering resentment which made it impossible. He had been deeply hurt and humiliated by the events of October 1922, and forgiveness did not always come easily for Austen Chamberlain. Even had he known what events lay six months in the future, it is unlikely he would have behaved one iota differently – a rigidity which of course much affected the direction of British politics in the inter-war years.

For the balance of Bonar Law's public life it was Birkenhead who was the most unreconciled of the Tory former coalitionists. His whipping-boy of choice was his fellow peer, Curzon, whom he considered the greatest 'rat' at the Carlton Club, and harassed at every turn. In December his desire to embarrass the Government, more particularly to humiliate the Foreign Secretary, led him to stumble into a trap which he had laid for others. It was a reminder to Conservatives that such mischief damaged not only Bonar Law's Cabinet, but the entire party.

On 3 December Beaverbrook published in the *Sunday Express* a letter which had come rather mysteriously into his hands. Dated 15 February

1922 and addressed to Curzon by Venizélos's successor as Greek premier, Demetrios Gounaris, it appealed in the most desperate terms for additional British assistance in the ill-fated Greek struggles against the Turks. Scapegoats for the failed war, Gounaris and five of his ministers were executed soon afterwards, following a military coup which also overthrew King Constantine. Birkenhead insisted that *he* had never heard of such a letter and, equally dazzled by the prospect of embarrassing Curzon, Lloyd George, Chamberlain, Horne and Worthington-Evans expressed similar ignorance.[37]

In the Lords on 7 December Birkenhead launched a brutal attack on the Foreign Secretary – then in the throes of the Lausanne Conference – reading out both the Gounaris letter and Curzon's reply in which he advised that the Greeks 'hold on'. 'F.E.' charged that the Cabinet had not been shown the letter and that Curzon was the author of a real-life Greek tragedy. If true, the accusations would surely have caused Curzon's resignation, endangered the Lausanne negotiations, and shaken the new Government to its foundations. Like General Maurice in 1918, however, the former coalitionists failed to reckon with Hankey: the Cabinet Secretary located the correct confidential file and before the end of the day was able to demonstrate that the letter had been circulated to the Cabinet by Curzon and even bore Birkenhead's initials.[38] Salisbury in the Lords and Bonar Law in the Commons put out the fire with a great show of magnanimity but in fact at terrible cost to the mischief-makers. 'Our friends, your late colleagues,' Bonar Law wrote to Curzon in Lausanne 'have made almost as big a mess of it as I have seen in my whole political experience.'[39]

On 11 December Birkenhead offered an apology, 'frigidly received' by their Lordships,[40] and a week later Lady Curzon was delighting in the opportunity to cut him at a ball – although, as she lamented to her husband, 'I am afraid he was too drunk to notice.'[41] Bonar Law had no time for revenge, however, and this *opéra bouffe* simply made it more difficult for him to accomplish his goal of co-opting the former coalitionists into his Government. An old friend reported him to have said at the time of the Carlton Club meeting, 'I must have Austen and F.E. back at the first possible opportunity. But there will have to be an interval. Tell them not to let it be protracted by unnecessary bitterness.'[42] The pleasure many Tories took in Birkenhead's humiliation did not amend Bonar Law's priorities in the slightest, but it was clear that an excess of 'unnecessary bitterness' stood in his way. Hankey, who saw him daily, was disturbed by the implications of this: 'Bonar Law ... has the whole burden on his shoulders ...,' he noted in his diary in November. 'I really don't know what will happen to them if Bonar's health cracks.'[43]

II

On 20 November Parliament assembled for a three-week session to pass the Irish Free State Bill enacting the constitutional arrangements of the December 1921 treaty. There was no question that the Bill would pass, but it was a melancholy affair for many Conservatives – particularly in view of the twilight war which raged on among Irish supporters and opponents of the new Free State. Despite the rumblings of Ulster Unionists and British Die-Hards, Bonar Law skilfully piloted the bill through the time-honoured proceedings with multi-partisan support. The last Lord-Lieutenant, Lord Fitzalan,[44] retired from the Viceregal Lodge – his place taken by Tim Healy, the first Governor-General of the Irish Free State – and within a very few months an uneasy peace had settled over the troubled island; it was to last for a half-century. Although it gave him no pleasure, this was the greatest parliamentary moment of Bonar Law's brief premiership. One observer has put it well: 'He had to placate the extreme elements of his own Party and avoid accusations of betrayal. This he succeeded in doing, and his performance was generally recognized as masterly.'[45]

Despite the few inevitable rough patches, this brief session was an impressive start for the new Government. With a solid Conservative majority – many of whom viewed him as the saviour of their party – Bonar Law's command of the House was as assured as ever it had been. It was true that his voice was never strong during this time, and the diaries and letters of parliamentarians often refer to the 'colds' which left him hoarse and rasping. However, the House of Commons – where making oneself heard was so often a trial – listened considerably when he rose to speak. While Salisbury had to contend with Birkenhead in the Lords, Bonar Law had no such antagonist, and he and the eclipsed giants Lloyd George, Chamberlain and Churchill customarily treated each other with respect.

This Parliament witnessed a remarkable innovation, in the introduction of a large Labour Party contingent, many of them impatient radicals who took particular delight in baiting the luminaries among their elders and opponents. Remarkably, Bonar Law was spared this. As Sanders recalled,

There has been a certain amount of Labour rowdiness but it has been not so pronounced as the papers make out; ... but we have been asking the House to do too much in the time; there has been little real obstruction. Bonar has got hold of the House already; the Labour men are never offensive to him as they were to L.G.[46]

The admiring Davidson was obviously delighted to be able to write to Lord Stamfordham in February: 'the Prime Minister himself has completely mastered the House, and has delivered a series of speeches which have impressed his parliamentary enemies on the Labour benches almost more than they have his friends ...'[47] Davidson was certainly no unbiased observer, but there is no shortage of evidence to support his view: the veteran socialist George Lansbury told the House of his regard for Bonar Law, and also for Balfour, '... not because I agree one bit with what either of them do ... but because I could understand what they meant when they got up to speak ...' Andrew McLaren, a loyal Independent Labour Party man, heard only approval on his own side of the aisle when he said: 'There is no man who has impressed me more than the Prime Minister ... I cannot get away from his personality. He seems to be very honest and very anxious to do something for the country.'[48] The 'Wee Free' Liberal Samuel Pattinson told his constituents in Horncastle in December 1922, according to the *Yorkshire Post*, that

The Conservatives had the finest leader the House of Commons had seen for a very long time. Mr Bonar Law was a perfectly wonderful man, and held the House in the hollow of his hand. He admired him exceedingly, although he differed with him. Mr Bonar Law was honest, and it was his honest intention to do his best for the country.[49]

Politics is a very rough game, however, and there were those prepared to test the mettle of the new Government. Only a week after the election, a delegation of unemployed workers marched to London (mostly in motor-lorries, Neville Chamberlain quipped) to demand a meeting with the premier and to place before him their ultimatum that the Government should assume direct responsibility for the grave unemployment situation. There can be no doubt of the sincerity of Bonar Law's often-expressed concern about the economic 'slump' and the hardship which it caused to the unemployed, yet he felt equally strongly that a Government deeply in debt and elected on a programme which roundly rejected the state interventionist promises of the Lloyd

George era could not meet such demands. Furthermore, as he had said repeatedly during the election campaign, he absolutely repudiated the notion that all matters led in the first instance to Number 10. He refused to budge from his belief that the delegation must take their complaints to the responsible Ministers – of Labour and of Health – and the Cabinet agreed. Predictably, the deputation expressed threatening outrage; but the Prime Minister held his ground.[50]

Several of the leaders of the march were famous radicals familiar to the police for their violent rhetoric: when it became known that, as a precautionary measure in the tense atmosphere of the time, their police records had been delivered to Number 10, both the marchers and their supporters on the Labour benches were angered. The final twist was given to the tale at the end of this somewhat tumultuous week, when a news conference was held at Number 10 and the reporter for the Labour *Daily Herald* was excluded. As he had denied asking for the police records, so Bonar Law denied having given such a provocative order, and asserted privately that he would have countermanded both instructions had he known of them; but on the central issue in question he stood firm: delegations, be they from the trade unions or the Federation of British Industry, had every right to petition their representatives, but they must not, he believed, presume that the Prime Minister could solve all their problems. Furthermore, he declared, it was well within the right – even the responsibility – of the Prime Minister's office to ascertain whether men who were well known for the extremism of their behaviour had police records. His explanation, delivered with his usual calm and candour, disarmed criticism and the crisis faded.[51]

A few weeks later Bonar Law defused another potentially explosive episode in Glasgow. He declined as Prime Minister to see a delegation of the Glasgow unemployed, but then announced that he would be pleased to hear them *as their Member of Parliament*.[52] Though he had insisted on his ground rules rather than theirs in meeting these men, the patience and courtesy with which he then treated them lowered the political temperature considerably. This crisis, too, melted away, and several Labour Members later privately expressed approval of what the Prime Minister considered a necessary defence of the freedom of Government from intimidation.[53]

Bonar Law resisted any idea of 'presidential' government, and had explained to public and Parliament often during the electoral campaign that he saw his administrative role as rather like that of the chairman of a large enterprise, with ministers truly in charge of their own departments, subject to his supervision. Thus Sanders, the Agriculture Minister, was expected to deal with the difficulties over the import of Canadian cattle, while Neville Chamberlain, having replaced the unfortunate Griffith-Boscawen at the Ministry of Health, was let alone to conceive his successful housing programme. Ministers who demonstrated initiative could expect Bonar Law's support, though if they ignored what he considered to be prudence – as did Amery, in relocating a naval squadron from Constantinople to Malta during the Lausanne Conference without notifying either Prime Minister or Foreign Office – they could expect to feel his tug on their coat-tails.[54]

Party officials were trusted in similar fashion; but, once again, if the need arose he acted both firmly and swiftly. The aged party treasurer Lord Farquhar, for example, had become mentally unstable, and there was evidence that he had funnelled monies intended for the Conservative war chest into the infamous Lloyd George fund, and refused during the election to sign cheques from the Conservative coffers which he controlled.[55] When this was brought to his attention, Bonar Law summarily removed the protesting Farquhar without a second thought.[56] Similarly, when the newly ennobled Viscount Younger was moved to the party treasurer's office to sort out the chaos, Bonar Law ignored the demands of the Die-Hards to install Gretton in his place and appointed Colonel F.S. Jackson as party chairman.[57]

Not surprisingly, perhaps, the minister most determined to act as independently as possible was Curzon. Bonar Law's Foreign Secretary had hated what he considered the interference with foreign affairs of Lloyd George and his legions of advisers at Number 10. The new Prime Minister's vision of his own role suited his aristocratic colleague, as did the fact that foreign policy was the element of Government responsibility in which he had in the past taken least interest. Nor, to Curzon's joy, had Bonar Law any intention of replicating the international conference-hopping agenda of his predecessors. Given the staggering problems of international relations which faced the Great Powers in the 1920s, however, Bonar Law knew he could not responsibly stand completely aside – even had he wished it.

III

The Lausanne Conference began on 18 November 1922, and here the frequently difficult Curzon was at his most brilliant. His lack of tact with his colleagues at home ran true to form, however, as he accused the Cabinet of cowardice over the issue which divided Britain and the Turks – the Kurdish territory of Mosul, demanded by Constantinople. Curzon was determined to face down the Turks but convinced that Bonar Law favoured surrender: in a phrase of immortal cruelty he complained to Harold Nicolson that the Prime Minister's feet were 'glacial. Positively glacial.'[58] It was not fear of the Turk which motivated Bonar Law, but anxiety lest the Foreign Secretary should stray from the policy outlined in his October letter to *The Times* and which had helped to win the recent election.[59] Backed by the Cabinet he repeatedly pointed this out to Curzon, who ultimately orchestrated a successful conclusion to the problem.[60]

It was another continuing dilemma, the vexed question of German reparations, which brought Bonar Law to the centre stage of foreign affairs – and in this matter his reputation for pessimism was entirely appropriate. The core of the problem lay in the fact that France and Belgium, so badly damaged by the German occupation of 1914–18, demanded that Germany should make the payments to them required of her under the Treaty of Versailles. Successive German governments had claimed they simply were unable to do so. Earlier in the year, Poincaré for the French had pressed the International Reparations Commission (the British delegate abstained) to declare Germany in default of her legal obligations, as under the terms of the Treaty she certainly was. By the time Bonar Law's Government had taken office, the French were bent on occupation of the Ruhr district to seize minerals and timber in lieu of the overdue payments. Bonar Law was troubled by the prospect, believing that such a policy would harm the fledgling Weimar Republic without doing much good for France. He explained his distaste to Neville Chamberlain: 'We having together knocked Germany down, one of us is going to kick her while she is on the ground, and the others will let her.'[61] On 9 December, the premiers of Britain's three main wartime European Allies arrived in London to discuss the problem. Poincaré's proposal was simple: Germany paid up, or the French occupied the Ruhr.

Bonar Law's début on the international stage went remarkably smoothly. The three premiers – Poincaré, Belgium's George Theunis, and the recently installed Italian *Duce*, Benito Mussolini – were friendly, and seemed impressed. Derby no doubt passed on Poincaré's remark that the French much preferred dealing with M. Bonar Law because, unlike Lloyd George, he listened to them.[62] Hoping to avoid a breach with France, the Prime Minister played for time in the age-old way of diplomacy – by telling his Allies just enough to raise their hopes of British co-operation in their efforts to squeeze the reluctant Germans, while stopping short of any pledge. Hankey, who had once feared his new master was a babe in the diplomatic woods, recorded his amusement in his diary:

> Bonar Law is more tricky than I suspected. Before the meeting [on 10 December] he wanted to meet the Belgians alone … and asked them to Downing St, and for some reason he did not want Poincaré to know that they were conspiring … I met them all coming downstairs together. Theunis and Jaspar [the Belgians] entered the Cabinet room by the usual entrance from the hall. Bonar came in through another door from the private secretary's room. Seeing M. Poincaré in the Cabinet room he turned to the Belgians (whom he had just left at the bottom of the stairs) and greeted them effusively, *shaking them by the hand*. And the *Morning Post* and other papers this morning are contrasting the 'straightness' of Bonar Law with the obliquity of Ll.G.![63]

All Bonar Law gained, however, was agreement from the Powers that none would act until after additional discussions had been held in Paris in the New Year. Recognizing the inevitable when he saw it, he told the Cabinet that nothing was likely to stop a French invasion of the Ruhr.[64] Nevertheless, he did not give up, and took with him to Paris a proposal to settle the reparations controversy. The plan was conceived by Keynes and Bradbury, Bonar Law's wartime Treasury advisers, and encompassed a four-year moratorium on reparations, followed by annual payments of £100 million per year, to be financed by a complicated series of bond issues and with the incentive of reduced liability for prompt payment. Britain's own contribution was to be the cancellation of the majority of the Allied war debts owed to herself.[65] Bonar Law presented the plan as though the minds of the French and Belgians were completely open, but he knew better. During the three days of meetings, 2–4 January, he soon came to realize that he had been right all along: the French were determined upon occupation. He was accompanied in Paris by the President of the Board of Trade, Sir Philip Lloyd-Greame, who recalled being told by him:

> We can't do anything at this meeting except agree to go our own ways for the time being and to do that in as friendly a way as we can and with as little prejudice as possible to future relations.[66]

Yet if Bonar Law had won nothing in his sole foray onto the international stage, he could take some comfort in the truism that no British representative could have done better. Lloyd-Greame wrote to his father that 'Bonar was wonderful. Clear as crystal, firm and friendly.'[67] Victor Cazalet, Lloyd-Greame's private secretary, remarked in his diary that Bonar Law's undramatic personal style made the rupture between the Allies less vicious than it might otherwise have been. Much of the reason for this, Cazalet concluded, was that there was a marked absence of intrigue or gossip surrounding the British Prime Minister: 'But then Bonar refuses to indulge in either.'[68]

Bonar Law led an electorate and a party largely pro-French in their sympathies and, despite the hopelessness of the conference, he was determined not to allow the reparations crisis to escalate into a crisis in Anglo-French relations. The French were entirely within their rights in demanding what was owed to them under the Treaty of Versailles. The British zone of military occupation in the Rhineland lay between the French zone and the Ruhr, and the Government had no real choice but to permit the French to move troops across the British sector. Bonar Law was a realist, but he was also angered by what he saw as Poincaré's stubbornness. In his days as Chancellor of the Exchequer Davidson had accompanied him to Paris for Anglo-French negotiations which had been similarly frustrating and fruitless. The same Poincaré, then President of the Repubic, had seen the British delegation off from the Gare du Nord; Bonar Law, smiling wryly, waved through the window of his coach. 'And you can go to hell,' he had said, as the train left the station.[69] Can he have felt very differently in December 1922?

On 11 January, French troops occupied the Ruhr. Berlin declared a policy of passive resistance, pledged to make good the wages of striking workers from a treasury already bankrupt, and the predictable result was economic and social chaos. It was the disaster Bonar Law had expected and, though the alliance survived, Anglo-French relations were markedly strained. Bad as this was, it was neither the last nor the worst of Bonar Law's war debt troubles.

Before 1914 Britain had been the greatest creditor nation in the world, but the debts of her wartime Allies proved as uncollectable as Germany's reparations payments – and the Great War left her £900 million in debt to the United States. Much of this had, of course, been amassed while Bonar Law was Chancellor, and businessman that he had been, he took it much to heart. The repayments question had remained in a kind of fiscal limbo while fruitless negotiations were carried on between the Lloyd George and Wilson governments. Then in 1920 Americans had turned their backs on the brilliant internationalist Woodrow Wilson, and placed their faith in a new President, Warren Gamaliel Harding, who a few months before Bonar Law's assumption of the premiership had invited a British delegation to Washington to settle the matter. The new Chancellor, Baldwin, finally sailed for America in late December 1922, just as Bonar Law was making ready for his rendezvous with Poincaré in Paris.

Bonar Law subscribed to the celebrated Balfour Note of August 1922, published shortly before the fall of the coalition, which laid down that Britain would collect payment from her debtors only in the amount which was demanded by her own creditor.[70] Since it was obvious that she could expect no repayments from her Allies for the foreseeable future, it seemed to Bonar Law a grotesque injustice that Britain should be asked to repay her war debt to America. He explained to the House in mid December:

> I am sure there is no one in the world who will doubt that, from the point of view of justice, it cannot be right that we alone should make payment as the result of this ... I am convinced that to make that payment without receiving anything from outside sources would reduce the standard of living in this country for a generation, and would be a burden upon us, which no one who talks of it now has any conception of.[71]

Now, in 1923, the American government intended to have their money, and it was in this climate of opinion that Stanley Baldwin, accompanied by the Governor of the Bank of England, Montagu Norman, arrived in Washington on 4 January. As Chancellor of the Exchequer Baldwin came with great prestige, but he came without plenipotentiary powers – to negotiate, but not to effect agreement to any terms.

Convinced that America would come to her senses, Bonar Law believed delay to be the best policy. Baldwin disagreed, concerned about the short-term damage non-co-operation might do to British credit, her international stature, and his remaining hopes that the US would play a role in the reconstruction of Europe. Bonar Law told him that he himself was only willing to swallow repayment in the form of an annual annuity of £30 million and for a period not to exceed fifty years – terms the new British Ambassador, Sir Auckland Geddes, thought the Americans would accept. The American Debt Commission had something very different in mind, however: there would be no annuities, and Britain's debt must be paid off at an interest rate of 3 per cent for ten years and 3½ per cent for a further fifty-two years. Including the interest already deferred, this amounted to annual payments of principal and interest of between £161 million and £187 million. The official American attitude came to be characterized by Harding's successor Calvin Coolidge's observation that 'They hired the money, didn't they?' Bonar Law found this simply intolerable, and immediately telegraphed to Baldwin: 'If a settlement is not obtainable on terms which seem to us reasonable, you have no alternative but to ask for further time for consideration, and to return.'[72]

Baldwin wished to press for a reduction of the rate of interest to 3 per cent, with a sinking fund of ½ per cent, but Bonar Law – in view of the other American terms – declared anything over 2½ per cent positively extortionate. He agreed to summon the Cabinet to consider Baldwin's plan, but he would endorse it only if the Americans would remit the unpaid interest. He continued to stress to the Chancellor that 'time is on our side in this matter', and reminded him not to imply agreement to any terms. The actual American demand was announced on 14 January: annual payments at 3 per cent or $161 million for ten years, and at 3½ per cent or $184 million thereafter, with the creation of a sinking fund at ½ per cent with back interest to be paid at 4½ per cent. Baldwin came away convinced this was the best deal that could be made, and members of the Debt Commission had convinced him that prompt acceptance was the key to the desired Anglo-American co-operation.

Bonar Law thought the US offer nothing less than usurious. In the business world, he believed, such an approach would be seen as a concerted effort by a creditor to ruin a debtor, without regard for actual repayment. He continued to believe that to accept would be to shackle future generations to an obligation which would menace economic recovery, and he was shocked that Baldwin, himself a former businessman, could not see as much. He immediately sought the advice of the banker and former Chancellor Reginald McKenna, who indicated his complete agreement with the Prime Minister.[73] Keynes concurred, reminding Bonar Law that, in the end, America had no more power to collect from Britain than Britain had from France or, for that matter, from Germany.[74]

Bonar Law rejected the idea that this was a matter of national honour, and the proposed terms also offended his ethical values. Britain had indeed 'hired' the money but, he reminded the House, 'It is an undoubted fact that we were in that position because we had used up all our securities and pledged them already to secure munitions for carrying on the war; and we had pledged them without any regard whatever to whether it was for the British Armies or the Armies of our Allies ...'[75] Britain had expended her own wealth in a great common cause – much of it, of course, in cash paid directly to American industries. When she began to borrow heavily from the United States, much of the principal came to Britain because she was the broker America preferred over France, Italy and Russia; and much of the borrowed wealth never left America, but simply enriched her manufacturers. With the Balfour Note Britain had pledged herself to a generous policy towards her wartime creditors, and Bonar Law expected Washington to behave in a similar spirit.

He also believed the European Allies had paid in other ways. The United States came officially into the Great War in April 1917, but took little part for more than a year – a year in which Britain and France had fought through some of the most terrible battles of the conflict in the name of all the Allied and Associated Powers, expending their blood and wealth to bring down the common enemy. Now Britain, above all others, was expected to pay handsomely for the privilege. Baldwin later recalled that in the disagreement Bonar Law 'saw the blood of his two sons. "We paid in blood: they did not: you can't equate that with a cash payment" – that was Bonar's view.'[76] And so it was.

Because of the Christmas recess, ministers were scattered across the country, and Bonar Law hastily assembled what colleagues he could on 15 January to secure their agreement to withholding acceptance of the American terms.[77] Baldwin's delegation arrived home on the twenty-seventh, to be met at Southampton by a large party of journalists, whetted by leaks in the American press and hungry for an important story of their own. The Chancellor, quite unprepared, replied to their queries with appalling frankness, suggesting that he had brought back the best possible offer, one which the Government would be well advised to take. He believed that he was speaking 'off the record', but of course his words – or versions of them – were soon splashed across the nation's newspapers. It was a disaster, and Baldwin acknowledged the enormity of his error later, saying that 'he would rather that his tongue had been torn out than have talked to the press at Southampton.'[78]

The full Cabinet met on Tuesday, 30 January, and Baldwin repeated the arguments members had already read in the press. US interest rates were regrettably higher than those to which the City was accustomed.[79] The US Senate meant business, however, and its members were largely ignorant of the niceties of international finance. The payment schedule was daunting, but it was better than allowing the debt to accumulate until it reached unmanageable proportions. They could expect no better offer: refusal to settle would be as bad as defaulting on the debt, and was inconceivable – particularly in light of the Anglo-American co-operation for which they all hoped. Britain's national honour and international credit were at stake, and to fail to settle the matter now would inevitably lead to future fiscal problems which would certainly be worse. Baldwin was heard in silence, and the initiative then passed to the Prime Minister.

In his private record of the decisive Cabinet meeting, Derby noted that after Baldwin had finished,

> Bonar Law then did an extraordinary thing. Instead of asking for expression by each of us of our opinions he produced the same arguments as he had used to me the day before, said his mind was quite made up and that nothing would induce him to remain the head of a Government which consented to sign.

This was, of course, a demand for the surrender of Baldwin and those who agreed with him, as Derby immediately recognized:

> We were all aghast at this, and the Lord Chancellor [Lord Cave] really voiced our opinions when he made in a very tactful way a remonstrance against a pistol being put to our heads. Bonar agreed that he had done this and thought it best to let us know his views ...[80]

The Prime Minister explained that he was not suggesting the British Government should repudiate the debt (a point often misunderstood by historians), but rather that they should continue to pay interest on the principal in the presumption that in a few years Washington would come to its senses. For the American methods of negotiation he had only contempt: 'To treat us as badly as that must strike anyone as absurd ...'[81]

His colleagues were unmoved, however, and there was near unanimity in favour of acceptance. It is difficult to be certain exactly who supported Bonar Law's position: Amery recalled that only Lord Novar, the Scottish Secretary, did so.[82] Derby's recollection was that, except for the Prime Minister and Lloyd-Greame, 'we were absolutely unanimous in saying that we ought to accept the terms.'[83] Hankey, who was present, told Tom Jones that both Novar and Lloyd-Greame supported Bonar Law.[84] In any event, it was frighteningly clear that the Prime Minister was unable to support the policy of the overwhelming majority of his own Government – and the room fell absolutely silent for a moment. Before anything even more destructive could be said, Novar hastily suggested an adjournment until the following day. The Prime Minister consented, rose, and left the room.

There is a curious footnote to this meeting. In *The Times* that morning there had appeared a letter, over the pseudonym 'Colonial', addressing the American debt question and stressing precisely the arguments with which Bonar Law failed to sway the Cabinet. Though the Prime Minister had admonished his colleagues only the week before against writing letters or articles for the press, the letter was written by Bonar Law himself.[85] He had seen Wickham Steed the evening before the Cabinet meeting, and may well have discussed with him his intention to send the letter.[86] It is possible that Beaverbrook knew of the ploy, but Davidson did not. Whatever else it may have meant, it certainly speaks to Bonar Law's desperation to bring his colleagues around to his perspective.

The Prime Minister had seldom felt so isolated, and during the long night that followed the Cabinet meeting he came very close to resignation. His health, so promising a few months before, now troubled him, and his eight weeks in office had been worrisome and exhausting. He had argued in Cabinet in terms as clear to him as any in his long career, and he was stunned by the total rejection of his position. He remembered well how only months before these very men had pleaded with him to be their political saviour, and the memory made his disappointment that much greater. But most of all, Bonar Law was haunted by the certainty that his colleagues were absolutely wrong: the US terms were bad for Britain.

The peace that resignation might bring would come at a high cost, however: abandoning his Sovereign and his nation after such a short innings was a distasteful prospect. Furthermore, the potential damage to his party of an early retirement weighed heavily on him. Who, after all, would succeed him? The former coalitionists continued in their alienation from the Government, thus ruling out as possible successors Chamberlain, Balfour or Horne. It was unlikely that Curzon, senior among his Cabinet colleagues, could unite the party and lead from the Lords. If Bonar Law resigned because he disagreed with him over the

American debt terms, it would taint Baldwin's chances. Could the veteran Derby save Government and party – surely that was also unlikely?

With the Prime Minister's approval, a group of senior ministers met privately the following morning in the Lord Chancellor's room to discuss the impasse.[87] Cave and Baldwin, who had argued most strongly for the American terms, recommended capitulation to Bonar Law.[88] The rest, led by Derby and Bridgeman and excepting only the steadfast Novar, insisted that to reject the US terms in the glare of national and even world publicity was impossible. After an hour they could think of nothing more constructive than to send a deputation of the Prime Minister's old friends Devonshire and Cave, as well as Baldwin himself, to implore Bonar Law not to resign.

In the meantime, McKenna reported that opinion in the City was uniformly in favour of acceptance, and changed his own advice accordingly: the moment for rejection of the terms had passed, he said, and he recommended surrender.[89] Beaverbrook continued to hate the terms, but also begged Bonar Law to give in.[90] Perhaps this made it easier for the Prime Minister to do what those who knew him best might have expected – to compromise over the terms, and keep the Cabinet and the party together.

It is unknown what the three emissaries said to him, but – as other Tory ambassadors had found in the past – it is unlikely that they had to proceed much beyond the call of party loyalty. Their personal fealty may have failed him, but it was his decision at the Carlton Club that had put them in power in the first place, and he accepted the responsibility thus incurred. The four certainly spoke as friends, and Bonar Law confessed that he could not stand against so solid a majority of his colleagues. He would climb down – the alternatives were so much worse.

In a five-minute meeting of the Cabinet the following afternoon, the Prime Minister announced his surrender. The official record noted only 'That the proposal of the United States Funding Commission should be accepted in principle.'[91] As Derby recalled, '[Bonar Law] said he had slept on it and come to the conclusion he was asking his colleagues to make too great a sacrifice and although he still held the same opinion he gave way and agreed to the American proposal. A great relief to us all.'[92]

Their relief was purchased at Bonar Law's expense. He had struggled against the burden of chronic depression all his life, and was unable to view this affair as a simple disagreement in the normal course of Cabinet politics. He felt abandoned by his colleagues, wondering whether he was master of the Government his sacrifice had made possible. Tom Jones concluded simply: 'I have never seen him so depressed.'[93] Beaverbrook's recollections of the episode are both credible and affecting:

> In any case his self-confidence *did* receive a severe shock by his absolute failure to carry his Cabinet. He had seen [Lloyd] George wangle a Cabinet so often, that he had not perhaps realised that [Lloyd] George never undertook the task without calculating well in advance, that the effort would be successful. The blow to his prestige and influence struck him hard.[94]

Bonar Law was wounded, but he lost neither his perspective nor his humanity, and part of the reason for this was certainly the fact that only weeks before Lady Sykes had given birth to his first grandchild, and namesake. The man who had always taken great pleasure in an affectionate and easy relationship with his children when they were small enjoyed elaborate and animated 'conversations' with the infant Bonar Hugh Sykes, known within the family as 'Ptoly'. Early in 1923, holding the baby in his arms, Bonar Law pronounced his final word on these events: 'Poor little chap, you'll still be paying off the debt when you are my age.'[95]

IV

By early 1923 Bonar Law was again a very sick man. His physicians seemed unable to do anything about his failing voice, though they diagnosed nothing more than a 'relaxed throat'. This discomfort was only part of what appeared to be a rising tide of troubles which reached its zenith in the weeks following the war debt crisis. The problems of French ambitions in the Ruhr and of Turkey in Mosul remained before the Government; conditions in Egypt were unsettled; and the conference at Lausanne had reached no conclusion. At home, the high level of unemployment gnawed away at public confidence, and Griffith-Boscawen's inability to find a parliamentary seat did nothing to forward his promised housing programme. Hankey, a master of understatement, noted in his diary in February that this litany of anxieties had '. . . in combination produced a state of affairs which cannot be very attractive to [Bonar Law].'[96]

A new parliamentary session began in mid February, and the King's Speech revealed that the Government planned few initiatives for the coming months. For the time being, Bonar Law would have been satisfied merely to win the by-elections scheduled for early March.[97]

According to Hankey, the Government were 'knocked endways' by the results:[98] on 3 March, Griffith-Boscawen was defeated at Mitcham, as was George Stanley, Under-Secretary at the Home Office, at Willesden East. Three days later J.W. Hills, Financial Secretary to the Treasury, lost Liverpool, Edge Hill. The whips had been optimistic about the contests; the losses were laid to the account of intervention by Tory former coalitionists, and the hostile Rothermere press. The defeats were distressing, and that at Mitcham – involving an already once-defeated Cabinet minister – little less than humiliating.[99]

The House rose for the Easter recess on 29 March, amid much concern on the Government benches over the fact that their leader – who continued to attend every sitting of the House – could speak only in a hoarse whisper. On doctor's orders Bonar Law retreated to Torquay for a fortnight's rest, which served to provide fodder for press speculation that his health was breaking and that he meant to resign.[100] Various scenarios were offered: the former coalitionist Austen Chamberlain would succeed, or perhaps even Birkenhead; or Baldwin. Inevitably, such speculation reached Curzon in Switzerland, and the Marquess, as he had become, fired off to Bonar Law a letter of frustration and surpassing vainglory: should the Prime Minister have to go – which, he carefully noted, would be calamitous – he could not possibly consider serving under any of their colleagues. He recited the litany of his own undoubted qualities and accomplishments, and his iron-clad claim to the succession.[101] Given what was already preying on his mind, Bonar Law was unimpressed by Curzon's self-serving initiative. He returned fire tersely from his Devon retreat: 'The rumour is without foundation. I have not been up to the mark for a month or six weeks but I have no intention of resigning unless my health should make it impossible for me to continue.'[102]

Parliament reassembled on 10 April, and the Prime Minister returned to his place on the Treasury Bench, insisting that he felt better than he had in weeks. His throat, however, would not respond to treatment; and as he attempted to respond to the first question directed to him – Number 44, it happened to be – he struggled hard to make himself heard. Nourah Waterhouse, the wife of Bonar Law's secretary, observed from the Strangers' Gallery, and later recalled the scene:

'Speak up!' cried someone from the Opposition Benches, and immediately the whole House turned upon the interrupter in marked resentment. Bonar stood still, his lips moved, but no sound came. Then he smiled wistfully, and actually articulated, 'I will do my best.' But he failed. Mr Baldwin, the Deputy Leader, took his place, and Bonar left the Chamber.[103]

Although the Government were beaten on a snap vote the very day of this poignant scene,[104] their fortunes now turned markedly upward. Bonar Law's quiet dignity in the House despite his obvious discomfort roused the sympathy of Members, and there was much criticism when the *Observer* retailed the resignation rumours. Birkenhead, most vengeful among the former coalitionists, savaged Bonar Law and the Government in a biting article in the *Sunday Times*, expressing disdain for a Cabinet which staggered only, he said, 'from discredit to discredit'.[105] But the erstwhile Lord Chancellor's attack backfired, as usual, and Sanders reported with delight that 'the effect has been rather to pull the party together.'[106]

Baldwin introduced his only Budget on 16 April, and it was widely praised as a successful performance filled with encouraging news. Expenditure was £97 million less than anticipated, and revenue £3 million over estimate. The Chancellor's explanation of Treasury efforts to manage the huge debt pleased the House (who among its Members had anything convincingly better to offer?), and his anticipation of an income surplus for the following fiscal year allowed him to propose reductions in certain other taxes, including sixpence off income tax and small decreases in selected excise taxes.[107] Like the House, the press cheered the Budget – even the Rothermere newspapers abandoned their customary hostile tone.[108]

After a difficult winter, feeling in Westminster was that the Bonar Law Government had ridden out the storm. Curzon's efforts in Lausanne finally bore fruit, and pressures in Asia Minor eased. The by-election defeats had not foreshadowed disaster for the Government, and Neville Chamberlain had seized with both hands his opportunity at the Health Ministry afforded by Griffith-Boscawen's misfortune. The tailing-off of press attacks, Birkenhead's clumsy belligerence and the rousing success of the Budget also played a part in buoying up the Prime Minister's spirits. Continuing difficulties with his throat and his doctors' inability to diagnose the cause hung over him, however: though he seldom missed a session, by now he could not speak at all in the House. In view of the feelings he had expressed the previous October about the length of time he might hold office, it is inconceivable that he was not considering at this time the question of how long he might be able to go on.

Austen Chamberlain certainly became convinced that this was the case,[109] for he revealed to a few close associates that he had once again been offered the succession to the premiership, this time apparently by Bonar Law – or at least (and this is a significant point), in Bonar Law's name. His story was that on 10 April he was invited to dine with Birkenhead, Horne, Guest and Oliver Locker-Lampson at Rothermere's London house. Their host was indisposed, and his son Esmond took his place. Birkenhead was taken up to speak to Rothermere, who told him to relay to Chamberlain a question which came from Beaverbrook but supposedly had originated with Bonar Law. Chamberlain repeated it to his sister Hilda:

> Will I join Bonar's Govt as Privy Seal & Leader of the House taking at the moment only Horne in with me but with Bonar's verbal understanding that he will resign on August 1st in my favour with the clear understanding that I shall then reconstruct the Govt on my own lines – a thorough reconstruction. A strange world my masters![110]

This is a curious tale from beginning to end – that Bonar Law should authorize Beaverbrook to take such an offer to Rothermere, for him to relay it, through Birkenhead, to Chamberlain! Strange indeed, for Bonar Law distrusted Rothermere, and Rothermere knew Birkenhead was vengeful against Bonar Law. Chamberlain felt nothing but distaste for both Beaverbrook and Rothermere, and his reactions were precisely in character: first, he would receive no overtures through agents, particularly those agents; second, agreement would mean betrayal of his friends; and finally, the offer itself was discreditable, and would bring dishonour upon all parties. He concluded that it was morally and politically objectionable.[111]

This offer – and the idea that it originated with Bonar Law – has often been reported at face value by historians.[112] There seems to be no reason to doubt that an offer was made, but there are good reasons to doubt Chamberlain's explanation of what it meant. Beaverbrook certainly claimed to have brought Rothermere and Bonar Law together on 13 April, though this cannot be corroborated.[113] If a meeting at which the succession was discussed between these distinctly antipathetic men did take place, it is difficult to envisage the Prime Minister involving Rothermere in such a circuitous plot to snare Chamberlain as his successor.

In his unpublished memorandum of these events Beaverbrook mentions only that his two guests discussed the forthcoming Budget.[114] It is true that the Rothermere press became uncharacteristically favourable towards the Government from the time of the Budget speech, but it seems unlikely that this was related to the question of the succession. In fact, Rothermere indicated in a rather absurd letter written to Beaverbrook some days after these events that he assumed Bonar Law would serve another three years and be remembered as 'one of the most successful Prime Ministers in history'. This was conditional, however: 'If Bonar places himself in my hands.'[115]

It is likely that the clarification of this episode lay with Neville Chamberlain, who was the only figure at this time intimate both with his elder brother Austen, and with the Prime Minister. When he became aware of these machinations he went straight to the Prime Minister and told him all that he knew of the affair. Bonar Law was precise in his reply: he had sent *no* such message to Austen Chamberlain through *any* agent. He went further: while Conservatives, he believed, were perhaps willing at this moment to have Horne back in the Cabinet, they were not yet ready to be reconciled with Austen Chamberlain, much less with the disgraced Birkenhead. For Beaverbrook or Rothermere to suggest that the majority of Conservatives were prepared to accept the prompt succession of Austen Chamberlain to the premiership was 'grotesque'.[116] Perhaps to save face, Austen wrote to Neville a few days later that he had known at the time the two press lords were speaking without the authority of Bonar Law.[117] This might have been the case; but it is more likely he thought that once again he had chosen to be right rather than Prime Minister.

By this point the deterioration in the Prime Minister's health was obvious. Cabinet meetings, always concise and businesslike affairs when Bonar Law was in the chair, by April had become almost perfunctory, with the premier all but unable to take part in discussion because of his inability to make himself easily heard. He managed to struggle into the Privy Council uniform he so loathed, in order to attend the wedding of the Duke of York – the future King George VI – on 26 April; and though he stood straight and dealt patiently with well-wishers, his drawn and grey appearance alarmed all who saw him. No one was more concerned than Beaverbrook, who for weeks had been advising him to go abroad to rebuild his strength. Bonar Law resisted, arguing that since his doctors had been unable to identify any particular ailment, his place was on the Treasury Bench – whether he could speak or not.[118]

Beaverbrook enlisted the help of Bonar Law's family and of his physician, Sir Thomas Horder, who stressed that another sabbatical could only improve the Prime Minister's condition. The patient, however, continued to resist. 'The whole of this business of inducing the Premier to hand over command and go abroad for a time', Beaverbrook recalled, 'was an absolute death grapple with his unwillingness to do anything of the kind and cost hours of time.' Finally Bonar Law gave in, and on 26 April informed his colleagues that 'he was neither resting his throat nor doing any good in the House and that he had consequently decided to go away for a complete rest until after Whitsuntide.' Certainly it must have chilled his Cabinet, in office only six months, to hear his conclusion: 'If that did no good,' Amery recalled, 'he said he would seriously have to think of resigning.'[119] In the meantime, Curzon would deputize for him, and Baldwin would lead in the Commons.

Bonar Law was received by the King the next day, and they discussed the possibility of the Prime Minister visiting North America.[120] In the event, the sunshine of the Mediterranean had more appeal; and, accompanied only by his son Dick, Bonar Law sailed from Southampton on 1 May on the Dutch liner *Princess Juliana*. After stopping briefly in Algiers, the ship docked in Genoa on the eighth. Though *The Times* correspondent in Italy patriotically reported of the Prime Minister that 'his face is very brown and his step active',[121] the ship was also met by Davidson, who noted neither a tanned face nor a lively step, and drew his own sober conclusions: 'Those of us who were close to him feared, but never mentioned, that his disease might be incurable and his fate sealed.'[122]

16

Coda

Bonar law's generation set great store by the hygienic potency of sea air and Mediterranean sun, and for the first few days of his voyage he expressed some confidence in their healing powers.[1] It was obvious, however, that a week at sea had done nothing to relieve the increasing discomfort in his throat. When Davidson and the devoted Berry joined the party in Genoa on 8 May 1923, Dick Law confirmed their conclusion that his father was suffering from something far more serious than fatigue and a 'relaxed throat'.[2] Bonar Law chose to abandon the cruise, and the party moved on to the comfort of Aix-les-Bains.

In this fashionable watering-spot they encountered Bonar Law's old friends the Kiplings, and the poet was so shocked by the premier's appearance and state of mind that he telegraphed to Beaverbrook to come out immediately.[3] In his unpublished memorandum of the period, Beaverbrook noted that he had already been summoned by a message sent from Genoa by Bonar Law himself.

> It was an alarming letter, one of the most alarming letters I have ever received, and brought me post-haste to see him ... If anything he was worse rather than better. Depression seemed to have settled down on him like a cloud, and he also complained of pain in his head.[4]

Beaverbrook hurried to Aix and, like the Kiplings, was stunned by what he found. According to Tom Jones,

From Aix, B.L. sent a 'de profundis' letter to B[eaverbrook] begging him to come out or he would throw himself under a train. When B. got there he found B.L. taking about 10 doses of anti-carnia daily to keep down the pain he was suffering.[5]

Having been convinced that his friend was suffering primarily from exhaustion and a nagging sore throat, Beaverbrook became acutely aware of how wrong he had been: he shepherded the party (now also including Mrs Davidson) to Paris, after arranging for Sir Thomas Horder to meet them there. On Wednesday, 16 May, Bonar Law and his friends arrived in Paris and Beaverbrook, hoping it would raise his spirits, insisted that they attend a dinner party given by Lord and Lady Granard. He watched Bonar Law slip during the course of the evening into deeper pain and silence, and understood that he required more than cheerful company.[6] Horder visited the Prime Minister in his suite in the Hôtel Crillon the following afternoon; he said little, prescribed further medicines to ease the pain, and discreetly withdrew. In those days it was widely considered kinder to withhold the worst news from the very ill, and Horder indicated nothing to his patient of what he had learned.

Beaverbrook had installed himself in another hotel, and there he awaited the verdict. He did not wait long. Horder summoned him by telephone immediately after leaving his patient, and confided as they walked in the Paris sunshine what had somehow escaped his detection for many months: Bonar Law was suffering from cancer of the throat. The two immediately returned to the Crillon; without explaining the gravity of his affliction, Horder merely told the Prime Minister that his illness justified his immediate resignation. Beaverbrook, who had stubbornly resisted the possibility, now did an about-face and encouraged his friend to retire from office. He recalled that Bonar Law 'was almost lighthearted in his relief at the idea of laying down a burden which had been crushing his failing vitality.'[7]

A sort of Tory Moses, Bonar Law had led the party from servitude to the coalition, through a triumphal election and the initial trials of office. But although he had entered into the Promised Land, it was not for long. Politics is fraught with cruel ironies, and he and his followers were soon caught up in the question of who would be his Joshua.

Yet life and the business of the State had to go on. Accompanied by Horder, Beaverbrook returned to London the following morning to prepare the press for the resignation announcement.[8] Bonar Law, his son and the Davidsons followed on Friday morning, with Davidson under orders to 'prepare the way at the Palace and with some of his senior colleagues.'[9] Bound for an alpine holiday, L.S. Amery had arrived in Paris on Thursday evening and met Bonar Law's party. He soon learned of the impending resignation and hurried back to London on the same boat-train.[10] Between Davidson and Amery, the task of spreading the word among the Tory politicians was dealt with swiftly.

The news of the Prime Minister's affliction spread across Whitehall over that Whitsun weekend, and the question of the succession pushed aside all other matters in public life. The Conservative Party continued to enjoy a healthy parliamentary majority, and he was to resign for reasons independent of politics and without a designated heir apparent: in such a case, Bonar Law anticipated, his advice to the King would be of the highest importance – and the prospect of giving it filled him with dread.

Though the former leader, Austen Chamberlain, was still ambitious for the premiership, he and his friends remained aloof from the Government and unacceptable to the majority of the party faithful. Within the Cabinet only three possible candidates were seriously mentioned: Lord Derby, Lord Curzon, and Stanley Baldwin.

Eddie Derby possessed long experience in office, and his popularity and prestige within the party were formidable. Though apparently when Bonar Law's impending resignation became known he was encouraged by the press lords Beaverbrook and Rothermere, even by Birkenhead and Austen Chamberlain, to consider himself a possible successor, Derby refused to be their candidate.[11] Sensing a 'stop Baldwin' campaign, he went immediately to the party chairman, Colonel Jackson, made his non-candidacy plain, and added that he would in no circumstances serve under Curzon, 'his *bête-noire* in public life'.[12] The two readily agreed that when it came to it, 'Baldwin was the right man.'[13] The potential contest was therefore promptly reduced to only two runners: Curzon and Baldwin.

In his shattered state of health and faced with such a choice, Bonar Law wished above all to avoid the responsibility of making one or the other candidate the favourite. In this too Beaverbrook had attempted to come to his friend's aid: in Paris on the afternoon of 17 May, he had revealed the truth and the problem to the Liberal statesman Lord Crewe, the newly-appointed Ambassador; their conclusion was that sufficient precedents existed to allow Bonar Law to avoid the awful duty on which his mind was now becoming fixated. Crewe recalled that neither Gladstone in 1894, nor Campbell-Bannerman fourteen years later, had recommended a successor to his Sovereign, and the examples sounded authoritative enough to cheer Bonar Law when he was told them over bridge at the Embassy that afternoon.[14]

In fact these historical anecdotes were mere placebos: they eased the Prime Minister's mind, but were the King to request his advice, it would have been unthinkable for him to refuse it.[15] Though he was gravely ill, Bonar Law was in full control of his faculties; he was not bedridden; his voice was weak, but not inaudible in close conversation – and how could a resigning minister able to play bridge be considered too incapacitated to offer counsel to his Sovereign? In the event, his wish to remain uncommitted was honoured by George V, out of his respect and consideration for a very sick man. Amery, when he dined with Bonar Law on the evening of 17 May, found his leader's appearance alarming but his spirits far better than he had expected. The temporary passage of the cloud was almost certainly due to the fact that Bonar Law's mind had been eased by his conversation with Crewe, and he was now quite willing to discuss possible candidates for the succession to the premiership with his younger colleague, in general terms.[16]

The question remains: why was Bonar Law determined to avoid offering a recommendation to the King, and unyielding in his resolve to offer no explanation for that determination? Several points are worthy of consideration. Bonar Law had never enjoyed an easy relationship with the King, who was quite capable of doggedly arguing against advice he did not particularly wish to hear – a possibility the Prime Minister would not have wanted to face. It is also possible that Bonar Law had no advice to give – that this deeply forthright and very ill man could not, knowing the strengths and faults of each, in honesty recommend one aspirant over the other. A third possible explanation is that he simply found both available candidates wanting and the circumstances impossible. Seniority and experience made Curzon the obvious choice, but while Bonar Law admired his talents he feared he was too overbearing to be able to form a Government or hold it together. Baldwin was popular with the party and, if Chamberlain remained in the wilderness, certainly destined one day to be Prime Minister. His experience as Chancellor and as Leader of the House was scant, however, and his handling of the US debt affair had shaken Bonar Law. Yet he was in the Commons, the political base of choice in the post-war world, and he also possessed humility and common sense – attributes which were seldom reckoned among Curzon's many undeniable qualities.

When faced with important decisions not only had Bonar Law often been slow to make up his mind – he had on occasion reversed himself after taking time to 'sleep on it'. Once convinced, however, he had never before shrunk from making a decision, and now he did. The historian cannot fail to conclude that whatever other reasons existed, his broken health – coupled with the chronic depression which in his weakened condition he found so much harder to resist – played the greatest part in causing him to act as he did.

When he returned to London on Saturday 19 May, the crowd of newspaper reporters and admirers who welcomed him at Victoria Station obviously felt little doubt of the seriousness of his condition. An official and rather bleak announcement issued by his doctors later that day dashed all hope: 'In spite of rest the Prime Minister's voice is still unsatisfactory. We are unable to promise improvement within a reasonable time.'[17] Awaiting the official inevitable, the press men – apparently in respectful silence – clustered around the ailing statesman's house in Onslow Gardens throughout Saturday and Sunday.

These events occurred as the King and Queen were at Aldershot for Whitsuntide. It was apparently Beaverbrook who suggested that the thirty-seven-mile journey, and Bonar Law's obvious illness, furnished plausible reasons for him to resign by letter rather than in the course of the usual personal audience – and obviated the possibility of any discussion about the succession.[18] The King, of course, had little choice in the matter; but as he struggled to do the right thing he noted in his diary, 'it is not easy to make up my mind whether to send for Curzon or Baldwin'.[19] It seems likely that Bonar Law composed his short letter of resignation that Saturday, dating and signing it the following day.[20] He also wrote briefly to Curzon, who continued to chair the Cabinet, explaining only that he had resigned, and that he would not be offering a recommendation regarding the succession.[21]

Responsibility for delivering Bonar Law's resignation letter to the King was entrusted to his son-in-law Sir Frederick Sykes and his Principal Private Secretary Colonel Waterhouse. Lord Beaverbrook, who was present at Onslow Gardens on the Sunday, offered this explanation:

> I insisted, however, on Sykes going and taking the principal part because I knew that he realised far better than anyone how absolutely necessary it was that matters should not take a turn which would entangle Bonar Law once more in the 'nomination' issue we had just escaped from.[22]

On a page attached to this same unpublished typescript and headed 'Alternative Ending', he also gave a slightly different version of events:

To Col. Ronald Waterhouse, as Principal Private Secretary to the Prime Minister, fell the duty of delivering the letter to the King, who was in Aldershot.

He did not hold the confidence of Bonar Law's family. Sir Frederick Sykes, Bonar Law's son-in-law, offered to accompany the Secretary.

Davidson, who also was present, claimed thirty years later that he had suggested Sykes should present Bonar Law's letter, 'rather than let it be conveyed by the hand of his official secretary.' He added: 'I have no recollection that there was distrust of Waterhouse or fear of his misrepresenting Bonar Law.'[23]

One cannot help but wonder: if Waterhouse was so distrusted that Sykes was charged with presenting the letter to the King at Aldershot – the sole purpose of the journey – what possible reason can there have been for Waterhouse to make the journey at all? The reason, as we shall see, was that he and Davidson were pursuing an agenda unknown either to Sykes or to the Prime Minister.

However it came about that they were travelling together, Sykes and Waterhouse set out for Aldershot in Bonar Law's rather shabby motor-car shortly after 11 a.m. They were received by Lord Stamfordham, who at once took Sykes to the King to hand over the melancholy letter. After a thirty-minute audience, Sir Frederick collected Waterhouse and returned directly to Onslow Gardens with His Majesty's regretful acceptance of the resignation.[24] On 20 May 1923, Bonar Law's premiership effectively came to an end: the news was immediately released to the press.[25]

Events moved quickly from this point, and within forty-eight hours Stanley Baldwin was Prime Minister. For the biographer of Bonar Law, however, there remain two additional matters worthy of consideration, and about which both participants in and historians of these events have disagreed. The first involves the question of precisely what information was transmitted to the King in Bonar Law's name, and by whom. The other is this: though he went to great lengths to avoid recommending a successor, did Bonar Law in fact express a preference between the two aspirants, Curzon and Baldwin?

The subject of what the King was told, by whom, and in what circumstances was raised first by Lord Blake, who discovered a long-overlooked memorandum in the Royal Archives when he was preparing his biography of Bonar Law in the early 1950s.[26] Unsigned and undated, the four-page document is a powerful argument in favour of Baldwin, subtly dismissing the candidacy of Curzon because, in the first place, he did not

> ... inspire complete confidence in his colleagues, either as to his judgment, or as to his ultimate strength of purpose, in a crisis. His methods, too, are inappropriate to harmony. The prospect of his receiving deputations as Prime Minister from the Miners' Federation or the Triple Alliance, for example, is capable of causing alarm for the future relations between the Government and Labour – between moderate and less moderate opinion.

The memorandum also stressed the fact that Curzon was a peer:

> The time, in the opinion of many Members of the House of Commons, has passed when the direction of domestic policy can be placed outside the House of Commons, and it is submitted that, although foreign and imperial affairs are of vital importance, stability at home must be the basic consideration. There is also the fact that Lord Curzon is regarded in the public eye as representing that section of privileged conservatism which has its value but which, in this democratic age, cannot be too assiduously exploited.

Lord Blake concluded that the anonymous document had been written by Davidson, who when approached – though no doubt surprised to see it again after thirty years – acknowledged authorship.[27] He explained that Bonar Law's secretary, Miss Watson, had typed the memorandum directly from his dictation; it was then sealed into an envelope and entrusted to Waterhouse to give to Lord Stamfordham, whom Davidson claimed had requested of him a confidential evaluation 'from the point of view of the average backbencher'.[28] None of the other members of Bonar Law's circle, including Sykes, expressed to Lord Blake any knowledge of the memorandum; and he therefore concluded that Waterhouse must have placed the sealed envelope into Stamfordham's (or perhaps even the King's) hands 'behind Sykes's back'.[29]

Colonel Waterhouse did more than simply give Stamfordham the paper, for attached to it is a brief note by the Royal Secretary: 'This is the memorandum handed to the King on Sunday 20th May: and which Colonel Waterhouse stated practically *expressed the views of Mr Bonar Law*.'[30] To summarize the episode as it has been accepted by most historians: the document was written by Davidson at Stamfordham's request and surreptitiously handed to the Royal Secretary by Waterhouse, who added the fiction that it represented the judgement of the Prime Minister.

New evidence now suggests that the memorandum was not com-posed solely by Davidson and discreetly typed by Miss Watson directly from his dictation.[31] A.J. Sylvester, another of Bonar Law's secretaries, wrote his own record of the events of Sunday, 20 May 1923, and placed it in his private files, where it remained for many years after these events.[32] He recalled that when he arrived in the room the three men shared at Number 10 on Sunday morning, he found Davidson and Waterhouse poring over a draft of the memorandum. Sylvester, asked to type a final copy of the 'very personal and secret document which was urgently required', did so as the others smoked and discussed the mem-orandum and to whom it might be sent. It was, they decided, to be delivered by Waterhouse to Lord Stamfordham – who, they agreed, *was not to know the exact origins of the document, which was to be identified only as coming from 'a mutual friend'.*

Sylvester's version has the ring of truth about it: in later life Davidson often spoke disparagingly of Waterhouse, but they were good friends at this time and shared both a devotion to Bonar Law and great hopes for Baldwin – and themselves. Davidson's explanation that Stamfordham had personally requested the memorandum of him is not borne out either by any corroborating evidence or by the note appended to it, which mentions only Waterhouse's actions – and in any case, it is unlikely that the King's secretary would ask for the views of an 'average backbencher' from a member of the Prime Minister's inner circle. The fact that Davidson, Waterhouse and Sylvester all retained copies of the memorandum dispenses with the inference that Miss Watson typed the only version of the document directly from Davidson's dictation and that no one else saw it. Likewise, suggestions by historians that Amery or Jones or Bridgeman played some part in its preparation do not appear to be in any way verifiable.[33] In fact, Jones's diary indicates that he was shown a copy of the memorandum by Sylvester on Sunday evening and that he, Jones, knew little of its origins.[34] Finally, while Davidson or Waterhouse perhaps wished to hide their roles in this affair, Sylvester had no such motivation – he composed his account, based on his contemporary diary, only after the other principals were dead, and did not release it during his own very long lifetime.

The question of Bonar Law's own preference between the contest-ants for the position he himself wished only to escape is equally inter-esting: did he favour Curzon, Baldwin, or some other aspirant? Since Lord Blake's discovery of the document historians seem generally agreed that Waterhouse was inaccurate in his claim to Stamfordham that the so-called Davidson memorandum expressed Bonar Law's opinion.[35] There is little reason to doubt that the Prime Minister presumed Curzon's impressive credentials would prevail, and that he would be chosen to form a Government. According to Beaverbrook, Bonar Law said as much to Baldwin himself, when the three met as Sykes and Waterhouse were making their way to Aldershot: Curzon would probably become premier, Baldwin was told, but his turn would come. The Chancellor seemed untroubled by this, and indicated (unlike Curzon) that he would serve under anyone who could hold the party together.[36] Similarly, Amery recorded in his diary that when he had spoken to the Prime Minister in Paris two days earlier, Bonar Law had indicated that he was 'inclined to doubt the possibility of displacing Curzon against his will.'[37]

Yet, of this very same conversation, Amery also noted that, though he recognized Curzon as the favourite, 'Bonar's view on the whole [was] leaning toward Baldwin.'[38] The former editor of *The Times*, Wickham Steed, recalled that he saw Waterhouse and Davidson at Number 10 on the Sunday morning, and claimed the three were in agreement that Bonar Law had said, 'I suppose it will have to be Baldwin.'[39] Even Beaverbrook, who favoured Curzon, wrote later of Bonar Law's opinion: 'Privately, I have no doubt that he intended to nominate Curzon, if he had to nominate anyone, and that he wanted ... in his heart to nominate Stanley Baldwin.'[40] Finally, there is the recollection of Tom Jones, who saw the ailing Prime Minister at Onslow Gardens on Sunday afternoon and later noted in his diary that the two had talked privately of the succession: 'His voice was a loud whisper. "If the King asked for his advice as to a successor he would put Baldwin first."'[41]

Not surprisingly, the most fascinating testimony is that of the enigmatic Colonel Waterhouse. According to his wife, his explanation was that early that Sunday morning he had breakfasted alone with Bonar Law, and they discussed the succession question. Waterhouse was soon to deliver his master's resignation letter to the King. What, he asked, if the Sovereign demanded a recommendation? Nourah Waterhouse later published her husband's report of the conversation:

B.L.: 'I do not want to be asked that.'

Ronald: 'But you may find it inevitable.'

B.L.: 'Then I shall refuse.'

Ronald: 'You are placing me in an impossible position. It is like asking a Press Reporter to publish certain half-facts without giving him the full context and telling him exactly what to suppress. You send me to represent you on an extremely difficult and delicate mission; you completely reserve the substance; provide me only with the shadow; and then expect me to succeed. You *must* tell me what your answer would be, if you had to give it.'

B.L.: 'But I would not, and I will not.'

Ronald: 'If I give you my word of honour to preserve your confidence.'

B.L.: 'In that case ... I am *afraid* ... I should have to say – Baldwin.'[42]

Nourah Waterhouse's memoir was to have been published in 1940. It only progressed as far as the printing of a handful of proof copies, however, before being withdrawn under threat of prosecution for violation of the Copyright and Official Secrets Act; and was finally published two years later after parts of the text had been deleted.[43] In the suppressed version Lady Waterhouse said her husband was received alone by the King and Queen on 20 May and that he urged Baldwin's case, emphasizing the arguments contained in the Davidson memorandum, which the King had not yet read. King George, Waterhouse said, resisted his endorsement of Baldwin and pressed Curzon's claims, to the point where Waterhouse, exasperated and embarrassed, finally blurted out his most powerful argument: Bonar Law's confession made at breakfast earlier in the day that he thought Baldwin the better choice.[44] This was the most important portion of the original text to have been deleted before Lady Waterhouse's book was published in 1942.

There is, of course, no conclusive evidence that the exchange occurred – certainly it was never confirmed by the King and Queen, nor was it ever mentioned by Sir Frederick Sykes. What seems clear is that Waterhouse delivered precisely this argument to Lord Stamfordham, who summoned him to the Palace the following day, 21 May. According to Stamfordham, Waterhouse told him the tale of his breakfast with Bonar Law. He also left Lord Stamfordham with the quite false impression that the contents of the memorandum were known to and confirmed by Sir Frederick Sykes as an accurate summary of the opinions of his father-in-law, and added furthermore that he had consulted the Law family and in particular Mary Law, who also confirmed its accuracy.[45] It is, however, as certain as anything else in this bizarre episode that these conversations between Waterhouse and Sykes and the Laws never occurred.[46]

Waterhouse adhered to his story, as did his wife, throughout their lives; and the appearance of Lord Blake's *Unknown Prime Minister* motivated certain of his friends to defend Waterhouse's memory by recounting the story of the mysterious royal audience.[47] Whether either the conversation with the King and Queen or the earlier breakfast interrogation actually took place will probably never be known. The balance of the available evidence suggests that they were figments of Colonel Waterhouse's imagination – like his conversations with Sykes and Mary Law.

In the end, what is certain is that whatever the machinations of these conspirators, they made little difference. Since the resignation occurred on Whit Sunday, most of the men of power whom the King might have consulted were, like him, away from the capital. He asked Sykes during the Sunday interview whom the Prime Minister would recommend he consult, and word came later in the day from Onslow Gardens that Lord Salisbury would offer good counsel.[48] Summoned from the country by Bonar Law, he travelled to London in his frock-coat and silk hat in the guard's van on a milk train, arriving at Onslow Gardens on Monday at 8 a.m. The two men were agreed on the contrasting virtues of the two candidates, and also that it was difficult to imagine Curzon's credentials could be overlooked – so long, of course, as senior Conservatives would agree to serve under him. Then Salisbury went to the Palace, where Stamfordham had hurried from Aldershot to receive him. He repeated his conclusion that Curzon's claim appeared to be too strong to resist, of which Stamfordham – who agreed – took polite note.[49]

The King also wished to consult the last Conservative Prime Minister, Lord Balfour, who was in Sheringham in Norfolk recovering from an attack of phlebitis. With expressions of regret for the long drive he would have to make, on Sunday Stamfordham nevertheless summoned the septuagenarian to London.[50] The two met on both Monday and Tuesday, and Balfour's advice contrasted with that of his cousin Salisbury: Curzon's claims were strong, but the wisest counsel was that the premiership should remain in the Commons.[51] Unlike Salisbury, Balfour also saw the King, and repeated the advice he had already given.[52]

Stamfordham continued to collect what opinion he could during these anxious hours, seeing on Monday and Tuesday the retired senior civil servant, Sir George Murray;[53] the editor of *The Times*, Geoffrey Dawson (who had changed his surname from Robinson in 1917); the

Conservative Chairman, Colonel Jackson; and, of course, Colonel Waterhouse.[54] Only Dawson favoured Curzon, all other advice was fatal to his hopes: his isolation from the Lower House and his unpopularity within his own party were points stressed too repeatedly to be ignored.[55] On Monday morning Stamfordham also found himself unable to evade the unsought advice of Amery and Bridgeman, who captured him outside his house and marched him around St James's Park, pleading Baldwin's case.[56]

While advice and testimony continued to pile up, it appears that in fact the King had already made up his mind. According to his own memorandum, when Stamfordham saw the editor of *The Times* on Monday,

> I told him frankly that the King so far was convinced that his responsibility to the country made it almost imperative that he should appoint a Prime Minister from the House of Commons. For were he not to do so and the experiment failed the country would blame the King for an act which was entirely his own, and which proved that His Majesty was ignorant of and out of touch with public opinion.[57]

On Monday evening the rivals were alerted that they would be wanted in London the following day – Curzon by telegram to Montacute House in Somerset, where he refused to install a telephone – but only Baldwin was summoned to the Palace.[58] The poignant story of Curzon's journey, almost certainly under the delusion that he was to achieve his ambition of the premiership, is sadly familiar.[59] He was seen not by the King but by Stamfordham, and not at Buckingham Palace but at his own house in Carlton House Terrace. The news that he had been passed over was devastating; outraged, he subjected Stamfordham – who had supported his candidacy – to a positively incendiary interview.[60] Baldwin accepted the King's charge to form a Government, and continued the Cabinet in essentially the form in which he inherited it – with Curzon at the Foreign Office.[61]

Bonar Law's premiership lasted 211 days, the shortest-lived Government of this century. There can be no doubt that he approved of the King's choice, though it is also true that he was surprised by it.[62] His relationship with Baldwin, strained by the American debt affair, had returned to its old easiness, and it is surely true that the issue of the premiership remaining in the House of Commons was a matter of concern to him.

About Curzon he had numerous reservations: although the two had been colleagues for many years, it is all but impossible to locate any letter written by him to Curzon which demonstrates true warmth, while Curzon's bullying letters to him are now the stuff of legend.[63] As noted in the last chapter, in early April 1923, when Bonar Law was already a very sick man, Curzon wrote to him in a manner surpassing even his usual level of unfeeling self-importance:

> I have been asked three times within the last week whether it is true that you are about to resign, and to recommend that Baldwin be appointed P.M. in your place.
>
> I have replied that I believe there is not the smallest foundation for this canard, and I need hardly add that in my view your retirement would be a national calamity, which should not be permitted to occur.
>
> Moreover, I am sure that if you contemplated such a step, you would do me the favour of consulting me in advance. For my own position would be directly involved.
>
> I have never sought to push myself or my claims, and have done what work was allotted to me. But I am your senior colleague, I have been Leader of the House of Lords for over 6 years. I am the sole member of the Cabinet who as served continually since 1915. I have a certain record and a certain public reputation, having filled high offices of state for over thirty years. I think that I even assisted materially to form your administration.[64]

The letter continued in this vein for several more paragraphs, and it is not difficult to imagine its impact on an ailing man whose character was distinguished by quiet dignity and an almost excessive modesty. One observer has suggested the cumulative effect of such letters: 'All combined to alter Bonar Law's assessment of Curzon's sense of proportion.'[65] If an insight is wanted into Bonar Law's intense desire to avoid offering a recommendation, perhaps it can be drawn from evidence such as this. Baldwin was transparently honest, and popular in the party, though perhaps – as the US debt settlement affair indicated – without sufficient experience to prepare him for the premiership; Curzon, so long on the top rungs of power and so oppressively self-assured, perhaps had too much. Whatever the rights and wrongs of the succession question, it had all now ceased to be Bonar Law's affair.

During his last hours as Prime Minister he turned to a duty which must have given him some small pleasure – his Resignation Honours List. His contribution was only four names: his physicians Sir Thomas Horder and Chichester Gould May received respectively a baronetcy and a knighthood; his secretary, Geoffrey Fry, was appointed Companion of the Order of the Bath; and Colonel Waterhouse, the man historians have often insisted was disliked by his master, he recommended to be appointed Knight Commander of the Bath.[66]

The outpourings of regret for Bonar Law's resignation and good wishes for his recovery were remarkable. In the House his Honourable Friends extolled him in generous terms, and perhaps something can be learned of the man from the recollections of old adversaries of all parties:[67] Ramsay MacDonald noted that he wrung from the Opposition 'a strange mysterious sympathy, because we saw in him much less of a party leader than of a strong, courageous, devoted man, doing his duty in almost impossible circumstances.' Asquith for the moment put aside old resentments and recalled 'His uncanny power of grasp and assimilation; his admirable[,] and in some ways unique, faculty in debate; his fine sensitivity to the parliamentary atmosphere; his generous devotion to the House of Commons; his strong, unfailing sense of duty and his entire personal unselfishness.' Among the most touching words were those of Austen Chamberlain: 'It is of his personal and private character that I speak – that simplicity, that unselfishness, that devotion to work and duty which won the affection and confidence alike of his colleagues and of his countrymen outside.'

It is impossible to judge at what point Bonar Law realized the seriousness of his illness. His daughter Lady Sykes, who was closest to him in these last months, remained convinced that at least during the summer he was unaware of his true condition, apparently accepting the explanation that he suffered from 'enlarged glands'.[68] He was never told either by his physicians or his family that he had an advanced malignancy, almost certainly the direct product of fifty years of heavy smoking; but surely with the coming of autumn, he knew he was dying.

The most pressing immediate concern was that as the cancer spread, he suffered terrible pain in his throat, head and face which was alleviated only by ever-stronger drugs. Almost immediately following his resignation an operation was performed on his throat in an unsuccessful attempt to remove the diseased tissue, followed by 'deep ray' – that is, X-ray – treatments to attack the malignancy, which also proved ineffective. This was the extent of the medical orthodoxy of the day, but in view of the advanced state of the disease by the time it was diagnosed, it is unlikely that much more could be done today.

During the summer months Bonar Law's condition seemed for a time to improve, but he was little seen in London, preferring Brighton.

At last freed of the demands of office, he spent as much time as possible with his family and continued to take special pleasure in his grandson and namesake. Though he faced them stoically, the X-ray treatments led to further pain, which called for increasingly stronger analgesics; and he remarked in one of his mock soliloquies to the infant: 'Oh, Ptoly, I do hope you don't have to have deep ray treatments when you are old.'[69]

He endeavoured to go on with his life nevertheless, and behaved as though his affliction were temporary. Just as he had walked out of the Referendum Pledge crisis in 1913 to buy a new overcoat, in late June he sent the faithful Sweeney out to buy a new motor-car – admitting finally that his old one was indeed as disreputable in appearance as his sister had long insisted it was.[70] He was able to return for a few weeks to a long-favoured haunt in France, the Golf Hotel at Le Touquet, and even played several holes on sunny afternoons. Here, as in London and Brighton, his companion was often his friend Beaverbrook, who amused him for hours with talk of politics, of great men and, inevitably, of the past. Beaverbrook arranged bridge and chess partners (in London, a regular at bridge once again was McKenna) and supplied him with the news of the hour in Westminster. It was even said that he manipulated his friend's stock portfolio, making large purchases himself in order to be able to report a rise in the value of his shares.[71] Whatever the truth may be about the enigmatic Max Aitken, his love for his friend seemed unconditional as he 'proved himself once more the foul-weather friend.'[72]

Perhaps the most remarkable of Beaverbrook's gifts, only weeks before his friend's death, was a luncheon at which he brought Bonar Law and Lloyd George together for the last time. Old quarrels were forgotten in recounting tales of wartime partnership. In a letter following the luncheon Lloyd George told him: 'I have just written a preface to a book in which I slang everybody with perfect impartiality. I was delighted to see you once more & see you looking ever so much better than I did when I passed through a similar experience.'[73] The first two declarations were quite true, the third was not: Bonar Law looked a dying man.

He returned to Onslow Gardens in October, and continued to receive a small number of visitors and even to play chess as long as his deteriorating vitality allowed. He read the newspapers daily almost until the end, and politics of course remained his favourite subject of conversation – as men of politics continued to be his only guests. He saw Baldwin on 24 October for half an hour, but on the following day contracted what soon revealed itself to be pneumonia.[74] Beaverbrook, of course, was his last visitor: 'You are a curious fellow,' he said to his old friend.[75] On 30 October 1923, his daughter Kitty's seventeenth birthday, Andrew Bonar Law died in his sleep in the early hours of the morning.

Bonar Law's will decreed that his property should be divided in equal parts among his children, and it revealed that he died a man of substance, if not wealth. The gross principal value of his investments was reported as £61,800, with creditors payable £2,200 and debtors owing £6,000.[76] He stipulated that all his papers were to be left to Beaverbrook, on the understanding that his son Dick was to have full access to them in the event that he should wish to write a biography of his father.[77] The house in Onslow Gardens was sold, as were most of its furnishings – including the beloved billiard table – and the new motorcar.[78]

Bonar Law stated in his will that it was his wish to be buried beside his wife in Helensburgh, but this was not to be. Throughout their long association Beaverbrook had insisted, to Bonar Law's amusement, that his friend was a great man. 'I wanted him to go out in a big way and with all the glory that could possibly be bestowed on him,' he wrote years later.[79] A family funeral in a Scottish churchyard clearly would not meet the case, and Beaverbrook hastily organized a campaign in the press and in the Conservative Party in favour of a State Funeral, followed by burial in Westminster Abbey. The Government were pleased to honour the man who was the author of their good fortune; Beaverbrook talked the family around, the Dean and Chapter of the Abbey extended the appropriate offer, and the late Prime Minister's final wish was set aside. On 5 November his ashes were interred beneath the floor of the Abbey, and there is no memorial apart from a simply-inscribed paving stone:[80]

Andrew Bonar Law

1858–1923

Sometime Prime Minister

Thus we reach the scene with which this book began. Perhaps it is fitting that the final comment on that bleak November day should not be any of the famous barbs of Asquith or Curzon, but from one who did not rise so high. Some days after the funeral, 'Peter' Sanders confided to his diary:

> Ten days ago Bonar died. Very generally mourned. The crowd on the day of his funeral was remarkable when one remembers how little he advertised himself or was advertised in his lifetime ... He certainly did a big thing for the party a year ago.[81]

Bonar Law would have wished for no better epitaph.

II

Many historians writing about these years have embraced the image of Bonar Law as a grimly partisan, even brutal politician – the author of the 'new style', who flirted with treason and threatened civil war. Those willing to grant him a measure of rehabilitation because of his service in the Great War have often been inclined to concede him only the status of Lloyd George's gun-bearer, the 'fixer' who arranged Cabinet and Parliament to do as the Wizard wished. Even the last pages of his story – when he finally mounted the top rung of the political ladder, his body already poisoned with cancer – are tainted for many and still regarded as a regrettable tale of a man who roused the 'second eleven' to prepare the way for Baldwin to neutralize the first-class men, mismanage the 'Slump' and lay the groundwork for Appeasement.

The reality is something different. The embittered anti-Catholic bigot of the 'sick Canadian–Ulster brain' would countenance no religious prejudice, and entrusted his own children to the care of an Irish Catholic nanny. The 'gilded tradesman' proved to be a perceptive and open-minded Chancellor who earned the admiration of Treasury professionals famous for their harsh judgements of their political masters. The firebrand who held the House in his grip with his menacing anti-Home Rule speeches struggled to force a reluctant Liberal Government to place the issue before the electorate, and constrained his own party to pledge that they would obey the result. When this campaign was successfully resisted by Asquith and Redmond, he shifted his energies towards constructing a compromise which would be tolerable to all Irish and British opinion. The cold man with neither passion nor aesthetic was actually an ardent husband, a tender and indulgent father and grandfather. He was a generous brother and friend, much loved in return, and in his time among the most popular Members in the House, among men of all parties. The man modest 'to the point of simplicity' in fact possessed redoubtable ambition, but this was tempered by a strain of realism which – as in the years of the Great War – always led him to subordinate his aspirations to what he was certain was the national good.

Whatever else he was, in his public life Bonar Law was the very model of the good party man – as Lloyd George and Churchill so brilliantly were not – for he believed that progress, under the British constitution, could be made only through party, and that in general the nation was better off in the hands of Conservatives.[82] This belief was, as we have seen, both a burden and a comfort throughout his public life. He sought a life in politics not merely because he possessed a keen will to power, but because, like Peel and Gladstone and Lloyd George, he wished to drive the nation in the direction he believed it ought to go. Unlike them, however, he made few promises, and strove primarily to adhere to Burke's simple assay of statecraft: to possess a 'disposition to preserve and an ability to improve'. Greater men than he achieved only a measure of success, much leavened with failure, and this was certainly true of the life of Bonar Law.

He made mistakes which he regretted – renunciation of the Referendum Pledge, the delay in speaking out against the Dardanelles campaign and the US debt settlement crisis are but examples – yet he was able to recover from them in a way which affords some insight into his character. Even great men stumble, and when they do they are saved in different ways from their errors, or not saved at all. Bonar Law found it easier than some to overcome his pride, accept compromise (often devised by others), and press on towards a greater goal. It would be misleading to label success of this sort genius, but it is no less important in politics and sometimes saved his country from great trouble.

These chapters describe an extraordinary career lived out in fascinating times – and a man who surely would have been unremarkable had he not been drawn to the world of politics. In that rarefied sphere he was not a brilliant cynic like Disraeli, a self-obsessed moralist like Gladstone or a magnificent innovator like Lloyd George. He would have resisted any comparisons at all, and sincerely opposed being described as a great man – nor, by any usual measure, was he.

His greatest legacies were two: the first is the existence of Northern Ireland as a part of the United Kingdom – a constitutional arrangement that will survive into the twenty-first century. His second gift, certainly more important to him than anything else in politics, was to the British Conservative Party, which he believed with all his heart could govern the nation better than any other. His leadership left it renewed and strengthened, and set on the path towards generations of electoral success. By any standard, he has few peers in modern times as a political party leader.

Discussions of greatness held little interest for Bonar Law. Speaking of such things once with Clemenceau, with a smile he told the Tiger of France: 'All great men are humbugs.' Perhaps that is why, though there were those who could not forgive him his shortcomings, there were many more who loved him and still more who gladly followed him. For himself, he would have been satisfied to be able to say at the end, like St Paul: 'I have fought a good fight, I have finished my course, I have kept the faith.' And that he certainly had.

Notes

ABBREVIATIONS

HHAP – Asquith Papers
SBP – Baldwin Papers
AJBP – Balfour Papers (British Library)
AJBPW – Balfour Papers (Whittinghame Papers, Scottish Record Office, Edinburgh)
BBKP – Beaverbrook Papers
RABP – Blumenfeld Papers
SJBP – Brodrick (Midleton) Papers
WBP – Bull Papers
RCP – Lord Robert Cecil Papers
ACP – Austen Chamberlain Papers
NCP – Neville Chamberlain Papers
WSCP – Churchill (Chartwell) Papers
CP – Curzon Papers
JCCDP – Davidson Papers
GDP – Dawson Papers
FP – Fisher Papers
MFP – Fraser Papers
JLGP – Garvin Papers
EGP – Goulding (Wargrave) Papers
GBP – Griffith-Boscawen Papers
HAGP – Gwynne Papers
KP – Kitchener Papers
LP – Lansdowne Papers
BLP – Bonar Law Papers
BLP/372 – Bonar Law Papers (House of Lords Record Office Historical Collection 372)
LGP – Lloyd George Papers
WLP – Long Papers (British Library)
WLPT – Long Papers (Wiltshire Record Office, Trowbridge)
LMP – Maxse Papers
TMP – Melville (Tugander) Papers

AMP – Milner Papers
EPP – Pollock (Hanworth) Papers
RA – Royal Archives
GRD – Riddell Diary
RP – Rothermere Papers
HSP – Samuel Papers
JSP – Sandars Papers
SP – Selborne Papers
AJSP – Sylvester Papers
SMP – Steel-Maitland Papers
SLSP – Strachey Papers
WBP – Willoughby de Broke Papers
HWP – Wilson Papers
WEP – Worthington-Evans Papers

PREFACE AND ACKNOWLEDGEMENTS
1. George Dangerfield, *The Strange Death of Liberal England* (New York, 1961 edn), p. 80.
2. *Daily Express*, 8 November 1922.

CHAPTER I: EARLY DAYS
1. RA, King George V's Diary.
2. A copy of the funeral service may be found in WLP, Add. MSS. 62440/117–21.
3. This remark is frequently quoted and was taken as the title for Lord Blake's biography: *The Unknown Prime Minister: The Life and Times of Andrew Bonar Law, 1858–1923* (London, 1955).
4. He was kinder to Bonar Law in his memoirs, *Memories and Reflections* (London, 1928), Vol. II, p. 246.
5. Curzon to Lady Curzon, 5 November 1923, CP, MSS. Eur. F 112/797. The letter is printed in Lady Curzon's *Reminiscences* (London, 1955), pp. 180–3, and part of it is in Lord Beaverbrook, *Men and Power, 1917–1918* (London, 1960 edn), p. 321.
6. In addition to Blake, other studies of his life are H.A. Taylor, *The Strange Case of Andrew Bonar Law* (London, n.d. [1932]) and, more recently, Mary Peck, *The Image and the Source: A Study of Andrew Bonar Law* (Fredericton, New Brunswick, 1976). I am grateful also to Mr Stephen Schollom for providing me with a copy of his unpublished paper 'Parents and Grandparents of Andrew Bonar Law'.
7. In order to avoid confusion with the Kingston Peninsula, the town was renamed Rexton in 1900.
8. It is possible that James Law was preceded to Kingston by an uncle, Ronald McDonald, and for that reason chose to accept the call to St Andrew's, Kingston, over other congregations seeking his services. Schollom, 'Parents and Grandparents of Andrew Bonar Law'.
9. Peck, *Image and the Source*, p. 8.
10. *Ibid.* The house and barn stand today as a New Brunswick historic site.
11. This tale was much doted on in Canada: see the *Sackville [New Brunswick] Tribune*, 11 November 1916, and Peck, *Image and the Source*, p. 15.
12. W.F. Somerville in 1911 recalled how a mishap during their boyhood play with an old muzzle-loading rifle had almost robbed the Conservative Party of its new-found chief: 12 November 1911, BLP 12/2/2.
13. Blake, *Unknown Prime Minister*, p. 21.
14. After the Reverend James Law retired to Maddybenny in Ulster in 1877, Bonar Law

– a notoriously bad sailor – braved the Irish Sea to visit him on every available weekend until the elder Law's death five years later.

15. Eventually two of Bonar Law's brothers, William and John, as well as his sister Mary, also emigrated to Great Britain.

16. This, probably to one Archdeacon Armitage, of 1 January 1924, is preserved in the Public Archives of Nova Scotia. See Peck, *Image and the Source*, p. 14, where due to a typographical error it is dated 1824.

17. R.D. Blumenfeld, *R.D.B.'s Diary* (London, 1930), pp. 78–9.

18. A.E. O'Leary argues against this conclusion, based on the testimony of a 'long time Richibucto resident': *Memory Lane With Characters I Knew* (New Brunswick, privately printed, 1937).

19. See Blake, *Unknown Prime Minister*, p. 25.

20. Sir Henry Campbell-Bannerman and Lord Bryce also attended the Glasgow High School.

21. Augustine Birrell, *Things Past Redress* (London, 1937), p. 275.

22. See H.A. Taylor, *Bonar Law*, p. 25, and Blake, *Unknown Prime Minister*, p. 27.

23. These were his words in his own inaugural speech as Rector, on 11 March 1921.

24. H.A. Taylor, *Bonar Law*, p. 34.

25. *Ibid.*, pp. 30–1.

26. *Ibid.*, p. 33.

27. Thomas Jones, *Whitehall Diary, Vol. I: 1916–1925*, Keith Middlemas, ed. (London, 1969), entry of 28 January 1921, p. 128.

28. First elected for Leith in 1885, he retired from the seat in 1886 in favour of W.E. Gladstone. He was returned to the House for Stirlingshire in 1892 and sat until 1895.

29. BLP 8/10.

30. The loan was approximately £7,500.

31. Blake, *Unknown Prime Minister*, p. 34.

32. BLP 15/13.

33. H.A. Taylor, *Bonar Law*, p. 42.

34. BLP 6/5. He also inherited £3,000 from William Kidston and a contingent interest in the will of Charles Kidston. See also Lord Beaverbrook's 'Peroration' on Bonar Law's background and character, BBK G/13/V.

CHAPTER 2: ENTERPRISE AND AMBITION

1. Little evidence survives of his life, and what remains records Robert Law's financial difficulties, his drinking problem and the assistance he received from his brother. See Robert Law to Bonar Law, 24 February 1894, BLP 1/1/2. Bonar Law also corresponded with James Jardine, the local banker who apparently held Robert Law's debts. James Jardine to Bonar Law, 2 Mar 1894 and 16 April 1894, BLP 1/1/3 and 1/1/4; and Bonar Law to James Jardine, 28 April 1898, BLP 12/1/66. These indicate that Bonar Law paid his brother's debts and continued to subsidize him at a rate of £250 per year.

2. A. Chisholm and M. Davie, *Lord Beaverbrook: A Life* (London, 1993), p. 93.

3. Lord Winterton, *Orders of the Day* (London, 1953), p. 59; Kenneth Rose, *King George V* (London, 1984) pp. 151–2.

4. Their children were James (Jim) born in 1893, Isabel (Tizzie) 1896, Charles (Charlie) 1897, Harrington (Tony) 1899, Richard (Dick) 1901, and Catherine (Kitty) 1906.

5. Bonar Law to Mr Grieve, 1 February 1897, BLP 12/1/2. This correspondence occurred some months before what has been accepted to have been his first steps in politics.

6. Bonar Law to Col. King, 29 April 1897, BLP 12/1/9.

7. H.A. Taylor, *Bonar Law*, pp. 50–1.
8. The totals were Bonar Law 4,140 and Provand 3,140. The Unionists secured a majority of 134 seats over the combined Opposition.
9. Ian Malcolm, *Vacant Thrones: A Volume of Political Portraits* (London, 1967 edn), p. 67.
10. Austen Chamberlain, *Down the Years* (London, 1935), p. 54. He wrote to another friend that before entering the Board of Trade he was 'so miserable for want of something to do that I [was] more than once on the point of giving up my seat.' Bonar Law to [Sir Alexander] Henderson, 5 December 1905, TMP, Hist. Coll. 200.
11. Alfred Gollin, *Balfour's Burden* (London, 1965), p. 24.
12. Middlemas, ed., *Whitehall Diary*, entry of 28 January 1921, p. 127.
13. H.A. Taylor, *Bonar Law*, p. 67.
14. Malcolm, *Vacant Thrones*, p. 59.
15. Beaverbrook to Robert Blake, 20 August 1951, BBK C/42.
16. Speech delivered to the Constitutional Club on 11 April 1907. For the delight this brought to the Tariff Reformers, see Austen Chamberlain to Mary Chamberlain, 12 April 1907, ACP 4/1/164.
17. L.S. Amery, *My Political Life*, Vol. I (London, 1953), p. 387.
18. *Ibid.*
19. *Daily Express*, 20 March 1921.
20. Blumenfeld, *R.D.B.'s Diary*, pp. 78–9, entry of 7 October 1900.
21. Malcolm, *Vacant Thrones*, p. 59.
22. Thomas Jones, *A Diary with Letters, 1931–1950* (Oxford, 1954) p. xxvii.
23. Polling began on 12 January and ended 7 February.
24. J. Chamberlain to Bonar Law, n.d. [January 1906], BLP 21/1.
25. Not surprisingly, Bonar Law sought bridge partners wherever he travelled in Canada: see Philip Dansken Ross, *Retrospects of a Newspaper Person* (Toronto, 1931), pp. 146–7. Other such visits to North America were discussed and even planned but never undertaken.
26. 133 Conservatives and 24 Liberal Unionists were returned.
27. See Chris Cook and John Stevenson, eds, *The Longman Handbook of Modern British History, 1714–1980* (London, 1983), p. 68.
28. For the Compatriots see, for example, Robert Scally, *The Origins of the Lloyd George Coalition* (Princeton, 1975), pp. 110–32.
29. See Amery's two letters to Bonar Law of 2 March 1906, BLP 18/2/15 and 18/2/16; and the negative reply, 9 April 1906, BLP 18/8/3.
30. The most thorough examination of the Confederates is Larry L. Witherell, *Rebel on the Right: Henry Page Croft and the Politics of Edwardian Britain, 1903–1914*, (Newark, Delaware, 1997), on which the following paragraphs are based.
31. J.S. Sandars to Wilfrid Short, 28 October 1907, AJBP, Add. MSS. 49765/76–7.
32. Cecil to Balfour, 13 January 1908, AJBP, Add. MSS. 49737/84.
33. Lord Ridley, however, wrote to Austen Chamberlain, 22 January 1909: 'The "Confederates" make an awful lot of noise, which is good; but don't let us tell the Free Fooders how little the Confederates really do!' ACP 17/3/79.
34. Dr Witherell accepts that neither Collings, Duncannon, Garvin, Goulding, Parker nor Bonar Law were Confederates: *Rebel on the Right*, Appendix 1, pp. 214–20.
35. Bonar Law denied any knowledge of a book of essays, *The New Order*, published in 1909 by the Confederates. See Bernard Wise to Bonar Law, 12 November 1911, BLP 24/3/16. On 20 June 1912, after he had become Leader, Croft and several of his closest associates wrote to Bonar Law protesting their loyalty and wishing an audience to explain the activities of the Confederacy: BLP 33/2/20.
36. See Neil Blewett, 'Free Fooders, Balfourites, Wholehoggers: Factionalism Within

the Unionist Party', in *Historical Journal*, XI (1974), pp. 117–18, n. 103; and Witherell, *Rebel on the Right*, ch. 5.

37. Sir Charles Petrie, *The Life and Letters of the Right Hon. Sir Austen Chamberlain* Vol. II (London, 1940), pp. 202–3; Alan Sykes, *The Tariff Reform Movement in British Politics* (Oxford, 1979), pp. 125–6.

38. Austen Chamberlain to Mary Chamberlain, 11 February 1907: Austen Chamberlain, *Politics from Inside: An Epistolary Chronicle, 1906–1914* (London, 1936), pp. 48–51.

39. See Stephen Koss, *The Rise and Fall of the Political Press in Britain, Vol. II: The Twentieth Century* (Chapel Hill, 1984), p. 108; Matthew Fforde, *Conservatism and Collectivism* (London, 1990), p. 91. The plan was probably drafted by Richard Jebb, chief leader-writer for the *Morning Post*.

40. Sykes, *Tariff Reform Movement*, pp. 196–9.

41. Bonar Law had deep reservations about the appropriateness of the publication of the programme. See Bonar Law to Fabian Ware, 29 September 1908, BLP 18/8/10; see also Sykes, *Tariff Reform Movement, ibid.*

42. H.A. Taylor, *Bonar Law*, p. 108.

43. 2 February 1906, BLP 18/3/28.

44. Deakin, an imperial preference enthusiast, was a hero to British Tariff Reformers. See John Hutcheson, *Leopold Maxse and the National Review, 1893–1914* (New York, 1989), pp. 270–4.

45. See J.S. Sandars to Balfour, 13 January 1907, AJBP, Add. MSS. 49765, and Deakin to Maxse, 7 August 1908, LMP, 457/s560. Portions of this letter are printed in Hutcheson, *Maxse*, p. 274.

46. See Austen Chamberlain to Mary Chamberlain, 12 April 1907, ACP 4/1/64; and John Grigg, *Lloyd George: The People's Champion, 1902–1911* (London, 1978), p. 197.

47. He did not include Balfour in his estimate: Petrie, *Austen Chamberlain*, Vol. II, pp. 203–4.

48. John Vincent, ed., *The Crawford Papers: The Journals of David Lindsay, Twenty-Seventh Earl of Crawford and Tenth Earl of Balcarres During the Years 1892 to 1940* (Manchester, 1984), diary entry of 29 June 1907, p. 102.

49. See Sykes, *Tariff Reform*, pp. 141–4.

50. 17 January 1908, BLP 18/8/6.

CHAPTER 3: 'THE COMING MAN'

1. Always financially prudent, he sold his Helensburgh property before buying the remaining 34 years of the lease on Pembroke Lodge.

2. 17 November 1922, BLP 108/9/21. McLean led the Liberals in the Commons briefly, from February 1919 to February 1920.

3. This legendary club included Edward Goulding, Waldorf Astor, Lord Charles Beresford, J.E.B. Seeley and Frederick Guest. Also members were the Unionist and Liberal party managers Arthur Steel-Maitland and the Master of Elibank, and the aristocratic Lord Esher, Lord Kitchener, and Lord Stamfordham. See Campbell, *F.E. Smith* (London, 1983), pp. 268–9. See also Colin R. Coote, *The Other Club* (London, 1971).

4. Grigg, *Lloyd George; The People's Champion*, pp. 102–3.

5. 14 April 1908, *ibid*, p. 155.

6. BLP 1/2 contains a large collection of letters of condolence from notables of all political stripes. Additional letters, uncatalogued at this time, have recently been added to the Bonar Law Papers.

7. 30 November 1909, AMP, 36/167–8.

8. See Steel-Maitland to Bonar Law, 3 July 1913, BLP 29/6/14.

9. H.A. Taylor, *Bonar Law*, p. 120.
10. Roy Jenkins, *Mr Balfour's Poodle* (London, 1968 edn), p. 36. See also Ruddock F. Mackay, *Balfour: Intellectual Statesman* (Oxford, 1985), pp. 229–30.
11. Sir Henry enjoyed the unusual distinction of being both Prime Minister and Father of the House in 1907–8.
12. Bonar Law to [George A.] Gibbs, 3 April 1912, BLP 33/4/28.
13. E.H.H. Green, *The Crisis of Conservatism: The Politics, Economics and Ideology of the British Conservative Party, 1880–1914* (London, 1995), p. 274.
14. The vote totals were Bonar Law 8,472 and Cotton 6,054.
15. The Unionists received 46.9 per cent of the popular vote, the Liberals 43.2 per cent, and the minor parties and independents 9.9 per cent: Butler and Freeman, *British Political Facts*, p. 122.
16. Unsigned draft, Bonar Law to Salisbury, 4 February 1910, BLP 20/34.
17. See Alfred M. Gollin, *The Observer and J.L. Garvin, 1908–1914* (London, 1960), p. 185.
18. Liberal representatives included Asquith, Lloyd George, Lord Crewe, the Liberal leader in the Lords, and Ausgustine Birrell, the Irish Secretary. For the conference see Corinne Comstock Weston, 'The Liberal Leadership and the Lords' Veto, 1907–1910', in *Historical Journal*, XI (1968).
19. 3 August 1910: Jeremy Smith, 'Andrew Bonar Law and Conservative Strategy towards the Third Home Rule Bill, 1911–1914' (unpublished Ph.D. thesis, London School of Economics and Political Science, 1994), p. 20.
20. Several early drafts as well as two copies of the final version of the memorandum are in LGP, C/16/9. A copy also may be found in ACP 49/6/1, though this did not come into his possession until 1915. The memorandum was first printed in Sir Charles Petrie, *The Life and Letters of Austen Chamberlain*, Vol. I (London, 1939), pp. 381–8.
21. JSP, Ms. Eng. hist. 762/300. Except for Balfour himself, it is unlikely that the other Unionist leaders actually saw the document itself, but were merely told of its contents. Memorandum by Austen Chamberlain, 29 January 1915, ACP 13/2/2.
22. Austen Chamberlain to Lord Cawdor, 21 Oct. 1910, ACP 10/2/15. This is printed in Chamberlain, *Politics from Inside*, p. 286.
23. Austen Chamberlain's letter to F.E. Smith of 21 October 1910 implies that Bonar Law joined Smith among those favourable to devolution: *Politics From Inside*, pp. 283–5.
24. Gollin, *Observer and J.L. Garvin*, p. 231.
25. BLP 21/3/10.
26. Derby to Bonar Law, BLP 21/3/11.
27. Bonar Law to Goulding, 9 September 1910, EGP 2/66.
28. Balfour to Bonar Law, 15 October 1910, BLP 21/3/15.
29. Bonar Law to Balfour, 19 October 1910, BLP 22/4/1.
30. Vincent, ed., *Crawford Papers*, p. 167.
31. For the origins of the referendum idea see Corinne Comstock Weston, *The House of Lords and Ideological Politics: Lord Salisbury's Referendal Theory and the Conservative Party, 1846–1922* (Philadelphia, 1995).
32. See Neal Blewett, *The Peers, the Parties and the People*, (London, 1972), pp. 176–7.
33. *Ibid.*, p. 177.
34. Gollin, *Observer and J.L. Garvin*, p. 265.
35. Balfour to Austen Chamberlain, 28 November 1910: Chamberlain, *Politics from Inside*, pp. 303–4.
36. Gollin, *Observer and J.L. Garvin*, pp. 258–9, and Blewett, *Peers, Parties and the People*, p. 183.
37. BLP 18/8/14. Bonar Law sent a copy of this letter to Austen Chamberlain and, as

Dr Blewett points out in *Peers, Parties and the People*, p. 446, n. 73, neither the original nor that copy has survived.

38. He reiterated the idea of reciprocity in a letter to Lord Derby of 19 December 1910, BLP 18/8/16.
39. 29 November 1910, AJBP, Add. MSS. 49693/6–9.
40. The results were: Liberals 272, Unionists 272, Labour 42, Irish Nationalists 84. More than fifty seats changed hands, though the result affected the make-up of the House not at all.
41. This may be found in Blake, *Unknown Prime Minister*, p. 67, and in many later works which cite (or fail to cite) this. Its origins are unclear.
42. Derby to Col. Rutherford (forwarded to Bonar Law), 27 February 1911, BLP 21/4/21.
43. H.A. Taylor, *Bonar Law*, p. 144.
44. Bonar Law to Lansdowne, 11 February 1911, BLP 18/8/17.
45. This is usually recalled as the 'Cecil Scene' because of the organizational hand played in it by Lord Hugh Cecil, yet another son of Lord Salisbury and future Provost of Eton. Though his friends Smith and Goulding did, Bonar Law neither participated in nor approved of the 'scene'. See the diary of Lord Balcarres, who became Chief Whip in June: Vincent, ed., *Crawford Papers*, entry of 24 July 1911, pp. 198–9.
46. To the disgust even of many 'Hedgers', 37 Unionist peers voted with the Government to ensure passage of the Bill.
47. See Churchill to Bonar Law, 4 June 1911, BLP 18/7/174.
48. Undated typescript by Lord Beaverbrook: BBKP, G/13/V.

CHAPTER 4: PARTY LEADER
1. Vincent, ed., *Crawford Papers*, diary entry of 16 December 1911, p. 258.
2. The Revd William Aitken went to Newcastle, New Brunswick as a minister of the Church of Scotland, the 'Auld Kirk', from which James Law's Reformed Church had dissented – a fact which Max Aitken misunderstood, to Bonar Law's annoyance.
3. Aitken always stressed the almost accidental nature of their first meeting; in fact, he had planned it well in advance and had sought out appropriate introductions for the occasion: Anne Chisholm and Michael Davie, *Lord Beaverbrook: A Life* (London, 1993), p. 64.
4. Bonar Law had already invested a sizeable amount in the Canadian iron and steel market: see Anne Airth-Kindree Kelsch, 'Politicians, the Press and Power: Lord Beaverbrook's Introduction to British Politics, 1910–1918', unpublished Ph.D. thesis, Texas A&M University, 1993.
5. A.J.P. Taylor, *Beaverbrook* (London, 1972), p. 31.
6. Aitken was in London for a short time in April 1910 and apparently met Bonar Law briefly: see A.J.P. Taylor, *Beaverbrook*, p. 39.
7. Aitken to Bonar Law, 18 Oct 1910, BBKP C/201. Bonar Law replied, with 'the enclosed form filled up for $100,000', on 20 October 1910: C/201.
8. Many men in British public life benefited from Aitken's financial advice, including H.H. Asquith, Winston Churchill and Timothy Healey, as well as Goulding (whom he made Chairman of Rolls-Royce Ltd), F.E. Smith and Walter Long; among many non-politicians were Rudyard Kipling and J.L. Garvin. See Kelsch, 'Politicians, the Press and Power', pp. 16 and 122.
9. Bonar Law to Aitken, 6 October 1910, BBKP, C/201.
10. Bonar Law to Maj. Pownall, 14 November 1910, BLP 18/8/13.
11. See Vincent, ed., *Crawford Papers*, diary entry of 12 November 1911, p. 252.
12. Acland-Hood informed Aitken that the honour was for 'services to come and to

the Unionist Party and not to the Canadian [Conservative] party': Chisholm and Davies, *Lord Beaverbrook*, p. 91. Early in the year he had saved the financially troubled *Daily Express* with an unsecured loan of £25,000, and later in 1911 he purchased the *Globe* newspaper – perhaps these were the 'services'. See A.J.P. Taylor, *Beaverbrook*, pp. 60–3; and Kelsch, 'Politicians, the Press and Power', pp. 111–21.

13. N.d. (June 1911), BLP 18/7/181.
14. Bonar Law to Aitken, 28 July 1911, BBKP C/201.
15. Chisholm and Davies, *Beaverbrook*, p. 93.
16. Bonar Law to Sir Robert Borden, 9 December 1911, BLP 33/3/32.
17. 12 June 1910, Witherell, *Rebel on the Right*, p. 118.
18. See John Ramsden, *The Age of Balfour and Baldwin, 1902–1940* (London, 1978), pp. 56–62.
19. See Blewett, *Peers, Parties and the People*, pp. 266–8.
20. Ramsden, *The Age of Balfour and Baldwin*, pp. 57–61.
21. *Ibid.*, p. 59.
22. See Sykes, *Tariff Reform Movement*, p. 226; and Witherell, *Rebel on the Right*, Ch. 7.
23. 11 October 1911, Austen Chamberlain to Mary Chamberlain, ACP 4/1/714.
24. Entry of 16 July 1911, WBP 4/4.
25. Diary entry of 25 July 1911, WBP 4/4.
26. 6 October 1910, Witherell, *Rebel on the Right*, p. 128.
27. Vincent, ed., *Crawford Papers*, Balcarres to Lady Wantage, 6 February 1911, pp. 175–6.
28. See Hutcheson, *Maxse*, pp. 380–1; and Sykes, *Tariff Reform*, pp. 248–51.
29. Vincent, ed., *Crawford Papers*, diary entry of 26 July 1911, p. 173.
30. Vincent, ed., *Crawford Papers*, diary entry of 30 September 1911, p. 224. On 29 September 1911 Walter Long sent to Balfour a brutally frank eight-page memorandum which all but accused him of failing in his leadership of the party. It may have been the culminating example of a series of last straws. JSP, MSS. Eng. hist. 784/128–37.
31. See the memorandum by Walter Long regarding this meeting, 24 October 1911, WLP Add. MSS. 62415/224; and Vincent, ed., *Crawford Papers*, diary entry of 27 October 1911, pp. 237–8.
32. Chisholm and Davies, *Beaverbrook*, p. 110.
33. 11 October 1911, ACP 4/1/714.
34. A.T.Q. Stewart, *Edward Carson* (Dublin, 1981), p. 75.
35. Austen Chamberlain to Mary Chamberlain, 27 October 1911, ACP 4/1/721. See also David Dutton, *Austen Chamberlain: Gentleman in Politics* (Bolton, 1985), pp. 92–4; and Petrie, *Walter Long*, p. 170.
36. Goulding originally intended to support Chamberlain but was brought into Bonar Law's camp by Aitken: Aitken to Bonar Law, n.d. [early October 1911], BLP 18/7/198. This letter is the first in which Aitken addressed his friend by the salutation 'Dear Bonar'. According to Balcarres, Bonar Law was asked to stand for the leadership also by the two Benns, Remnant, Worthington-Evans, Gilbert Parker, Griffith-Boscawen and William Peel: Vincent, ed., *Crawford Papers*, 'note of 12 November 1911', p. 247.
37. See Chisholm and Davies, *Beaverbrook*, p. 111. The estimate was Aitken's.
38. John Ramsden, ed., *Real Old Tory Politics: The Political Diaries of Sir Robert Sanders, Lord Bayford, 1910–35* (London, 1984; hereafter cited as *Sanders Dairies*), diary entry of 12 November 1911 and W.C. Bridgeman to Sanders, 7 November 1911, pp. 34–5. Austen Chamberlain to Mary Chamberlain, 4 November 1911, ACP 4/1/723.
39. See Vernon Bogdanor, 'The Selection of the Party Leader', in *Conservative Century*, Anthony Seldon and Stuart Ball, eds (London, 1994), pp. 69–73.

40. Vincent, ed., *Crawford Papers*, diary entry of 7 November 1911, p. 241; Philip Williamson, ed., *The Modernisation of Conservative Politics: The Diaries and Letters of William Bridgeman, 1904–1935* (London, 1988; hereafter cited as *Bridgeman Diaries*), entry of 7 November 1911, p. 52.
41. Balcarres initially wished a single conclusive vote with the leader to be selected by true majority. That was unlikely, of course, given the fact that there were three candidates. See Vernon Bogadanor, 'Selection of the Party Leader', Seldon and Ball, eds, *Conservative Century*, p. 72.
42. Bonar Law indicated as much to Balfour, 11 November 1911, AJBP Add, MSS. 49693/17–18. This also was Balcarres's initial assumption: Vincent, *Crawford Papers*, diary entry of 10 November 1911, p. 246.
43. N.d. [early October 1911], BLP 18/7/198.
44. See, for example, Aitken's recent biographers: A.J.P. Taylor, *Beaverbrook*, p. 46, and Chisholm and Davies, *Beaverbrook*, p. iii.
45. Bonar Law to Aitken, 15 August 1911, BBKP C/201.
46. 27 October 1911, ACP 4/1/721.
47. Bull noted in his diary on 9 November 1911: 'BL's friends let out the secret of running him. "Come with us Bull [,] he never forgets his friends."' WBP, 4/4.
48. Goulding to Bonar Law, 9 November 1911, BLP 24/1/1. This letter is printed in Blake, *Unknown Prime Minister*, pp. 79–80.
49. Chamberlain, *Politics from Inside*, diary entry of 9 November 1911, p. 387.
50. BLP 24/1/1.
51. *Ibid.*
52. A typed copy of the draft letter survives in the Bonar Law Papers, making less believable Aitken's dramatic story of casting the paper on the fire: BLP 39/1/1.
53. See, for example, A.J.P. Taylor, *Beaverbrook*, p. 70; and Chisholm and Davies, *Lord Beaverbrook*, p. 112.
54. Lord Beaverbrook, *The Decline and Fall of Lloyd George* (London, 1963), p. 198.
55. A.J.P. Taylor, *Beaverbrook*, p. 70. The biographer indicates in the same paragraph that the tales of Aitken's elaborate lobbying are mythical.
56. BLP 117/21/15. The letter is printed in Blake, *Unknown Prime Minister*, p. 82.
57. According to Chamberlain, Balcarres thought that he (Chamberlain) could win if the vote were to be held on Saturday, 11 November, but that Long's strength was growing daily and that he could possibly win by Monday: Chamberlain, *Politics From Inside*, diary entry of 10 November 1911, p. 388. However, on 9 November Balcarres noted in his diary: 'At Carlton [Club] betting is 6 to 4 in W. Long's favour': *Crawford Papers*, p. 244. William Bull also thought that Long would win easily in the secret ballot at the Carlton Club: diary entry of 31 December 1911, WBP 4/4. Robert Sanders noted in his diary that on 9 November 'I went round the 1900 Club and was surprised to find that men were mostly for Long': *Sanders Diaries*, entry of 12 November 1911, p. 34. J.L. Garvin agreed, writing to Waldorf Astor on 10 November that Long appeared 'to be developing strength enough to beat both Austen & Bonar. Walter's victory seemed certain': Gollin, *Observer and J.L. Garvin*, p. 359.
58. Vincent, ed., *Crawford Papers*, 'Notes', 9 November 1911, p. 244. On 31 January 1918 Austen Chamberlain told William Bridgeman that he and Long had agreed on a fight to the end, with the loser to support the winner, but that Bonar Law's candidacy made that impossible. This recollection is not corroborated at any other point in the documents seen by the current author. Williamson, ed., *Bridgeman Diaries*, addendum to entry of 10 November 1911, p. 54.
59. See John Kendle, *Walter Long, Ireland and the Union: 1905–1920* (Montreal, 1992), pp.

66–7, for Long's remark that a victory in the contest would have killed him within two years.

60. According to his biographer, Long claimed that he had asked Harry Samuel to write to Henry Chaplin, the senior Tory MP, to request that Balcarres engineer just such a compromise: Sir Charles Petrie, *Walter Long and His Times* (London, 1936), pp. 171–2. Sir William Bull also noted that Long suggested the mutual withdrawal: diary entry of 10 November 1911, WBP 4/4. Chamberlain denied any knowledge of this: Chamberlain, *Politics from Inside*, p. 389; and Balcarres's diary makes no mention of it.

61. Sandars wrote to Balfour on 10 November that Long's supporters planned to vote for Bonar Law if it appeared that Chamberlain had a plurality on 13 November: BBKP (copy) G/13/VI.

62. Vincent, ed., *Crawford Papers*, 'Notes', 10 November 1911, p. 246.

63. 1 November 1911, ACP 4/1/726.

64. He has had much support from historians. See Gollin, *Observer and J.L. Garvin*, p. 358.

65. BLP 24/1/3. See also Vincent, ed., *Crawford Papers*, 'Notes', 10 November 1911, p. 246.

66. Williamson, ed., *Bridgeman Diaries*, entry of 10 November 1911, p. 53.

67. Balcarres to Bonar Law, 11 November 1911, BLP 24/3/8.

68. Vincent, ed., *Crawford Papers*, diary entry of 13 November 1911, p. 249. Copies of the minutes of the meeting may be found in ACP 9/4/3 and BLP 24/3/69.

69. Only Sir Frederick Banbury, Long's fellow Wiltshireman who disapproved of the compromise, remained seated: Vincent, ed., *Crawford Papers*, diary entry of 13 November 1911, p. 250.

70. BLP 24/4/3.

71. Versions of the anecdote may be found in H.A. Taylor, *Bonar Law*, pp. 157–8, and Blake, *Unknown Prime Minister*, p. 85.

72. Williamson, ed., *Bridgeman Diaries*, entry of 13 November 1911, p. 54.

73. Vincent, ed., *Crawford Papers*, 'Notes', 11 November 1911, p. 247.

74. Alan Clark, ed., *A Good Innings: The Private Papers of Viscount Lee of Fareham* (London, 1974), p. 127. The son of a Dorset rectory, Lee was extremely sensitive about the source of his wealth and never forgave Bonar Law for teasing him by suggesting that 'The trouble with you is that your wife has too much money': *ibid.*, p. 76.

75. Henry Chaplin to Bonar Law, 31 December 1911, BLP 24/5/166.

76. 13 November 1911, BLP 24/3/7. H.A. Gwynne noted that the chagrin of the Liberals revealed that the Unionists had made the correct choice of leader: Phillips, *Diehards*, p. 148.

77. 'Sunday', 19th [November 1911], SLSP 11/7/39.

78. Undated diary entry [December 1911], WBP 4/4.

79. 16 November 1911, RA GV 01608A/2.

80. Croft to Bonar Law, BLP 24/4/92.

81. Fisher to 'Annie' [Goulding], 24 November 1911, GP 2/43.

82. Philips, *Diehards*, p. 148.

83. 11 November 1911, BLP 24/3/9.

84. Ramsden, *Age of Balfour and Baldwin*, p. 67.

85. See David Dutton, *'His Majesty's Loyal Opposition': The Unionist Party in Opposition, 1905–1915* (Liverpool, 1992), pp. 117–26.

86. See Ramsden, *Age of Balfour and Baldwin*, pp. 68–9; and Dutton, *Loyal Opposition*, Ch. 6.

87. See Robert Blake, *The Conservative Party from Peel to Thatcher* (London, 1985), pp.

19–23; Dutton, *Loyal Opposition*, pp. 138–40; and Ramsden, *Age of Balfour and Baldwin*, pp. 70–1.

88. Austen Chamberlain to Mary Chamberlain, 19 February 1912, ACP 4/1/752; Vincent, ed., *Crawford Papers*, diary entry 12 February 1912, p. 260.

89. Conservative Party Archives, *Report of a Special Conference*, 9 May 1912. The meeting was held at the Queen's Hall, London; the Liberal Unionists held a similar meeting at the same time at the Memorial Hall. With the amalgamation the Liberal Chief Agent, William Jenkins, became the deputy to John Boraston, Principal Agent of the combined party. Memorandum, n.d. (May 1912?), MFP, MS.Eng., c.4788/49.

90. Bogdanor, 'The Selection of the Party Leader', in Seldon and Ball, eds, *Conservative Century*, p. 94.

91. Vincent, ed., *Crawford Papers*, diary entry of 16 December 1911, p. 258.

CHAPTER 5: UNFINISHED BUSINESS

1. *Minutes and Reports of the Conservative Party Conference*, 17 November 1911.
2. See, for example, that incomparable limning of Edwardian politics, Dangerfield, *Strange Death*, p. 80 and *passim*.
3. *Ibid.*, p. 100.
4. See Ramsden, *Age of Balfour and Baldwin*, p. 67.
5. Vincent, ed., *Crawford Papers*, 22 February 1912, pp. 261–2.
6. Ramsden, *Age of Balfour and Baldwin*, p. 67.
7. Lord Oxford and Asquith, *Memories and Reflections*, Vol. I (New York, 1928), p. 239. This rather irresistible quote has been printed many times by many different authors.
8. Williamson, ed., *Bridgeman Diaries*, entry April–August 1912, p. 59.
9. Butler and Freeman, eds, *British Political Facts*, pp. 127–8.
10. Bonar Law to Arnold Ward, 15 January 1912, BLP 33/4/1.
11. Bonar Law to F.E. Smith, 31 July 1913, BLP 33/5/48.
12. See Matthew Fforde, *Conservatism and Collectivism, 1886–1914* (Edinburgh, 1990), ch. 3. Early in his career Steel-Maitland had been secretary to Lord Milner.
13. See Ramsden, *Age of Balfour and Baldwin*, pp. 76–7. The USRC overplayed their hand with Bonar Law, and he tightened the reins on the committee in late 1912. As it was, their energies were channelled into the Irish debate: *ibid.*, p. 50.
14. Bonar Law to Garvin, 9 November 1907, JLGP.
15. See Ramsden, ed., *Sanders Diaries*, entry of 19 February 1912, p. 411.
16. See Garvin to Bonar Law, 16 February 1912, BLP 25/2/26.
17. Vincent, ed., *Crawford* Papers, diary entry of 3 December 1911, p. 257.
18. See Green, *Crisis of Conservatism*, p. 294; and Sykes, *Tariff Reform*, p. 262.
19. *The Times*, 27 January 1912.
20. Chamberlain, *Down the Years*, p. 224.
21. See the letters between Thomas Comyn Platt and Walter Long, forwarded to Bonar Law, 20–21 June 1912, BLP 26/4/29.
22. Bonar Law to Salisbury (draft), 4 February 1910, BLP 20/34.
23. Bonar Law to Derby, 14 November 1911, BLP 33/3/4.
24. Bonar Law to Lady Primrose, 26 February 1912, BLP 33/4/17, quoted in Sykes, *Tariff Reform*, p. 256.
25. BLP 25/2/34.
26. Vincent, ed., *Crawford Papers*, diary entry of 20 February 1912, p. 261.
27. Attending were the Duke of Devonshire and Lords Lansdowne, Ashbourne, Derby, Halsbury, Midleton, Londonderry, Selborne and Chilston. The Commons leaders were Bonar Law, Chamberlain, Long, Steel-Maitland, Smith and Chaplin, as

well as George Wyndham, Alfred Lyttelton and Sir Robert Finlay. Though invited, Lord Curzon and Sir Edward Carson were unable to attend. Balcarres could not resist observing of the rather elderly gathering: 'All the obsolete mandarins were present ...' For the meeting, see Balcarres's memorandum, 29 February 1912, Vincent, ed., *Crawford Papers*, pp. 264–5. Bonar Law had hoped to exclude certain peers, including Londonderry and Halsbury, but relented on Lansdowne's protestations: Lansdowne to Bonar Law, 23 February 1912, BLP 25/2/49.

28. See Chamberlain, *Down the Years*, pp. 432–6.
29. 14 March 1912, BLP 25/3/32.
30. Salisbury to Bonar Law, 1 May 1912, BLP 26/3/2, and reply, 3 May 1912, BLP 33/4/34.
31. Bonar Law informed the King in September 1912 that, upon taking office, his party would face a need for increased sources of revenue for defence and social expenditures, and the Unionist Govt would have no new source of taxation open to them except by means of a Tariff: 'Notes of Observations made to H.M. by Mr Bonar Law, 27 September 1912', Lord Stamfordham, RA GV 2553 (1).
32. Salisbury replied immediately to Bonar Law, pleading: 'Please don't talk of not going on as Leader': 6 May 1912, BLP 26/3/14.
33. Lansdowne to Bonar Law, 20 June 1912, BLP 26/4/31.
34. Despite his distaste for formal entertainments, Bonar Law hosted a lavish banquet at the Carlton Hotel in honour of the Canadian visitors: Bonar Law to Lord Lansdowne, 1 June 1912, BLP 33/4/40. He also took advantage of his new popularity with Lady Londonderry to inspire an invitation to Londonderry House: Bonar Law to Lady Londonderry, 1 June 1912, BLP 33/4/41. For the Carlton Hotel dinner see Vincent, ed., *Crawford Papers*, diary entry of 8 July 1912, p. 277.
35. Bonar Law to Borden, 26 October 1912, BLP 33/4/61. See also Bonar Law to Lord Graham, 6 August 1912, BLP 33/4/51.
36. The Confederates announced their intended vigilantism in *The Times* on 15 June 1912. Five days later, in response to an angry retort from Bonar Law, Croft and his colleagues protested their total loyalty to the leader and begged an interview to explain their position: Croft, Basil Peto and Ronald McNeill to Bonar Law, BLP 33/2/20. See also Witherell, *Rebel on the Right*, pp. 182–3.
37. (Copy) BBKP, C/201.
38. Bonar Law employed the argument that Borden was a powerful pro-tariff force applying pressure on the British Unionists: see Stamfordham's memorandum of Bonar Law's conversation with the King, 27 September 1912, RA GV 2553 (1)/1.
39. Bonar Law to Aitken, 3 September 1912, BBKP, C/201.
40. Lansdowne to Bonar Law, 10 October 1912, BLP 27/3/28.
41. Lansdowne to Bonar Law, 13 October 1912, BLP 27/3/34. Bonar Law also wrote again to Borden to encourage him to announce his pledge of tariff co-operation: 26 October 1912, BLP 33/4/61. Borden replied explaining that he would do so in early 1913, but events overtook his need to redeem the promise: 3 December 1912, BLP 28/1.
42. Ramsden, ed., *Sanders Diaries*, entry of 17 November 1912, p. 52.
43. See Randolph S. Churchill, *Winston Churchill*, Vol. II, *Young Statesman, 1901–1914* (London, 1967), pp. 456–7. Churchill apparently kept the volume as a souvenir of battle.
44. Ramsden, ed., *Sanders Diaries*, entry of 17 November 1912, p. 52.
45. For the episode see Violet Bonham Carter, *Winston Churchill as I Knew Him* (London, 1965), pp. 300–1.

46. *Report of the Annual Conference,* 14–15 November, 1912.
47. For the remarkable reception, see Vincent, ed., *Crawford Papers,* Balcarres to Lady Wantage, 15 November 1912, p. 284.
48. *Report of the Annual Conference,* 14–15 November 1912.
49. 28 November 1912; see also Salvidge's similar letter of 6 December 1912, both in WLP, 446/5.
50. SLSP, 5/9/8/3.
51. Vincent, ed., *Crawford Papers,* diary entry of 30 November 1912, p. 289.
52. 9 December 1912, marked 'Private', SLSP 9/8/4.
53. See Blake, *Unknown Prime Minister,* p. 112 and Witherell, *Rebel on the Right,* p. 185.
54. Witherell, *Rebel on the Right,* p. 185.
55. Edward Goulding, a Vice-President of the Tariff Reform League, suggested to Bonar Law on 20 December 1912 that he was willing to circulate a petition among members of the League calling for a reinstatement of the Referendum Pledge: ACP 10/3/33, quoted in Sykes, *Tariff Reform,* pp. 113–14. Yet he played something of a double game in writing to Garvin on 11 January 1913 suggesting that it was Bonar Law who had lost his nerve, while under the influence of Aitken: see Gollin, *Observer and J.L. Garvin,* p. 383. He did not mislead Chamberlain, who was well informed about his correspondence with Bonar Law: A. Chamberlain to Bonar Law, 24 December 1912, BLP 28/1/86.
56. Bonar Law to Selborne, 20 December 1912, SP 73/75. See also Bonar Law to Lansdowne, 25 December 1912, LP 88/31.
57. 9 December 1912, SLSP 9/8/4.
58. Lord Northcliffe could not have been wider of the mark when he observed as this crisis waned that Bonar Law was much under the influence of the Great Families: see Vincent, ed., *Crawford Papers,* diary entry 9 January 1913, p. 301.
59. Randolph S. Churchill, *Lord Derby, 'King of Lancashire'* (London, 1959), p. 154.
60. Derby to Bonar Law, 21 December 1912, BLP 28/1/72.
61. Bonar Law to Derby, 24 December 1912, BLP 33/4/81.
62. Bonar Law to Balcarres, 24 December 1912, BLP 33/4/81. Derby had written to Balcarres as early as 5 September 1912 complaining: 'I am coming out against Food Taxes. I can't stand them any longer': R. Churchill, *Derby,* p. 163. See also Balcarres's letter to Bonar Law of the same date, BLP 27/2/7, noting that Derby's action was in spite of the conclusion of the Shadow Cabinet, to which he was a party. The Unionist elder statesman Henry Chaplin wrote to Long on Boxing Day 1912 that Derby was obviously 'doing mischief' in Lancashire: WLPT 947/446/34. See also Dutton, *Loyal Opposition,* p. 190.
63. Bonar Law to Lansdowne, 25 December 1912, BLP 33/4/83. Northcliffe had recently begun a major campaign in his newspapers against what he termed 'stomach taxes'.
64. Churchill, *Derby,* pp. 175–6.
65. Derby to King George V, 16 November 1911, RA GV 01608 A/2.
66. Derby to Balfour, 21 December 1912, AJBP Add. MSS. 49743.
67. R. Churchill, *Derby,* pp. 169–70.
68. Derby to Long, 25 December 1912. WLPT 446/23.
69. Vincent, ed., *Crawford Papers,* diary entry of 29 December 1912, p. 293.
70. BLP 33/4/86.
71. 1 January 1913, BLP 33/5/1A.
72. Bonar Law to Long, 4 January 1913, WLP, Add. MSS. 62404/29; Ramsden, ed., *Sanders Diaries,* entry of 5 January 1913, p. 58.
73. Vincent, ed., *Crawford Papers,* diary entry of 1 January 1913, p. 294.
74. *Ibid.,* p. 297. When he got wind of the crisis Long wrote to Bonar Law, pleading

that he must not consider resignation, which would 'mean ruin for our cause': 2 January 1913, WLPT 947/446/37.

75. Chamberlain, *Politics from Inside*, pp. 511–13.

76. John Barnes and David Nicholson, *The Leo Amery Diaries* (London, 1980), entry of 1 January 1913, p. 89.

77. When the *Observer* on 22 December printed the rumour that Bonar Law would resign and be succeeded by Carson, Garvin was rebuked by the Ulster leader, who promised that he would back Bonar Law through 'thick and thin': Gollin, *Observer and J.L. Garvin*, p. 375.

78. Ramsden, ed., *Sanders Diaries*, entry of 12 January 1913, p. 59.

79. See, for example, Blake, *Unknown Prime Minister*, p. 115; Gollin, *Observer and J.L. Garvin*, p. 381; Sykes, *Tariff Reform*, p. 271.

80. Vincent, ed., *Crawford Papers*, diary entry of 7 January 1913, p. 298.

81. *Ibid.*, p. 299.

82. Waldorf Astor explained that he and Hewins, Goulding, Amery, Page Croft, Smith and Carson shaped Carson's original draft into a form acceptable to most Members; then Lord Hugh Cecil and McNeill, perhaps with Astor's assistance, further revised it: Gollin, *Observer and J.L. Garvin*, p. 382. See also Witherell, *Rebel on the Right*, pp. 187–8.

83. The earliest drafts of the Memorial may be those retained by Malcolm Fraser, the party publicity chief: MFP, Ms. Eng. c. 4789/20–23. Several drafts as well as a copy of the final version of the Memorial are in BLP 41/M/9; other copies of drafts are in file BLP 41/M/11. Copies of the final text are also to be found in ACP 9/5/46 and the papers of Lord Balcarres. Copies of the document were not made available, even to most members of the party. It was made public only on 10 February 1914, when it appeared in *The Times* and the *Morning Post*, and was published once again twenty-five years later in Sir Charles Petrie, *The Life and Letters of Sir Austen Chamberlain*, Vol. I (London, 1939), pp. 330–2.

84. Amery, Lloyd and Winterton were Confederates, while Archer Shee had been a member of the Reveille: Witherell, *Rebel on the Right*, Appendices 1 and 2.

85. It has often been reported that six MPs failed to sign: see, for example, Blake, *Unknown Prime Minister*, p. 118; and David Ayerst, *Garvin of the Observer* (London, 1985), p. 131; Julian Amery, in his *Joseph Chamberlain and the Tariff Reform Campaign* (London, 1951), p. 983, listed five names. Aitken claimed that despite his admiration for Bonar Law, he did not sign the Memorial: *Politicians and the Press* (London, 1925), pp. 120–1. Historians have long accepted this at face value, yet the original copy of the document in the Crawford papers bore his signature: see Balcarres's tally of signatures, BLP 41/M/9; and the comment of Professor John Vincent, *Crawford Papers*, p. 305.

86. In Edinburgh on 24 January he repeated these terms and reminded Unionists that the party remained committed to a modest tariff on imported manufactured goods; this came to be called the Edinburgh Compromise: see Steel-Maitland to Lord Robert Cecil, RCP, Add. Mss. 51071B/25–9. Bonar Law's original draft of the speech and the letter to Balcarres were retained by Malcolm Fraser, MFP, MS. Eng. c. 4789/50–64 and 31.

87. Bonar Law to Balcarres, 13 January 1913, BLP 41/M/11.

88. N.d., BLP 41/M/12.

89. A copy of the minutes was retained by Long: WLPT 947/451.

90. 8 January 1913, BLP 33/5/6.

91. Balcarres, 'Comments on the recent Crisis, 19 January 1913', Vincent, ed., *Crawford Papers*, p. 304. See also Lord Stamfordham to King George V, 31 December 1912, RA GV K588/1. Claude Lowther wrote to Bonar Law at the height of the crisis: 'If

you could but realize how the party has been heartened and stimulated by your leadership . . .': 2 January 1913, BLP 28/2/9.

92. Lansdowne himself noted years later that Bonar Law's position 'necessarily overshadowed' his own: Lansdowne to Bonar Law, n.d. [March 1917], LP 88/51.

93. Vincent, ed., *Crawford Papers*, p. 289.

CHAPTER 6: IRELAND: 'WE ARE IN FOR TROUBLOUS TIMES'

1. In the 20 by-elections in which seats changed party hands between April 1911 and the coming of the Great War, 14 Unionists defeated Liberals or Labourites; Liberals took one seat from the Unionists, and one Independent Conservative defeated the official Unionist candidate.

2. See Patricia Jalland, *The Liberals and Ireland* (London, 1980), pp. 50–1, and George Dangerfield, *The Damnable Question* (New York, 1976), pp. 70–1. A by-election in Londonderry City in January 1912 reversed the ratio.

3. Dutton, *Loyal Opposition*, p. 211.

4. Robert Sanders noted in his diary on 13 October 1912; '[Bonar Law] has said both publicly and privately that in . . . case [of an election] he would not support resistance. There he differs from Carson.' Ramsden, ed., *Sanders Diaries*, p. 51.

5. 8 August 1911. For the significance of this speech, see Smith, 'Bonar Law and Conservative Strategy', p. 93.

6. *The Times*, 8 December 1911.

7. *The Times*, 27 January 1912. For this speech see H.A. Taylor, *Bonar Law*, p. 167, and Dangerfield, *Strange Death*, p. 96.

8. The story told by Edward Marjoribanks, that the Carsons had Italian origins and were originally called Carsoni, is unfortunately a myth: see his *Life of Lord Carson*, Vol. I (London, 1932), p. 5, but also H. Montgomery Hyde, *Carson: The Life of Sir Edward Carson, Lord Carson of Duncairn* (London, 1953), p. 5.

9. See Smith, 'Bonar Law and Conservative Strategy', pp. 86, 99–101.

10. Stewart, *Carson*, p. 77.

11. Entry of 14 April 1912, GRD, Add. MSS. 62970.

12. On 6 December 1911 he wrote to W.H. Clemney advising that he would not address the Ulster Orange Lodges if they insisted on wearing their quasi-religious regalia: BLP 33/3/28.

13. 7 Oct 1912, BLP 33/4/58.

14. Stewart, *Carson*, p. 73.

15. Asquith to King George V, 6 February 1912, HHAP 6/95–6.

16. Carson to Lady Londonderry, 14 April 1912, quoted in Hyde, *Carson*, p. 312; see also Riddell's diary entry of 14 April 1912, GRD, Add. MSS. 62970.

17. *National Union Gleanings*, Vol. XXXVIII, p. 359.

18. On 12 November 1912, it will be recalled, Asquith was tripped up with a defeat on a snap division on a financial amendment to the Bill.

19. Stephen Mark Duffy, '"No Question of Fighting": The Government, the Army and the Curragh Incident, 1914' (unpublished Ph.D. thesis, Texas A&M University, 1993), p.18. Belfast magistrates ruled that since the UVF existed to maintain 'the constitution of the United Kingdom as now established', it was legal: Hyde, *Carson*, p. 298.

20. Dangerfield, *Damnable Question*, p. 93.

21. Unionist Central Office estimated that less than half the Liberal candidates had even mentioned Home Rule in their campaign speeches: see Blewett, *Peers, Parties and the People*, p. 326, and Ramsden, *Age of Balfour and Baldwin*, pp. 78–9.

22. Ramsden, *Age of Balfour and Baldwin*, p. 79.

23. 11 April 1912, quoted in Smith, 'Bonar Law and the Conservative Strategy', p. 119.

24. See H.J. Hanham, ed., *The Nineteenth Century Constitution, 1815–1914* (London, 1969), p. 197; Ramsden, *Age of Balfour and Baldwin*, pp. 78–9; and Smith, 'Bonar Law and Conservative Strategy', pp. 119–20.
25. *Gleanings and Memoranda*, Vol. XL, p. 349.
26. Chamberlain, *Politics From Inside*, pp. 486–7.
27. Rose, *King George V*, pp. 138–9.
28. Malcolm, *Vacant Thrones*, p. 62. Bonar Law more than once used this same phrase to describe himself, beginning with the Albert Hall speech of January 1912.
29. See Nicolson, *King George the Fifth* (London, 1953), p. 223. Balfour advised the King similarly (though more gently) in 1913: see his memorandum of 16 September 1913, AJBP, Add.MSS. 49693. See also Dutton, *Loyal Opposition*, p. 218.
30. See Roy Jenkins (London, 1966), *Asquith*, p. 279; and Jalland, *Liberals and Ireland*, pp. 102–3.
31. Unionists took the formerly Liberal seats of Hanley, on 13 July, and Crewe, on 26 July. The storied North-west Manchester fell to them in a by-election of 8 August.
32. *The Times*, 29 July 1912, emphasis added. A draft of the speech was retained by Malcolm Fraser: see MFP, MS., Eng. c. 4789/7–19.
33. Dangerfield, *Strange Death*, p. 106.
34. Jenkins, *Asquith*, p. 278.
35. Jalland, *Liberals and Ireland*, p. 103.
36. Bonar Law to Joseph Welch, 26 July 1913, BLP 33/5/46.
37. An excellent new interpretation of the campaign is offered by Dr Jeremy Smith, 'Bluff, Bluster and Brinkmanship: Andrew Bonar Law and the Third Home Rule Bill', in *The Historical Journal*, Vol. XXXVI, Mar. 1993.
38. *The Times*, 8 February 1913.
39. 18 October 1913, BLP 33/6/84.
40. 1 January 1913, *Gleanings and Memoranda*, Vol. XL, p. 119.
41. In 1912 MP for St Austell, Cornwall, Agar-Robartes had been unseated by petition from his previous seat in Bodmin.
42. Entry of 14 April 1912, GRD, Add. MSS. 62955.
43. See Long to Bonar Law, 4 June 1912, BLP 26/4/7, wherein he declared that he could 'not assent to H.R. in any form' – yet he voted with Bonar Law in favour of the amendment.
44. 28 June 1912, Smith, 'Conservative Strategy', p. 126.
45. Hyde, *Carson*, pp. 326–7.
46. 18 June 1912: *National Union Gleanings*, Vol. XXXIX, p. 80.
47. For this episode, see Hyde, *Carson*, pp. 291–2. The five were Ulster Unionist MPs James Craig and Col. Robert Sharman-Crawford, and Ulster notables Thomas Andrews, Edward Sclater and Col. R.H. Wallace.
48. Stewart, *Carson*, p. 78. Not to be left out, 234,046 women signed a similar 'declaration' on the same day.
49. Brendan Mac Giolla Choille, ed., *Intelligence Notes, 1913–16* (Dublin, 1966), p. 19.
50. 30 Sept. 1912, HAGP, Dep. 20. The characteristically Bonar Law-esque bit of humour referred, of course, to Maxse's 'BMG' campaign of 1911.
51. RA, King George V's Diary.
52. 'Notes of Observations made to H.M. by Mr Bonar Law', 27 September 1912, RA GV K2553 (1) /2.
53. The two Royal servants had been joint Private Secretaries from the time of the King's accession.
54. Bonar Law maintained a regular correspondence with Stamfordham, who was the King's trusted personal adviser. In this period the Unionist leader regularly pressed with Stamfordham his case for Royal intervention: see, for example, his letter of 16

November 1912, BLP 33/4/65.

55. Hyde, *Carson*, p. 325; Jalland, *Liberals and Ireland*, p. 106.
56. Edinburgh, 10 September; and Bow and Bromley, 26 November.
57. Milner to F.S. Oliver, 23 October 1913, quoted in Sykes, *Tariff Reform*, p. 284.

CHAPTER 7: 'ULSTER, ULSTER, ALL THE TIME'

1. A. Chamberlain to M. Chamberlain, 16 March 1913, ACP 4/1/952. See also see T. Comyn Platt to Long, forwarded to Bonar Law, BLP 26/4/29.
2. As examples of Bonar Law's troubles with these Unionists, see Lord Robert Cecil to Bonar Law, 21 March 1913, BLP 29/2/32; Bonar Law to Page Croft, 10 November 1913, BLP 33/6/97; and Clark, *Good Innings*, Lee's diary entry of 5 February 1913, p. 131. See also Bonar Law's comment upon Lord Hugh's search for a Parliamentary seat: '[I] would rather let twenty men into the Commons than so troublesome a Tory as Hugh Cecil': Kenneth Rose, *The Later Cecils* (London, 1975), p. 241.
3. Bonar Law truly feared Lloyd George's potential to distract the public from Home Rule with his proposed Land Campaign: see Ramsden, ed., *Sanders Diaries*, entry of 8 July 1913, p. 66.
4. 19 January 1913, RA GV K808/1.
5. The standard work on the affair remains Frances Donaldson, *The Marconi Scandal* (London, 1962). Valuable recent correctives may be found in Bentley B. Gilbert, *Lloyd George: Organizer of Victory, 1912–1916* (London, 1997), pp. 32–55; John Grigg, *Lloyd George: From Peace to War, 1912–1916* (London, 1985), Ch. II. See also H. Montgomery Hyde, *Lord Reading* (London, 1967), pp. 120–67.
6. Koss, *Rise and Fall of the Political Press*, Vol. II, p. 175.
7. Italics added.
8. *Le Matin* inaccurately attributed as its source Maxse's *National Review*, but then recanted its entire story before the libel suit was pressed.
9. Entry of 22 March 1913, GRD, Add. MSS. 62972.
10. Of the three Unionist barristers, only Campbell had consulted Bonar Law prior to accepting a Marconi-related brief.
11. For the relevant and angry correspondence, see BLP 29/4.
12. See Baird to Bonar Law, 4 April 1913, BLP 29/3/4. It is also true that Carson and Smith, both Unionist Privy Councillors and members of the Shadow Cabinet, might have pleaded conflict of interest and so avoided the controversy.
13. Smith attacked his critics in a long letter to *The Times* in June: Campbell, *F.E. Smith*, p. 336. Carson was more philosphical about the anger of colleagues who did not understand the 'traditions of the Bar': Carson to Gwynne, June 1913, HAGP, Dep. 17. See also Hyde, *Carson*, p. 333.
14. Murray's stockbroker went bankrupt in May 1913, and only then was the news of his party share purchases revealed. Unionists leaked this to the press only after efforts to work it into the Chesterton trial failed: see Oliver Locker-Lampson to Bonar Law, 9 June 1913, BLP 29/5/12. Murray did not testify before the Select Committee because he was in Colombia at the time; on the slightest provocation Unionists in the House therefore put up a howl of 'Bogata! Bogata!', which amused Bonar Law enormously.
15. See Ramsden, ed., *Sanders Diaries*, entry of 22 June 1913, pp. 66–7.
16. *Gleanings and Memoranda*, Vol. XLI, pp. 62–4.
17. Upon becoming leader, he resigned his directorships and thus reduced his income by £2,000 a year: Vincent, ed., *Crawford Papers*, diary entry of 28 November 1911, p. 257. See also the undated notes of 1909 by Bonar Law's secretary, Miss Sarah Tugander: MP, Hist. Coll. 200.

18. As in the diary entry of 10 October 1934, by Robert Bruce Lockhart, quoted in B. Gilbert, *Lloyd George: Organizer of Victory*, p. 49.
19. Diary entry of 14 July 1912, GRD, Add. MSS. 62971.
20. Duff Cooper, *Old Men Forget* (London, 1953), p. 35.
21. Diary entry of 9 August 1913, GRD, Add. MSS. 62973.
22. Bonar Law to Aitken, 23 June 1913, BBKP, C/201.
23. Londonderry was lost 30 January: see the entry of 16 February 1913, Ramsden, ed., *Sanders Diaries*, p. 60; and B. Gilbert, *Lloyd George: Organizer of Victory*, p. 95. On 16 May the Unionists took Newmarket from the Liberals, followed by Reading on 8 November and S. Lanarkshire on 12 December.
24. BLP 29/6/33.
25. Dicey to Bonar Law, n.d. [March 1913], 11 June 1913 and 13 June 1913, BLP 29/2/42, 29/5/22, and 29/5/25; see also Dicey to Strachey, 18 August 1913, SLSP 5/6/12.
26. The King's daily post contained a regular flood of letters on the subject, many from Ulster and most opposing Home Rule: Nicolson, *King George the Fifth*, p. 221.
27. *Ibid.*, p. 222. For a spirited defence of Asquith's 'relative inactivity', see Jenkins, *Asquith*, p. 282.
28. HHAP 38/120–1. This is printed in Nicolson, *King George the Fifth*, pp. 223–4.
29. HHAP 38/158–173. Both are printed in Jenkins, *Asquith*, pp. 538–44.
30. Nicolson, *King George the Fifth*, pp. 225–9.
31. Patricia Jalland correctly points out that Loreburn, once an uncompromising Gladstonian Home Ruler, mentioned neither devolution nor Ulster exclusion as proposals for settlement: *Liberals and Ireland*, p. 127.
32. For Lansdowne's report of his own talk with the King, see BLP 39/E/7.
33. 18 September 1913, BLP 33/5/56. Enclosed with this was Bonar Law's *aide-mémoire* of his various talks at Balmoral. His handwritten draft, dated 16 September, is included in this file, and a finished copy is in LP 1/12. He forwarded a copy to Carson, BLP 33/5/57.
34. Lord Roberts, the senior Field Marshal of the British Army, wrote to Bonar Law on 14 September 1913, protesting that the employment of troops to enforce Home Rule in Ulster would 'strain discipline to almost a breaking point, and have a most disastrous effect on the Army generally': BLP 30/2/11.
35. Dutton, *Loyal Opposition*, p. 204.
36. Bonar Law to Lansdowne, 27 September 1913, BLP 33/5/61.
37. Hyde, *Carson*, p. 340.
38. 20 September 1913, BLP 30/2/15.
39. BLP 30/2/17. Lansdowne had also tried to dissuade the King from pressing for a compromise based on any form of Ulster exclusion: n.d., Lansdowne to Bonar Law, BLP 39/E/7.
40. 23 September 1913, BLP 30/2/20 and 21; also 26 September 1913, 30/2/27; 27 September 1913, 30/2/29, and 30 September 1913, 30/2/37.
41. 24 September 1913, BLP 33/5/59.
42. Bonar Law to Lansdowne, 27 September 1913, BLP 33/5/61.
43. See Stamfordham's letters to Bonar Law of 26 September 1913, BLP 30/2/28; 1 October 1913, 30/3/1; and 7 October 1913, 30/3/10; and Bonar Law's replies of 1 Oct 1913, RA GV K2553 (2)46; and 4 October 1913, BLP 33/5/66. By this time the Palace considered Bonar Law the more reasonable among the Unionist leaders of the two Houses: Jalland, *Liberals and Ireland*, p. 147.
44. See Balfour to Bonar Law, 23 September 1913, BLP 30/2/20, and Stamfordham to Bonar Law, 26 September 1913, BLP 30/2/28: Campbell, *F.E. Smith*, pp. 338–9.

45. BLP 33/6/69.
46. Long to Bonar Law, 5 October 1913, BLP 30/3/7. For this see Smith, 'Andrew Bonar Law and Conservative Strategy', p. 247.
47. Hyde, *Carson*, p. 343.
48. 8 October 1913, and 'Appendix', LP 1/41, copy in BLP 33/5/68.
49. Ronan Fanning, '"Rats" versus "Ditchers": The Diehard Revolt and the Parliament Act of 1911', in Art Cosgrove and J.I. McGuire, eds, *Parliament & Community, Historical Studies 14* (Belfast, 1983), p. 206.
50. For devolution and the 'Home Rule all round' ideas, see John Kendle, *Ireland and the Federal Solution: The Debate Over the United Kingdom Constitution, 1870–1921* (Montreal, 1989).
51. 10 October 1913, BLP 30/3/16.
52. Kitchin to BL, 30 September 1913, BLP 30/2/35. Lloyd George suggested to T.P. O'Connor that the Irish Nationalists consider this – a notion which, predictably, fell on deaf ears: Jalland, *Liberals and Ireland*, p. 150.
53. *The Times*, 9 October 1913.
54. Marked 'secret', BLP 30/3/11. Bonar Law was amused at the idea that Churchill had apparently told Asquith the request for a meeting was raised by him and not the First Lord: Bonar Law to Lansdowne, 10 October 1913, LP 1/48.
55. 10 October 1913, HHAP 38/224.
56. 10 October 1913, BLP 30/3/17. On the following day Lansdowne forwarded a letter from Carson refusing to consider any offer of the exclusion of only the four Protestant counties: BLP 30/3/23.
57. Bonar Law to Asquith, 10 and 11 October 1913, HHAP 38/224, 38/230; and Asquith's reply of 11 October, BLP 30/2/22. On 13 October Asquith telegraphed to Bonar Law an agreed code word, 'Tomorrow', meaning all was ready: BLP 30/3/27.
58. Lansdowne to Bonar Law, 13 October 1913, BLP 30/3/29; and, similarly, Midleton to Bonar Law, 11 October 1913, BLP 30/3/23.
59. Bonar Law to Lansdowne, 15 October 1913, enclosing 'Notes of Conversation with the P.M.': LP 1/55; also in BLP 33/6/80.
60. Jenkins, *Asquith*, p. 289.
61. 15 October 1913, HHAP 38/231.
62. For an alternative interpretation see Jalland, *Liberal and Ireland*, p. 154.
63. 18 October 1913, BLP 33/6/84.
64. *Newcastle Daily Journal*, 30 October 1913.
65. Asquith to Bonar Law, 30 October 1913, BLP 30/3/75; and reply, 2 November 1913, HHAP 39/1. Linlithgow was successfully defended and Reading captured from the Liberals.
66. 'Memorandum of meeting with the Prime Minister of 6 November 1913', 7 November 1913, BLP 33/6/93. For examples of such hostility, see Salisbury to Bonar Law, 31 October 1913, BLP 30/3/80; and Chamberlain to Lansdowne, 29 October 1913, Chamberlain, *Politics from Inside*, pp. 567–9.
67. BLP 33/6/93.
68. 7 November 1913, WLP, Add. MSS, 62404/35.
69. Bonar Law to Long, 8 November 1913, WLP, Add. MSS. 62404/37.
70. Bonar Law to Lansdowne, 26 November 1913, BLP 33/6/102.
71. Bonar Law to Balfour, 18 November 1913, BLP 33/6/98; and Bonar Law to Long, 21 November 1913, WLP, Add. MSS. 62404/38.
72. Bonar Law to Carson, 3 December 1913, BLP 33/6/106.
73. Asquith to Bonar Law, 3 December 1913, BLP 31/1/5; and reply, 3 December 1913, HHAP 39/40.

74. See Blake, *Unknown Prime Minister*, pp. 171–2, and Jenkins, *Asquith*, pp. 292–3, for differing views. Patricia Jalland concludes that Bonar Law was 'somewhat naïve' to assume that Asquith would go forward with an exclusion proposal: *Liberals and Ireland*, pp. 156–7.
75. B. Gilbert, *Lloyd George: Organizer of Victory*, p. 97.
76. Asquith to King George V, 14 November 1913, HHAP 7/71–2.
77. Edward David, ed., *Inside Asquith's Cabinet: From the Diaries of Charles Hobhouse* (London, 1977; hereafter cited as *Hobhouse Diaries*), entry of 25 November 1913, p. 151.
78. 'Notes of Conversation with the P.M.', 10 December 1913, enclosed in his letter to Lansdowne of the same date, BLP 33/6/111.
79. The two devolutionists had been in contact, hoping to gain a hearing for such a plan: see Chamberlain's memorandum of 26 November 1913, *Politics from Inside*, pp. 572–7.
80. Lansdowne to Bonar Law, 11 December 1913, BLP 31/1/25, 'Possibility of a Settlement', 16 December 1913, BLP 31/1/38. Suspicion of the compromise debate in the party is also indicated in Selborne to Bonar Law, BLP 31/1/47; and Long to Bonar Law, 15 December 1913, WLP, Add. MSS. 62404/40.
81. Chamberlain, *Politics from Inside*, p. 588.
82. *Ibid.*, p. 591.
83. Bonar Law wrote to Lansdowne 22 December 1913: BLP 33/6/115.
84. Asquith to Carson (copy), 23 December 1913, BLP 31/1/52.
85. See Jenkins, *Asquith*, p. 295. A draft of the reply, in Bonar Law's hand on Cherkley notepaper, survives: BLP 33/6/117.
86. 27 December 1913, BLP 33/6/119. Dr Jalland has written that one of Asquith's objectives in this curious exercise was '... to confuse the opposition as to his real intentions and gain further time': *Liberals and Ireland*, p. 185. He apparently had failed to confuse Bonar Law.
87. Carson to Asquith (draft in Carson's hand), 7 January 1914, BLP 34/1/7. See Hyde, *Carson*, p. 344, and David, ed., *Hobhouse Diaries*, entry of 23 January 1914, pp. 156–7.
88. 22 December 1913, BLP 33/6/115.
89. 27 December 1913, BLP 33/6/120. This curious meeting has previously been overlooked by historians.
90. Asquith agreed to this: see his letter to Bonar Law, 10 January 1914, sent on to Lansdowne, LP 2/107.
91. *The Times*, 16 January 1914.
92. RA GV, K2553(3)/77, 26 January 1914.
93. Rose, *King George V*, pp. 150–1.
94. 22 December 1913, SP 77/64.

CHAPTER 8: TO THE BRINK
1. Bonar Law to Lansdowne, LP 2/101.
2. *Gleanings and Memoranda*, Vol. XLII, pp. 97–100.
3. Lord Milner's diary entry of 13 January 1914, AMP 85.
4. Amery, *My Political Life*, Vol. I, p. 441. Undated drafts may be found in AMP 157/192, and LP 2/109.
5. 17 January 1914, LP 2/108; copy in BLP 34/1/14.
6. Supporters insisted the crowd numbered as many as a million. This was probably an exaggeration, but there is little doubt that it was enormous. A copy of the flyer advertising the meeting survives as WLP, Add. MSS. 62436/82. See Amery, *My Political Life*, Vol. I, pp. 441–2.

7. Lord Long of Wraxall, *Memories* (London, 1923), p. 203. For the Covenant campaign, see William S. Rodner, 'Leaguers, Covenanters, Moderates: British Support for Ulster, 1913–1914,' in *Eire–Ireland*, 17, no. 3; Gregory Phillips, 'Lord Willoughby de Broke and the Politics of Radical Toryism, 1909–1914', in *Journal of British Studies*, Vol. 20, no. 1; and Kendle, *Walter Long*, pp. 78–83.

8. Gollin, *Proconsul in Politics: A Study of Lord Milner in Opposition and in Power* (London, 1964), p.189; Dangerfield, *Strange Death*, p. 336.

9. Gollin, *Proconsul in Politics*, p. 189.

10. *The Times*, 26 July 1911.

11. 20 July 1912, BLP 26/5/34.

12. Copies of the unsigned memorandum may be found in BLP 32/3/1, dated 4 June 1913, and SP 77/21–22, dated 5 June 1913. It is printed in George Boyce, ed., *The Crisis of British Unionism: The Domestic Political Papers of the Second Earl of Selborne, 1885–1922* (London, 1987), pp. 94–9, without attribution but with speculation that the author might have been Willoughby de Broke. For the correct attribution of the document, see Corinne C. Weston, 'Lord Selborne, Bonar Law, and the "Tory Revolt"', in R.W. Davis, *Lords of Parliament* (Stanford, 1995), pp. 163–77.

13. This accompanied a letter from Louis Coward to Fellowes, 2 December 1913, forwarded to Bonar Law by Fellowes on 5 December: BLP 31/1/7. Copies were sent to Lansdowne and Balfour.

14. Bonar Law to Sir Henry Craik, 16 March 1914, BLP 34/2/39.

15. Bonar Law to Lansdowne, 15 October 1913, BLP 33/6/80; and to Carson, 18 September 1913, BLP 33/5/57.

16. Lord Roberts to Bonar Law, 14 September 1914, BLP 30/2/11.

17. A draft of such a letter survives, written for Roberts's signature by Bonar Law, with amendments by Carson and dated 27 January 1914: BLP 34/1/21. It was, however, never sent.

18. On 26 January 1914 he wrote to Willoughby de Broke, who also favoured amendment of the Army Act, that he attached 'great importance' to the amendment proposals he had seen: WBP 7/14.

19. In conversation on 26 January: Blake, *Unknown Prime Minister*, p. 175; Weston, 'Tory Revolt', pp. 169–70. He followed this with a letter four days later; if there was any response, no copy survives: LP 2/115.

20. Bonar Law to Lansdowne, 30 January 1914, LP 2/115. A copy of the letter was sent to Balfour, AJBP, Add. MSS. 49693/141–5.

21. See Lansdowne to Bonar Law, 1 February 1914, and Bonar Law's reply of 2 February, BLP 31/3/1 and 34/1/28; and Balfour to Bonar Law, 3 February 1914, BLP 31/3/7.

22. Bonar Law to Lord Robert Cecil, 3 February 1914, BLP 34/1/29, and to J.H. Howell, n.d. [early February 1914], BLP 34/2/37.

23. 'Proposed Clause in Army (Annual) Bill', 2 February 1914: BLP 31/3/2.

24. R. Cecil to Bonar Law, 2 February 1914, and Bonar Law to Balfour, BLP 31/3/3 and BLP 34/1/31.

25. The committee included one former and two future Lord Chancellors (Halsbury, Finlay and Cave), and a future Lord of Appeal (Carson), and Nobel Peace Prize laureate (Cecil).

26. For the unsigned and undated [6 March 1914] report, see MFP, MS. Eng. c. 4790/132–8. See also Lansdowne to Balfour, AJBP, Add. MSS. 49730/270. Felix Cassell advised similarly: n.d. [February 1914?] MFP, MS. Eng. c. 4790/127–31.

27. Vincent, ed., *Crawford Papers*, diary entry of 12 March 1914, p. 328.

28. Anonymous letter (Geoffrey Robinson) to Milner, 18 March 1914, AMP 40/58. The authorship of the letter is revealed in Gollin, *Proconsul in Politics*, p. 190.

Malcolm was Secretary of the Union Defence League, a British Covenanter and loyal supporter of Bonar Law.

29. Ramsden, *Sanders Diaries*, entry of 19 March 1914, p. 74.
30. Strachey to Curzon, 19 March 1914, SLSP 4/17/17.
31. BLP 34/2/44.
32. A brief perusal of *Who's Who* of the time reveals that many Unionist MPs were themselves former officers, or held Territorial commissions, or were related to serving officers.
33. See Jenkins, *Asquith*, p. 301.
34. Carson to Bonar Law, 5 March 1914, BLP 31/4/5.
35. In this regard, see Weston, 'Tory Revolt', pp. 171–7.
36. Jalland, *Liberals and Ireland*, p. 199.
37. *The Times*, 20 March 1914.
38. Nicolson, *King George the Fifth*, p. 233.
39. 28 November 1913, *Unionist Gleanings and Memoranda*, Vol. XLII, p. 21.
40. 14 March 1914: Randolph S. Churchill, *Winston Churchill, Vol. II, Young Statesman, 1901–14* (London, 1967), p. 472.
41. *Unionist Gleanings and Memoranda*, Vol. XLII, p. 278.
42. Though precautionary warrants had apparently once been made out, there was no intention to arrest Carson or his lieutenants: Hyde, *Carson*, p. 359.
43. *Ibid.*, p. 351, and Dangerfield, *Damnable Question*, p. 89. See also Long to Bonar Law, 20 March 1914, BLP 32/1/6.
44. 14 March 1914, copy, HHAP 40/5–6. See also Cmd. 7329, 14 April 1914.
45. See Sir James Fergusson, *The Curragh Incident* (London, 1964); A.P. Ryan, *Mutiny at the Curragh* (London, 1956); Jalland, *Liberals and Ireland*, ch. VII; I.F.W. Beckett, ed., *The Army and the Curragh Incident, 1914* (London, 1986); and Duffy, 'No Question of Fighting'.
46. Duffy, 'No Question of Fighting', pp. 64–5.
47. The deployment of ships had been approved by the Cabinet committee of Birrell, Churchill, Crewe, Seely and Simon, overseeing questions of Irish security. Asquith also approved and informed the King accordingly on 18 March. See R. Churchill, *Churchill, Young Statesman*, p. 474.
48. In discussions at the War Office on 19 March regarding the possible consequences of troop movements, Paget blurted out 'in a wild kind of way: "I shall lead my army to the Boyne."' Sir John French told him not to be a 'bloody fool': Gwynne to Bonar Law, n.d. [April 1914], BLP 39/2/25; see also Blake, *Unknown Prime Minister*, p. 187.
49. Fergusson, *Curragh Incident*, pp. 67–9, and Duffy, 'No Question of Fighting', pp. 109–12. For the Government version, see Cmd. 7329, 1914.
50. Duffy, 'No Question of Fighting', p. 164.
51. *Ibid.*
52. Though he either forgot, or simply denied, the existence of the telegram to Charles Hobhouse, he as Postmaster-General had responsibility for inland wireless telegraphy, and access therefore to records of such communications. The message read 'General and all cavalry officers Curragh Division resigned today', and was successfully delivered at 5.46 p.m. See David, ed., *Hobhouse Diaries*, 168–9.
53. See, for example, Bonar Law's notes of his conversation with Lt-Gen. Wilson, n.d. BLP 32/1/49; and the 'Message from General Wilson', 23 March 1914, BLP 32/1/50. See also A. Chamberlain to M. Chamberlain, 20 and 21 March 1914, *Politics from Inside*, pp. 624–7.
54. Bernard Ash, *The Lost Dictator: Field Marshal Sir Henry Wilson* (London, 1968), p. 96.
55. See R.J.Q. Adams and Philip P. Poirier, *The Conscription Controversy in Great Britain, 1900–18* (London, 1987), chs 1–3.

56. The correspondence from these and other sources relating to the first days of the crisis may be found in BLP 32/1/36–93. Perhaps the most useful informant was Walter Long: see his memoranda of 28 March and 22 April 1914, both in file BLP 39/2/22.

57. BLP 34/2/45. Asquith's reply predictably suggested delaying discussion of the crisis until Wednesday; Bonar Law indicated he would have none of it: Asquith to Bonar Law, 23 March 1914, BLP 32/1/51, and reply, 24 March 1914, BLP 34/2/49.

58. *Unionist Gleanings and Memoranda*, Vol. XLII, p. 417.

59. Until 1918, MPs were required to seek the approval of their electors upon taking office.

60. Cmd. 7318 and Cmd. 7329.

61. See David, ed., *Hobhouse Diaries*, entry of 1 April 1914, p. 168. A year later, Lord Crewe and Charles Hobhouse agreed that Churchill had in fact attempted to engineer a plot against Ulster in 1914, relying on naval power: entry of 20 May 1915, p. 246.

62. Even the eminently reasonable Lord Crawford believed that an 'elaborate plot' was afoot, although probably unknown to 'Asquith and the respectable members of the Cabinet': Vincent, ed., *Crawford Papers*, p. 330. Save for the remark about the premier, Chamberlain agreed: Petrie, *Austen Chamberlain*, Vol. I, p. 360. Amery believed in the 'pogrom' for the remainder of his life: *My Political Life*, Vol. I, p. 445.

63. There was some misunderstanding, and Davidson apparently reported to Asquith that Bonar Law agreed to his proposal; there was, of course, no further mention of it. See Asquith, *Letters to Venetia Stanley*, edited by Michael and Eleanor Brock (Oxford, 1982), p. 60, n. 3.

64. Dutton, *Loyal Opposition*, p. 223; Jalland, *Liberals and Ireland*, p. 239.

65. An Army order was issued on 27 March 1914 to prevent any such choices as Paget made ever again being offered to British officers, and reiterating the inviolacy of all lawful orders: BLP 93/2/21.

66. Ronald McNeill wrote to Bonar Law in late 1921 asking if he had known Crawford or had advance knowledge of his plan. Bonar Law denied familiarity with either, though he noted that he stood by his statement of approval, in 1914. This seems to have been corroborated by Sir Henry Wilson: 21 December 1921, and reply of the same date, BLP 107/1/107 and 107/4/18.

67. Kendle, *Ireland and the Federal Solution*, pp. 172–5.

68. Bonar Law received at least two such documents encouraging consideration of a federal solution; both are undated but are from the period between February and June. BLP 39/4/32 was signed by 22 Members, and BLP 39/4/33 by 51. Asquith received a similar petition signed by 78 Liberals: May 1914, HHAP 39/159–60. Sanders noted that Bonar Law wished to receive no more memorials: Ramsden, ed., *Sanders Diaries*, entry of 6 May 1914, p. 77.

69. Ramsden, ed., *Sanders Diaries*, entry of 30 April 1914, p. 77.

70. *Ibid.*, diary entry of 6 May 1914, p. 77.

71. Chamberlain to M. Chamberlain, 5 May 1914, *Politics from Inside*, pp. 643–5.

72. Hyde, *Carson*, p. 367.

73. See Bonar Law to Balfour, 5 May 1914, AJBP, Add. MSS. 49693/166–8, and Chamberlain to M. Chamberlain, 6 May 1914, *Politics from Inside*, p. 645.

74. After the death of the Revd James Law she retired to Bath, where she lived out her life.

75. Unionist Whip Robert Sanders noted in his diary on 18 June: 'That row was not got up by the whips. [L.S.] Amery did more than anyone else to promote it.' Ramsden, ed., *Sanders Diaries*, pp. 77–8.

76. Sir Almeric Fitzroy, *Memoirs* (London, 1923), Vol. II, p. 550, quoted in Dutton, *Loyal Opposition*, p. 248, n. 179.
77. R.B. Finlay to Bonar Law, 22 May 1914, BLP 32/3/40. This file contains a selection of congratulatory letters about the episode.
78. See the memoirs of Lowther (Viscount Ullswater), *A Speaker's Commentaries* (London, 1925), pp. 159–60.
79. 18 June 1914, BLP 39/4/38.
80. *Ibid.*
81. The Unionists retained Grimsby on 15 May and took North-East Derbyshire and Ipswich from the Liberals on the 18th and 23rd.
82. Ramsden, ed., *Sanders Diaries*, entry of 6 May and 16 July 1914, pp. 77–8.
83. See Jalland, *Liberals and Ireland*, p. 252.
84. Harold Harmsworth, Lord Rothermere, was the brother of Lord Northcliffe.
85. Memorandum by Bonar Law, 17 July 1914, BLP 39/4/43. Murray apparently reported that the Unionists demanded abolition of the plebiscite by county and the time limit on exclusion, and creation of an 'exclusion Ulster' consisting of the four counties and portions of Fermanagh and Londonderry City, all in exchange for their support for Home Rule for the rest of Ireland and a pledge not to seek repeal when they came into office.
86. 6 July 1914, *Gleanings and Memoranda*, Vol. XLIII, p. 176.
87. Rothermere may have been present at this meeting as well: see Asquith to Venetia Stanley, 15 [actually 16] July 1914, Asquith, *Letters to Venetia Stanley*, Brock and Brock, eds, p. 105; Asquith to Bonar Law, 16 July 1914, BLP 33/1/29, written after the Bonar Law–Carson–Murray meeting.
88. BLP 39/4/43.
89. BLP 33/1/29.
90. See David, ed., *Hobhouse Diaries*, entry of 18 July 1914, p. 173. Bonar Law replied similarly in an informal note to Lord Stamfordham on 20 July 1914, RA GV K2553(6)/26.
91. There is among Asquith's papers an undated page in the handwriting of King George V, no doubt given to the Prime Minister, suggesting as possible members of the conference Asquith and Crewe, and Redmond and Dillon, with Lloyd George's name followed by a query; for the Opposition: Lansdowne, Bonar Law, Carson and Craig, with Balfour's name also followed by a query: HHAP 39/226.
92. 21 July 1914, BLP 39/4/44. For Asquith's remarks to the Cabinet on the conference, see David., ed., *Hobhouse Diaries*, entry of 23 July 1914, pp. 174–5.
93. 22 July 1914, Asquith, *Letters to Venetia Stanley*, p. 109.
94. *Ibid.*, p. 109.
95. Jalland, *Liberals and Ireland*, p. 253.
96. 24 July 1914, Asquith, *Letters to Venetia Stanley*, p. 122.
97. R. Churchill, *Churchill: Young Statesman*, p. 489.

CHAPTER 9: THE LIBERALS' WAR
1. Asquith, *Letters to Venetia Stanley*, p. 136.
2. Undated memorandum, BBKP, G/57/29.
3. Campbell, *F.E. Smith*, pp. 372–3.
4. Amery, *My Political Life*, Vol. II, p. 17.
5. Wishing to deflect criticism that he was intriguing with the pro-war element of the Cabinet, Bonar Law refused an invitation to dine that evening with Grey, Churchill and Smith.
6. Amery, *My Political Life*, Vol. II, pp. 17–18; Chamberlain's memorandum, 1–5 August 1914, AC 14/2/2.

7. AC 14/2/2.

8. *Ibid.* In his *Politicians and the War* Lord Beaverbrook indicated that the letter was drafted by Bonar Law and 'despatched to Downing Street': p. 31. A.J.P. Taylor claimed that Beaverbrook drafted the letter, an anecdote probably based upon a much later recollection by Aitken: *Beaverbrook*, p. 84.

9. In 1918 Asquith recalled to Strachey that the letter had had no effect on the Cabinet: Asquith, *Letters to Venetia Stanley*, p. 147, n. 6. See also Blake, *Unknown Prime Minister*, p. 233 and Hazlehurst, *Politicians At War*, pp. 40–1. For another interpretation, see the essay by K.M. Wilson in *British Journal of International Studies*, 1 (1975), pp. 148–59.

10. Asquith to Bonar Law, 2 August 1914, BLP 34/3/3.

11. Four ministers initially resigned – Lord Beauchamp, Simon, Morley and John Burns – but only the latter two persisted.

12. *Unionist Gleanings and Memoranda*, Vol. XLIII, p. 211.

13. A.J.P. Taylor, *Beaverbrook*, p. 86.

14. Adams and Poirier, *Conscription Controversy*, p. 61. The Irish Nationalists did not participate: HHAP 26/13.

15. Bonar Law to Grey, marked 'Confidential', 6 August 1914, HHAP 36/66.

16. Three from each to the other; these may be found in BLP 34/3, and HHAP 13.

17. Harcourt to Bonar Law, 14 and 15 August 1915, BLP 34/3/41–44.

18. See Petrie, *Chamberlain*, Vol. II, p. 5.

19. See Hazlehurst, *Politicians at War*, p. 136.

20. Memorandum, n.d., BLP 34/3/16.

21. HHAP 13/210.

22. *Unionist Gleanings and Memoranda*, Vol. XLIII, p. 355.

23. See Younger to Bonar Law, 5 September 1914, BLP 34/5/16.

24. *Ibid.*, pp. 374–5.

25. Asquith wrote to Venetia Stanley remarking that the Unionists resembled a group of 'middle-aged gentlemen trying to look like the early French revolutionists in the Tennis Court'; but the Unionist Whip William Bridgeman noted that the departure was quite undramatic 'as everyone else was coming out too.' Both on 15 September 1914, Asquith, *Letters to Venetia Stanley*, p. 239; Bridgeman to Caroline Bridgeman, Williamson, ed., *Bridgeman Diaries*, p. 83.

26. Asquith, *Letters to Venetia Stanley*, 15 September 1914, p. 239.

27. Hazlehurst, *Politicians at War*, p. 142.

28. See *War Memoirs of David Lloyd George* (2 vol. edn London, 1938), Vol. I, p. 138.

29. Lord Roberts died in November 1914, in St Omer, *en route* to visit troops of the Indian Army in France.

30. Hazlehurst, *Politicians at War*, p. 128.

31. 27 January 1915, BLP 36/2/46.

32. BLP 36/2/45.

33. *The Times*, 9 and 12 January 1915. See also Bonar Law to Lansdowne, 12 January 1915, BLP 37/5/2.

34. Memorandum by Austen Chamberlain, 29 January 1915, LGP, C/3/14/8.

35. Bonar Law to Curzon, 29 January 1915, CP, MSS. Eur. F. 112/96.

36. Memorandum by Robinson, 20 December 1914, GDP 119–22.

37. Asquith agreed afterwards to circulate War Council papers to Bonar Law and Lansdowne, but only four were delivered between 17 March and the beginning of the coalition in May: Hazlehurst, *Politicians at War*, p. 231.

38. 10 March 1915, Asquith, *Letters to Venetia Stanley*, p. 469; Churchill to Lord Fisher, 15 March 1915, quoted in Hazlehurst, *Politicians at War*, pp. 230–1.

39. 27 March 1915, BLP 36/6/37.

40. *Politicians and the War* (1960 edn), p. 68.
41. Bonar Law to R. Cecil, 1 April 1915, RCP, Add. MSS. 51161/221; and to Lansdowne, 2 April 1915, LP 88/40.
42. Bonar Law to Strachey, 19 April 1915, SLSP 9/8/14.
43. See John Stubbs, 'The Impact of the Great War on the Conservative Party', in Gillian Peel and Chris Cook, eds, *The Politics of Reappraisal* (London, 1975), p. 26.
44. An introduction to the episode should begin with Martin Pugh, 'Asquith, Bonar Law and the First Coalition', in *Historical Journal*, XVII (1974), no. 4; and Hazlehurst, *Politicians at War*.
45. See R.J.Q. Adams, *Arms and the Wizard: Lloyd George and the Ministry of Munitions, 1915–1916* (London, 1978), pp. 31–6.
46. 21 March 1915, BBKP, C/318.
47. W.A.S. Hewins, *The Apologia of an Imperialist: Forty Years of Empire Policy*, Vol. II (London, 1929), p. 25.
48. See Adams and Poirier, *Conscription Controversy*, p. 74.
49. George H. Cassar, *Asquith as War Leader* (London, 1994), p. 88. Asquith's source of information for this assertion was Kitchener.
50. Stephen Koss, *Asquith* (New York, 1976), p. 181.
51. See Adams and Poirier, *Conscription Controversy*, p. 75.
52. Hewins, *Apologia of an Imperialist*, Vol. II, p. 29.
53. See Beaverbrook, *Politicians and the War*, p. 87.
54. Adams and Poirier, *Conscription Controversy*, pp. 76–7.
55. Viscount French, *1914* (London, 1919), pp. 358–61.
56. Hewins, *Apologia of an Imperialist*, Vol. II, pp. 30–1.
57. Chamberlain Diary fragment, 14–18 May 1915, ACP 2/2/25.
58. Adams and Poirier, *Conscription Controversy*, p. 75.
59. 15 May 1915, BLP 117/1/19.
60. Capt. B.H. Liddell Hart, *The Real War, 1914–1918* (London, 1964 edn), p. 122.
61. He succeeded Prince Louis of Battenberg, who was driven from the post in October 1914 because of the dangerous combination of his German birth and the popular anti-German hysteria.
62. *Ibid.*, p. 438. Fisher went to a suite in the Charing Cross Hotel, where he was soon located by agents of the infuriated Prime Minister.
63. This irresistible imagery originates with Lord Beaverbrook, as does so much of the conventional wisdom of this story; but see also Jenkins. *Asquith*, p. 355.
64. Beaverbrook, *Politicians and the War*, pp. 105–6. Bonar Law received a letter from Fisher on 17 May, written in such extreme language that it convinced him the Admiral had to retire from the stresses of public life. BLP 37/2/34.
65. See Bonar Law to Fisher, 20 May 1915, FP 1/19/1026 and 1027; 22 May 1915, FP 1/20/1034; and Fisher to Bonar Law, 22 May 1915, BLP 50/2/31.
66. Lloyd George, *War Memoirs*, Vol. I, p. 136.
67. *Ibid.* The story is told in Beaverbrook, *Politicians and the War*, pp. 106–7.
68. The list of subscribers is very long and has included the current writer.
69. See Peter Fraser, 'Lord Beaverbrook's Fabrications, in *Politicians and the War, 1914–1916*', in *The Historical Journal*, XXV (1982). Col. Hankey's 1920 diary seems approximately to confirm Beaverbrook's version of events, though the Cabinet Secretary wrote in 1960: 'The statement that Bonar Law and Lloyd George "there and then" went to Asquith also lacks confirmation'. *The Supreme Command*, Vol. I (London, 1961), p. 319.
70. Memorandum by Chamberlain, 14–18 May 1915, ACP 2/2/25.
71. *Ibid.*
72. The Treaty of London, under which Italy agreed to join the War on the side of the

Allies, had been signed only three weeks earlier. Italy had not yet declared her belligerency. For this bright spot in what was otherwise a bleak time for Asquith, see Cassar, *Asquith as War Leader*, p. 89. However, the brightness was perhaps less than it might have been, for the Italian Government fell on 13 May, giving Asquith an additional subject for concern.

73. LGP, C/5/8/5. Copies of the letter may be found in the papers of most of the central figures in this episode.

74. Bonar Law sent to Lloyd George, presumably by messenger, a copy of his letter to Asquith. Attached to this was a brief note: 'I enclose a copy of the letter. You will see we have altered it to the extent that we do not definitely offer Coalition[,] but the substance is the same.' LGP, C/5/8/5. It is quite likely, as Peter Fraser points out, that when he wrote his memoirs years later, Lloyd George relied heavily on Beaverbrook for details he did not himself recall. By the time the *War Memoirs* appeared, both Bonar Law and Asquith were dead. Fraser, 'Lord Beaverbrook's Fabrications', p. 156.

75. His denial of any interest in coalition came in response to a query by a Liberal MP, F.H. Booth, on 12 May.

76. For this episode see, for example, Jenkins, *Asquith*, pp. 363–6, M. Gilbert, *Churchill: Challenge of War*, pp. 446–7, and Hazlehurst, *Politicians at War*, pp. 262–3, who emphasize its importance in Asquith's decision-making at this time; and Koss, *Asquith*, pp. 186–7, Michael and Eleanor Brock, the editors of Asquith, *Letters to Venetia Stanley*, pp. 598–9, and Cassar, *Asquith as War Leader*, pp. 99–100, do not.

77. Bonar Law had indicated as much to John Redmond in mid March: Gwynn, *John Redmond*, pp. 467–8, cited in Hazlehurst, *Politicians at War*, p. 265, n. 1.

78. 17 June 1915: Robert Rhodes James, *Memoirs of a Conservative: J.C.C. Davidson's Memoirs and Papers, 1910–1937* (London, 1969), p. 25.

79. Bonar Law said in his letter to Buxton that the idea was Asquith's: Rhodes James, *Memoirs of a Conservative*, p. 25; Lloyd George told Frances Stevenson that 'the Tories demanded a national government': A.J.P. Taylor, ed., *Lloyd George: A Diary, by Frances Stevenson* (London, 1971, hereafter cited as *Stevenson Diary*), entry of 18 May 1915, p. 51. In his *Memories and Reflections*, p. 116, Asquith wrote that the decision for coalition came to him 'quite independently in the exercise of my own judgment.'

80. ACP 2/2/25.

81. These letters are printed in Asquith's *Memories and Reflections*, Vol. II, p. 118.

82. ACP 2/2/25. Lord Stamfordham also presumed that Bonar Law would become Chancellor and Lloyd George War Secretary: Stamfordham to the King, 20 May 1915, cipher telegram, RA GV K770/6.

83. On 21 May Balfour wrote to Bonar Law that Kitchener presumed that he would be removed and that he preferred to be succeeded by Bonar Law: AJBP, Add. MSS. 49693/208. Stamfordham indicated that Kitchener soon changed his mind: Stamfordham's memorandum, 25 May 1915, RA GV K770/12.

84. An unattributed Cabinet list is preserved among the papers of Malcolm Fraser, showing Bonar Law as Home Secretary, Carson as Lord Chancellor and Balfour as Lord President: MFP, MS. Eng. c.4790/146–7.

85. Memorandum by Lord Stamfordham, 25 May 1915, RA GV K770/12.

86. This was Lloyd George's henchman, Dr Christopher Addison: Cassar, *Asquith as War Leader*, p. 105.

87. *Politicians and the War*, p. 134.

88. Jenkins, *Asquith*, p. 367.

89. Memorandum of 26 May 1915, HHAP 27/216–17. Lord Blake pointed out that

portions of the memorandum were printed by Asquith's official biographers, but they excised this key phrase. The full text, though with a slight mis-transcription, was published in *Unknown Prime Minister*, p. 251. Lord Jenkins published it in full in *Asquith*, pp. 368–9.

90. A letter from Lord Crewe, Asquith's favourite confidant in the Cabinet, to Lloyd George of 24 May 1915 indicates: '... our plan would place only one Unionist Minister in the inner circle [Balfour at the Admiralty] and him not one of their inner circle as it now exists': LGP, C/4/1/22.

91. For this episode see Grigg, *Lloyd George: From Peace to War*, pp. 254–5; and B. Gilbert, *Lloyd George: Organizer of Victory*, pp. 202–5.

92. Rhodes James, ed., *Memoirs of a Conservative*, p. 25.

93. See Hazlehurst, *Politicians at War*, p. 265.

94. For the difficulty caused by this and similar cases, see John McDermott, 'Trading With the Enemy: British Business and the Law During the First World War', in *The Canadian Journal of History*, Vol. XXXII, No. 2.

95. George H. Robb (chief counsel to William Jacks and Co.) to Bonar Law, 19 May 1915, BLP 37/2/40.

96. N.d. [June 1915], BLP 64/D/3.

97. 15 February 1915, Asquith, *Letters to Venetia Stanley*, p. 432.

98. As suggested by Lord Jenkins, *Asquith*, pp. 369–70.

CHAPTER 10: COLONIAL SECRETARY

1. Aitken held the honorary rank of Lieutenant-Colonel. In May 1915 Bonar Law had attempted to secure for him the baronetcy he desired, but the Canadian Government refused to support the nomination. He succeeded only in July 1916, without much enthusiasm on the part of either the Canadians or the King: see A.J.P. Taylor, *Beaverbrook*, pp. 87, 108; and Chisholm and Davies, *Beaverbrook*, p. 137. For Davidson's view of the relationship between Bonar Law and Aitken, see Rhodes James, *Memoirs of a Conservative*, pp. 26–7.

2. Baird (created Baron Stonehaven 1925, Viscount Stonehaven 1938) regularly apprised Bonar Law of events at the Front. See, for example, Baird to Bonar Law, 3 January 1915 and 18 January 1915, BLP 36/1/3 and 28.

3. Information from Mrs Betty Boyd-Maunsell.

4. Rhodes James, *Memoirs of a Conservative*, p. 30.

5. During this period Bonar Law's secretary, Miss Sarah Tugander, wrote out her recollections of Bonar Law's confidential remarks to her. He indicated to her on 8 June 1915 that his military knowledge was insufficient to justify an 'independent line': Notes, 8 June 1915, MP.

6. 8 June 1915, JCCD, DAV 19.

7. Selborne replied that he was not so pessimistic as Bonar Law: 8 June 1915, JCCDP, DAV 19. Bonar Law indicated to Maj.-Gen. Henry Wilson – an unrelenting critic of the Dardanelles Campaign – on 15 July 1915: 'I am afraid we cannot abandon it': BLP 53/6/33. See also Blake, *Unknown Prime Minister*, p. 265.

8. Notes, 19 August 1915, MP.

9. Adams and Poirier, *Conscription Controversy*, p. 103.

10. M. Gilbert, *Churchill: Challenge of War*, p. 522.

11. Notes, 2 September 1915, MP.

12. Beaverbrook, *Politicians and the War*, p. 142.

13. For this episode, see Adams and Poirier, *Conscription Controversy*, pp. 104–12.

14. These letters are printed in Blake, *Unknown Prime Minister*, p. 263. Asquith wrote a second letter on the same day asking Bonar Law to serve, but the Colonial Secretary remained adamant: 12 August 1915, BLP 51/12/12.

15. Beaverbrook's Notes of Conversations with Bonar Law, 12 August [1915], BBKP, G/5/VII.
16. 15 September 1915, BLP 117/1/20.
17. 15 September 1915, LGP, D/17/8/7.
18. See A.J.P. Taylor, ed., *Stevenson Diary*, entry of 17 September 1915, pp. 60–1: and Grigg, *Lloyd George: From Peace to War*, p. 318.
19. Notes of Conversations, 15 September 1915, BBKP, G/5/VIII. See also his remark to Miss Tugander: Notes, 27 August 1915, MP.
20. See his brief paper submitted to the Cabinet, 12 October 1915, CAB 37/135/23.
21. See Long to Bonar Law, 12 October 1915, BLP 51/4/7; and Trevor Wilson, ed., *The Political Diaries of C.P. Scott* (London, 1970), entry of 14–15 October 1915, p. 143. Bonar Law's Under-Secretary, Steel-Maitland, indicated in a letter to Lord Milner of 15 October 1915 that he also contemplated resignation at this time: Gollin, *Proconsul in Politics*, p. 307.
22. BLP 51/4/16.
23. See Asquith's paper, 'Conduct of the War', 28 October 1915, CAB 37/136/36.
24. M. Gilbert, *Churchill: Challenge of War*, pp. 558–9. Remarkably, McKenna was an exception.
25. 1 November 1915, LGP, D/17/8/9.
26. Wilson, ed., *Scott Diaries*, entry of 1–2 November 1915, p. 153.
27. 2 November 1915, HHAP 15/91.
28. Asquith wrote to Lloyd George on 3 November: 'I suppose even B.L. would hardly object to such a plan': LGP, D/18/2/12.
29. Aitken's 'Notes', 2–3 November 1915, BBKP, G/5/7.
30. 5 November 1915, HHAP 15/125.
31. CAB 37/137/6. See Asquith's reply to Bonar Law, 5 November, 1915, HHAP 15/95.
32. 8 November 1915, BLP 53/6/47; and, on the same day, Bonar Law to Lloyd George, BLP 53/6/46.
33. Also 8 November 1915, and found in the same file as his resignation letter, BLP 53/6/47. Lord Jenkins, *Asquith*, p. 381, describes this as a letter of 'withdrawal rather than of victory'. Perhaps it is neither, and means precisely what it says.
34. Beaverbrook says that he had made sure of such a pledge before he wrote either letter: *Politicians and the War*, p. 162. Lord Jenkins points out the absence of evidence to support this claim, *Asquith*, p. 381; and this is reiterated in Cassar, *Asquith as War Leader*, p. 259, n. 38. It is unlikely that there would be evidence of such an agreement.
35. Beaverbrook, *Politicians and the War*, p. 163.
36. Notes of conversation between Aitken and Bonar Law, 12 November 1915, BBKP, G/5/VIII. See also Cassar, *Asquith as War Leader*, p. 134.
37. In fact Grey attended regularly and Chamberlain (India Secretary and chairman of the new Manpower Board) and Curzon (chairman of the Shipping Control Board) soon did the same, as did the First Sea Lord and CIGS: Grigg, *Lloyd George: From Peace to War*, p. 320, fn. 1.
38. Bonar Law advised Asquith against an over-hasty rejection of the idea! Carson agreed with him: 12 November 1915, BBKP, G/57/29; a second copy may be found in folder C/202. This is printed in M. Gilbert, *Churchill: Challenge of War*, p. 565.
39. Bonar Law to Long, 6 August 1915, WLPT 947/498.
40. Adams and Poirier, *Conscription Controversy*, pp. 67–9. For a defence of Kitchener's position on conscription, see George H. Cassar, *Kitchener: Architect of Victory* (London, 1977), ch. 21.

41. KP, PRO 30/57/73/16.
42. No admirer of either Asquith or Lloyd George, Haig considered Bonar Law 'a straight and honourable man, indeed, so honest that he is too much so for the crowd he is with': Gerard J. De Groot, *Douglas Haig, 1861–1928* (London, 1988), pp. 227–8.
43. 18 December 1914, BLP 37/4/39.
44. See Long's angry letter and memorandum to Bonar Law of 27 January 1915, BLP 36/2/47, indicating that he sought the immediate imposition of mandatory military service.
45. In the four weeks from mid May, only nine editorials and four published letters touched on the issue in the major metropolitan dailies. In the month following the formation of the coalition, 79 editorials and 105 letters addressed conscription: Adams and Poirier, *Conscription Controversy*, p. 85.
46. BLP 117/1/19.
47. David, ed., *Hobhouse Diaries*, entry of 17 June 1915, pp. 247–8. Charles Hobhouse mistakenly believed that Lloyd George had thrown in his lot with the Unionists over conscription. It is unlikely that Hobhouse knew that Grey, of all people, had drafted (but did not distribute) a memorandum calling for the discussion of mandatory service: FO 800/100.
48. BLP 37/2/39. Maj.-Gen. Henry Wilson noted with satisfaction in his diary on 18 May 1915: '... with the new Government ought to come conscription': HWP.
49. 20 May 1915, BLP 117/1/12.
50. Without advice from the Imperial General Staff, Kitchener arrived at the figure, based on population, as an approximation of the French effort.
51. CAB 137/134/9, 3 and 5 respectively.
52. See R.J.Q. Adams, 'Asquith's Choice: The May Coalition and the Coming of Conscription, 1915–1916', in *Journal of British Studies*, 25 (1986).
53. 8 October 1915, CAB 37/135/15.
54. For the unrealistic nature of Kitchener's expectations, see Keith Grieves, *The Politics of Manpower* (Manchester, 1988), p. 22.
55. BLP 51/4/7.
56. Wilson, ed., *Scott Diaries*, entry of 14–15 October 1915, p. 143.
57. Talbot to Bonar Law, 16 October 1915, BLP 51/4/16. This was endorsed by Long, the arch-conscriptionist, 17 October 1916, BLP 51/4/18.
58. This memorandum indicated that these were also the views of Lansdowne, Curzon, Selborne, Chamberlain, Long, Carson, Lloyd George and Churchill: KP, PRO 30/57/73/36.
59. 25 October 1915, CAB 37/136/30. A draft of this paper in Bonar Law's hand is in BLP 63/A/5.
60. HHAP, 28/179–80. See Adams, 'Asquith's Choice'.
61. Adams and Poirier, *Conscription Controversy*, p. 130. On 11 November Derby announced unequivocally that if bachelors failed to attest in adequate numbers, it meant conscription for them.
62. They demanded the additional numbers by 31 March 1916: CAB 22/80.
63. Asquith to Chamberlain, ACP 19/1/7. Curzon had already drafted a bill weeks earlier: 15 September 1915, LGP, D/16/10/5. Curzon's version essentially became the first National Service Bill.
64. 17 December 1915, SLSP 9/8/15.
65. On 10 January Bonar Law told C.P. Scott that he favoured military conscription for married men but that, in the interests of national unity, industrial conscription was impossible: Wilson, ed., *Scott Diaries*, entry of 10–11 January 1916, p. 170.
66. 16 and 23 December 1915, in CAB 42/6/14.

67. 4 February 1916, CAB 37/142/11.
68. See Bridgeman's letters to his wife of 14, 15 and 19 December 1915, Williamson, ed., *Bridgeman Diaries*, pp. 93.
69. M. Gilbert, *Churchill: Challenge of War*, p. 689.
70. A number of Unionist back-benchers, including Amery, Younger, Banbury and McNeil, had written to Bonar Law on 2 December 1915, stating their opposition to a continuance of the sitting Parliament beyond another year, if necessary. Their enthusiasm for an election, which Bonar Law wished to avoid, caused their leader great anxiety: BLP 52/1/6.
71. See Stubbs, 'Impact of the Great War', p. 27. A much smaller Liberal War Committee was formed at the same time. See John Turner, *British Politics and the Great War: Coalition and Conflict, 1915–1918* (New Haven, 1992), p. 77.
72. See Amery, *My Political Life*, Vol. II, pp. 79–80; Hyde, *Carson*, p. 397; and Gollin, *Proconsul in Politics*, Ch. XIII. They were often joined by Philip Kerr, Dr Leander Starr Jameson (of the famous 'Raid' of pre-Boer War days) and, occasionally, even Lloyd George.
73. 1 April 1916, BLP 53/6/69.
74. 31 March 1916, BLP 53/6/68. In June 1915 Wilson was appointed KCB and promoted to the rank of Lieutenant-General.
75. Bonar Law to Carson, 4 April 1916, BLP 53/6/70.
76. CAB 37/145/35.
77. CAB 17/159.
78. Memorandum, 16 April 1916, RA GV K951/2.
79. 17 April 1916, BLP 53/1/14.
80. 17 April 1916, HHAP 16/147–53.
81. CAB 27/3.
82. *Daily Mail*, 19 April 1917.
83. See Stamfordham's memorandum, 19 April 1916, RA GV K951/7.
84. Hankey, *Supreme Command*, Vol. II, 475.
85. For Hankey's notes for Asquith's speech, see HHAP 491/185234.
86. Wilson to Maxse, 19 April 1916, LMP, 472.
87. Roskill, *Hankey*, Vol. I, p. 265.
88. See Adams and Poirier, *Conscription Controversy*, p. 167.
89. For this affair see Gollin, *Proconsul in Politics*, p. 344.
90. Dutton, *Austen Chamberlain*, p. 127.
91. Balfour theorized as much to Lord Salisbury, 17 June 1916: AJBP, Add. MSS. 49758.
92. Beaverbrook, *Politicians and the War*, ch. XV. Lloyd George outlined the conclusions of the meeting to Riddell: entry of 11 June 1916, GRD, Add. MSS. 62977.
93. Blake, *Unknown Prime Minister*, pp. 289–300. Lord Blake was severely criticized by Asquith's daughter, Lady Violet Bonham Carter, for publishing what she considered a scurrilous story: letter to *The Times*, 9 January 1956. There was of course, and remains, no evidence conclusively to prove or refute the event. Lord Beaverbrook set his research assistants on the case at the time of the Blake–Bonham Carter controversy, and they also could not settle the matter: BBKP, G/5/X.
94. 'Telephone Note' from Lord Beaverbrook, n.d., BBKP, G/5/X.
95. *Ibid.*
96. Bonar Law always thought Asquith's wartime social life a bit too full. See Miss Tugander's undated recollection of August 1915, MP.
97. For Lloyd George's considerations at the time, see B. Gilbert, *Lloyd George, Organizer of Victory*, pp. 338–42.
98. Turner, *British Politics and the Great War*, p. 91.

99. Asquith also tried to sack the Viceroy, Lord Wimborne, but gave in to his remonstrance: Jenkins, *Asquith*, p. 396.
100. See his Cabinet papers of 19 and 21 May 1916, CAB 37/148/13 and 21.
101. Kendle, *Long, Ireland and the Union*, pp. 96–7.
102. B. Gilbert, *Lloyd George: Organizer of Victory*, p. 323; Hyde, *Carson*, p. 403.
103. See Kendle, *Long, Ireland and the Union*, p. 115; and B. Gilbert, *Lloyd George: Organizer of Victory*, pp. 322–3.
104. See John D. Fair, *British Interparty Conferences: A Study of the Procedure of Conciliation in British Politics, 1867–1921* (Oxford, 1980), p. 134.
105. Williamson, *Bridgeman Diaries*, entries of 21 and 22 June 1916, p. 102. The Die-Hard Sir Frederick Banbury chaired the meeting.
106. Bonar Law to Lord St Audries (Sir Alexander Acland-Hood), 27 June 1916. This is printed in Beaverbrook, *Politicians and the War*, pp. 267–8.
107. CAB 37/150/23. Asquith to King George V, 27 June 1916, HHAP 8/171–8.
108. Williamson, ed., *Bridgeman Diairies*, entry of 27 June 1916, pp. 104–5.
109. 'Notes', Meeting of the Unionist Party, 7 July 1916: BLP 63/C/64.
110. Williamson, ed., *Bridgeman Diaries*, entry of 7 July 1916, pp. 107–8. Bridgeman much disliked the settlement.
111. See Dangerfield, *Damnable Question*, pp. 238–9.
112. 17 July 1916, CAB 37/151/37. See Kendle, *Long, Ireland and the Union*, p. 128.
113. Bonar Law to Asquith, 28 May 1916, BLP 53/6/12. Ivor Guest, 1st Viscount Wimborne, like his cousin Winston Churchill, was a former Unionist.
114. 17 July 1916: Petrie, *Long*, pp. 204–5.
115. See his undated 'pen portraits' of his colleagues, written after his resignation in July: SP 80/287.
116. Williamson, ed., *Bridgeman Diaries*, entry of 10 July 1916, p. 108. Bridgeman was far angrier with Bonar Law than this indicates. He wrote to Leo Maxse on 14 July: 'It's this d——d cleverness ... the more you get so-called businessmen & pushers into politics the more you will have of it': *ibid.*
117. Beaverbrook, *Politicians and the War*, p. 272.

CHAPTER 11: THE DECEMBER CRISIS

1. Trevor Wilson, *The Myriad Faces of War: Britain and the Great War, 1914–1918* (Cambridge, 1986), pp. 309–12. French losses at Verdun exceeded 500,000 men, and the attacking Germans' over 400,000.
2. The French lost 190,000 men on the Somme, the Germans 465,000.
3. See Jenkins, *Asquith*, pp. 414–15.
4. Wilson, *Myriad Faces of War*, p. 396.
5. Grigg, *From Peace to War*, pp. 435–8; Cassar, *Asquith as War Leader*, pp. 200–1; Roskill, *Hankey*, Vol. I, p. 279.
6. Scott to L.T. Hobhouse, 23 April 1915: Wilson, ed., *Scott Diaries*, p. 121.
7. For these connections see Koss, *Rise and Fall of the Political Press*, Vol. II, pp. 298–9. See also B. Gilbert, *Lloyd George: Organizer of Victory*, pp. 386–7.
8. J.M. McEwen, 'The Press and the Fall of Asquith', in *Historical Journal*, Vol. XXI (1978).
9. At issue was the lucrative palm-oil trade, control of which was much desired by a group of Liverpool interests who had recently gained a monopoly in the West African trade. Bonar Law supported his Colonial Office experts who wished to break the power of the Liverpool ring: John Stubbs, 'The Impact of the Great War on the Conservative Party', in Gillian Peele and Chris Cook, eds, *The Politics of Reappraisal* (London, 1975), pp. 28–30; see also Peter J. Yearwood, 'Expatriate Firms and the Colonial Economy in Nigeria in the First World War', in *Journal of Imperial*

and Commonwealth History, Vol. 21, No. 1 (1998). I am grateful for the insights of Dr Yearwood regarding the background of the Nigeria affair.

10. 27 May 1915, *The Times*.
11. Lord Beaverbrook confused these two occasions in *Politicians and the War*, p. 288. See J.O. Stubbs, 'Beaverbrook as Historian: "Politicians and the War, 1914–1916" Reconsidered', in *Albion*, Vol. 14, nos 3–4 (1982); and Peter Fraser, 'Lord Beaverbrook's Fabrications in *Politicians and the War*', in *The Historical Journal*, Vol. XXV, No. 1 (1982).
12. The Government majority was 231 to 117, with 73 Unionists in support and 65 voting with Carson. Eleven Liberals including Winston Churchill also voted against the Government.
13. See H.A. Taylor, *Robert Donald* (London, n.d.), pp. 128–33, where there is printed most of the text of Bonar Law's remarkably candid interview with Donald of 29 December 1916.
14. See Bonar Law's memorandum regarding the fall of the coalition, prepared at the suggestion of Aitken, 30 December 1916. The existence of the document remained secret for many years after Bonar Law's death. Aitken used it for his ends in his *Politicians and the War* but did not acknowledge it. Lord Blake saw it and cited it.
15. BLP 85/A/1.
16. *Ibid.*
17. This in an interview with the American journalist, Roy Howard, on 29 September 1916: see B. Gilbert, *Lloyd George: Organizer of Victory*, p. 369.
18. CAB 37/159/32.
19. Beaverbrook, *Politicians and the War*, pp. 372–5.
20. See B. Gilbert, *Lloyd George: Organizer of Victory*, pp. 376–8.
21. Beaverbrook, *Politicians and the War*, p. 308.
22. Aitken's version of events paid little attention to the roots of co-operation between the three which did not involve himself: Beaverbrook, *Politicians and the War*, Ch. XXIV.
23. A.J.P. Taylor, ed., *Stevenson Dairy*, entry of 13 November 1916, p. 122.
24. Beaverbrook, *Politicians and the War*, p. 312.
25. Hyde, *Carson*, p. 406. In this exchange Carson defended the character of Lloyd George but attacked Asquith.
26. After the Nigeria debate, Bonar Law muttered to Hankey that Lloyd George was 'at the same time the right hand to the P.M. and the leader of the opposition': John F. Naylor, *A Man and an Institution: Sir Maurice Hankey and the Custody of Cabinet Secrecy* (Cambridge, 1984), p. 13.
27. A.J.P. Taylor, ed., *Stevenson Diary*, entry of 18 November 1916, p. 124. The only other guests were Sir Henry Wilson and his wife. See Bonar Law to Lloyd George, 17 November 1916, suggesting a private meeting, LGP, E/2/17/2.
28. H.A. Taylor, *Donald*, p. 129, emphasis added. Aitken wrote that he had pressed Sir Reginald Brade, the Permanent Secretary at the War Office, to convince Bonar Law of the desirability of a small war council: *Politicians and the War*, p. 326. Fraser, 'Lord Beaverbrook's Fabrications in *Politicians and the War*', has shown that this quite probably never happened. Bonar Law did not need Brade's coaxing.
29. H.A. Taylor, *Donald*, pp. 129–30, emphasis added; BLP 85/A/1.
30. BLP 85/A/1.
31. Beaverbrook, *Politicians and the War*, p. 340.
32. See A.J.P. Taylor, *Beaverbrook*, p. 111, and Grigg, *Lloyd George: Peace to War*, p. 447.
33. See Gilbert, *Lloyd George: Organizer of Victory*, p. 389; and H.A. Taylor, *Donald*, p. 110.
34. 25 November 1916, BLP 63/A/3.
35. Bonar Law wrote on 30 December: 'Before Carson and Lloyd George came I had

written out the following statement ...': BLP 85/A/1. See also Fraser, 'Beaverbrook's Fabrications in *Politicians and the War*', p. 157.

36. BLP 85/A/1.

37. In his 30 December memorandum, Bonar Law writes that 'he sent me' the letter. John Grigg points out correctly that it was shown him personally by Asquith before it was actually sent: *Lloyd George: Peace to War*, p. 448. Bonar Law almost certainly sanitized his account to spare the explanation that Asquith's first draft included hurtful remarks about Carson and Lloyd George. Asquith was willing, at Bonar Law's prompting, to amend only his criticism of Carson. See Asquith to Bonar Law, 26 November 1916, BLP 53/4/24.

38. *Asquith*, p. 425.

39. John Turner, *British Politics and the Great War*, p. 131.

40. BLP 85/A/1.

41. A.J.P. Taylor, ed., *Stevenson Diary*, 27 Nov 1916, p. 129.

42. This is printed in Asquith's *Memories and Reflections*, vol. II, pp. 175–8.

43. The first use of this now-standard term to describe the three ministers may have have been in the diary of Lord Crawford, the recently appointed Agriculture Minister. Perhaps it was common currency among Westminster insiders: Vincent, ed., *Crawford Papers*, memorandum, 2 December 1916, p. 369.

44. Chamberlain, *Down the Years*, p. 115; Vincent, ed., *Crawford Papers*, memorandum of 2 December 1916, p. 369.

45. Long to Bonar Law, 2 December 1916, BLP 53/4/28. See Beaverbrook, *Politicians and the War*, p. 368, where this letter is printed but erroneously dated '2.10.16'.

46. BLP 85/A/1.

47. *Ibid.*

48. Asquith to Lloyd George, 1 December 1916 (copy), BLP 53/4/27. *Politicians and the War*, pp. 186–7.

49. 2 December 1916, BLP 117/1/30.

50. Hyde, *Carson*, p. 410.

51. According to Crawford, attending were Bonar Law, himself, Curzon, Chamberlain, Long, Smith and H.E. Duke. Lansdowne was absent, and Balfour remained on his sickbed: *Crawford Papers*, memorandum, 3 December 1916, pp. 369–70. Lord Blake, *Unknown Prime Minister*, p. 314, adds the names of Derby and Cecil. Randolph Churchill names only Curzon, Cecil, Chamberlain and Long: *Derby*, p. 229. In his memoir, Austen Chamberlain does not indicate who attended: *Down the Years*, p. 114.

52. *Reynolds's News*, 3 December 1916. This weekly was owned by Sir Henry Dalziel, a Liberal MP and staunch Lloyd George man.

53. Bonar Law indicated as much to Hankey on Saturday: Roskill, *Hankey*, Vol. I, pp. 332–3.

54. Vincent, ed., *Crawford Papers*, memorandum of 3 December 1916, p. 370.

55. BLP 85/A/1.

56. Chamberlain to Lord Chelmsford, 8 December 1916, ACP 15/3/8.

57. BLP 85/A/1.

58. N.d. [3 December 1916], BLP 64/H.

59. *Politicians and the War*, pp. 410–18. See, for example, Fraser, 'Lord Beaverbrook's Fabrications in *Politicians and the War*'; Fair, *British Interparty Conferences*, p. 145; and A.J.P. Taylor, *Beaverbrook*, pp. 116–17.

60. ACP 15/3/8. Chamberlain to Lord Robert Cecil, 30 May 1932, ACP 39/5/39. Crawford's account also does not support Aitken's version: Vincent, ed., memorandum of 3 December 1916, *Crawford Papers*, pp. 370–2.

61. *Asquith*, p. 435.

62. Aitken wrote that Bonar Law later summoned F.E. Smith back to Edwardes Square to offer an opinion – apparently he also dismissed Aitken's protests: see Beaverbrook, *Politicians and the War*, pp. 318–9. This is not mentioned in either Lord Birkenhead, *'F.E.': F.E. Smith, First Earl of Birkenhead* (London, 1959); or John Campbell, *F.E. Smith: First Earl of Birkenhead* (London, 1983).

63. BLP 85/A/1.

64. Spender and Asquith, *Asquith*, Vol. II, pp. 258–9; Blake, *Unknown Prime Minister*, pp. 318–19.

65. *Asquith*, p. 440.

66. *Unknown Prime Minister*, pp. 317–20.

67. *Politicians and the War*, pp. 425–8.

68. BLP 85/A/1; emphasis added in quotation from this document which follows.

69. Memorandum of 3 December 1916, Vincent, ed., *The Crawford Papers*, p. 371. Bonar Law offered the same explanation to Robert Donald in his interview of 29 December 1916: H.A. Taylor, *Donald*, p. 131.

70. Asquith demonstrated no confusion at the Unionists' meaning and sought no clarification from any of them. Two days later, Robert Cecil gave him a copy of the resolution, at which the Prime Minister expressed no surprise – and it changed nothing.

71. The Liberal journalist A.G. Gardiner outdid these others when he wrote in 1932 that Bonar Law had placed 'one of the darkest blots on the page of history': H.A. Taylor, *Donald*, pp. 143–5.

72. Chamberlain to Lord Chelmsford, 8 December 1916, ACP 15/3/8. This is printed with commentary in Chamberlain, *Down the Years*, pp. 115–28.

73. Chamberlain, *Down the Years*, p. 120.

74. There is no doubt that Asquith was told the contents of the Unionist resolution: see the memorandum titled 'The Break-Up of the First Coalition', by Lord Crewe, printed in Asquith's *Memories and Reflections*, Vol. II, pp. 155–7. See also Cassar, *Asquith as War Leader*, p. 218.

75. Balfour was still indisposed, and Curzon and Long had left for the country. Crawford reported as present himself, Cecil, Smith, Chamberlain and Duke: Vincent, ed., *Crawford Papers*, diary entry of 3 December 1916, p. 371. It was to this group Bonar Law explained that he had not handed Asquith the Unionist resolution. This conclave was not mentioned in print by either Aitken or Chamberlain.

76. Bonar Law to Asquith, 3 December 1916, HHAP 31/16–17.

77. BLP 85/A/1.

78. The information which inspired Robinson came primarily from Carson, though Northcliffe had spoken to Lloyd George on 3 December and almost certainly had a hand in the article. I am grateful to Dr J. Lee Thompson for allowing me to read his discussion of this episode in his forthcoming book, *Politicians, the Press and Propaganda: Lord Northcliffe and the Great War, 1914–1919* (Kent, Ohio, 1999). See also the discussion in Grigg, *Lloyd George: From Peace to War*, pp. 458–9. Lord Blake correctly reminds us that the facts were not beyond the gathering skills of other correspondents: *Unknown Prime Minister*, p. 328. The *Manchester Guardian* and the *Morning Post* also published articles on that morning critical of Asquith and containing inside information.

79. These were McKenna, Harcourt, Runciman and Grey: *Politicians and the War*, p. 439.

80. *Ibid.*, pp. 441–2. Lord Crewe, in his contribution to Asquith's *Memories and Reflections*, p. 158, also says that the Unionist trio met the Prime Minister in the morning.

81. Undated [5 December 1916] memorandum by Viscount Samuel, HSP, A/56/1.

They were staunchly in favour of resignation and against compromise with Lloyd George and the Unionists.

82. Vincent, ed., *Crawford Papers*, entry of 4 December 1916, p. 373. Cecil's letter to Chamberlain of 30 May 1932 indicates that those two 'Cs' denied that the meeting with Asquith took place: ACP 39/5/39.
83. Vincent, ed., *Crawford Papers*, Memorandum of 4 December 1916, p. 372.
84. BLP 85/A/1.
85. *Ibid.* Portions of this passage are printed in Blake, *Unknown Prime Minister*, p. 331, where there are minor inaccuracies in the transcription.
86. Vincent, ed., *Crawford Papers*, Memorandum of 4 December 1916, p. 373.
87. Beaverbrook, *Politicians and the War*, pp. 461–3.
88. BLP 85/A/1. Bonar Law scribbled in the margin of Aitken's own record of the crisis that after he read Asquith's letter: 'I definitely decided to back L.G. and I at once told him so': A.J.P. Taylor, *Beaverbrook*, p. 119.
89. *Politicians and the War*, Ch. 37.
90. Dutton, *Austen Chamberlain*, p. 133.
91. Chamberlain wrote to Florence Amery on 9 December 1916: 'Bonar Law is not seeking my advice and has not sought it at all in recent times': Barnes and Nicholson, eds., *Amery Diaries*, Vol. I, p. 132.
92. Beaverbrook's description of Bonar Law's furious reaction is as well known as it is well told: *Politicians and the War*, pp. 479–80. Chamberlain's memoir discreetly acknowledges the outburst of temper – and unconvincingly denies there was reason for it: *Down the Years*, p. 123.
93. Beaverbrook, *Politicians and the War*, *ibid.* See Chamberlain to Long, 11 December 1923, noting soon after Bonar Law's death his conclusion that the leader suspected him – Chamberlain – of seeking the party leadership: ACP 15/3/21.
94. Chamberlain to Lord Chelmsford, 8 December 1916, ACP 15/3/8.
95. It was at this meeting Cecil provided Asquith with a copy of the 3 December resolution: Stanfordham, n.d., 'Memorandum on the Circumstances relating to the Fall of Mr Asquith's Administration', RA GV K1048A/2.
96. Once again, all the Unionist ministers except Balfour were present.
97. Balfour sent Bonar Law copies of two letters to Asquith refusing to withdraw his resignation; both of 5 December 1916, BLP 53/4/32 and 53/4/33.
98. Memorandum of 5 December 1916, Vincent, ed., *Crawford Papers*, pp. 373–6.
99. Bonar Law to Asquith, 5 December 1916, HHAP 31/43.
100. HSP, A/56/1.
101 Vincent, *Crawford Papers*, diary entry of 5 December 1916, p. 376.
102. Bonar Law may have seen Lloyd George after the meeting of Unionist ministers, perhaps with Aitken, who reported that they agreed that Bonar Law would try to form a Cabinet including both Asquith and Lloyd George: *Politicians and the War*, pp. 483–6; Blake, *Unknown Prime Minister*, pp. 334–5. Yet a note from Bonar Law to Lloyd George, undated but written at this time, indicates: 'The King has agreed to [Asquith's] resignation. I suppose you ought not to see me. I have nothing special to say.' LGP, E/2/17/6. In his memorandum of the crisis, Bonar Law makes no mention of seeing Lloyd George. BLP 85/A/1.
103. Memorandum by Lord Stamfordham, 5 December 1916, RA K1048A/1. See also Nicolson, *King George the Fifth*, pp. 288–9, and Rose, *King George V*, p. 198.
104. BLP 85/A/1.
105. 'Report of the Conference held Wednesday 6 December 1916', RA GV K1048A/1. Apparently the King saw Balfour privately before the conference began: entry of 6 December 1916, RA, King George V's Diary.
106. Asquith to Bonar Law, 6 December 1916, BLP 81/1/1.

107. Vincent, ed., *Crawford Papers*, diary entry of 7 December 1916, p. 376.
108. Jones, *Diary With Letters*, entry of 17 November 1934, p. 139.
109. BLP 85/A/1.
110. Bonar Law made no mention of offering the Foreign Office to Balfour earlier in the day: BLP 85/A/1. Years afterward Balfour told Aitken the story, which appears in a footnote in *Politicians and the War*, p. 502. Bonar Law told the 'pistol' anecdote to Robert Donald on 7 December, and Chamberlain repeated it to Lord Chelmsford and later published it in his memoirs: H.A. Taylor, *Donald*, p. 145; Chamberlain, *Down the Years*, p. 126. Mrs Dugdale thought the two Foreign Office stories cancelled out the Bonar Law anecdote with the delicious 'pistol to my head' remark. See Grigg, *Lloyd George: From Peace to War*, p. 477, n. 1.
111. Once again, Aitken's version for years held sway: see *Politicians and the War*, Ch. XL.
112. Vincent, ed., *Crawford Papers*, diary entry of 5 December 1916, p. 375.
113. Long to Lady Londonderry, 6 December 1916, quoted in Richard Murphy, 'Walter Long, the Unionist Ministers, and the Formation of Lloyd George's Government in December 1916', in *The Historical Journal*, Vol. XXIX, No. 3 (1986).
114. *Politicians and the War*, p. 515. See also Blake, *Unknown Prime Minister*, p. 340.
115. Bull's diary entry of 8 December 1916. WBP, 4/14.
116. Long to Chamberlain, 7 December 1916, ACP 15/3/20. Murphy, 'Walter Long and the Formation of Lloyd George's Government'.
117. Lord Curzon, 'Memorandum of Conversation between Lloyd George and Certain Unionist ex-Ministers', December 7th 1916, marked 'Very Secret', BLP 81/1/36.
118. Austen Chamberlain to Neville Chamberlain, 11 December 1916, NCP 1/27/6. See also his letter to Chelmsford of 8 December 1916, ACP 15/3/8.
119. Gollin, *Proconsul in Politics*, pp. 370–5.
120. Rose, *King George V*, p. 199.
121. See Hyde, *Carson*, pp. 413–15; Lloyd George, *War Memoirs*, Vol. I, p. 699. When he and Bonar Law met the senior Unionist ex-ministers on 7 December, Lloyd George resisted their opposition to Carson: ACP 15/3/8. This is not mentioned in Curzon's memorandum. BLP 81/1/36.
122. For the disappointed office-seekers, see Grigg, *Lloyd George: Peace to War*, p. 496.
123. *Politicians and the War*, pp. 504–8.
124. See A.J.P. Taylor, *Beaverbrook*, pp. 121–7. Aitken indicates he was offered the Post Office, *Politicians and the War*, p. 507, and Lord Blake that he turned down the under-secretaryship at the Munitions Office, *Unknown Prime Minister*, p. 346.
125. Chisholm and Davie, *Lord Beaverbrook*, p. 148.

CHAPTER 12: PARTNERSHIP

1. Long to Bonar Law, 18 December 1916, BLP 65/2/6. Sir George Fiddes to Davidson, 11 December 1916, BLP 65/2/4.
2. Thomas Jones recalled: 'Miss W[atson] worships Bonar Law and will talk endlessly about him': Middlemas, ed., *Whitehall Diary*, entry of 30 April 1921, pp. 154–5. Miss Tugander in 1916 married James Melville, a future MP and Solicitor-General in Ramsay MacDonald's second Government.
3. Rhodes James, ed., *Memoirs of a Conservative*, p. 49.
4. See Keynes's touching recollection, 'Mr Bonar Law', written soon after the latter's retirement from public life in May 1923: *Essays in Biography*, ed. by Geoffrey Keynes (New York, 1963 edn), pp. 40–4.
5. Robert Skidelsky, *John Maynard Keynes: Vol. I, Hopes Betrayed, 1883–1920* (London, 1983), pp. 336–8.
6. Keynes wrote to the painter Duncan Grant on 21 March 1918: 'Bonar Law was

much amused at my wanting to buy pictures and eventually let me have my way as a sort of joke': *ibid.*, p. 349.

7. See Keith Middlemas and John Barnes, *Baldwin* (London, 1969), pp. 57–8.

8. R.D. Blumenfeld, Davidson and Beaverbrook are among those who later claimed to have placed Baldwin's name before Bonar Law. See Middlemas and Barnes, *Baldwin*, p. 58; Rhodes James, *Memoirs of a Conservative*, p. 58; and Beaverbrook, *Men and Power, 1917–1918* (London, 1960 edn), pp. x–xi.

9. For Lever's mission see Kathleen Burk, *Britain, America and the Sinews of War* (London, 1985), Ch. 5.

10. Margot Asquith to Bonar Law, 23 December 1916, BLP 12/2/39.

11. Pembroke Lodge was rented to a Col. Lewin in 1919–20, and then the remaining 22 years of the lease were sold to an American, Mrs Margaret Ellen Vine, in September 1920. The house was then pulled down: undated note, BLP 15/16.

12. Kitty Law was an energetic and inquisitive child. Left largely at this time in the care of her governess, the formidable Miss Duggan, she quite naturally felt deprived of her father's companionship during the war and post-war years – a time when the political demands on him were, of course, both enormous and irresistible. In 1926 she married an American investment banker, Kent Galbraith Colwell, and lived much of the remainder of her life in the United States. Information from Mrs Betty Boyd-Maunsell and Mrs Anne Catherine Menninger.

13. For this wonderful tale I am grateful to Mr Bonar Sykes.

14. Malcolm, *Vacant Thrones*, pp. 64–5.

15. Sir Arthur Griffith-Boscawen, *Memories* (London, 1925), p. 222.

16. Hankey's staff was unrelated to Lloyd George's personal secretariat, the so-called 'Garden Suburb': see John Turner, *Lloyd George's Secretariat* (Cambridge, 1980).

17. Roskill, *Hankey*, Vol. I, p. 376.

18. Harold Nicolson, *Diaries and Letters, 1930–1939*, Nigel Nicolson, ed. (London, 1966), entry of 6 July 1936, p. 268.

19. Lloyd George, *War Memoirs*, Vol. I, p. 612.

20. Peter Rowland, *Lloyd George* (London, 1975), pp. 373–4.

21. 27 December 1916, WLP, Add. MSS. 62404/101.

22. Hankey, *Supreme Command*, p. 578.

23. Lloyd George, *War Memoirs*, Vol. I, p. 609.

24. I am grateful to Dr Martin Horn of McMaster University for allowing me to read his unpublished paper 'Britain, Total War, and the External Financing of Russia and France'.

25. See Kathleen Burk, 'The Treasury: From Impotence to Power', in Kathleen Burk, ed., *War and the State: The Transformation of British Government, 1914–1919* (London, 1982).

26. For this crisis see Burk, *Sinews of War*, pp. 82–7, and for the entire problem, chs. 4–5; and also Skidelsky, *Keynes: Hopes Betrayed*, ch. 14.

27. The Governor was admired by Asquith, who arranged for his peerage in 1914, and by Lloyd George: *War Memoirs*, Vol. I, p. 68.

28. Beaverbrook thought Cunliffe simply a 'tyrant': *Men and Power*, p. 99; and Davidson recalled him as 'definitely a bully': undated memorandum, JCCDP, DAV 314.

29. See Rhodes James, *Memoirs of a Conservative*, pp. 58–61. Bonar Law pressed ministers to 'sell' war bonds in their speeches and brought in to the Treasury men experienced in advertising, including Hedley le Bas; Northcliffe's partner, Kennedy Jones; and the manager of the *Daily Mail*, George Sutton: see Wrench, *Struggle*, p. 335; and Bonar Law to Northcliffe, 20 February 1917, and Northcliffe's reply, 21 February 1917, NP, Add. MSS. 62158/39 and 62158/41.

30. Memorandum by Keynes, 9 April 1917, T 172/422/23.

31. Lever remained in the US until mid July. His diary of the period has been preserved: T 172/429.
32. Skidelsky, *Keynes: Hopes Betrayed*, p. 340.
33. Cunliffe to Bonar Law, 11 June 1917, T 172/422/25A.
34. 3 July 1917 (copy), BLP 65/2/26.
35. Bonar Law to Lever, 22 June 1917, T 172/429/103.
36. Bonar Law to Lloyd George, 9 July 1917, LGP, F/30/2/19.
37. Bonar Law to Lloyd George, 9 July 1917, BLP 65/3/20.
38. BLP 65/3/20.
39. JCCDP, DAV 314.
40. See Chamberlain, *Down the Years*, pp. 132–3. Buckmaster had been Lord Chancellor in Asquith's coalition.
41. Perhaps for consolation, Bonar Law appointed Cunliffe in 1919 to the inter-Allied committee on German reparations: Bonar Law to Cunliffe, 25 January 1919; and response, 26 January 1919, JCCDP, DAV 89.
42. *Unionist Gleanings and Memoranda*, Vol. XLVIII, p. 213.
43. Reports of this meeting appeared in the London dailies on 26 December 1917.
44. John Denny to Bonar Law, 29 December 1917, T 172/770.
45. 7 January 1918, T 172/770.
46. Bonar Law to Sir Robert Perks, 31 May 1919, BLP 101/3/94. On this point, Beaverbrook surely misled his biographer: A.J.P. Taylor, *Beaverbrook*, p. 166.
47. Bonar Law to Lloyd George, 18 September 1917, BLP 84/6/127.
48. File BLP 2/3/7 contains what few materials survive concerning the wartime deaths of Jim and Charlie Law.
49. Wilson, ed., *Scott Diaries*, entry of 29 August 1917, p. 302.
50. Ramsden, ed., *Sanders Diaries*, entry of 15 June 1917, p. 87.
51. 'Press release', n.d., BLP 3/3/19.
52. Wilson, ed., *Scott Diaries*, entry of 29 August 1917, p. 302.
53. Lord Riddell's diary entry of 14 July 1912, GRD, Add. MSS 62971.
54. See Younger to Davidson, 9 June 1917, BLP 82/1/11, enclosing copies of his letters of 8 and 9 June to Lloyd George, virtually threatening rebellion if Churchill returned to the Government.
55. This letter is printed in Beaverbrook, *Men and Power*, p. 131.
56. *War Memoirs*, Vol. I, p. 636.
57. Beaverbrook, *Men and Power*, pp. 136–7.
58. Hewins to Long, 24 July 1917, WASHP 65.
59. 3 August 1917, BLP 84/6/99. A week earlier Bonar Law had rejected the request of the Executive Committee of the National Union, infuriated over the Churchill appointment, for a party meeting.
60. Ramsden, ed., *Sanders Diaries*, entry of 20 July 1917, p. 88.
61. Smuts arrived in London in March for the meeting of another of Lloyd George's innovations, the Imperial War Cabinet.
62. See Curzon to Lloyd George, n.d., LGP, F/11/8/13; and Turner, *British Politics and the Great War*, p. 223.
63. Long to Bonar Law, 19 September 1917, BLP 82/4/19.
64. See W.D. Rubenstein, 'Henry Page Croft and the National Party, 1917–1922', in *Journal of Contemporary History*, IX (1974). The manifesto of the Party appeared in the *Morning Post* on 30 August 1917.
65. Dawson to Northcliffe, 1 September 1917, NP, Add. MSS. 62245/93–7; and Long to Bonar Law, 18 September 1917, BLP 82/4/17. See also Koss, *Rise and Fall of the Political Press*, Vol. II, p. 318.
66. Ramsden, ed., *Sanders Diaries*, entry of 3 October 1917, p. 89.

67. Lloyd George would have sacked Haig, had he found sufficient support; but only Bonar Law, according to Hankey, among the War Cabinet offered conditional backing. De Groot, *Haig*, pp. 301–2, 307–8.

68. War Cabinet Minutes, 8 June 1917, CAB 23/159. See David Woodward, *Lloyd George and the Generals* (Newark, Delaware, 1983), pp. 169–83.

69. *Lloyd George and the Generals*, pp. 183–5.

70. For the debate over the losses at Third Ypres, see Adams and Poirier, *Conscription Conflict*, p. 280, n. 44.

71. Maj. C.R. Cochran Patrick to Bonar Law, n.d. [21 September 1917], BLP 2/3/7.

72. Beaverbrook, *Politicians and the War*, p. 256.

73. Brig.-Gen. David Henderson to Bonar Law, 6 August 1915, BLP 2/1/5.

74. Capt. James Law's name appears on the monument to missing airmen at Faubourg d'Amiens Cemetery at Arras.

75. For Davidson's recollections, see Rhodes James, *Memoirs of a Conservative*, p. 57.

76. Stanley Salvidge, *Salvidge of Liverpool: Behind the Political Scene, 1890–1928* (London, 1934), p. 166.

77. See Beaverbrook's 'notes' enclosed in his letter to Davidson, 21 October 1963, JCCDP, DAV 314. For the episode, see Chisholm and Davie, *Beaverbrook*, p. 151, and Blake, *Unknown Prime Minister*, pp. 355–6.

78. Harrington Robley (Tony) Law survived the War. Like his elder brother Jim he came to love flying and qualified as a pilot. He never enjoyed robust health, never married, and led a life away from the public eye.

79. Woodward, *Lloyd George and the Generals*, p. 210.

80. Adams and Poirier, *Conscription Controversy*, pp. 220–9.

81. Minutes of the War Cabinet, 18 February 1918, CAB 23/348.

82. Lord Derby backed Robertson and was packed off to the Paris Embassy, while Milner took over the War Office.

83. Younger to Long, 19 October 1917, WLPT 947/599.

84. See the draft dated 6 November, AJBP, Add. MSS. 49730/291–9; and Max Egremont, *Balfour* (London, 1980), pp. 296–9.

85. No copy of the minutes of the conference survives.

86. See Turner, *British Politics and the Great War*, pp. 249–50, 253.

87. See Bonar Law to Lansdowne, 30 November 1917, BLP 84/6/133.

88. Lord Edmund Talbot reported to Philip Kerr that whatever sentiment existed among Unionists for Lansdowne's letter died with Bonar Law's condemnation: Kerr to Lloyd George, 4 December 1917, LGP, F/89/9.

89. *Gleanings and Memoranda*, Vol. XLVIII, p. 178.

90. Ramsden, ed., *Sanders Diaries*, entry of 1 December 1917, p. 93.

91. Ramsden, *Age of Balfour and Baldwin*, p. 119.

92. Ramsden, ed., *Sanders Diaries*, entry of 1 December 1917, p. 93.

93. See Thompson, *Northcliffe and the Great War*.

94. Beaverbrook reproduced the draft in *Men and Power*, following p. 288.

95. A.J.P. Taylor, *Beaverbrook*, p. 141.

96. His resignation was announced on 22 January 1918.

97. A. Chamberlain to N. Chamberlain, 12 April 1918, NCP 1/27/33. See also Dutton, *Austen Chamberlain*, pp. 140–2.

98. Trenchard persevered in his resignation and was succeeded by Maj.-Gen. Frederick Sykes. When Churchill added the Air Ministry to his responsibilities in 1919, he reversed the situation and in February reinstated Trenchard. Sykes, by this time Sir Frederick, became instead the first Controller-General of Civil Aviation.

99. Rhodes James, *Memoirs of a Conservative*, p. 69.

100. In his version of this story, Beaverbrook does not mention Bonar Law playing a role

– though he does reproduce Rothermere's letter to Bonar Law, without explanation: *Men and Power*, pp. 228–37.

101. Woodward, *Lloyd George and the Generals*, p. 305.
102. Minutes of the War Cabinet meeting of 16 May 1917, CAB 23/1/140. Irish separatists, most importantly the Sinn Féin organization, refused to participate: see Robert B. McDowell, *The Irish Convention, 1917–1918* (London, 1970); and Fair, *British Interparty Conferences*, Ch. X.
103. Carson to Bonar Law, 8 April 1918, BLP 83/2/9.
104. War Cabinet Minutes, 25 March 1918, CAB 23/5/372. See Adams and Poirier, *Conscription Controversy*, Ch. 11.
105. De Groot, *Haig*, p.378.
106. Sanders noted that even Carson 'said frankly that he did not know what to do': diary entry of 17 April 1918, Ramsden, ed., *Sanders Diaries*, p. 103.
107. The committee included Barnes, Chamberlain, Curzon and Smuts, as well as Addison, Cave, and H.E. Duke. Their draft bill was actually Long's creation, forwarded with committee approval.
108. War Cabinet Minutes of 23 April 1918, CAB 23/6/397. Long wrote to Bonar Law on 19 April that federalism was the only path to making easier the Unionist leader's task of harmonizing interests within the party. Bonar Law was not convinced: WLPT 947/563. For the federalism question, see Kendle, *Ireland and the Federal Solution*, pp. 197–209.
109. BLP 83/2/33.
110. Bonar Law to Carson, 28 April 1918, BLP 84/7/25.
111. War Cabinet Minutes, 19 June 1918, CAB 23/6/433.
112. Unlike Lansdowne's infamous letter, *The Times* published Maurice's, as did certain other London dailies. Maurice had clearly violated military regulations and was subject to severe punishment, though he was allowed to retire honourably. He became military correspondent of the *Daily Chronicle*, thus putting an end to Bonar Law's candid talks with Robert Donald. Lloyd George had his revenge when, a few months later, a group of his friends purchased the newspaper and turned out both Donald and Maurice: Koss, *Rise and Fall of the Political Press*, Vol. II, pp. 333–7.
113. Middlemas and Barnes, *Baldwin*, p. 68.
114. War Cabinet Minutes, 7 May 1918, CAB 23/6/406.
115. See Woodward, *Lloyd George and the Generals*, pp. 290–1.
116. War Cabinet Minutes, CAB 23/6/397.
117. Woodward, *Lloyd George and the Generals*, p. 291.
118. Maurice had spoken with Robertson and Col. Repington before writing to the press: see Robertson to Maurice, 4 May 1918, Maurice Papers, 4/5/24, quoted in Woodward, *Lloyd George and the Generals*, p. 298; and Turner, *British Politics and the Great War*, p. 298, n. 66. Yet in his notorious letter Maj.-Gen. Maurice insisted, 'It has been seen by no soldier.' This does little to strengthen his claim to the right to cast the first stone. For Maurice's side, see Nancy Maurice, ed., *The Maurice Case from the Papers of Major-General Sir Frederick Maurice* (London, 1972).
119. Lloyd George to Bonar Law, 7 May 1918, BLP 80/2/20.
120. War Cabinet minutes, 7 May 1918, CAB 23/6/406.
121. CAB 23/6/406. See also Lloyd George, *War Memoirs*, Vol. II, pp. 1786–7.
122. See Barnes and Nicholson, eds., *Amery Diaries*, Vol. I, entry of 7 May 1918, p. 219.
123. For the evidence collected by Hankey, see Roskill, *Hankey*, Vol. I, pp. 539–44, and for an admirable summary of the arguments see Woodward, *Lloyd George and the Generals*, pp. 299–304.
124. Before publishing his letter, Maurice had taken his allegations to Carson's successor as UWC Chairman, Salisbury, who spoke against the Government on the eighth: see

Stubbs, 'Impact of the Great War on the Conservative Party', p. 30, and Barnes and Nicholson, eds, *Amery Diaries*, Vol. I, entry of 8 May 1918, p. 219.

125. Barnes and Nicholson, eds, *Amery Diaries*, Vol. I, entry of 8 May 1918, p. 220.
126. For Asquith's possible motives, see Trevor Wilson, *The Downfall of the Liberal Party* (London, 1966), pp. 110–12.
127. Roskill, *Hankey*, Vol. I, pp. 543–5; and Woodward, *Lloyd George and the Generals*, pp. 300–3.
128. Astor to Garvin, 11 May 1918, JLGP.

CHAPTER 13: THE CHALLENGE OF PEACE

1. Entry of 27–28 September 1918, GRD, Add. MSS. 62982. Riddell had leased the house for Lloyd George's use.
2. Salvidge, *Salvidge*, p. 166.
3. See H.A. Taylor, *Bonar Law*, p. 239. See also Lord Riddell's diary entry of 10 November 1918, GRD, Add. MSS. 62982.
4. The other members were Long, Younger and James Clyde, Lord Advocate and MP for Edinburgh West: see Ramsden, ed., *Sanders Diaries*, entry of 3 March 1918, pp. 102–3.
5. See Sanders's minutes, annotated by Bonar Law, of the meeting of 19 July 1918, BLP 83/5/18; and also Ramsden, ed., *Sanders Diaries*, entry of 14 July 1918, p. 106.
6. Salvidge, *Salvidge*, p. 166.
7. Derby to Long, 5 July 1918, WLPT 947/547.
8. Younger to Long, 31 August 1918, WLPT 947/682. See also Younger to Bonar Law, 16, 20 and 23 September 1918, BLP 95/2.
9. Bonar Law to Balfour, 5 October 1918, AJBP, Add. MSS. 49693/272–81.
10. Carson to Lloyd George, 21 October 1918, LGP, F/6/3/18; Bonar Law to Carson, 25 October 1918, BLP 84/7/96.
11. See Long to Bonar Law, 29 October 1918, and the telegram of Curzon, R. Cecil, Chamberlain and Long to Bonar Law, 30 October 1918, BLP 84/2/11 and 84/2/13.
12. Bonar Law to Curzon, 31 October 1918, CP, MSS. Eur. F. 112/122A/14–17.
13. He was replaced temporarily by Sir Auckland Geddes and, in January 1919, by Dr Addison, who presided over the transformation of the Board into the new Ministry of Health.
14. Bonar Law to Lloyd George, 24 January 1919, LGP, F/30/3/4.
15. This note scrawled in red pencil was attached to the final draft of his letter of dismissal to Hayes Fisher. The priceless artefact has disappeared from the Bonar Law papers, though the letter to Hayes Fisher remains: BLP 84/3/1.
16. See Ramsden, *Sanders Diary*, entry of 27 October 1918, pp. 110–11.
17. Labour was represented in the postwar Coalition by a handful of Labour Party defectors to Victor Fisher's anti-socialist National Democratic Party, led in the House by George Barnes, who remained in the War Cabinet.
18. Kenneth O. Morgan, *Consensus and Disunity: The Lloyd George Coalition Government, 1918–1922* (Oxford, 1979), pp. 34–6.
19. These included Crawford, Balfour, Chamberlain, Long, Cecil, Eric and Auckland Geddes, Sanders, Younger and Rowland Prothero.
20. 2 November 1918, BLP 95/1.
21. This latter sentiment came, of course, almost directly from Carson's compromise proposal on 21 October 1918.
22. Lord Robert resigned his office: Cecil to Bonar Law, 11 November 1918, BLP 84/3/10. In the end High Churchmen, like the Church itself, accepted the arrangements: BLP 104/3.

23. Younger to Bonar Law, 8 Nov. 1918, BLP 95/1.
24. *Report of the Meeting of the Unionist Party*, 12 November 1918, BLP 95/3.
25. Ramsden, ed., *Sanders Diaries*, 16 December 1918, p. 113. See also Chaplin to Bonar Law, 14 November 1918 (and reply of the same date), BLP 95/3.
26. These were published on 18 November and 22 November, respectively. The copy of the manifesto from which Bonar Law read at the joint meeting survives: BLP 95/1.
27. Compare Wilson, *Downfall of the Liberal Party*, Ch. 6, and Morgan, *Consensus and Disunity*, Ch. 2.
28. The derisive term was Asquith's. Bonar Law retained his own 'coupon', dated 20 November 1918, and signed by Lloyd George and himself: BLP 21/6/64 (21).
29. According to H.A.L. Fisher, Bonar Law claimed on 23 November 1918 to have received that day at least ten 'abusive' telegrams from Unionists in Liverpool alone, who complained that their men had been required to surrender winnable seats to Liberal candidates: Turner, *British Politics and the Great War*, p. 321. See also Ramsden, *Age of Balfour and Baldwin*, pp. 140–1.
30. As Professor Wilson notes, organizational confusion ensured that the 'coupon' was withheld from some candidates who supported the coalition, and provided to others who did not: *Downfall of the Liberal Party*, pp. 157–8.
31. *Age of Balfour and Baldwin*, p. 141. In the end, nineteen independent Unionist candidates stood against couponed Liberals: one threw the seat to Labour, and five won handily.
32. The correspondence regarding the change and the constituency election is contained in BLP files 21/4–6. I am grateful to Professor Ramsden for pointing out to me the advantage to a Unionist in this district of the plural vote still granted to business occupiers until after World War II.
33. See Dutton, *Austen Chamberlain*, pp. 155–6; Chamberlain's *Down the Years*, pp. 132–43; and his letters to his brother Neville, 11 and 13 January 1919, NCP 1/27/45 and 46.
34. The phrase was used in the pro-coalition *Outlook*, April 1919: Morgan, *Consensus and Disunity*, p. 179.
35. The others were Lloyd George, Balfour, Barnes and a representative Dominion Prime Minister – various men held this appointment.
36. Chamberlain, *Down the Years*, pp. 141–2. Smuts also went to Paris as a member of the South African delegation, resigning from the War Cabinet in January 1919.
37. See Morgan, *Consensus and Disunity*, p. 177.
38. L.C.B. Seaman, *Post-Victorian Britain, 1902–1951* (London, 1993 edn), p. 108.
39. Lord Riddell's diary entry of 8 June 1919, GRD, Add. MSS. 62981. Bonar Law thought the total might reach £8 billion.
40. Skidelsky, *Keynes: Hopes Betrayed*, p. 357.
41. See Roskill, *Hankey*, Vol. I, p. 602.
42. Churchill to Bonar Law, 5 July 1919, BLP 97/5/4. See Paul Addison, *Churchill on the Home Front, 1900–1955* (London, 1993 edn), pp. 206–7.
43. Created by Act of Parliament, the committee of miners, mine owners and experts and chaired by a judge, Sir John Sankey, looked into the conditions of the mines. Their interim report in March 1919 recommended nationalization, but the final report in June consisted of four conflicting recommendations. With Bonar Law's agreement, Lloyd George rejected nationalization.
44. War Cabinet Minutes, 4 February 1919, CAB 23/9/525.
45. CAB 23/9/525. See also Roskill, *Hankey*, Vol. I, p. 190.
46. Kendle, *Long, Ireland and the Union*, p. 175.

47. This in a speech of 12 July 1919: George Boyce, *Englishmen and Irish Troubles: British Public Opinion and the making of Irish Policy, 1918–22* (London, 1972), p. 107.
48. Cabinet Minutes, 7 October 1919, CAB 23/12/628. Also serving were Birkenhead, Fisher, Horne and Sir Auckland Geddes; as well as the Attorney-General, Sir Gordon Hewart; Deputy Minister of Munitions, Frederick Kellaway; and Food Controller, George Roberts. For Long's position, see CAB 23/12/624 and Kendle, *Long, Ireland and the Union*, p. 176.
49. 9 October 1919, BLP 101/3/159.
50. *First Report of the Cabinet Committee on Ireland*, CAB 27/68/56.
51. Those who favoured the nine-county design argued that this would facilitate eventual Irish unification – those preferring a six-county Northern Ireland thought this more realistically governable by Belfast and less likely ever to come under a Dublin Parliament.
52. Lloyd George to Dame Margaret Lloyd George, 11 September 1920, Kenneth O. Morgan, ed., *Lloyd George: Family Letters, 1885–1936* (Cardiff and London, 1973), p. 193.
53. The Government declared martial law on 10 December in Counties Cork, Kerry, Limerick and Tipperary.
54. Diary entry of 10 September 1919, GRD, Add. MSS. 62984.
55. Morgan, *Consensus and Disunity*, p. 177; and for the 'fusion' question, Ch. 7.
56. Four were lost to 'Wee Free' Liberals, and the loss of the seat at Dover in January 1921 to an 'Anti-Waste' independent Conservative was even worse for pro-fusion coalitionists. In Woolwich East in March 1921, a coalition Unionist defeated a Labour candidate in a rare turn against the tide.
57. The Chairman was Oscar Guest, brother of the coalition Liberal Chief Whip, Frederick Guest; the Committee Secretary for the Liberals was Colin Coote, for the Unionists Oswald Mosley: Morgan, *Consensus and Disunity*, p. 178.
58. Ramsden, ed., *Sanders Diaries*, entry of 19 July 1919, p. 128.
59. 5 October 1919, AJBP, Add. MSS. 49693/272–80. See also Lord Riddell's diary entry of 1 February 1920, GRD, Add. MSS. 62985.
60. *The Times*, 15 October 1919.
61. *Gleanings and Memoranda*, Vol. L, pp. 536–7.
62. See Addison, *Churchill on the Home Front*, p. 214, and Morgan, *Consensus and Disunity*, p. 184.
63. Blake, *Unknown Prime Minister*, p. 416; Morgan, *Consensus and Disunity*, p. 176.
64. 10 March 1920, draft copy, BLP 96/4.
65. Ultimately a degree of harmony was restored when each coalition party nominated candidates acceptable to the other, and each won a seat on 27 March – an isolated triumph of the fusion movement: Morgan, *Consensus and Disunity*, p. 188.
66. Vincent, ed., *Crawford Papers*, diary entry of 15 March 1920, p. 406.
67. Bonar Law to Balfour, 12 March 1920, and to Lord Derby, 16 March 1920, BLP 96/4. See also Ramsden, *Sanders Diaries*, entry of 14 March 1920, p. 136.
68. A.J.P. Taylor, ed., *Stevenson Diary*, entry of 18 March 1920, p. 206.
69. *Ibid.*, entry of 16 March 1920, p. 205.
70. Vincent, ed., *Crawford Papers*, diary entry of 19 March 1920, p. 406.
71. 24 March 1920, BLP 96/4.
72. See Ramsden, *Age of Balfour and Baldwin*, p. 144; and the 'Minutes of the National Union Conference, Birmingham', 10 June 1920.
73. Ramsden, ed., *Sanders Diaries*, entry of 23 June 1920, p. 139.
74. *Ibid.*
75. See Younger to Bonar Law, 21 May 1920, BLP 99/1/15.
76. Greenwood, and later Kellaway, and Bonar Law were in charge of preparations to

maintain civil order: see Bonar Law to Sanders, 27 July 1920, Ramsden, ed., *Sanders Diaries*, p. 140.

77. For an indication of the pressure the Southern Unionists and their British allies kept on Bonar Law through the parliamentary progress of the Bill, see the report of his meeting with Lord Midleton and a deputation of Southern Unionists, as well as Neville Chamberlain, the newly elected MP for Birmingham, Ladywood, who chaired the Unionist Reconstruction Committee: 17 March 1920, SJBP, PRO 30/67/42. See also Ramsden, ed., *Sanders Diaries*, entry of 31 March 1920, p. 137.

78. Ramsden, ed., *Sanders Diaries*, entry of 10 July 1920, p. 140.

79. See Griffith Boscawen, *Memories*, p. 247.

80. Michael Kinnear, *The Fall of Lloyd George: The Political Crisis of 1922* (Toronto, 1973), p. 24.

81. See Page Croft to Bonar Law, 31 October 1918, BLP 84/2/15. See also Younger to Bonar Law, 2 January 1921, printed in Beaverbrook, *Decline and Fall of Lloyd George*, pp. 241–4.

82. Leith to Chamberlain, 4 March 1922, ACP 33/1/2, and reply of the same date, ACP 33/1/26c.

83. See Beaverbrook, *Politicians and the War*, p. 257; and Blake, *Unknown Prime Minister*, pp. 419–20. Information from Mr Bonar Sykes.

84. See Blake, *Unknown Prime Minister*, p. 402; Lord Jenkins, *Baldwin* (London, 1987), p. 188; Rhodes James, *Memoirs of a Conservative*, p. 100; and Middlemas and Barnes, *Baldwin*, pp. 165, 177. Beaverbrook disparaged Waterhouse's character to Lord Blake in 1954, BBKP C/44, but had requested his services at the Ministry of Information during the Great War. For the relevant correspondence of March and April 1918, see JCCDP, DAV 77.

85. He was a favourite of Lord Stamfordham; and, after Bonar Law's 1921 retirement, Waterhouse was appointed Private Secretary to the Duke of York. He later served both Baldwin and MacDonald as Principal Private Secretary.

86. Sir Frederick Sykes, *From Many Angles: An Autobiography* (London, 1942), p. 219.

87. Nourah Waterhouse, *Private and Official* (London, 1942), p. 215. For Waterhouse's equally warm reply, 26 March 1921, see BLP 107/1/6.

88. Wickham Steed wrote to Waterhouse on 27 December 1922: 'I do not want to bother the PM ... besides, in talking to you I feel I am, in reality, talking to him': JCCDP, DAV 139.

89. The friend was Beaverbrook, and the critic Mary Law – who ultimately succumbed to Beaverbrook's charm and became his good friend, too.

90. Middlemas, ed., *Whitehall Diary*, entry of 30 January 1921, p. 129.

91. Sir Donald MacAlister, Vice-Chancellor, Glasgow University, to Bonar Law, 25 October 1919, BLP 17/3/10. The results were: Bonar Law 1,073, Murray 726, and Russell, 80.

92. Middlemas, ed., *Whitehall Diary*, entry of 28 January 1921, p. 127.

93. A copy of the text of the speech survives, as well as the original draft corrected in Bonar Law's hand: BLP 17/5/7 and 17/5/5.

94. Vincent, ed., *Crawford Papers*, diary entry of 17 March 1921, p. 410.

95. Ramsden, ed., *Sanders Diaries*, entry of 13 March 1921, p. 149.

96. Bonar Law to Malcolm Fraser, 22 March 1921, BLP/372. Information from Mr Bonar Sykes.

97. Stamfordham to the King, 18 March 1921, RA GV K1681/8.

98. Bonar Law to Davidson, 21 March 1921, Rhodes James, *Memoirs of a Conservative*, p. 103. See also Waterhouse, *Private and Official*, p. 215. Information from Mr Bonar Sykes.

99. 15 March 1921, BLP 101/5/57.

100. See Dangerfield, *Damnable Question*, p. 328; Seaman, *Post-Victorian Britain*, p. 125; and Maurice Cowling, *The Impact of Labour, 1920–1924* (Cambridge, 1971), pp. 117–18. This is expressly rejected in Ramsden, *Age of Balfour and Baldwin*, p. 150. Miss Stevenson said as much: A.J.P. Taylor, ed., *Stevenson Diary*, entry of 11 November 1921, pp. 236–7. Mrs Lloyd George was convinced that Bonar Law's health had broken because of his friendship with Beaverbrook. Lord Riddell's diary entry of 17 April 1921: GRD, Add. MSS. 62987.

101. Baldwin wrote soon afterwards to Balfour: 'When he had once cast off his burden, he seemed more tranquilly happy than he has been for years': 22 March 1921, AJBPW, GD 344/2/19.

102. Copies of his letters of resignation, all dated 17 March 1921, to the King, the Prime Minister and the Unionist Chief Whip, Lord Edmund Talbot, may be found in BLP 101/5/58–60; to his constituency committee, BLP 2/4/38.

103. A.J.P. Taylor, *Stevenson Diary*, entry of 12 May 1921, pp. 215–16. See also Derby to Lloyd George, 21 March 1921, DP (17) 47/3.

104. 17 March 1921, BLP 100/3/24/48.

105. Vincent, ed., *Crawford Papers*, diary entry of 17 March 1921, p. 410.

106. Shortly thereafter, Miss Watson spoke for his entire former staff when she wrote to Bonar Law: '. . . at the moment you want me I am ready to come to you . . . We all hate this place without your presence & get more depressed each day': BLP 107/1/2.

107. It was a season of retirements: a month earlier Walter Long retired with a peerage, and in May Carson became a Lord of Appeal and thus a life peer.

108. Bonar Law to Beaverbrook, 4 June 1921, BBKP, C/204.

109. 1 June 1921, BLP 107/1/32.

110. 9 June 1921, BLP 117/1/33.

111. Ramsden, ed., *Sanders Diaries*, entry of 16 July 1916, p. 158.

112. BLP 107/3/3.

113. 30 April 1921 (copy), BBKP G/57/29.

114. 8 June 1921 (copy), BBKP G/57/29.

115. Bonar Law to Beaverbrook, 17 June 1921, BBKP C/204.

116. Beaverbrook asserts that Lloyd George offered Bonar Law the Foreign Office at this time: *Downfall of Lloyd George*, p. 65. This became a firm offer in January.

117. BBKP G/57/29; *Decline and Fall of Lloyd George*, p. 94.

118. The meeting was apparently held on 22–23 August 1921. For Bonar Law's renewed concerns about Ulster in the June and August conversations, see Kinnear, *Fall of Lloyd George*, p. 15.

119. Bonar Law to Goulding, 26 September 1921, GP 2/71. The house still stands and remains a private residence; since 1958 it has borne one of London's famous circular blue 'historic' plaques, noting his former residence.

CHAPTER 14: RENEWAL

1. Bonar Law to Croal, 12 November 1921. BLP 107/1/83. Parliament rose on 10 November and, except for a brief sitting from 14 to 19 December dedicated to the Irish negotiations, did not then face a regular session until February 1922.

2. *The Times*, 23 June 1921. See Boyce, *Englishmen and Irish Troubles*, pp. 136–9; and Rose, *King George V*, pp. 238–9. This was drafted by Sir Edward Grigg, Lloyd George's private secretary.

3. Craig had succeeded Carson as leader of Ulster Unionism and served as Prime Minister of Northern Ireland from 1921 until his death in 1940.

4. *Correspondence Between His Majesty's Government and the Prime Minister of Northern Ireland Relating to the Proposals for an Irish Settlement*, Lloyd George to Craig, 10 November 1921, Cmd. 1921/1561.

5. See A.J.P. Taylor, ed., *Stevenson Diary*, entry of 6 November 1921, pp. 234–5. This is confirmed by Tom Jones and contradicts the interpretation of St John Ervine, *Craigavon: Ulsterman* (London, 1949), pp. 444–5. For this minor mystery, see Boyce, *Englishmen and Irish Troubles*, p. 160.

6. A.J.P. Taylor, ed., *Stevenson Diary*, entry of 8 November 1921, p. 235.

7. Ervine, *Craigavon*, p. 444.

8. According to H.A. Taylor, the agent was the editor of the *Glasgow Herald*, Sir Robert Bruce: *Bonar Law*, p. 255.

9. 21 November 1921, BLP 107/1/83.

10. See A.J.P. Taylor, ed., *Stevenson Diary*, entry of 11 November 1921, p. 237. Bonar Law wrote in almost exactly the same terms to Lord Rothermere, 16 November 1921, BLP 107/4/6.

11. In late October Col. John Gretton tabled a resolution challenging the entire idea of negotiations with the Irish rebels. Lloyd George treated the uprising as a vote of confidence and was rewarded with a huge majority of 439 to 43.

12. Derby to Lloyd George, 18 November 1921, LGP, F/14/5/33; and Derby to Younger, 5 November 1921, quoted in R. Churchill, *Derby*, p. 422.

13. Salisbury to Bonar Law, 18 November 1921, printed in Beaverbrook, *Decline and Fall of Lloyd George*, pp. 119–20.

14. Gretton's resolution received only 70 votes from among the more than 1,800 delegates: see Kinnear, *Fall of Lloyd George*, p. 98; Salvidge, *Salvidge*, pp. 218–19; and Morgan, *Consensus and Disunity*, p. 248.

15. 12 November 1921, BLP 107/1/83.

16. Waldorf Astor wrote to Garvin on 17 November 1921 that the Government would not have received overwhelming support from the National Union '... if Bonar had made his bid and had a good seconder': Morgan, *Consensus and Disunity*, p. 249.

17. Ramsden, *Age of Balfour and Baldwin*, p. 157.

18. Frank Pakenham (Lord Longford), *Peace by Ordeal* (Cork, 1951 edn), p. 207.

19. *Ibid.*, pp. 274–5; and see also Fair, *British Interparty Conferences*, p. 258.

20. See Pakenham, *Peace by Ordeal*, pp. 204–5 and 207.

21. Bonar Law had long argued that dominion self-governance could turn to independence with the unilateral stroke of a pen in a 'colonial' capital. See his remarks to Lords Midleton and Oranmore, 18 March 1920. SJBP, PRO 30/67/42; and Milner to Bonar Law, 9 April 1920, SJBP 381/134.

22. Bonar Law to Croal, 12 November 1921, BLP 107/1/83.

23. Constituency and even Die-Hard sentiment praised Bonar Law's position: see the correspondence in BLP 107/1/96. Conservative anger was directed at Chamberlain: see Dutton, *Austen Chamberlain*, p. 172.

24. This was the inscription on a silver salver presented to Lloyd George in remembrance of these events by F.E. Guest.

25. Wilson had replaced Talbot as Chief Whip in March 1921.

26. Kinnear, *Fall of Lloyd George*, p. 101.

27. Salvidge, *Salvidge*, p. 225. Birkenhead agreed with this advice, and Churchill did not: see Beaverbrook, *Decline and Fall of Lloyd George*, p. 132.

28. See Kinnear, *Fall of Lloyd George*, Ch. 5; and Beaverbrook, *Decline and Fall of Lloyd George*, Ch. VII. For an alternative view, see Morgan, *Consensus and Disunity*, Ch. 11.

29. Chamberlain to Sanders, 22 December 1921, ACP 32/2/6. He sought opinion also from his brother Neville, and from Derby, Salvidge, Younger, Fraser and J.C. Williams, the Chairman of the National Union. All opposed an early election. See Dutton, *Austen Chamberlain*, pp. 172–3.

30. Frank Owen, *Tempestuous Journey: Lloyd George, His Life and Times* (London, 1954), p. 595.

31. Beaverbrook, *Decline and Fall of Lloyd George*, p. 132.
32. See the memorandum prepared for the party leader, 'A Short Diary of a Press Campaign', n.d., ACP 32/4/15.
33. This letter of 9 January 1922 is printed in Ramsden, ed., *Sanders Diaries*, pp. 171–2. Chamberlain complained of Younger's action, to him and to Lloyd George: Dutton, *Austen Chamberlain*, p. 73.
34. See Morgan, *Consensus and Disunity*, pp. 274–5; and Ramsden, *Age of Balfour and Baldwin*, p. 159. Younger was rebuked by an angry Birkenhead, who compared the party chairman to a cabin boy attempting to seize control of the ship. The Executive Committee of the National Union came close to passing a resolution of censure against the Lord Chancellor.
35. Salvidge, *Salvidge*, p. 227.
36. Blake, *Unknown Prime Minister*, p. 438.
37. 7 January 1922, ACP 5/1/223.
38. Chamberlain to Lloyd George, 4 January 1922, ACP 32/2/20.
39. After an informal lunch on 9 January, Lloyd George challenged Briand and Bonomi, the Italian, to a golf match with himself, Sir Edward Grigg, Riddell and Bonar Law, who also remained in Cannes. Briand had never played the game and hacked about hopelessly, voraciously photographed by members of the French press. When the photographs appeared in the Paris papers, Briand was humiliated and resigned, to be replaced by the hard-liner Poincaré. It marked the end of any hope of a conciliatory agreement between the Allies and Germany.
40. This remark was by Watkin Davies: Morgan, *Consensus and Disunity*, p. 276.
41. Petrie, *Sir Austen Chamberlain*, Vol. II, p. 173.
42. Ramsden, ed., *Sanders Diaries*, entry of 8 February 1922, pp. 172–3.
43. Diary entry of 12 February 1922, GRD, Add. MSS. 62989; A.J.P. Taylor, ed., *Stevenson Diary*, entry of 4 February 1922, p. 240.
44. Lloyd George to Chamberlain, 27 February 1922, printed in Petrie, *Sir Austen Chamberlain*, Vol. II, pp. 174–8.
45. Dutton, *Austen Chamberlain*, p. 176.
46. In February the Convervatives lost Manchester, Clayton and Camberwell North-west to Labour, and Bodmin to an Asquith Liberal. They expected to lose Wolverhampton West in early March, though they held it easily. In March, the Lloyd George Liberals lost Leicester East to Labour.
47. Ramsden, ed., *Sanders Diaries*, entry of 19 March 1922, p. 175.
48. Morgan, *Consensus and Disunity*, pp. 336–7.
49. Ash, *Lost Dictator*, pp. 2 and 280.
50. Wilson's personal courage was beyond doubt – he died facing his murderers, drawing his sabre. This was the last assassination of an MP until the murder of the Conservative Airey Neave by IRA terrorists in March 1979.
51. 25 June 1922, ACP 5/1/244.
52. Ramsden, ed., *Sanders Diaries*, entry of 2 July 1922, p. 177.
53. *The Times*, 27 June 1922.
54. Martin Gilbert, *Winston Churchill, Vol. IV: The Stricken World* (London, 1975), p. 738.
55. Ramsden, ed., *Sanders Diaries*, entry of 2 July 1922, p. 177.
56. Diary entry of 16 May 1922, DP 29/1.
57. See H.J. Hanham, 'The Sale of Honours in Late Victorian England', *Victorian Studies*, March 1960.
58. For this fascinating character, see Tom Cullen, *Maundy Gregory: Purveyor of Honours* (London, 1974).
59. See Nicolson, *King George the Fifth*, pp. 511–13; and Rose, *King George V*, pp. 251–2. Chamberlain wrote secretly to Lord Stamfordham on 3 May 1922 encouraging the

Palace to protest to Lloyd George against the length of his honours lists, ACP
23/5/12; the King's secretary was only too happy to oblige, ACP 23/5/14.

60. Vincent, ed., *Crawford Papers*, diary entry of 8 July 1922, p. 426.

61. Attending were the party whips, Wilson and George Gibbs. The under-secretaries
included: L.S. Amery (Admiralty), John Baird (Home Office), Clement Barlow
(Labour), Sir Bolton Eyres-Monsell (Admiralty), William Bridgeman (Board of
Trade), John Gilmour (Treasury), Sir William Mitchell-Thompson (Board of
Trade), Herbert Pike Pease (Post Office), Robert Sanders (War Office), Col.
George Stanley (War Office), Maj. George Tryon (Pensions), Lord Winterton
(India), and Edward Wood (Colonies). Also present were Sir Ernest Pollock, the
Attorney-General, who was not a member of the Cabinet, and Griffith-Boscawen,
the Agriculture Minister, who was: ACP 33/2/10.

62. 'Notes on conference with the Under-Secretaries', 20 July 1922, ACP 33/2/4; 'The
Fall of the Coalition in Oct 1922', memorandum by Sir Ernest Pollock (Lord
Hanworth), 14 September 1931, EPP, MSS. Eng. hist., 432/137–180; Ramsden,
ed., *Sanders Diaries*, entry of 21 July 1922, p. 179.

63. Ramsden, ed., *Sanders Diaries*, entry of 21 July 1922, p. 179.

64. EPP, MSS. Eng. hist. 432/145.

65. EPP, MSS. Eng. hist. 432/138.

66. 1 September 1922, ACP 33/2/12.

67. Chamberlain to Derby, 7 September 1922, DP 33.

68. Derby to Chamberlain, 9 September 1922, DP 33.

69. Salisbury to Bonar Law, 23 September 1922, BLP 107/2/61.

70. Wilson to Chamberlain, 'September 1922', ACP 33/2/26; Salisbury to Selborne, 26
September 1922, Boyce, ed., *Selborne's Political Papers*, pp. 235–6. See also Younger's
confidential memorandum of 27 September 1922, Ramsden, ed. *Sanders Diaries*, pp.
184–5.

71. A. Chamberlain to I. Chamberlain, 24 September 1922, ACP 5/1/249. Emphasis in
the original.

72. Lloyd George called Venizélos 'the greatest Greek statesman since Pericles'; Lord
Vansittart commented: '[He] was the worst influence in Lloyd George's life . . .',
but added, 'I admired and distrusted him immensely.' David Walder, *The Chanak
Affair* (London, 1969), p. 356.

73. M. Gilbert, *Churchill: Stricken World*, p. 827.

74. Walder, *Chanak*, pp. 224–32.

75. *Ibid.*, p. 282.

76. 'The Decision', undated memorandum by Lord Beaverbrook, BBKP, G/57.

77. DP 47/3.

78. Undated memorandum by Lucy Baldwin, 'The Recollections of a Cabinet-
Breakers's Wife on the Government Crisis of October 1922' (copy), JCCDP, DAV
314.

79. Fraser to Sanders, 22 September 1922, printed in Ramsden, ed., *Sanders Diaries*, p.
182.

80. ACP 23/2/28.

81. Beaverbrook, *Decline and Fall of Lloyd George*, p.165.

82. Ramsden, ed., *Sanders Diaries*, entry of 1 October 1922, p. 181.

83. Beaverbrook, *Decline and Fall of Lloyd George*, p. 166.

84. In *Decline and Fall of Lloyd George*, p. 168, Beaverbrook notes that this occurred at his
Fulham house, the Vineyard, on 6 October; but in an earlier undated memorandum
he wrote that the conversation occurred over the telephone: BBKP, G/57/29.

85. The letter also appeared in Beaverbrook's *Daily Express*. Steed apparently saw
Bonar Law in the evening and claimed later to have advised him to alter the

wording of the letter to make it appear less threatening. See his letter to the *Daily Express*, 2 November 1933. Beaverbrook confirms the contact with Derby: *Decline and Fall of Lloyd George*, p. 168.

86. Churchill also wrote on the same day to his constituency chairman: 'Broadly speaking, I agree with Mr Bonar Law': M. Gilbert, *Churchill: Stricken World*, p. 859.

87. Vincent, ed., *Crawford Papers*, diary entry of 7 October 1922, p. 446.

88. 7 October 1922, ACP 24/4/18.

89. David Dutton notes correctly that the letter 'was not endowed by contemporaries with the same significance as that attributed by some later historians': *Austen Chamberlain*, p. 192.

90. See Campbell, *F.E. Smith*, pp. 606–7; and Roskill, *Hankey*, Vol. II, p. 295.

91. See the examples in BLP 107/2/66.

92. Middlemas and Barnes, *Baldwin*, p. 114.

93. Beaverbrook, *Decline and Fall of Lloyd George*, pp. 172–8.

94. Attending with Chamberlain were Lords Balfour, Birkenhead, Crawford, Curzon, Lee and Peel, as well as Baldwin, Griffith-Boscawen, Horne, Worthington-Evans, and the Chief Whip, Wilson.

95. Vincent, ed., *Crawford Papers*, diary entry of 10 October 1922, p. 450.

96. 'Recollections of a Cabinet-Breaker's Wife', JCCDP, DAV 314.

97. *Ibid*; Rhodes James, *Memoirs of a Conservative*, p. 117.

98. Wilson to Sanders, 12 October 1922, Ramsden, ed., *Sanders Diaries*, p. 190; Wilson to Chamberlain, 11 October 1922, ACP 33/2/43.

99. Younger warned Churchill on 14 October: 'My party is likely to be in absolute revolt': WSCP 2/125/20.

100. Chamberlain to Birkenhead, 12 October 1922, ACP 33/2/52.

101. Rhodes James, *Memoirs of a Conservative*, p. 120; Beaverbrook, *Decline and Fall of Lloyd George*, p. 186.

102. Viscount Templewood, *Empire of the Air* (London, 1957), p. 19.

103. See Barnes and Nicholson, eds., *Amery Diaries*, Vol. I, entry of 24 October 1922, p. 295; for the effect on Curzon of Lloyd George's address, see David Gilmour, *Curzon* (London, 1994), p. 552.

104. 'The Break-Up of the Coalition – The Story of a Wonderful Week', undated memorandum by Griffith-Boscawen, GBP, MSS. Eng. hist, 396/119–23.

105. Middlemas and Barnes, *Baldwin*, p. 117.

106. Barnes and Nicholson, *Amery Diaries*, Vol. I, entry of 13 October 1922, p. 294; GBP, MSS. Eng. hist. 396/119–23.

107. Baldwin's co-conspirators were Amery and Philip Lloyd-Greame, Secretary of Overseas Trade at the Board of Trade.

108. In order to keep out Die-hard peers, only MPs and lords holding office were invited – some eight peers were admitted. Curzon did not attend, giving the general exclusion of the lords as his reason: Curzon to Chamberlain, 18 October 1922, ACP 33/2/90. To others he explained his absence by citing his personal loyalty to Chamberlain: Gilmour, *Curzon*, p. 554.

109. Barnes and Nicholson, *Amery Diaries*, Vol. I, entry of 16 October 1922, p. 296.

110. *Ibid*.

111. 'Recollections of a Cabinet-Breaker's Wife', JCCDP, DAV 314; Rhodes James, *Memoirs of a Conservative*, p. 123.

112. Beaverbrook, *Decline and Fall of Lloyd George*, pp. 195–6.

113. Gilmour, *Curzon*, p. 554.

114. BBKP G/57.

115. Draft letter, 18 October 1922, marked 'not sent', BLP 107/4/35.

116. 'Recollections of a Cabinet-Breaker's Wife', JCCDP, DAV 314. For Kipling's

friendship with Bonar Law, see Bonar Sykes, 'Memories of the Kiplings', in *Kipling Journal*, March 1996.

117. According to Hoare, 80 Conservative back-benchers were summoned to a meeting at his Cadogan Gardens house by Hoare, Lane-Fox, Walter Guinness and John Hills. See the announcement of the meeting, WBP, 5/6. Sanders suggests that only 35 MPs attended: Ramsden, ed., *Sanders Diaries*, entry of 19 October 1922, p. 191.

118. Chamberlain, *Down the Years*, p. 221.

119. Beaverbrook, *Decline and Fall of Lloyd George*, p. 198.

120. Earl of Ronaldshay, *The Life of Lord Curzon* (London, 1928), Vol. III, pp. 320–1.

121. In a letter to *The Times* on 16 December 1947, Arthur Mann claimed that Bonar Law told him at the Carlton Club on 19 October that Chamberlain was likely to carry the meeting, and also that on the preceding evening Baldwin had remained with him until he agreed to attend. Neither of these assertions rings true: first, his anxiety about the rebellion was based not on the fear that it might fail, but on the certainty that it would succeed; second, Baldwin did not appear at Onslow Gardens until midnight.

122. 6 November 1922, BLP 108/9/16. Tom Jones visited Onslow Gardens shortly after the Carlton Club meeting and noted in his diary that Bonar Law had said, and Miss Law had confirmed, that his sister had opposed his decision to attend: Middlemas, ed., *Whitehall Diary*, entry of 22 October 1922, p. 214. Davidson, a close friend of Miss Law, recalled that she supported the decision: Rhodes James, *Memoirs of a Conservative*, p. 126. A decade later, Jones recorded that Stanley Baldwin insisted Mary Law was responsible for her brother's attendance: *Diary With Letters*, entry of 18 September 1932, pp. 61–2.

123. Steed to the Editor, *The Times*, 18 December 1947.

124. 25 July 1922, WLP, Add. MSS. 62404/112–13. Long had retired and been created Viscount Long of Wraxall in May 1921.

125. This is Davidson's recollection of Beaverbrook's words: Rhodes James, *Memoirs of a Conservative*, p. 127.

126. For the best analysis of the contest, see John Ramsden, 'The Newport by-election and the fall of the Coalition', in Chris Cook and John Ramsden, *By-Elections in British Politics* (London, 1997).

127. Beaverbrook, *Decline and Fall of Lloyd George*, pp. 189–90.

128. Sanders to Wilson, 8 October 1922, Ramsden, ed., *Sanders Diaries*, p. 190.

129. Bonar Law was surprised and amused to receive warm support from Rothermere's newspapers. 'You are a queer creature,' he wrote to the press lord. 'You abuse me like a pickpocket, forget all about it & then write a most friendly letter for which notwithstanding I am obliged.' 19 October 1922, RP, AALR 005.

130. Vincent, ed., *Crawford Papers*, diary entry of 19 October 1922, p. 453.

131. Dutton, *Austen Chamberlain*, p. 197.

132. Middlemas and Barnes, *Baldwin*, p. 123.

133. Petrie, *Chamberlain*, Vol. II, p. 203.

134. These included the Die-Hard Sir Henry Craik, and Francis Mildmay, who spoke for the back-bench centre. The Chief Whip, Wilson, whom Chamberlain never forgave, supported the motion at length, though the question had already been called.

135. Vincent, ed., *Crawford Papers*, entry of 19 October 1922, p. 452.

136. *Gleanings and Memoranda*, Vol. LVI, pp. 491–3.

137. The abstention was that of Sir Robert Clough. The ballots passed into Davidson's possession and remain among his papers. Many historians have recorded erroneous results, no doubt misled by the incorrect count recorded in *Gleanings and Memoranda*, Vol. LVI, p. 495. More confusing is the fact that the wrapping paper which for many decades held the ballots is incorrectly marked '186–87'.

138. Williamson, ed., *Bridgeman Diaries*, entry of October 1922, p. 161.
139. See Stamfordham's undated memorandum, 'Resignation of Mr Lloyd George', RA GV K1814/1.
140. 'Of all ill-omened places', was Crawford's reaction. Vincent, ed., *Crawford Papers*, diary entry of 20 October 1922, pp. 454–5.
141. His speech was only some twelve minutes long, and he closed it with a reference to his recent medical examination, reminding his followers that he would resign immediately if his health required it and asking '[that] . . . you will not press me to remain if I ask you to set me free.' *Gleanings and Memoranda*, Vol. LVI, p. 501.
142. Diary entry of 20 October 1922, DP 29/1. See also entry of 20 October 1922, Barnes and Nicholson, *Amery Diaries*, Vol. I, pp. 307–8.

CHAPTER 15: 'A REAL OLD TORY CABINET'
1. Philip Ziegler, *Melbourne: A Biography of William Lamb, 2nd Viscount Melbourne* (London, 1976), p. 170.
2. Diary entry of 21 October 1922, DP 29/1.
3. The incoming Cabinet were unanimous on this point. Wickham Steed, whom Bonar Law consulted, agreed: Steed to Bonar Law, 19 October 1922, BLP 117/2/2.
4. Middlemas, ed., *Whitehall Diary*, entry of 30 October 1922, p. 219; Roskill, *Hankey*, Vol. II, 308; and Colin Cross, ed., *Life With Lloyd George: The Diary of A.J. Sylvester* (London, 1975), pp. 11–12.
5. *The Times*, 27 October 1922.
6. For this episode and its conclusion, see Roskill, *Hankey*, pp. 306–22; Naylor, *A Man and an Institution*, Ch. 3; and Cabinet minutes of 1 November 1922, CAB 23/32.
7. Bonar Law's request, for example, that the law officers retain their positions was declined: Pollock to Bonar Law, 23 October 1922, HP, MSS. Eng. hist. d. 432/27. See also Lord Derby's diary entry of 30 October 1922, DP 29/1.
8. See Lord Riddell's diary entry of 15 November 1922, GRD, Add. MSS. 62988.
9. Ullswater, *A Speaker's Commentaries*, p. 289. See also Roskill, *Hankey*, Vol. II, p. 301; and Barnes and Nicholson, *Amery Diaries*, Vol. I, entry of 21 October 1922, p. 308.
10. According to his nephew, McKenna was approached by Bonar Law but declined the offer of the Exchequer in order not to draw votes away from the new Government among Tories who remembered him as a Liberal minister: Stephen McKenna, *Reginald McKenna, 1863–1943* (London, 1948), pp. 318–19. Baldwin's biographers indicate that the offer was his idea and that the future Prime Minister accepted the post only after McKenna's refusal: Middlemas and Barnes, *Baldwin*, p. 124.
11. Cave had been Home Secretary, 1916–19, before becoming a Lord of Appeal.
12. 15 December 1922, *Gleanings and Memoranda*, Vol. LVI, pp. 7–8.
13. Campbell, *F.E. Smith*, p. 615.
14. Hankey's diary entry of 26 November 1922, quoted in Roskill, *Hankey*, Vol. II, p. 326.
15. The newcomer was Lord Novar, Secretary of State for Scotland.
16. Ramsden, ed., *Sanders Diaries*, entry of 25 October 1922, p. 192.
17. Vincent, ed., *Crawford Papers*, diary entry of 25 October 1922, p. 461.
18. *The Times*, 2 November 1922.
19. Vincent, ed., *Crawford Papers*, diary entry of 31 December 1922, p. 475.
20. Barnes and Nicholson, *Amery Diaries*, entry of 23 October 1922, p. 308.
21. See Amery, *My Political Life*, Vol. II, pp. 241–5; Middlemas and Barnes, *Baldwin*, p. 127; and Kinnear, *Fall of Lloyd George*, p. 157.
22. See Campbell, *F.E. Smith*, pp. 613–14. Birkenhead, not surprisingly, was the most vituperative of the Tory ex-coalitionists.

23. *The Times*, 3 November 1922.
24. Vincent, ed., *Crawford Papers*, diary entry of 29 October 1922, p. 463. Even Churchill recommended a period of 'stability and recuperation', but he was defeated at Dundee.
25. Kinnear, *Fall of Lloyd George*, p. 138, and for election Chs 7–8.
26. Michael Kinnear calculates that in 160 constituencies the two former coalition parties worked together, and in 55 others opposed one another. In the remaining 400, the two parties did not appear on the same ballot: *Fall of Lloyd George*, p. 144.
27. Kinnear, *Fall of Lloyd George*, p. 165.
28. 29 October 1922, BLP 108/9/11. Campbell's request at the time was to be appointed a Law Lord: Campbell to Bonar Law, undated [22 November 1922] BLP 108/22/16.
29. Bonar Law had already planned to and in fact did offer a junior office to Esmond Harmsworth. It was, quite understandably, rejected. See their exchange of correspondence of 24 October 1922, BLP 108/1/1. 108/9/3 and 108/1/2.
30. The elements of this episode may be found in Lord Derby's diary, entry of 24 October 1922, DP 29/1; Rhodes James, *Memoirs of a Conservative*, p. 135; Hankey's diary entry of 25 October 1922, Roskill, *Hankey*, Vol. II, pp. 310–11; and Sanders's diary entry of 25 October 1922, Ramsden, ed., *Sanders Diaries*, p. 192. As soon as Rothermere left him, Bonar Law apparently either dictated or wrote a memorandum giving the details of the interview. This has not survived, though both Davidson and Bonar Law's son Richard attested to its existence. Richard Law recalled to Lord Blake that the memorandum was dictated to him: Blake, *Unknown Prime Minister*, p. 472, n. 1; but Davidson noted thirty years after the event that the premier himself wrote it in his own hand: Rhodes James, *Memoirs of a Conservative*, p. 135. Davidson, on 7 October 1955, drafted but did not send a letter to the *Evening Standard* in which he insisted that Bonar Law sent a veiled message to Rothermere in his Drury Lane speech of 2 November 1922, in which he said that he would not 'make any bargain with the Press': JCCDP, DAV 310.
31. Middlemas, ed., *Whitehall Diary*, Vol. I, entries of 10–12 November 1922, p. 221.
32. The official Liberal candidate, Sir George Paish, ran a poor third. The race was made by the ILP man, himself a former Liberal, Edward Rosslyn Mitchell.
33. Wilson returned to the House in December, Hills not until 1925. Griffith-Boscawen retired from the House after his by-election defeat in March 1923.
34. *Decline and Fall of Lloyd George*, p. 222.
35. Barnes and Nicholson, eds, entry of 25 October 1922, *Amery Diaries*, Vol. I, p. 309. Neville Chamberlain became Postmaster General, and soon afterwards Minister of Health, in succession to Griffith-Boscawen.
36. A. Chamberlain to I. Chamberlain, 18 November 1922, ACP 5/1/250. See also Chamberlain to Wilson, 22 November 1922, ACP 33/2/95.
37. See Blake, *Unknown Prime Minister*, pp. 477–80; Roskill, *Hankey*, Vol. II, pp. 324–5; Campbell, *F.E. Smith*, pp. 621–2; and Gilmour, *Curzon*, pp. 560–1.
38. Hankey revealed Birkenhead to be correct in recalling that the Cabinet had not discussed the correspondence, but this was by their own choice: Hankey to Bonar Law, 8 December 1922, PREM 1/18; and Naylor, *Man and an Institution*, pp. 115–16, 348, n. 4.
39. 8 December 1922, BLP 111/12/42.
40. *The Times*, 12 December 1922.
41. Gilmour, *Curzon*, p. 561. Curzon was unappeased, writing to his wife on 12 December: 'Birkenhead had to apologise yesterday to the [Foreign Office], not to me!' CP, Mss. Eur. F.112/796/155–6.
42. Salvidge, *Salvidge*, p. 238.

43. Roskill, *Hankey*, Vol. II, p. 323.
44. This was Bonar Law's former Chief Whip, Lord Edmund Talbot.
45. Rhodes James, *Memoirs of a Conservative*, p. 138.
46. Ramsden, ed., *Sanders Diaries*, entry of 17 December 1922, p. 194.
47. 21 February 1923; JCCD, DAV 143. Gower wrote similarly to Stamfordham on 15 December: Blake, *Unknown Prime Minister*, p. 481.
48. For these references of 27 November and 5 December 1922, and other such examples, see *Gleanings and Memoranda*, Vol. LVI, p. 114.
49. *Yorkshire Post*, 22 December 1922.
50. Cabinet Minutes of 20 November 1922, CAB 23/32.
51. Under the advice of his colleagues, he agreed later to see representatives of the Miners' Federation and the National Farmers' Union. He rationalized his actions by seeing only officers of accredited organizations, and by noting that these deputations included MPs come to discuss issues before the House. He continued to argue that the Prime Minister should not deal directly with *ad hoc* pressure groups, whomever they claimed their constituency to be – a scruple his successors did not always share.
52. For this latter episode of December 1922, see the file BLP 22/2/2.
53. See David Dilks, *Neville Chamberlain, Vol. I: Pioneering and Reform, 1899–1929* (Cambridge, 1984), pp. 300–1.
54. Waterhouse called a note to Amery as stiff a letter as he had 'ever read from BL's pen & the fact of its being only about 7 lines made it all the stiffer!': Stamfordham to the King, 2 January 1923, RA GV M1835/24.
55. For examples of Farquhar's sad decline, see Fitzalan to Bonar Law, 12 February 1923; and Younger to Bonar Law, 12 March 1923, BLP 108/4/8 and 108/6/6.
56. Bonar Law to Farquhar, 15 February 1923, BLP 108/9/55.
57. A popular MP and former English cricket captain, Francis Stanley Jackson was joined at Central Office by Adm. Reginald 'Blinker' Hall, the former Chief of Naval Intelligence, who replaced Fraser as Chief Agent.
58. Harold Nicolson, *Curzon: The Last Phase* (London, 1934), p. 324.
59. Perhaps the unelected Curzon did not appreciate as did Bonar Law that a war was hardly a suitable beginning for a Government recently voted into office on a pledge of 'tranquillity': see Blake, *Unknown Prime Minister*, p. 487.
60. See the Cabinet minutes of 6 November 1922, CAB 23/32; also Bonar Law to Curzon, 8 January 1923, BLP 111/12/57. The Lausanne Conference adjourned on 4 February and resumed in April, completing its work with the signing of the treaty on 4 July 1923, after Bonar Law had left office. The dispute over Mosul dragged on officially until 1926, when the League of Nations awarded the territory to Iraq.
61. Dilks, *Neville Chamberlain*, p. 304.
62. Lord Derby's diary entry of 9 December 1922, DP 29/1. Mussolini's charm did not beguile Bonar Law, who remarked when asked what he thought of the first Fascist dictator: 'Sheer lunatic': Vincent, ed., *Crawford Papers*, diary entry of 25 August 1935, p. 564.
63. 12 December 1922: Roskill, *Hankey*, Vol. II, p. 127. Emphasis in the original.
64. Cabinet Minutes, 7 December 1922, CAB 23/32; and Lord Derby's diary entry of 11 December 1922, DP 29/1.
65. Robert Skidelsky, *John Maynard Keynes, Vol. II: The Economist as Saviour* (London, 1992), p. 123.
66. Lord Swinton, *I Remember* (London, 1948), p. 28.
67. J.A. Cross, *Lord Swinton* (Oxford, 1982), p. 46.
68. Robert Rhodes James, *Victor Cazalet: A Portrait* (London, 1976), p. 86.
69. Rhodes James, *Memoirs of a Conservative*, p. 143.

70. This was issued on 1 August 1922. See McKay, *Balfour*, pp. 337–9.
71. 14 December 1922.
72. 13 January 1923: Middlemas and Barnes, *Baldwin*, p. 140.
73. Undated unpublished paper by Lord Beaverbrook, BBKP, G/57/29.
74. Skidelsky, *Keynes: Economist as Saviour*, p. 124.
75. 14 December 1922.
76. Jones: *Diary with Letters*, entry of 27 February 1932, p. 31.
77. Minutes of Cabinet meeting of 15 January 1923, CAB 23/45. Attending were the Duke of Devonshire, Lord Derby and Lord Novar, and Amery, Barlow, Griffith-Boscawen and McNeil, representing Curzon. Geddes, the ambassador, as well as the former Chancellor, Horne, and the newspaper proprietor, Lord Burnham – all of whom were in the United States at the time – telegraphed recommending acceptance of the US terms: Middlemas and Barnes, *Baldwin*, p. 143.
78. K. Young, *Baldwin*, p. 41.
79. More revealing than the very brief Cabinet minutes are the unattributed detailed notes of the meeting to be found in JCCDP, DAV 143.
80. Diary entry of 30 January 1923, DP 29/1.
81. JCCDP, DAV 143.
82. Barnes and Nicholson, eds, *Amery Diaries*, Vol. I, entry of 29–31 January 1923, pp. 319–20. Davidson concurred: JCCDP, DAV 143. For this controversy, see Cross, *Swinton*, pp. 46–7. Novar wrote a letter a decade later to Sir Clive Wigram obliquely confirming this, and the fact that the deadlock was known about outside the Cabinet: 27 December 1932, RA GV L2317/51.
83. Diary entry of 30 January 1923, DP 29/1.
84. Middlemas, ed., *Whitehall Diary*, entry of 5 February 1923, pp. 227–8. Beaverbrook claimed that 'two colleagues' supported Bonar Law: BBKP, G/57/29. Lord Blake agreed: *Unknown Prime Minister*, p. 493.
85. See Lord Derby's diary entry of 30 January 1923, DP 29/1.
86. See Steed's article of 18 December 1932, in The *Sunday Times*. Geoffrey Dawson, Steed's successor, also confirmed the authorship: Rhodes James, *Memoirs of a Conservative*, p. 142.
87. Lord Derby's diary entry of 31 January 1923, DP 29/1; Novar to Wigram, 27 December 1932, RA GV L2317/51.
88. Ramsden, ed., *Sanders Diaries*, entry of 4 February 1923, pp. 199–200.
89. A.J.P. Taylor, *Beaverbrook*, p. 205. Bonar Law had been advised similarly as early as 11 January, before the terms were known: see Oswald Falk to Bonar Law, 11 January 1923, JCCDP, DAV 143.
90. BBKP, G/57/29. See also Beaverbrook to Blake, 5 April 1963, BBKP, C/45.
91. Cabinet Minutes, 31 January 1923, CAB 23/45.
92. Diary entry of 31 January 1923, DP 29/1. See also Ramsden, ed., *Sanders Diaries*, entry of 4 February 1923, p. 200.
93. Middlemas, ed., *Whitehall Diaries*, Vol., I, entry of 5 February 1923, p. 227.
94. BBKP, G/57/29.
95. Information from Mr Bonar Sykes.
96. 3 February 1923: Roskill, *Hankey*, Vol. II, p. 334.
97. See the related correspondence in files BLP 108/4 and 108/9.
98. Roskill, *Hankey*, Vol. II, p. 335.
99. Griffith-Boscawen lost to an 'Independent' Conservative run by Rothermere and Austen Chamberlain's associate, Oliver Locker Lampson: Ramsden, *Age of Balfour and Baldwin*, p. 173.
100. The speculation of the *Observer* on 15 April 1923 elicited an official denial from No. 10 on the following day.

101. 2 April 1923, CP, MSS. Eur. F. 112/320.
102. 5 April 1923, CP, MSS. Eur. F. 112/230/150–1.
103. Waterhouse, *Private and Official*, p. 256.
104. Ramsden, ed., *Sanders Diaries*, entry of 15 April 1923, p. 203.
105. 22 April 1923.
106. Ramsden, ed., *Sanders Diaries*, entry of 22 April 1923, p. 204.
107. See Middlemas and Barnes, *Baldwin*, pp. 156–7. Beaverbrook explained that the reduction in the income tax rate came as a result of the intervention of Bonar Law, McKenna and, of course, himself: BBKP, G/57/29.
108. The consensus among Conservative insiders was that Rothermere and Birkenhead had quarrelled and that this accounted for Rothermere's turn in favour of the Government: see Barnes and Nicholson, eds, *Amery Diaries*, Vol. I, entry of 17 April 1923, p. 324; and Ramsden, ed., *Sanders Diaries*, entry of 29 April 1923, p. 204.
109. See Chamberlain to Ida Chamberlain, 22 April 1923, ACP 5/1/271.
110. 14 April 1923, ACP 5/1/270. See also A. Chamberlain to N. Chamberlain, 22 April 1923, NCP 1/27/69; and Lord Derby's diary entry of 28 April 1923, DP 29/1.
111. ACP 5/1/270.
112. The classic biographies of both Bonar Law and Austen Chamberlain do so: Blake, *Unknown Prime Minister*, p. 509; Petrie, *Austen Chamberlain*, Vol. II, p. 213. Chamberlain's most recent biographer remains sceptical about the entire affair: Dutton, *Austen Chamberlain*, p. 203.
113. BBKP, G/57/29.
114. *Ibid.*
115. A.J.P. Taylor, *Beaverbrook*, p. 207. This massive work does not mention the offer of the succession.
116. N. Chamberlain to A. Chamberlain, 23 April 1923, NCP 1/27/70; N. Chamberlain, diary entry of 26 April 1923, NCP. For the younger Chamberlain's difficult position in this affair, see Dilks, *Neville Chamberlain*, p. 317.
117. A. Chamberlain to N. Chamberlain, 25 April 1923, NCP 1/27/71.
118. For Beaverbrook's recollection of this episode, see his undated paper, BBKP, G/57/29.
119. Barnes and Nicholson, eds, *Amery Diaries*, Vol. I, entry of 26 April 1923, p. 325.
120. RA, King George V's Diary, 27 April 1923.
121. 9 May 1923.
122. Rhodes James, *Memoirs of a Conservative*, p. 149.

CHAPTER 16: CODA

1. Bonar Law to Curzon, 5 May 1923, CP, MSS. Eur. F. 112/230/153.
2. Davidson and Berry, without escort, carried with them for the Prime Minister's personal use a new cipher key for the decoding of encrypted messages – a proceeding which would horrify modern security agencies.
3. Rhodes James, *Memoirs of a Conservative*, p. 149.
4. BBKP, G/57/29. Later, Beaverbrook could not recall whether he had been summoned by letter or telegraph: 'Notes by Lord Beaverbrook for Mr Blake', March 1954, BBK G/13/VI.
5. Middlemas, ed., *Whitehall Diary*, Vol. I, entry of 10 June 1923, pp. 241–2.
6. BBKP, G/13/VI.
7. BBKP, G/57/29.
8. BBKP, G/13/VI.
9. Memorandum by Davidson, 19 May 1955, JCCDP, DAV 310.
10. Barnes and Nicholson, eds, *Amery Diaries*, Vol. I, entries of 18–19 May 1923, pp. 326–7.

11. Sir Philip Sassoon delivered these offers of support to Derby on 20 May. Beaverbrook subsequently denied involvement in the succession struggle, and his biographers have agreed, but there is no reason to disbelieve Derby's recollection that Sassoon at least claimed to speak for these men: Lord Derby's diary entry of 20–22 May 1923, DP 29/1.
12. R. Churchill, *Derby*, p. 259.
13. Lord Derby's diary entry of 20–22 May 1923, DP 29/1.
14. See Blake, *Unknown Prime Minister*, pp. 514–15; and A.J.P. Taylor, *Beaverbrook*, p. 208.
15. In 1894 Queen Victoria chose not to consult Gladstone and appointed Lord Rosebery to be her Prime Minister. In the latter case, Campbell-Bannerman was seriously ill and King Edward VII, who was in France at the time, appointed the uncontested successor – Asquith.
16. Barnes and Nicholson, *Amery Diaries*, Vol. I, entry of 18 May 1923, p. 326.
17. This was signed by an additional consultant, Douglas Harmer, as well as Bonar Law's regular physicians, Horder and Gould May: BLP 108/9/62.
18. See Rose, *King George V*, pp. 266–8.
19. RA, King George V's Diary, 20 May 1923.
20. Beaverbrook later noted that he had drafted a letter of resignation but that Bonar Law rejected it in favour of his own version: BBKP, G/13/VI.
21. 20 May 1923, CP, MSS. Eur. F.112/130/157. Bonar Law also wrote to Rothermere, whose newspapers had ceased their attacks against him, thanking him for this kindness and ending forever their past quarrels: 21 May 1923, BLP108/9/63.
22. BBKP, G/57/29.
23. Davidson to Blake, 19 May 1955, JCCD, DAV 310. Blake leaned towards the explanation in Beaverbrook's 'Alternative Ending': *Unknown Prime Minister*, p. 520.
24. Bonar Law to King George V, 20 May 1923, RA GV K1853/1; King George V to Bonar Law, 20 May 1923, GV K1853/3.
25. Press release, 20 May 1923, BLP 108/9/62.
26. RA GV K1853/5. Davidson retained a copy, JCCDP, DAV 143/84. This is printed in *Unknown Prime Minister*, pp. 520–21, with several minor errors of transcription. This version appears in Middlemas and Barnes, *Baldwin*, pp. 163–4, and in Rhodes James, *Memoirs of a Conservative*, pp. 154–5. In fact, Nourah Waterhouse had used her husband's copy of the memorandum in her *Private and Official*, pp. 259–62, more than ten years before the publication of Lord Blake's book. She did not identify it, however, and it went largely unnoticed by historians. See Cameron Hazlehurst, 'The Baldwinite Conspiracy', *Historical Studies*, Vol. 16, No. 63.
27. *Unknown Prime Minister*, p. 522.
28. This was Davidson's explanation in his unpublished memoirs: Rhodes James, *Memoirs of a Conservative*, pp. 153–5.
29. *Unknown Prime Minister*, p. 522. In his memoirs Sykes dealt only cursorily with the episode, and lamented years later than he had not paid closer attention at the time: *From Many Angles*, p. 317, and information from Mr Bonar Sykes.
30. RA GV K1853/4: emphasis added.
31. Maurice Cowling suspected that Davidson and Waterhouse worked together, *Impact of Labour*, p. 259; and Hazlehurst, 'The Baldwinite Conspiracy', concluded that Davidson and Amery wrote the memorandum, and that Bridgeman and Waterhouse were co-conspirators.
32. 'Baldwin Prime Minister, Davidson's Memorandum', July 1971, AJSP, B15.
33. See Hazlehurst, 'Baldwinite Conspiracy'. Neither Amery nor Bridgeman appears to have known of the Davidson memorandum, though the two pressed Baldwin's candidacy on Stamfordham, who seems to have ignored them.

34. Middlemas, ed., *Whitehall Diary*, Vol. I, entry of 20 May 1923, pp. 235–6. Jones guessed, incorrectly, that the memorandum was composed the night before by Davidson and Amery, and that both Bonar Law and Baldwin might have known about it.
35. See Blake, *Unknown Prime Minister*, pp. 521–2.
36. Beaverbrook to Blake, 18 March 1954, BBKP, C/44. Beaverbrook mistakenly recalled this as having occurred on Monday, 21 May.
37. Barnes and Nicholson, eds, *Amery Diaries*, Vol. I, entry of 18 May 1923, p. 326.
38. *Ibid.*
39. Steed to Davidson, 22 February 1952, JCCDP, DAV 308.
40. Chisholm and Davie, *Beaverbrook*, p. 199.
41. Middlemas, ed., *Whitehall Diary*, entry of 20 May 1923, p. 236.
42. Waterhouse, *Private and Official*, p. 263. Emphasis in the original.
43. See Hazlehurst, 'Baldwinite Conspiracy'; and Michael S. Howard, *Jonathan Cape, Publisher* (London, 1971), pp. 192–5. The proof copy belonging to Guy Chapman of Jonathan Cape, containing his explanation of the controversy and a brief manifesto by Waterhouse asserting the accuracy of his version of events, is now in the collection of the British Library. In May 1941 Waterhouse gave a statutory declaration before a Commissioner for Oaths to the same effect.
44. For this alleged conversation see Nourah Waterhouse, *Private and Official* (1940 edn), pp. 265–70; and Hazlehurst, 'Baldwinite Conspiracy'.
45. Memorandum by Lord Stamfordham, 22 May 1923, RA GV K1853/17.
46. Lady Sykes, when she learned of this claim many years later, rejected it because she remembered well that her aunt was never able to forgive Baldwin for his role in the US debt settlement affair and did not in any way approve of his succession to the premiership. Information from Mr Bonar Sykes.
47. See Jack E. Rose to the *Evening Standard*, 7 October 1955, which described these events – consistent with the 1940 version of *Private and Official*. Davidson preserved a cutting of this letter: JCCDP, DAV 310.
48. Sykes, *From Many Angles*, p. 317. Bonar Law considered recommending Neville Chamberlain, but his brief Front Bench experience, as Health Minister, made it impossible.
49. Memorandum by Lord Stamfordham, 21 May 1923, RA GV K1853/8.
50. Telegram, Stamfordham to Balfour, 20 May 1923, RA GV K1853/6.
51. Memoranda by Lord Stamfordham, n.d. [21 May 1923], and 22 May 1923, RA GV K1853/10 and K/1853/18. Stamfordham mentions that in the second meeting, on Tuesday morning, Balfour added that he had been struck by the argument in *The Times* of that morning that the absence of representation in the Lords of the official Opposition, the Labour Party, was an additional reason for the Prime Minister to be a member of the Lower House.
52. Lord Derby's diary, 29 May 1923, DP 29/1.
53. Murray served as Permanent Under-Secretary at the Treasury, 1903–11.
54. Memoranda by Lord Stamfordham, 21 May 1923, RA GV K1853/8, K1853/11, and K1853/19.
55. Col. Jackson reported that Central Office was being deluged by anti-Curzon sentiment, and that no more than 50 MPs would support Curzon: Memorandum by Lord Stamfordham, 22 May 1923, RA GV K1853/19. In his memoirs, Lloyd-Greame recalled this as a correct assessment: *Sixty Years*, p. 76.
56. Memoranda by Lord Stamfordham, 21 and 22 May 1923, RA GV K1853/9 and K1853/17; Barnes and Nicholson, eds, *Amery Diaries*, Vol. I, entry of 21 May 1923, p. 327.
57. Memorandum by Lord Stamfordham, 21 May 1923, RA GV K1853/11. Dawson

adjusted the editorial direction of *The Times*, to suit a pro-Baldwin decision. See also Rose, *King George V*, pp. 268–9.

58. Telegram, Stanfordham to Curzon, 21 May 1923, RA GV K1853/12. The date stamp on the telegram form is 23 May, but this is of course incorrect.
59. This is told most recently and very well in Gilmour, *Curzon*, pp. 584–6.
60. Memorandum by Lord Stamfordham, 22 May 1923, RA GV K1853/21. Curzon swallowed his disappointment and within a week made the speech nominating Baldwin as leader of the party.
61. The Government was little changed from the old: added were Lord Robert Cecil (Lord Privy Seal), Worthington-Evans (Postmaster-General), Joynson-Hicks (Financial Secretary to the Treasury), and Hoare (Secretary of State for Air). Davidson became Chancellor of the Duchy of Lancaster, though outside the Cabinet.
62. Davidson to Blake, 19 May 1955, JCCDP, DAV 310; Beaverbrook, 'Soundscriber Notes for Mr Blake', 18 March 1954, BBKP, G/13/VI. See also Hazlehurst, 'Baldwinite Conspiracy'.
63. For example, 9 April 1923, complaining about William Joynson-Hicks's speech touching on foreign policy ('this kind of thing will not do from subordinate ministers'), BLP 108/7/2; and 25 April 1923, protesting to Lord Winchester regarding investment in Turkey ('say that [he] should address himself to the F.O. and not to No. 10'), BLP 112/15/2. For the Winchester affair, see also Blake, *Unknown Prime Minister*, pp. 510–11.
64. 2 April 1923, CP, MSS. Eur. F. 112/320.
65. D.R. Thorpe, *The Uncrowned Prime Ministers* (London, 1980), p. 144.
66. 21 May 1923, PREM 2/34.
67. 28 May 1923.
68. Middlemas, ed., *Whitehall Diary*, Vol. II, entry of 10 June 1923, p. 241.
69. Information from Mr Bonar Sykes.
70. Waterhouse, *Private and Official*, p. 265.
71. For this tale see Chisholm and Davie, *Lord Beaverbrook*, pp. 199–200.
72. A.J.P. Taylor, *Beaverbrook*, p. 210.
73. Beaverbrook, *Decline and Fall of Lloyd George*, p. 233.
74. Middlemas, ed., *Whitehall Diary*, Vol. I, entry of 26 October 1923, p. 253.
75. A.J.P. Taylor, *Beaverbrook*, p. 210.
76. Bonar Law's principal debtor was William Jacks and Co., which was close to bankruptcy and unable to pay: BLP 17/2/20. As executor, Beaverbrook retained many of the documents related to the probate of Bonar Law's estate: BBKP, C/205d. Bonar Law's Will of 1 August 1916, amended later that month and in November 1919, December 1922 and September 1923, survives: BBKP, C/210.
77. Richard Law, later first Baron Coleraine, began but never completed a study; several early chapters were seen by Tom Jones and later by Lord Blake. They have not survived.
78. A portion of Bonar Law's personal library as well as certain pieces of the furniture of his study were given to the University of New Brunswick, where later Beaverbrook endowed a library building in the name of Bonar Law and Viscount Bennet, the former Canadian premier. The building today houses the Provincial Archives of New Brunswick.
79. BBKP, G/13/VI.
80. There are other monuments to Bonar Law, in additional to the library building detailed in n. 78, above. In 1929, through the generosity of the Tory MP Urban Broughton and the initiative of Davidson, the Conservative Party established a Bonar Law College at Ashridge in Hertfordshire, primarily for the training of party

workers. After 1954 it ceased to have any political ties, and ultimately became Ashridge Management College. It continues today in the hands of the Ashridge (Bonar Law Memorial) Trust. Finally, the farmhouse in Rexton in which Bonar Law was born has been restored and was rededicated as an historic site in 1997.

81. Ramsden, ed., *Sanders Diaries*, entry of 11 November 1923, p. 209.
82. See Keynes, 'Mr Bonar Law'. Keynes understood party feeling, but not the workings of a party machine.

Bibliographic Note

This study is based upon a number of collections of papers, public and private; upon the contemporary newspaper press and the *Parliamentary Debates*; as well as on published sources. The purpose of the endnote references is not only to show the origins of quotations or to provide evidence for the author's conclusions, but also to aid the reader who wishes to pursue further the lines of thought developed here. Perhaps this will be accepted as a defence by those who grow tired of the rather large number of notes which begin 'See ...' or 'In this regard ...'

Documentary sources consulted include the Prime Ministers' papers and those of the Cabinet, the Treasury, the Admiralty and the Foreign, War and Colonial Offices, as well as the *Parliamentary Debates*. All quotations in the text from speeches in Parliament are taken from this official source unless otherwise noted.

Other archival sources consulted include the papers of:
King George V, Royal Archives, Windsor
Leo Amery, courtesy of the late Lord Amery
H.O. Arnold-Forster, British Library
H.H. Asquith, Bodleian Library, Oxford
Waldorf Astor (Lord Astor), Reading University Library
Stanley Baldwin, Cambridge University Library
Arthur James Balfour, British Library and Scottish Record Office
Lord Beaverbrook, House of Lords Record Office
R.D. Blumenfeld, House of Lords Record Office
St John Brodrick (Lord Midleton), Public Record Office

Sir William Bull, Churchill College, Cambridge
Lord Robert Cecil (Lord Cecil of Chelwood), British Library
Austen Chamberlain, University of Birmingham
Neville Chamberlain, University of Birmingham
Winston S. Churchill (Chartwell Trust Papers), Churchill College, Cambridge
Lord Crewe, Cambridge University Library
Lord Curzon, Oriental and India Office Collections, British Library
J.C.C. Davidson (Lord Davidson), House of Lords Record Office
Geoffrey Dawson, Bodleian Library, Oxford
Lord Derby, Liverpool City Library
Master of Elibank (Lord Murray), National Library of Scotland
Lord Esher, Cambridge University Library
Lord Fisher, Churchill College, Cambridge
Malcolm Fraser, Bodleian Library, Oxford
J.L. Garvin, Harry Ransom Humanities Research Center, University of Texas
Sir Edward Goulding (Lord Wargrave), House of Lords Record Office
Sir Arthur Griffith-Boscawen, Bodleian Library, Oxford
H.A. Gwynne, Bodleian Library, Oxford
Sir Maurice Hankey (Lord Hankey), Churchill College, Cambridge
W.A.S. Hewins, University of Sheffield Library
Sir Samuel Hoare (Lord Templewood), Cambridge University Library
Lord Kitchener, Public Record Office
Lord Lansdowne, British Library
Andrew Bonar Law, House of Lords Record Office
David Lloyd Geroge (Lord Lloyd-George), House of Lords Record Office
Walter Long (Lord Long), British Library and Wiltshire Record Office
Leo Maxse, West Sussex Record Office
Reginald McKenna, Churchill College, Cambridge
Lord Milner, Bodleian Library, Oxford
Lord Northcliffe, British Library
Sir Ernest Pollock (Lord Hanworth), Bodleian Library, Oxford
Sir George Riddell (Lord Riddell), British Library
Field Marshal Lord Roberts, National Army Museum
Field Marshal Sir William Robertson, Liddell Hart Centre for Military Archives, King's College, London
J.S. Sandars, Bodleian Library, Oxford
Lord Selborne, Bodleian Library

Lord Stamfordham, Royal Archives, Windsor
A.J. Sylvester, National Library of Wales
Sir Arthur Steel-Maitland, Scottish Record Office
J. St Loe Strachey, House of Lords Record Office
Lady Melville (Sarah Tugander), House of Lords Record Office
Field Marshal Sir Henry Wilson, Imperial War Museum
Lord Willoughby de Broke, House of Lords Record Office
Sir Laming Worthington-Evans, Bodleian Library, Oxford

Index

Index

Wilson, F.M. Sir Henry (*cont.*)
181, 204, 268; rebuked by BL, 209;
hatred of Asquith, 212; diary quoted,
265; assassinated, 309–10, 313
Wilson, Col. Leslie, 306, 312, 319,
326; and election question (1922),
313, 319, 320, 322; election defeat,
338
Wimborne, 1st Viscount, 218
Winterton, 6th Earl of, 29, 91
Wood, Edward, 332

Worthington-Evans, Sir Laming, 286,
304, 306, 307
Wyndham, George, 79, 93

York, Duke of (King George VI), 357
Younger, Sir George, 303, 304, 306,
319, 321, 326; Chairman of Unionist
Party, 262; and election question
(1922), 307, 310, 312, 319, 320;
Treasurer of Unionist Party, 343
Ypres, Third Battle of, 260